2003 Edition

Bassing Bible®

The Ultimate Bass Fishing Reference

Stoeger Publishing Company · Accokeek, Maryland

Stoeger Publishing.
Great Outdoor Books Since 1925

STOEGER PUBLISHING COMPANY
is a division of Benelli U.S.A.

Benelli U.S.A.
Vice President and General Manager:
  Stephen Otway
Director of Brand Marketing and Communications:
  Stephen McKelvain

Stoeger Publishing Company
President: Jeffrey Reh
Publisher: Jay Langston
Managing Editor: Harris J. Andrews
Art Director: Cynthia T. Richardson
Imaging Specialist: William Graves
Copy Editor: Kate Baird
Publishing Assistant: Christine Lawton
Technical Illustrations: William Graves

Published by Stoeger Publishing Company
17603 Indian Head HIghway, Suite 200
Accokeek, Maryland 20607

BK0304
ISBN:0-88317-248-8

Library of Congress Control Number: 2002110066

Manufactured in the United States of America
Distributed to the book trade and
to the sporting goods trade by:
Stoeger Industries
17603 Indian Head Highway, Suite 200
Accokeek, Maryland 20607
www.stoegerindustries.com

OTHER PUBLICATIONS:
Shooter's Bible 2003 - 94th Edition
  The World's Standard Firearms
    Reference Book
Gun Trader's Guide - 25th Edition
  Complete, Fully-Illustrated
  Guide to Modern Firearms with
  Current Market Values

Hunting & Shooting
  Hounds of the World
  The Turkey Hunter's Tool Kit:
    Shooting Savvy
  Complete Book of Whitetail Hunting
  Hunting and Shooting with the Modern
    Bow
  The Ultimate in Rifle Accuracy
  Advanced Black Powder Hunting
  Labrador Retrievers
  Hunting America's Wild Turkey
  Taxidermy Guide
  Cowboy Action Shooting
  Great Shooters of the World

Collecting Books
  Sporting Collectibles
  The Working Folding Knife
  The Lore of Spices

Firearms
  Antique Guns
  P-38 Automatic Pistol
  The Walther Handgun Story
  Complete Guide to Compact Handguns
  Complete Guide to Service Handguns
  America's Great Gunmakers
  Firearms Disassembly with
    Exploded Views

Rifle Guide
Gunsmithing at Home
The Book of the Twenty-Two
Complete Guide to Modern Rifles
Complete Guide to Classic Rifles
Legendary Sporting Rifles
FN Browning Armorer to the World
Modern Beretta Firearms
How to Buy & Sell Used Guns
Heckler & Koch: Armorers
  of the Free World
Spanish Handguns

Reloading
  The Handloader's Manual of
    Cartridge Conversions
  Modern Sporting Rifle Cartridges
  Complete Reloading Guide

Fishing
  Ultimate Bass Boats
  The Flytier's Companion
  Deceiving Trout
  The Complete Book of Trout Fishing
  The Complete Book of Flyfishing
  Peter Dean's Guide to Fly-Tying
  The Flytier's Manual
  Flytier's Master Class
  Handbook of Fly Tying
  The Fly Fisherman's Entomological
    Pattern Book
  Fiberglass Rod Making
  To Rise a Trout

Motorcycles & Trucks
  The Legend of Harley-Davidson
  The Legend of the Indian
  Best of Harley-Davidson
  Classic Bikes
  Great Trucks
  4X4 Vehicles

Cooking Game
  Fish & Shellfish Care & Cookery
  Game Cookbook
  Dress 'Em Out
  Wild About Venison
  Wild About Game Birds

Contents

FOREWORD

Black bass are America's most popular game fish. Scores of books have been written describing the multitude of techniques for catching them and the many lakes and streams that serve up blue-ribbon fishing for largemouth, smallmouth and spotted bass. Until now, however, no bassing book ever encompassed detailed "how to, where to" information and a lengthy product information guide. The "Bassing Bible" does just that, in what will no doubt become the authoritative guide for bass fishing enthusiasts for many years to come.

Dive into these 400 pages, and learn new tactical tips and trip destinations in articles penned by some of the country's top angler-writers. In crisp, informative style, they tell you how to zero in on bass and entice them to strike, no matter what time of day, what season or what body of water you're fishing. Learn about night fishing, finesse techniques, selecting the right crankbait or spinnerbait, targeting trophy fish and analyzing your bassing hole. Pick up helpful hints for fishing oxbow lakes, rivers and other waters. Discover the fun of doodlesocking and the challenge of competitive fishing. Learn the history behind the fishing reels you use, and one veteran angler's picks for America's top bass lakes. And much, much more.

While you're sure to enjoy these delectable articles, they're just an hors d'oeuvre to whet your appetite. For an entrée, we've put together the most complete black bass fishing product information guide you've ever seen. You'll find complete specifications and up-to-date retail prices for boats, motors, electronics, rods, reels, lures and accessories. Whether you're in the market for a new fully outfitted, mega-bucks bass boat or just want to know the sizes and colors of a specific lure, you'll find it here in an easy-to-navigate guide made specifically with you—the bass angler—in mind. Browse the hundreds of pages and you'll discover products you didn't even know exist, all of which will help you catch more and bigger bass.

Last, but not least, we've included a manufacturer's directory, with mailing addresses, phone numbers and website addresses for all the U.S. and foreign businesses whose products are featured herein. When you need a catalog, want additional information or decide to make a purchase, it will serve as your guide for making contact with the companies you need to reach.

Enjoy the feast. Without doubt, the things you learn here will make you a better bass angler.

Hook 'em!

—Keith Sutton, Editor

FEATURE ARTICLES

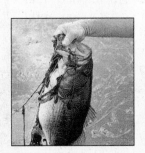

America's Best Bass Lakes
By John E. Phillips

How do you pick America's best bass-fishing lakes? I use two criteria—my own personal experience and the knowledge of some of the best bass fishermen in the world. Numbers of these lakes produce big bass, while other lakes primarily yield large numbers of bass. However, if you want to get your rod bent by some high-flying bigmouths, consider fishing these waters.

Fishing in the St. Lawrence River's crystal-clear water makes light line and little baits the primary tackle.

St. Lawrence River

I first fished the St. Lawrence River, which runs for 800 miles from Lake Ontario to the Gulf of St. Lawrence in the Atlantic Ocean, in 1980, when Bo Dowden won the BASS Masters Classic there. I'd never seen a lake that had as many smallmouths and largemouths in such clear water.

The Thousand Islands region of the river is home to some of the most pristine fishing waters you'll ever see. You'll enjoy fishing the waters around Boldt Castle, on one of the Thousand Islands near Alexandria Bay, for both the experience and the atmosphere. Where else in the United States can you catch bass while fishing around a castle? The St. Lawrence has numbers of both smallmouth and largemouth bass, and

provides a productive place to fish a tube jig. You also can catch bass there on a 1/2-ounce lead-head jig, a 3/4-ounce double willow-leaf spinnerbait and topwater lures. The lake has so much structure in the form of islands, grass, and rocky points that you can fish almost any way and catch bass. The crystal-clear water makes light line and little baits the primary tackle, but you can use bigger baits and fish deeper water and catch some really nice fish.

Southerners hear New York mentioned and think of New York City, but upstate New York, particularly the Thousand Islands regions of the St. Lawrence River, has some of the prettiest country, clearest water, and finest bass fishing you'll discover anywhere in the country.

For more information, contact: Thousand Islands International Tourism Council, P.O. Box 400, Alexandria Bay, New York 13607; call (800) 847-5263; or visit www.1000islands.org.

Although Kevin VanDam fishes all over the nation, he picks Lake St. Clair in Detroit, Michigan, as one of his favorite bass lakes.

Lake St. Clair

Kevin VanDam, winner of the 2001 BASS Masters Classic, picks Lake St. Clair, just outside Detroit, Michigan, as his favorite bass lake. This circular 26-mile-long lake spans an area of 430 square miles.

"I like to fish Lake St. Clair because it's shallow, with lots of vegetation, and a large number of big smallmouths in it," VanDam says. "The lake also houses numbers of big largemouths, but has built its reputation on giant smallmouth bass."

During the summer months, VanDam prefers to fish a plastic worm at Lake St. Clair. However, he says, fishing a tube jig will produce bass.

"To catch numbers of bass that will weigh 3- to 5-pounds each, I'll fish a 1/2-ounce tandem willow-leaf blade Strike King Premier spinnerbait with a shad-colored skirt," VanDam reports. "The spinnerbait will pull bass up to the surface that may have holed up 12- to 15-feet deep."

Even during the autumn, VanDam will fish the spinnerbait at Lake St. Clair to catch both largemouths and smallmouths.

"In the spring, I'll often catch and release 100 bass a day on this lake," VanDam explains. "I'll fish a tube jig, a lipless crankbait, a spinnerbait, and a jerkbait. I'll fish the shallow-water flats for aggressively feeding bass."

To learn more about Lake St. Clair, visit www.lakestclair.net.

Lake Champlain

You'd expect Floridian Shaw Grigsby to pick one of his own Florida lakes as his favorite. But Grigsby, host of the "One More Cast" television show and one of the nation's leading tournament bass fishermen, picks the Vermont side of Lake Champlain as his selection.

Grigsby chose Lake Champlain as one of America's best bass lakes because, he says, "I can catch a large number of smallmouths and largemouths, five pounds or more, there."

During the summer, Grigsby fishes with a topwater lure, like the Spit-N-King, along the edge of the grass to catch big largemouths and a few smallmouths as well.

"In the fall, I'll pitch a jig along the edge of the grass and into holes in the grass," Grigsby reports. "I'll fish a spinnerbait down the edge of the weeds. I like to fish a white-and-chartreuse, 1/2-ounce spinnerbait with either white- or chartreuse-colored blades."

Grigsby admits he most enjoys fishing Lake Champlain in spring, just after the ice melts. "At that time of year, I'll catch some really big smallmouths that will jump higher than my head," Grigsby says. "I like to target the shallow-water rocky shores with a tube jig, a spinnerbait or a jerkbait." For guide information, visit Lake Champlain Fishing Charters at: www.lakechamplaincharters.com

Although fishing in the South for lunkers like this is what Shaw Grigsby does for a living, he often travels north to Lake Champlain, where he can mix smallmouth and largemouth action.

Mississippi Oxbows

One of the most recognized bass fishermen in the nation, Bill Dance, of Memphis, Tennessee, selects the numerous oxbow lakes that parallel the Mississippi River, from St. Louis, Missouri, to Baton Rouge, Louisiana, as the best bass fishing in the nation. "I most like to fish along the Arkansas and Missouri state lines. The river levels dictate what bait you should fish and how you can catch bass there."

Dance says if you fish as the water level in the river falls, you can expect to catch plenty of 1- to 2-pound largemouths and an occasional seven-pounder in the oxbows.

When the water level falls, Dance depends on his topwater lures. He'll fish mud bars and sand bars early and late with topwaters. In midday, he'll fish these same regions with plastic worms. When he finds cover, whether visible or underwater, he prefers to fish a spinnerbait.

"Remember, even in hot weather when the surface temperature reaches 95 to 100 degrees, you still can catch bass using shallow-water patterns in these oxbow lakes," Dance reports. "I like river fishing, and I enjoy oxbow-lake fishing. I believe the oxbow lakes along the Mississippi River produce some of the finest bass fishing in the nation. You can fish one at any time of the year and catch bass."

For more information on the Mississippi River oxbows, visit: www.fishinglouisiana.com or call the Mississippi Department of Economic Development at 800-WARMEST or visit the website at: www.visitmississippi.org. To learn more about Arkansas, go to www.agfc.com or www.tourarkansas.com. For Missouri information, visit: www.conservation.state.mo.us/fish; for Tennessee information, go to: www.tennesseeanytime.org/main/travel/tourism

Although Bill Dance is known far and wide for catching big smallmouth, he enjoys fishing Mississippi River oxbows and believes they are home to some of America's best bass-fishing waters.

Even when the weather's rough, you still can find plenty of big bass at Lake Texoma.

Lake Texoma

Located on the border of Texas and Oklahoma, this 89,000-acre lake was created in 1944 by the damming of the Red River. The Texas Parks and Wildlife Division has worked hard to manage this lake toensure a population of trophy-size bass. Monster bass lurk among are abundant stick-ups and dead trees that dot the lake. No one gets really excited about a 6-pound largemouth at this lake. If a fish weighs less than ten pounds, you'll find that you don't get any respect if you choose to brag about it. Flipping a jig or casting a spinnerbait usually works best for catching Texoma's big bass.

If you're planning to fish Lake Texoma for the first time, I highly recommend you hire a guide. This large lake has so much cover and structure that you can cast all day around visible targets and still not find bass. But when you're searching for a place to catch one of the biggest bass of your life, fish Lake Texoma.

To learn more about fishing Lake Texoma, contact the Lake Texoma Association, P.O. Box 610, Kingston, Oklahoma, 73439, (405) 564-2334, or visit: www.resourcedesignassoc.com/lake-texoma

Lake Guntersville

Lake Guntersville, on the Tennessee River in northeastern Alabama, has produced some of the biggest catches of largemouth bass ever recorded during professional bass fishing tournaments. Over 66,000 acres in area, with 950 miles of winding shoreline, the lake first gained national recognition in 1978 when Rick Clunn, now a four-time BASS Classic winner, brought in a three-day total of 59 pounds, 15 ounces of bass and won one of the early B.A.S.S. tournaments on this lake.

Today, the lake is a popular site for bass fishing. In summer, many anglers like to fish plastic frogs and plastic rats on top of the miles of milfoil which house bass. The swimming worm also works effectively around the grass.

Fall and winter months see catches of some of the biggest bass along the edges of the main river channel using crankbaits, jigs and spoons. January and February provide the best times to catch big bass at Lake Guntersville. Some anglers even catch lunkers over ten pounds each.

If you plan to fish Lake Guntersville, spool up with 14- to 25-pound-test line, but beware; you still may get your line broken. Spinnerbaits also work well on this lake; fish them along the edge of the grass in spring and fall, and on humps and along the river channel in winter.

To learn more about Lake Guntersville, write: Lake Guntersville State Park, 7966 Alabama Hwy. 227, Guntersville, Alabama 35976-912, or call 800-ALA-PARK; visit the website at: www.dcnr.state.al.us.

If you fish during the spring, rubber rats like this one are good choices to catch bass out of Lake Guntersville's grass.

The Watchmaker's Reels
By Soc Clay

The very first double-multiplying geared baitcasting reel was made by George Snyder of Paris, Kentucky, in 1810. He became the first of the great Kentucky reel makers who dominated the market for nearly 100 years.

The original Snyder reels would establish the fashion of reel making in America that continues today with similar body designs.

The very first "baitcasting" reel ever made looks a lot like the ones we use today. The same design, the same way it fits on a reel—these things haven't changed all that much since George Snyder invented his "fine casting instrument" in his Paris, Kentucky, watchmaker's shop in 1810.

The story of this amazing invention, which would eventually allow every angler in the world to go fishing without buying a then-expensive flyrod, began on the banks of a quiet, picturesque stream that flowed through the new frontier town of Paris, Kentucky.

Stoner Creek was (and still is) a beautiful stream filled with shimmering riffles and long, placid pools. The stream supported an excellent population of smallmouth and spotted bass. Fish in the two- and three-pound class sunned themselves near the surface during the warming days of springtime. Folks who wandered by pondered ways to catch them. Fresh fillets for the table would have been a welcome relief from the sparse menus of the time.

But the fish were lying a good distance from the bank, too far away for a common sapling and line to reach. That's probably what watchmaker George Snyder, president of the Bourbon County Anglers Association, thought as he went about his work of building fine timepieces and hammering out silver objects in his shop back in town.

Throughout the cold winter days of 1810, he continued to think about the problem as he tinkered at his work bench. This gentleman of European descent had not yet heard terms such as "hawg", "lunker", "wall-hanger", or even "them old brown fish" at that early date in North American angling history. Nevertheless, he was well aware of the sporting qualities of the black bass, even though he had difficulty catching them.

Snyder had learned angling techniques fishing the trout and salmon streams of Europe, and this fly-fishing background caused him to yearn for a way to deliver a tempting morsel to the fish that lived in the deep, clear pools of the nearby stream. But fly fishing was out of the question. The shores bordering the waterway were woolly with growth, and there was no room to make the back cast necessary to deliver a fly or tiny live creature out into the current where the bass lay.

Other than fly fishing equipment, there was hardly any fishing tackle available. There was the all-wood Nottingham reel, a popular fishing instrument used in England during the period, but it was designed for retrieving and storing line. In his book *The History Of Angling*, noted author Charles Waterman referred to the old Nottingham reels as being the "durable forerunner of modern winches."

While there were some reels with multiplying gear systems available in the early 1800s, they could not be used for casting because the gear ratio was to low to let line out without creating a backlash.

Socially, Snyder considered himself an aristocrat and believed it to be totally improper for a gentleman to deliberately get his feet wet while angling. Yet, he knew that the fish in Stoner Creek would bite, if only he could "cast" his offering out to where they lay finning in the current. Wet-legging it was out of the question, and there were no wading boots in those days.

Little is recorded about how Snyder decided to make a device featuring a "double-multiplying" gear ratio that would permit a spool to turn fast enough to cast a line and a hook loaded with bait out to the fish, but it's safe to assume that all of the above-mentioned factors came into play. Eventually, Snyder was able to assemble an instrument, still effective today, that solved many of the problems he and the rest of the angling world faced in casting live bait. History notes that Snyder's fishing apparatus was called, appropriately enough, a "baitcasting instrument." A watchmaker by trade, Snyder advertised his multiplying-geared reels in an 1812 edition of the *Western Citizen*, a newspaper in his home town.

Benjamin Meek's famous Bluegrass reels (circa 1835) were a marked improvement over the first baitcasters made by Snyder.

All of the Kentucky reels were handmade by silversmiths and watchmakers.

Word of Snyder's invention spread slowly out of the Bluegrass region. It was not until about 1830 that Mason Brown, a judge and an avid angler, acquired a Snyder reel. He fished with it for a while, but decided it needed improvements. He consulted with his watchmaker friend and fellow angler Benjamin Meek, who worked in nearby Frankfort, Kentucky, to see if he could improve upon Snyder's unique casting device.

Meek accepted the challenge and copied Snyder's invention, adding his own refinements to the reel. By 1835, Meek and his younger brother, Benjamin, had become so good at building baitcasting reels by hand that they began manufacturing and marketing what became the world-famous "Bluegrass" line of baitcasting reels for the then-expensive sum of $50.00 each.

While both the Snyder and Meek reels featured double-multiplying

The Bluegrass 33 reel featured watch jewels for bearings and construction that kept oil from leaking out of the reel. It became the most famous of all the early Kentucky reels.

gears (four to one ratio), the Meek brothers were the first reel makers to use jeweled watch bearings at the ends of the spool for smoother turning. They also added spiral gearing and were the first to develop a bear--ing seal to prevent oil from leaking from the reel.

Throughout the mid-to-late 1800s, reels made by many famous watchmakers followed. Most of them were built by Kentuckians who had been apprentices to Meek between 1830 and 1850. Meek's apprentice B.C. Milan became a highly-respected reelmaker who taught his son John the trade. The Milan reels won the international first prize at the 1893 World's Fair in Chicago, captured first place at the 1889 Fisheries exposition in Bergin, Norway, and took top honors for design and functionality at the 1904 World Exposition in Paris, France. John Milan continued to manufacture fine baitcasting reels until 1927.

The Kentucky reel replaced all manner of line-storing reels in the 19th Century.

From 1850 to 1925, other Kentucky watchmakers began building their own reels. One was William H. Talbot, who moved from Frankfort, Kentucky, to Nevada, Missouri, where he continued to build some of the finest and most expensive baitcasting reels of the period. Talbot later moved his operation to Kansas City and built fine casting instruments into the 1920s. George W. Gayle, also an apprentice of Ben Meek, began building handmade casting reels of superior quality in 1882. His son Clarence continued his father's business until the 1940s.

J.L. Sage, of Lexington, Kentucky, was a Connecticut-born gunsmith who may have served an apprenticeship in reelmaking under Ben Meek when Meek's partner, B.C. Milan, was fighting in the 1846 war with Mexico. Sage's reels displayed a superior level of craftsmanship, but were very similar in design to the Meek and Milan reels. In all, Sage made about 350 reels between 1850 and 1885. They were praised for their small size and excellent workmanship. The Sage reels featured German silver or brass construction. Buffalo horn was used for the reel handle grasp on the Kentucky-style crank, which featured only one knob.

Most of the Kentucky reels made from 1850 to 1900 were constructed from brass and German silver, using the same careful craftsmanship of the very best watches of the period.

When Jonathan and Benjamin Meek started making baitcasting reels for the marketplace, they sent to Switzerland for special tools that were not available in the U.S. At the time, there was only one gear-cutting machine in Kentucky. It is believed that all of the gears for the early Kentucky reels were produced on this one machine in Danville, Kentucky, just south of Lexington.

The era of Kentucky's watchmakers reels began to slowly crumble in 1898 when William Shakespeare, a Michigan-based reelmaker, introduced the first truly workable level-wind device for a Kentucky reel.

Shakespeare had become dissatisfied when he learned that, unless the caster used careful thumb control during the retrieve, the line would bunch up on one part of the spool and create a major backlash on the next cast.

The level-wind mechanism on the Shakespeare reel became so popular with anglers around the

The watchmakers' reels of the 19th century allowed anglers to "cast" bait out into the water, but it required the addition of Bill Shakespeare's "level-wind" device to allow anglers to cast out and retrieve artificial lures.

Garcia's red reel, the Ambassadeur, marketed to American anglers in the early 1950s, re-established baitcasting reels as a favorite among fishermen in North America.

No doubt, George Snyder, the old watchmaker in Paris, Kentucky, never could have dreamed of terms such as "flippin'", "pitchin", or such descriptions as "titanium-plated", "anti-reverse", "synchronized level-wind" and "fascast thumbar." And he never could have imagined that the offsprins of his invention would shift from the broad green fields of the Bluegrass to Asia, where a multi-billion dollar industry has developed in reel-making. It is equally doubtful that few of the reel makers today are aware that the product they export to all corners of the globe came about simply because a member of central Kentucky's gentry wanted to fish desperately, but couldn't stand the thought of getting his feet wet!

The first ads for the spinning reel appeared in a few American magazines in 1937.

Spinning Steps In

Level-wind baitcasting reels dominated American angling history until the mid-1930s, and the advent of a new fishing style called "spinning." While Peter Malloch of Perth, Scotland, made a spinning reel as early as 1884, it was Alfred Holden Illingsworth, scion of the Bradford Worsted trade in England, who obtained the first patent on a reel that resembled the open-face spinning reels of today.

Later, the Hardy brothers of England and Pezon-Mitchel in France redesigned Illingsworth's model. Bache Brown introduced the Luxor reel to the U.S. angling market in 1935. The Luxor reel was advertised in *Field & Stream*, and many anglers decided to give it a try. However, by the time a market developed for the strange-looking fishing device, World War II cut off distribution.

Hence it would not be until 1947 that spinning tackle received broad public acceptance in America.

It was this acceptance, along with the ease of no-backlash casting, that forced demand for conventional baitcasting tackle to a national low ebb. nationwide spinning reels suddenly showed up in almost every fisherman's tackle box. Not only was the reel easy to cast, anglers could suddenly remain far away from targeted cover, use very small lines, and cast tiny lures into areas where it had been impossible to do so with standard baitcasting reels.

Spinning is credited for expanding sport fishing world-wide. The reels are so easy to cast that even a small child has no trouble tossing bait or lures into productive waters.

Five Finesse Tactics For Tough Conditions

By Larry Larsen

In the spring, bass often get finicky. A relatively-thin, curl-tail plastic worm, rigged Texas-style with a very light slip sinker, fished "dead" in the water, will trigger a very subtle strike.

The largemouth slowly mouthed the tiny worm. The fish wasn't moving, nor was the strike highly detectable, but when I set the hook, the seven-pounder jumped for the clouds. The spawn-heavy female bore for nearby brush, but snubbed short, she again erupted on the surface and tried to spit out the morsel that fooled her.

Largemouth bass of this size don't give up easily. She powered her way into a submerged tree beneath my boat as I struggled to force her back out. Steady pressure worked the bass free of the entanglement, and after another half-hearted airborne attempt to give up the wiggler affixed to her jaw, she was led into the net. On a spring day of very tough fishing during the height of the spawn, I gained further satisfaction by releasing her.

The battle was normal for springtime trophy bass trying to escape from an unpleasant 3/0 "hookup." But, when largemouth bass are quick to hit a lure and eject it, it was a pleasant surprise that this fish held the bait for ten seconds or so. "Short" strikes are a common occurrence to frustrated bass anglers trying to fool largemouths when largemouths are trying to spawn.

While other anglers experienced undetectable strikes or the usual "tap/spit" action with a hook set only through water, I had come across a lure and presentation the finicky fish would fall for. A small, 6-inch, attractant-impregnated worm, coupled with the "dead worm" technique, proved successful in those challenging conditions.

Weather affects how bass bite, or, in this case, their spawning pre-occupation. Wise anglers have a bag of tricks to use in specific weather conditions. When conditions turn harsh and slow down the bite, several finesse-type baits and presentations may unlock bass jaws. Most veteran anglers turn to lightweight tackle and lighter line, but the lure offering is also extremely important. So is patience. The five following tactics may save the day when fishing is slow.

Dead-Wormin' For Preoccupied Spawners

The scented worm, fished almost "dead" in the water, is an old technique called "dead-sticking" or "dead-worming," but it was the key to breaking the short-strike syndrome established by bedding largemouth everywhere on my spring trip. In spring, bass are often finicky. A relatively-thin, curl-tail plastic worm, rigged Texas-style with a very light slip sinker, will trigger a very subtle strike. Use a sharpened 3/0 worm hook and a 1/8-ounce bullet sinker.

The visible worm, as it lies motionless on the bottom, uses scent as the attractant to entice the bass to pick it up. 14-pound test monofilament line is usually adequate for bass in and around sparse cover. For areas with little cover, clear water and smaller bass, line size can be adjusted downward.

For best results, the worm should be tossed slightly beyond the target. On the initial cast, let the lure settle or glide to the bottom on a semi-taut line, and be ready for a strike. To best interpret any resistance, keep the rod tip about 60 degrees above the water and in front of you. Watch your line closely for a twitch or slight movement to the side. Set the hook at the slightest twitch.

Give the worm time to settle to the bottom, then let it rest at least 20 seconds. Slowly lower the rod tip and take in most of the slack. Leave a slight bow in the line so any critical movement can be seen without the bass getting suspicious or feeling you. Most strikes softly transmitted through the rod will be of a bass mouthing the bait gently. Remain alert, and place a sensitive finger on the line to aid in detection of the lightest pick-up.

Tube-Jigging for High-Pressure Spring Bass

In spring, under extreme high-pressure conditions with cloudless skies and a slow bite, a small soft-plastic tube and jighead combo may be the key. Sheffield, Alabama guide Barry Holt opts for a 3- to 3-1/2-inch tube married to a 1/8- to 1/4-ounce jig when such conditions exist. If lake

DEAD-WORM RIG

"Dead-sticking", or "dead-worming", as the technique is called, may be the key to short strikes from spawning bass. It does require plenty of patience, however.

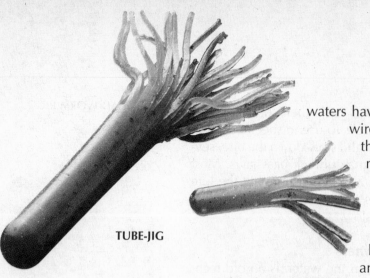

TUBE-JIG

waters have a minimal current, this rig with single wire weed guard can be worked very slowly through bottom rocks to entice small-mouths or largemouths. Holt recommends working the rig on spinning gear spooled with 6-to-8-pound test monofilament line so it connects with the bottom by employing small twitches rather than larger motion jerks. Just barely lift the bait and try not to get hooked, he suggests.

Holt, who has guided anglers on the Tennessee River impoundments in northwest Alabama for over 17 years, frequently deals with currents, so his casts are made quartering upstream (from which any current might be coming). The 42-year-old guide will then pick up the slack and crawl the bait very slowly along the bottom through any rocks and stumps that may be present. The jig and tube combo will effectively mimic crawfish.

Big, 12- to 30-inch-diameter chunk rocks that allow the bass get out of current and conserve energy are ideal spots to use the ploy, according to Holt. In extreme high-pressure conditions, and even in a dead-water situation, he finds he gets a lot more bites in such places, versus the pea-gravel flats more predominant on the river chain of reservoirs. The bass are lethargic and are more apt to hit the bait if they can find some structure to rest behind.

"The high-pressure frontal conditions can affect the fishing almost any time of the year, but the presence has more affect on bass in March through May than does the same weather in the fall," he says. "The post-frontal conditions in the spring will slow down the fishing for a couple of days, but it all depends on how strong the front is and how high the pressure is behind it."

"When these conditions exist, any current helps tremendously, because the fish tend to scatter and go deeper," explains Holt. "That makes them harder to catch. Look at creek mouths the day after a rain, or at the dam schedule for generating power (and, correspondingly, current) to help find the best place to throw the tube and jig."

Trick Wormin' for the Finicky Fall Malaise
A "trick" worm is just the right finesse bait to draw attention from finicky largemouths inhabiting hydrilla and milfoil expanses. When bass get

Weight and Color Adjustments For Tough Times

When conditions are unfavorable for active fish, a weight or color change may be wise. "Let the conditions tell you how to modify your fare," suggests Alabama guide Barry Holt. When you return to places where you caught fish before a weather front, you may want to fish a little deeper and tighter to structure, with a slower presentation of the tube and jig combo. Since the fish are positioned differently, a darker silhouette on a jig hopped high off the bottom won't generate the same amount of strikes it would under normal conditions.

"When my bait is being dragged along the bottom, I prefer lighter bait colors, such as watermelon or clear smoke," Holt advises. "But if there is no current, go to the 1/8-ounce jig head. You may also need to use a heavier line, so the bait falls even slower. If you can find the current, then go to a slightly-heavier jig head, such as 1/4 ounce. But be ready for hang-ups, because even with a weed guard, the jig may be carried by the current under a rock."

When fishing under high-pressure conditions for slow-biting largemouths, Holt opts for a slightly larger bait such as a 4- or 4 1/2-inch tube rigged texas-style with a 3/0, wide-gap hook and a 1/8 to 1/4-ounce slip sinker.

lethargic in the fall as waters cool, and nothing seems to be productive, the belly-hooked worm rig, also called a Wacky Worm or a Finesse Worm, could be the key to action. The rig, which has been around quite a few years, usually consists of a 5-inch, straight-tail plastic worm and exposed 3/0 hook.

Place the hook through the mid-section of the worm, leaving it exposed. Do not add a weight. To be balanced, the hook should go right through the middle, so each tail wags and twists, or spinning is minimized.

When fishing this rig, use a long rod, keep the tip high and have plenty of patience. Cast the lightweight fare high to softly land in weedy pockets, let it sink into the deep and drift along, and give it little twitches ever so subtly as you slowly crank in the lure. Move the bait very slowly and watch the line for movement. The hits may be faint, so line watchers catch more fish with this rig. Some strikes can be felt and slack can be quickly given, if needed. When a worm temporarily hangs on a weed and then comes free, give it slack to minimize its movement out of the strike zone.

Pause in the retrieve and let the Trick Worm rig sink into pockets in the vegetation. The bait can often be slowed considerably to entice a "follower" or one of the more

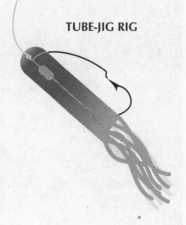

TUBE-JIG RIG

A "trick" worm is just the right finesse bait to draw attention from finicky large-mouth inhabiting aquactic vegetation. To rig the "trick" or "wacky" worm, *inset*, place the hook through the mid-section of the worm, leaving it exposed, and do not add a weight.

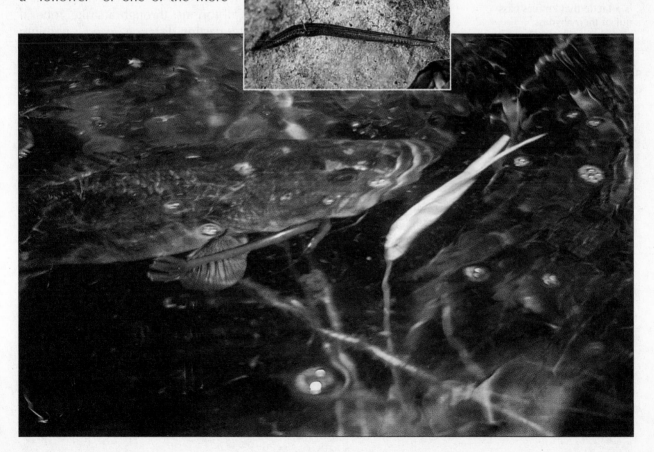

When waters are clear, bass are more cautious. Doodling is a tactic that entices bass out of their shyness.

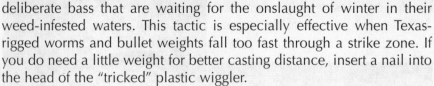

TRICK WORM RIG

DOODLE RIG

deliberate bass that are waiting for the onslaught of winter in their weed-infested waters. This tactic is especially effective when Texas-rigged worms and bullet weights fall too fast through a strike zone. If you do need a little weight for better casting distance, insert a nail into the head of the "tricked" plastic wiggler.

Drop-Shotting for Suspended Bass

The newest technique to gather notoriety for catching bass with a subtle, finesse-type presentation is called "drop-shotting" or "down-shotting". The rig, which employs an artificial bait, appeared on the bass fishing scene nationwide in the early 1990s. It is a search tool that allows the angler to better locate the strike zone when bass have moved off structure and are suspending in the water column. The tactic can be productive in deep or relatively shallow waters, as long as the water is fairly clear. When fronts turn off the bass, and instead of moving deeper or tighter to cover, they move laterally in the water column, this rig can be a salvation.

The drop shot rig consist of a 3/8- to 1/2-ounce, bell-type or specific drop-shot, release-type sinker, a small, light-wire No. 1 hook tied 12-18 inches above the weight, and a small, nose-hooked, soft-plastic bait. The hook is tied to the line first with a palomar knot, making sure to create a loop long enough so the tag-end of the finished knot is 18 to 30 inches long. The sinker is then tied or attached to that tag-end to complete the rig.

The sinker allows the rig to maintain bottom contact while the line back to the reel is kept taut. That allows the lure to dance slowly in place in the water column above bottom obstructions. Many anglers

use 4-inch fluke-type or soft jerkbaits. Others use special drop-shot minnows or tiny 3- to 5-inch finesse worms. Tiny tubes with additional floatation to suspend the bait away from the line also may be employed.

The rig is fished on 8-to-12-pound test, low-stretch, low-visibility monofilament by shaking the rod tip so the soft plastic twitches without moving the weight. When the rig is lifted and moved a few feet, the sinker falls back to the bottom, and the bait darts for the bottom and abruptly stops to suspend, like an errant minnow might do. When bass are suspended, it is most productive to cast to shallower water and drag the presentation out to deeper water.

Doodling The Clearest, Cool Waters

Many finesse tactics now in common use originated in the western U.S. in deep, clear canyon reservoirs. The "doodle rig," perhaps the most famous transplant, now catches bass in extremely clear waters throughout the country. As sediments settle and water visibility substantially increases, when summer winds subside and/or sunny skies diminish plankton growth with the onset of winter, bass become more finicky. If the waters are heavily fished, then it may be time for the doodle rig.

Fishing the drop-shot rig near vertical presents challenges even to light-tackle anglers. Light lines and small lures are the key to action here.

The rig consists of a thin, 4- or 5-inch worm with minimum tail size that is rigged Texas-style on a No. 1 fine-wire hook combined with a 1/8- or 3/16-ounce slip sinker and a glass bead. It requires such a relatively-small weight because too much will dampen the bait's action. The bead is threaded on the line between the sinker and the hook. To prevent the soft plastic from sliding down the hook, peg it in place by pushing a short section of stiff wire through the head and buried hook eye. Clip off the excess peg wire.

Doodling is a shaking technique that seems to attract a bass to the bait when other tactics fail. The bait is normally worked through relatively deep waters with a short, fast pulsating movement of the rod tip. This causes the rig to dance enticingly and the sinker to clatter against the glass bead. Although the bait is wiggling erratically, the strikes are usually soft and the angler may only feel an increase in pressure on the terminal end of his line.

When you are searching for an answer to tough conditions, try one of these rigs for an attitude adjustment. Go home happy!

Can't We All Just Get Along?
Facts About Black Bass

By Bob Borgwat

Collectively grouped as black bass, the largemouth, smallmouth and spotted basses have a lot in common: aggressive natures, voracious feeding habits, widespread distribution, and a nationwide following of dedicated, fervent anglers who have made black bass the most sought-after, important gamefish in North America.

Individually, these basses are historically recognized and separated by their original ranges:

• Largemouth bass (Micropterus salmoides) originally were indigenous to southeastern Canada, the Great Lakes, and south into the Mississippi Valley to Mexico and Florida. This northern largemouth also ranged northward up the Atlantic Coast to Maryland. A subspecies, the Florida largemouth bass (Micropterus salmoides floridanus) originally was found only in peninsular Florida and as genetic intergrades with the largemouth bass of southern Georgia.

• Smallmouth bass (Micropterus dolomieu) originally ranged with abundance from Minnesota to Quebec and south to northern Alabama, then west to eastern Kansas and Oklahoma.

• Spotted bass (Micropterus puntulatus) are native fish of the low gradient tributaries of the Ohio-Mississippi drainage from Ohio south to the Gulf states and west to Texas, Oklahoma and Kansas. The species ranges eastward, too, into western Florida.

LARGEMOUTH BASS
(Micropterus salmoides)

Description: The largemouth is the largest member of the sunfish family. It generally has light greenish to brownish sides with a dark lateral line that tends to break into blotches toward the tail. Often confused with smallmouth and spotted bass, it is easily distinguishable because the upper jaw extends beyond the rear edge of the eye. Also, its first and second dorsal fins are almost separated by an obvious deep dip, and there are no scales on the soft-rayed second dorsal fin or on the anal fin. Locally, the largemouth bass is tagged with a variety of names, including largemouth, black bass, green bass, bigmouth, bucketmouth and green trout.

Subspecies: Two are recognized: the northern largemouth (M. s. salmoides) and the Florida largemouth (M. s. floridanus). The two look much the same, but the Florida largemouth has 69-73 scales along the lateral line compared to the northern largemouth's 59-65 scales. Florida bass grow to trophy size more readily than northern largemouth in warm waters.

Age and Growth: Growth rates are highly variable, with differences attributed mainly to food supply and length of growing season. Female bass live longer than males and are much more likely to reach trophy size. By age two or three, females grow much faster than male bass. Males seldom exceed 16 inches, while females frequently surpass 22 inches. At five years of age, females may be twice the weight of males. One-year-old bass average about seven inches in length and grow to an adult size of 10 inches in about 1-1/2 to 2-1/2 years. Generally, trophy bass (10 pounds and larger) are about 10 years old. The world-record largemouth weighed 22 pounds, 4 ounces and was caught in 1932 at Montgomery Lake in Georgia.

**SMALLMOUTH BASS
(Micropterus
salmoides)**

Description: The smallmouth bass is generally green with dark vertical bands rather than a horizontal band along the side. Small yellow to gold flecks of color pepper the skin. There are 13-15 soft rays in the dorsal fin, and the upper jaw never extends beyond the eye. Micropterus is Greek meaning "small fin." The species epithet dolomieu refers to the French mineralogist M. Dolomieu. Water quality and bottom substrates can cause the smallmouth to appear more bronze in color. Depending on the location, smallmouths may be called brown bass, brownie, bronze bass or bronzeback.

Subspecies: None; however, identification of the shoal bass and Suwanee bass is sometimes confused with the smallmouth bass.

Age and Growth: The growth of smallmouth bass depends upon the amount and kind of feed, the temperature of the water and the length of the growing season. In some infertile streams, it takes four years for the bass to reach 9 inches. In the larger fertile rivers, 9 inches will be reached during the second summer; it requires 7 to 10 years in these rivers for a smallmouth to attain 18-20 inches. The world-record smallmouth weighed 11 pounds, 15 ounces and was caught in Dale Hollow Lake, Tennessee, in 1955.

SPOTTED BASS (Micropterus punctulatus)

Description: The species epithet punctulatus, Latin for "dotted," refers to rows of dark spots on the fish's pearly lower sides. Overall coloration is more contrasting and striking than that of the largemouth bass. The lateral line is commonly a series of short, almost-black blotches. They may also be called spots, Kentucky spotted bass, or spotted black bass.

Subspecies: Alabama spotted bass (M. p. henshalli) and the Wichita spotted bass (M. p. wichitae).

Age and Growth: Young of the year grow from 1-1/2 to 4 inches long, depending on water quality and forage availability. Smaller and slower-growing than the largemouth, a 3-to-4-pound spotted bass is a big fish, with 5-pound-plus weights true trophies. Full-grown adult weights are similar to those of smallmouth bass. The world-record spotted bass, a 10-pound, four-ounce fish, was caught at Pine Flat Reservoir, California, in 2002.

OTHER BLACK BASSES

Redeye Bass (Micropterus coosae)…also known as the Coosa bass, shoal bass, Flint River smallmouth, Chipola bass, black bass. It originally ranged in the watershed of the Apalachicola and Chipola river systems in Florida.

Shoal Bass (Micropterus cataractae)…common to Florida's Apalachicola and Chipola rivers where shoals exist; also found in the Chattahoochee and Flint rivers drainages of Georgia.

Suwanee Bass (Micropterus notius)…sometimes confused with the smallmouth bass, redeye bass or spotted bass. Restricted to the Suwannee and Ochlockonee rivers systems of Florida and Georgia. Also occupies the spring-fed lower reaches of Florida's Santa Fe and Ichetucknee rivers, tributaries of the Suwannee River.

Guadalupe Bass (Micropterus treculi)...found only in Texas and has been named the official state fish. It is endemic to the northern and eastern Edwards Plateau, including the headwaters of the San Antonio River, the Guadalupe River above Gonzales, the Colorado River north of Austin, and portions of the Brazos River drainage.

Today, distribution of largemouth, smallmouth and spotted basses is nationwide. Some of the finest individual bass fisheries are in locations where bass were once not found. With the expansion of railroads in the late 1880s, largemouths were moved west of the Rockies and introduced to the Columbia River system of Washington and Oregon. Railroads also provided means to import smallmouths east of the Ohio River system, and eventually smallmouths from Lake Ontario arrived in California, Oregon and Washington. Relatively speaking, spotted bass are newcomers to many waters across the nation, with widespread distribution occurring during the late 1970s and into the 1980s.

Distribution--both manmade and natural--of the basses also results in restrictions that frequently limit local bass-fishing opportunities to the single species most adaptive to the local environment. But largemouth, smallmouth and spotted bass also co-exist in impoundments

Author with largemouth bass in woody cover in north Georgian impoundment.

The quiet backwaters of cypress and tupelo swamps in the Deep South are favorite destinations for anglers pursuing largemouth bass.

and riverways, frequently sharing habitats while also occupying specific habitat features that can separate them both horizontally and vertically in the water column. Where all three species are found, the preferred habitat of the black basses often allows anglers to focus their efforts to target individual species or fish with potluck tactics and techniques that can result in mixed catches of these closely-related game fish.

Like many relatives, however, the black basses do not always complement each other. For example, fisheries biologists in California, Missouri and Georgia have documented displacement or replacement of smallmouth bass by spotted bass. Because spotted bass prefer much of the same deep, rocky, clear-water environments favored by smallmouth bass, spots are frequently blamed for the demise of the smallmouth fisheries where they have been introduced by fisheries stocking programs, as well as illegal importation by anglers who favor the aggressive nature of the spotted bass.

For many fisheries officials and anglers alike, the spotted bass has been recognized as an "intermediate" bass--a fish whose favored habitat ranges between that of the largemouth bass and smallmouth bass, but which is more likely to share the deep, rocky, clear-water environs of the smallmouth bass, where it is found in impoundments. Indeed, spotted bass and largemouth bass appear to get along quite nicely in both impoundments and moving waters. It's likely a matter of preferred habitat that allows both fish species to keep their numbers strong in shared waters. Largemouths favor shallow water--20 feet or less--combined with heavy vegetation and/or timber and still backwaters. Likewise, where largemouths and smallmouths co-exist in impoundments, the fish are commonly separated by almost identical preferred habitat characteristics. Pitch a plastic worm or top-water plug into the back of a cove where weedbeds, reeds or laydowns "thicken" the environment, and the bass likely to inhale the offering is a largemouth. But where spots and/or smallmouths co-exist with large-mouths, those same lures are likely to produce jarring strikes from these more aggressive basses when cast to steep, main-lake points of that same cove where gravel, boulders and other rocky substrate is found. Few anglers will argue that it will most likely be a smallmouth or spotted bass that smashes a gurgling plug or gulps a plastic worm fished off a rocky shoreline from shallow to deep water.

Exactly why spotted bass appear to displace/replace smallmouths is not clearly understood by fisheries officials. The key factors in the displacement of smallmouths by spotted bass appear to be water quality and shared habitat, but the data are inconclusive. Where found in rivers and streams, fisheries biologists say spotted bass seem to prefer silted pools in slow water. But those same biologists have found spotted bass also will occupy the riffles and deep pools preferred by the smallmouth. Where they are found in lake environments, spotted bass frequently are caught off the same deep, rocky structures where smallmouth are found. And it is the spots' inclination to occupy the gravel points and humps, steep shorelines and rock walls inhabited by smallmouths that results in many anglers' disappointment when it seems that the smallmouth bass has been replaced by its vigorous cousin.

Spotted bass in impoundments also are not always limited to rocky environs and can overlap their range with largemouth bass, especially during the spawning season. Whereas water temperature defines all three species' preferred spawning periods, it is shallow water, 2- to 5-feet deep, where spots, largemouths and smallmouths prefer to build their nests. Cover is likely to be abundant wherever a bass spawns, and water quality and vegetation will affect the specific locations of bass nests. Largemouths are more likely to spawn in areas of weeds and dingy water than will spotted bass or smallmouth bass. Spots and smallmouths prefer gravel and clay bottoms for nest building, but hard bottoms are required for all three species, and it is not out of the question to find spawning spotted bass alongside their brethren.

Diet, too, could be among the factors that lead

Stump fields on the gravel beds of Lake Shasta in Northern California are favored spawning grounds for spotted bass.

to overlap in the ranges of the basses, which share nearly identical forage preferences. The foods of small largemouth, smallmouth and spotted bass are small crustaceans and invertebrates in larval, intermediate and adult stages. As each of the species grows larger, so do their food requirements. Soon, large insects, small fish, crawfish, frogs, salamanders and worms become the preferred foods of the basses. These forage species progressively grow larger as the bass itself grows larger and more dominant in its environment. Forage of outsized largemouths also might include crabs, snakes, mice, turtles and even birds. Some of the heaviest largemouth bass (in excess of 10 pounds) are fooled by huge crankbaits, stickbaits, jigs and jerkbaits.

Deep, slow-moving pools on rivers in the middle-South offer cool midday hideouts for smallmouth bass during the heat of summer.

LARGEMOUTH BASS

Because largemouths tolerate a wide range of water clarities and bottom types, bass fishermen are fortunate to find largemouths in watersheds in almost every state and many countries. Certainly, largemouths are the most widely-distributed bass, including worldwide distribution. Largemouths swim in nearly all suitable waters in Mexico, Central America and South America. Anglers in Japan, South Africa, Australia and other nations appreciate the fish's aggressive nature and willingness to strike an artificial lure that results in thrilling fights above and below the waterline.

Largemouths prefer clear, slow or still waters where aquatic vegetation provides both forage and cover for the bass, such as the environ-

ments found at Clear Lake in California and Lake Fork in Texas. Freshwater habitats include rivers, impoundments, swamps and ponds, but largemouths also occupy the brackish waters common on the northern and eastern coasts of the Gulf of Mexico. They prefer water temperatures from 65 to 85 degrees and are usually found at depths of less than 20 feet.

Depending on local weather and water conditions, largemouth bass spawn from December through May. Peak spawning commonly occurs in February and March in the southern tier of states and from March to April in the mid-to-northern tiers of states. Key water temperature for spawning is 58 to 65 degrees and continues as temperatures rise into the 70s. Male bass build the nests and direct the females into hard-bottom areas along shallow shorelines or in protected areas,

Top-Notch Black Bass Waters

Bass, whether spots, largemouths and small-mouths, are the nation's most sought-after gamefish. Quality fisheries for each species are found in virtually every state, and in some cases all three species of bass co-exist in a single impoundment or river in good, or maybe even great ,numbers.

Certainly, bass anglers in every state can name their top local bass fisheries, but some waters across the country arguably produce better bass fishing opportunities than others. Qualifying such a list is a matter of considering historical catches, record-book catches, current catch rates, fishing pressure, and individual weights of the top catches, as well as the weights of tournament-winning stringers.

With those stated qualifications (and some unstated qualifications) two of the nation's top bass experts--Dave Precht, editor for Bassmaster magazine, and Dave Washburn, editor for FLW Outdoors magazine--helped build the following list of the top five bass fishing waters, in no particular ranking, individually identified by the three top species of black bass.

LARGEMOUTH BASS

Lake/River	Location
Clear Lake	California
Sacramento/ San Joaquin Delta	California
Lake Walk-In-Water	Florida
Stick Marsh/Farm 13	Florida
Lake Fork	Texas

SMALLMOUTH BASS

Lake/River	Location
Dale Hollow Lake	Tennessee
Lake St. Claire	Michigan
Lake Champlain	New York Vermont
Lake Erie	Ohio Pennsylvania New York
Pickwick Lake	Alabama Mississippi Tennessee

SPOTTED BASS

Lake/River	Location
Pine Flat Reservoir	California
Lake Perris	California
Lake Lanier	Georgia
Lake Martin	Alabama
Lake Shasta	California

such as canals and coves. Female bass are typically larger than the male, which will aggressively attack anything that approaches the nest and eggs, as well as the fry, which remain in tight schools until growing to about an inch in length.

SMALLMOUTH BASS

Because of its reputation as a strong, acrobatic fighter, the smallmouth bass has been distributed across the United States and into other countries where high-quality water conditions are found. Actually a stream fish, the smallmouth has adapted quite well to many impoundments, especially those that feature riverine environments with abundant gravel. They do best in large impoundments with depths of more than 30 feet.

In rivers and streams, they inhabit riffle areas that flow over gravel, boulders or bedrock and are separated by deep pools, such as Oregon's Umpqua River. But deep tailwater runs below large dams also prove the smallmouth's affinity for current. Wheeler Reservoir, on the Tennessee River in Alabama, is a classic example of the smallmouth's affinity for current in big water. Both rivers are recognized as leaders among smallmouth bass fisheries. Smallmouth bass are not found in Florida and Louisiana.

As springtime water temperatures near 60 degrees, males locate nests near shorelines in lakes. Stream- and river-bred smallmouths spawn downstream from boulders or some other obstruction that offers protection against strong current in streams. Males may spawn with several females on a single nest, then guard the nest from the time eggs are laid until fry begin to disperse, a period of up to a month.

SPOTTED BASS

Unofficially, and certainly unscientifically, the spotted bass could be described as a "cross" between the largemouth and smallmouth bass. This acrobatic, extremely aggressive and hard-fighting bass has relatively recently gained huge popularity with U.S. bass anglers. Commonly diminutive in its largest sizes in comparison to the largest largemouth bass, the spot makes up for its weight and length shortfalls by its power and what some anglers describe as a beligerent attitude. It is an attacker, a marauder, that at times will school by the hundreds.

Spotted bass inhabit areas of more current than do largemouth bass, and water that is more eutrophic, or fertile, than water preferred by smallmouth bass. However, spots are frequently accused of displacing or replacing smallmouth bass populations, as noted above, but solid evidence as to why has been elusive. California's Lake Shasta and Georgia's Lake Chatuge are two examples of the issue. Over a period of 10 years, both these waters that once supported outstanding smallmouth bass fisheries appear to have lost the smallmouth due to spotted bass that grew to high numbers following introduction of the species. The loss of smallmouths notwithstanding, anglers at these impoundments and elsewhere are eager to fish for spotted bass, which assail many of the same lure selections chosen for targeting largemouth bass and smallmouth bass.

Spotted bass typically reach 3 to 4 years of age before they prepare to spawn. Rock and gravel is the preferred substrate for the nests, which are built somewhat smaller than that of a largemouth but in shallow depths consistent with the spawning habits of its big-mouthed cousin. Males build nests when the water temperature ranges from 57 to 74 degrees, and continue to guard the eggs during incubation and for up to four weeks after they have hatched. As young fish grow, their diet shifts from zooplankton to insects, and finally to fish and crayfish.

Understanding Oxbows:
A Bass Angler's Guide

By Keith Sutton

Belly boats (float tubes) provide excellent means for fishing small, out-of-the-way oxbows seldom visited by anglers.

It was a perfect bass hideout. Buckbrush lined a ditch coursing across the bottom of the oxbow. Adjacent to the brush was a long log, the upper end of which was suspended atop two cypress knees. The bottom end projected into the brushy edge of the little ditch, creating a shady hiding place ideal for a big bass.

A bass was home, alright. But when my buddy Jim knocked on its door with a spinnerbait, he wasn't prepared for the fish's response.

Jim's cast was exemplary; the lure fell right beside the log, sinking into the shadowy recess below. He hadn't turned his reel handle a full revolution when the fish struck. The bass inhaled the spinnerbait, shot for cover, and did a perfect loop-de-loop around the butt of the log. It mattered not that a 190-pound man held the end of the line opposite the bass. The fish, a six- or seven-pounder, broke the water's surface, made one flip of its tail and was gone.

Jim reeled in his slack line and laid down his rod. He pulled out a bandanna and wiped beads of sweat from his forehead.

"I hate to whine," he said. "But that son-of-a-gun didn't really play fair."

It's true; the term "fair play" seldom enters the oxbow bassin' equation. Bass in these waters are brawlers. They fight dirty and make their relatives in bigger, man-made lakes look like a bunch of wimps.

Maybe it's the extraordinary fertility of oxbow lakes that gives bass the upper hand. In these natural waters, every fish seems to have an extra measure of strength and stamina.

Maybe it's the marriage of confined living space, generally shallow water and dense cover that makes oxbow bass so good at line-busting and throwing hooks. These fish know every inch of their home territory, and they use that familiarity to discomfit their human antagonists.

Maybe it's the beauty of oxbows that causes these problems. When you're fishing in the shade of 500-year-old cypress trees, the serenity of it all can lull you into a state of total relaxation. Reflexes get sluggish, and consequently, lots of bass are lost.

Who knows? And more to the point, who cares? Oxbow lakes serve up exceptional bass fishing, and if oxbow bass get the jump on us more often than usual, it's a small price to pay for the privilege of being there.

For many inexperienced anglers, catching oxbow bass is like trying to read a secret message. Try as they might, it seems impossible to break the code, and many go away frustrated, vowing never again to fish an oxbow.

But contrary to the opinions of some unfortunate fishermen, the only real "secret" to oxbow bass fishing is preparing yourself with an in-depth knowledge of oxbow dynamics. In many physical respects, oxbows are vastly different than man-made lakes, and each oxbow has characteristics making it different from other oxbows. Unless one knows and understands these differences, fishing for bass may be nothing more than a waterhaul.

Let's examine the origins and physical attributes of oxbow lakes. Knowing what to look for, and when, and where, will increase your chances for success.

Oxbow Origins

A lowland river left to its own devices will twist in its valley like a head-shot snake. The river erodes earth in one place, only to deposit it somewhere else, and though a river may always look the same to a casual visitor, it's never the same two days in a row.

Over the years, a lowland river plows a new channel here and abandons an old one there, always following the path of least resistance. Sometimes, when a meandering stream erodes the shores of its broad bends, loops of water are severed from the main stream. The ends of the loops are blocked by sediments deposited by the parent stream, and a crescent-shaped lake is left behind. The shape of these lakes resembles the U-shaped piece of wood on an ox yoke; thus they are called oxbow lakes. Oxbow lakes are also known as "cut-offs" or "river lakes."

When an oxbow is severed from the river, its character immediately begins changing. The absence of continually flowing water allows sediment carried in from seasonal flooding to

Anglers willing to make the extra effort required to access remote oxbows often find superb bass fishing in picturesque settings far from the beaten path. Hiking in may be the only way to reach some of these extraordinary waters.

build on the bottom. The old meander scar becomes shallower and relatively flat-bottomed. Water-tolerant plants like cypress, tupelo, buckbrush and willow take root along the lake's edges. In years of drought, some shallow oxbows dry up, allowing plants to gain a foothold and encroach still farther into the lake. It's because of this cyclic process that many oxbows have large cypress trees growing in the middle of the lake, or have a ring of living trees and shrubs extending 100 feet or more from dry land.

Many oxbows provide fantastic bass fishing. The annual cycle of winter/spring flooding that gradually chokes these lakes with silt also figures heavily in making them the outstanding bass fisheries they are.

The annual flooding cycle stimulates oxbow bass to go on a feeding binge as waters recede to normal levels. The feeding binge puts them in excellent spawning condition, and because of the fertility of river oxbows, heavy spawns usually follow each winter/spring flooding cycle. Spawning still occurs in years of drought, when flooding is absent, but it doesn't happen with the gusto that characterizes post-flood spawns.

For many oxbow anglers, beauty is the primary drawing card. If they catch a few bass while visiting these scenic honeyholes, so much the better.

Oxbow Types

Mastering oxbow bass fishing requires knowledge of the types of oxbow lakes. Some oxbows remain connected to the parent stream; some do not. Some lie within the floodplain of major streams, while others lie outside the floodplain. Differing conditions on each type of oxbow dictate the manner and amount of planning necessary to enjoy a productive bass fishing trip.

Oxbows that remain connected to the main river normally provide the best fishing for big bass. When the river floods the oxbow, inflowing nutrients enrich the water and help sustain thriving communities of forage animals on which bass feed. This yearly overflow cycle also provides temporary, but important, spawning habitat for oxbow bass.

Unfortunately, severe water level fluctuations also make river-connected oxbows the trickiest to fish. When the river rises, the lake rises. When

the river falls, the lake falls. Changing water conditions dramatically affect fishing, and anglers must monitor water levels closely to pick the most productive days.

There are no hard-and-fast rules for fishing river-connected oxbows; fish are caught under all conditions. But as a general rule, bass seldom bite when the water is on a fast rise. Fishing runout areas—the cuts connecting oxbow and river—can be outstanding during a fast fall. But the best fishing on these oxbows is usually when the water level is steady or slowly rising or falling.

On river-connected oxbows, bass anglers should also know the depth at which the river moves in and out of the oxbow being fished. This information is usually available at local baitshops or from area anglers, and once you know it, you can monitor the river level in local newspapers to plan a trip during peak fishing periods. When the river is entirely out of the oxbow, fishing conditions are likely to be more stable and predictable. When the river overflows into the oxbow, anglers must know the intensity of water level fluctuations—fast rise, slow fall, etc.—to determine the best bass fishing days.

Many oxbows are no longer connected to the river proper but still lie within the stream floodplain. These lakes are subject to flooding and rapidly changing water levels during wet

Though most oxbow lakes are small with poor access, some provide means by which larger bass boats may be launched, if you are willing to fish with only a trolling motor for propulsion.

Oxbow Tackle

The tackle best applied to oxbow bassing varies considerably from the standards of big-lake anglers. Most oxbow anglers prefer bait-casting rigs with shorter rods; about 5-1/2 feet is generally the best length, because of the cramped quarters of the boat and the tight, brushy fishing conditions. You don't need big heavy tackle boxes, either. Take a small tackle box with a dozen 1/4- to 1/2-ounce spinnerbaits, an assortment of 6- to 8-inch plastic worms, a couple of chartreuse or crawfish-colored crankbaits, and two or three of your favorite surface lures. If you can drive close to the bank, you may want to haul a trolling motor, but if you face a longer haul into the lake, take a short sculling paddle instead.

The lighter the boat, the better it's suited for this type of fishing. I prefer lightweight 10- or 12-foot johnboats, but canoes, inflatables and belly boats work well, too.

Many bass anglers know the "Coal Pile," an oxbow on the lower Arkansas River in Arkansas, known for producing trophy largemouths. This oxbow hotspot has long been a favorite of tournament pros fishing this huge river.

months, and here again, bass fishermen should scrutinize water fluctuations when planning a visit.

Some oxbows lie outside the river floodplain, isolated by levees or dams. These lakes usually provide the most predictable fishing opportunities, since water fluctuations are less dramatic and have less influence on overall fishing conditions.

Finding Oxbow bass

Finding oxbow bass isn't unusually complicated. Work all available cover carefully, probing every nook and cranny in the brush and every likely log and cypress tree, changing baits and presentations until you find what works best.

One thing to remember is that even though most oxbows are relatively flat and of uniform depth, the outside bend of the lake is usually somewhat deeper than the inside bend. This is important when water temperature rises above the bass's 70 to 75 degree comfort range. When this happens, bass concentrate on the deeper side of the lake where the temperature is more to their liking.

When bass are shallow, they relate to some sort of cover. Cypress trees skirt the banks of many oxbows, and working crankbaits, spinnerbaits or plastic worms around their broad bases and knees is a good way to catch bass. Buckbrush and willows are also common on oxbows, and many bass are caught in the thickest of such cover available. Other prime fishing spots include fallen trees, beaver lodges, sunken Christmas tree shelters, lily pads, shoreline riprap, stump fields and boat docks.

If you're on an oxbow when flood waters are receding, try fishing around run-out chutes between oxbow and river. These attract fish with the promise of an easy meal. Look for areas where out-flowing water is

Mississippi River Oxbows

Superb bass fishing is available in many oxbow lakes along the lower Mississippi River:
- Kentucky: Swan and Long lakes near Paducah
- Tennessee: Everett's Lake west of Dyersburg, Chisolm Lake west of Ripley, Hathright Pocket and Crutcher Lake west of Henning
- Arkansas: Island 40 Chute and Dacus Lake near West Memphis, Midway Lake south of Hughes, Old Town Lake at Wabash, Lake Chicot at Lake Village

- Mississippi: Tunica Cutoff at Tunica, Lake Whittington at Benoit, Lake Ferguson at Greenville, Albermarle Lake at Fitler, Eagle Lake west of Redwood, Lake Mary north of Ft. Adams
- Louisiana: Lake St. Joseph at Newellton, Lake Concordia at Ferriday, Old River Lake at Innis, False River Lake at New Roads

Other states have oxbow largemouth havens as well. Your state fisheries agency is a good source for information.

constricted—like sloughs and natural cuts—then work a lure around surrounding woody cover. Key your efforts to periods when water is falling three to six inches a day; a faster fall makes it hard to locate fish.

One final note: when you're considering where to go, think small. Although some oxbows cover several thousand acres, the real jewels are much smaller. It's harder to pinpoint bass on the larger oxbows, and fishing them isn't much different than fishing the nearest Corps of Engineers mega-lake.

For the true oxbow experience, visit small lakes off the beaten path. It's not uncommon to fish all day on one of these little oxbows and never see another boat. The scenery is splendid, and when the bass are biting, there's only one way to describe it — heaven on earth.

Understanding oxbow lakes and how to fish them will add a whole new dimension to your fishing. The facts presented here should help you get off to a good start, so you, too, can enjoy the magic and majesty of these blue-ribbon bass lakes.

This scene is reminiscent of many oxbow bass fishing excursions—two buddies in a small johnboat fishing a lake of magnificent beauty far from the madding crowds.

Crankbaits: Choose the Right One

By Keith Sutton

Crankbaits are available in hundreds of different styles, sizes, colors and actions. This presents a dilemma for anglers who use crankbaits when fishing for bass. How do you select the lure that will catch the most fish? Are there certain conditions when one crankbait is preferred over another? When are big crankbaits more appropriate? Small ones? How does one choose the best color from the astounding variety available? Is a floating bait best or one that dives deep? Should I crank it fast or slow?

There are no pat answers to any of these questions. But don't fret. Help is available. One of America's premier crankbait experts has developed a list of crankbait characteristics that can help you cope with "crankbait confusion." Understanding these characteristics can greatly improve your fishing success.

Joe Hughes, of Fort Smith, Arkansas, is known in fishing circles as "The Doctor of Diving Plugs." He has spent many days working with lure designers and fishing with professionals to exchange ideas useful in product development. His knowledge of crankbaits and crankbait fishing is unexcelled in the world of angling.

Hughes has developed a list of crankbait characteristics that can help put more fish in your boat.

"The versatility a crankbait has, the way you can use it to catch a lot of different types of fish under many different situations, is based upon some of its characteristics," Hughes says. "I sat down one day and tried to make sense of what allowed these baits to perform under various conditions. The word 'characteristic' kept popping up. It has a characteristic of sinking, a characteristic of high buoyancy, a characteristic of the depth it attains. I put these on paper and came up with nine basic characteristics."

The first characteristic is depth. "Depth is where the fish are," Hughes says. "You must select a lure that works at the depth the fish are to be a successful crankbait angler."

Hughes says many anglers are misled into thinking crankbaits can work deeper than they actually will. "You have to take time to determine what depth a crankbait will run, or at least trust the information you're given by the manufacturer," he says. "The best thing to do is to go out and determine how deep the bait runs on the length of cast you make, the size line you use, and how fast a reel you own. Typically, if you work a deep-diving crankbait with your rod pointed down into the

Spotted, or Kentucky, bass are suckers for crankbaits placed in their strike zones.

water, the bait will run deeper with longer casts, lighter line and slow retrieves. Do everything you can to allow the bait to attain its maximum depth."

To select a bait that runs at the proper depth, anglers must first know the depth where fish are likely to be holding. "When people go to a marina for fishing information, they tend to ask, What are they biting?" says Hughes. "That's the wrong question. The question to ask is, How deep are they? That's the first thing you need to know. If you trust the information you're given, you know exactly what ball park you're in, as far as selecting a lure."

The second crankbait characteristic, speed, is closely tied to depth. "Speed affects depth," Hughes says. "That's why it's important to look on your reel to determine its speed. Some reels are slower, like 3.8 to 1 (line circles the spool 3.8 times for every return of the reel handle). Others are high-speed reels with a 7 to 1 ratio. Others fall in between the extremes. The way these reels affect the depth a bait swims is based on the fact that most people turn the handle about the same speed. So the reel takes over for them. To get the bait to its maximum depth, visually appraise its action in the water. When you see the lure giving a good action, that's the speed you want to crank it. Once you get it down there, you can speed it up, stop and start it, but first look at the bait in the water to see how to best retrieve it."

Action is another important crankbait characteristic. "Action relates to two different areas," says Hughes. "First, action is the action the bait has—the side to side action, the wobble. The other action is what you do from a mental standpoint with the lure, like fishing a topwater for instance. You twist and jerk and think about how to get the fish to hit on top. If you take this same mental involvement you have with a topwater plug and use it in plugs that work down out of sight, you'll enhance your productivity. A steady retrieve only catches fish about 10 percent of the time. Other times, the things you do to provide erratic action to the lure mean the difference in catching fish and not catching fish. Put the same effort into running a deep-diving crankbait you would with a topwater."

Characteristic number four is buoyancy. This determines whether a

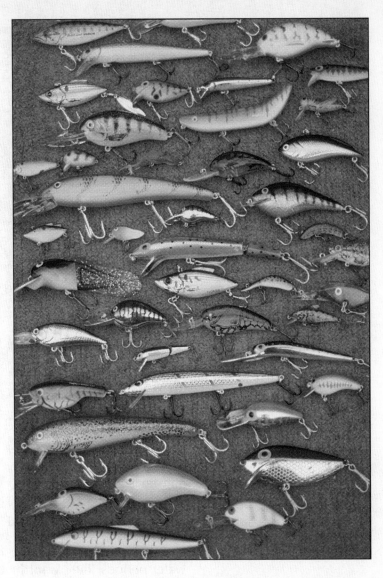

Crankbaits are available in hundreds, perhaps thousands, of style/color/size/action combinations. To avoid "crankbait" confusion, anglers must understand the characteristics of each lure, and how those characteristics can be applied in particular fishing situations.

Size is one characteristic of crankbaits. According to "The doctor of Diving Plugs," Joe Hughes, big bass often strike tiny crankbaits, despite popular misconceptions.

bait floats (positive buoyancy), sinks (negative buoyancy) or suspends (neutral buoyancy).

"Buoyancy is something professional anglers are very attuned to," Hughes says. "When fishing heavy cover, they want baits that back up and float and have a degree of buoyancy. When fishing during cool-water periods, they want baits that can be stopped without popping back to the surface, baits that stay where they are, suspended. Negative buoyancy baits like vibrating, lipless crankbaits allow you to fish all depths. You can fish them on bottom, near the top or in between. Be attuned to buoyancy to know which baits to select for certain fishing conditions."

Color is the characteristic anglers probably give the most consideration when selecting a crankbait. "Color, as a characteristic of fishing lures, got a great boost from research conducted by Dr. Loren Hill," says Hughes. "There are colors anglers find very productive that most would never have tied on had it not been for the impact of Dr. Hill's Color-C-Lector. The color gray, for instance, is a color that doesn't sell well. But, it's a great fish catcher. Gray, according to Loren's research, was the number one color overall. It wasn't always the most visible to bass, but it was always up there, the second or third or fourth most visible color under a tremendous number of conditions. The fact that gray catches fish makes sense when you consider that most forage fish are some shade of gray."

According to Hill's research, red is also a top color, a fact borne out by angler response to certain lures. "Red signifies blood or circulation," says Hughes, "Like something that can be easily captured because it's injured. Red has reproductive connotations, too. To show how important it is to anglers, consider this example. Several years ago, someone at PRADCO said, look, if we don't paint these little red mouths on our Rebel minnows, we can save a lot of money. So we quit doing it. The consumers went out of their skulls! We got dozens of letters saying, 'What happened to the red mouth? These baits don't produce as well.' So we went back to putting red on our lures. You'll notice that many lures have a red gill, throat or belly. It's not there for decoration, it's there because fishermen said the baits don't work as well without it."

Crankbaits can be categorized according to the depth at which they work, such as this group of medium-diving crankbaits.

Black also ranks high on the color list. "Black rates high, because it's a predominant color at night," Hughes says. "It has strong applications in clear and stained water as well. As far as other strong colors, Loren's research says fluorescent colors tend to give you more visibility than regular colors of the same hue in all kinds of water."

Tips for Fishing Lipless Crankbaits

There are few bass lures that offer the versatility of lipless crankbaits, such as the Bill Lewis Rat-L-Trap and Cordell Spot. Anglers are able to use them at all depths, in muddy water and clear, during all seasons and in almost any cover. Without changing lures, you can jig over deep-water humps, count down to bass suspended by bridge pilings, or buzz across the top of a weedbed. Best of all is their simplicity; anyone can fish these lures.

Lipless crankbaits come in floating and sinking models, and are available in sizes that range from tiny (1/10 ounce) to large (over 1 ounce). Each has a line-tie eye on the back, which makes the lure run with its head angled down. Water pressure on the flat forehead produces a convulsive shimmy that resembles a small baitfish zipping through the water. Bass find this action irresistible. Most models contain rattles that add the additional enticement of sound.

Tips for fishing lipless crankbait,
1. For the best action, attach lipless crankbaits with loop knots. Never use snap swivels or heavy leaders.
2. Use a soft-tipped rod to better feel the vibration of the lure in the tip, and calibrate your retrieval speed to get the heaviest vibration and loudest rattle possible.
3. Use light lines (4- to 8-pound-test) for the smallest lipless crankbaits (less than 1/4 ounce), 10- to 12-pound-test line for 1/4-ounce lures, 12- to 15-pound for 1/2-ounce models, and up to 20 for 3/4- to 1-ounce versions.
4. Small hooks on some lipless crankbaits cause lost fish. If necessary, change to a larger hook size to overcome this problem.
5. When fishing debris-strewn bottoms, clip off one or both of the downward-turned trebles on the hooks. You'll still hook plenty of fish but avoid many snags.

Understanding crankbait characteristics and applying those characteristics to various fishing situations can help anglers catch more black bass.

Hughes' thoughts on size, the sixth characteristic, also offer new insights for crankbait anglers. Though many of us were taught that catching big fish requires big lures, Hughes says it ain't necessarily so.

"If you use a big lure, all you'll catch is a big fish," he continues. "But big fish are just as likely to hit a small bait as a big one, if it's presented at the proper depth, the right speed, the right color, if you do the right things, as far as action is concerned. Get into the smaller bait philosophy, and you can say, I'm fishing for every predator fish in this body of water. You'll have a lot more fun."

Shape is less important than most other characteristics. "Shape is basically a way to match the hatch," Hughes says. "If you fish where crawfish are the primary forage animals, use a bait resembling a crawfish. If you're fishing where there are lots of shad, use a shad- or minnow-type lure. Still, this is probably the one characteristic where you can arbitrarily make a choice and not hurt your fishing success. If you're at the right depth and use the right speed, action and color, then, other than in some clear-water situations, shape may not be terribly important."

Sound and vibration are the eighth characteristic of crankbaits. This is an area where Hughes expects to see many new innovations.

"Sound hasn't been exploited to the maximum by lure manufacturers," says Hughes. "Still, there is definitely something important about sound. A predator fish will make the final decision on what he eats according to what he sees, even in muddy water. He'll either accept or reject your lure based on what he sees. But sound could be the enticement that gets him to look."

Hughes included scent as the final characteristic on his list. "Scent is a minimal characteristic in reference to most crankbaits," he says. "If you're working the lure properly, fish will likely strike it before they smell it. Once they taste it, they're hooked."

Lipless crankbaits, often called vibrators, are dynamite bass lures when fished correctly.

Human scent may have a negative effect, however, especially on slow-moving or suspending lures. "You can eliminate this with a shot of the 'real' scents," Hughes says, "scents like Real Craw or Real Baitfish that are extracts of the forage you're trying to duplicate."

Hughes notes that developing his list of nine crankbait characteristics wasn't done without a lot of thought and research. "It was a process of probably nine or ten years of fishing the products we make and trying to learn more about them." he says. "I can't just walk up to someone and say, 'This great fishing lure catches fish.' People want to know how it catches fish. The depth it runs, the size and shape and all those other things are important characteristics. So it was an educational evolution, if you will."

The vast array of crankbaits on today's market can leave you bewildered. But when you buy crankbaits, when you fish with them, take Joe Hughes' list of crankbait characteristics and give them some thought. You'll find you've put an end to crankbait confusion. Employ the nine characteristics of crankbaits as part of your angling game plan, and it's a sure bet your fishing will improve.

Can't Miss Prop Bait Tips

1. Cast a prop bait and start reeling it back, with props spinning, the instant it touches the water. Get the reel in gear and start cranking fast just as the lure settles. Bass see what looks like a struggling baitfish.
2. Where bass cover is dense, cast to the cover's edge, and let the lure sit until all ripples subside. Twitch it just enough to rotate the props a time or two. If no strike comes, start a steady retrieve. The idea is to get the bass' attention so it will swim over for a look. Once it does, you want to make the lure appear as if it has seen the fish and is trying to escape.
3. Another variation is to retrieve the lure with a series of wiggles and jerks. This type of retrieve can be combined with the same "walk the dog" rhythm used with stick baits.
4. Many bassers overlook prop baits when fishing rivers, but the effectiveness of these lures increases where heavily oxygenated water and current keep bass active.

The Lost Art of Doodlesocking

By Charles Bridwell

Modern bass anglers have some preconceived notions about the best way to hook, fight and land a lunker bass. Some feel they need a specialized boat, the latest gear, most expensive tackle, and a suitcase full of lures to be effective. While technology has provided us with marvelous electronic equipment, amazingly powerful and stable boats, and an unbelievable assortment of rods, reels and lures, catching bass still boils down to one very basic element—getting the fish to strike. Modern anglers flip, pitch, skip or otherwise cast lures in hopes of drawing the attention of bass, but all these techniques have one major drawback—the lure is tossed into a good spot, then it's retrieved.

Wouldn't it be better to put the lure in a good spot close to cover where a bass is likely to hide and make it dance and sputter long enough to arouse the fish's predatory instinct? Back in the 1800s, such a method came to be known as doodlesocking. It remains one of the best ways to catch a bass and is so effective it is banned in many bass tournaments. Out of vogue, it may be in danger of becoming a lost form of angling.

No one is certain how or when doodlesocking came into existence. Variations of doodlesocking have probably been practiced since man first picked up a pole and used it to place a lure in front of a fish. In

Fish should be brought alongside the boat by extending the pole behind the angler in a hand-over-hand motion.

fact, there remains some disagreement even today about the term and the technique it describes. Similar techniques, called dabbling and jigger-doodling, use an up-and-down jigging motion and can be effective, but they're not to be confused with doodlesocking.

In its pure form, doodlesocking is extremely simple. It can be done from a boat, the bank, or while wading. The essential tackle is a stout pole, a short length of heavy line and some sort of lure. The only other gear needed for doodlesocking is a good stringer and a skillet, for this isn't a tournament sport; it's a technique developed by hungry men with limited equipment.

A long pole like this 16-footer will reach far back into cover, but can cause fatigue. Note that the angler is supporting the butt of the pole under his forearm and elbow to compensate.

The first item of business for the aspiring doodlesocker is to acquire a pole. It could be a cane pole cut green from a bamboo grove or purchased in a bait shop. Good results can also be had using a stout fiberglass pole. Avoid thin, whippy poles that don't have the strength to handle the task. Some anglers favor a pole as short as eight feet. Others may select one twice that long. Choose a pole that can be handled comfortably for long periods.

Tie a length of stout fishing line securely to the pole's tip, then leave a couple of feet of line onto which the lure will be tied. Some prefer the lure to be only six or eight inches from the pole's tip, but a foot or two is probably the average. Use monofilament or braided line of at least 20-pound test and there will be less likelihood of losing a good fish.

With pole and line ready, the final task is to decide on a lure. The time-tested favorite is a topwater lure that makes noise. Chuggers, like the Lucky 13 and Pop-R, will work fine. Also good are propeller baits like the Devil's Horse and Tiny Torpedo. Luhr Jensen's Jerk-N-Sam has a fine darting motion and makes a gurgling splash bass find irresistible. Even the "cigar" baits like the Zara Spook and Puppy give good results when used properly.

The object is not to plop a lure down quietly and make it twitch. Instead, it should be worked with vigorous jerks and pops that will alert any bass in the area to the presence of a potential meal. The lure should be bumped into trees, stumps, rocks and other structure. Make furious figure eights and circles, or try jerking quickly one way and then the other to create a frantic zigzag motion with the lure. One unusual technique that can produce good results is to tap the water vigorously with the pole's tip ahead of the lure. This creates an illusion that the lure is

Even battle-scarred lures like this worn Jerk-N-Sam by Luhr Jensen produce good results.

chasing something.

Doodlesocking isn't so much a style of presentation as it is a form of commotion. It's a disruption in the scheme of nature, and it signals bass to investigate. Generally, the most aggressive and largest bass are the ones that will be attracted to strike. Some believe doodlesocking makes bass mad and that they strike in anger.

When a bass takes the lure, it may make a hole in the water that looks like someone flushed a toilet. Or, it may simply suck the lure under with little warning. Normally, the strikes are aggressive and heart-stopping.

It's not unusual for a bass to miss the lure. It's moving rapidly and, even though they're efficient predators, bass sometimes have a hard time homing in and inhaling the lure on the first try. The good news is that, once enticed to attack, it's not unusual for a bass to hit repeatedly, slashing at the lure three or more times in quick succession.

The angler must be aware of this trait and use it to his advantage. It takes some practice to avoid jerking the lure away from the fish. The angler must steel his nerves and wait until the fish is felt pulling before the hook is set. Once the fish is hooked, the angler should pull the pole toward him, hand over hand, until the fish is alongside, where it can be netted or lipped. The pole must be arched some to allow the bow of the rod to fight the fish, with the handle of the pole going well behind the angler.

The beauty of doodlesocking, aside from its inherent simplicity, is that it allows the angler to whip the water to a froth in a very small area that likely holds a bass. Heavy cover is transformed from a place to avoid into a spot to try one's luck. A small hole in a patch of weed, moss, or lily pads can be easily fished, even if the opening is no larger than a washtub. Rock piles, logjams, and boat docks can be effectively probed.

A stealthy approach is important, but not as much as one might think. Anglers know they can get fairly close to bass and catch them by flipping jigs into cover, and the same holds true for doodlesocking. In fact, with a pole of medium length, say 10-12 feet, anglers can easily approach close enough to catch bass without spooking them. As with any other approach, water clarity and sunlight may be factors to be considered.

One disadvantage of doodlesocking is that it can be somewhat tiring. By choosing a pole they can easily handle and by taking turns with a buddy, anglers can reduce fatigue. One trick is to grasp the pole about two feet above the end and allow the butt of the pole to extend under the forearm to the elbow. This greatly increases leverage and reduces fatigue.

Although doodlesocking is traditionally done on the water's surface, it's a mistake to limit lures only to topwater plugs. A buzzbait or other spinners can be run in maddening circles above a bass and elicit some savage strikes. For variety, try sub-surface lures. Diving lipped baits works well, as do worms, grubs, jigs, and other lures.

Almost any waters can be fished by the doodlesocking method, but it is traditionally reserved for quiet backwaters, slow-moving rivers, streams, and farm ponds. The key is to find areas where fish are feeding on or near the surface.

One advantage of doodlesocking is that it allows coverage of every inch of the bank. In shallow oxbows lined with cypress, anglers can move slowly along and work their lures around every tree, limb, stump and cypress knee. In farm ponds, bass can often be found near shoreline cover, along weeds or holding near fallen trees. Anglers can approach quietly from the bank in many waters, but may be better off in a small aluminum boat, if conditions are not too windy.

The good news about doodlesocking is that it's a sport almost anyone can enjoy, and it works for many species of game fish. It costs almost nothing to get started, but it can be as addictive as any drug habit. It may be outlawed for tournament professionals and even scorned by elitist anglers, but it's a great way to spend a day on the water and one of the oldest, most productive techniques for bass fishing known to man.

Anglers can fish a lure completely around cover like this with the doodlesocking method.

How To Analyze A Fishing Hole

By Vernon Summerlin

"Catching bass is simple," says Bill Dance. "Know what bass like and find it on the lake." This axiom is simple, but applying it proves to be difficult, because bass are a puzzle.

PIECES OF THE PUZZLE

With enough pieces of information, you can put a picture together of daily bass behavioral patterns so you will have a good day of fishing. Where bass are holding, what baits they want, how they want them presented, weather conditions and water conditions, are essential pieces of the mystery. Let's start with ten important pieces of the puzzle that help you locate bass.

1. Structure and cover mean different things, but many anglers use them interchangeably. To avoid confusion, follow these definitions.

Bridges, submerged or not, span a depression, usually have riprap and roadbeds associated with them, and provide bass with cover and food.

Structure is the bottom, be it a point, hump, or flat. Simply put, it is the shape of the bottom.

Cover refers to all the other things that may be in the water, including tires, logs, weeds, trees, docks, bridges, brush piles, and so on. Cover refers to anything that a bass can hide in, next to, or under.

2. Active bass are in a feeding mood and willing to strike. Bass are active when they are migrating and holding along their migration route. **Inactive,** or neutral, bass are not in a feeding mood but can be tricked into striking your bait. They are usually inactive when in their sanctuary.

3. Sanctuary is a safe place in deep water where bass rest. Bass may find sanctuary in heavy cover in shallow water.

4. Migration route is the path bass take when they move from their sanctuary to shallow water and back. Bass are said to be migrating when moving along this route.

5. A **contact point** is a place where migrating bass encounter different structure or cover away from their sanctuary and may pause there before moving again. These contact points are also like road signs to bass.

6. A **break** is an abrupt, horizontal or vertical change in otherwise constant stretches of bottom, or structure. On a topographical map, it is the interruption of the smooth flow of contour lines. A contact point is usually on a **breakline,** which is a break in an orderly pattern. Breaks in the breakline are thought to be the best places to hold larger bass.

Breaklines may also occur where dissimilar features or conditions meet, such as where a straight rock formation changes direction, where clear water meets dingy water, where a weedline begins, and where there is a change in temperature. Where these and other dissimilar features or conditions meet, there is an edge.

7. **Edges** are breaks, and bass love edges and their transition zones. The **transition zone** is the area between the meeting of distinct features or conditions. These zones may be sharp or diffuse. Differences in temperature, light and dark, pH, dissolved oxygen, where gravel meets sand, where water meets aquatic plants and where swift meets slack current are a few examples where edges and transition zones form.

9. The end of the migration route is the **scatter point**, where bass separate into smaller groups or individuals to go about their business in the shallows.

Once you locate bass and their migration routes, with experience you can predict their movements when conditions change.

10. **Weather** is often a strong factor influencing bass behavior. Conditions can change drastically with the passage of a weather front, especially in the spring. A weather front is the line between two air masses, usually a cold one meeting a warm one. Warm, moist air is ahead of the front with cold, dry air behind it. The barometric pressure is lower ahead of the front, and bass are active. A change in the wind direction lets you know the front has reached you.

After the passage, the barometric pressure rises, the sky clears, but humidity and temperatures usually drop. Bass become inactive and bury themselves in cover after the frontal passage.

Don't overlook docks, piers, and boat houses that have vertical and horizontal cover. These structures, particularly when located near deep water, are often more attractive to bass.

Waterfalls are especially cool areas to fish in summer, but they draw bass year-round due to well-oxygenated waters and an abundant food source.

Active bass will be over cover or structure looking for forage. Less active fish may suspend or concentrate along breaklines or be close to or in cover.

Putting these and other puzzle pieces together (various conditions and features) gives you a picture of where bass are likely to be.

U.S. FISHING WATERS

Depending on where you live, your black bass angling takes place in rivers, natural lakes, or manmade reservoirs. Each one is different. Geographic location, shape of the basin, and water fertility are three factors that determine a lake or reservoir type.

Northern waters are cooler and experience severe winters, limiting the growing season of bass, and favor the smallmouth bass. Warmer southern waters usually favor the largemouth, except in highland areas such as in the Appalachians, Ouachitas, and Cumberlands, where the smallmouth tends to dominate. Waters impounded in the western mountains are cool-to-cold water and are more suited to trout than bass. Western coastal states have a variety of reservoir types, from flatland to canyon. Lake Castaic, a canyon reservoir in southern California, favors world-class Florida-strain largemouth bass weighing greater than 20 pounds.

NATURAL LAKES

Natural lakes fit into three categories, based on water fertility: eutrophic, mesotrophic, or oligotrophic.

Eutrophic lakes are fertile, and are old lakes, usually shallow, favoring plant life. They range from the Atlantic Ocean to the Rocky Mountains, from the third tier of states from the Canadian border south through Florida and Texas. Their surrounding soils are nutrient-rich, supplying nitrogen, phosphorus, and other nutrients ordinarily found in agricultural areas. Eutrophic lakes are well suited for black bass, with the largemouth bass usually dominant.

Mesotrophic lakes have medium fertility. Most of these lakes range from New England to the Dakotas. Coolwater species dominate these

middle-aged waters. Smallmouths tend to succeed better than large-mouths in these lakes.

Oligotrophic lakes have few nutrients. Most oligotrophic lakes are located on the Canadian Shield, a rock-bound area that extends throughout eastern Canada and the first tier of states from Maine to Minnesota. Smallmouths tend to persist in these waters.

RIVERS

Rivers support largemouth, smallmouth and spotted bass, and usually offer distinct habitats for bass. Few free-flowing rivers exist today; most are dammed and manipulate current.

The main channel usually has current with a bottom of rock, sand, or silt. The sides of the channels may have wing dams of rock, like those found along the Mississippi River. They force the current toward mid-stream to keep sediment from settling, and offer good habitat for bass in the slack current behind the rock piles. Smallmouths and spots are likely to hold here.

Backwater areas consist of cuts, side channels and sloughs that appeal more to the largemouth bass because of the calm-to-moderate current. Backwater sloughs with no

Currents, even those caused by wind, sweep food along banks and over points. The stained streaks show the areas likely to hold active bass.

Bass love transition zones. Where the dirt bank meets the rocks is a bass hot spot, but the abandoned barge in the same area makes it even more inviting to bass.

Bass move into flooded areas to take advantage of different foods that can be found there.

current often have muck bottoms, and may have vegetation, another largemouth predilection.

Dammed rivers' swiftest waters are in their tailraces. The bottoms are usually scoure ,leaving only rock. Gravel, sand, and silt are deposited, in that order, at the edges of the current and downstream as the current slows.

Largemouths may hold close to the current in eddies and slack water, whereas smallmouths and spots will hold at the edge of current and in the current behind a current break, such as a boulder.

RESERVOIRS

Much like natural lakes, manmade reservoirs range from fertile to nutrient-poor. It is the shape of their basins that lend themselves to classification. The more fertile reservoirs are typically flatland reservoirs. Hilland and highland reservoirs are moderately fertile. Canyon reservoirs are nutrient-poor.

Flatland reservoirs are among the shallowest of reservoir types, reaching about 50 feet deep near the dam. Many manmade features are found submerged in flatland reservoirs, such as roadbeds, bridges, railroad beds, house foundations, ponds, and many more features that

Underwater Features

Lake features are varied, be it structure or cover. Some structures are associated with the shoreline, while others are offshore and isolated. Both onshore and offshore features may be capable of providing food, sanctuary and spawning areas for bass. Bass living on offshore features may have never seen a lure.

Some features are obvious, while others will require a topo map and sonar to locate. If you mark or outline features with marker buoys, it will help you fish the feature more effectively.

The three most bass-favored features:
- FLATS, submerged flood plains, figure prominently as bass habitat because logs, aquatic plants, and debris accumulate on them, and they provide spawning areas.
- POINTS are easy to see and probably the most-often fished feature in a lake. They are one of the best places to locate fish because they are often part of migration routes.
- HUMPS are large bumps on the bottom. Doug Hannon says bass prefer structure with a large surface area. Humps offer sides and top as surface area. They attract bigger bass because there is more food available in one area.

A few of the best manmade structures are roadbeds, bridges, and docks. Roads and old railroad beds are excellent features for holding bass. Bass use them for spawning and migration routes. These features normally have deeper water in the form of ditches beside them. Bass like to be near deeper water, even if it's only a foot or two.

Bridges are hot spots because vertical shapes meet a sloping bottom. These sites also attract baitfish because rubble and riprap usually accompany a bridge.

Docks, marinas, and boat slips provide excellent bass habitat. These manmade structures have cover, shade, vertical pilings, or other objects that accommodate the base of the food chain. Owners often enhance their docks by adding brush piles. What could be better? Being near deep water would make it perfect.

Flooded bushes frequently attract bass to dine on worms, insects, and other food items trapped there.

Warm-water discharge canals are "must fish" places in winter because they attract baitfish and predators alike.

remain after the area was flooded. The shoreline has few, if any, steep bluffs, many large flats, and broad, gentle sloping points, coves, and submerged feeder creek junctions, usually far from the shoreline, because the main channel doesn't run close to shore. These are the best reservoirs for largemouth bass.

Examples of flatland reservoirs are Kentucky Lake in Kentucky and Tennessee, Ross Barnett in Mississippi, and Lake Toho in Florida.

Hill-land reservoirs are deeper near their dams, from 50 to 180 feet, and contain many of the same submerged features as the flatland reservoirs. They may have some steep bluffs, many rounded points, flats, coves, and the main channel rarely comes close to the shoreline. You will usually find about a 50-50 mix of largemouths and smallmouths in these reservoirs.

Examples of hill-land reservoirs are Toledo Bend in Texas, Kinzua in Pennsylvania and Shelbyville in Illinois.

Highland reservoirs range from 60 to 200 feet deep at their dams and contain about the same submerged features as the previous reservoir types. Points are steeper and less round, fewer flats, more steep bluffs, coves are steeper and longer, and the main channel often runs close to the shoreline. Smallmouths are more prevalent than largemouths.

Migrant Bass vs Homebody Bass

It's commonly thought bass relate to structure, but does that make it true? Bass that remain near structure and ambush prey from hiding places are home range, or territorial bass. They spend most of their lives within a hundred-yard area.

Studies show, however, that there is a small population of migrant bass in some lakes that doesn't relate to structure but to depth and forage instead. These bass move with baitfish and don't seem to pay any attention to the bottom, shorelines or breaklines. They don't hide and ambush prey; they follow baitfish and eat when the opportunity is right.

Bass tagged with radio transmitters show that some home range bass move farther than others but they tend to stay in a range they define for themselves. They are more predictable and easier to catch.

Home range bass often rest in a deep-water sanctuary or in heavy cover in the shallows. They migrate to feed. Breaks and contact points are the signposts that bass have learned to read like road signs along their migration routes.

Sometimes they move for the fun of it, sort of like taking a stroll. These are active bass, and active bass are likely to strike your bait.

After a period of time in the shallows, they begin moving back to their deep-water home. They may use the same route or a different one but they follow established routes.

Examples of the highland reservoirs are Broken Bow in Oklahoma, Sidney Lanier in Georgia and Bull Shoals in Arkansas and Missouri.

Canyon reservoirs may be 600 feet deep at the dam with few of the submerged features found in the previously-mentioned reservoir types. These are mostly rocky impoundments along steep, deep river canyons in the West. This type of reservoir has many sheer walls, very long feeder rivers and creeks, is narrow along the main channel that may run close to the shoreline, but has no significant flats. These reservoirs are poor habitat for black bass, even the smallmouth.

Examples of canyon reservoirs are Mead in Nevada and Arizona, Powell in Utah and Flaming Gorge in Wyoming and Utah.

Plateau reservoirs range from 50 to 200 feet deep at their dams, but do not contain many of the submerged features. The steepness and roundness of points varies widely among these reservoirs. Shorelines in deep coves are generally steep, may have aquatic plants in upper regions, and the main channel has few meanders and does not run close to the shoreline. Most reservoirs of this type are in the western USA and offer only borderline habitat for smallmouth bass.

Examples of plateau reservoirs are Clear in California, Peck in Montana, and Roosevelt in Arizona.

No place is better for bass than vegetation; it's their number one hangout. It provides cover for bass and various links of the food chain are also present.

Scratching the Surface
By Alan Clemons

Maybe no greater thrill exists than to experience the heart-stopping explosion of a scrappy largemouth, smallmouth, or spotted bass blasting a topwater lure before trying to escape with it.

It can happen on a peaceful morning with water smooth as glass or on a windy day when the lure appears to be surfing on the chop. From around visible shoreline cover such as downed treetops, submerged cover such as stumps or brush piles, and over deep humps or in shallow water with vegetation, nothing else compares to catching a bass on topwater baits.

The varieties of topwater lures seem endless, but there are a few distinct differences. Buzzbaits have at least one cupped propeller blade that turns when retrieved. Chuggers, or spitters, have a concave face that spits water with a sharp snap of the rod tip. Prop baits are fat cigar-shaped hard baits with noisy propellers on one or both ends. Slim prop baits such as the Smithwick Devil's Horse do the same but offer a smaller profile.

Some anglers also use stickbaits, such as the legendary Rapala minnow, and retrieve them slowly to create a tantalizing wake. Stickbaits can be retrieved with a snap of the rod tip to stay within 6-8 inches of the surface before suspending or floating back to the top. Soft plastics such as the Slug-Go, Zoom Super Fluke and floating worm can be rigged weedless and worked on top.

Topwater lures come in all shapes and sizes. In late spring a 1/8- or 1/4-ounce buzzbait can be deadly around shoreline cover. At night, a

You're going to get snagged fishing around thick cover, but that's where the bass like to hide.

Jitterbug may be the ticket. When bass are deep and need a wake-up call, a massive Luhr-Jensen Woodchopper may be what you need.

Bass will hit topwater lures year-round and all day long. Don't believe it if someone says they won't. Bass are opportunistic feeders, taking advantage of the easiest meal they can get. During the doggiest days of summer in the South, a big dog-walking lure such as an Excalibur Super Spook will call them up. In the waning days of winter up north, even with ice ringing the shoreline, smaller chuggers cast on the ice and worked off the edge may yield surprising results.

Quite possibly, there's no better time to fish topwater lures than during the spawn and postspawn periods. That varies throughout the country, although the major spawn occurs in spring from late February through May. In Florida, it's much earlier—late November through January—and in the extreme northern states it may be as late as May and June.

Bass protecting their beds and then feeding on baitfish following the spawn offer great opportunities to catch consistent numbers. They may hit large lures with noisy retrieves or smaller versions with a subtle action. Begin with the downsized lures—a Storm Chug Bug, Strike King Spit'n King, Excalibur Pop'n Image, Rebel P60 Pop-R—and increase the size according to the fish's reactions as the forage grows.

Pro angler Zell Rowland of Texas is widely known for his love of topwater lures, primarily the Pop-R. His use of them in the late 1980s on the tournament circuits provided a resurgence in topwater hard baits, which had for some reason fallen from grace with many anglers. Rowland modifies his baits by sanding the sides and changing the dimension of the concave water-spitting face, adding chicken feathers on the rear treble hook, and sometimes adding a prop for more noise.

"After a week or so following the spawn when the bass have recovered, they start to get aggressive again," Rowland said. "When their fry hatch, they'll often return to those areas to eat their fry. That's when you really can wear them out. The feathers add so much. Chicken feathers are pretty water-resistant. When you pop the lure, they come

Even giant bass, such as this 9-pounder, will come up in summer to hit topwater lures worked over milfoil, hydrilla, or other aquatic vegetation.

together and flare back out. If a bass is watching it, or has missed it and still is looking at it, that little flare often is more than they can stand.'"

One great thing about topwater lures is the variety that can be offered. If the bite is slow, a subtle walk-the-dog motion can be employed with a Zara Spook or Slug-Go. If the bass are aggressive, a fast buzzbait, prop bait or noisy chugger may be the best option. One day, they may want a small-profile bait. The next, it may take a super-sized lure to rattle their cage.

Longtime angler Chase Ross of Alabama favors two topwater lures during the postspawn and throughout summer: a Mann's Chug'n Spit and a Zara Spook. If the bass aren't taking either lure very well, he'll follow up with a Mann's Baby 1-Minus crankbait, which runs just a few inches under the surface or can be waked on top.

"With the Chug 'n Spit, I like to make it `bloop' and let it sit until the ripples stop," Ross said. ``The lure has a deeper sound. I change the back hooks to add one with larger feathers. The fish will jump out to kill it. With the 1-Minus and Baby 1-Minus, you can work them just under the surface and around cover without making a lot of noise. They're great to use with traditional topwater lures in order to effectively cover a lot of territory."

Buzzbaits are one of the easiest topwaters to use and are among the most popular. They can be cast and retrieved quickly, similar to a spinnerbait, and are great search baits to locate fish or help establish a pattern. The cup in the blades on a buzzbait or prop bait can be modified by gently bending it to make it run faster or be noisier. Slightly bending

Hollow, soft-plastic topwater lures that float are excellent for fishing around weedy cover that may hold bass.

the wire arm on buzzbaits so the blade will tick the body helps create a clacking noise that may drive bass wild.

"During the summer when it's hot, I don't want anything slow. I want it fast, so I'll open the blades up to make it faster," said George Cochran of Arkansas, a longtime tournament pro. "I want the blades to squeak, too, because fish are curious and they'll come investigate. Through our tournament experiences, we've determined that squeaking makes a difference."

Topwaters around Vegetation

The expanding invasion of exotic aquatic vegetation such as milfoil, hydrilla, and water hyacinth presents a double-edged sword: bass and forage fish love the habitat, but anglers often cannot get to some areas or are afraid of using treble-hooked lures around the thick jungles of matted weeds.

There are ways to get around the problems of hooking the vegetation. Weedless topwater lures such as the venerable Mann's Rat, Strike King Pop'n Frog and Snag Proof Tournament Frog offer relief, along with your best chance of hooking up with a lurking lunker. These soft-plastic, hollow-bodied baits have one or two large hooks rigged through the body that prevent all bu,t the occasional snag while presenting the image of a critter trying to swim across the surface.

Before the vegetation reaches the surface and creates a thick mat, all kinds of topwater lures can be

Topwater lures are great search baits when trolling along shorelines, especially if there is a lot of cover or vegetation growing off the bank.

Chuggers have a concave face that spits water but can also be worked side-to-side.

61

The legendary Arbogast Jitterbug has a very wide wobble, when retrieved slowly.

employed to call up bass from their hidey-holes. In many cases, bass will concentrate on patches of milfoil or hydrilla, even the dead or dying stems from the previous season, instead of the thickest areas where even fish may have a hard time navigating. Searching for these scattered areas often can be productive. Ditto for water hyacinths or lily pads; smaller patches of these surface plants may yield better results when attacked with a weedless topwater, buzzbait or weedless spoon like the Johnson Minnow.

Around thick vegetation on Southern waterways like Guntersville Lake in Alabama, the Mississippi River Delta in Louisiana, or Lake Okeechobee in Florida, anglers must be prepared. Fishing in these areas is no time to have light line or wimpy tackle. Battling a brute that takes your lure and dives for cover in a stand of hydrilla requires heavy artillery.

Alabama angler Hadley Coan fishes regularly on Guntersville Lake, where in late summer the hydrilla and milfoil may cover a third of the 67,000-acre impoundment. Coan favors a big Snag Proof Tournament Frog on a 7-foot-6 heavy action G.Loomis flipping stick with 30-pound test Berkley Fireline on a Shimano Curado reel. When a bass hits, he sets the hook hard to keep it from burying in the vegetation. If a fish hits away from his lure, the reel's fast ratio allows him to wind in and cast quickly.

"The rod's fast tip lets me work the lure better and I like the Fireline because there's no stretch involved when you set the hook," Coan said. "You have to get the fish's head up out of the grass and coming to you as quickly as possible. Sometimes you're making long casts if a fish is out in a mat, maybe a 20-30 yard cast to get to it. With monofilament, that's a lot of line and stretch."

When fishing around vegetation, look for small cuts, openings and

Dance In Spring, Spit In Autumn

Topwater baits can be fished all year in most parts of the country, but there are some subtle differences in seasonal attitudes of bass that may increase your chances of success.

Professional angler Mark Rose of Arkansas believes spring is the time for "walking the dog" when bass are feeding and spawning in shallow water. Rose, a member of the Strike King Lures pro staff, opts for a Spit'n King chugger.

"During early spring I like the side-to-side movement to keep the bait in the same place and give it an erratic action," he said. "You think of a spitting bait as a chugging lure, but I've found in spring that the walking action really attracts bass that may not come up and eat a spitting bait."

Chugging baits sound like a bass chasing or eating a minnow, Rose said. The erratic walking sashay allows him to keep the lure around cover longer, unlike a buzzbait.

"In fall, I like the chugging action with a faster retrieve," he said. "If you can give it the wounded shad effect, it can attract a lot of strikes. You also can give it a louder pop, which sounds like another fish feeding, and may make a bigger fish come see what is going on."

Rose opts for a 5- or 6-foot medium-action G.Loomis rod and Shimano reel for topwater lures, with 12- or 14-pound test Stren. The shorter rod lets him make longer or more precise casts and work the lure better with tighter strokes.

"The whole key is short twitches, short and quick, with your wrist and a low rod tip," he said. "The bait will spin around and actually lose ground. You're not moving it forward. You're turning the head and keeping the tail in basically the same area."

---

points where it may be growing on an underwater feature such as a sloping point. Work each area carefully, dancing the bait and stopping it at the edge of the mat before pulling it off into an opening. On windy days, vegetation lines may be excellent areas to target. Baitfish can be pushed against the wall of milfoil or hydrilla and bass will be lurking around the edges.

Modifying Your Lures

Perhaps no other outdoors arena involves more tinkering with equipment than fishing, and topwater lures are among the most changed.

Anglers may add or remove feathers or Mylar tinsel on hooks, different-sized hooks, propellers, blades, skirts, and employ color designs that resemble something from an explosion at a paint factory.

With his Snag Proof frogs on Guntersville, Coan clips the trailing skirts from the frog's legs, slips a few BB shots inside the hollow body and plugs the leg openings with plastic rattles. The added weight makes the bait's rear end sit lower, putting the massive hooks at a better angle for a high-percentage hookup.

Another option is to remove the paint on a lure by carefully scratching it with a knife blade or medium-grit sandpaper. Some anglers believe a duller appearance may be more productive if a bass believes the lure, imitating a wounded minnow, already has been whacked once or twice.

Using split rings and tying your line directly to the lure can make a difference in its action and is worth a test. Replacing the split rings on each treble hook with a larger ring, which allows the hook to swing more freely, may provide better hook-ups and reduce the chances of losing a fish.

When topwater action heats up on your lake, experiment with these tactics and hang on for one of the best bass experiences you can have.

Propeller baits, such as the Heddon torpedo, often work when bigger, louder lures won't.

Sights Set on Hawgs
By Jeff Samsel

A black and blue Riverside Flip-N-Jig dressed with a blue sapphire Beavertail Chunk is a good sight-fishing bait for Mark Davis because the bait is very visible to him in the water.

Pitching a bait to a bedding bass is like going into a bar and slapping a stranger in the face, according to Mark Davis of Pflueger fishing tackle.

"Do it 20 times and you'll get 20 different reactions," said Davis, who has been bass fishing as long as he has been able to hold a rod and who has "slapped the faces" of a bunch of heavyweight largemouths. "You have to learn how to read the fish and to figure out what to do next, based on how they react and how they have been acting."

Davis lives within a few minutes' drive of South Carolina's Lake Murray, a big, clear impoundment that has a national reputation for the heavyweight bass it produces. Every spring, he gets the opportunity to match wits with some of Murray's biggest largemouths. In addition, Davis' job carries him to prime fishing destinations all over the country. Therefore, he has had opportunities to set his sights on spawning fish in all different types of rivers and lakes.

"The first thing someone has to figure out about sight-fishing is that there is no 'one, two, three' process that always works," Davis said. "Every bass is different, and things like rising and falling water levels and water temperatures and water clarity all affect the spawn."

Variables acknowledged, understanding a few things about the normal spawning behavior of largemouths provides a big head start toward finding fish and figuring out how to catch them. Knowing the basics makes it much easier for an angler to determine which variables might come into play and to adjust accordingly.

For starters, largemouth bass prefer to spawn when the water temperature is 68 degrees and within a day or two before or after a full moon, according to Davis. However, surface temperatures and bottom temperatures sometimes vary from one another, he warned, and rising or falling water temperatures can cause fish to spawn at different times or even to absorb eggs and not spawn in a season.

The most common bedding areas are in shallow water in the backs of coves, creeks and pockets, but some fish will spawn several feet below the surface, at times over offshore structure. Davis said that fishermen should look for fish around cover, especially vertical cover, like docks pilings or stumps, which spawning bass really relate to.

The upper ends of many reservoirs warm more quickly than their lower ends, Davis pointed out, because there tend to be more shallow flats. Also, the north shores of lakes tend to warm up fastest. Late-winter/early-spring weather patterns commonly bring cold north winds, and north-shore waters are protected from those winds. Also, a north shore has a southern exposure and typically will get the most direct sunlight on a lake during a day.

At Lake Murray, Davis begins looking for fish early in the spring in those areas that warm fastest. He always looks hard for fish in areas where he has seen spawning fish in the past, knowing that fish will use those areas again. "They may not spawn around the exact same dock or at the same time, but if some spawned there one year, some will spawn there another year," he said.

In unfamiliar waters, Davis will look in as many different types of places as possible. If he looks in the back of a stump-filled pocket off the main lake and finds no fish, he'll head halfway up a creek arm and search around some docks. Then he'll go all the way to the back of a creek and look around some other kind of cover. As he moves from spot to spot, he continually watches the temperature gauge, as temperatures will often vary several degrees in different types of areas, even in the same lake.

One thing Davis won't do is abandon the search. "You have to commit to sight-fishing, if that's what you want to do," he said. "If you want to look a while and then do other stuff or fish while you look, you probably won't find fish--or not the best fish, anyway."

When he does find fish on beds, the first thing Davis typically will do is to stop and pull out his lake map. If he's in a cut off the creek channel near the second point back in a creek on the north side of the lake, he'll look for other spots that fit that exact description.

Bass often bed around vertical structure, such as dock posts.

Often, getting bedding bass to respond calls for going after them with a variety of offerings.

When Davis searches for bass, the main thing he looks for is a distinctive vertical line, which is the outline of the tip of the bass' tail. "You're looking for something vertical in a horizontal world," he said. "Often, all you'll see at first is that vertical line. Keep staring at it, and the rest of the bass will start taking shape."

When Davis finds a fish, he gets in the best position possible and watches the area for a while. He looks at the actual bed. If the bass are just cruising, they aren't quite ready to spawn and may be tough to catch. If they are around a bed but not staying on it, that's better, but only a little. The ideal scenario is to find a male and a female together on a bed that are "locked down" on that bed. That means they are staying right on the bed, returning immediately if they run something away, and they are not easily spooked.

Davis can tell a lot about how catchable fish are by their positioning and movements before he ever pitches a bait that way. "That's a big part of what makes sight-fishing so fun. You really have to read the fish and figure out how to approach them."

Once Davis has watched the fish for a while, he will begin making pitches into and around the bed and see how they react. "A fish may run from it, or swim slowly up to it, or bluff-charge it and stop," he said. "Whatever the fish does, you have to figure out what it will take to make it strike. Basically, you're looking for each fish's hot button."

He'll cast to the bed and around it, will swim baits through, drop them in, drag them along the bottom and pull them into the bed and leave them. At times he'll even bump a bass that's really locked in to try to make it mad. "If the bass keeps running from the bait but isn't going far, sometimes a good strategy is to just keep pitching where the bass is heading and cutting it off. Everywhere the fish goes, the bait is in front of it," Davis said.

Again there's no single technique that is easy to detail. It takes persistence, trial and error, and an ability to gauge the fish, the last of which comes only with experience doing this kind of fishing.

When a male and a female are locked down on a bed, the male is almost always easiest to catch, Davis said. "You'll catch the male first 90 percent of the time. When you do, put the male in the live well. Pitch the bait back in there, and, if the female doesn't leave, you're probably going to catch that fish."

As for how long to spend on any given fish or pair of fish, Davis said that simply depends on how long an angler has to spend. "In a tournament setting, you also have to consider how many fish--and how many big fish--you think that you will need to compete and think about how many fish you have located," he said.

Davis pitches a variety of different types of baits at bedding bass, and sometimes he will change several times while working the same fish to try to figure out what will do the trick for that particular bass. He noted that some very good anglers consider certain types of lures--jigs, lizards, or whatever--as the bait you must fish with. He has found that different fish respond best to different lures, however, just like different fish respond best to different presentations.

All else being equal, the most important characteristic of a sight-fishing bait for Davis is visibility to him.

"I want to see that bait at all time, if at all possible, to know just how the fish is responding to it," David said. "I even know guys who sight-fish with nothing but white jigs and white trailers for that exact reason."

More often than not, Davis gears up pretty

Making the Pitch

Pitching, either underhanded casting that begins with the bait in hand to create the proper momentum and swing, or pitching, which uses only the amount of line that has been pulled from the reel, each have their place in sight fishing.

Most situations call for pitching, which allows a bait to be propelled a modest distance, placed accurately, and landed with almost no splash. Efficient pitchers can lay baits right where they want, time and time again.

Most pitchers hold the bait at about waist level, about even with them or just behind them and slightly out to the side. Some pinch the bait between a thumb and forefinger; others lay it on extended fingers. The rod is pointed almost straight out, usually with the reel turned inward, and with the pitching arm not quite fully-extended. The actual pitching motion is simply a gentle lift and extension of the arm.

Some anglers keep their reels quite open and rely heavily on thumb pressure. Others keep reels very tight. Likewise, various anglers have their own preference in terms of rod actions. However it's done pitching isn't particularly difficult. However, as in any type of cast, getting the timing and motion down does require practice.

Wise anglers practice at home, pitching to targets at a variety of distances before they get to the lake. They pay attention to accuracy and to delicacy and adjust motions and tension settings as needed. Waiting until you have a double-digit-weight largemouth locked down on a bed is a poor time to be missing the mark on pitches or making unnecessarily big splashes.

Flipping generally comes into play only when the type of cover prohibits pitching and conditions allow an angler to work extremely close.

If bass are locked down, catching them comes down to persistence and an ability to read the fish and figure out what will aggravate them into taking a bait.

Inset:
Sight-fishing begins with doing a lot of searching to locate fish on the beds.

heavily when he sight-fishes. "When a boat hovers around a bed for an hour and someone makes cast after cast to the same place, the fish knows something's up. That fish is there for a reason--to protect that bed--so I'm not really worried about spooking it with my line," he explained.

Davis typically uses 20- or 25-pound-test line, spooled on a Pflueger Trion LP baitcast reel and matched with a Trion flippin' stick, which is 7 feet long and has a medium-heavy action. He keeps his drags pretty tight, wanting to be able to get a heavyweight fish away from docks or other nearby cover if he needs to.

Sight-fishing, while fun, requires a lot of figuring and persistence, both for finding fish and for getting the right one to bite. When Davis does hook one, especially one he has watched for hours and knows is an absolute hawg, the last thing he wants to do is to lose that fish because he was fishing with gear that was too light.

Spinnerbaits Bag Bass From Top To Bottom

By John N. Felsher

Probably no other lure in a bass buster's arsenal approaches the versatility of a spinnerbait. Spinnerbaits don't look like anything a bass should ever see, much less eat, but they entice bass by the bushel from the surface to deep holes through a variety of presentations.

If 100 professional bass anglers lined up and each named his or her top three baits, each one would probably put spinnerbaits somewhere on that list. In fact, spinnerbaits rank second on the list of all-time "champion" lures. According to the Bass Anglers Sportsman Society, spinnerbaits accounted for 76 victories in 375 major tournaments from the late 1960s to the late 1990s. Only plastic worms, with 89 victories, scored higher during that time.

"A spinnerbait is without a doubt one of the most versatile baits on the market," said two-time B.A.S.S. Angler of the Year Gary Klein of Weatherford, Texas. "Not only can you use it shallow or deep, but you can use it in dingy water or clear water. It can catch all three species of bass. I generally fish spinnerbaits shallow, but I have

Leroy Sutterfield of Vienna, Mo., admires a 5.5-pound largemouth bass he caught on a spinnerbait at Toledo Bend Reservoir on the Texas-Louisiana state line.

caught fish down to 30 feet deep."

Spinnerbaits come in various sizes from micro to macro. Most bass anglers in North America use 1/4- to 3/4-ounce versions. A few anglers use spinnerbaits up to 1-ounce for deep-water presentations. Some even use tiny spinnerbaits to catch small bass, crappie, and assorted panfish.

"The key to fishing spinnerbaits at any depth is to use the right weight and the right blade size and configuration," said Denny Brauer of Camdenton, Missouri, the 1998 Bassmasters Classic champion. "In clear shallow water with finicky fish, I use a 1/8-ounce spinnerbait. I use a 1-ounce spinnerbait for deep water in heavy cover. I might use a heavy spinnerbait in 12 to 14 feet of water along a weed line. For the majority of shallow water spinnerbait fishing, I recommend a 1/4- to 3/8-ounce spinnerbait."

Many anglers use spinnerbaits in shallow, weedy, or woody areas. Not entirely weedless or snag-proof, nevertheless spinnerbaits slip through broken weed patches and structure extremely well. With long, thin blades, willow-leaf spinnerbaits move most easily through thick vegetation, but even they won't work in solid vegetation mats.

In thick weeds, anglers often "buzz" spinnerbaits with a steady retrieve across the surface. Blades make a commotion that resembles shad popping on the surface as spinnerbaits sputter through weedy patches. Sometimes skillful anglers can even run them across the tops of floating lily pads. Bass often explode through vegetation to attack spinnerbaits in thick weeds.

Spinnerbaits probably perform best in woody or rocky cover. On a "safety-pin" style spinnerbait, a bent wire holding the blades makes it almost snag-proof. In tangled masses of branches from fallen trees or standing timber, wires deflect off hard structure. Often, the thumping of a spinnerbait striking wood attracts fish.

Around thick cover, anglers may retrieve spinnerbaits steadily just below the surface, or use a "stop-sink-and-go" method. With the latter method, pull a spinnerbait a few feet and then allow it to sink for a few moments. Blades continue turning as the bait sinks, resembling dying shad. Frequently, bass strike as lures fall.

Many people toss spinnerbaits at visible cover, ripping baits through structure. This method certainly catches fish, but might spook shy bass. To catch those wary, cover-hugging bucketmouths, add one more notch on the spinnerbaits' versatility resume—finessing!

Tweaking Spinnerbaits To Perfection

After more than three decades of professional bass fishing, one would think that every improvement in lure design has already hit the market. However, Americans love to tinker with their toys.

"I modify everything I fish," said Gary Klein, a professional bass angler from Weatherford, Texas. "I like a high-speed retrieve. In a high-speed retrieve, a spinnerbait will roll unless the wire is bent correctly. Where the wire comes out of the head, I put my thumb and bend the wire up. I'm actually pushing the eyelet back so the blade hangs farther toward the back of the hook, but does not touch the hook."

Besides changing the shape of spinnerbait wires, anglers might shorten the wires or change the configuration of blades. A few add extra blades. Some add a dash of color, especially bleeding red, around the head for extra enticement. Others add weights or rattles to increase the noise, sink rate, or vibration.

Many anglers add a second, or trailer, hook to normally single-hooked spinnerbaits. Although these snag more frequently in heavy cover, they also hook more fish. To keep a trailer hook attached, cut a plastic disk from a milk jug with a hole punch. Push the hook through the plastic disk above the trailer hook to hold it in place.

Some anglers go to more trouble than just adding a hook. Some anglers change the hook configuration entirely, turning a single hook upside down. Many anglers change the way a spinnerbait looks. Anglers can adopt these highly versatile baits quickly as conditions vary.

Danny Welch buzzes a spinnerbait near cypress trees in Lake St. John near Vidalia, Louisiana.

"If you cast a spinnerbait behind cover, the bass will feel the vibration and know it's coming," said 2001 Bassmaster Classic champion Kevin VanDam of Kalamazoo, Michigan. "It gives them time to think about whether they should hit it. My idea is to get the reaction strike before they know what's happening. You can get a fish that's not in an active mood to bite that way."

VanDam hones a delivery style that combines the finesse of pitching or flipping worms with the famous spinnerbait versatility. Striving for accuracy over distance, VanDam tosses spinnerbaits with a gentle, low-arcing sidearm maneuver. As the bait floats toward his intended target, he keeps his thumb lightly on the spool of a bait-casting reel and one eye glued to the lure wafting through the air.

As the bait nears the preferred impact point or passes directly over it, he lightly presses down with his thumb to stop the bait just above the water. Instead of ker-plunking down into the water and possibly spooking bass, the bait stops and settles into the water with hardly a ripple. Surprised by this sudden "invasion" of its territory, a bass strikes out of anger, not necessarily hunger.

"Finessing" a spinnerbait works particularly well in tight cover, such as that found around logjams, blow-downs, lily pads, dock pilings, rocky banks, riprap, stump fields, or similar places with visible cover to use as targets. Tree-lined rivers rich in woody cover or small coves in major lakes provide ripe conditions for finessing Ol' Mossbacks. Any place where anglers can get close to cover without spooking fish would also work for finessing spinnerbaits.

"It's the same basic presentation as pitching a worm, but I use a short rod for spinnerbaits," VanDam said. "With a spinnerbait, you can cover so much more water in a day. With a worm or jig, cast it by the target and move it out. It's not an effective lure for the rest of the cast. With a spinnerbait, fish might strike it two or three feet away from the target. It covers more water effectively."

Finessing works especially well in stained or muddy water conditions. In stained water, bass won't spook as easily and they stick as close to cover as possible. Anglers can usually approach within a short distance without scattering the fish.

In muddy or stained water, use brighter colors. In darker water or at night, use dark colors. Oddly, black makes a better silhouette at night. Use light colors in clear water. At times, anglers can catch bass on nearly any color combination. To narrow down the selection, stick with a few basics.

Homer Humphreys unhooks a bass he caught along the Red River in northwestern Louisiana.

"I like to throw white or some form of white such as pearl, or a shad type pattern," said former B.A.S.S. Angler of the Year, Mark Davis from Mount Ida, Arkansas. "In slightly off-color water, it's tough to beat white and chartreuse. Another favorite of mine is black and yellow. I also use blue and chartreuse."

Try to simulate natural forage with color selection. If bass feed mostly on shad, use white or shad colors. If bass feed mostly on panfish, use reds, golds or chartreuse. If bass feed heavily upon crawfish, use reddish colors, especially in early spring when crawfish emerge from mud. In late spring, many bass feed heavily upon their fellow bass fingerlings. Use green and white combinations. Baits that mimic those morsels that bass devour provoke the most strikes.

Spinnerbaits work extremely well on windy days. When fishing a wind-swept shoreline, a larger, heavier spinnerbait might cut through gusts better to allow more accurate casting. Bigger blades create more disruption and underwater noise, necessary to compete with the natural noise generated by wave action.

"As a general principle, if the wind is blowing 20 miles per hour or more, a spinnerbait fisherman is going to catch bass better in any season under any other conditions," said Alton Jones, a bass pro from Waco, Texas. "The harder the wind blows, the better bass bite spinnerbaits. One of my favorite techniques is to run a

Shane Allman lips a bass that struck a spinnerbait in thick flooded brush at Lake Sam Rayburn near Jasper, Texas.

This bass struck a Cabela's Living Eyes spinnerbait at Wilson Lake, an impoundment of the Tennessee River near Sheffield, Alabama.

spinnerbait as fast as possible along a steep rocky bank. I use a 1/2- or 3/4-ounce willow-leaf spinnerbait because I want speed without lift. I like white and chartreuse with double No. 4 and No. 3 gold willow-leaf blades. I reel fast and steady. When bass hit, they practically knock the rod out of my hands."

While most people probably use spinnerbaits in water less than 10 feet deep, spinnerbaits can also produce quality fish in deeper waters. In deeper water, throw spinnerbaits near shorelines or isolated structure and run them out across the drop-offs. At the drop-offs, stop cranking and let the spinnerbait fall to the bottom.

At the bottom, "slow-roll" spinnerbaits with a slow, steady retrieve, barely moving the blades as it bumps along the bottom contours. Slow-rolling makes an excellent late winter or early spring presentation when cold water makes fish less active. Slow-rolling works exceptionally well when run parallel to deep drop-offs, banks or other vertical structure.

"In deep water, I fish a spinnerbait for suspended fish," said Randy Blaukat, a professional bass fisherman from Joplin, Missouri. "In the summer and winter, fish suspend at about 10 to 20 feet deep. I make a long cast with a 3/4-ounce spinnerbait and count it down until it reaches the right depth. To test it, get into an area where you know the depth and drop it to the bottom. Count to see how long it takes to hit bottom to give a good idea of how quickly it sinks. In clear water, suspended fish chase a bait up or down. It doesn't have to be at the exact depth as long as it's in the neighborhood."

Some deep-water spinnerbait enthusiasts use the jigging, "yo-yo" or "helicopter" method for active deep bass. After the bait touches bottom, pop it off the bottom several feet and let it fall back to the bottom. Rotating blades "helicopter" down, spinning and flashing with fish-attracting effectiveness. Keep repeating this rising and falling pattern.

"In deeper water, I work down the contour of the cover with a single Colorado or Indiana blade," Brauer said. "A spinnerbait has a tendency to lift off the bottom even when retrieved slowly. Slow the retrieve and let the bait sink all the way to the bottom at times and yo-yo it. Stop the retrieve and let it flutter back down to the bottom. Let it make contact with the vegetation or the bottom and start the retrieve again. Bump the cover whenever possible. That's a dynamite winter or early spring technique when fish are staging along points, humps or old roadbeds."

In water deeper than 20 feet, few methods can compete with vertical jigging. Scan for fish along humps or drop-offs with electronics. Position the boat over a school of fish and drop a heavy spinnerbait with a single Colorado blade straight to the bottom. Use spinnerbaits that weigh 3/4- to 1-ounce for a good steady fall. Once it hits bottom, jig it up and down repeatedly directly below the boat. Keep the bait in the water bouncing up and down off the bottom, but move the boat slowly to reposition the bait.

If an angler can only own one bass bait and wants to fish from top to bottom in any water body in the country all year long, few offerings can beat a spinnerbait.

Russ McVey of Southpaw Guide Service shows off a bass he caught on a spinnerbait along the Red River near Shreveport, Louisiana.

River Smallmouth Lures: From Top To Bottom
By Gerald Almy

THIN-MINNOW PLUG

The author lands a five-pounder in the New River, West Virginia.

Shafts of golden sunlight slant through the canopy of oaks and sycamores lining the rocky river bank as a pair of anglers drifts quietly downstream with the flow. With a gentle splat, a small surface lure alights on the emerald water, then gurgles with a tug of the line. Tiny waves lap outward from the plug, then all is still.

With a suddenness that is both exhilarating and unnerving, the tranquility of the scene disintegrates like a hammer shattering glass. A bundle of taut muscle and predatory instinct--the smallmouth bass--crashes through the stream's surface, engulfs the lure and arches skyward.

The thought crystallizes again: the smallmouth bass may well be the ultimate North American gamefish, particularly in its river habitat. Yes, some would claim that honor belongs to a more glamorous species such as salmon, steelhead or tarpon. But those fish, intriguing though they are, do not offer the broad distribution and wide availability that makes the smallmouth such a grand sportfish for everyone.

One of the most important things to keep in mind when choosing a selection of lures for smallmouths is how different they are from their larger relative, the largemouth. They're almost

a totally different quarry in terms of habitat preferences, feeding style and personality. Where the largemouth is pot-gutted and plodding, susceptible to heavy tackle and large, noisy lures, the smallmouth displays just the opposite characteristics. Strong, yet quick, sometimes stocky, but never fat, the bronze bass demands subtle offerings, delicate tackle, a stealthy approach and finesse in presentation.

In truth, the fish is more like a wary stream brown trout than a largemouth. This is true of its habitat preferences and diet, as well as the types of offerings and approaches that pay off for the angler. Smallmouths prefer cold, clear water and thrive in currents. In terms of diet, they often feed on compact, trout-sized fare, including aquatic insects, such as caddis flies, mayflies, stoneflies, damsel flies, and hellgrammites, as well as terrestrial insects, such as ants, grasshoppers, beetles, and crickets. They also relish crayfish and small baitfish like dace, shiners, darters, mad toms, and chubs.

In spite of these refined tastes, river smallmouths can actually be taken on a wide variety of lures worked at every level from the very surface to crawling across the rubble-strewn bottom. To some extent you'll want to change which lures you select for a day on the water according to the time of year, water temperature, and insect and baitfish activity, but with the selection described below you'll be equipped for virtually any season and any conditions you might encounter--short of muddy, raging torrents following a prolonged, heavy rain.

A Rapala thin-minnow took this Arkansas fish.

Topwater

Few would deny that working lures on the surface provides the most angling excitement, and that seems like the prime place to start.

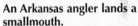

An Arkansas angler lands a smallmouth.

Bronzebacks often feed at this level when waters are warm, chasing damsel and dragonflies, snatching up grasshoppers that plop in from land, and grabbing large mayflies. But working the top doesn't just mean imitating insects. I've seen 3-pound smallmouths literally explode out of the water and grab baitfish in midair that they've chased to the surface.

Because of the wide variety of foods they'll take on top, you don't have to "match the hatch" when surface fishing for bronzebacks. They aren't that selective. But you do want a compact lure that lands gently on the water and one that doesn't create too much of a ruckus when you retrieve it.

Topwater lures come in a variety of styles, and I like to stock a few of each type. The propellor lure belongs in every

Bill Rooney fishes the Rappahannock River, in Virginia

smallmouth tackle box. The Heddon Tiny or Teeny Torpedo is a classic. The Bagley SPM2 Mighty Minnow is also good. A stickbait, such as the Zara Pooch, Zara Puppy or Poe's Jackpot, is another good bet. Also, stock a few poppers, such as a small version of the Rebel Pop R. Finally, add one wobbling lure, such as the famous Jitterbug, in one of the two smallest sizes it's made in. These lures can be especially good for night fishing.

With prop lures, stick baits and poppers, try gentle twitches first. If this doesn't produce, go to a more violent jerking, with pauses in between. The Jitterbug can be fished erratically, but usually a slow, steady retrieve is best. Work these lures around rock piles, wood structure, weeds, eddies and the tail-outs of pools.

POPPER OR CHUGGER

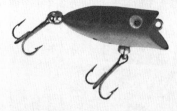

Near-Surface

If lures worked on the surface don't score, go slightly lower. The two best lures for bridging the gap from the top to mid-levels are floater-diver minnow plugs and soft plastic jerkbaits. The Rapala is the most famous of the thin-minnow lures, but other good models are made by

TINY TORPEDO

A topwater lure, Heddon's Tiny Torpedo, fooled this New River 5-pounder for Richard Aide.

Berkley, Bagley, Rebel, Manns, Yo-Zuri, Storm, Cordell, Bomber, and Smithwick. For most situations, I like 2- to 4-inch models, but occasionally I'll use a 5-inch version if I think big fish are in the area. For low summer waters, stick to the smaller versions. Silver with a black back is the standard color, but also try colors, such as orange and chartreuse, if the water is murky.

These lures can actually be fished as topwater offerings. Cast to likely smallmouth hangouts such as eddies, logs near shore or ledges, let the ripples settle, then twitch them lightly. Pause, then twitch again. If nothing takes the lure, crank it back very slowly so it makes a v-wake on the surface.

Only after these topwater approaches fail to produce do I switch to a steady reeling retrieve, which makes them dive about 12-24 inches, depending on the model you're using. Sometimes fish just won't nail the lures on top, where it's most fun, but will slam into these offerings a foot below the surface with the simple steady retrieve. It may seem boring, but it's actually produced more big fish for me than the erratic twitching method has.

Soft plastic jerkbaits can also be fished on top or down a few feet. The Slug-O was the first soft plastic jerkbait, but now many companies make their own versions in various shapes. The two main attractions of these lures are their life-like, erratic motion and pliable feel once a fish grabs them. Twitch the lures with a fluttering, darting motion on the surface first. If that doesn't produce, let them sink a

Tackle & Extras

You can use a very light baitcasting outfit for smallmouths in rivers, but the choice of most experienced bronzeback specialists across the country is a light spinning rig. Some downsize even further to ultralight and others scale upward a bit to medium action. All will work fine. Just choose which feels best for your personal tastes and the waters you fish.

If most of the smallmouths are in the 8-12 inch range, ultralight will fit the bill for almost all of the lures discussed above. If you regularly encounter fish in the 3-pound plus range, a medium weight rig isn't out of place to make sure you can set the hooks firmly and pressure bass away from snags that could break the line.

I like a rod of 5½-6½ feet, equipped with a light reel with a butter-smooth drag. Buy an extra

spool and keep one filled with four pound monofilament, one with six pound. For very large fish, you might even keep a third spool ready with eight pound test. If you go with a levelwind, you can opt for 8 pound in one of the braided lines. For most of my river smallmouth fishing, I keep two outfits rigged and ready, one with four pound, one with six, so I can quickly probe any likely spot with at least two prime offerings without retying.

Besides rod and reel, you'll need a tackle box for boat fishing and a vest or compact box you wear on your shoulder or around your neck when wade fishing. Other important items to bring include polarized sunglasses, hat with a brim, sunscreen, line clippers, insect repellent, drinks, lunch and camera.

The New River, a great smallmouth river in West Virginia

MID-LEVEL CRANKBAIT

foot or two, then work them with the same tantalizing motion, only underwater. Try pausing next to ledges, logjams or large rocks, so the lure sinks briefly, tempting bass that might be holed up near the structure.

Mid-Level

If fish aren't cooperating on topwater or near-surface lures, it's time to think about mid-level offerings. Several selections fit the bill. A traditional spinner is an excellent choice. Versions such as the Mepps, Panther Martin or Rooster Tail are very effective minnow imitations and can be deadly when fished with just a straight retrieve. Small spinnerbaits, such as the famous Beetle Spin, and models made by Riverside, Blue Fox, and Mister Twister are also good choices. You can actually work these at whatever level you choose from just under the surface to bumping the bottom, but it's for active fish in the mid-level zone that I find them most valuable.

My main choice for these transition-zone smallmouths, however, is the crankbait. Three types are worth stashing in your tackle box. The first is simply the smallest versions of regular crankbaits made by companies such as Bomber, Worden, Rapala, Storm, Berkley, Manns,

Grubs are great smallmouth producers.

Norman, Bagley, Cordell, and Luhr-Jensen. The second type is the crayfish-shaped crankbait. The third category consists of the specialty mini-crankbaits such as the Creek Creature, Crick Hopper, and Cat'R Crawler by Rebel, and several of Yo-Zuri's smaller models.

Probe deep holes, tail-outs of pools, eddy water and structure such as ledges, rock piles, undercut banks and logjams. Bounce the lures off of rocks and ledges to try to draw instinct strikes and use both steady and stop-and-go retrieves.

Bottom Bouncing

When fish are hovering right smack on or just above the bottom, several lures are standouts. Grubs are cheap, humble lures, but may be the best offering of all for this situation. Rig them on a $\frac{1}{16}$- to $\frac{1}{8}$-ounce jighead or fish them Carolina-style with the last $\frac{1}{8}$-inch of the head impaled on a size 4-8 Octopus style hook, 18-24 inches behind a split shot or egg sinker and swivel. Pumpkinseed, watermelon, smoke, avocado, motor oil,, and chartreuse are good colors. Try both steady reeling and lift and drop retrieves.

Live bait fishermen score on some of the largest fish with tiny catfish called madtoms or stonecats. Charlie Case (Riversmallies.com; 804/374-0335) makes the most realistic soft plastic imitation of these that I've tried. They even include fake whiskers! Rig them on the jigheads that are included in the package or fish them Texas-style with a sliding weight in front.

Though often thought of as largemouth lures, plastic worms in the 4-5 inch size are also great for crawling across the bottom over rocks and rubble to stir up jumbo smallmouths. Top colors are blue, purple, black and green. Rig them either Texas-style or with multiple exposed hooks if hang-ups aren't too much of a problem.

Try these proven lures on river smallmouths and I think you'll agree with those who rate this acrobatic bronze battler as the gamest of all North American sportfish.

Top Retrieves for River Smallmouths

A variety of retrieves will work, depending on which lure you choose. Here, though, are three basics that can be varied slightly and put to work with almost any artificial.

- **SLOW AND STEADY.**
  This is an easy way to fish that is surprisingly effective. In fact, it probably accounts for more smallmouths than all other retrieves put together. Hold the rod steady, point it at the lure and reel slowly and smoothly. Spinners, crankbaits, thin-minnow lures, grubs, plastic worms, spinnerbaits, wobbling surface lures--all are prime candidates for this presentation. It's an especially good method for early season, late fall and winter, when the fish's metabolisms are running slow and water temperatures are low.

- **FAST AND STEADY.**
  This is similar to the technique above, except you speed things up a bit. It's very useful when fish are in an aggressive mood and pays off well from spring through early fall. All of the lures listed above, except grubs and worms, can be fished at this more lively pace.

- **ERRACTIC.**
  This covers lots of ground, but basically involves moving the lure with anything from a tiny twitch, to a sharp jerk, to sweeping the rod forward six feet. It also includes the tactic of simply pausing occasionally to let the lure rest motionless on the surface, suspend or drift lower if it's a sinking offering, such as a grub or spinnerbait.

  Twitching is often best with surface lures and worms; jerking works well at times with thin-minnow plugs and crankbaits. Lifting and dropping the rod is another good method for grubs, worms and spinnerbaits. Try a variety of these erratic techniques whenever smoother, traditional presentations come up cold.

The Dark Side of Bass Fishing

By Jim Spencer

I t was dark.

Not the kind of dark where you can sort of see things, but actually, really, dark. It started as a regular midsummer moonless night, with clear skies and a million stars up there to shed at least enough light to enable a fellow to see the guy in the other end of the boat. But as we drove to the boat ramp at 10 p.m., the stars started winking out as a band of clouds rolled in from the west. By the time the boat was in the water, we were enveloped in a blackness so complete, so impenetrable, we might as well have been blind.

"I'm not sure I can fish in this," came Ted's voice out of the void as we groped around in the back of the truck for our fishing gear. "I couldn't see my own knuckles if I was punching myself in the eye. I know it's supposed to be dark at night, but this is ridiculous."

I didn't admit it, but I shared my buddy's sentiments. It was darker than the inside of a black Angus bull. But after all, we'd come here to fish, and the stubborn streak that's always been part of my nature took over from whatever good sense and logic I possess.

"Oh, it'll be fine once we get on the water," I said, with a confidence I didn't feel.

This was a small, private lake, and there were no nearby lights. Although we wanted to let our eyes get accustomed to

The big 'uns go on the prowl when it gets dark.

the dark, we couldn't find our way to the boat without our flashlights. Then we had to use the lights to get the boat away from the bank, and then to select our lures. Ted chose a surface plug with fore-and-aft propellers; I opted for a spinnerbait.

Once the knots were tied, Ted switched off the flashlight. The night wrapped around us like a shroud.

Conventional sight fishing, as in casting to specific targets, was impossible. There were no targets. There was only the void. All we could do was make random, on-faith casts in the stumpy cove, being careful to keep the arcs of our fishing rods well away from each other.

Inevitably, one or the other of us would drape his line across an unseen stump or log and get hung, necessitating much heaving and pulling and cursing. But in between the hang-ups and the curses, we caught fish. The bite was on, as the walleye guys say, and before midnight we'd stopped counting, with 25 bass brought to the boat. Since I was catching as many fish as Ted and getting hung up a lot less, after the first 30 minutes he switched from his treble-hooked topwater to a spinnerbait. By the time the action tapered off just before dawn, we'd caught and released close to 100 bass.

That inaugural trip, more than thirty years ago, was a revelation, and it gave the lie to what I'd always been told about night fishing before I gave it a try for myself--that the fishing is better around the full moon. Sure, you can catch bass at night when the moon is full (I've done it many times), but the best action is the week or so surrounding the new moon. It's not that the fishing is better when the moon is full, it's just that it's easier to fish then because you can see what you're doing. Therefore, night anglers tend to limit their efforts to those times when the moon is in the sky, and so they have no idea whether the fish are active during the dark of the moon or not.

That's not to say you should limit your night fishing to the week around the new moon. As with bass fishing in the daylight hours, the best time to go bass fishing at night is on the night you have the time and opportunity to go, regardless of the moon phase.

One other possible reason there aren't more night bass anglers is because the first hour or two after sundown is generally a pretty unproductive time. All three species of bass tend to feed fairly heavily during the last hour of daylight, but between sundown and full dark the action

Lights on, or Lights Off?

There are three theories regarding the use of lights for night fishing.

One is, "Just say no." These anglers wouldn't turn on a flashlight when night-fishing for any reason. They believe shining a light on the water scares the fish. Whether this is true can be debated, with anecdotes to lend support to both sides. What can't be debated is the fact that turning on a light wrecks night vision for a few minutes, and since night vision is important, using a light too often isn't a good idea.

This second theory says shining a light on the water doesn't hurt andma, in fact, even help if it's a steady light, as it attracts insects, which attract small fish, etc. this theory works for crappie, white bass, walleyes, and catfish, but doesn't seem to work for bass. Anglers who fish for crappies and other species under lights catch very few black bass.

The third school of thought involves using low-intensity "black lights." These are mounted over the side of the boat and cast a faint purple light over the fishing area. Proponents of this system claim the black light doesn't alarm bass, and the angler can see where he's casting. I've tried black light fishing three times, and while we caught fish each trip, the action was below average. Whether that was coincidence or not is questionable, but I'm suspicious. Few serious night fishermen use black lights; maybe that should tell you something. No question, though, a black light makes it much easier to fish in the dark.

The closest many anglers get to night fishing is staying on the water through dusk until it gets too dark to see. Actually, this is the slowest period of the day for bass activity.

usually tapers off considerably and stays that way for a while. Since many anglers who decide to try night fishing begin by fishing in late afternoon and staying on the water as night falls, they get a false impression. They enjoy the fast action near sundown, then continue to fish as the bite tapers off. After an hour or so of casting in the early part of the night, they get disgusted and leave--just about the time they ought to be hitting the water.

Once the fish do begin to feed, the action usually continues until sunrise or a little after, but it's been my experience that the heaviest feeding occurs between midnight and 2 a.m. Although many anglers scoff at the notion, I've had good results by timing my night fishing expeditions to be on the water during the peak periods listed in the Solunar Tables.

Night fishing while a front is approaching can produce fantastic action, but the downside is that you're liable to get caught in the storm. If you're fishing ahead of a front, it's best to concentrate your efforts within a reasonable distance of shelter, so you can make a run for it when the bad stuff arrives.

Fishing at night is a dark art in more ways than one. While it's a very popular form of fishing in warm weather on many of the large Southern and Midwestern and Western reservoirs, those of us who do it are still in the minority, and the whole business is still shrouded in mystery. Even those of us who do it don't talk much about it.

There are two good reasons for this close-mouthed attitude. One is the vague sense of embarrassment felt by many of us who are night anglers. It's unreasonable, but it's there; I've talked to too many other night fishermen to doubt it. Bass fishermen are a goofy enough bunch, and I think maybe we subconsciously decide that night fishing is even goofier.

The other reason we don't talk much about it is because we catch fish. Big fish, sometimes. On hard-fished waters, the big ones become largely nocturnal, and those who restrict their efforts to the daytime hours rarely have much of a chance at them. It's no accident that a large percentage of the largemouth, smallmouth and spotted bass in the IGFA, National Freshwater Fishing Hall of Fame, and individual state fishing records were taken at night.

The old phrase "As different as night and day" takes on a whole new meaning when you're on the water in the dark. Even the simplest things

Tying One On

One of the knottiest problems associated with night fishing, for many anglers, is tying their lures to their lines when they can't see either the lure or the line. Some anglers use a snap on the end of the line, but opening and closing a snap is also a problem in the dark, and it adds a potential weak place to your tackle, as well as hampering the action of some lures.

This problem is easily solved. The accompanying photos illustrate the steps involved in tying a simple knot that retains nearly 100 percent of the line strength. It's a knot that anyone with average coordination can tie in the dark in five seconds, with a little practice.

1. Thread the line through the lure and bring the tag end of the line up and over the extended thumb and index finger of your left hand.

2. Bring the tag end down and wrap it four or five times around the loop on which your lure is hanging.

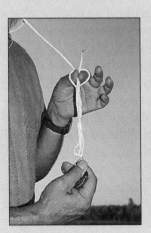   

3. Bring the tag end up to your left hand and grasp the end of the line between thumb and forefinger.

4. Release the tag end with your right hand and carefully grasp the lure, then pull your left hand and the tag end of the line through the loop you laid over your thumb and forefinger.

5. Grasp the main line in your left hand and pull, maintaining your right-handed grip on the lure. The knot will pull down snug.

6. Trim the excess and you're done.

Dark lures are the ticket for night fishing. The theory is, the darker lures produce a sharper silhouette and are easier to see, although research has proven bass feed at night mostly by sound and vibration.

are difficult when you can't see what you're doing. But there are a few things you can do to make night fishing a little less frustrating and a little more rewarding.

Having a spare rod (or two) rigged and ready to go is a good idea for night fishing, because you can switch to another rig if you break off or get a tough backlash. But make sure they're secure and out of the way when they're waiting their turn. I've broken a couple of rods and kicked one overboard before learning this lesson.

The arrangement of the seats, tackle boxes, rods and other equipment in your boat becomes much more important at night. Keeping a clear place for your feet is not only easier on your equipment, it's also an important safety factor. If you've ever stuck a foot in a tackle box and either rammed a treble hook past the barb into your toe or stumbled and fallen out of the boat--or both simultaneously, as I did one dark night about ten years ago--you know the truth of that statement. Develop a system, and make sure everything stays in its assigned spot so you can both find it when you need it and avoid it when you don't.

Put together a simpler, smaller tackle box for night fishing. You don't need a wide selection of lure designs or colors. A sack of plastic worms, five or six assorted sizes and styles of spinnerbaits, a couple crankbaits, and two each of three surface lures (popper, propeller and Jitterbug-style), all in dark colors, are all in the world you'll ever need. If you like jig-fishing, add a handful of jigs and a bottle of pork rind to that list. You might feel naked at first, but anything else is excess baggage.

Go a little heavier than normal on line size. In the first place, the darkness lets you get away with it, and in the second place, you'll be getting hung up more than normal, so you'll need the heavier line. Come to think of it, an extra spool of mono is a good item to add to that pared-down night fishing box.

Throw in a pair of sturdy needle-nosed pliers with a strong cutting surface, too, for hook removal from both fish and (if you're unlucky) fishermen.

On big water, even on familiar big water, always carry a map and compass, or map and GPS unit. Things look different at night, and islands and brushpiles crop up where they've never been before. Don't fish alone at night and always tell someone where you're going and approximately when you intend to be back. A cell phone may be intrusive on a fishing trip, but it might save your bacon. Carry one!

None of this is meant to scare you or discourage you from giving bass fishing's dark side a try. It's an enjoyable, effective and productive way to beat the summer heat. Just keep your wits about you, and don't get into risky situations.

There's a lot to be said for being left in the dark.

Not enough dark-colored lures in your tackle box? A can of gloss black enamel spray paint can quickly convert any lure you need for night fishing.

ALUMACRAFT BASS BOATS

INVADER 185

Weight: 1300 lbs.
Hull Type: Pad-V
Livewells: 1 aerated- 22 gal.
Battery Storage: aft
Trolling Motor: opt
Storage: 4 dry, 1 rod, 1 tackle.

INVADER 175
Length: 17' 5"
Width: 88", 64"
Side Height: 23"
Transom: 22", 88"
Horsepower: 50-115
Capacity: 4-1200 lbs.
Weight: 1200 lbs.
Hull Type: Pad-V
Livewells: 1 aerated- 22 gal.
Battery Storage: aft
Trolling Motor: opt
Storage: 4 dry, 1 rod, 1 tackle.

MV SUPER HAWK
Length: 15' 0"
Width: 62", 42"
Side Height: 20"
Transom: 20", 60"
Horsepower: 15-40
Capacity: 4-795#
Weight: 467#
Hull Type: Mod V
Livewells: 1 aerated
Battery Storage: aft
Trolling Motor: opt

CRAPPIE DELUXE
Length: 15' 0"
Width: 64", 42"
Side Height: 20"
Transom: 20", 62"
Horsepower: 15-25
Capacity: 3-745 lbs.
Weight: 467lbs.
Hull Type: Mod V
Livewells: 1 aerated
Battery Storage: aft
Trolling Motor: opt
Storage: 2 aft 1 fwd

CRAPPIE JON
Length: 14' 0"
Width: 64", 42"
Side Height: 20"
Transom: 15", 62"
Horsepower: 10-25
Capacity: 3-740 lbs.
Weight: 330 lbs.
Hull Type: Mod-V
Livewells:1
Battery Storage: fwd

Trolling Motor:
Storage: 1 fwd

BASS PRO 165
Length: 16' 8"
Width: 74", 52"
Side Height: 23"
Transom: 22"/74"
Horsepower: 50-90
Capacity: 4-1100 lbs.
Weight: 852 lbs.
Hull Type: Step-V
Livewells: 1 aerated-18 gal.
Battery Storage: aft
Trolling Motor: opt
Storage: 2 dry, 1 rod, 1 tackle.

INVADER 195
Length: 19' 4"
Width: 92"/67"
Side Height: 23"
Transom: 22"/92"
Horsepower: 50-150
Capacity: 4-1400 lbs.
Weight: 1350 lbs.
Hull Type: Pad-V
Livewells: 1 aerated- 22 gal.
Battery Storage: aft
Trolling Motor: opt
Storage: 4 dry, 1 rod, 1 tackle.

INVADER 185
Length: 18' 4"
Width: 92", 67"
Side Height: 23"
Transom: 23"/92"
Horsepower: 50-135
Capacity: 4-1300 lbs.

MAGNUM 175 CS
Length: 17' 11"
Width: 88"
Depth: 41"
Transom: 88"/20"
Horsepower: 130
Capacity: 5-1310 lbs.
Weight: 1175 lbs.
Fuel Tank: 34 gal.
Livewells: 2
Trolling Motor System: 12/24v.
Battery Storage: 2
Trolling Motor: opt

MAGNUM 175
Length: 17' 11"
Width: 88"
Depth: 41"
Transom: 88"/20"
Horsepower: 80
Capacity: 5-1310 lbs.
Weight: 1135 lbs.
Fuel Tank: 34 gal.
Livewells: 2
Trolling Motor System: 12/24v.
Battery Storage: 2
Trolling Motor: opt

MAGNUM 165
Length: 16' 5"
Width: 81"
Depth: 36"
Transom: 81"/20"
Horsepower: 65
Capacity: 5-1250 lbs.
Weight: 840 lbs.
Fuel Tank: 22 gal.
Livewells: 1

BOATS

ALUMACRAFT BASS BOATS

Trolling Motor System: 12v.
Battery Storage: 1
Trolling Motor: opt

MV TEX SPECIAL CS
Length: 16' 8"
Width: 70", 48"
Side Height: 21"
Transom: 20"/69"
Horsepower: 15-55
Capacity: 5-1010 lbs.
Weight: 425 lbs.
Hull Type: Mod-V
Livewells: 1 aerated
Battery Storage: aft
Trolling Motor: opt
Storage: 2 fwd, 1 aft.

TOURNAMENT PRO 185 CS
Length: 18' 11"

Width: 96"
Depth: 43"
Transom: 95"/20"
Horsepower: 200
Capacity: 6-1750lbs.
Weight: 1510 lbs.
Fuel Tank: 41 gal.
Livewells: 2
Battery Trolling Motor System: 12/24v.
Trolling Motor: opt

TOURNAMENT PRO 185
Length: 18' 11"
Width: 96"
Depth: 43"
Transom: 95"/20"
Horsepower: 100
Capacity: 6-1750lbs.
Weight: 1475 lbs.
Fuel Tank: 41 gal.

Livewells: 2
Battery Storage: 2
Trolling Motor System: 12/24v.
Storage: fwd
Trolling Motor: opt

TOURNAMENT PRO 175 CS
Length: 17' 11"
Width: 96"
Depth: 43"
Transom: 95"/20"
Horsepower: 175
Capacity: 5-1550 lbs.
Weight: 1415 lbs.
Fuel Tank: 34 gal.
Livewells: 2
Battery Storage: 2
Trolling Motor System: 12/24v.
Storage: fwd
Trolling Motor: opt

ASTRO BOATS

1850 SF
Ski or fish? If that is the question, then the answer is the ASTRO® 1850 SF. The 1850 SF is an 18' boat that brings performance, style, comfort and function together in an I/O design for both skiing and fishing without compromises to either. The boat's high-performance hull with a 90" beam and the standard-package 3.0-liter Mercruiser® engine offer a perfect blend of power and performance for deep-water ski starts, a wide-range of towing speeds and positive boat handling stability for skiing or racing to the next fishing spot.

Passengers can enjoy a comfortable ride from any of the boat's many seating options, including two in the open bow area and several behind the walk-thru windshield – a swivel seat, two removable fishing chairs or the bench seat in between. The driver's seat is adjustable. But what really sets the 1850 SF apart from all other so-called "ski and fish" models is the boat's user-friendly design and the seemingly-endless list of standard features. Included are a ski tow ring, fold-away boarding ladder, full-width swim platform, removable aft deck cushion, removable fishing chairs, removable

bow cushions, drink holders and a 25 quart cooler. There's also an aerated livewell, full-dash instrumentation, AM/FM cassette with two speakers, tilt-steering wheel, glove box, port side cooler, horn, paddle and fire extinguisher.

The 1850 SF comes pre-wired for a 12-volt trolling motor. An optional special package includes a removable trolling motor that fits easily and out of the way into the boat's in-floor storage area. Removal of the bow and aft-deck cushions reveals the two fishing decks, each with a seat base that fits

the two fishing chairs that are moveable from the aft seating area.

The boat comes standard on a color-keyed single axle trailer with surge brakes, tongue jack and 14" tires with chrome wheels and "EZ" lube hubs.

The ASTRO 1850 SF is available in Off-White and Mediterranean Blue or Off-White and Diablo Red color schemes.

MSRP: The standard package of boat, 3.0-liter Mercruiser engine and trailer retails for around $17,295, plus applicable dealer prep and destination charges.

BASS CAT BOATS

COUGAR

The Cougar's 20'3" hull is based on the "top of the line" Jaguar. This model has stable handling, rock solid fishing platforms and lighter weight than the Jaguar, yet agile handling as it corners, even in rough water. Bass Cat "All Fiberglass" quality construction throughout. Vinyl ester resins combined with new manufacturing techniques provide a structure that carries a Transferable Lifetime Structural Warranty. Tournament anglers will appreciate the stability of the massive decks both front and rear, which offer plenty of room for two flippin' tight cover. At the bow is Bass Cat's patented recessed basin, which holds the trolling motor foot control. It's flush with the deck, out of the way, puts the fisherman 10-12" closer to the action, as it helps relieve back and foot strain associated with a day's fishing. This recessed area also provides space for a digital graph. Up front, two full-length rod boxes will keep all rods and reels organized and out of the way. Plus, convenient partner rod storage is accomplished with a built-in rod holder beside the passenger seat. Both front and rear storage compartments with additional under the bench seat storage provide plenty of room for tackle and accessories. Two ice chests, one at the front and one at the rear between the seats, keep lunch and drinks easily accessible to all.

SPECIFICATIONS
Length: 20' 3"
Min. storage length: 24' 10"
With swing away tongue: 22' 2"
Beam: 93"
Approx. weight: 1395 lbs.
Approx. weight (dual console): 1455 lbs.
Fuel capacity: 36 gal.
Max. horsepower range: 175-285

JAGUAR

The Jaguar's 20' 3" hull glides over and thru the water with ease. It's stable, yet agile, even in rough water. Tournament fishermen and their partners will never get in one another's way, nor stumble over equipment getting to the net. A master rod box and a separate partners rod box in the rear deck keeps all rods and reels organized and out of the way. Front and rear deck storage compartments provide all the additional tackle and accessory storage any fisherman could need or want. At the bow, fishermen will find Bass Cat's patented recessed basin, which holds the trolling motor foot control. It's flush with the deck, puts fishermen 10-12" closer to the action, plus helps relieve back and foot strain associated with a day's fishing. This recessed area also provides space for a digital graph. Three front storage compartments plus an ice box keep everything close and offer plenty of floor space for two "flippin'" close covers. A dual console (DC) model is also available for those who prefer the looks and passenger convenience offered by two consoles.

SPECIFICATIONS
Length: 20' 3"
Min. storage length: 24' 10"
With Swing Away Tongue: 22' 2"
Beam: 93"
Approx. weight: 1665 lbs.
Approx. weight (dual console): 1725 lbs.
Fuel capacity: 52 gal.
Max. horsepower range: 175-285

PANTERA CLASSIC

The Pantera Classic offers a superior rough water ride in a low profile design. Dual rod boxes, a new center line trolling motor mount with recessed trolling motor pedal basin, aerated and recirculating livewells, 36-gallon fuel tank, tilt steering and aluminum lids are just a few of the standard features. A modular console includes a BP400 with VDO tach/speed/fuel gauges. Dual full-length rod boxes and front deck storage areas hold all the rods and tackle needed for a serious day of fishing for you and your partner. Additional storage is found under the seats, with an ice chest between the driver and passenger seats. Behind the seats is a rear deck large enough for your partner to move around with greater ease. A Class dual console is also available for those who use their boat for both skiing and fishing, or just prefer the appearance of the dual console boats.

SPECIFICATIONS
Length: 19'
Min. storage length: 23' 11"
With swing away tongue: 21' 3"
Beam: 92"

Approx. weight: 1245 lbs.
Approx. weight (dual console): 1295 lbs.
Fuel capacity: 36 gal.
Max. horsepower range: 115-200

PANTERA III

From the deeper eight stringer hull to the BP101 LCD Digital Dash, the Pantera III is pure perfection in quality, craftsmanship and boating innovations. The patented recessed trolling motor pedal basin in the bow helps reduce back, knee and ankle stress while placing fishermen 10-12" closer to the action. This deck modification allows for an additional rod box, larger storage areas and a console design that allows even the largest anglers ample room and comfort behind the Momo tilt steering wheel. Better comfort also is found in the bench seats, with higher backs for additional support. Between the seats is a convenient additional ice chest. Passengers will find a convenient, secure rod storage shelf beside the bench seat. The roomier rear section of the deck has smooth rounded corners, which are more aerodynamic and allow motor control cabling to exit at the center of the splashwell and enter the engine with less binding and kinking as they link to the console control. The deeper hull design provides a smoother ride and allows for reduced backwash on shutdown. A Pantera III DC is available with dual consoles for

those who prefer the looks and added protection from the elements for their passengers. The passenger's console has a large glove box for added storage.
SPECIFICATIONS
Length: 19' 3"
Min. storage length: 23' 11"
With swing away tongue: 21' 3"

Beam: 93"
Approx. weight: 1395 lbs.
Approx. weight (dual console): 1445 lbs.
Fuel capacity: 52 gal.
Max. horsepower range: 135-200

BASS CAT BOATS

PHELIX

Bass Cat's Phelix is perfect for those anglers desiring a fiberglass boat that is very affordable. Great for small lakes, this "All Fiberglass" boat is made from vinyl ester resins with vacuum compression manufacturing techniques. Economical, easy maintenance, quality construction and a lifetime transferable structural warranty all add up to a lifetime of fun on the water. Standard features include bow and transom lights, a custom trailer with a 3" channel welded frame, 2 interior deck compartments that can be used for livewells or ice chests, and a storage compartment at the bow.

SPECIFICATIONS
Length: 17'
Beam: 64"
Approx. weight: 525 lbs.
Max. horsepower: 25

ermen will appreciate the added front and rear deck space as well as the recessed trolling motor basin to help relieve knee and ankle stress. Comes with a long list of standard features, including dual steering, hydraulic lid openers and a dual aerated livewell with removable divider. Available options include a Flippin' Deck, allowing added storage beneath the deck. Made with vinyl ester resins and "All Fiberglass Construction" techniques.

SPECIFICATIONS
Length: 18'
Min. storage length: 22'
With swing away tongue: 19' 6"
Beam: 91"
Approx. weight: 1175 lbs.
Approx. weight (dual console): 1225 lbs.
Fuel capacity: 27 gal.
Max. horsepower range: 115-175

SABRE

The Sabre features a low profile with smooth aerodynamic contours, and a price tag aimed at those efficiency-minded fishermen. A quick throttle response will keep you in the fast lane right from the instantaneous "hole shot." Plus, the Sabre handles like a dream. It will take a turn smoothly, no hopping or skipping. Tournament fish-

Summer Boat Deals
Looking for a used fishing boat? The middle of the summer is one of the best times to find a bargain. Boat dealers and boat owners are more anxious to strike a deal before the end of the fishing season, when they may have to keep the boat through the winter.

BULLET BASS BOATS

MODEL 20CC

20CC

The Bullet 20CC is designed around a center console flanked by step-up carpeted storage areas and an extra large front casting platform. Like all Bullet boats, the 20CC offers amenities like generous tackle storage areas, a built-in insulated ice chest, and large divided livewell. Standard features include: step saver bow panel, large front casting platform, step up - opens to carpeted storage areas, driver console and dash, passenger seats (removable w/storage), drivers seat with insulated ice chest underneath, dry storage compartments, divided livewell with two lids, battery and fuel storage.

SPECIFICATIONS
Length: 20' 1"
Beam: 91"
Weight: 1175 lbs.

20XD

The Bullet 20XD delivers great acceleration and tremendous top speed. An extended deck on this 20-foot boat improves maneuvering on board without sacrificing floor or storage space. Standard features include: step saver bow panel, extended deck, carpeted rod box, step up - opens to carpeted storage area, carpeted tackle storage/rod box, driver console and dash, 3 piece bench seat with storage under outside seats, insulated ice chest, dry storage compartment, divided livewell with 2 lids, battery and fuel storage.

SPECIFICATIONS
Length: 20' 1"
Beam: 91"
Weight: 1200 lbs.

20XDC

The Bullet 20XDC is 20 feet of sheer fishing pleasure. Built from the mold of its big brother, the 21XDC, the extended, raised deck design allows for ample casting room. This high performance rig features dual consoles and dash, plus generous amounts of carpeted storage for all of your rods and tackle. Standard Features include:

SPECIFICATIONS
Length: 20' 1"
Beam: 91"
Weight: 1220 lbs.

20XF

The Bullet 20XF was designed for the fisherman who wanted more floor space. Built from the mold of the 20XD, the extended floor design allows for ample room for tackle and/or a live bait tank, as well as storage under the front casting deck. As with all Bullet boats, this 20 footer will get you there in a hurry. Standard features include: step saver bow panel, casting deck, carpeted rod box, hatch to carpeted storage area, carpeted tackle storage and rod box, driver console and dash, 3 piece bench seat with storage, insulated ice chest, dry storage compartment, divided livewell with 2 lids, battery and fuel storage.
Specifications
Length: 20' 1"
Beam: 91"
Weight: 1175 lbs.

20XRD

The Bullet 20XRD has an extended, raised deck design. The casting platform is raised slightly higher, providing a deck area that is 8" longer. Standard features include: step saver bow panel, extended deck, carpeted rod box, carpeted tackle storage/rod box, driver console and dash, 3 piece bench seat with storage under outside seats, insulated ice chest, dry storage compartment, divided livewell with 2 lids, battery and fuel storage.

SPECIFICATIONS
Length: 20' 1"
Beam: 91"
Weight: 1200 lbs.

21XD

Improve your vantage point from the extended deck of the Bullet 21XD. With 21 feet 10 inches of tournament ready hi-technology, this Bullet beauty delivers a rock-steady ride. Deep, roomy, carpeted storage units line the deck to house an arsenal of tackle. Standard features include: step saver bow panel, extended raised deck, carpeted tackle, storage and rod box, step up - opens to carpeted storage area, passenger and driver console with dash, 3 piece bench seat with storage, insulated ice chest, dry storage compartment, divided livewell with 2 lids, battery and fuel storage.

SPECIFICATIONS
Length: 21' 10"
Beam: 91"
Weight: 1300 lbs.

BUMBLE BEE BOATS

2100 PRO SPORT

2100 PRO SPORT
2100 SUPER VEE

Standard Features: 12" jackplate, adjustable foot throttle, front deck dual rod lockers, third rear rod locker (super vee), over 25 cubic feet of dry storage, all fiberglass storage boxes, divided rear fiberglass livewell, timed aeration, recirculation, and pro-air livewell systems, livewell pumpout system, livewell remote valve, windshield(s), 36# high density composite transom, high-performance dash, full instrumentation, lighted rotary switches, auxillary power outlet, 1000 g,p.h. auto bilge pump , 46 gallon aluminum fuel tank, seat cargo net storage, custom hi-dry seats, full locking storage, lighted storage, rod lockers, and livewell, instant on courtesy lights, recessed bow panel with step saver switches, custom boat, carpet, cupholders, pull up cleats, carpet trim, easy access mechanical area.
SPECIFICATIONS
Length: 21' 6"
Beam: 90" Approx.
Weight: 1400 lbs.
Rec'd horsepower: 225-250
Fuel capacity: 46 gal.

Storage capacity: 25 cu. Ft (exc. Rod box)
Livewell: 31 gal.

278 PRO FD

Standard Features: 6" jackplate, all fiberglass storage boxes, rear fiberglass 30 gallon livewell, timed aeration, and recirculation livewell systems, 36# high density composite transom, speed, tach, and fuel gauges, bilge pump , custom hi-dry seats, front and rear fold down fishing seats, full locking storage, carpet, and seat vinyl colors, high-performance dash, recessed bow panel, windshield.
SPECIFICATIONS
Length: 17' 8"
Beam: 82"
Approx. Weight: 1000 lbs.
Rec'd horsepower: 115-150
Fuel capacity: 25 gal.
Storage capacity: 12 cu. Ft (exc. Rod box)
Livewell: 30 gal.

270 PRO FD

Standard Features: 6" jackplate, all fiberglass storage boxes, rear fiberglass 30 gallon livewell, timed aeration, and re-circulation livewell systems, 36# high density composite

transom, speed, tachometer, and fuel gauges, bilge pump, custom hi-dry seats, front and rear fold down fishing seats, full locking storage, carpet, high-performance dash, recessed bow panel, windshield.
SPECIFICATIONS
Length: 16' 4"
Beam: 82" Approx.
Weight: 900 lbs.
Rec'd horsepower: 75-135
Fuel capacity: 20 gal.
Storage capacity: 10 cu. Ft (exc. Rod box)
Livewell: 30 gal.

280 PRO FD

Standard Features: 10" jackplate, foot throttle, single rod locker, 10 cubic feet of dry storage, all fiberglass storage boxes, divided fiberglass 31 gallon livewell, timed aeration and re-circulation livewell systems, livewell remote valve, 36# high density composite transom, full instrumentation, 1000 g.p.h. auto bilge pump, 31-gallon aluminum fuel tank, custom hi-dry seats, full locking storage, carpet, easy access mechanical area.
SPECIFICATIONS
Length: 18' 0"

Beam: 84"
Approx. Weight: 1,100 lbs.
Rec'd Horsepower: 150-175
Fuel capacity: 31 gal.
Storage capacity: 10 cu. Ft (exc. Rod box)
Livewell: 31 gal.

290 SUPER VEE/290 PROSPORT (DUAL CONSOLE)

Standard Features: 10" jackplate, foot throttle, front deck dual rod lockers, over 13 cubic feet of dry storage, all fiberglass storage boxes, divided rear fiberglass 31 gallon livewell, timed aeration, recirculation, and Pro-Air livewell systems, livewell pumpout system, livewell remote valve, windshield(s), 36# high density composite transom high-performance dash, full instrumentation, lighted rotary switches, auxillary power outlet, 1000 g,p.h. auto bilge pump, 40 gallon aluminum fuel tank, custom hi-dry seats, full locking storage, instant-on courtesy lights, recessed bow panel with step saver switches, custom boat, carpet, cupholders. easy access mechanical area

SPECIFICATIONS
Length: 19' 1"
Beam: 90"
Approx. Weight: 1,200 lbs. Rec'd
Horsepower: 200
Fuel capacity: 40 gal.
*Storage capacity:*13 cu. Ft (exc. Rod box)
*Livewell:*31 gal.

200 PRO VEE AND 200 PROSPORT

Standard Features: 10" jackplate, foot throttle, single rod locker, over 13 cubic feet of dry storage, all fiberglass storage boxes, divided rear fiberglass 31 gallon livewell, timed aeration, re-circulation, and Pro-Air livewell systems, livewell remote valve, 36# high density composite transom, full instrumentation, 1000 g,p.h. auto bilge pum p. 40 gallon aluminum fuel tank, custom hi-dry seats, full locking stor-

age, carpet, cupholders, easy access mechanical area, bucket seats with adjustable driver's

SPECIFICATIONS
Length: 20' 4"
Beam: 90"
Approx. Weight: 1,300 lbs.
Rec'd horsepower: 200-225
F*uel capacity:* 40 gal.
Storage capacity: 13 cu. Ft (exc. Rod box)
Livewell: 31 gal.

180 PRO SPORT

Standard Features: 10" jackplate, foot throttle, single rod locker, over 10 cubic feet of dry storage, all fiberglass storage boxes divided rear fiberglass 31 gallon livewell, timed aeration, and re-circulation livewell systems, livewell remote valve, 36# high density composite transom, full instrumentation, 1000 g.p.h. auto bilge pump, 31 gallon aluminum fuel tank, custom hi-dry seats, front pro pole and rear fold down, full locking storage, carpet, easy access mechanical area

SPECIFICATIONS
Length: 18' 0"
Beam: 90"
Approx. Weight: 1,100 lbs.
Rec'd horsepower: 150-175
Fuel capacity: 33 gal.
Storage capacity: 10 cu. Ft (exc. Rod box)
Livewell: 31 gal.

180 PRO VEE

Standard Features: 10" jackplate. foot throttle, single rod locker, over 10 cubic feet of dry storage, all fiberglass storage boxes divided rear fiberglass 31 gallon livewell, timed aeration, and re-circulation livewell systems, livewell remote valve, 36# high density composite transom, full instrumentation, 1000 g,p.h. auto bilge pump , 31 gallon aluminum fuel tank, custom hi-dry seats, front pro pole and rear fold down, full locking storage, custom boat, carpet, easy access mechanical area.

SPECIFICATIONS
Length: 18' 0"
Beam: 90"
Approx. Weight: 1,100 lbs.
Rec'd horsepower: 150-175
Fuel capacity: 33 gal.
Storage capacity: 10 cu. Ft (exc. Rod box)
Livewell: 31 gal.

254

STANDARD FEATURES: DELUXE FOLD DOWN SEATS. BILGE PUMP. AERATED LIVEWELL.
SPECIFICATIONS
Length: 15' 4"
Beam: 74"
Approx. Weight: 650 lbs.
Rec'd horsepower: 50-80
Fuel capacity: 14 gal.
Storage capacity: 8 cu. Ft (exc. Rod box)
Livewell: 19 gal.

154

Standard Features: Fiberglass deck, Rod box, Storage boxes, Aerated livewell, Switch panel, Electronics platform, Carpeted interior, Composite transom
SPECIFICATIONS
Length: 15' 3"
Beam: 69"
Approx. Weight: 600 lbs.
Rec'd horsepower: 25-40
Fuel capacity: 8 gal. Built-in tank.

STINGER

Standard Features: deluxe fold down seats, speed, tachometer, fuel, fiberglass deck, rod box, storage boxes, aerated livewell, switch panel, electronics platform, carpeted interior, composite transom, bilge pump, aerated livewell.
SPECIFICATIONS
Length: 15' 3"
Beam: 69"
Approx. Weight: 650 lbs.
Rec'd horsepower: 40-80
Fuel capacity: 12 gal.
Livewell: 12 gal.

CHARGER BASS BOATS

296 TF

595 XLF

Charger's 595 XLF is a truly large bass boat for the amateur or professional angler looking for a smooth ride with more deck space and larger storage compartments. Load the 595 XLF with a wide range of options or take it factory equipped, and you'll be boss of the lake. The 595 XLF features a built-in jack plate, raised forward and rear casting decks, and a 4-inch thick transom.

SPECIFICATIONS
Length: 21' 9"
Beam: 96"
Weight: 1800 lbs.
Horsepower: all v-6's
Molded Depth: 41"
Capacity: 6 person/900 lbs. 1500 lbs. Persons, motor, gear

496 TF

Enjoy a relaxed day on the water with our new 496. The big broad deck space allows you to get to fore and aft in a split second. The cockpit rests down in the hull for added comfort and reliability. This boat is a solid choice for the avid angler. The 496 TF features a built-in jack plate, raised forward and rear casting decks, and a 4-inch thick transom.

SPECIFICATIONS
Length: 20' 6"
Beam: 95"
Weight: 1650 lbs.
Max. Horsepower: All V-6's
Molded Depth: 41"
Capacity: 6 person/900 lbs. 1500 lbs. persons, motor, gear.

395 TF

All Charger bass boats are loaded with dry and wet storage compartments and the 395 TF and 395 VF are no exceptions. The professional angler likes the convenience of a Charger bass boat "when the going gets fast". No fumbling or stumbling just a lot of convenient storage for all the items that are his "tricks of the trade" to catch the big fish. The 395TF features a built-in jack plate, raised forward and rear casting decks, and a 4-inch thick transom.

SPECIFICATIONS
Length: 19' 6"
Beam: 96"
Weight: 1425 lbs. (VF), 1475 lbs. (TF)
Max. Horsepower: 225 Molded *Depth*: 41"
Capacity: 6 person/750 lbs. 1400 lbs. persons, motor, gear.

375 T

You can have your choice of outboard power . . . add a trolling motor and take off for the day. You say you want to go for a refreshing dip or maybe water ski and then picnic? With the 375 T it's your choice. There is plenty of storage room for all the "stuff" you need for your fun on the water. For the family . . . Compliments of Charger innovation and design.

SPECIFICATIONS
Length: 19' 4"
Beam: 93"
Weight: 1550 lbs.
Max. Horsepower: 200
Molded Depth: 39"
Capacity: 5 person/750 lbs. 1350 lbs. persons, motor, gear.

296 TF

This smooth and easy riding 296 TF Charger comes equipped with loads of storage. The front deck features 2 huge storage organizer compartments while the rear holds 2 additional tackle utility boxes. Huge deck and storage boxes provide space for all the gear storage you can imagine. This 19' 3" boat gives you that "easy" and smooth Charger ride. The 296 TF features a built-in jack plate, raised forward and rear casting decks, and a 4-inch thick transom.

SPECIFICATIONS
Length: 19' 3"
Beam: 94"
Weight: 1450 lbs. (VF), 1500 lbs. (TF)
Max. Horsepower: 200
Molded Depth: 41"
Capacity: 6 person/900 lbs. 1400 lbs. persons, motor, gear.

195 VF

Like all other Charger models you can add the "Pro-Air livewell cooling system" (only the model 195 VF features this system as standard equipment). Fish keep cool in the pro-air, suffer less stress, and enjoy a more successful release. The boat interior needs no configuration change as the pro-air fits neatly into the present design. Ask your dealer for details and be a leader in fish conservation. The 195 VF features a built-in jack plate, raised forward and rear casting decks, and a 4-inch thick transom.

SPECIFICATIONS
Length: 19' 3"
Beam: 94"
Weight: 1400 lbs. (VF), 1450 lbs. (TF)
Max. Horsepower: 200
Molded Depth: 41"
Capacity: 6 person/900 lbs. 1400 lbs. persons, motor, gear.

CHARGER BASS BOATS

186 TF

Fishability is great with a huge floating platform. Serious tournament anglers and guides will appreciate the extra large deck. Storage spaces provide ample room for all the gear you need for a full day of fishing. There are a huge number of color selections to choose from. The 186 TF features a built-in jack plate, raised forward and rear casting decks, and a 4-inch thick transom.

SPECIFICATIONS
Length: 18' 6"
Beam: 92"
Weight: 1250 lbs. (VF), 1300 lbs. (TF)
Max. Horsepower: 175
Molded depth: 41"
Capacity: 5 person/825 lbs. 1300 lbs. Persons, motor, gear.

182 TF

The 182 TF dual console Charger is a shade smaller than the biggest model, the 182, but still boasts the quality found on all Charger boats. You can rig this beauty up to 150 big horses and really take off. For the new boater or the old pro the ride will amaze you. The 182 TF features a built-in jack plate, raised forward and rear casting decks, and a 4-inch thick transom.

SPECIFICATIONS
Length: 17' 10"
Beam: 90"
Weight: 1225 lbs. (VF), 1250 lbs. (TF)
Max. Horsepower: 150
Molded Depth: 40"
Capacity: 5 person/675 lbs. 1250 lbs. persons, motor, gear.

180 VF

All the features that come with Charger bass boats can be found or added to our 180 series models. An old favorite in the Charger line of boats, this boat will perform and handle with ease when launching or on the water. Go see your Charger dealer to see all the different models. The 180 VF features a built-in jack plate, raised forward and rear casting decks, and a 4-inch thick transom.

SPECIFICATIONS
Length: 17'10"
Beam: 86"
Weight: 1150 lbs. (VF), 1200 lbs. (TF)
Max. Horsepower: 150
Molded Depth: 41"
Capacity: 5 person/625 lbs. 1200 lbs. Persons, motor, gear.

169 VF

This boat is for the serious or casual sportsman. It's packed with ample storage compartments. It has your choice of horsepower with no loss of performance or speed. You can track and catch big fish from this medium sized rig. The 169 VF features a 3-inch thick transom.

SPECIFICATIONS
Length: 16' 9"
Beam: 88"
Weight: 1000 lbs.
Max. Horsepower: 135
Molded Depth: 41"
Capacity: 4 person/550 lbs. 1100 lbs. persons, motor, gear.

CONNECT-A-DOCK BOATS

BASS BABY

Bigger is not always better—especially when an angler is trying to launch his fishing boat into a shallow pond or backwater. Modular dock distributor Connect-A-Dock solves the problem with its Bass Baby, a unique fishing boat with wheels that can be transported in the back of a pickup truck, and then hand-carried or rolled to the water's edge for launching. The Bass Baby is a two-person boat that offers extreme durability and the convenience of fishing in small bodies of water. At 96" long x 54" wide x 18" tall, the 143-pound boat drafts only 2½" to 3" when empty. It meets strict Coast Guard safety regulations and has a maximum flotation of 475 pounds. By setting a bow- or stern-mounted trolling motor for minimum depth, a fully-loaded Bass Baby can operate in waters only 9" deep. Since the boat is rotationally molded of impact-resistant polyethylene, its seamless hull is virtually leakproof and puncture-resistant. Contact with submerged stumps, branches and rocks will not harm the boat's hull while operating in shallow waters. The Bass Baby is ideal for fishing those hard-to-get spots where the big ones hide. It comes with a two-year warranty.

SPECIFICATIONS
Overall hull length: 96"
Beam: 54"
Horsepower: rated for a 2-hp gasoline motor or an electric trolling motor

Transom height: 18"
Total persons, motor, gear: 475 lbs.
MSRP: $499 plus freight, without motor

FISHER BOATS

PRO HAWK 1860V

This is a serious boat for some serious fishing. Designed to take on big waters or small lakes, the Pro Hawk's 18' 6" performance mod-V hull is capable of handling up to a powerful V6, 150 horsepower outboard. Combine that with a durable design featuring .125 thick (⅛ inch) all-welded aluminum construction, backed by

FISHER's exclusive "Fish Forever" Warranty, and the end result is a boat built to last a lifetime.

This boat sports a 92" beam and a whopping 72" bottom width. That means a super stable ride on the water and spacious fishing decks and storage compartments above water. Bow and aft decks are carpeted aluminum and come complete with bike seat and

clamshell fishing chair. The bow deck also has two locking rod boxes.

The Pro Hawk 1860V standard package includes a gas stingy, yet powerful 115 ELPTO Mercury® outboard, 24-volt, 67 pound thrust MotorGuide® electric trolling motor and a Zercom® in-dash depth finder with surface temperature. Other standard features include a huge 34 gallon aerated livewell with timer, a molded fiberglass console with smoked plexiglass windscreen, Quicksilver® Classic 3000 control box and full dash instrumentation – tachometer, speedometer, voltmeter, fuel, trim and water pressure gauges.

The Pro Hawk 1860V comes on a factory-matched, color-keyed, welded tubular frame single axle trailer. Standard features include surge disc brakes, swing-away tongue, submersible lights, loading guides, 14 inch tires with chrome wheels, bearing protection, motor support and tie downs. All necessary cranking and deep cycle batteries are included, making this water ready package a true turn-key deal.

MSRP: The single console version of the 1860V rigged with a 125 hp ELPTO retails at about $17,750, plus applicable dealer prep and destination charges.

Get Ready at the Ramp
When waiting in line to launch your boat, load all your gear, disconnect your boat straps, take off your motor-tote and be ready to launch when you get to the ramp. The line will move much quicker if everyone does this.

HP190 SE

The HP190 Special Edition high performance bass boat from G3 gives aluminum bass boats a bold and distinctive look other manufacturers only dream about. Two-tone black and platinum paint, Special Edition graphics, bonus features and a 175 horsepower rating make the HP190 Special Edition feel like a family member. With all aluminum materials for the hull, floor and deck, and welded construction from bow to transom, these boats won't rattle apart even in the roughest conditions. The high performance pad hull jumps out of the hole quickly and achieves speeds nearing 70 mph. The HP 190 Special Edition is available in single or double console models. The 90-inch beam creates a front casting deck large enough for two anglers. Under the front deck lids are two roto-molded rod lockers with built in rod storage tubes plus two roomy front deck storage compartments to stow gear and tackle. The Special Edition includes a step for the front deck with storage access that extends the length of the deck.

SPECIFICATIONS
Boat Length: 19';
Length on Trailer: 23'2"; *Beam:* 90";
Width on Trailer: 94"; *Bottom Width:* 61"; *Transom Height:* 20"; *Side*

Depth: 20"; *Hull Gauge:* .100, welded;
Max. Horsepower: 175 h.p.
Fuel Capacity: 27 gals.
Livewell Dimensions: 14" x 41" (19 gal.)
MSRP: $18,995 to $23,495

PRO 185

Bass boats should be built to handle tough conditions yet laid out to compliment the angler's fishing abilities. The Pro 185 from G3 is on the mark for both categories with a hull welded with .100 gauge aluminum and features designed with fishing in mind. The 18½ foot long Pro 185 is rated for a 115-horsepower Yamaha outboard and the improved "New Generation" modified-V step hull calms choppy water for a smooth ride and maximum performance at all speeds. The ³⁄₁₆ inch extruded longitudinal stringer system runs the full length of the hull, adding strength and providing truer hull alignment.

SPECIFICATIONS
Boat Length: 18'5"
Length on Trailer: 22' 6"; *Beam:* 72"
Width on Trailer: 80"
Bottom Width: 56"
Transom Height: 20"; *Side Depth:* 20"

Hull Gauge: .100, welded
Max. Horsepower: 115
Fuel Capacity: 21 gals.
Livewell Dimensions:
14" x 41" (19 gal.)
MSRP: $12,495 to $15,495

JAVELIN BASS BOATS

170 SC

170 SC

Features: 10-year hull warranty with a 3-year protection plan on selected components: 100% composite construction, Armorcote gelcoat, real-time in-dash flasher with water temperature, two aerated livewells, Motorguide 743 four 12-volt 42" 43-lb thrust foot controlled trolling motor, bilge pump, built-in ice chest, driver's console with: tachometer, speedometer, fuel and trim gauges, high impact rub rail, lockable water resistant latches on all storage compartments, Teleflex no-feedback steering system

SPECIFICATIONS
Length: 16'8"
Beam: 83"
Persons/Capacity: 5 / 610 lbs Max
Weight Capacity: 1160 Max
Horsepower Power: 115 Approximate
Fuel Capacity: 26 gals.

180 SC & 180 DC

Features: 10-year hull warranty with a 3-year protection plan on selected components, 100% composite construction, Armorcote gel coat, real-time in-dash flasher with water temperature, divided / aerated live well, Flowrite 3 position livewell system with timer, Motorguide 743 four 12-volt 42" 43 lb thrust foot controlled trolling motor, bilge pump, built-in ice chest, driver's console: tachometer, speedometer, fuel and trim gauges, "high flow" anti-airlock aerator pump, real-time in-dash flasher with water temperature, Teleflex no-feedback steering system

SPECIFICATIONS
Length: 17' 5"
Beam: 86"
Persons/Capacity: 4 /510 lbs Max
Weight Capacity: 1080 lbs Max
Horsepower: 135
Approximate Fuel Capacity: 29 gal.

185 S-C & 190 DC

Features: Limited lifetime warranty on the hull with 3 year protection plan on selected components, 100% composite construction, Armorcote gel-coat, Lowrance X-51 graph flush mount, divided / aerated livewell Flowrite 3 position, livewell system with timer, "high-flow" anti-airlock aerator pump, Minn-Kota Max 65 42" 24-volt foot control bilge pump, built-in ice chest, driver's console with tachometer, speedometer, fuel and trim gauges, Teleflex Baystar hydraulic steering system.

SPECIFICATIONS
Length: 18' 6"
Beam: 91"
Persons/Capacity: 4 / 530 lbs Max
Weight Capacity: 1110 lbs Max
Horsepower: 150 Approx Fuel
Capacity: 36 gal

200 SC & 200 DC

Features: 10-year hull warranty with a 3-year protection plan on selected components, 100% composite construction, Armorcote gelcoat, real-time in-dash flasher with water temperature, Teleflex Sea Pro hydraulic steering, divided/aerated livewell, Flowrite 3-position livewell system with timer, driver's console with: tachometer, speedometer, fuel and trim gauges, lighted rocker switches at bow and console, Motorguide 764 24-volt 42" 64 lb thrust foot controlled trolling motor, 12-volt accessory plug, automotive style circuit breaker electrical system, bilge cover, bilge pump, built-in ice chest, cargo net, dual rod lockers with gas-assist lid shocks, javelin fish measuring board with storage sleeve, non-skid bow and stern mats, real-time in-dash flasher with water temperature.

SPECIFICATIONS
Length: 19' 10"
Beam: 95"
Persons/Capacity: 5 / 645 lbs Max
Weight Capacity: 1300 lbs Max
Horsepower Power: 225
Approx Fuel Capacity: 48 gal.

1652 V SPORT

2370 GUIDE BOAT

1860

LEGEND CRAFT BOATS

Legend's heavy built construction and high quality are quickly gaining recognition by bass fishermen. Standard boats are available, or have one custom built to meet your needs.

STANDARD EQUIPMENT:
Short bow seat
17" center seat
20" rear seat or
48" extended deck with 20" rear seat
Green, flat black or unpainted

Options:
48" extended deck
Drop deck
Extra knee brace

16"-27" transom
Extra cross seat with 1 or 2 livewells
Standard splash pan
4'-8' gun/rod box
4'-8' square bottom box for truck
Livewell or dry storage:
16"x18"-24"-30"-36"
Diamond Tread Plate for decks and floors
1'-3' deck extensions
Consoles: side and center
Hand or foot trolling motor brackets
Full seat commercial livewell
Under deck storage with/without door
1' extra deck storage extension
Full seat storage

Pedestal base
Rear deck
Pontoons
Smooth bottom boats
Mud Buddy motors (2.5-29 hp) and blinds
Paints: metallic gray or camo
PICTURED:
Model 2370:
V Hull Guide Boat
Model 1860:
Flat Floor & Sides, Center Console With Livewell, 7 Ft. Rod/Gun Box
Model 1652:
V Sport

LOWE BASS BOATS

180W

SPECIFICATIONS
Length: 17'
Beam: 76"
Bottom Width: 56"
Transom Height: 21" Max.
Person Weight: 495 Approx.
Hull Weight: 995 Max.
Weight/Capacity: 1075 Max.
Horsepower Capacity: 115
Fuel Capacity: 20 gal.

STINGER

This all-welded Stinger series of professional level bass classics is changing the way experienced anglers think about aluminum. Computer-assisted CAD engineering and all-welded SuperLock™ construction techniques have produced a high-performance, custom Pro-Trac hull design that maximizes handling, durability and, of course, fishability. This totally wood-free series includes spacious forward and rear TufDeck™ aluminum casting decks with all the built-in fishing features you demand. And, the Stinger series is the ultimate go anywhere, anytime bass power tool built with heavy duty 5052 H-34 marine grade aluminum alloy, tough extruded center keel, bow stem, gunnels and rub rail, plus a composite no-wood transom, all for extra long life.

180W 8°–18° ALL-WELD MODIFIED V-SIDE CONSOLE BASS

Standard package includes a 50 hp. base outboard* and painted bunk trailer. Important features include TufDeck™ aluminum floor liner and decks, .100" heavy-duty all-weld hull and bow 30" live well and an extra large 50" stern live well with bait well dividers and timer.
Features: pedestal seats, fuel gauge, tilt/trim gauge, 24v electric trolling motor, 11.4 gal.\24.8 gal. aerated livewell, Humminbird fish finder, raised casting decks with storage, 12 volt receptacle, lockable rod storage, molded console, speedometer, tachometer, voltmeter.

SPECIFICATIONS
Length: 17'10"
Beam: 85.5" Transom
Height: 21" Max.
Person Weight: 725 Approx.
Hull Weight: 1050 Max.
Weight/Capacity: 1380 Max.
Horsepower Capacity: 150
Fuel Capacity: 20 gal

70W VARIABLE 8°–18° ALL-WELD MODIFIED V-SIDE CONSOLE BASS

Standard package includes 40 hp. base outboard and painted bunk trailer. Important features include TufDeck™ aluminum floor liner and decks, .100" heavy-duty all-weld hull and bow and stern 30" live wells with dividers and timer.
Features: pedestal seats, fuel gauge, tilt/trim gauge, 12v electric trolling motor, 2-11.4 gal aerated livewells, Humminbird fish finder, raised casting decks with storage, 12 volt receptacle, lockable rod storage, molded console, speedometer, tachometer, voltmeter

160W VARIABLE 8°–18° ALL-WELD MODIFIED V-SIDE CONSOLE BASS

Standard package includes a 25 hp. base outboard and painted bunk trailer. Important features include TufDeck™ aluminum floor liner and decks, .100" heavy-duty all-weld hull and extra wide/deep lockable rod storage.
Features: pedestal seats, fuel gauge, tilt/trim gauge, 12v electric trolling motor, 11.4 gal aerated livewell, Humminbird fish finder, casting decks with storage, 12 volt receptacle, lockable rod storage, molded console, speedometer, voltmeter.

SPECIFICATIONS
Length: 16'
Beam: 76"
Transom Height: 21" Max.
Person Weight: 550 Approx.
Hull Weight: 975 Max.
Weight Capacity: 1025 Max.
Horsepower Capacity: 70 Fuel
Capacity: 20 gal.

BASS STRIKER SERIES

Bass Striker series comes fish-ready with all the serious fishing features and equipment. Strikers feature large aerated livewells with rounded corners, lockable rod and tackle storage, bow mount trolling motor, a 71" beam for large casting decks forward and aft, and a console located Hummingbird fish finder. These feature packed Bass Strikers also deliver exceptional durability with TufDeck™ aluminum floor liners, 5052 H-34 marine grade aluminum hand riveted SuperLock™ hulls, stainless steel fasteners, rot-free roto-molded seat construction and a sharp looking composite helm console.

NX 896

Measuring in at 19'6" and having a 92" beam, the NX 896 is just the right size and has all the right features and moves to meet almost every bass angler's needs. From its hand laid fiberglass hull to the fiberglass stringer system, this boat is quality and value at its finest. The NX 896 standard package includes a Mercury® XR6 200 horsepower outboard, stainless prop, MotorGuide® 24-volt, 67 pound thrust trolling motor, TRACKER® Pro 160 SX LCR by Humminbird® and a color coordinated drop axle trailer.

A massive bow and aft deck with bike seat and molded fold-down fishing seat provide lots of fishing room and comfort. And the decks have roomy, lockable rod boxes, dry storage compartments, rod tie-down straps, ice chest and an insulated 33 gallon livewell with round corners, two fill pumps, recirculation system with timer and remote drain controls.

All the lids are made from aluminum for strength and are insulated to keep catches lively. A full bench seat provides seating for three. There's a partner's rod ramp on the port side.

On the inside, the NX 896's electrical system features a two bank on-board battery charging system, cour-

tesy light, 12-volt accessory outlet and 1500 GPH bilge pump. Also standard is dual rack and pinion steering and full dash instrumentation including tachometer, speedometer, voltmeter, fuel, water and trim gauges.

The NX 896 rests on a welded frame, color-coordinated, drop axle, drive-on trailer equipped with a handy swing-away tongue so the trailer can fit in most garages. There's also a folding tongue jack, transom saver, transom tie-downs, carpeted bunks and 14" tires on chrome wheels with "EZ"

lube hubs.

This standard package is water ready, including a cranking battery and two Interstate deep cycle trolling motor batteries. Upgrades with additional options and accessories are also available. Among these are Mercury EFI or OptiMax outboards, hydraulic steering, MotorGuide 36-volt trolling motor, jack plates, Hot Foot throttle controls and more.

MSRP: $22,595 (single console version), $22,895 (dual console)

PATRIOT 929 DC

The Patriot 929 DC is decorated in a tasteful red, white and blue color scheme, complete with stars and stripes. The look is neither gaudy, nor faddish. But it does make a statement about American pride. Appropriately, the 929 is the flagship of NITRO's much heralded 9 Series. And while the company is proud to salute those at the helm in Washington for their fine job, "DC" in this case stands for double console. That means driver and passenger are both in for a comfortable ride, rain or shine.

The Patriot 929 DC is 20'9" in length and has a 96" beam. Its PerforMax™ hull is so tough it's backed by NITRO's unique 9-lives Limited Lifetime Warranty. The standard Patriot package includes a NITRO 225 EFI outboard,

MotorGuide® 24-volt, 67 pound thrust trolling motor, Zercom® flasher with surface temp and a color coordinated tandem-axle, drive-on trailer with 14" radial tires, custom wheels, disc brakes and swing-away tongue. There's also hydraulic tilt steering, a

deep split-level cockpit, 10" jack plate, two-bank on-board battery charger, front bike seat and rear fishing chair on power pedestals, retractable rod straps, two 18-gallon livewells and more.

MSRP: $30,395 for standard package

POLAR BOATS

1896 AND 1788 SKIFFS

Each of these Polar Skiff models is designed with a spacious bow casting deck and an optional fold-down casting chair for an additional fisherman onboard. To keep gear safe and dry, items can easily be stored in a lockable compartment. To maintain the freshest catch and bait, the aerated baitwell/livewell with radius corners is located under a cushioned seat on the console. The console area also has six rod holders to prevent lines from tangling and keep clutter off the deck. A removable cooler with a cushioned seat can also be used as a fishbox.

SPECIFICATIONS

1896 model
Length: 18' 1"
Beam: 7' 10"
Front deck: 6' 6"
Floor width: 6' 10"
Max. horsepower rating: 120
Fuel capacity: 19 gal.
MSRP: $13,925
with a Yamaha 90 TLRA outboard

1788 MODEL
Length: 17' 7"
Beam: 7' 5"
Front deck: 5' 9"
Floor width: 6' 10"
Max. horsepower rating: 115
Fuel capacity: 19 gal.
MSRP: $12,063
with a Yamaha 60 TLRA outboard

PROCRAFT BOATS

PRO 185

This 18'2" high-performance fiberglass hull features an 88" beam and is rated for up to a 175 horsepower outboard. The hull is backed by an amazing Pro Guard 10 Year Hull Warranty, made possible because of PROCRAFT's unique all composite stringer construction.

The standard Pro 185 package includes a Mercury® 115 ELPTO power plant, 24-volt MotorGuide® trolling motor, in-dash Zercom® C.I.D. graph with surface temperature, Quicksilver® stainless prop and a factory-matched trailer.

Like any quality bass boat, the Pro 185 features both a bow and aft raised fishing deck, complete with pro fishing seat up-front and a fold-down fishing chair in the back. Beneath the compartment lids on the decks are molded-plastic dry storage boxes and dual rod compartments that can be locked. The larger lids are fitted with gas-assisted lifts. Also found in these spacious decks are two 14 gallon livewells equipped with "auto-timed" aeration and recirculation systems, remote drain controls, insulated lids and the PROCRAFT Max Air Induction system.

A full bench seat offers comfortable seating for three. Marine grade 16 ounce carpet is used on all deck and floor surfaces. And as an extra bonus and for further proof that PROCRAFT design engineers understand fishing, the bow carpet has an edge trim. The inside workings of the Pro 185 include heavy duty 24-volt trolling motor wiring and harnesses, remote tilt, anchor and navigation light switches, 800 GPH bilge pump and a console equipped with a full complement of marine gauges and circuit breaker protection. Dual anti-feedback steering is standard, as is a Quicksilver flush mount throttle control.

The trailer package is just as well equipped as the boat. A single axle 4" steel tube trailer frame comes color-matched to the boat and features a polyurethane finish and accent stripe. The trailer has submersible lights and reflectors, heavy duty winch, deluxe diamond step plates, 14" radial tires on chrome wheels with "EZ" lube hubs, transom tie-downs and motor support.
MSRP: under $17,000.00, plus freight and destination charges

175VS

Rated for a top end of 130 horses, the 175 enjoys the responsive handling of no-feedback steering. A 10-inch engine setback is built into the stern for faster, shallower hole shots and accelerated performance. Coupled with Ranger's exclusive Rite-Track Keel™ design, the 175 is geared for optimum maneuverability and a solid, one-piece feel to the ride and handling. Inside, fishing decks are broad and spacious. Platforms are extremely stable. And the layout is literally honeycombed with lockable storage. At the helm, the console is equipped with a full array of electronics and instrumentation, including speed, tach, fuel and trim gauges. A MinnKota trolling motor is standard as well as a Garmin 160 fishfinder and an on-board charger. Matched to a custom RangerTrail® trailer with a spare tire and wheel.

SPECIFICATIONS
Overall hull length: 17' 5"
Beam: 87"
Horsepower: 70-130
Transom height: 22"
Inside depth: 20"

Total persons, motor, gear: 1,145 lbs.
Approx. boat wt.: 1,370 lb. SVS, 1,395 lb. DVS
Rod box lengths: port 7'; starboard 7'
MSRP: $17,000 to $21,000

185VS

Turning heads as well as rpm's, the new 185VS takes the all-time most popular-sized tournament rig and gives it an even more popular price. Combined with Ranger's exclusive Rite-Track hull design, maneuverability is solid and responsive. Spread over a super-wide 92-inch beam, the 185 touts a world of room for multiple anglers on either deck. Broad beam stability minimizes rocking from quick, sudden movements and provides a superior platform for stalking fish in the shallows. In the cockpit, the high performance bench seating is specially contoured for greater leg, lateral and lumbar support. Custom molded footrests provide even more comfort on long runs. And, at the console, speed, tach, fuel, trim and water pressure gauges are all standard.

SPECIFICATIONS
Overall hull length: 18' 5"
Beam: 92"
Horsepower: 150-175
Transom height: 23"
Inside depth: 20"

Total persons, motor, gear: 1,365 lbs.
Approx. boat wt.: 1,560 lb. SVS, 1,585 lb. DVS
Rod box lengths: port 7'3", starboard 6'8"
MSRP: $23,000 to $27,000

RANGER BOATS

BOATS

195VS

Tournament-engineered with a passion to excel, the single and dual console 195s feature the smooth, solid handling of Sea Star Pro fluid steering. Designed with a 10-inch integrated engine set-back, the 195 delivers quicker, more responsive hole shots. Combined with a low profile layout, the 195's flared hull contours and extra wide 92-inch beam mean less wind resistance and an even drier ride. In the cockpit, speed, tach, fuel, trim and water pressure gauges are positioned for easy visibility. Additional electronics include a Garmin 160 fishfinder and a built-in, multi-bank battery charger. Custom footrests add to the comfort of longer runs and seating features the extra security of additional leg and lumbar support. Rod compartments are extremely spacious and include a port side organizer, oversized openings and gas shocks on the lids. Further equipped with a MinnKota trolling motor and a custom RangerTrail® trailer with brakes.

SPECIFICATIONS:
Overall hull length: 19' 5"
Beam: 92"
Horsepower: 150-200
Transom height: 23"
Inside depth: 20"
Total persons, motor, gear: 1,430 lbs.
Approx. boat wt.: 1,635 lbs. SVS, 1,660 lbs. DVS
Rod box lengths: port 7'3", starboard 6'11"
MSRP: $30,000 to $33,000

205VS

Loaded with standard equipment, this tournament-level powerhouse is factory rigged, rated for 225 horses, and priced to give you an instant head start. The 205 is available in both single and dual console models. Its 92½ inch beam is among the broadest in Ranger's entire freshwater line. With such a large beam, the 205 not only enjoys a world of lockable storage and optimum stability, but deck area and fishing space has also increased. Smooth Sea Star Pro® fluid steering centers the helm, complementing the 205's solid, one-piece feel. Elsewhere, performance instrumentation fills the console while molded-in footrests and a wealth of legroom work to eliminate the stress and fatigue of long-distance running. Further equipped with an on-board battery charger, MinnKota trolling motor, Garmin electronics and a tandem axle trailer with brakes and swing-away tongue.

SPECIFICATIONS:
Overall hull length: 20' 5"
Beam: 92½"
Horsepower: 175-225
Transom height: 23"
Inside depth: 19¾"
Total persons, motor, gear: 1,470 lbs.
Approx. boat wt.: 1,705 lb.SVS, 1,730 lb.DVS
Rod box lengths: port 8', starboard 7'
MSRP: $34,000 to $38,000

519VX

With larger, lower profile fishing decks the 518VX Comanches are built for full scale tournament action. Fluid, Sea Star Pro® steering centers the helm while an integrated engine set-back accelerates hole shots and virtually eliminates backwash from quick stops. Twin fuel tanks are centered below the seating for greater stability and faster planing. Elsewhere, the increased bow flare helps ensure an extremely dry ride in the roughest waters. Lockable rod storage covers both sides of the front deck while a runnin' rod rack keeps your favorite rods close at hand. At the helm, the electronics center includes the added convenience and dependability of a backlit digital switching system.

Leg room is plentiful and molded-in footrests reinforce the total performance atmosphere. Running on more than three decades of tournament bred refinements, the single and dual console 518VX Comanches are built to take up the slack and take home the winnings.

SPECIFICATIONS:
Overall hull length: 19'
Beam: 91½"
Horsepower: 150-200
Transom height: 23"
Inside depth: 19¾"
Total persons, motor, gear: 1,400 lbs.
Approx. boat wt.: 1,590 lb. SVX, 1,615 lb. DVX
Rod box lengths: port 7'6", starboard 7'
MSRP: $32,000 to $36,000

Light Check
Your boat trailer's electrical components are subjected to a variety of adverse conditions, so check them periodically. Have someone stand behind the boat to make sure tail lights, brake lights and turn signals are working properly. If signals are dim, you may have a bad connection, or could need a more powerful flasher unit on the tow vehicle. An occasional shot of WD-40 into the pig tail wiring connector will reduce corrosion.

RANGER BOATS

520VX

With larger, lower profile fishing decks, the single and dual console 520s run on a wide open 20' 9" hull design and carry Ranger's exclusive "VX" high performance seal. The smooth, responsive handling of Sea Star Pro® steering guides up to 225 horses of factory-rigged outboard power while an integrated 15-inch engine set-back accelerates hole shots and virtually eliminates backwash from quick stops. Elsewhere, VX designers positioned the 92½" beam farther forward, creating a front deck so large that similarly sized rigs pale in comparison. The resulting increase in bow flare also helps ensure an extremely smooth, dry ride through the roughest of waters. Further equipped with a three-bank on-board charging system, a built-in insulated cooler, recessed tie cleats, automotive-style carpet trim and upright, level foam flotation.

SPECIFICATIONS:
Overall hull length: 20' 9"
Beam: 92½"
Horsepower: 200-225
Transom height: 23"
Inside depth: 20½"
Total persons, motor, gear: 1,500 lbs.
Approx. boat wt.: 1,775 lb. SVX, 1,800 lb. DVX
Rod box lengths: port 8', starboard 7'
MSRP: $37,000 to $41,000

522VX

With more deck space, more lockable storage, more fuel capacity and more all-out performance from start to finish, the 522VX Comanche has more of everything you need to take high performance angling to the next level. Ultra smooth, Sea Star Pro® steering guides a maximum outboard rating of 250 horses. Combined with a patented pultruded fiberglass transom, fiberglass stringers and multiple layers of zone-tempered fiberglass, the 522 carries an exceptional balance of power and performance. Even the largest of rods are pampered in this rig. Centering the front deck, the bi-level rod box is equipped with individual rod tubes and contoured rests to cradle the handles. The oversized port rod compartment stretches over 9 feet in length and features the added convenience of an oversized opening and airshock support on the lid.

SPECIFICATIONS:
Overall hull length: 22' 3"
Beam: 92½"
Horsepower: 200-250
Transom height: 23"
Inside depth: 20½"
Total persons, motor, gear: 1,600 lbs.
Approx. boat wt.: 1,925 lb. SVX, 1,950 lb. DVX
Rod box lengths: port 9'6"; center row 1, 7'6"; center row 2, 7'
MSRP: $38,000 to $42,000

SeaArk Boats of Monticello, Arkansas, builds a line of all-welded aluminum boats especially designed for the fisherman who does not want to spend a lot of money on a bass rig. The "P" line features the fishing basics in an extremely durable modified vee hull. SeaArk's "P" models are available from 16' to 20' in length and in bottom widths from 52" to 72". All models in the line come standard with a console fitted with steering, an aerated livewell which features a molded plastic liner, storage box, two stainless seat bases and an extra-wide rear bench seat.

The "P" series offers both side and center console models. The center console models have a .125 gauge aluminum treadplate floor as standard. The same floor is available as an option on the side console models. The "P" line also includes several low deck models which feature a lower, extended bow deck.

SeaArk offers many options for the "P" line, including upgraded paint and graphics, fold-down fishing seats, cushions for livewells, Gator-Hide interior finish, fishing packages, camouflage paint schemes, windshield, grab rail, flotation pods, rod boxes and additional storage boxes.

1652-PLD

SPECIFICATIONS
"P" MODEL
Model: 1652-P
Length Overall: 16'
Beam: 72"
Bottom Width: 52"
Side Depth: 20"
Gauge: .100
Maximum Horsepower Rating: 50
Weight Capacity: 1100 lbs.
Approximate Weight: 415 lbs.
Transom: 20"

Model: 1652-PLD
Length Overall: 16'
Beam: 72"
Bottom Width: 52"
Side Depth: 20"

Gauge: .100
Maximum Horsepower Rating: 50
Weight Capacity: 1100 lbs.
Approximate Weight: 460 lbs.
Transom: 20"

Model: 1652-PCC
Length Overall: 16'
Beam: 72"
Bottom Width: 52"
Side Depth: 20"
Gauge: .100
Maximum Horsepower Rating: 50
Weight Capacity: 1100 lbs.
Approximate Weight: 460 lbs.
Transom: 20"

MSRP: $3,450 to $6,375 (boat only)

Practice Trailer Backing
Backing a trailer into tight places or down a launch ramp is easier than it looks, but it does take practice. Start by practicing in a parking lot in a vehicle that allows you to see the trailer through the rear window. Vans, trucks, and campers that have obstructed rear views require more practice and the use of side mirrors. Be patient, and make steering adjustments slowly and a little at a time.

SEA ARK "P" BOATS

2072-PCC

Approximate Weight: 780 lbs.
Transom: 20"

Model: 1872-PCC
Length Overall: 18'
Beam: 95"
Bottom Width: 72"
Side Depth: 28"
Gauge: .125
Maximum Horsepower Rating: 130
Weight Capacity: 2075 lbs.
Approximate Weight: 875 lbs.
Transom: 20"

Model: 2072-P
Length Overall: 20'1"
Beam: 95"
Bottom Width: 72"
Side Depth: 28"
Gauge: .125
Maximum Horsepower Rating: 130
Weight Capacity: 2300 lbs.
Approximate Weight: 840 lbs.
Transom: 20"

Model: 1860-PLD
Length Overall: 18'
Beam: 82"
Bottom Width: 60"
Side Depth: 24"
Gauge: .100
Maximum Horsepower Rating: 80
Weight Capacity: 1240 lbs.
Approximate Weight: 515 lbs.
Transom: 20"

Model: 1860-PCC LD
Length Overall: 18'
Beam: 82"
Bottom Width: 60"

Side Depth: 24"
Gauge: .100
Maximum Horsepower Rating: 80
Weight Capacity: 1240 lbs.
Approximate Weight: 615 lbs.
Transom: 20"

Model: 1872-P
Length Overall: 18'
Beam: 95"
Bottom Width: 72"
Side Depth: 28"
Gauge: .125
Maximum Horsepower Rating: 130
Weight Capacity: 2075 lbs.

Model: 2072-PCC
Length Overall: 20'1"
Beam: 95"
Bottom Width: 72"
Side Depth: 28"
Gauge: .125
Maximum Horsepower Rating: 130
Weight Capacity: 2300 lbs.
Approximate Weight: 950 lbs.
Transom: 20"

MSRP: $3,450 to $6,375 (boat only)

Vehicle Towing Power

Your tow vehicle may have ample power to pull a loaded boat trailer down the road, but that doesn't mean it has the guts to haul the same piece of equipment up steep launching ramps, or that the brakes can hold everything safely on a steep incline. Follow manufacturer's towing guidelines, and never exceed tow limits. Too much trailer weight can cause an accident, or pull the tow vehicle into the lake on a steep ramp.

ST15

ST15

The ST15 delivers as the perfect boat for the first-time buyer who has decided the time to get on the water is now. Retiring hobbyists love the ST15 too - primarily for its easy trailering size and its equally pleasing value-based price. It's easy to handle, easy to get into, and a pleasure to own.

SPECIFICATIONS

Length on Trailer: 20'
Width on Trailer: 88"
Length Overall: 15' 7"
Beam: 78"
Transom Height: 24"
Height Overall: 46"
Interior Depth: 24"
Draft: 12"

Dry Weight: 1,050 lbs
Max H.P.: 70 h.p.
Max Weight Capacity: 931 lbs.
Max Persons Capacity: 3/391 lbs.
Fuel Capacity: 20 gals.
MSRP: $9,995 w/ Yamaha 40

SX200

For nearly 20 years, Skeeter's SX line of bass boats have been setting the standard for innovation, quality and value. The SX200 is top of the line. It features the legendary hydrodynamic design, speed and maneuverability of a Skeeter, as well as a list of features that will make you wonder how you went this long without one.

SPECIFICATIONS

Length on Trailer: 25'0"
Length on Trailer (w/Swing-away tongue): 22'10"
Width on Trailer: 101"
Length Overall: 19'6"
Beam: 94"
Transom Height: 24"
Height Overall: 44"
Interior Depth: 20"
Draft: 14"
Dry Weight: 1,550 lbs
Max H.P.: 200 h.p.
Max Weight Capacity: 1,350 lbs.
Max Persons Capacity: 5/775 lbs.
Fuel Capacity: 47 gals.
MSRP: $26,995 w/ Yamaha VX200

Hot Hubs Need Work
Each time you stop for gas when pulling a boat, place your hand on the boat trailer's wheel hubs. If the hubs are cool or slightly warm to the touch, the bearings are all right. If the hubs are hot, the bearings need to be replaced or repacked.

SKEETER BOATS

SX190

SX190

This eighteen and a half feet of pure fishing pleasure is easy to trailer and ready to go. This comfortable family fishing boat has everything you need, and nothing you don't. Classic Skeeter livewell system, roomy front and rear fishing platforms, and comfortable bench seating for up to three people.

SPECIFICATIONS
Length on Trailer: 22'9"
Length on Trailer (w/Swing-away tongue): 20'5"
Width on Trailer: 98"
Length Overall: 18'5"
Beam: 89"
Transom Height: 22"
Height Overall: 43"
Interior Depth: 19"
Draft: 12"
Dry Weight: 1,390 lbs
Max H.P.: 150 h.p.
Max Weight Capacity: 1,290 lbs.
Max Persons Capacity: 5/715 lbs.
Fuel Capacity: 36 gals.
MSRP: $20,995 w/ Yamaha V150

ZX225

One trip behind the wheel and you'll understand why the ZX225 is the choice for tournament anglers. From the sequin finish and pin-striped charms to a digital Cockpit Command Center, this baby ensures top advantage - a work horse that fits the bill whether fishing for sport or leisure.

SPECIFICATIONS
Length on Trailer: 26'6"
Length on Trailer (w/Swing-away tongue): 23'3"
Width on Trailer: 101"
Length Overall: 20'2"
Beam: 92"
Transom Height: 23"
Height Overall: 46"
Interior Depth: 19"
Draft: 16"
Dry Weight: 1,680 lbs
Max H.P.: 225 h.p.
Max Weight Capacity: 1,484 lbs.
Max Persons Capacity: 6/900 lbs.
Fuel Capacity: 50 gals.
MSRP: $40,995 w/ Yamaha VZ225

ZX250

It's love at first sight for the discriminating angler who wants the biggest, baddest, most tricked-out Skeeter we make. This is one fast and fancy fishin' machine. Every luxury we've ever dreamed up, loaded into one superior performance bass boat.

SPECIFICATIONS
Length on Trailer: 27'4"
Length on Trailer (w/Swing-away tongue): 23'10"
Width on Trailer: 101"
Length Overall: 21'
Beam: 92"
Transom Height: 23"
Height Overall: 46"
Interior Depth: 19"
Draft: 16"
Dry Weight: 1,760 lbs
Max H.P.: 250 h.p.
Max Weight Capacity: 1,484 lbs.
Max Persons Capacity: 6/900 lbs.
Fuel Capacity: 50 gals.
MSRP: $43,995 w/ Yamaha VZ250

SX190

201 PRO XL
Length: 20'8"
Beam: 95"
Persons/capacity: 5/695 pounds
Max. weight capacity: 1350
Max. horsepower: 250
Approx. fuel capacity: 50 gal.

200 PRO XL
Length: 20'1"
Beam: 95"
Persons/capacity: 5/695 pounds
Max. weight capacity: 1350
Max. horsepower: 220
Approx. fuel capacity: 50 gal.

17 XL
Length: 17'5"
Beam: 86"
Persons/capacity: 4/510 pounds
Max. weight capacity: 1080

Max. Horsepower: 135
Approx. fuel capacity: 29 gal.

18 XL
Length: 18'4"
Beam: 91"
Persons/capacity: 4/640 pounds
Max. weight capacity: 1215
Max. horsepower: 150
Approx. fuel capacity: 38 gal.

19 XL
Length: 19'1"
Beam: 92"
Persons/capacity: 5/640 pounds
Max. weight capacity: 1295
Max. horsepower: 200
Approx. fuel capacity: 42 gal.

20 XL
Length: 20'1"

Beam: 92"
Persons/capacity: 5/695 pounds
Max. weight capacity: 1350
Max. horsepower: 225
Approx. fuel capacity: 42 gal.

21 XL MAGNUM
Length: 20'8"
Beam: 92"
Persons/capacity: 5/695 pounds
Max. weight capacity: 1350
Max. horsepower: 250
Approx. fuel capacity: 50 gal.

290 SKI-N-FISH
Length: 21'4"
Beam: 95"
Persons/capacity: 7/1060 pounds
Max. weight capacity: 1635
Max. horsepower: 225
Approx. fuel capacity: 40 gal.

TRACKER BOATS

BOATS

AVALANCHE

The Avalanche is the world's first formed aluminum bass boat. Formed aluminum refers to a unique manufacturing process that bridges the gap between aluminum's durability and fiberglass's performance and stylish looks. TRACKER has modified and patented the process for building fishing boats. The hull, sides and cap of the Avalanche are formed from .125 (⅛ inch) thick aluminum alloy sheets, 20% thicker than that of ordinary aluminum boats. All metal-to-metal connections are welded to yield optimum strength and bonding. As a result, the Avalanche looks more like a fiberglass boat than an aluminum one at first glance. And its ride sure won't have you thinking metal construction. But aluminum it is and you get all of aluminum's finest qualities in strength and durability.

The 18'2' hull sports a generous 96" beam and weighs-in at an amazingly light 1400 pounds. The boat has a 175 horsepower maximum power rating. The hull design makes for an impressive hole-shot and the dual rack and pinion steering puts the driver in total boat-handling control.

Because the aluminum hull is several hundred pounds lighter than that of comparable 18' fiberglass boats, the Avalanche offers outstanding performance with a gas-stingy 115 horsepower outboard. It also makes it more tow-friendly for a wider range of vehicles.

The standard Avalanche package consists of a single or dual console boat with a Mercury® 115 ELPTO outboard, a 24-volt, 67 pound thrust MotorGuide® trolling motor, and a color coordinated drive-on trailer with a swing-away tongue jack, 14" tires on chrome wheels and "EZ" lube hubs. There's also full dash instrumentation including tachometer, speedometer, voltmeter, fuel, water pressure and trim gauges. And a TRACKER Pro 160 SX LCR by Humminbird® sonar unit comes on the console. Other standard features include a 41 gallon fuel tank, port and starboard aft storage, bench seat with storage, spacious front fishing deck with bike seat, built-in ice chest, two-bank on-board battery charger, 1100 GPH bilge pump and twin insulated livewells with fill and recirculation pumps and timers.
MSRP: $18,795 for standard package and a 115 hp outboard

PRO GUIDE V-16

Built for fishing from the trailer up, this impressive package starts with a 16'2" hull built from .080 5052 marine grade alloy. The beam is an amazing 86" and the running surface is a rock stable 69" making the V-16 among the widest and most stable boats in it's class. The extended heavy duty gunnel provides plenty of space for accessories such as rod holders, downriggers and other fishing essentials. The floors and decks are made of marine tech pressure treated plywood that includes a limited lifetime warranty.

The standard package includes a TRACKER 40 ELPTO Pro Series outboard with aluminum prop, 12-volt 40 pound thrust foot controlled Minn Kota® trolling motor, TRACKER Pro 128 DX LCR by Humminbird® and a drive-on Trailstar™ trailer. Other standard equipment includes six pedestal seat base locations, bow battery storage, lockable rod box, lockable side storage, marine grade carpeting throughout, insulated hatch lids, taper lock seat pedestals and bases, three deluxe fold-down seats and aft battery storage. The rear fishing deck is as angler-friendly as the one in front, with a raised platform and a seat base for a fishing chair. Wired for a 12-volt electric motor, all wiring and plumbing is sheathed for protection. A self-priming 500 GPH bilge pump and aerated livewell with timer are also standard. Among the other features are a bow baitwell, a deluxe molded fiberglass reinforced console and full instrumentation including speedometer, tachometer, voltmeter, fuel gauge and windshield. The boat rests solidly on a welded frame Trailstar™ trailer that features 13" tires and wheels, "EZ" lube hubs, transom saver, tie-downs and tongue jack.
MSRP: $9,495 for standard package, plus dealer prep and destination charges

TUNDRA™

The Tundra is available in three models: The 18SC single console, the 18DC dual console and the 18WT walk-thru windshield. All three are built tough from the ground up. Each model features an 18' hull that is formed from two sheets of .125 thick aluminum alloy into a Deep V design featuring a high performance running pad. The sides and top deck are formed from the same materials, using the same process. All major metal-to-metal connections are welded using robotic welders for the most uniform and strongest bonding possible. The hull, sides, top deck, transom and fishing decks all come together with the tightest of tolerances. Inside the exterior skin, an aluminum stringer system fits like a glove. A maximum horsepower rating of 175 and a generous 96" beam combine to provide all the space and power needed for serious fishing or serious fun.

The standard package for each Tundra model includes a 115 ELPTO

Mercury® outboard, bow, aft and in-floor storage, four deluxe fold-down seats, six pedestal locations, port and starboard lockable rod boxes, and a 12-volt, 52 pound thrust MotorGuide® electric trolling motor with a 50" shaft. There's also dual cable steering, full dash instrumentation, 1100 GPH bilge pump and color coordinated swing-away trailer with surge disc brakes, tongue jack, transom saver, 14" tires on chrome wheels and "EZ" lube hubs. All three Tundra models have bow and aft livewells and baitwells.

MSRP: Tundra SC, $19,595; Tundra DC, $19,995; Tundra WT, $20,995 (with standard packages featuring 115 hp outboards)

TX 17

The TX 17 starts with a proven modified V hull that's constructed of a single sheet of .072 thick aluminum for uncompromising strength. This boat's 16'10" hull features a generous 71" beam meaning there's plenty of fishing room on the topside for up to four anglers and all their gear.

The standard package includes a TRACKER 25 EL Pro Series electric start outboard with aluminum prop, 12-volt, 43 pound thrust

MotorGuide® electric trolling motor and a TRACKER Pro 128 DX LCR sonar unit by Humminbird®. An extruded aluminum gunnel adds to the boats strength and good looks. Inside you'll find fold-down driver and passenger seats, front and rear casting decks with fold-down seats, lockable rod storage, rod-holder straps, marine grade decks with a limited lifetime warranty, a large aerated livewell with divider, plus plenty of dry storage for tackle and other gear. The custom console offers a plexiglass windscreen, simulated burlwood switch panels, a Classic 3000 control box by Mercury® and full dash instrumentation with speedometer, tachometer, volt and fuel gauges. The whole package rests on a custom Trailstar™ drive-on trailer that features 13" tires and wheels, powder coat finish, load guides, "EZ" lube hubs, dolly wheel, transom saver and safety strap.

MSRP: $7,295, plus dealer prep and destination charges

TRITON BOATS

BASSMASTER CLASSIC

BASSMASTER CLASSIC LIMITED EDITION

B.A.S.S. and Triton come together in this limited edition bass boat. Triton's Bassmaster Classic Limited edition offers the performance and reliability of a Triton coupled with some very special features and the graphic look of bass fishing's premier tournament. This is the same rugged comfortable boat the Classic anglers use. The overall package encompasses both the feel and fishing quality of the Classic itself. And it's available in all models from Tr-19 to Tr-22 with dual or single consoles. This is a unique and surprisingly affordable way for anglers to be a part of the Classic. And who knows, with a boat like this, maybe they'll end up fishing the Classic themselves. It can happen; just ask one of the record fifteen Triton fishermen in this year's Classic.

TR-185/DC

Triton's design ingenuity has really come to the forefront in this sleek-looking, stellar-performing 18 footer. It is roomy, racy and loaded to the gills with the kind of features you would only expect on much larger boats - like generous dry storage, oversized hatch openings, huge rod lockers and divided hi-capacity aerated livewells. If fast hole shots and a teary-eyed top end are the kind of performance you're looking for, Triton will deliver beyond your expectations.

Fishing Features: Lowrance X-51 fish finder, MotorGuide 756 trolling motor, livewell pump-out system, aerator pump.

SPECIFICATIONS
Length: 18'6"
Beam: 91"
Horsepower Rating: 175 Approx.
Hull Weight: 1,431 lbs
Fuel Capacity: 36 gal
Livewell Capacity: 36 gal
Rear Storage Boxes: 168 qts
Front Storage Box: 300 qts
Built-in Ice Chest: 27 qts Max
Persons Capacity: 4 or 525 lbs.

TR-176/DC

A high quality, fully rigged, tournament-ready bass boat priced within reach of the majority of anglers. That's precisely what the new Triton 176 delivers in both single and dual-console designs. Loaded with features, these performance fishing machines feature a level of fit, finish, and fishability rivaling boats priced thousands of dollars more.

Fishing Features: 12/24-volt Motorguide trolling motor, 6-gauge, all copper trolling motor wiring, 1-"rodbuckle" rod hold-down strap, 2-oversized rod lockers, locking storage boxes, 3-pro-active lure storage, electric bilge pump - 625 g.p.h Lowrance X-51 fish finder, surface temp probe for X-51. divided hi-capacity rear insulated livewell, tackle and accessory storage trays, livewell

pump-out system, passenger-side rod ramp, totally recessed (flush) pedestal floor plates, 1-750 gph freshwater livewell pump, 1-750 g.p.h. livewell recirculation pump.

SPECIFICATIONS
Length: 17'3"
Beam: 86.5"
Horsepower Rating: 130
Approx. Hull Weight: 1,200 lbs
Fuel Capacity: 36 gal
Livewell Capacity: 36 gal
Rear Storage Boxes: 168 qts
Front Storage Box: 100 qts
Built-in Ice Chest: 27 qts Max
Persons Capacity: 4 or 525 lbs.

TR-176/DC

A fully-rigged, tournament-ready bass boat priced within reach of the majority of anglers. That's precisely what the new Triton 176 delivers in both single and dual-console designs. Loaded with features, these performance-fishing machines feature a level of fit; finish and fishability rivaling boats priced thousands of dollars more.

Fishing Features: 12/24-volt Motorguide trolling motor, 6-gauge, all copper trolling motor wiring, 1-"rodbuckle" rod hold-down strap, 2-oversized rod lockers, locking "oversized" storage boxes, 3-pro-active lure storage, electric bilge pump - 625 g.p.h. Lowrance x-51 fish finder, surface temp probe for x-51, divided hi-capacity rear insulated livewell, tackle and accessory storage trays, livewell pump-out system, passenger-side rod ramp, totally recessed pedestal floor plates, 1-750 g.p.h. freshwater livewell pump, 1-750 g.p.h. livewell recirculation pump.

SPECIFICATIONS
Length: 17'3"
Beam: 86.5"
Horsepower Rating: 130 Approx.
Hull Weight: 1,200 lbs.
Fuel Capacity: 36 gal.
Livewell Capacity: 36 gal
Rear Storage Boxes: 168 qts.
Front Storage Box: 100 qts. Built-in
Ice Chest: 27 qts. Max
Persons Capacity: 4 or 525 lbs.

TR-175

A high-quality, fully-rigged, tournament-ready bass boat priced within reach of the majority of anglers. That's precisely what the new TR-175 delivers in both single and dual-console designs. Loaded with features, these performance fishing machines feature a level of fit, finish and fishability rivaling boats priced thousands of dollars more.

Fishing Features: Lowrance X-51fish finder, MotorGuide 736 trolling motor, 6-gauge 12 volt trolling motor wiring, 1-aerator pump, livewell pump-out system.

SPECIFICATIONS
Length: 17'3"
Beam: 86.5"
Horsepower Rating: 130 Approx.
Hull Weight: 1,200 lbs Boat, Motor, Trailer Length Overall w/o Jackplate (without retractable tongue) 20'8" (with retractable tongue) 18'8"
Fuel Capacity: 28 gal Livewell
Capacity: 36 gal
Rear Storage Boxes: 168 qts

Front Storage Box: 100 qts
Built-In Ice Chest: 27 qts Max
Persons Capacity: 4 or 525 lbs.

TR-165

This exciting model delivers legendary Triton fishability and performance at a price weekend anglers can afford. The Triton TR-165 offers fishing features and riding comfort other rigs can't touch. Our TR-165's are the roomiest 16½ footers on the water, perfect for bass club competition and family fishing. They all run great with outboards from 75-100 hp.

Fishing Features: 6-gauge 12 volt trolling motor wiring, Lowrance X-51depth finder, MotorGuide 736 trolling motor, 12-volt battery charger.

SPECIFICATIONS
Length: 16'7"
Beam: 86"
Horsepower Rating: 100Approx.
Hull Weight: 1,150 lbs Boat, Motor, Trailer Length Overall w/o Jackplate (without retractable tongue) 20'6"(with retractable tongue) 18'6"
Fuel Capacity: 26 gal
Livewell Capacity: 36 gal
Rear Storage Boxes: 112 qts
Front Storage Boxes: 240 qts
Persons: 4 or 500 lbs

TR-19PD

A superbly designed bass boat that's brimming with serious fishing features. The forward Pro Deck is a spacious casting platform with massive dry storage boxes, dual oversized rod lockers, a huge built-in ice chest and Triton's custom tackle management system. Everything is right where the fisherman wants it, and like all Triton Pro Deck models, there's easy-in, easy-out access to the helm seat with

our convex console design.

Fishing Features: battery on-off switch, 12/24-volt Motorguide trolling motor, 6-gauge all copper trolling motor wiring, 12-volt power tap, 2-"rodbuckle" rod hold-down straps, 2-oversized rod lockers, locking "oversized" storage box, 3-pro-active lure storage, tackle and accessory storage trays, rod storage rack (built into rod locker), power lift lid pistons for front storage box and rod lockers, automatic electric bilge pump - 500 g.p.h. electric bilge pump, Lowrance 1240A in-dash flasher, twin hi-capacity rear insulated livewells, 1-large livewell w/ removable divided to accept longer species of fish (tx series only), livewell pump-out system - 500 g.p.h. passenger-side rod ramp, totally recessed pedestal floor plates, automatic aerator timer system, 2-750 gph freshwater livewell recirculation pumps, 2-750 gph livewell recirculation pumps,, T&H "Max-Air" livewell aeration system, 1-rear starboard baitwell (TX series only).

SPECIFICATIONS
Length: 19'6"
Beam: 93"
Approximate Hull Weight: 1,435 lbs
Horsepower Rating: 200Boat, Motor and Trailer Length Overall without jack-plate (without Retractable Tongue) 22'6" (with Retractable Tongue) 20'6"
Fuel Capacity: 47 gal
Livewell Capacity: 43 gal
Rear Storage/Baitwell: 84 qts/21 gal (TX model only)
Rear Storage Boxes: 168 qts
Built-In Ice Chest: 28 qts
Front Storage Box: 300 qts
Persons: 4 or 525 lbs.

Boat Positioning Is Critical
Proper boat positioning can determine your success when bass fishing. Many anglers prefer fish with the wind or current for convenience sake, but this is a mistake when fishing visible cover. A bass in cover usually faces into the current or wind, and you're more likely to catch that fish if you bring your lure with the natural flow of water. Also, by working into the wind, you can better control your boat and are less likely to pass up good targets.

WAR EAGLE BOATS

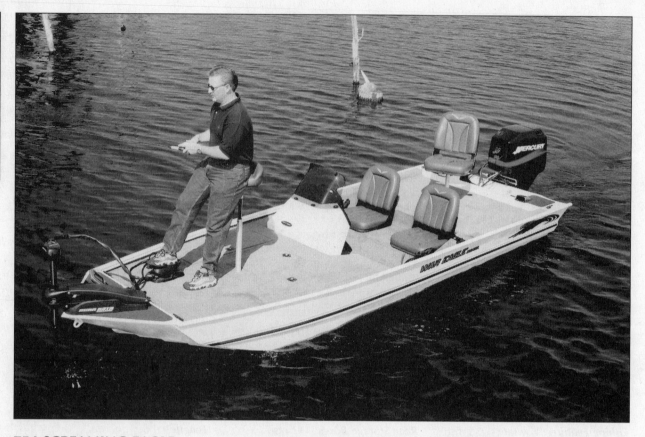

754 SCREAMING EAGLE

War Eagle 754 models have 12° V hulls built of .100 gauge aluminum and quarter inch extruded aluminum center keels. The 54" wide bottom is well proportioned for these 17 foot boats. Many 754s come with aluminum floors and side panels that can be covered with vinyl or carpet. Floors braces are doubled and strengthened with aluminum gussets. Gas resistant foam flotation, factory steering and a higher transom permit increased horsepower ratings for these boats. Side or Center Consoles and Trolling Motor Brackets are popular accessories. Spot Lights, Courtesy Lights, Q-Beam and Running Lights are available for night running. Seventeen foot and larger models have a Set Back Transom, another Team Ward design innovation. Positioning the motor further back, raises the bow and decreases drag on the hull for better performance.

SPECIFICATIONS
Length: 17'
Bottom Width: 54"
Beam: 72"
Side Depth: 22"
Hull Gauge: .100
Transom: 21"
Horsepower Rating: 90
Hull: 12 degrees

Rope a Boat When Launching Alone
If you don't have a helper when launching your boat, try tying the craft to your trailer (around the winch works well) with about 10-20 feet of rope. Back up until the boat starts to float, and tap the truck brakes. Drive forward a few feet. The boat should now float off the trailer, but not away. Untie it and walk it back to the shore or dock. This way you can launch fast and stay dry.

OUTBOARD MOTORS

HONDA MARINE MOTORS

OUTBOARD MOTORS

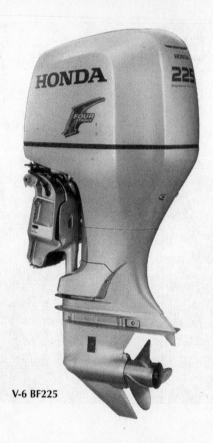

V-6 BF225

V-6 BF225

Fishermen who not only enjoy the solitude of freshwater fishing but also the feeling of 225 hp and instant response can get both from Honda Marine's V-6 BF225 4-stroke outboard. Derived from perhaps the most advanced 4-stroke technology, the BF225's ability to put a boat on plane at low rpm and perform above other 4-strokes at high rpm is virtually unmatched. Honda's Variable Valve Timing and Lift Electronic Control (VTEC), adapted from the company's world-class automobile racing engines, optimizes air/fuel mixture at both ends of the performance spectrum.

The engineering tolerances that make the BF225 nearly noise- and vibration-free are comparable to the standards for airplane engines. This, in addition to stainless steel components, strategically placed sacrificial anodes and Honda's exclusive 4-Front Corrosion Protection system, makes it one of the most reliable powerplants ever built.

The BF225's Engine Command Module (ECM) receives input from 18 sensors to ensure correct air/fuel mix and ignition curve, while maximizing long-term durability. The ECM also monitors the engine alert system for oil pressure, engine temperature, battery condition, water in fuel and other vital engine functions. Add the facts that the BF225 has a CARB 3-star rating and a comprehensive 3-year warranty, and this outboard becomes the best choice for enjoying many years of fishing.

High Performance Props
A high-performance prop on your outboard can help get your boat "out of the hole" faster, gives it extra stability and makes it handle better. These props usually are a little larger than regular props and may have four or more blades instead of the normal three.

JOHNSON-EVINRUDE MOTORS

MODEL 6 (1-CYLINDER)
Shaft Length: 15" **Weight:** 68 lbs.
Engine Type: Four-cycle 1-cylinder
in-line SOHC, 2-valve
Bore x Stroke: 2.22 x 2.01 in.
Displacement: 7.8 Cu. In. **Starting:**
Auto-rewind, **Manual Trim Method:**
Manual Trim & Tilt, Shallow-water
Drive, **HP:** 6 Full Throttle, **Operating
Range:** 5500-6500 RPM, **Gear Ratio:**
13:29 F-N-R, **Fuel Induction:** Single,
Carburetor Alternator: 5 Amp
Accessory Cooling: Pressure &
Temperature-Controlled,
Water-Cooled Steering: Tiller w/
Twist-Grip Throttle

MODEL 15 (2-CYLINDER)
Shaft Length: 15", **Weight:** 97 lbs.,
Engine Type: Four-stroke 2-cylinder
in-line SOHC, 2-valve,
Bore x Stroke: 2.28 x 2.24 in.,
Displacement: 18.4 Cu. In.,
Starting: Manual or Electric Choke,
Compression Reduction, **Trim
Method:** 5 tilt-pin positions, **HP:** 15,
Full Throttle Operating Range: 5400-
6000 RPM, **Gear Ratio:** 1.92:1 F-N-R,
Fuel Induction: Single Carburetor,
Alternator: Elec. 12V/80W,
Cooling: Temperature-Controlled
Water Cooling, **Steering:** Tiller
(Remote Opt.)

MODEL 25 (2-CYLINDER)
Shaft Length: 20", **Weight:** 120 lbs.,
Engine Type: Cross-flow 2-cylinder
in-line, **Bore x Stroke:** 3.000 x 2.250
in., **Displacement:** 32 Cu. In.
Starting: Electric/Manual, **Trim
Method:** Manual Trim, Programmed
Tilt & Shallow-water Drive, **HP:** 25
Full Throttle, **Operating Range:** 4500-
5500 RPM, **Gear Ratio:** 13:28 F-N-R,
Fuel Induction: Single carburetor,
Alternator: Electric 4 Amp Std.,
Cooling: Auto Pressure-Temperature-
Controlled, Water-Cooled, **Steering:**
Remote or tiller w/ Twist-Grip

MODEL 60 (4-CYLINDER)
Shaft Length: 20", **Weight:** 359.3 lbs.,
Engine Type: 4-stroke, 4-cylinder in-
line DOHC, 2-valve, **Bore x Stroke:**
2.91 x 2.97 in., **Displacement:** 49.7
Cu. In., **Starting:** Electric, **Trim
Method:** Power, Trim & Tilt, **HP:** 60
Full Throttle, **Operating Range:** 4700-
5300 RPM, **Gear Ratio:** 2.42:1 F-N-R

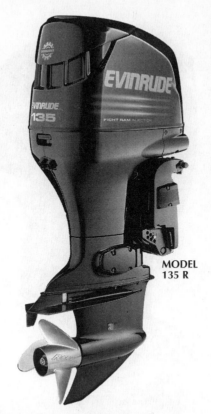

**MODEL
135 R**

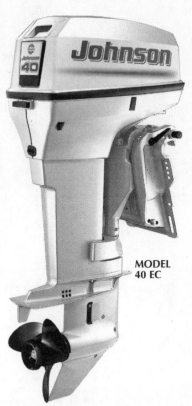

**MODEL
40 EC**

Fuel Induction: Digital Sequential
Multi-port Fuel Injection, **Alternator:**
Elec. 12V/216W, **Cooling:**
Temperature-Controlled Water
Cooling, **Steering:** Remote (tiller opt.)

MODEL 90 (V-4)
Shaft Length: 20", **Weight:** 319 lbs.,
Engine Type: Loop-charged V-4, 60°
Oil Injection, **Bore x Stroke:** 3.600 x
2.588 in., **Displacement:** 105.4 Cu.
In., **Starting:** Electric/Manual, **Trim
Method:** FasTrak Power Trim & Tilt,
HP: 90 Full Throttle, **Operating
Range:** 4500-5500 RPM, **Gear Ratio:**
13:26 F-N-R, **Fuel Induction:** Two
Dual-throat, **Carburetors Alternator:**
A5/20 Amp w/ Voltage Regulator,
Cooling: Auto Pressure-Temperature-
Controlled, Water-Cooled, **Steering:**
Remote

MODEL 150 (V-6)
Shaft Length: 25", **Weight:** 375 lbs.,
Engine Type: Loop-charged V-6, 60°
Oil Injection, **Bore x Stroke:** 3.600 x
2.588 in., **Displacement:** 158 Cu. In.

Starting: Electric/Manual, **Trim
Method:** FasTrak Power Trim & Tilt,
HP: 150 Full Throttle, **Operating
Range:** 4500-5500 RPM, **Gear Ratio:**
14:26 F-N-R, **Fuel Induction:** Two
Triple-throat Carburetors, **Alternator:**
Top Charge 35 Amp w/ Voltage
Regulator, **Cooling:** Auto Pressure-
Temperature-Controlled, Water-
Cooled, **Steering:** Remote

MODEL 175 (V-6)
Shaft Length: 25", **Weight:** 375 lbs.,
Engine Type: Loop-charged V-4, 60°
Oil Injection, **Bore x Stroke:** 3.600 x
2.588 in., **Displacement:** 158 Cu. In.,
Starting: Electric/Manual, **Trim
Method:** FasTrak Power Trim & Tilt,
HP: 175 Full Throttle Operating,
Range: 4500-5500 RPM, **Gear Ratio:**
14:26 F-N-R, **Fuel Induction:** Two
Triple-throat Carburetors, **Alternator:**
Top Charge 35 Amp w/ Voltage
Regulator, **Cooling:** Auto Pressure-
Temperature-Controlled, Water-
Cooled, **Steering:** Remote

MERCURY OUTBOARD MOTORS

OPTIMAX 200XS

OptiMax 135

Propshaft Horsepower: 135-hp **Max RPM (W.O.T.):** 5000-5600 **Cylinders/ Configuration:** 60 degree V-6 **Displacement:** 153 cu.in. **Bore & Stroke:** 3.5 in. x 2.65 in. **Fuel Induction System:** 2-Stage Direct Fuel Injection **Exhaust System:** Through Prop **Lubrication System:** Electronic multi-point variable ratio oil injection **Cooling System:** Water cooled with thermostat and pressure controlled **Ignition System:** Digital Inductive **Starting System:** Electric (turnkey) **Alternator:** Belt-driven 60 amp (756 watt) with voltage regulator, **Gear Ratio:** 2.0:1 **Gear Shift:** F-N-R **Steering:** Remote **Trim System:** Power Trim **Shaft Length:** 20 in. (508mm **Weight-Dry:** 443 lbs. (201 kg) **Operator Warning Systems:** Overheat, low oil level, water in fuel, check engine

OptiMax 200XS

Propshaft-rated Horsepower: 200 **Full Throttle RPM Range:** 6000-6500 **Displacement:** 153 cu. in. **Cylinders:** V-6 (60° vee), **Bore (in/mm):** 3.50/89 **Stroke (in/mm):** 2.65/67 **Induction System:** Direct Fuel Injection **Ignition:** Digital Inductive (SmartCraft compatible) **Alternator System:** 60-amp (846-watt) w/ Voltage Regulator **Gear Ratio:** 1.87:1 (SM) (TM)* **Fuel/Oil Ratio:** Electronic Multipoint Oil Injection **Recommended Fuel:** 92 Octane Minimum (R+M)/2 (99 RON), **Rotation:** Left- or right-hand (SM), right-hand (TM) **Shaft Length:** 15 in. or 20 in. **Weight-Dry:** 400 lbs.

OptiMax 250XS

Propshaft-rated Horsepower: 250 **Full Throttle RPM Range:** 5300-5800 **Cylinders:** V-6 (60° vee) **Displacement:** 185 cu. in. **Bore (in/mm):** 3.63/92 **Stroke (in/mm):** 3.00/76 **Induction System:** Direct Fuel Injection **Ignition:** PCM 555 Digital Inductive **Alternator System:** 60-amp (846-watt) w/ Voltage **Regulator Gear Ratio:** 1.62:1 (SM)* 1.75:1 (TM)* or (FM)* **Fuel/Oil Ratio:** Electronic Multipoint Oil Injection **Recommended Oil:** Mercury Premium Plus (TC-W3) **Recommended Fuel:** 92 Octane Minimum (R+M)/2 (98 RON) **International Rotation:** Left or right-hand (FM) right-hand (SM), (TM) **Shaft Length:** 20 in. (508 mm), 25 in. (635 mm) or 30 in. (762 mm) **Weight-Dry:** (L) = 497 lbs., (XL) = 512 lbs., (XXL) = 528 lbs.

MERCURY OUTBOARD MOTORS

2.5 EFI SPORT

PRO MAX 300X

Propshaft-rated Horsepower: 300.
Full Throttle RPM Range: 6100-6800
Cylinders: V-6 (60° vee)
Displacement: 185 cu. in. **Bore (in):**
3.63, **Stroke (in):** 3.00 **Induction
System:** Electronic Fuel Injection.
Ignition: Digital Inductive (SmartCraft
compatible) **Alternator System:** 60-
amp (846 watt) w/dual Voltage
Regulator **Gear Ratio:** 1.62:1 (SM)
1.75:1 (TM) or (FM) **Fuel/Oil Ratio:**
Electronic Multipoint Oil Injection
Required Fuel: 92 Octane Leaded or
Unleaded (R+M)/2 (98 RON)
Rotation: Left or Right Hand (SM)
(FM), Right-Hand (TM) ** **Shaft
Length:** 20 in./508mm (SM) (TM), 25 in.
635mm (FM) **Weight (lbs/kg):** 467

2.5 EFI SPORT

Propshaft Horsepower: 280 Full
Throttle RPM Range: 7200-7500
Cylinders: V-6 (60° vee)
Displacement: 153 cu. in, **Bore (in):**
3.50/89 **Stroke (in/mm):** 2.65
Induction System: Electronic Fuel
Injection **Ignition:** Inductive Coil
w/Computer Control **Alternator
System:** 60-amp (846-watt) w/dual
Voltage Regulator **Gear Ratio:**
1.87:1 (SM) **Fuel/Oil Ratio:** 40:1
2-Cycle Outboard Required Fuel:
92 Octane Leaded or Unleaded
(R+M)/2 (98 RON) **Rotation:** Left or
Right Hand Shaft **Length:** 20 in.
Weight (lbs/kg): 375 lb.

60 EFI

Cylinders/Configuration: 4 (in-line)
Gear Shift: F-N-R, **Trim System:**
Power Trim **Operator Warning
Systems:** Overheat, low oil pressure,
overrev **Weight-Dry:** 248 lbs.
Propeller Options: Black Max,
Vengeance, QA3, QSS, **Steering:**
Tiller or Remote **Bore & Stroke:**
2.56 in. x 2.95 in. **Alternator:** 20
amp (252 watt) **Propshaft
Horsepower:** 60-hp, **Gear Ratio:**
1.83:1 **Shaft Length:** 20 in. Optional
22.5 in. **Cooling System:** Water
cooled with thermostat and fresh
water flush **Ignition System:**   ECM
555 Digital Inductive **Max RPM
(W.O.T.):** 5500-6000 **Displacement:**
60.8 cu. in. **Exhaust System:**
Through Prop **Starting System:**
Electric **Lubrication System:** Wet
sump with pressurized lube system

MERCURY OUTBOARD MOTORS

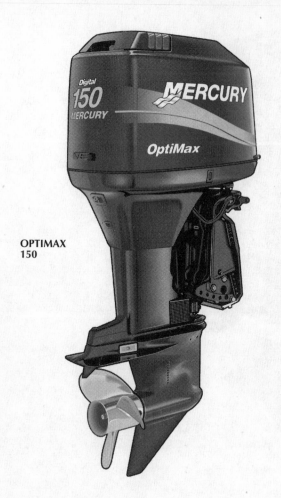

OPTIMAX 150

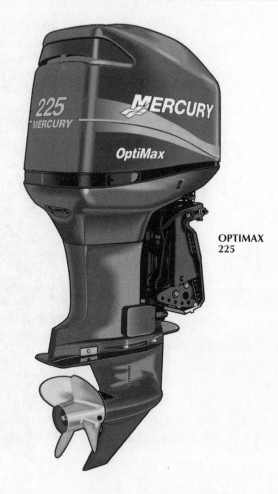

OPTIMAX 225

OptiMax 150

Propshaft Horsepower: 150-hp (112 kW) **Max RPM (W.O.T.):** 5000-5600 **Cylinders/Configuration:** 60 degree V-6 **Displacement:** 153 cu.in. (2507cc) **Bore & Stroke:** 3.5 in. x 2.65 in. (89mm x 67mm, **Fuel Induction System:** 2-Stage Direct Fuel Injection **Exhaust System:** Through Prop **Lubrication System:** Electronic multi-point variable ratio oil injection **Cooling System:** Water cooled with thermostat and pressure controlled **Ignition System:** Digital Inductive **Starting System:** Electric (turnkey) **Alternator:** Belt-driven 60 amp (756 watt) with voltage regulator **Gear**

Ratio: 1.87:1 **Gear Shift:** F-N-R **Steering:** Remote **Trim System:** Power Trim **Shaft Length:** 20 in. (508mm) **Weight-Dry:** 443 lbs. (201 kg) **Operator Warning Systems:** Overheat, low oil level, water in fuel, check engine **Propeller Options:** Black Max, Vengeance, Laser II, Mirage Plus, Tempest Plus, Trophy Plus, High Five, Offshore P.S., QA3, QSS, QS2000, QS3000

225

Propshaft Horsepower: 225-hp, **Max RPM (W.O.T.):** 5000-5750, **Cylinders/Configuration:** 60 degree V-6 **Displacement:** 185 cu.in., **Bore &**

Stroke: 3.63 in. x 3.00 in., **Fuel Induction System:** 2-Stage Direct Fuel Injection **Exhaust System:** Through Prop **Lubrication System:** Electronic multi-point variable ratio oil injection **Cooling System:** Water cooled with thermostat and pressure controlled **Ignition System:** Digital Inductive **Starting System:** Electric (turnkey) **Alternator:** Belt-driven 60 amp (756 watt) with voltage regulator **Gear Ratio:** 1.75:1 **Gear Shift:** F-N-R, **Steering:** Remote **Trim System:** Power Trim **Shaft Length:** 20 in. **Weight-Dry:** 516 lbs. **Operator Warning Systems:** Overheat, low oil level, water in fuel, check engine

NISSAN/TOHATSU OUTBOARD MOTORS

90 HP TLDI

90 HP TLDI

Standard Features: low-pressure direct injection system, user-controlled variable idle speed, onboard self-diagnostics system, water temperature sensor, dual throttle position sensors, electronic fuel pump, 18.5-amp charging system, analog tachometer & oil level gauge, power tilt/trim, LCD ignition system.

SPECIFICATIONS

Engine: 3-cylinder
Starting: Electric
Controls: Remote Control
Gear Shift: Forward-Neutral-Reverse
Propeller: 11" - 21"
Transom Height: 20", 25"
Fuel Mix: Variable Auto-mixing (120:1-50:1)
Weight: 314 lbs. (143 kgs)
Lighting: 12V 220W 18.5A
RPM Range: 5150-5850
Displacement: 1267cc (77.3 cu.in.)
Bore & Stroke: 86x72.7 (3.39 x 2.86in)
Gear Ratio: 2.0:1

70 HP TLDI

Standard Features: low-pressure direct injection system, user-controlled variable idle speed, onboard self diagnostics system, water temperature sensor, dual throttle position sensors, electronic fuel pump, 18.5-amp charging system, analog tachometer & oil level gauge, power tilt/trim, LCD ignition system.

SPECIFICATIONS

Engine: 3-cylinder
Starting: Electric
Controls: Remote Control
Gear Shift: Forward-Neutral-Reverse
Propeller: 11" - 21"
Transom Height: 20"
Fuel Mix: Variable Auto-mixing (120:1-50:1)
Oil Type: Premium TCW3
Fuel Tank: Optional 25 Liters (6.6 US gals)
Separate Tank Weight: 314 lbs. (143 kgs)
Lighting: 12V 220W 18.5A
RPM Range: 5150-5850
Displacement: 1267cc (77.3cu.in.)
Bore & Stroke: 86x72.7 (3.39 x 2.86in)
Gear Ratio: 2.3:1

50 HP TLDI

Standard Features: low-pressure direct injection system, user-controlled variable idle speed, onboard self diagnostics system, water temperature sensor, dual throttle position sensors, electronic fuel pump, 18.5 amp charging system, analog tachometer & oil level gauge, power tilt/trim, LCD ignition system.

SPECIFICATIONS

Engine: 3-cylinder
Starting: Electric
Controls: Tiller Handle or Remote Control
Gear Shift: Forward-Neutral-Reverse
Propeller: 7" - 15"
Transom Height: 15", 20"
Fuel Mix: Variable Auto-mixing (120:1-50:1)
Oil Type: Premium TCW3
Fuel Tank: Optional 25 Lit. (6.6 US gals)
Separate Tank Weight: 211 lbs. (96kgs)
Lighting: 12V 220W 18.5A
RPM Range: 5150-5850
Displacement: 697cc (42.5 cu. in.)
Bore & Stroke: 68 x 64mm (2.68 x 2.52in.)
Gear Ratio: 1.85:1

NISSAN/TOHATSU OUTBOARD MOTORS

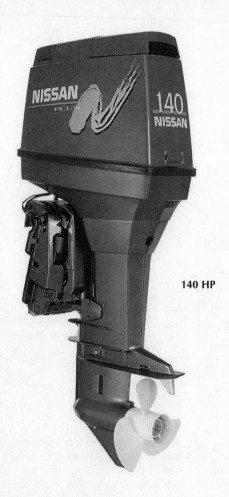

140 HP

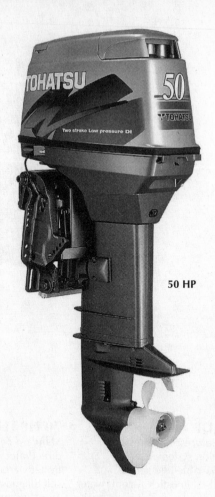

50 HP

140 HP

Standard Features: loop-charged induction, CD ignition system, stainless steel water pump housing, start-in-gear protection, thermostatically-controlled cooling system, through-the-prop exhaust, auto-mixing with integral tank, power trim/tilt, audible overheat monitor, LCD tachometer/oil pressure/T&T gauge, water pressure sensor.

SPECIFICATIONS

Engine: 4-cylinder
Starting: Electric
Controls: Remote Control
Gear Shift: Forward-Neutral-Reverse
Propeller: 11" - 21"
Transom Height: 20"
Fuel Mix: Variable Auto-mixing (120:1-50:1)
Oil Type: TCW3
Fuel Tank: Optional 25 Liters (6.6 US gals)
Separate Tank Weight: 360.8 lbs (164 kgs)
Lighting: 12V 330W 27.5A

RPM Range: 5200-5700
Displacement: 1768cc (107.9cu.in.)
Bore & Stroke: 88x72.7mm (3.46x2.86in)
Gear Ratio: 2:1.

120 HP

Standard Features: loop-charged induction, CD ignition system, stainless steel water pump housing, start-in-gear protection, thermostatically controlled cooling system, through-the-prop exhaust, auto-mixing with integral tank, power trim/tilt, audio overheat monitor, LCD tachometer/oil pressure/T&T gauge, water pressure sensor.

SPECIFICATIONS

Engine: 4-cylinder
Starting: Electric
Controls: Remote Control
Gear Shift: Forward-Neutral-Reverse
Propeller: 11" - 21"
Transom Height: 20", 25"
Fuel Mix: Variable Auto-mixing

(120:1-50:1)
Oil Type: TCW3
Fuel Tank: Optional 25 Liters (6.6 US gals)
Separate Tank Weight: 360.8 lbs (164 kgs)
Lighting: 12V 330W 27.5A
RPM Range: 5,200-5,700
Displacement: 1768cc (107.9cu.in.)
Bore & Stroke: 88x72.7mm (3.46x2.86 in)
Gear Ratio: 2:1

70 HP

SPECIFICATIONS

Engine: 3-cylinder
Starting: Electric
Controls: Remote Control
Gear Shift: Forward-Neutral-Reverse
Propeller: 11" - 21"
Transom Height: 20"
Fuel Mix: Variable Auto-mixing (120:1-50:1)
Oil Type: TCW3

NISSAN/TOHATSU OUTBOARD MOTORS

30 HP

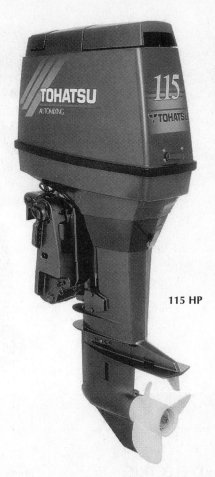

115 HP

Fuel Tank: Optional 25 Liters (6.6 US gals)
Separate Tank Weight: 231 lbs. (105 kgs)
Lighting: 12V 130W 11A
RPM Range: 5150-5850
Displacement: 938cc (57.2cu.in.)
Bore & Stroke: 74x72.7mm (2.91x 2.86in)
Gear Ratio: 2.3:1.
Standard Features: loop-charged induction, CD ignition system, stainless steel water pump housing, start-in-gear protection, thermostatically controlled cooling system, through-the-prop exhaust, auto-mixing with integral tank, power trim/tilt, audio overheat monitor, analog tachometer and oil level gauge, optional water pressure sensor.

40 HP
Standard Features: loop-charged induction, CD ignition system, stainless steel water pump housing, start-in-gear protection, thermostatically controlled, cooling system, through-the-prop exhaust, dual swirl combustion, chamber heads, auto-mixing with integral tank, power trim/tilt, analog tachometer and oil level gauge, (remote control model only).

SPECIFICATIONS
Engine: 3-cylinder
Starting: Electric Start
Controls: Tiller Handle or Remote Control
Gear Shift: Forward-Neutral-Reverse
Propeller: 7"- 16"
Transom Height: 15", 20"

Fuel Mix: Variable Auto-mixing (120:1-50:1)
Oil Type: TCW3
Fuel Tank: Optional 25 Lit. (6.6 US gals)
Separate Tank Weight: 158 lbs. (72 kgs)
Lighting: 12V 130W 11A
RPM Range: 5000-5700
Displacement: 697cc (42.5 cu. in.)
Bore & Stroke: 68 x 64mm (2.68 x 2.52in.)
Gear Ratio: 1.85:1

OUTBOARD ELECTRIC MOTORS

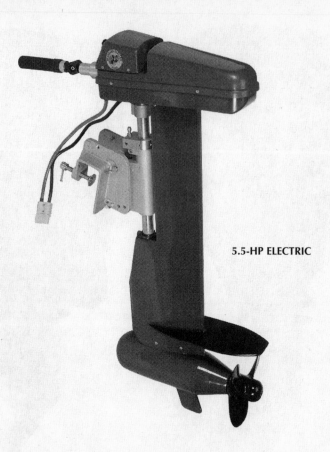

5.5-HP ELECTRIC

OUTBOARD ELECTRIC CORPORATION
OUTBOARDS 5.5-HP ELECTRIC

Producing approximately 198 pounds of sustained thrust, Outboard Electric Corporation's 5.5-hp electric outboard is designed as the main propulsion motor for pontoon boats, small fishing vessels, sailboats and other watercraft. Unlike many electric outboards with pre-set motor speeds, the Outboard Electric unit contains a lever-type speed control to permit continuous throttle adjustment. This provides instant response to changes in speed and direction, allowing for safe docking and maneuvering. In contrast to conventional electric motors with operating efficiencies of 65-70%, the unit's 85-90% efficiency is achieved by proprietary motor windings, which improve efficiency and heat dissipation. Any thermal buildup quickly conducts to the water, lowering the operating temperature. Electronic components are further protected from temperature buildup by special heat-conducting material. The electric outboard motor appeals to boaters on inland lakes, ponds, reservoirs and waterways where gasoline outboard operation is often prohibited due to air and water pollution restrictions. *MSRP:* $4,495

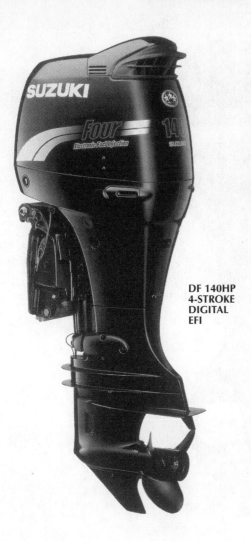

DF 140HP
4-STROKE
DIGITAL
EFI

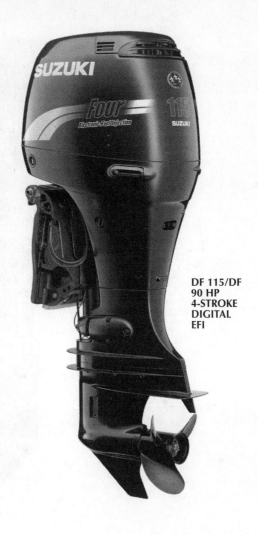

DF 115/DF
90 HP
4-STROKE
DIGITAL
EFI

OUTBOARD MOTORS

DF 140HP 4-Stroke Digital EFI

Features: dual overhead cams, four valves per cylinder, tuned intake manifold and 4-into-2-into-1 exhaust system, overall 2.38:1 gear ratio, large induction port on engine cover, two-stage cam drive, offset drive shaft, oil cooler and air flow cooling to key components.

SPECIFICATIONS

Prop shaft horsepower: 140
Cylinders: I-4
Displacement: 124.7 cu. in. (2044 cc)
Shaft length: Long 20" x Long 25"
Counter Rotation Available

DF 115/DF 90 HP 4-Stroke Digital EFI

SPECIFICATIONS

Prop shaft horsepower: 115/90
Cylinders: I-4
Displacement: 118.9 cu. in. (1950 cc)
Shaft length: Long 20" x Long 25"
Features: 2.59:1 gear ratio, solid-state ignition.

DF 70/DF 60 HP 4-Stroke Digital EFI

SPECIFICATIONS

Prop shaft horsepower: 70/60
Cylinders: I-4
Displacement: 79.2 cu. in. (1298 cc)
Shaft length: Long 20"
Features: digital sequential fuel injection, pulse-tuned, water-cooled intake manifold, dual cooling system.

SUZUKI OUTBOARD MOTORS

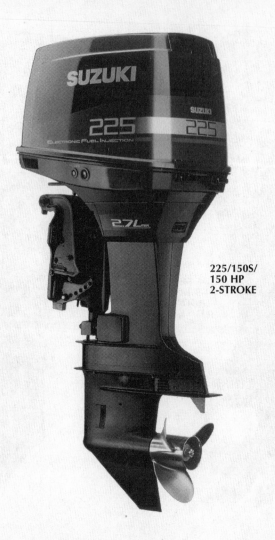

225/150S/
150 HP
2-STROKE

DF50/DF40 4-Stroke Digital EFI
SPECIFICATIONS
Prop shaft horsepower: 50/40
Cylinders: I-3
Displacement: 49.7 cu. in. (815 cc)
Shaft length: Long 20"
Features: Solid-state ignition, multi-point sequential fuel injection, tuned intake manifold, enclosed timing chain and automatic chain tensioner.

DF30/DF25 HP 4-Stroke
SPECIFICATIONS
Prop shaft horsepower: 30/25
Cylinders: I-3
Displacement: 36.4 cu. in. (597 cc)
Shaft Length: Short 15" Long 20"
Features: 3-cylinder, single overhead cam powerhead, triple Mikuni carburetors with accelerator pumps, digital CDI ignition, automotive-type timing chain and automatic chain tensioner.

DF 15/9.9 HP 4-Stroke Digital EFI
SPECIFICATIONS
Prop shaft horsepower: 15/9.9
Cylinders: I-2
Displacement: 18.4 cu. in. (302 cc)
Shaft length: Short 15" Long 20"
Features: three-stage baffle chamber and through-the-hub exhaust, conveniently located indicator light and shift lever, manual or electric start, tiller handle or remote setup.

225/150S/150 HP 2-Stroke
SPECIFICATIONS
Prop shaft horsepower: 225/150S/150
Cylinders: V-6 (60 Degrees)
Displacement: 164.3 cu. in.
Shaft length: Long 20" (DT150S) X Long 25" (DT225/ DT150)
Features: digital electronic fuel injection, Microlink ignition system, gravity-fed oil injection, engine monitor gauge, corrosion protection system of coatings, bonding wires and sacrificial anodes.

YAMAHA OUTBOARD MOTORS

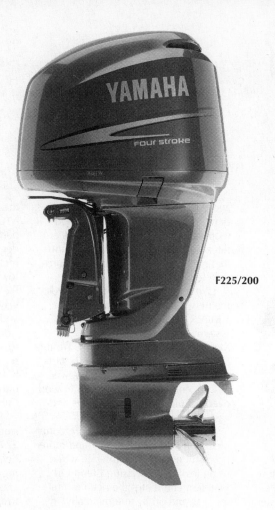

F225/200

OUTBOARD MOTORS

F225 AND F200

With Yamaha's F225 or F200, boaters will be able to enjoy the V6 power and performance they need and gain the additional benefits of clean-running performance, outstanding fuel efficiency, exceptional range and quiet operation that four-stroke outboards provide. The Yamaha F225 and F200s also eliminate the need for two-stroke oil to be mixed with fuel. This advantage further reduces operating expense and increases onboard storage space because a separate oil tank is no longer needed.

The F225 and F200 were designed to revolutionize outboard performance with their compact and lightweight configuration. To accomplish this standard, Yamaha engineers developed an "In-Bank Exhaust System" which is a Yamaha exclusive and patented innovation that reverses the intake and

exhaust system layouts when compared to conventional four-stroke V6 engines. Additionally, the fuel injectors are located on the inside of the intake tracks to further save space and also keep the injector electrical wiring away from the cowling for further durability. These new V6 four-stroke motors even feature a marine-inspired alternator system located underneath the flywheel on top of the engine. This unique 45-amp alternator is compact and enhances reliability with its lightweight design and protected location.

The F225 and F200 both feature a unique new 3.3-liter 60-degree V6 DOHC power unit designed to deliver high combustion efficiency and high power output to exceed the performance requirements for marine power applications. They also feature Yamaha's award-winning DOHC Double Overhead Cam technology

that includes 24 valves for more precise valve timing and outstanding fuel economy. The intake and fuel injection system feature six tuned intake tubes that boost torque in the low-to-middle rpm range, providing power and acceleration that is truly exceptional. This unique system includes six independent throttle valves and six individual inside track fuel injectors.

The F225 is available in 25"- and 30"-shaft models, with the F200 available in 25"-shaft model only. Counter-rotation models are available on both the F225 and F200 models for twin installations. These outboards also feature a unique idle speed controller and idle noise reduction system that provides quiet operation throughout the entire RPM range.

MSRP: **Model F225** $17,620
Model F200 $16,990

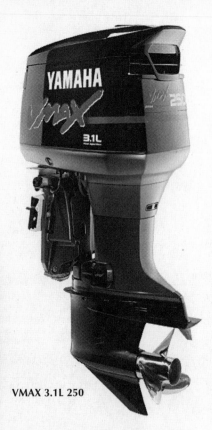

VMAX 3.1L 250

OUTBOARD MOTORS

YAMAHA VMAX 3.1L 250

With a 3.1-liter displacement, the VMAX 3.1L 250 features Yamaha's OX66 advanced fuel injection system on a 76-degree loop-charged engine block, making it one of the most powerful bass outboards available today. The heart of the VMAX 3.1L 250 is its fuel-injection system - OX66. The OX66 advanced fuel injection system sports a feedback fuel-injection system with quad filtration that injects fuel after the throttle valves to help increase fuel efficiency and power throughout the throttle range. A Yamaha-exclusive Oxygen Density Sensor enhances performance by continually monitoring oxygen density in the exhaust gases which the electronic control unit (ECU) then measures to adjust the correct fuel quantity for optimum efficiency and power.

The new outboard also features six independent throttle valves and injectors coupled with the ECU to provide instant throttle response. To supply fuel to the injectors, the system utilizes a two-speed electric fuel pump that reduces low-speed operational amper-age by 33 percent, resulting in less draw on batteries. Yamaha's closed-loop system also features four system filters to clean out any contaminants that may enter the system and to provide long-term durability.

Like all of Yamaha's V6 outboards, the new 250 features Yamaha's S.M.A.R.T. microcomputer ignition system. S.M.A.R.T. (Starting, Management, Alert, Reliability, Trouble Shoot) ignition allows for quick starts hot or cold, optimum engine power output, engine protection with low oil, overheat and over-rev warnings and easy maintenance.

Loop charging provides more complete combustion efficiency and more powerful engine performance while using less fuel. Precision Blend Oil Injection eliminates the need to pre-mix gas and oil by automatically injecting oil. This oil injection system responds to the motor's precise oil demands at different engine speeds by varying the amount of oil injected ensuring efficiency and engine durability.

Special exhaust tuning improves low- to mid-range torque and offers a higher top end while a high-performance gearcase with a streamlined, longer bullet and a new 1.81:1 gear ratio offers less drag in the water. Lower water intakes allow the engine to run cool and smooth at higher mounting heights while a wide-span mounting bracket, featuring rubber motor mounts that are 22 percent stronger than last year's, dampens vibration for smooth operation and superior handling. Weight for this new engine is 493 lbs.

The 250 features a 20" shaft, electric start for effortless starting, remote steering and power trim and tilt that ranges from a -4 degree trim that gets the boat quickly out of the hole to a +16° for optimum speed and top-end performance. The motor tilts up 70 degrees for ease of trailering and includes an extra tilt switch on the lower engine pan for easy use while the boat is trailered. And once underway, the High Output Charging System and Multi-Charge System with battery isolator produce from 20 amps at idle to 35 amps at 5500 rpm to keep the batteries fully charged, even with multiple accessories running. This feature only requires an optional Isolator Cable to be installed.

The VMAX 3.1L 250 fights corrosion with features like Yamaha's ACP-221 paint application process, a technologically-advanced process featuring five layers of paint, including a clear coat with UV inhibitors applied to Yamaha's corrosion-resistant, high-strength aluminum alloy - YDC 30. The 250 also features replaceable anti-corrosion anodes strategically placed in the engine block, transom bracket and on the lower unit where they sacrifice themselves to protect the other metal components from corrosion. Freshwater flushing is also standard.

Thermostatic cooling monitors and controls proper engine temperature for consistent performance, increased efficiency and reliability, while through-propeller exhaust helps to keep engine noise to a minimum. A pilot water hole provides visual assurance of engine water flow. The Yamaha VMAX 3.1L 250 is a standard and stock VMAX model, not a specialty racing motor, like many 250 horsepower outboards offered by some competitors. Being a stock model of the Yamaha VMAX series, the VMAX 3.1L 250 is backed by Yamaha's Two-Year Factory Limited Warranty at no extra cost.

MSRP: $17,620

TROLLING MOTORS

MINN KOTA TROLLING MOTORS

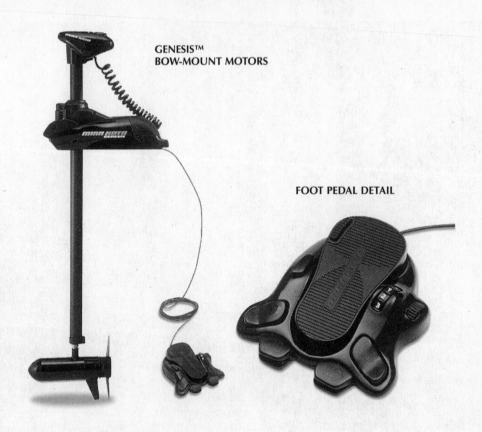

**GENESIS™
BOW-MOUNT MOTORS**

FOOT PEDAL DETAIL

GENESIS™ BOW-MOUNT MOTORS

Minn Kota's® most advanced trolling motor, Genesis™ features automatic stow and deploy with push of a button. Automatic power trim raises and lowers the motor, providing optimal shaft length, for all conditions.

Control features on the ergonomically-designed foot pedal include momentary on, master on/off switch, mode select (AutoPilot™/stow and deploy), fine adjust speed control, speed control, trim up/down, momentary steer left, momentary steer right and constant on. Other Genesis features include double-tube shaft, RealTime Battery Gauge (displays running time remaining at current power), Weedless Wedge™ and power steering. Genesis comes standard with AutoPilot (automatic navigation) and Universal Sonar (fully integrated transducer and wires compatible with most major fish-finders) features.

SPECIFICATIONS

Model: Genesis 74/AP-US (AutoPilot-Universal Sonar)
Mount: Integrated Impact Protection System
Control: Low Profile
Maximum Thrust: 74
Maximum Amp Draw: 45
Volts: 24
Speed (Forward/Reverse): Variable
Shaft Length: 45", 60"
Weedless Wedge: Yes
Composite Shaft: Yes
Maximizer: Yes
Battery Meter: Realtime
Maximum Boat Length: 25'
MSRP: $1480 - $1510 (45)
$1550 - $1580 (60)

Model: Genesis 74/AP (AutoPilot)
Mount: Integrated Impact Protection System
Control: Low Profile
Maximum Thrust: 74
Maximum Amp Draw: 45
Volts: 24
Speed (Forward/Reverse): Variable
Shaft Length: 45", 60"
Weedless Wedge: Yes
Composite Shaft: Yes
Maximizer: Yes
Battery Meter: Realtime
Maximum Boat Length: 25'
MSRP: $1350 - $1380 (45)
$1429 - $1450 (60)

Model: Genesis 74
Mount: Integrated Impact Protection System
Control: Low Profile
Maximum Thrust: 74
Maximum Amp Draw: 45
Volts: 24
Speed (Forward/Reverse): Variable
Shaft Length: 45", 60"
Weedless Wedge: Yes
Composite Shaft: Yes
Maximizer: Yes
Battery Meter: Realtime
Maximum Boat Length: 25'
MSRP: $1350 - $1280 (45)
$1320 - $1350 (60)

MINN KOTA TROLLING MOTORS

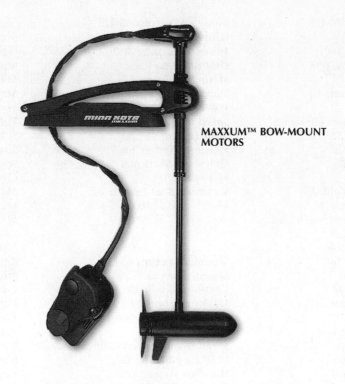

MAXXUM™ BOW-MOUNT MOTORS

Model: Genesis 55/AP-US (AutoPilot-Universal Sonar)
Mount: Integrated Impact Protection System
Control: Low Profile
Maximum Thrust: 55
Maximum Amp Draw: 45
Volts: 12
Speed (Forward/Reverse): Variable
Shaft Length: 45", 52""
Weedless Wedge: Yes
Composite Shaft: Yes
Maximizer: Yes
Battery Meter: Realtime
Maximum Boat Length: 21'
MSRP: $1330 - $1360 (45)
$1380 - $1400 (60)

Model: Genesis 55/AP (AutoPilot)
Mount: Integrated Impact Protection System
Control: Low Profile
Maximum Thrust: 55
Maximum Amp Draw: 43
Volts: 12
Speed (Forward/Reverse): Variable
Shaft Length: 45", 52"
Weedless Wedge: Yes
Composite Shaft: Yes
Maximizer: Yes
Battery Meter: Realtime

Maximum Boat Length: 21'
MSRP: $1200 - $1230 (45)
$1250 - $1280 (60)

Model: Genesis 55
Mount: Integrated Impact Protection System
Control: Low Profile
Maximum Thrust: 55
Maximum Amp Draw: 43
Volts: 12
Speed (Forward/Reverse): Variable
Shaft Length: 45"
Weedless Wedge: Yes
Composite Shaft: Yes
Universal Sonar: No
Maximizer: Yes
Battery Meter: Realtime
Maximum Boat Length: 21'
MSRP: $1100 - $1130 (45)

MAXXUM™ BOW-MOUNT MOTORS
Designed specifically to provide hard-core bass anglers with rugged durability and maximum power needed for a long day on the water. The Bowguard 360° breakaway mount breaks away from any direction and automatically resets itself. Maxxum has the highest

power available at 101 pounds of thrust (also 74, 65 and 55) and shaft lengths of 42", 52" and 62". Maxxum motors are backed by a 3-year warranty, while the indestructible composite shafts have a lifetime warranty. Other key features on Maxxum include Maximizer™ (solid-state circuitry that delivers up to five times more running time on a single battery charge) and overload sensing circuitry that protects the motor from overheating when accidentally engaged in the stowed position.

SPECIFICATIONS
Model: Maxxum 101
Mount: Bowguard 360
Control: Wide Track
Maximum Thrust: 101
Maximum Amp Draw: 37
Volts: 36
Speed (Forward/Reverse): Variable
Shaft Length: 42", 52", 62"
Weedless Wedge: Yes
Composite Shaft: Yes
Maximizer: Yes
Maximum Boat Length: 25'
MSRP: $810 - $840 (42),
$830-$860 (52), $840 - $870 (62)

MINN KOTA TROLLING MOTORS

**Model: Maxxum 74-US
(Universal Sonar)**
Mount: Bowguard 360
Control: Wide Track
Maximum Thrust: 74
Maximum Amp Draw: 45
Volts: 24
Speed (Forward/Reverse): Variable
Shaft Length: 42", 52", 62"
Weedless Wedge: Yes
Composite Shaft: Yes
Maximizer: Yes
Maximum Boat Length: 25'
MSRP: $820 - $850 (42),
$840-$870 (52), $850 - $880 (62)

Model: Maxxum 74
Mount: Bowguard 360
Control: Wide Track
Maximum Thrust: 74
Maximum Amp Draw: 45
Volts: 24
Speed (Forward/Reverse): Variable
Shaft Length: 42", 52", 62"
Weedless Wedge: Yes
Composite Shaft: Yes
Maximizer: Yes
Maximum Boat Length: 25'
MSRP: $740 - $770 (42),
$760-$790 (52), $770 - $800 (62)

**Model: Maxxum 65-US
(Universal Sonar)**
Mount: Bowguard 360
Control: Wide Track
Maximum Thrust: 65
Maximum Amp Draw: 38
Volts: 24
Speed (Forward/Reverse): Variable
Shaft Length: 42", 52"
Weedless Wedge: Yes
Composite Shaft: Yes
Maximizer: Yes
Maximum Boat Length: 23'
MSRP: shaft $740 - $770 (42),
shaft $760 - $790 (52)

Model: Maxxum 65
Mount: Bowguard 360
Control: Wide Track
Maximum Thrust: 65
Maximum Amp Draw: 38
Volts: 24
Speed (Forward/Reverse): Variable
Shaft Length: 42", 52"
Weedless Wedge: Yes
Composite Shaft: Yes
Maximizer: Yes
Maximum Boat Length: 23'
MSRP: shaft $660 - $690 (42),
shaft $680 - $710 (52)

**Model: Maxxum 65/SC
(Speed Coil)**
Mount: Bowguard 360
Control: Wide Track
Maximum Thrust: 65
Maximum Amp Draw: 38
Volts: 12/24
Speed (Forward/Reverse): 10
Shaft Length: 42"
Weedless Wedge: Yes
Composite Shaft: Yes
Maximizer: No
Maximum Boat Length: 23'
MSRP: $600 - $630

**Model: Maxxum 55/SC
(Speed Coil)**
Mount: Bowguard 360
Control: Wide Track
Maximum Thrust: 55
Maximum Amp Draw: 43
Volts: 12
Speed (Forward/Reverse): 5
Shaft Length: 42", 52"
Weedless Wedge: Yes
Composite Shaft: Yes
Maximizer: No
Maximum Boat Length: 21'
MSRP: $510 - $540

TROLLING MOTORS

Keep Batteries Charged
If you wait too long to charge trolling motor batteries, or fail to charge them for a proper amount of time, you'll be faced with replacing those batteries sooner than you'd like. Deep-cycle batteries should be charged within 24 hours of use and should be kept fully charged while stored. Check your battery dealer or manufacturer for specific charging requirements.

MINN KOTA TROLLING MOTORS

Model: Maxxum 55
Mount: Bowguard 360
Control: Wide Track
Maximum Thrust: 55
Maximum Amp Draw: 43
Volts: 12
Speed (Forward/Reverse): Variable
Shaft Length: 42", 52"
Weedless Wedge: Yes
Composite Shaft: Yes
Maximizer: Yes
Maximum Boat Length: 21'
MSRP: $580 - $610 (42),
$600 - $630 (52)

Model: Maxxum 101H
Mount: Bowguard 360
Control: Tilt Twist Tiller
Maximum Thrust: 101
Maximum Amp Draw: 37
Volts: 36
Speed (Forward/Reverse): Variable
Shaft Length: 52"
Weedless Wedge: Yes
Composite Shaft: Yes

Maximizer: Yes
Maximum Boat Length: 21'
MSRP: $750 - $780

**Model: Maxxum 74/H
(Hand Control)**
Mount: Bowguard 360
Control: Tilt Twist Tiller
Maximum Thrust: 74
Maximum Amp Draw: 45
Volts: 24
Speed (Forward/Reverse): Variable
Shaft Length: 42", 52"
Weedless Wedge: Yes
Composite Shaft: Yes
Maximizer: Yes
Maximum Boat Length: 23'
MSRP: $650 - $680 (42),
$670 - $700 (52)

**Model: Maxxum 65/H
(Hand Control)**
Mount: Bowguard 360
Control: Tilt Twist Tiller
Maximum Thrust: 65

Maximum Amp Draw: 38
Volts: 24
Speed (Forward/Reverse): Variable
Shaft Length: 52"
Weedless Wedge: Yes
Composite Shaft: Yes
Maximizer: Yes
Maximum Boat Length: 23'
MSRP: $570 - $600

**Model: Maxxum 55/H
(Hand Control)**
Mount: Bowguard 360
Control: Tilt Twist Tiller
Maximum Thrust: 55
Maximum Amp Draw: 43
Volts: 12
Speed (Forward/Reverse): Variable
Shaft Length: 42"
Weedless Wedge: Yes
Composite Shaft: Yes
Maximizer: Yes
Maximum Boat Length: 21'
MSRP: $490 - $520

Quick Check
When you lift your trolling motor out of the water when preparing to move to another spot, check for fishing line and other obstructions around the prop. Before you crank up your outboard, be sure the trolling motor is completely in the stow position so it won't bounce up and possibly get broken.

MINN KOTA TROLLING MOTORS

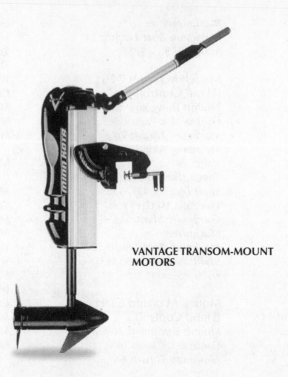

VANTAGE TRANSOM-MOUNT MOTORS

VANTAGE TRANSOM-MOUNT MOTORS

With the push of a button, Vantage automatically lowers or raises the motor to the engaged or stow position. And, with articulated 4:1 steering and up to 101 lbs. of continuous thrust, you get the power and control to go anywhere anytime. From top to bottom, this is a one-of-a-kind transom-mount motor which shares no equal.

FEATURES

- Automatic Stow and Deploy: Simply press the "down" button and the motor automatically lowers into the water. Press "up" and the motor raises to the stowed position. No manual lifting required.
- Articulated Steering: With a 4:1 steering ratio, Vantage is ultra-responsive. Slight handle movements are all that are required to make pinpoint adjustments in boat position.
- Weedless Wedge Prop: The only true 100% weedless prop. Patented swept-back design pushes weeds away without draining power.
- Breakaway Mount: Unique mounting bracket breaks away, protecting the motor from damage should an

underwater obstacle be hit.
- Dual-Purpose Directional Indicator: Shows the direction of travel, and can be instantly turned on the water for backtrolling. No tools or physical effort required. Simply lift and turn the indicator 180 degrees to change trolling direction.
- Extra-Long Telescoping Tiller: The industry's longest. Fully extends up to 31" and tilts up or down for ergonomic comfort and control.
- Maximizer: Advanced, solid state circuitry delivers up to five times more power on a single battery charge. Stay out longer, stronger.
- Cool Power: Stays cool under the most demanding conditions to give you greater sustained thrust and motor life.

SPECIFICATIONS

Model: Vantage 101
Mount: Metal Breakaway
Control: Extension Tilt Twist Tiller
Maximum Thrust: 101
Maximum Amp Draw: 37
Volts: 36
Speed (Forward/Reverse): Variable
Shaft Length: Variable
Weedless Wedge: Yes
Maximizer: Yes

Maximum Boat Length: 25'
MSRP: $1100 - $1130

Model: Vantage 74
Mount: Metal Breakaway
Control: Extension Tilt Twist Tiller
Maximum Thrust: 74
Maximum Amp Draw: 45
Volts: 24
Speed (Forward/Reverse): Variable
Shaft Length: Variable
Weedless Wedge: Yes
Maximizer: Yes
Maximum Boat Length: 25'
MSRP: $1000 - $1030

Model: Vantage 55
Mount: Metal Breakaway
Control: Extension Tilt Twist Tiller
Maximum Thrust: 55
Maximum Amp Draw: 43
Volts: 12
Speed (Forward/Reverse): Variable
Shaft Length: Variable
Weedless Wedge: Yes
Maximizer: Yes
Maximum Boat Length: 21'
MSRP: $900 - $930

TROLLING MOTORS

MOTORGUIDE TROLLING MOTORS

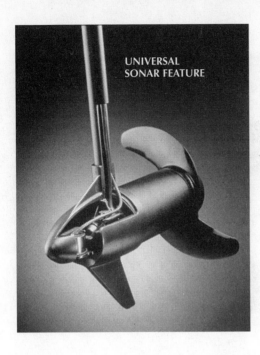

UNIVERSAL
SONAR FEATURE

COPILOT™ FEATURE

UNIVERSAL SONAR FEATURE

Available on select Minn Kota trolling motor models, Universal Sonar features a high-frequency transducer integrated into the lower unit of the motor with wiring that runs up and inside the composite shaft, meaning these components are fully protected. Plug-in accessory adapters provide compatibility for Universal Sonar with select models of fish-finders from the following companies: Bottom Line®, Eagle®, Garmin®, Humminbird®, Lowrance® Vexilar® and Zercom®.
MSRP: $80.00

COPILOT™ FEATURE

CoPilot™ is a patented wireless remote steering system, designed specifically to work with selected Minn Kota electric steer motors (PowerDrive™ and Riptide®). It features a small wireless remote, similar to an automobile keyless entry remote, that allows the operator to control the boat's steering and speed from any location on the boat. The remote, which floats, can be attached to a fishing rod (with any of the three brackets that come standard), wrist or belt for easy use.

CoPilot can be added to existing

Minn Kota PowerDrive, PowerDrive with AutoPilot and Riptide with AutoPilot motors by simply attaching the receiver to the ride side plate. An optional plug is available to allow the control to be switched back and forth between CoPilot or foot pedal control operation.

Stay Sharp
When you anticipate you might be fishing in heavy grass, be sure before leaving home that your trolling motor prop is smooth and sharp. A sharp prop usually will slice through the grass, even at low speeds.

MOTORGUIDE TROLLING MOTORS

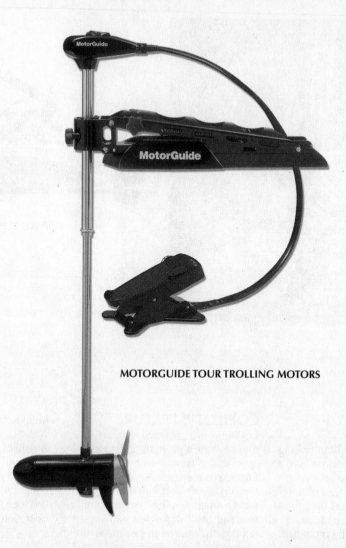

MOTORGUIDE TOUR TROLLING MOTORS

MOTORGUIDE TOUR TROLLING MOTORS

Tour motors have super-tough, super-strong stainless steel shafts and feature the pull-pull steering system, the easiest to use of all mechanical cable steering systems for high-thrust trolling motors, reducing steering torque and foot fatigue. There's also Soft-Start™ technology built-in to ensure that a touch to the pedal's on-switch doesn't catch you or your partner by surprise when in the highest power settings.

Other Features:
- 2-part, double-dipped conformal acrylic coating on all electronic boards and components.
- From 82 to 109 romping, stomping pounds of thrust with 36-volt or 24-volt power options.
- Two cable, pull-pull steering always keeps a cable in pull mode virtually eliminating torque.
- Soft-Start feature says "adios" to awkward starts.
- Pinpoint ready models feature a patented interference-free transducer built right into the lower unit, eliminating the need for messy cables and clamps.
- All-new and stronger Gator™ Spring mount with spring-return breakaway feature.
- Built-in weed ring, extended skeg, and 3-blade Machete® prop for weed-free performance.

SPECIFICATIONS

Model TR82 FB:
82-lb. thrust, 24 volts, variable speed control, 45" shaft, foot steering control #21 Gator Spring mount style (available in 50" and 60" shaft)
MSRP: $789.00

Model TR82P FB:
82-lb. thrust, 24 volts, variable speed control, 45" shaft, foot steering control #21 Gator Spring mount style (available in 50" and 60" shaft)

Model TR109 FB:
109-lb. thrust, 36 volts, variable speed control, 45" shaft, foot steering control #21 Gator Spring mount style (available in 50" and 60" shaft)
MSRP: $889.00

Model TR109P FB:
109-lb. thrust, 36 volts, variable speed control, 45" shaft, foot steering control #21 Gator Spring mount style (available in 50" and 60" shaft)
MSRP: $989.00

MOTORGUIDE TROLLING MOTORS

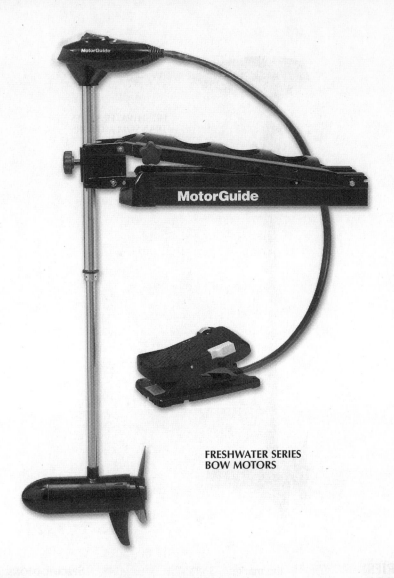

**FRESHWATER SERIES
BOW MOTORS**

FRESHWATER SERIES
BOW MOTORS

Freshwater Series Bow motors deliver power and performance. 12 and 24-volt models with up to 71 pounds of thrust – the most dependable motors ever built.

Features:

- 2-part, double-dipped conformal acrylic coating on all electronic boards and components.
- MotorGuide's innovative Gator Breakaway mount delivers strength and protection up front.
- HyperDrive™ lower unit delivers quiet, efficient power.
- Lighted directional indicator is like GPS for the eyes.
- 3-blade Machete® prop.
- Satisfy your need for speed in fixed or variable speed models.
- All stainless steel components.
- Available in 12 and 24-volt models, every motor is ready to deliver proven and dependable performance.

SPECIFICATIONS

Model FW54 HB (Freshwater Bow Mount, Hand-Control):

54-lb. thrust, 12 volts, 5/2 speed control, 50" shaft, hand steering control, Twist-Tiller foot pedal style, 360-degree steering response time: instant, #16 Breakaway mount style (available in 54-, 71- and 82-lbs. thrust)
MSRP: $399.00

Model FW46 FB (Freshwater Bow Mount, Foot-Control):

46-lb. thrust, 12 volts, 5 speed con-trol, 36" shaft, foot steering control, Rack and Pinion foot pedal style, 360-degree steering response time: instant, #07 Standard Bow mount style (available in 54- and 109-lbs. thrust; 42", 50", 45" and 60" shaft)
MSRP: $359.00

**Model FW71 HP
(Freshwater Bow Pontoon):**

54-lb. thrust, 12 volts, 5/2 speed con-trol, 50" shaft, hand steering control, Ext. Twist-Tiller foot pedal style, 360-degree steering response time: instant, #1P Pontoon mount style (available in 71-lbs. thrust
MSRP: $499.00

MOTORGUIDE TROLLING MOTORS

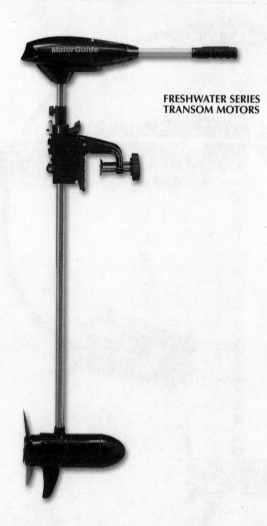

**FRESHWATER SERIES
TRANSOM MOTORS**

FRESHWATER SERIES TRANSOM MOTORS

Freshwater Series Transom handles are the longest extending twist-tillers on the market.

Features:

- 2-part, double-dipped conformal acrylic coating on all electronic boards and components.
- The longest twist-tiller handle on the market.
- In-handle forward and reverse control.
- 3-blade Machete® prop (46 pounds and up).
- Stainless steel shafts.
- All-metal mounts. How strong is your transom?
- Kill switch on variable-speed models.

SPECIFICATIONS
Model FW30 HT:

30-lb. thrust, 12 volts, 5/2 speed control, 30" shaft, hand steering control, Twist-Tiller foot pedal style, 360-degree steering response time: instant, #03 Transom mount style (available in 46-, 54- and 82-lbs. thrust; 42" and 45" shaft)
MSRP: $119.00

Oiling Reduces Noise
From time to time, oil the hinge points on your trolling motor bracket. This will keep the bracket quiet and help you avoid unnecessary noise that could spook bass.

TROLLING MOTORS

MOTORGUIDE TROLLING MOTORS

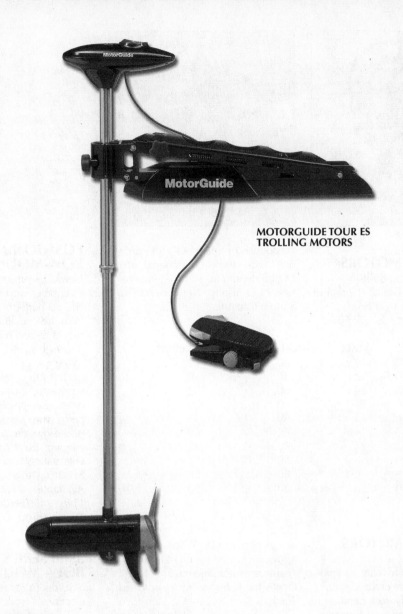

MOTORGUIDE TOUR ES TROLLING MOTORS

MOTORGUIDE TOUR ES TROLLING MOTORS

Tour ES motors capture the heel/toe functionality and steering speed of a cable-controlled motor, without the torque. And with the optional 16' soft-wire extension cable you can maintain control, even from the back of the boat

Features:
- 2-part, double-dipped conformal acrylic coating on all electronic boards and components.
- Servo Positioning Steering captures heal/toe functionality and steering speed of a cable-controlled motor.
- Gator™ Spring mount provides

breakaway peace of mind and hinged access door (60" shaft models come standard with Gator™ Spring XL).
- Pinpoint-ready models feature a patented interference-free transducer built right into the lower unit, eliminating the need for messy cables and clamps.
- 1.8 second 360° steering response time (24 volt 2.0 sec.)
- Stow/run switch on pedal puts lower unit in appropriate stow or run position.

SPECIFICATIONS

Model TR ES82P FB:
82-lb. thrust, 24 volts, variable speed

control, 45" shaft, electric steering control, ES Servo foot pedal style, 360-degree steering response time: 2 seconds, #21 Gator Spring mount style (available in 50" and 60" shaft) *MSRP*: $989

Model TR ES109P FB:
109-lb. thrust, 36 volts, variable speed control, 45" shaft, electric steering control, ES Servo foot pedal style, 360-degree steering response time: 1.8 seconds, #21 Gator Spring mount style (available in 50" and 60" shaft) *MSRP*: $1089

PINPOINT TROLLING MOTORS

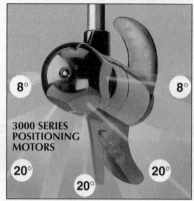

2000 SX SERIES POSITIONING MOTORS

Features: Depth Track. Built-in 240kHz transducer. Digital depth and surface temperature. LCD display. 12V, 24V, or 36V models. 40, 60, or 80 pounds of thrust. 42", 50", 56", or 60" shafts. Backlit directional arrows. Digital depth and surface temperature. LCD display. Network Fishing System Capable

Model	Volts	Thrust (lbs.)	Shaft Length
2300SX-42	12	40	42
2300SX-50	12	40	50
2700SX-42	24	60	42
2700SX-50	24	60	50
2700SX-56	24	60	56
2700SX-60	24	60	60
2900SX-42	24	80	42
2900SX-50	36	80	50
2900SX-56	36	80	56
2900SX-60	36	80	60

3000 SERIES POSITIONING MOTORS

Pinpoint's 3000 series feature five built-in transducers that relay information to a high-speed microprocessor. You can automatically track depth contours, the shoreline, or submerged creek channels at the touch of a finger. Pinpoint™ Positioning Motors are the ultimate boat positioning system for every angler. Each of these models has a low-profile "rocker" style foot pedal, an oversize LCD display that shows digital depth and surface temperature at a glance. The LCD display and arrow are backlit for night fishing.
Features: Automatic tracking for Depth Track, Shore Track and Creek Track. 5 Built-in 240kHz transducer. 12V, 24V, or 36V models. 40, 60 or 80 pounds of thrust. 42", 50", 56" or 60" shafts. Backlit directional arrow. Digital depth and surface temperature LCD display. Network Fishing System Capable.

Model	Volts	Thrust (lbs.)	Shaft Length
3300-42	12	40	42
3300-50	12	40	50
3700-42	24	60	42
3700-50	24	60	50
3700-56	24	60	56
3700-60	24	60	60
3900-42	24	80	42
3900-50	36	80	50
3900-56	36	80	56

POSITIONING 3700 BOW-MOUNT MOTOR

Network Compatible means all of your electronics work together as a system. You get performance and reliability from the Pinpoint 3000 series. Bow-mount motors have five built-in transducers that relay information to a high-speed microprocessor to automatically track depth contours, the shoreline, or submerged creek channels. Motors also have a low-profile rocker style foot pedal. The oversize liquid crystal display shows digital depth and surface temperature at a glance. Motor has 24 volts with 60 pounds of thrust.

SPECIFICATIONS
Available: 42", 50", and 60" shaft.
Volts: 24, *Thrust:* 60 lbs.
Depth Track: 3, *Shore Track:* 3
Creek Track: 3

3900 SERIES BOW- MOUNT MOTOR

Network Compatible means all of your electronics work together as a system. You get performance and reliability from the Pinpoint 3000 series. Bow-mount motors have five built-in transducers that relay information to a high-speed microprocessor to automatically track depth contours, the shoreline, or submerged creek channels at the touch of a finger. Motors also have a low-profile rocker style foot pedal. The oversize liquid crystal display shows digital depth and surface temperature at a glance. Motor is 36 volts and has 80 pounds of thrust.

SPECIFICATIONS
Available: 42", 50", or 60" shaft.
Volts: 36, *Thrust:* 80 lbs.
Depth Track: 3, *Shore Track:* 3
Creek Track: 3

ELECTRONICS

ELECTRONICS

BOTTOM LINE ELECTRONICS

TOURNAMENT NCC 6300

TOURNAMENT 1101

The Bottom Line Tournament 1101 is a versatile fish finder with 128 vertical pixels, built-in digital surface temperature, and the option of digital boat speed, all in one low-priced package. Straight from the box, the unit can be positioned on the console or front deck just like all Bottom Line Tournament Series fishfinders. But with the optional installation bracket, the Tournament 1101 can be easily mounted in the dash of the console with the look of factory rigging.

Standard features on the Tournament 1101 include automatic operation, zoom and bottom track, adjustable night light, built-in simulator, screen contrast adjustment, automatic gain control, voltage meter and much more. Fish located on the multi-level Fish D'Tect are identified for depth. The saltwater-protected case measures 5 inches by 5.3 inches by 2.5 inches. The 7.2 square-inch screen with 1200 pixels per square inch delivers a sharp screen image down to 240 feet deep.

The Tournament 1101, like all Bottom Line products, carries a one-year full warranty and a limited lifetime service policy.
MSRP: $69.95

TOURNAMENT NCC 6300

The Bottom Line Tournament NCC 6300 has a wide-format 22.75 square inch screen that displays 153,600 pixels (that's 6,751 pixels per square inch). Now anglers can see even more detail to better distinguish soft or hard bottoms, to better identify the various types of underwater structure, and to find fish resting on the bottom that were previously overlooked.

The Tournament NCC 6300 has Bottom Line's patented Sidefinder® technology. Sidefinder offers side scanning capabilities, allowing anglers to see not only below the boat but also to the side. With the optional Sidefinder upgrade, multiple side views are available. The unit detects fish that other sonars just can't find, like those hiding under docks, suspended beside a submerged tree trunk or along a rip-rap bank.

Bottom Line's split screen capabilities allow a combination of views. For example, both the LCD bottom-reading Sidefinder and a flasher mode can be seen at the same time, offering the angler additional sonar capabilities and range. Moreover, sonar pictures can be viewed at the same time as the map. All these variations are just standard features of the Tournament NCC 6300.

C-Map card reading capabilities literally point out every nook and cranny on the water with highly detailed maps. Using Computrol's Tournament GPS module and built-in multi-track 12-satellite receiver, the Tournament 6300 can pinpoint thousands of hot fishing spots in GPS vernacular.
MSRP: around $950

ELECTRONICS

FISHEASY™ 2

FISHEASY™ 2 PORTABLE

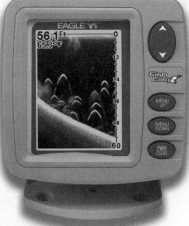

FISHEASY™ 2T

FISHEASY™ 2

From innovative Eagle® technology comes the FishEasy 2, a high-power, high-resolution, feature-rich sonar that's made easy-to-use even for newcomers to LCD fish-finding, and at a price that's easy to afford.

SPECIFICATIONS

- Super-sharp 4" diagonal 240x160 pixel Film Super Twist display reveals fantastic underwater detail and target separation
- Excellent viewing in direct sunlight; backlit screen and keypad for night/low light use
- 1,500 watts peak-to-peak power for depths to 800 feet
- 200 kHz Skimmer® transducer for up to 60 degrees of fish detection area using high sensitivity settings; operates at boat speeds up to 70 mph
- Operating ease - Advanced Signal Processing (ASP™) features automatic fine tuning for the best sonar picture in nearly all water conditions
- Unique FishReveal™ feature uses 10 levels of gray tones to expose fish hidden in clutter and cover
- New HyperScroll™ feature displays fish targets at higher boat speeds
- Advanced Fish I.D.™ displays targets in different sizes of fish symbols; FishTrack™ gives depth readings above each symbol
- Patented GRAYLINE® separates fish and structure on or near the bottom from the actual bottom, and defines bottom composition/hardness.
- Fish/depth/shallow alarms
- Advanced receiver design gives enhanced resistance to electrical interference
- Instant screen updates during depth range changes for uninterrupted underwater viewing
- Optional sensor for water temp/trolling speed/distance display
- Completely sealed and waterproof and features
- Full one-year warranty.

MSRP: $129.99

FISHEASY™ 2 PORTABLE

For go-anywhere anytime fish finding. Features handy Porta-Power Pack case with molded-in sonar bracket and shoulder strap. Includes portable 200 kHz Skimmer® transducer with suction cup mounting. Uses eight D-cell batteries or one compatible rechargeable gel-cell battery (batteries not included).

MSRP: $149.99

FISHEASY™ 2T

Features a 200 kHz Skimmer® transducer with a built-in sensor for accurate digital display of water surface temperature.

MSRP: $159.99

ELECTRONICS

EAGLE® ELECTRONICS

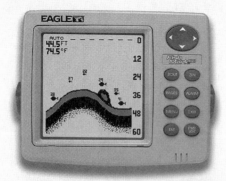

FISHMARK™ 160

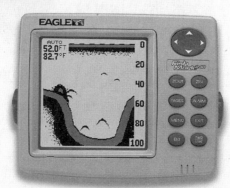

FISHMARK™ 240

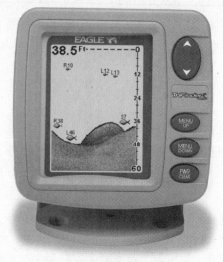

TRIFINDER™ 2

FISHMARK™ SERIES

Eagle® presents high-performance, pro-grade LCD sonar (including water temp) for the avid angler in two highly-affordable choices that make FishMark™ fish finders America's hottest deal in performance, versatility, and price.

FISHMARK"™160
SPECIFICATIONS
- High-contrast 5" diagonal Film SuperTwist LCD offers eye-pleasing 160x160 pixel resolution for enhanced target detail and separation
MSRP: $219

FISHMARK™ 240
SPECIFICATIONS
- High-definition 5 diagonal Film SuperTwist display renders super-sharp 240x240 pixel resolution for superior underwater picture detail
- Features internal back-up memory that automatically saves user's custom sonar settings between uses
- Accepts optional sensors for adding livewell and baitwell temp readings.
MSRP: $319

Eagle® FishMark™ 240 & 160 Shared Features
- Excellent screen viewing in direct sunlight; backlit screen and keypad for night/low light use
- 1,500 watts peak-to-peak power for depths to 800 feet
- 200 kHz Skimmer® transducer with built-in temp sensor for up to 60 degrees of fish detection coverage using high sensitivity settings; operates at boat speeds up to 70 mph
- Operating ease - Advanced Signal Processing (ASP™) features automatic "fine-tuning" for the best sonar picture in nearly all water conditions
- Unique Windows feature offers choices of critical sonar information displays in easy-to-read split-screen panels
- Split-screen zoom, multiple zoom ranges, automatic bottom tracking, and instant display updates during range changes
- Popular FasTrack™ feature displays instantaneous flasher-style sonar returns in a vertical bar
- Advanced Fish I.D.™ displays targets in different sizes of fish

symbols; FishTrack™ gives depth readings above each symbol
- Patented GRAYLINE® separates fish and structure on or near the bottom from the actual bottom, and defines bottom composition/hardness.
- Fish/depth/shallow/zone alarms
- Optional sensor for trolling speed/distance display
- Completely sealed and waterproof
- Full one-year warranty.

TRIFINDER™ 2
Enjoy triple the fish-finding coverage plus all the power, performance, and easy operation features of the FishEasy™ 2 at an economical price.
SPECIFICATIONS
- Features the exclusive Eagle® 3-Beam BroadView™ transducer for up to 150-degrees of fish-finding coverage with high sensitivity settings
- Special TargetTrack™ feature displays depths of fish symbol targets AND indicates their locations - left, right, and directly under the boat
MSRP: $179

LOWRANCE ELECTRONICS

**GLOBALMAP®
100**

**GLOBALMAP®
2400**

GLOBALMAP® 100

Here's one handheld mapping GPS that goes to any extreme on land or water, and is tough to beat. The award-winning GlobalMap® 100 is extremely precise, durable, and waterproof. Best of all, it's extremely affordable.

SPECIFICATIONS

- Large 2.5 diagonal high-contrast Film SuperTwist LCD display
- High-definition 160(V) x 104(H) resolution for excellent mapping detail
- Excellent viewing in direct sunlight; backlit screen for night/low light navigation
- Internal antenna for precision 12-parallel channel GPS with strong satellite lock-ons even in tree cover.
- Built-in custom Lowrance background map with enhanced water, shoreline, coastal, and highway detail from southern Canada to northern Mexico, plus Hawaii and the Bahamas
- Optional MapCreate™ custom mapping software allows user to make unlimited high-detail maps of any area, any time, without unlock codes or additional fees of any kind
- Compatible with optional Navionics® charts
- Easy point-and-map cursor navigation and route planning
- Storage for up to 750 waypoints, 1,000 event markers, and 99 routes (up to 99 waypoints per route)
- 3 savable and retraceable plot trails with up to 3,000 points per trail

- 28 different graphic icons to mark locations
- 32 map zoom display ranges 0.1- 2,000 miles with one-touch zoom-in/zoom-out control
- Internal back-up memory keeps GPS data safe and accessible for years
- Operates on four AA batteries (not included)
- Completely sealed and waterproof
- Full one-year warranty

MSRP: $209

GLOBALMAP® 2400

The compact, wide-screen, high-res GlobalMap®2400 mapping GPS+WAAS with digital recording and custom mapping option. On the dash, or in the console, it's how any angler can improve their sense of direction affordably.

SPECIFICATIONS

- 5" diagonal high-contrast Film SuperTwist LCD display
- High-detail 240x240 pixel resolution; excellent viewing in direct sunlight
- Brilliant, enhanced cold cathode backlit screen with adjustable brightness for use in low light or at night
- Waterproof drawer for one compact, rewritable memory card to record/playback GPS trip details, and to load custom mapping for navigational display
- External receiver/antenna for precision 12-parallel channel GPS and WAAS reception
- Built-in custom Lowrance background map with enhanced

water, shoreline, coastal, and highway detail for the continental U.S. and Hawaii
- Mega-memory storage for up to 1,000 waypoints, 1,000 event markers, and 100 routes (up to 100 waypoints per route)
- 10 savable and retraceable plot trails with up to 10,000 points per trail
- 42 different graphic icons to mark locations
- 34 map zoom display ranges 0.1-4,000 miles with one-touch zoom-in/zoom-out control
- Optional MapCreate™ custom map-mapping software allows user to make unlimited high-detail maps of any area, any time, without unlock codes or additional fees of any kind
- MapCreate™ maps include an expansive, searchable Points-of-Interest database to easily locate features and services (marinas, hotels, emergency services, airports, etc.) by cursor placement or menu selection
- MapCreate™ maps are created by the user on a PC, saved to an MMC or SD memory card, and loaded into the unit for navigational display
- Compatible with optional Navionics® XL Charts and HotMaps™
- Internal back-up memory keeps GPS data safe and accessible for decades
- Completely sealed and waterproof
- Full one-year warranty

MSRP: $429

LOWRANCE ELECTRONICS

**GLOBALMAP®
3000MT**

GLOBALMAP® 3000MT

Whether on the water, or on your way to and from the water, the GlobalMap® 3000 MT puts a wider world of big-screen, high-detail GPS+WAAS mapping performance with digital recording at your fingertips.

SPECIFICATIONS

- 6.54" diagonal super-high-definition Monochrome Transflective LCD display
- High-detail 480(H)x350(V) resolution; excellent viewing in direct sunlight
- Brilliant, enhanced cold cathode backlit screen with adjustable brightness for use in low light or at night
- Waterproof drawer for up to two compact, rewritable memory cards to record/playback GPS trip details, and to load custom mapping for navigational display
- External receiver/antenna for precision 12-parallel channel GPS and WAAS reception
- Background map with enhanced water, shoreline, coastal, and highway detail for the continental U.S. and Hawaii
- Mega-memory storage for up to 1,000 waypoints, 1,000 event markers, and 100 routes (up to 100 waypoints per route)
- 10 savable and retraceable plot trails with up to 10,000 points per trail
- 42 different graphic icons to mark locations
- 34 map zoom display ranges 0.1-4,000 miles with one-touch zoom-in/zoom-out control
- Includes MapCreate™ custom mapping software to make unlimited high-detail maps of any area, any time, without unlock codes or additional fees of any kind
- MapCreate™ maps include an expansive, searchable Points-of-Interest database to easily locate features and services (marinas, hotels, emergency services, airports, etc.) by cursor placement or menu selection
- MapCreate™ maps are created by the user on a PC, saved to an MMC or SD memory card, and loaded into the unit for navigational display
- Compatible with optional Navionics® XL Charts and HotMaps™
- Internal back-up memory keeps GPS data safe and accessible for decades
- Completely sealed and waterproof
- Full one-year warranty

MSRP: $799.99

Chart Speed

The rate at which the 'picture' travels across the screen of a fish-finder unit is called the "chart speed," or sometimes "sweep speed." The chart speed is adjustable on most units. If the top-end chart speed is high enough, you can run your boat fast and still graph fish. But if the top-end speed is too slow, the marks won't be wide enough to interpret.

ELECTRONICS

LOWRANCE ELECTRONICS

iFINDER™

iFINDER™ ATLANTIS

iFINDER™ EXPRESS

iFINDER™ PLUS

iFINDER™

Sleek. And Ye Shall Find with precise mapping GPS+WAAS performance in a powerful, pocket-size handheld with digital memory card recording/playback capability, colorful cover options, and choices in specialty marine and travel models.

SPECIFICATIONS

- Large 2.9" diagonal high-contrast Film SuperTwist LCD display
- Sharp 160(V)x120(H) pixel resolution for excellent mapping detail
- Superb viewing in direct sunlight; backlit screen for night/low light navigation
- Optional colorful FaceOffs™ covers in red, blue, yellow and camouflage
- Internal antenna for precision 12-parallel channel GPS and WAAS reception
- Built-in custom Lowrance background map with enhanced water, shoreline, coastal, and highway detail for the continental U.S. and Hawaii; includes interstate exit services database for U.S. only
- Internal slot for MMC memory card (not included with standard model) for recording/playback of GPS trip details, and to load optional user-created MapCreate™ enhanced-detail mapping up to

128MB for navigational display
- Storage for up to 1,000 waypoints, 1,000 event markers, and 100 routes (up to 100 waypoints per route)
- 10 savable and retraceable plot trails with up to 10,000 points per trail
- 42 different graphic icons to mark locations
- 37 map zoom display ranges .05-4,000 miles with one-touch zoom-in/zoom-out control
- Internal back-up memory keeps GPS data safe and accessible for decades
- Operates up to 12 hours on two AA batteries (not included)
- Water-resistant to IPX2 standards; includes durable, transparent travel pouch with adjustable lanyard for waterproof navigation
- Full one-year warranty

MSRP: $219

iFINDER™ ATLANTIS

The specialty iFINDER™, enhanced for marine voyagers. Comes pre-loaded with a 16MB MMC memory card with detailed mapping of U.S. coastal and Great Lakes waters, featuring over 60,000 navigational aids and 10,000 wrecks and obstructions and features unique white FaceOffs™ cover.
MSRP: $299

iFINDER™ EXPRESS

The specialty iFINDER™, ideal for off-the-water travel with a distinctive warm grey FaceOffs™ cover. Comes pre-loaded with a 32MB MMC memory card featuring a searchable Points-of-Interest database to find key locations and services - like airports, hotels, restaurants, marinas, emergency services, and more - in the continental U.S. and Hawaii.
MSRP: $299

iFINDER™ PLUS

The standard iFINDER™, with the added plus of including the Lowrance GPS Mapping Accessories Pack to create unlimited, enhanced-detail mapping of any location in the continental U.S. and Hawaii, anytime on a PC (without unlock codes or added costs) for loading to MMC card for iFINDER™ navigational display. Includes MapCreate™ custom mapping software on two CDs, 16MB MMC card, and memory card reader/interface with high-speed USB connector. Comes with standard black FaceOffs™ cover.
MSRP: $429

LOWRANCE ELECTRONICS

LCX-15 CI

LCX-16 CI

THE INNOVATIVE LOWRANCE LCX SERIES

Introducing the "next generation" and technology leap beyond the legendary X16 and X15 paper graph recorders of yesteryear. Only the Lowrance LCX Series now provides inland anglers affordable choices in big-screen, ultra-high resolution sonar—including color—with optional GPS+WAAS/ mapping capability, plus innovative digital recording/playback of sonar graphs and GPS trip details using Multi-Media Card or Secure Digital memory cards.

For the truly serious angler who demands performance and versatility, the Lowrance LCX Series is loaded with advanced features, with the best LCD resolution, detail, and target separation ever achieved with Color Illuminated (CI) or Monochrome Transflective (MT) displays.

LCX Series Shared Sonar Features

- Dual frequency selectivity – separate 50 kHz or 200 kHz operation, or both simultaneously in split-screen display mode
- Depth capability with bottom tracking to 3,000 feet and beyond
- High-performance, dual-frequency, Skimmer® transducer with 4,000 watts peak-to-peak power @ 200 kHz, and 8,000 watts @ 50 kHz
- Programmable "Windows" feature allows users to compile their favorite sonar information for display in easy-to-read, split-screen panels
- Screen choices: full sonar, split zoom, split frequency, split sonar-data, split GPS-sonar, and custom display selections
- Patented GRAYLINE® (15 MT) and COLORLINE™ (16 & 15 CI models) separates fish and structure on or near the bottom from the actual bottom, and defines bottom composition/hardness.
- Advanced Signal Processing (ASP™) features automatic "fine tuning" for the best sonar picture in nearly all water conditions
- Advanced Fish I.D.™ displays targets in different sizes of fish symbols; FishTrack™ gives depth readings above each symbol
- Continuous depth and depth scale readouts; selectable upper and lower depth limits
- Instant zoom display ranges and zoom bottom tracking with easy zoom-in/zoom-out control
- Fish/depth/shallow/zone alarms
- Optional sensor for trolling speed/distance display

LCX SERIES SHARED GPS+WAAS/MAPPING FEATURES

Note: optional Lowrance GPS Mapping Accessories Pack used for GPS/WAAS operation on LCX Series models. Includes receiver/antenna, plus MapCreate™ custom map-making software on two CDs, one 16MB digital rewritable MMC memory card (loaded with background map of the continental U.S. and Hawaii), and MMC reader/interface with USB connector for PCs.

- Precision 12-parallel channel GPS and WAAS reception
- Custom background map displays enhanced water, shoreline, coastal and highway detail for the continental U.S. and Hawaii
- Mega-memory storage for up to 1,000 waypoints, 1,000 event markers, and 100 routes (up to 100 waypoints per route)
- 10 savable and retraceable plot trails with up to 10,000 points per trail
- 42 different graphic icons to mark locations
- 34 map zoom display ranges 0.1–4,000 miles with one-touch zoom-in/zoom-out control
- MapCreate™ custom mapping software allows user to make unlimited high-detail maps of any area, any time, without unlock codes or additional fees of any kind
- MapCreate™ maps include an expansive, searchable Points-of-Interest database to easily locate features and services (marinas, hotels, emergency services, airports, etc.) by cursor placement or menu selection
- MapCreate™ maps are created by the user on a PC, saved to an MMC or SD memory card, and loaded into any LCX Series unit with a GPS/WAAS antenna for navigational display
- Compatible with optional Navionics® XL Charts and HotMaps™

LCX-15 CI
SPECIFICATIONS

- 5.66" diagonal color illuminated, 256-color liquid crystal, TFT display

LOWRANCE ELECTRONICS

LCX-15 MT

LMS-240

- High-definition 320(H)x240(V) pixel resolution
- Brilliant, enhanced cold-cathode backlit screen with adjustable brightness for high visibility in direct sunlight, in low light or at night
- Waterproof drawer for up to two compact, rewritable memory cards to record/playback sonar graphs and GPS trip details, and to load custom mapping for navigational display
- back-up memory keeps sonar settings and GPS data safe and accessible for decades
- Completely sealed and waterproof
- Full one-year warranty

MSRP: $1,299 (sonar only)
$1,699 (sonar/GPS + mapping)

LCX-15 MT
SPECIFICATIONS
- 6.54" diagonal super-high-definition Monochrome Transflective LCD display
- High-detail 480(H)x350(V) pixel resolution
- Excellent viewing in direct sunlight
- Brilliant, enhanced cold-cathode backlit screen with adjustable brightness for use in low light or at night
- Waterproof drawer for up to two compact, rewritable memory cards to record/playback sonar graphs and GPS trip details, and to load custom mapping for navigational display
- Internal back-up memory keeps sonar settings and GPS data safe and accessible for decades
- Completely sealed and waterproof
- Full one-year warranty

MSRP: $799 (sonar only)
$1,199 (sonar/GPS + mapping)

LCX-16 CI
SPECIFICATIONS
- 6.38" diagonal color illuminated, 256-color, full VGA LCD TFT display
- High-definition 640(H)x480(V) pixel resolution
- Brilliant, enhanced cold-cathode backlit screen with adjustable brightness for high visibility in direct sunlight and in low light or at night
- Waterproof drawer for up to two compact, rewritable memory cards to record/playback sonar graphs and GPS trip details, and to load custom mapping for navigational display
- Internal back-up memory keeps sonar settings and GPS data safe and accessible for decades
- Completely sealed and waterproof
- Full one-year warranty

MSRP: $1,949 (sonar only)
$2,249 (sonar/GPS + mapping)

LMS-240
With the new LMS-240 sonar/GPS+WAAS unit with digital recording and custom mapping option, anglers can count on high performance, high power, and high detail to help fishing success where it really counts - to find fish, mark hot spots, and find their way to and from any place, any time, in any weather. Comes complete at a price as nicely compact as its case.
SPECIFICATIONS

- High-contrast 5" diagonal Film SuperTwist LCD display with excellent viewing in direct sunlight; backlit screen and keypad for night/low light use
- Super-sharp sonar and mapping detail with 240x240 pixel resolution with programmable gray scale to customize display to viewing preferences
- Waterproof drawer for one compact, rewritable memory card to record/playback sonar graphs and GPS trip details, and to load custom mapping for navigational display
- Full-screen and split-screen sonar-data-mapping viewing choices
- Internal back-up memory keeps sonar settings and GPS data safe and accessible for decades
- Completely sealed and waterproof
- Full one-year warranty

MSRP: $579

Sonar Features:
- 200 kHz Skimmer® transducer—with built-in temp sensor—with up to 60 degrees of wide fish-finding coverage; operates at boat speeds up to 70 mph
- Unique FishReveal™ feature employs 10 levels of gray tones to expose fish hidden in clutter and cover
- New HyperScroll™ feature displays fish targets at higher boat speeds
- Advanced Signal Processing (ASP™) features automatic "fine tuning" for the best sonar picture in nearly all water conditions
- Advanced Fish I.D.™ displays

ELECTRONICS

LOWRANCE ELECTRONICS

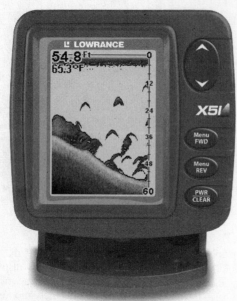

LOWRANCE X51

targets in different sizes of fish symbols; FishTrack™ gives depth readings above each symbol
- Patented GRAYLINE® separates fish and structure on or near the bottom from the actual bottom, and defines bottom composition/hardness.
- Advanced Fish I.D.™ displays targets in different sizes of fish symbols; FishTrack™ gives depth readings above each symbol
- Programmable "Windows" feature allows users to compile their favorite sonar information for display in easy-to-read, split-screen panels
- Continuous depth and depth scale readouts; selectable upper and lower depth limits
- Instant zoom display ranges and zoom bottom tracking with easy zoom-in/zoom-out control
- Internal back-up memory saves user's custom sonar settings for up to 10 years
- Fish/depth/shallow/zone alarms
- Instant screen updates during depth range changes for uninterrupted underwater viewing
- Optional sensor for trolling speed/distance display
- Completely sealed and waterproof
- Full one-year warrant

GPS/WAAS/Mapping Features:
- External receiver/antenna for precision 12-parallel channel GPS and WAAS reception
- Built-in background map with enhanced water, shoreline, coastal, and highway detail for the continental U.S. and Hawaii
- Mega-memory storage for up to 1,000 waypoints, 1,000 event markers, and 100 routes (up to 100 waypoints per route)
- 10 savable and retraceable plot trails with up to 10,000 points per trail
- 42 different graphic icons to mark locations
- 34 map zoom display ranges 0.1-4,000 miles with one-touch zoom-in/zoom-out control
- Optional MapCreate™ custom map-mapping software allows user to make unlimited high-detail maps of any area, any time, without unlock codes or additional fees of any kind
- MapCreate™ maps include an expansive, searchable Points-of-Interest database to easily locate features and services (marinas, hotels, emergency services, airports, etc.) by cursor placement or menu selection
- MapCreate™ maps are created by the user on a PC, saved to an MMC or SD memory card, and loaded

into the unit for navigational display
- Compatible with optional Navionics® XL Charts and HotMaps™

X51
The X51 gives the biggest LCD fish finder performance "bang" for the fewest bucks. This mighty finder with a surprisingly mini price is studded with features that tournament pros prefer, yet with simplified operation even for the first-time sonar user.

SPECIFICATIONS
- Renders super-sharp detail with a 240x160 pixel, 4" diagonal. Film Super Twist display
- Excellent viewing in direct sunlight; backlit screen and keypad for night/low light use
- 1,500 watts peak-to-peak power for depths to 800 feet
- 200 kHz Skimmer® transducer – with built-in temp sensor – with up to 60 degrees of wide fish-finding coverage; operates at boat speeds up to 70 mph
- FasTrack™ full-screen LCD flasher screen mode
- Operating ease - Advanced Signal Processing (ASP™) features automatic "fine-tuning" for the best sonar picture in nearly all water conditions
- Unique FishReveal™ feature employs 10 levels of gray tones to expose fish hidden in clutter and cover
- New HyperScroll™ feature displays fish targets at higher boat speeds
- Advanced Fish I.D.™ displays targets in different sizes of fish symbols; FishTrack™ gives depth readings above each symbol
- Patented GRAYLINE® separates fish and structure on or near the bottom from the actual bottom, and defines bottom composition/hardness.
- Instant zoom display ranges and zoom bottom tracking with easy zoom-in/zoom-out control
- Internal back-up memory saves user's custom sonar settings when unit is turned off
- Fish/depth/shallow/zone alarms
- Advanced receiver design maximizes sonar sensitivity and minimizes electrical interference

LOWRANCE X71

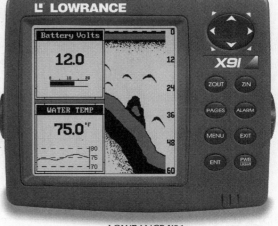

LOWRANCE X91

- Instant screen updates during depth range changes for uninterrupted underwater viewing
- Optional sensor for trolling speed/distance display
- Completely sealed and waterproof
- Full one-year warranty

MSRP: $199

X71

Packed with enhanced power and performance, plus proven Lowrance features galore, the new X71 is both a really great fishing companion and a really great value.

SPECIFICATIONS

- High-contrast 5" diagonal Film SuperTwist display delivers 160x160 pixel resolution for excellent sonar detail and target separation
- Excellent viewing in direct sunlight; backlit screen and keypad for night/low light use
- 1,500 watts peak-to-peak power for depths to 800 feet
- Unique FasTrack™ full-screen LCD flasher screen mode
- Handy "Windows" feature offers choices of data/sonar displays in easy-to-read split-screen panels

MSRP: $199

X91

Leading the way in high-performance fish finders, the X91 is the most complete package of popular Lowrance features that pro anglers demand in a dedicated sonar, and at a very

popular price. For experienced anglers who want fishing success no other sonar in its class does a better job than the X91.

SPECIFICATIONS

- High-definition 5" diagonal Film SuperTwist display with eye-popping 240x240 pixel resolution renders superb detail and target separation
- Beefy 3,000 watts peak-to-peak transmit power
- Dependable depth capability to 1,000 feet
- Popular FasTrack™ feature displays instantaneous flasher-style sonar returns in a vertical bar
- Enhanced cold-cathode backlighting for night/low light fish finding; excellent screen viewing in direct sunlight
- Unique FasTrack™ full-screen LCD flasher screen mode
- Programmable Windows feature allows users to compile their favorite sonar information for display in easy-to-read, split-screen panels

MSRP: $469

X71 / X91 SHARED FEATURES

200 kHz Skimmer® transducer – with built-in temp sensor –with up to 60 degrees of wide fish-finding coverage; operates at boat speeds up to 70 mph

- Advanced Signal Processing (ASP™) features automatic "fine tuning" for the best sonar picture in nearly all water conditions

- Patented GRAYLINE® separates fish and structure on or near the bottom from the actual bottom, and defines bottom composition/hardness.
- Advanced Fish I.D.™ displays targets in different sizes of fish symbols; FishTrack™ gives depth readings above each symbol
- Continuous depth and depth scale readouts; selectable upper and lower depth limits
- Instant zoom display ranges and zoom bottom tracking with easy zoom-in/zoom-out control
- Internal back-up memory saves user's custom sonar settings for up to 10 years
- Fish/depth/shallow/zone alarms
- Instant screen updates during depth range changes for uninterrupted underwater viewing
- Optional sensor for trolling speed/distance display
- Completely sealed and waterproof
- Full one-year warranty

PINPOINT ELECTRONICS

7320

7420

7520

7320 STANDALONE SONAR DISPLAY WITH TRANSDUCER

Pinpoint's Standalone Sonar Imaging Displays offer 160 x 160 pixels for unmatched resolution and target presentation. They have 3,600 watts of transmit power, custom-matched 20°/200 kHz transducers, and the most sensitive, noise-free receivers in the business. -Pinpoint's SYSTEM 7™ operating system 32-bit RISC based microprocessors and 2MB of high-speed memory give, you the processing power to make these displays operate faster than ever.

MaxAutoGain™ provides optimum performance whether fishing shallow or deep water. Automatic chart speed (18 pixels per second), power/gain and automatic or fixed range control are user-friendly and simplify operation. Other features include: 20°/200 kHz Transom Mount Transducer and adjustable backlight with Nightview™ adjustable split-screen zoom options; Grayband™ easy-to-use soft-key menus; deep, shallow and fish alarms, and split-screen views for transducer networking. Units are flush-mount capable. All units are Pinpoint network-compatible. Pinpoint has developed an advanced networking protocol called IN-SYNC SONAR™ that enables two or more Pinpoint Standalone SYSTEM 7™ High-Speed, Sonar Imaging Displays operating at the same frequency to be in use at the same time without interfering with each other. Anyone with two or more Pinpoint SYSTEM 7™ High-Speed, Sonar Imaging Displays and a SYNC 20 expansion cable can achieve multiple sonar views anywhere in the boat without interference. The 7320 is

designed with features to offer extremely crisp, clear and definitive images for superior fish-finding information. With a high-contrast 3.5" x 3.5" Super-Twist LCD screen, it offers 1.5" target separation for a clean view of underwater habitat.

7420 STANDALONE SONAR DISPLAY WITH TRANSDUCER

Pinpoint Standalone Sonar Imaging Displays feature 3600 watts of transmit power, custom-matched 20°/200 kHz transducers, and the most sensitive, noise-free receivers in the business. Pinpoint's New SYSTEM 7™ operating system 32-bit RISC based microprocessors and 2MB of high-speed memory gives you the processing power to make these displays operate faster than ever.

MaxAutoGain provides optimum performance whether fishing shallow or deep water. Automatic chart speed (18 pixels per second), power/gain and automatic or fixed range control are user-friendly and simplify operation. Pinpoint has developed an advanced networking protocol called IN-SYNC SONAR that enables two or more Pinpoint Standalone SYSTEM 7™ High-Speed, Sonar Imaging Displays operating at the same frequency to be in use at the same time without interfering with each other. Anyone with two or more Pinpoint SYSTEM 7™ High-Speed Sonar Imaging Displays and a SYNC 20 expansion cable can achieve multiple sonar views anywhere in the boat without interference. Utilizes a high contrast 3.5-inch x 3.5-inch Super-Twist LCD screen. The 7420 is designed with 240 vertical and

horizontal pixels with 4,702 pixels per square inch and 1-inch target separation for unmatched clarity. Comes with a 24-month Tournament-Tough warranty.

7520 STANDALONE SONAR DISPLAY

Pinpoint Standalone Sonar Imaging Displays feature 3600 watts of transmit power, custom-matched 20°/200 kHz transducers, and the most sensitive, noise-free receivers in the business. And, Pinpoint's New SYSTEM 7™ operating system 32-bit RISC based microprocessors and 2MB of high-speed memory gives you the processing power to make these displays operate faster than ever.

MaxAutoGain provides optimum performance whether fishing shallow or deep water. Automatic chart speed (18 pixels per second), power/gain and automatic or fixed range control are user-friendly and simplify operation. Pinpoint has developed an advanced networking protocol called IN-SYNC SONAR that enables two or more Pinpoint Standalone SYSTEM 7™ High-Speed, Sonar Imaging Displays operating at the same frequency to be in use at the same time without interfering with each other. Now you can view multi-transducer views of underwater structure by networking Pinpoint's Sonar Imaging Displays together. Anyone with two or more Pinpoint SYSTEM 7™ High-Speed Sonar Imaging Displays and a SYNC 20 expansion cable can achieve multiple sonar views anywhere in the boat without interference.

TECHSONIC INDUSTRIES ELECTRONICS

100SX

105SX

200DX

HUMMINBIRD 100SX

The 100SX utilizes a precise 24-degree beam transducer to locate bottom structure and show fish directly below your boat. Exclusive Structure ID™ grayscale displays detailed views of bottom hardness and underwater structure where fish hide. ID+™ Fish Identification marks the size and depth of detected fish, eliminating guesswork. Additional features include depth and fish alarms; zoom/auto zoom; quick disconnect swivel mount.

SPECIFICATIONS
Depth Capability: 600 feet
Operating Frequency: 200 kHz
Transducer (Standard): XHS-6-24 with 20 foot cable
Power Output: 250 Watts (RMS), 2000 Watts (peak to peak)
Transducer Area of Coverage: 24 degrees @ -10db
Power Requirement: 12 VDC
Display Type: FSTN Liquid Crystal Display
Display Matrix & Size: 128 V x 64 H Pixels, 2.90 inches x 2.35 inches
Unit Size (installed): 6¼ inches H x 6¼ inch W x 4¾ inch D

HUMMINBIRD 105SX

The full-featured, single beam 105SX comes complete with a water surface temperature sensor that enables you to find more fish, and a quick connect tilt and swivel mount for easy and adjustable mounting with no cables to plug in. Structure ID™ Grayscale reveals bottom locations where fish hide. 2000/250 watts (ptp/rms) output power maximizes bottom, fish & structure definition. The high-definition, high-contrast display provides clear viewing at any angle and in tough lighting. Selectable Fish ID+(target identification identifies fish targets and their depth or view sonar data. Also features zoom with auto zoom, depth alarm to 99 feet, backlit display, 3 button menu system with Smart Menus, adjustable sensitivity, clear view lens, waterproof construction, protective bezel with recessed lens, diagnostic mode with battery voltage, Smart Start with transducer recognition, bottom black option for high visibility, dual power mode for prolonged battery life, feature memory, 3 level fish alarm and simulator mode.

SPECIFICATIONS
Depth Capability: 600 ft
Display Size: 2.9" V x 2.35" H
Display Matrix: 128 V x 64 H
Display: FSTN Liquid Crystal
Size Installed: 6¾" x 6¼" x 4⅛"
Power Source: 12 VDC
Operating Frequency: 200 kHz
Sonar Coverage: 24° @ -10db
Transducer: Single Beam
Speed/Temperature: Capable, Temp Included
Power Output: P2000 Watts (Peak to Peak), 250 Watts (RMS)

HUMMINBIRD 200DX

The 200DX dual beam system uses two sonar beams at the same time for better performance. A precise enter beam locates fish and detailed bottom structure wider beams cannot show, while a wide beam locates fish around your boat in an area equal to your depth. In 20 feet of water, the wide beam covers an area 20 feet wide. Fish in the center beam are solid; fish in the wide beam are hollow. The unit is water temperature sensor capable. Additional features include quick disconnect swivel mount; depth and fish alarms; split screen zoom.

SPECIFICATIONS
Depth Capability: 600 feet
Operating Frequency: 200 kHz and 83 kHz
Transducer (Standard): XT-6-20 with 20 foot cable
Power Output: 250 Watts (RMS), 2000 Watts (peak to peak)
Transducer Area of Coverage: 53 degrees continuous @ -10db
Power Requirement: 12 VDC
Display Type: FSTN Liquid Crystal Display
Display Matrix & Size: 128 V x 64 H Pixels, 2.90 inches x 2.35 inches
Unit Size (installed): 6¼ inch H x 6¼ inch W x 4¼ inch D

TECHSONIC INDUSTRIES ELECTRONICS

300TX

400T

405SX

HUMMINBIRD 300TX

The 300TX tri-beam system uses three sonar beams to form a continuous 90-degree area of uninterrupted coverage. A precise center beam locates fish and detailed bottom structure, while two wide beams look to left and right to cover an area twice your depth. In 20 feet of water, the wide beams cover an area 40 feet wide. Fish in the center beam are solid; fish in the wide beams are hollow and point left or right indicating location. Additional features include optional side-looking sonar; Structure ID®; ID+™ Fish Identification and Depth; quick disconnect swivel mount; depth and fish alarms; split screen zoom. The unit is water temperature sensor capable and temperature/speed sensor capable.

SPECIFICATIONS
Depth Capability: 600 feet
Operating Frequency: 200 kHz and 455 kHz
Transducer (Standard): XT-6-TB-90-P with 20 foot cable
Power Output: 200 watts (RMS), 2400 watts (Peak to Peak)
Transducer Area of Coverage: 90 degrees continuous @ -10db
Power Requirement: 12 VDC
Display Type: FSTN Liquid Crystal Display
Display Matrix & Size: 128 V x 64 H pixels, 2.90" x 2.35"
Unit Size (installed): 6¾" H x 6¼" W x 4¼" D

HUMMINBIRD 400TX

The 400TX tri-beam system uses three sonar beams to form a continuous 90-degree area of uninterrupted coverage. A precise center beam locates fish and detailed bottom structure, while two wide beams look to the left and right to cover an area twice your depth. In 20 feet of water, the wide beams cover an area 40 feet wide. Fish in the center beam are solid, fish in the wide beams are hollow and point left or right indicating location. Additional features include 4-level grayscale display; 160 V x 160 H pixel High Definition FSTN display; optional side looking sonar; Structure ID®; ID+™ Fish Identification and Depth; quick disconnect swivel mount; Tru-Zoom with AutoZoom; depth and fish alarms; Total Screen Update™. Unit is water temperature sensor capable and temperature/speed sensor capable.

SPECIFICATIONS
Depth Capability: 600 feet
Operating Frequency: 200 kHz and 455 kHz
Transducer (Standard): XT-6-TB-90-P with 20 foot cable
Power Output: 300 Watts (RMS), 2400 Watts (Peak to Peak)
Transducer Area of Coverage: 90 degrees continuous @ -10db
Power Requirement: 12 VDC
Display Type: FSTN Liquid Crystal Display, 4 Level Grayscale
Display Matrix & Size: 160 V x 160 H pixels, 3" x 4"
Unit Size (installed): 7¾" H x 7⅞" W x 4¼" D

HUMMINBIRD 405SX

The extra-large Super-Twist LCD display on the 405SX boasts 160 vertical and horizontal pixels for high visibility and incredibly clear viewing from any angle. It sports a concise 2D view, and you can increase the size of the digital readout to create big, easy-to-read information. Plus, there's a bottom black option and three-level backlit display to ensure high-contrast and superior target detection. Innovative TruZoom™ technology reveals all structure and fish in incomparable detail on the bottom or at any depth, and it also features auto zoom. Additional features include 24° Hydrodynamic Transducer, quick access view button, depth alarm to 99 feet, clear view lens, waterproof construction, protective bezel with recessed lens, enhanced diagnostic mode with battery voltage, Smart Start with transducer recognition, 3-level fish alarm that sounds at the presence of fish, simulator mode to get you started immediately, and quick connect tilt and swivel mount.

SPECIFICATIONS
Depth Capability: 600 ft
Display Size: 3" V x 4" H Pixels
Display Matrix: 160 V x 160 H
Display: FSTN Liquid Crystal
Size Installed: 7¾" H x 7⅞" W x 4"D
Power Source: 12 VDC
Operating Frequency: 200 kHz
Sonar Coverage: 24° @ -10db
Transducer: Single Beam
Speed/Temperature: Capable, Temp Included
Power Output: 2400 Watts (Peak to Peak), 300 Watts (RMS)

3D PARAMOUNT

NS25 GLOBAL POSITIONING SYSTEM

HUMMINBIRD 3D PARAMOUNT

This unit includes all the Humminbird features and technology, plus 3D capability. Features include 3D bottom depiction; GraphLook™ Film Super-Twist LCD Display; fish location with left/right/center fish; water temperature and speed gauge; ID+™ Fish Identification and Depth; split screen zoom; depth and fish alarms; quick disconnect swivel mount.

SPECIFICATIONS

Depth Capability: 240 Feet (1000 Feet with optional 2D transducer purchase)

Operating Frequency: 455 kHz

Transducer (Standard): SHS-7W with 20 Foot Cable

Power Output: (455 kHz) 600 Watts (RMS), 4800 Watts (Peak to Peak)

Transducer Area of Coverage: 53 degrees Continuous Side-to-Side Coverage @ -10db

Power Requirement: 12 VDC

Display Type: FSTN GraphLook™ LCD Display

Display Matrix & Size: 240 V x 320 H Pixels, 3.40 inches x 4.53 inches

Unit Size (installed): 7⅝ inches H x 7⅞ inches W x 4⅜ inches D

HUMMINBIRD LEGEND FISHFINDERS

Humminbird's Legend™ fishfinders deliver the performance and clarity seasoned bass anglers seek. With three models available, each in either 600" or 2000" depth capabilities, you can choose the right fishfinder with the right capabilities for your serious fishing.

Legend™ fishfinders' exclusive Liquid Paper Graph™ display technology reveals bottom, structure, thermoclines and fish with clarity. Plus, 500 watts (RMS) of raw sonar power punches through tough water and bottom conditions so you don't miss a thing. RTS™ Real Time Sonar, with up to 30 sonar updates per second, catches all the action instantly. Combined with the precision knobs that place controls at your fingertips - you spend your time fishing, not punching buttons. Plus, a totally new intelligent temperature monitor audibly alerts you to water temperature changes to locate the zone where fish are hiding.

Each Legend fishfinder comes standard with trolling speed and water surface temperature. Each offers totally manual upper and lower range control with advanced second echo track, bottom lock zoom and automatic or manual operation, plus a full complement of advanced controls, including Whiteline™ bottom identification, adjustable Surface Clutter and RTS™ (Real Time Sonar) window.

HUMMINBIRD NS25 GLOBAL POSITIONING SYSTEM

This state-of-the-art unit combines GPS and chart plotting capabilities with Humminbird's latest sonar features. Utilizes C-Map NT Coastal and Inland Cartography (not included). Go to www.c-map.com for more information on C-Map. Features include 250 permanent waypoints, 50 temporary waypoints, 20 routes; 12-channel GPS receiver; full-screen North Up view, Course Up view, and Sonar view; split-screen combo view, showing chart and sonar information simultaneously; dimmable electroluminescent backlit display and keypad; Structure IDTM; automatic transducer recognition; 3-Size Fish Alarm; ID+ Fish Identification and Depth; TruZoomTM; quick-disconnect mounting system.

SPECIFICATIONS

Depth Capability: 1000 feet

Operating Frequency: 200 kHz

Transducer (Standard): XT-6-20 with 20 foot cable

Power Output: 300 watts (RMS), 2400 Watts (peak to peak)

Transducer Area of Coverage: 20 degrees @ -10db

Power Requirement: 12 VDC

Display Type: FSTN 4 Level Grayscale

Display Matrix & Size: 240 V x 320 H pixels, 3.40 inches x 4.53 inches

Unit Size (installed): 7⅝ inch H x 7⅞ inch W x 4⅜ inch D

TECHSONIC INDUSTRIES ELECTRONICS

LEGEND 1000

LEGEND 3000

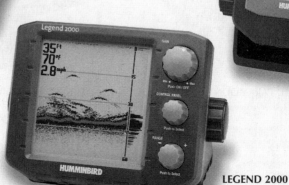

LEGEND 2000

LEGEND 1000
SPECIFICATIONS
Depth Capability: 600 ft.
Display Size: 3⅝" V x 3⅝" H x 5⅛" Diag.
Display Matrix: 160 V x 160 H pixels
Display: High Contrast FSTN
Grayscale: 8 Levels
Unit Size: 4¹³⁄₁₆" x 6³⁄₁₆" x 2¾"
Power Source: 12 VDC
Sonar: 200 kHz Single Beam
Sonar Coverage: 24° @ -10db
Target Separation: 2½ inches
Power Output: 500 watts RMS; 4000 watts (Peak to Peak)
Transducer: Transom Mount
Speed/Temperature: Included

LEGEND 2000
SPECIFICATIONS
Depth Capability: 600 ft.
Display Size: 3⅝" V x 3⅝" H x 5⅛" Diag.
Display Matrix: 240 V x 240 H pixels
Display: High Contrast FSTN
Grayscale: 16 Levels
Unit Size: 4¹³⁄₁₆" x 6³⁄₁₆" x 2¾"
Power Source: 12 VDC
Sonar: 200 kHz Single Beam
Sonar Coverage: 24° @ -10db
Target Separation: 2½ inches
Power Output: 500 watts RMS; 4000 watts (Peak to Peak)
Transducer: Transom Mount
Speed/Temperature: Included

LEGEND 3000
SPECIFICATIONS
Depth Capability: 600 ft.
Display Size: 4⅝" V x 3½" H x 5¾" Diag.
Display Matrix: 320 V x 240 H
Display: High Contrast FSTN
Grayscale: 16 Levels
Unit Size: 8⅝" x 8⅛" 2⅞"
Power Source: 12 VDC
Sonar: 200 & 200 kHz Dual Beam
Sonar Coverage: 24° & 18° @ -10db
Target Separation: 2½ inches
Power Output: 500 watts RMS; 4000 watts (Peak to Peak)
Transducer: Transom Mount
Speed/Temperature: Included

Store Electronics Safely
If your boat is outfitted with detachable electronics, remove them when traveling to your fishing spot. Sonar fish-finders and other electronics can be damaged by lengthy pounding received during trailering. And after being exposed to dust and grit under high wind pressure, they may not function as intended. When you return home, store electronics indoors to guard against damage from weathering, condensation and temperature extremes.

ELECTRONICS

TECHSONIC INDUSTRIES ELECTRONICS

LEGEND 1000 DEEP

LEGEND 3000 DEEP

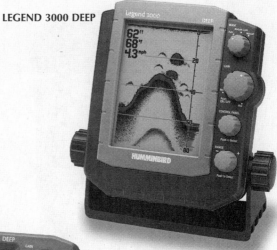

LEGEND 2000 DEEP

LEGEND 1000 DEEP
SPECIFICATIONS
Depth Capability: 2000 ft.
Display Size: 3⅝" V x 3⅝" H x 5⅛" Diag.
Display Matrix: 160 V x 160 H pixels
Display: High Contrast FSTN
Grayscale: 8 Levels
Unit Size: 4¹³⁄₁₆" x 6³⁄₁₆" x 2¾"
Power Source: 12 VDC
Operating Frequency: 200 & 50 kHz Dual Beam
Sonar Coverage: 20° & 74° @ -10db
Target Separation: 2½ inches
Power Output: 500 watts RMS. 4000 watts (Peak to Peak)
Transducer: Transom Mount
Speed/Temperature: Included

LEGEND 2000 DEEP
SPECIFICATIONS
Depth Capability: 2000 ft.
Display Size: 3 ⅝" V x 3 ⅝" H x 5 ⅛" Diag.
Display Matrix: 240 V x 240 H pixels
Display: High Contrast FSTN
Grayscale: 16 Levels
Unit Size: 4 ¹³⁄₁₆" x 6 ³⁄₁₆" x 2¾"
Power Source: 12 VDC
Operating Frequency: 200 & 50 kHz Dual Beam
Sonar Coverage: 20° & 74° @ -10db
Target Separation: 2½ inches
Power Output: 500 watts RMS, 4000 watts (Peak to Peak)
Transducer: Transom Mount
Speed/Temperature: Included

LEGEND 3000 DEEP
SPECIFICATIONS
Depth Capability: 2000 ft.
Display Size: 4⅝" V x 3½" H x 5¾" Diag.
Display Matrix: 320 V x 240 H pixels
Display: High Contrast FSTN
Grayscale: 16 Levels
Unit Size: 8⅝" x 8⅛" x 2⅞"
Power Source: 12 VDC
Operating Frequency: 200 & 50 kHz Dual Beam
Sonar Coverage: 20° & 74° @ -10db
Target Separation: 2½ inches
Power Output: 500 watts RMS, 4000 watts (Peak to Peak)
Transducer: Transom Mount
Speed/Temperature: Included

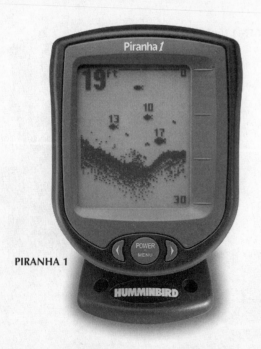

PIRANHA 1

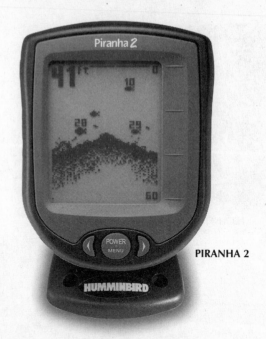

PIRANHA 2

HUMMINBIRD PIRANHA™ SERIES FISHFINDERS

Piranha fishfinders have a radical, sleek design, and One-Touch™ automatic control for incredible ease of use. All units deliver high levels of performance with such features as Structure ID™ Grayscale, Fish ID+™, fish alarm, depth alarm, zoom, sensitivity, depth range, memory remember settings, display backlight, waterproof construction and protected bezel with recessed lens.

Piranha 1 and 2 both feature an easy-to-read display with 128 vertical pixels. Piranha 1 has a maximum 240-foot depth capability, while Piranha 2 has a 600-foot depth capability and the added value of Bottom Black View. Piranha 3, 4 and 5 feature a larger, high-resolution FSTN display with 160 vertical pixels, and advanced Whiteline™ bottom identification. Piranha 4 also includes the popular Water Surface Temperature capability. Piranha 5 features the exclusive Humminbird Dual Beam Sonar to cover a wider area with superior structure definition, as well as Water Surface Temperature.

PIRANHA 1
SPECIFICATIONS
Depth Capability: 240 ft.
Display Size: 3 ¹/₁₆" V x 2 ½" H
Display Matrix: 128 V x 64 H pixels
Display: STN Liquid Crystal
Size Installed: 4⅜" W x 6⅛"
H x 3¼"D
Power Source: 12 VDC
Operating Frequency: 200kHz
Sonar Coverage: 24° @ -10db
Transducer: Transom Mount
Temperature: Capable
Power Output: 800 watts
(Peak to Peak), 100 watts (RMS)

PIRANHA 2
SPECIFICATIONS
Depth Capability: 600 ft.
Display Size: 3¹/₁₆" V x 2½" H
Display Matrix: 128 V x 64 H pixels
Display: STN Liquid Crystal
Size Installed: 4⅜" W x 6⅛"
H x 3¼"D
Power Source: 12 VDC
Operating Frequency: 200kHz
Sonar Coverage: 24° @ -10db
Transducer: Transom Mount
Temperature: Capable
Power Output: 800 watts
(Peak to Peak), 100 watts (RMS)

ELECTRONICS

TECHSONIC INDUSTRIES ELECTRONICS

PIRANHA 3

PIRANHA 4

PIRANHA 5

PIRANHA 3
SPECIFICATIONS
Depth Capability: 600 ft.
Display Size: 3⁷⁄₁₆" V x 2½" H
Display Matrix: 160 V x 65 H pixels
Display: High Contrast FSTN
Size Installed: 4⅜" W x 6⅛" H x 3¼"D
Power Source: 12 VDC
Operating Frequency: 200 kHz
Sonar Coverage: 24° @ -10db
Transducer: Transom Mount
Temperature: Capable
Power Output: 800 watts
(Peak to Peak), 100 watts (RMS)

PIRANHA 4
SPECIFICATIONS
Depth Capability: 600 ft.
Display Size: 3⁷⁄₁₆" V x 2½" H
Display Matrix: 160 V x 65 H pixels
Display: High Contrast FSTN
Size Installed: 4⅜" W x 6⅛" H x 3 ¼"D
Power Source: 12 VDC
Operating Frequency: 200 kHz
Sonar Coverage: 24° @ -10db
Transducer: Transom Mount w/ Temp
Temperature: Included in Transducer
Power Output: 800 watts
(Peak to Peak), 100 watts (RMS)

PIRANHA 5
SPECIFICATIONS
Depth Capability: 600 ft.
Display Size: 3⁷⁄₁₆" V x 2½" H
Display Matrix: 160 V x 65 H pixels
Display: High Contrast FSTN
Size Installed: 4⅜" W x 6⅛" H x 3¼"D
Power Source: 12 VDC
Operating Frequency: 200/83 kHz
Sonar Coverage: 53° & 20° @ -10db
Transducer: Transom Mount w/ Temp
Temperature: Included in Transducer
Power Output: 800 watts
(Peak to Peak), 100 watts (RMS)

GPS Puts You on the Fish Again
If you often fish on big reservoirs, consider purchasing a GPS unit. These devices use satellite signals to calculate your position. When you catch a fish, simply press a button to electronically mark the spot. After landing the fish, you can use that marker to take you back to the spot.

TECHSONIC INDUSTRIES ELECTRONICS

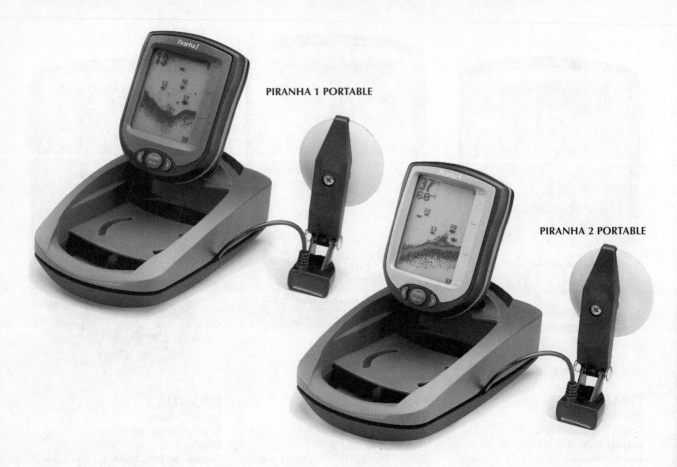

PIRANHA 1 PORTABLE

PIRANHA 2 PORTABLE

HUMMINBIRD PIRANHA PORTABLE FISHFINDERS

Like all Piranha units, the Piranha 1 and 4 Portables deliver high levels of performance, with such features as Structure ID™, Grayscale, Fish ID+™, fish alarm, depth alarm, sensitivity, depth range, memory remember settings, display backlight and waterproof construction. Both portable systems are ultra compact and lightweight enough to travel anywhere. They are ideally suited for use on fly-in trips where weight and space can be critical, and for use on canoes, kayaks, john boats, car toppers and rental boats. The fishfinder folds out for quick set-up, and folds in for protection during storage and transport. The rugged, protective case has a carry handle. Anti-skid rubber bottom keeps the unit solidly in place. Built-in transducer cable wrap keeps your system organized. Each uses 8 AA batteries. Suction cup transducer quickly and easily attaches to most boat hulls, for use at trolling speeds.

The Piranha 1 Portable features a display matrix of 128 vertical by 64 horizontal pixels and has a depth capability of 240 feet. The Piranha 4 Portable features 160 vertical by 65 horizontal pixels and has a depth capability of 600 feet. It also features water temperature with the sensor built into a 24 degree MicroDynamic transducer.

PIRANHA 1 PORTABLE
SPECIFICATIONS
Depth Capability: 240 ft.
Display Size: 3¹/₁₆" V x 2½" H
Display Matrix: 128 V x 64 H pixels
Display: STN Liquid Crystal
Size Installed: 4⅜" W x 6⅛" H x 3¼"D
Power Source: 12 VDC
Operating Frequency: 200 kHz
Sonar Coverage: 24° @ -10db
Transducer: Transom Mount
Temperature: Capable
Power Output: 800 watts (Peak to Peak), 100 watts (RMS)

PIRANHA 4 PORTABLE
SPECIFICATIONS
Depth Capability: 600 ft.
Display Size: 3⁷/₁₆" V x 2½" H
Display Matrix: 160 V x 65 H pixels
Display: High Contrast FSTN
Size Installed: 4⅜" W x 6⅛" H x 3¼"D
Power Source: 12 VDC
Operating Frequency: 200 kHz
Sonar Coverage: 24° @ -10db
Transducer: Transom Mount w/ Temp
Temperature: Included in Transducer
Power Output: 800 watts (Peak to Peak), 100 watts (RMS)

ELECTRONICS

ABU GARCIA RODS

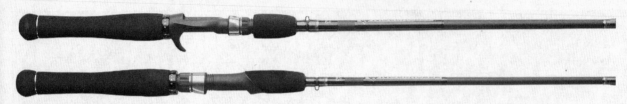

WORKHORSE RODS

With the Workhorse series, there are no tradeoffs between durability and action. A unidirectional, solid E-glass tip gives you extreme durability, while the powerful graphite butt section retains the sensitivity and action you'd expect from a graphite rod. Hard chromium SS304 guides are up to 55 percent lighter and 20 times stronger than conventional guides, making superline abrasion a distant memory.

SPECIFICATIONS

Spinning models (6):
Ultralight to medium action; 1-piece or 2-piece, 5' to 7' lengths.
MSRP: $34.95-$39.95.

Casting models (6):
medium to medium-heavy action; 1 piece; 5'6" to 7' lengths.
MSRP: $34.95-$39.95.

BERKLEY® RODS

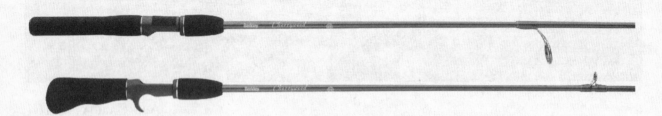

CHERRYWOOD®SPINNING AND CASTING RODS

Cherrywood rods have been around longer than any other Berkley rod made. All ten spinning and three casting models have received enhancements. Included in the upgrades is a rod blank with high graphite content. The lightweight graphite material deliver a level of sensitivity and responsiveness that rivals higher-priced rods. The sensitivity benefits of graphite are greater, but the strength characteristics of E-Glass fiberglass are retained. The handle construction delivers a powerful performance. Also, cork has replaced the EVA materials on the handle for improved grip during casting and fish handling. The positive lock-down reel seat holds reels securely in place. Each rod has its very own hook-holder built in.

Hard chromium SS304 guides are now used on Cherrywood rods instead of aluminum oxide guides. SS304 guides are up to 55% lighter than comparable conventional ceramic guides, yet are 20 times tougher. These guides reduce line friction and dissipate heat better so that monofilament line will last 10 times longer than with other guides.

SPECIFICATIONS

One-piece ultra-light spinning rods are available, including 4'6" model and a 5'0" model. There is also a two-piece light action rod that measures 5'6" long. Three six-foot rods are available, including a one-piece medium action, a two-piece medium action, and a one-piece medium-light action rod.

Two-piece spinning rods that measure 6'6" are available in both a medium-light action and a medium action. Also included in the Cherrywood rods are 7'0" and 10'0" medium action two-piece rods.

Cherrywood casting rods include a two-piece 5'6" medium action rod, a one-piece 6'0" medium heavy action rod and a one-piece 6'6" medium action model.
MSRP: $24.95

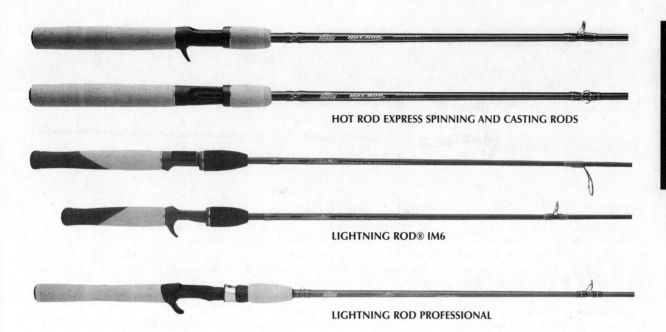

HOT ROD EXPRESS SPINNING AND CASTING RODS

LIGHTNING ROD® IM6

LIGHTNING ROD PROFESSIONAL

HOT ROD EXPRESS SPINNING AND CASTING RODS

Hot Rod Express spinning and casting rods are created with durable components. The frustrations and irritations usually experienced by young and novice anglers because of inferior equipment are now a thing of the past. Each is built on a graphite composite blank with E-Glass fiberglass support that maximizes the sensitivity benefits of graphite but has the strength characteristics of E-Glass fiberglass. The blank through handle design and quality components separates this rod from the rest of the class. The positive lock-down reel seat holds reels securely in place. The cork handle adds comfort for casting and cranking. The casting rods include a trigger handle for an improved grip. Aluminum oxide guides are lightweight yet strong and dependable cast after cast. There's even a hook holder conveniently located just in front of the handle.

SPECIFICATIONS

The six spinning rods include a two-piece light action rod that measures 5'6" in length, a 6'0" medium action rod that is also two-piece, a one-piece medium-heavy action 6'0" model, a 6'6" medium-light action two-piece rod and two medium action two-piece rods with one measuring 6'6"

and the other 7'0".

The three one-piece casting rods include a 5'6" medium action rod, a 6'0" medium-heavy action model and a 6'6" medium action rod.
MSRP: $14.95

LIGHTNING ROD® IM6

More Berkley graphite Lightning Rods IM6 have been sold in America than any other graphite rod by any other manufacturer. The Lightning Rod's famed high-modulus IM6 blank has the unique fast flex lightning tip for exceptional fish-fighting performance. Now the rod has the hard chromium SS304 guide system. SS304 guides are up to 55% lighter than comparable conventional ceramic guides, yet are 20 times tougher. These guides reduce line friction and dissipate heat better so that monofilament line will last 10 times longer than with other guides, 5 times longer with superlines. The handles are now made from cork replacing the cork/EVA combination handles of before. There's a convenient hook keeper added just above the handle. The rod also has a dynamic new look. The rod is black-chrome with black and red highlights. The attractive wraps on the SS304 guides include a third wrap for improved performance and longevity.

SPECIFICATIONS

Models: 17 models from ultra-light to heavy actions
Lengths: from 5'0" to 7'6"
Style: Every freshwater fishing technique is covered including casting plugs, worms, spinnerbaits, light jigs and grubs, flipping and live bait.
MSRP: $39.95 for the trigger casting rods, $44.95 for the flippin' rod and $34.95 for all other models

LIGHTNING ROD PROFESSIONAL

Sensitive IM7 graphite blank actions have been custom designed by leading professional anglers. IM7 graphite action fiber blank design strategically positions the high-modulus graphite material, reducing rod weight, increasing performance and sensitivity without sacrificing strength. The world's top professional fishermen have incorporated their own personal requirements to create a unique tournament-tested series of rods with technique-specific actions.

SPECIFICATIONS

28 styles, from the Roach 5', one-piece ultralight to the Roach 8'6" trolling model. Available with a variety of grip styles. Casting, spinning and flipping.
MSRP: $54.95-$79.95

BERKLEY® RODS

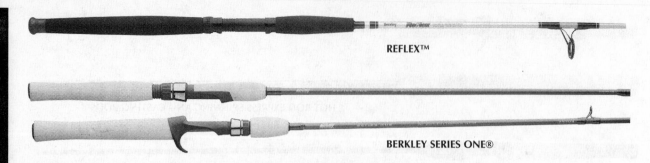

REFLEX™

BERKLEY SERIES ONE®

REFLEX™

The Berkley ReFlex lets you read and react like no rod you've ever fished — especially at night. ReFlex is constructed with super-strong E-glass for power, and is the only rod to use 3M™ Scotchlite™ reflective material under the guide wraps, reflecting up to 1500 times more light than white surfaces when viewed at night. Optical brighteners throughout the entire rod blank increase night visibility. With the Berkley ReFlex, you'll see every nibble, day or night, and have the power to put big fish in the boat.

SPECIFICATIONS
Spinning and Casting Models
Length: 7', 8', 9"
Pieces: 2
Action: medium, medium heavy
MSRP: $27.95-$38.95

BERKLEY SERIES ONE®

The incredibly-lightweight IM7 blank features a multi-bias laminate lay-up blank construction, which incorporates several graphite patterns individually rolled to maximize fiber alignment and reduce pattern overlap. This reduces the amount of graphite needed to produce a performance action, reduce's the rod's overall weight and enhances its sensitivity. With the pattern overlap areas distributed evenly around the blank, instead of around one narrow area, the spine of the Series One is greatly reduced, but its ultimate strength isn't. Equipped with Titanium SS304 Guide System—20 times tougher, 55% ligher and as hard as SIC guides for super smoothness and increased durability. These rods also featue cork handles and custom reel seats.

SPECIFICATIONS
Spinning models
Length: 5'6", 6', 6'6", 7'
Actions: light, medium light, medium, medium heavy
Pieces: all one piece
MSRP: $109.95-$114.95

Casting models
Length: 6', 6'6", 7'
Actions: medium, medium heavy
Pieces: all one piece
MSRP: $109.95-$119.95

Flipping model
Length: 7'6"
Action: medium
Pieces: telescopic
MSRP: $119.95

No High Sticking
When fighting a fish or trying to unsnag your line, don't "high stick" your rod. "High sticking" is pointing your rod straight up so only the tip bends, or bringing the rod past a 90° angle with the water. Many fishing rods are broken this way because high sticking overloads the tip area, which can easily cause the tip to break.

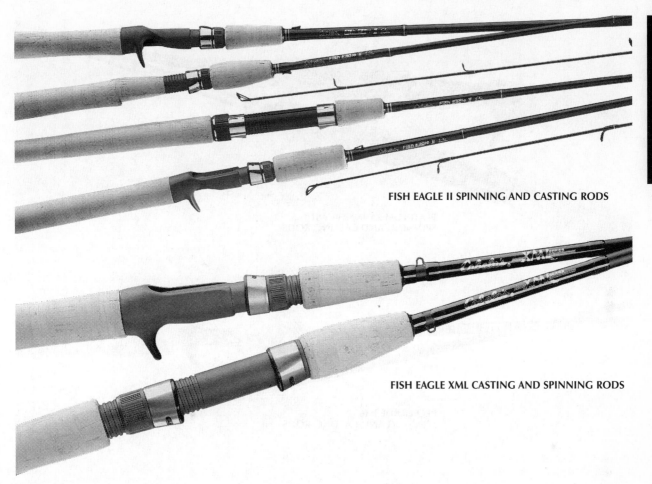

FISH EAGLE II SPINNING AND CASTING RODS

FISH EAGLE XML CASTING AND SPINNING RODS

FISH EAGLE II SPINNING AND CASTING RODS

In 1989, Cabela's introduced fishermen to IM6 graphite with the new Fish Eagle II rods. From that humble beginning, with only four models, until now, with 54 models ranging from ultra light to muskie, these legendary rods remain as some of the most sensitive, well-designed rods available. Plus the upgraded CX2 IM6 graphite blanks are stronger, lighter, and more powerful than ever. Today, many other manufacturers have followed Cabela's lead, and offer their version of IM6 graphite. But compared to Cabela's Fish Eagle II rods, it may as well be 1989 all over again.

Compare the craftsmanship, quality and price of these casting rods with comparable rods from any of today's top manufacturers and you'll find that, feature for feature, there is no better rod value on the market. Using the highest quality components, including high-grade Portuguese cork handles, Fuji aluminum-oxide guides and the highest quality of CX2 IM6 blanks, one of the world's premier rod builders crafts this exceptional series of rods exclusively for Cabela's. The actions are what really set these rods apart from the rest. Each was custom-designed by members of the Cabela's staff with input from some of the most knowledgeable professional anglers in the world. Cabela's built its reputation for quality with the Fish Eagle II Series and year after year they continue to be one of the company's best sellers. Built with CX2 IM6 graphite rated at 38 million modulus, they offer excellent strength and sensitivity in a reduced-weight, easy-handling rod.

30 spinning models, 24 casting models
MSRP(all rods in the series): *$79.99.*

FISH EAGLE XML CASTING AND SPINNING RODS

From the first touch one can feel the uncompromising quality and workmanship that define Cabela's XML casting rods. The non-glare, charcoal colored 44 million modulus XML graphite blanks are made from the finest materials available, using the latest construction techniques to insure these rods are the strongest you've ever fished with. The Fuji "Y"-frame, Hardloy guides reduce line slap and increase casting distance. Fuji reel seats feature frosted, stainless-steel hoods to hold reels tightly and provide you with years of trouble-free performance. Cabela's uses only the finest, select-grade Portuguese cork for the grips.

10 casting models, 17 spinning models
MSRP: *$99.99-$119.99*

CABELA'S RODS

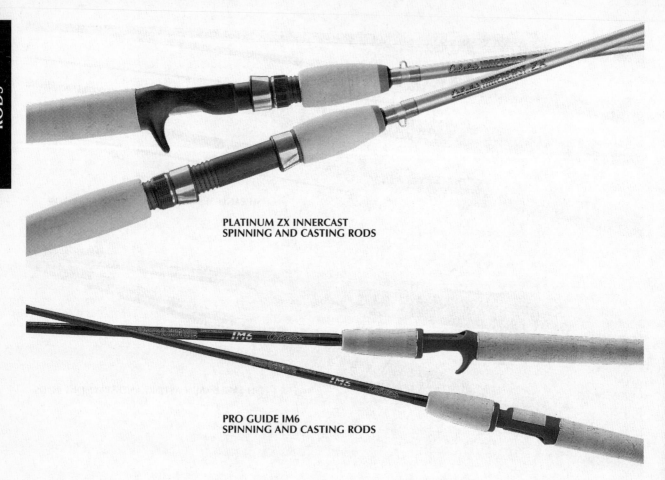

**PLATINUM ZX INNERCAST
SPINNING AND CASTING RODS**

**PRO GUIDE IM6
SPINNING AND CASTING RODS**

PLATINUM ZX INNERCAST SPINNING AND CASTING RODS

Cabela's took their popular line of Innercast rods to a whole new level with the addition of the ZX series. Like the originals, the line runs through the center of the high-modulus silver-colored, graphite blank, eliminating the need for rod guides and the problems associated with them. More line contact points makes them super-sensitive. Plus, there's fewer flat spots caused by rigid guide feet and no line slap or tip tangles allowing for superior castability. Fuji silicone-carbide entry guides and tiptops provide smooth performance and resist cuts and wear often caused by modern braided lines. High-grade Portuguese cork handles provide a comfortable grip and are equipped with blank-exposed Pac Bay graphite 661 reel seats that provide increased sensitivity. Also features a handy hook keeper and a line threader. All rods are one-piece.

Because the line actually passes through the inside of the rod, it follows the curve of the blank when you're fighting a fish and eliminates the stress which occurs when line passes through the guides. And because they bend in a nearly perfect arc, they do away with the flat spots caused by guide feet resulting in higher strength and better distribution of casting and fighting energy.
5 casting models, 3 spinning models
MSRP (all models): $79.99

PRO GUIDE IM6 SPINNING AND CASTING RODS

The IM6 rods pack features that you might find in rods that sell for twice as much. Each rod is constructed around an IM6 100% graphite blank that provides all the strength and sensitivity that has made them the top-selling blank in history. Fast tip actions allow quick, precise casts and rapid hooksets. Portuguese cork handles and lightweight graphite reel seats provide all-day comfort and fishability. Available in a wide range of actions.
20 spinning models, 9 casting models
MSRP (all rods in the series): $39.99

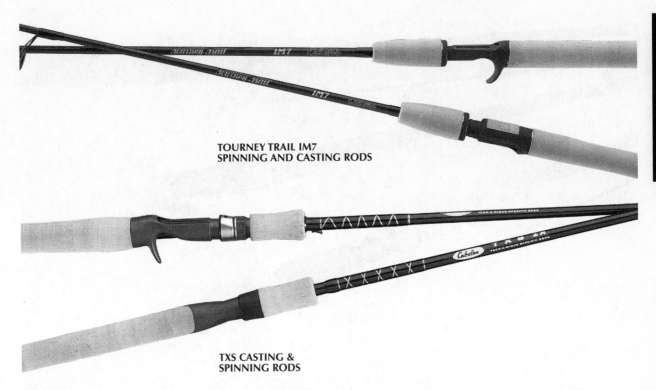

**TOURNEY TRAIL IM7
SPINNING AND CASTING RODS**

**TXS CASTING &
SPINNING RODS**

TOURNEY TRAIL IM7 SPINNING AND CASTING RODS

These IM7 rods have features you might find in rods that sell for twice as much. Constructed from 100% IM7 graphite, they feature fast tip-sensitive actions with enough backbone to handle anything that you may encounter. Tourney Trail rods feature cork handles for all-day fishing comfort, graphite reel seats and Blank-Through-Handle construction.
12 spinning models, 8 casting models
MSRP (all models): $59.99

TXS CASTING & SPINNING RODS

From the first "feel" you can tell that these are not your everyday fishing rods. Each action has been carefully designed and crafted to satisfy your every specific bass fishing technique need. Cabela's uses only the finest components available in the construction of these rods. The ultra-high strain modulus XR-III graphite is impregnated with Generation III bonding resin. This results in a extremely durable rod blank with ultra sensitivity strength and incredible lightness. The rods also feature premium Portuguese cork grips for all-day fishing comfort and Fuji SiC guide. They are available in select two-piece models, for spinning or casting.

TXS Casting Series

- The TXS I makes an excellent top-water or twitching rod, yet has enough backbone to haul the big ones out of cover.
- The TXS II has a moderate tip that makes it an excellent choice for shallow-running crankbaits.
- The TXS III is a fast tip rod that has plenty of backbone for use with worms or jigs.
- The TXS IV is a 6' 10" rod, rated up to 1 ounce, for pitching around heavy cover or docks.
- The TXS V has a 7' fast action, making it a great spinnerbait or all-around bass rod.
- The TXS VI is a 7' moderate tip rod to handle deep running crankbaits.
- The TXS VII, rated for up to 2 ounce, is the ultimate jigging/worming rod.
- The TXS VIII is a 7'6" telescopic rod makes an excellent flipping stock for dense cover and is rated for up to a 2½ ounce lure weight.
MSRP: $99.99

TXS Spinning Series

- At 6'3", the TXS IX is the ultimate finesse rod for fishing tubes. It has a moderate/fast tip and is one of the best feeling rods you'll ever fish.
- The TXS X, at 6' 6", is a medium-heavy power rod. It makes an excellent worm or rattle trap-style crankbait spinning rod.
- The TXS XI is an excellent twitching, or topwater type, rod or good all-around rod. The 6' 6" length helps to make long casts with 8-14 lb. line.
- The TXS XII is for the angler who likes Carolina or Slug O type fishing. The 7' rod is rated for up to 1½ oz.
MSRP: $99.99

CABELA'S RODS

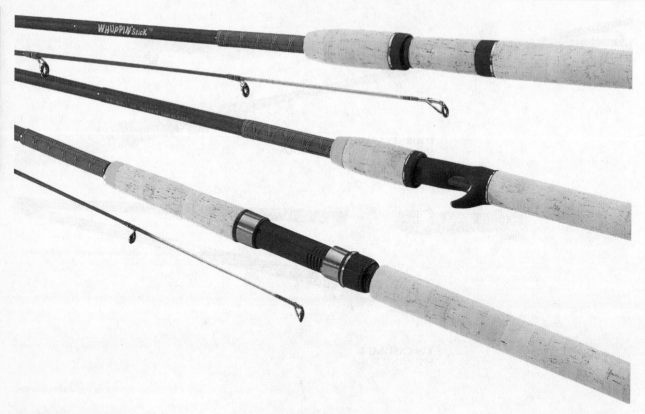

WHUPPIN' STICK CASTING RODS

When you're carrying your rods, every doorway, car door and obstacle represents a possible hazard. That's why Cabela's came up with the WHUPPIN' Stick, a nearly indestructible casting rod that doesn't sacrifice sensitivity and feel. Advanced polymer technology greatly enhances the strength of the fiberglass blank. The graphite twist lock reel seat keeps the reel snugly fastened to the rod for smooth operation with no wobble. Cork handles are easy to grip and remain comfortable throughout the longest days of pulling deep-diving crankbaits or bringing in monster fish. Stainless steel guide frames are as tough as the rest of the rod, so you can concentrate on fishing, not whether your rod can handle the fight. So if you're planning to go after tackle-busting lunkers, bust out an advantage, bring a WHUPPIN' Stick.
5 models
MSRP: $19.99

Two-Piece Rod Connections
When using a two-piece rod, it's important to seat the tip section firmly on the butt. This is easier if you first apply a coat of paraffin to the tip of the butt section to lubricate the taper. Don't worry that you might put the tip on too firmly; it can always be removed with a twisting action.

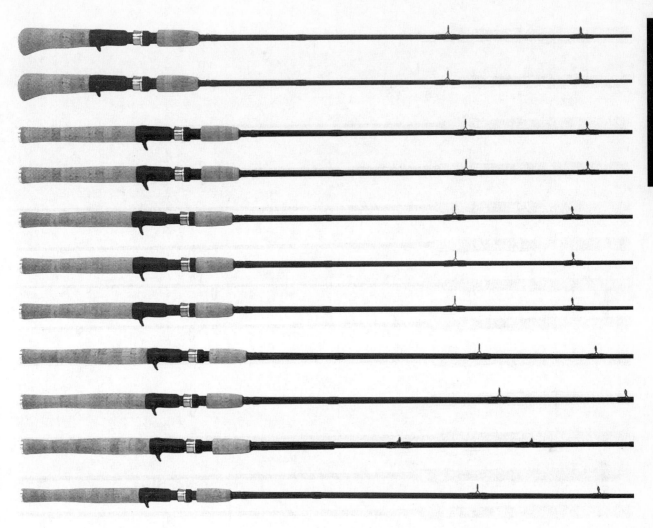

ARISTOCRAT "G2" IM7 CASTING RODS

Eagle Claw's popular Aristocrat™ rod is back, and better than ever.

"Generation 2" features IM7 blanks, SIC T-ring guides, comfortable high quality cork handles, and excetional actions. Designed by pro staff members, the ultra sensitive, but powerful "G2" is the right rod whether you're fishing the pro circuit or your favorite fishing hole.

SPECIFICATIONS

Model#	Length	Type	Sections	Action	Line	Lure Wt.	MSRP
AGC561MH	5'6"	CASTING	1	MH	8-17	¼-½ oz.	$45.95
AGC562M	5'6"	CASTING	2	M	6-12	¼-½ oz.	$45.95
AGC601M	6'0"	CASTING	1	M	8-15	³⁄₁₆-½ oz.	$49.95
AGC601MH	6'0"	CASTING	1	MH	8-17	¼-½ oz.	$50.95
AGC601H	6'0"	CASTING	1	H	12-20	⅜-¾ oz.	$51.95
AGC661M	6'6"	CASTING	1	M	8-17	¼-⅝ oz.	$52.95
AGC661MH	6'6"	CASTING	1	MH	10-20	¼-½ oz.	$53.95
AGC661H	6'6"	CASTING	1	H	12-20	⅜-¾ oz.	$55.95
AGC701MH	7'0"	CASTING	1	MH	8-17	¼-½ oz.	$56.95
AGC701THF	7'0"	CASTING	1	H	20-30	½-1 oz.	$59.95
AGC701H	7'0"	CASTING	1	H	12-20	⅜-¾ oz.	$59.95

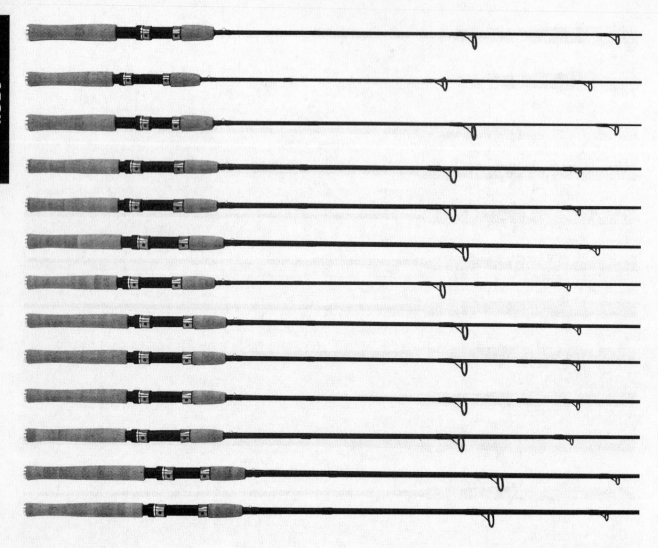

ARISTOCRAT "G2" IM7 SPINNING RODS

Eagle Claw's popular Aristocrat™ rod is back, and better than ever.

"Generation 2" features IM7 blanks, SIC T-ring guides, comfortable high quality cork handles, and excetional actions. Designed by pro staff mem-

bers, the ultra sensitive, but powerful "G2" is the right rod whether you're fishing the pro circuit or your favorite fishing hole.

SPECIFICATIONS

Model#	Length	Type	Sections	Action	Line	Lure Wt.	MSRP
AGS501UL	5'0"	SPINNING	1	UL	2-6	¹/₃₂-¼ oz.	$44.95
AGS562ML	5'6"	SPINNING	2	ML	2-8	¹/₁₆-¼ oz.	$44.95
AGS581LW	5'8"	SPINNING	1	L	4-8	¹/₁₆-³/₈ oz.	$45.95
AGS601M	6'0"	SPINNING	1	M	8-15	¹/₈-³/₈ oz.	$49.95
AGS601MH	6'0"	SPINNING	1	MH	8-17	¼-½ oz.	$50.95
AGS601H	6'0"	SPINNING	1	H	10-20	³/₈-¾ oz.	$51.95
AGS602M	6'0"	SPINNING	2	M	6-15	¹/₈-³/₁₆ oz.	$49.95
AGS662MH	6'6"	SPINNING	2	MH	8-17	¼-½ oz.	$52.95
AGS661M	6'6"	SPINNING	1	M	8-17	¼-⁵/₈ oz.	$52.95
AGS661MH	6'6"	SPINNING	1	MH	8-17	¼-½ oz.	$53.95
AGS661H	6'6"	SPINNING	1	H	10-20	¼-½ oz.	$56.95
AGS701MH	7'0"	SPINNING	1	MH	8-17	¼-½ oz.	$57.95
AGS701H	7'0"	SPINNING	1	H	12-20	³/₈-¾ oz.	$59.95

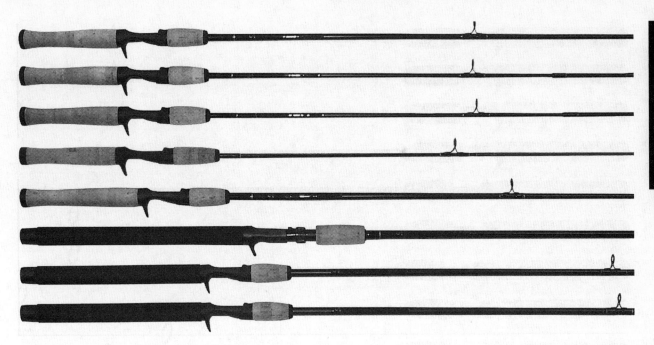

BLACK EAGLE™ GRAPHITE CASTING RODS

The new Black Eagle™ Graphite takes the classic Black Eagle to the next level. Graphite construction, full cork handles (cork/EVA on specialty mod-els), alumina oxide guides and Eagle Claw® quality. Available in casting, cranking, salmon/steelhead, live bait, and poppin' actions. Whatever the need, the Black Eagle™ graphite fits the bill.

Features:
• Alumina Oxide Guides
• Specie Cork Handles (Specie/EVA Handles on Specialty Models)
• FDC Screw Down Casting Reel Seat

SPECIFICATIONS

Model#	Length	Type	Sections	Action	Line	Lure Wt.	MSRP
BEG100	5'6"	CASTING	1	MH	6-12	¼-¾ oz.	$24.95
BEG101	5'6"	CASTING	2	M	6-12	¼-⅝ oz.	$24.95
BEG101G	5'6"	CASTING	2	M	6-12	¼-⅝ oz.	$25.95
BEG104	4'10"	CASTING	2	UL	2-6	¹⁄₁₆-¼ oz.	$24.95
BEG106	6'0"	CRANKIN'	1	H	8-20	½-1½ oz.	$26.95
BEG500	8'6"	SALMON/STEELHEAD	2	M	8-17	¼-1¼ oz.	$36.95
BEG501	7'0"	LIVE BAIT	1	M	8-17	⅜-1¼ oz.	$36.95
BEG502	7'0"	POPPIN'	1	MH	8-20	½-1½ oz.	$36.95

After-Fishing Rod Care

Your rod finish will last longer and look better if you always clean and dry your rod as soon as possible after returning from a fishing trip. Wipe the rod occasionally with silicone to remove grime and protect the finish. Avoid storing your rod in a damp bag or tube; the finish could be damaged by the combination of high humidity and heat.

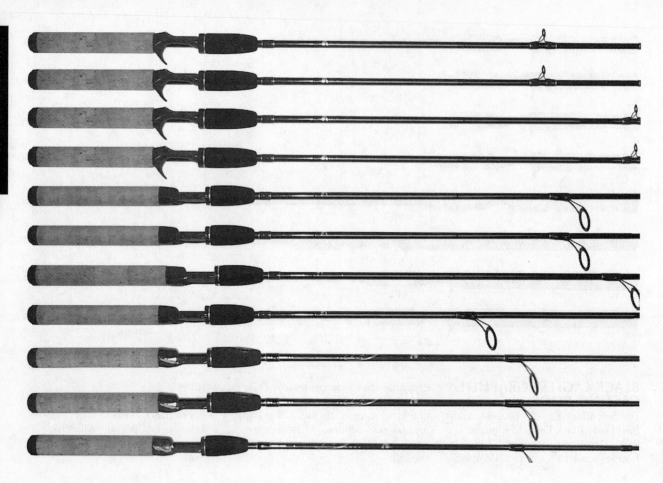

FLEX EAGLE® SERIES

Designed for optimum strength and flexibility, the new Flex Eagle series by eagle Claw offers superb back bone and power. Made of nearly indestructible E-Glass, the Flex Eagle is available in eleven models in both spinning and casting styles, and features alumina oxide guides, cork butt grips and touch type reel seat.

Features:
- Durable E-Glass Construction
- Alumina Oxide Guides
- Combination Cork and EVA Grip
- Deep Green Blanks With Matching Exposed Blank Reel Seat for Sensitivity

SPECIFICATIONS

Casting Model#	Length	Type	Sections	Action	Line	Lure Wt.	MSRP:
ECFX100	5'6"	CASTING	1	MH	10-20	¼-⅝ oz.	$21.95
ECFX101	5'6"	CASTING	2	M	8-14	⅛-⅜ oz.	$21.95
ECFX106	7'0"	CASTING	1	MH	10-25	⅜-1 oz.	$27. 95
ECFX106H	6'6"	CASTING	1	H	6-17	¼-⅝ oz.	$27. 95

Spinning Model#	Length	Type	Sections	Action	Line	Lure Wt.	
ECFX200	6'0"	SPINNING	2	M	6-12	⅛-⅜ oz.	$21.95
ECFX200	6'6"	SPINNING	2	M	8-17	⅛-⅝ oz.	$21.95
ECFX200LT	6'6"	SPINNING	2	L	6-12	¹⁄₁₆-⅜ oz.	$21.95
ECFX201	5'0"	SPINNING	1	UL	2-8	¹⁄₆₄-⅛ oz.	$21.95
ECFX201M	6'0"	SPINNING	1	M	4-12	⅛-½ oz.	$21.95
ECFX201H	6'0"	SPINNING	1	H	6-17	¼-⅝ oz.	$24.95
ECFX202	5'6"	SPINNING	2	UL	2-6	¹⁄₁₆-⅜ oz.	$21.95

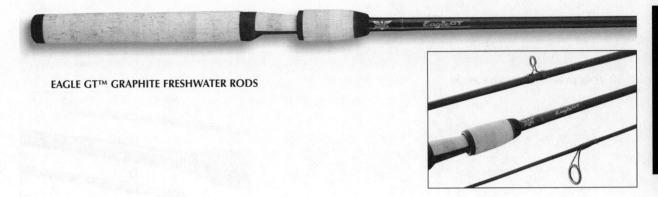

EAGLE GT™ GRAPHITE FRESHWATER RODS

EAGLE GT™ GRAPHITE FRESHWATER RODS

So you've decided it's time to take your passion up a level. We've been waiting, and we're ready to arm you with the multi-tapered Fenwick Eagle GT series.

Modeled after our HMG series, the Eagle GT is perfect for anyone who wants to enter the realm of performance rods and find actions tailored specifically for the applications they're fishing. You'll improve your casting distance and accuracy, feel the lightest bites and collect a few more fish stories. Better bring a camera.

SPECIFICATIONS

1-Piece Spinning
EGT 49SUL
Length: 4'9"
Power: Ultra Light
MSRP: $54.95

EGT 53SL
Length: 5'3"
Power: Light
MSRP: $54.95

EGT 59SM
Length: 5'9"
Power: Medium
MSRP: $54.95

EGT 60SML
Length: 6'0"
Power: Medium Light
MSRP: $54.95

EGT 60SM
Length: 6'0"
Power: Medium
MSRP: $54.95

EGT 60SMH
Length: 6'0"
Power: Medium Heavy
MSRP: $54.95

EGT 66SML
Length: 6'6"
Power: Medium Light
MSRP: $54.95

EGT 66SMH
Length: 6'6"
Power: Medium Heavy
MSRP: $54.95

EGT 70SM
Length: 7'0"
Power: Medium
MSRP: $67.95

2-Piece Spinning
EGT 56SUL-2
Length: 5'6"
Power: Ultra Light
MSRP: $54.95

EGT 60SL-2
Length: 6'0"
Power: Light
MSRP: $54.95

EGT 66SL-2
Length: 6'6"
Power: Light
MSRP: $54.95

EGT 66SM-2
Length: 6'6"
Power: Medium
MSRP: $54.95

EGT 70SL-2
Length: 7'0"
Power: Light

MSRP: $54.95
EGT 70SM-2
Length: 7'0"
Power: Medium
MSRP: $54.95

4-Piece Spinning
EGT 70SML-4
Length: 7'0"
Power: Medium Light
MSRP: $67.95

1-Piece Casting
EGT 56CMH
Length: 5'6"
Power: Medium Heavy
MSRP: $54.95

EGT 60CM
Length: 6'0"
Power: Medium
MSRP: $54.95

Triggerstik®
EGT 66TM
Length: 6'6"
Power: Medium
MSRP: $67.95

EGT 66TMH
Length: 6'6"
Power: Medium Heavy
MSRP: $67.95

EGT 70TM
Length: 7'0"
Power: Medium
MSRP: $67.95

EGT 70TMH
Length: 7'0"
Power: Medium Heavy
MSRP: $67.95

FENWICK® RODS

FENGLASS® FRESHWATER RODS

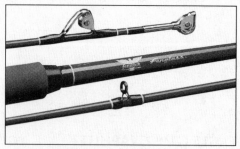

FENGLASS® FRESHWATER RODS (DETAIL)

FENGLASS® FRESHWATER RODS

Your time on the water is framed with goals. Expectations. That makes for a pretty frenetic pace. Thankfully, fast-tapered Fenglass rods can compensate.

Constructed with Fenwick's own E-glass, these rods possess qualities unlike any other fiberglass rods. Because they're built with faster actions, they should. They're highly durable, yet softer than graphite. More forgiving. And ideal in quick-retrieve applications like spinner and crankbait fishing where a softer rod aids in hooking and holding power.

SPECIFICATIONS
2-Piece E-Glass Spinning
FS 53
Length: 5'3"
Power: Ultra Light
MSRP: $84.95

FS 61
Length: 6'0"
Power: Ultra Light
MSRP: $84.95

FS 65
Length: 6'6"
Power: Medium
MSRP: $84.95

PLS 65
Length: 6'6"
Power: Medium Heavy
MSRP: $84.95
PLS 70
Length: 7'0"

Power: Medium Heavy
MSRP: $89.95

4-Piece E-Glass Spin/Fly
SF74-4
Length: 7'0"
Power: Light
MSRP: $109.95

1-Piece S-Glass Triggerstik®
FT 70
Power: Medium
Length: 7'0"
Power: Medium
MSRP: $109.95

HMG® AV™ FRESHWATER RODS

Far too many times you've been forced to choose between durability, high sensitivity and smooth, swift actions. For you, we offer the multi-tapered, intermediate-modulus Fenwick HMG AV series.

Built with a range of fast and moderate actions desired by today's anglers, yet with the strength necessary to lean on the biggest fish, the HMG AV series offers anglers Aramid Veil hoop fiber technology in a quickly tapered rod. The HMG AV is built with the Concept Guide Spacing and Sizing System for lightweight durability that transmits even the lightest taps without hampering strength. In fact, it increases it. This results in hooksets that hold and add control over the fish during the fight.

SPECIFICATIONS
1-Piece Spinning
GSVS 56 XLM
Length: 5'6"
XPower: Light
MSRP: $144.95

GAVS 60MF
Length: 6'0"
Power: Medium
MSRP: $144.95
GAVS 63MHM
Length: 6'3"
Power: Medium Heavy
MSRP: $144.95

GAVS 66MF
Length: 6'6"
Power: Medium
MSRP: $144.95

GAVS 66MHF
Length: 6'6"
Power: Medium Heavy
MSRP: $144.95

GAVS 69MM
Length: 6'9"
Power: Medium
MSRP: $144.95

GAVS 70MM
Length: 7'0"
Power: Medium
MSRP: $144.95

GAVS 70MLM
Length: 7'0"
Power: Medium Light
MSRP: $144.95

FENWICK® RODS

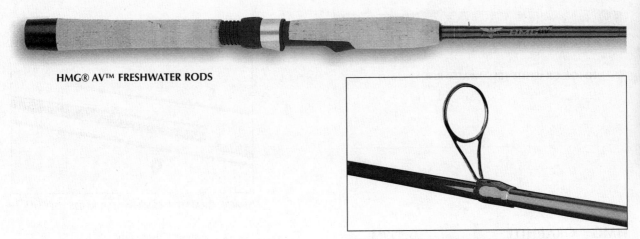

HMG® AV™ FRESHWATER RODS

HMG® AV™ FRESHWATER RODS (DETAIL)

GAVS 70MHM
Length: 7'0"
Power: Medium Heavy
MSRP: $144.95

GAVS 70MHF
Length: 7'0"
Power: Medium Heavy
MSRP: $144.95

2-Piece Spinning
GAVS 56 ULM2
Length: 5'6"
Power: Ultra Light
MSRP: $144.95

GAVS 60ULM-2
Length: 6'0"
Power: Ultra Light
MSRP: $144.95

GAVS 66MLM-2
Length: 6'6"
Power: Medium Light
MSRP: $144.95

GAVS 66MF-2
Length: 6'6"
Power: Medium
MSRP: $144.95

3-Piece Spinning
GAVS 66 LM3
Length: 6'6"
Power: Light
MSRP: $144.95

4-Piece Spinning
GAVS 70 MLM4
Length: 7'0"
Power: Medium Light
MSRP: $154.95

1-Piece Triggerstik
GAVT 60MM
Length: 6'0"
Power: Medium
MSRP: $144.95

GAVT 66MM
Length: 6'6"
Power: Medium
MSRP: $144.95

GAVT 66MF
Length: 6'6"
Power: Medium
MSRP: $144.95

GAVT 66MHF
Length: 6'6"
Power: Medium Heavy
MSRP: $144.95

GAVT 70MF
Length: 7'0"
Power: Medium
MSRP: $144.95

GAVT 70MHF
Length: 7'0"
Power: Medium Heavy
MSRP: $144.95

GAVT 70MHM
Length: 7'0"
Power: Medium Heavy
MSRP: $144.95

GAVT 70HF
Length: 7'0"
Power: H
MSRP: $144.95

1-Piece Triggerstik® with Carboloy tip top
GAVT 63 HMC
Length: 6'3"
Power: H
MSRP: $174.95

GAVT 66MH
Length: 6'6"
Power: Medium Heavy
MSRP: $174.95

GAVT 70MH
Length: 7'0"
Power: Medium Heavy
MSRP: $174.95

GAVT 76MH
Length: 7'6"
Power: Medium Heavy
MSRP: $174.95

2-Piece Triggerstik®
GAVT 76 HM-T
Length: 7'6"
Power: H
MSRP: $174.95

FENWICK® RODS

HMG® GRAPHITE FRESHWATER RODS

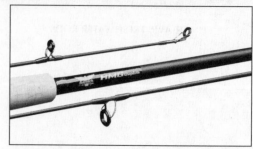

HMG® GRAPHITE FRESHWATER RODS (DETAIL)

HMG® GRAPHITE FRESHWATER RODS

You're loose. Limber. And at the top of your game. That's apparent in your fishing style. Here's over 40 freshwater rods to match it: The multi-tapered Fenwick HMG series.

Known as the rod that started the graphite craze, the HMG series is still built with legendary actions tailored specifically to the right application. For example, an HMG crankbait rod's action is slower than that of a jigging rod. An HMG worming rod will be much faster than an HMG spinnerbait rod, and so on. No matter what you're fishing for, you'll make a wise choice with the HMG series. Over a million other serious anglers have.

SPECIFICATIONS

1-Piece Spinning

G 145
4' Length: 6'
Power: Ultra Light
MSRP: $99.95

G 601
Length: 5'0"
Power: Ultra Light
MSRP: $99.95

G 953
Length: 5'3"
Power: Light
MSRP: $109.95

G 959L
Length: 5'9"
Power: Light
MSRP: $109.95

G 959M
Length: 5'9"
Power: Medium
MSRP: $109.95

G 960M
Length: 6'0"
Power: Medium
MSRP: $109.95

G 960ML
Length: 6'0"
Power: Medium Light
MSRP: $109.95

G 966L
Length: 6'6"
Power: Light
MSRP: $109.95

G 966M
Length: 6'6"
Power: Medium
MSRP: $114.95

G 966MH
Length: 6'6"
Power: Medium Heavy
MSRP: $114.95

G 970M
Length: 7'0"
Power: Medium
MSRP: $114.95

G 970MH
Length: 7'0"
Power: Medium Heavy
MSRP: $114.95

2-Piece Spinning
GFS 55
Length: 5'6"

Power: Ultra Light
MSRP: $109.95

GFS 61
Length: 6'0"
Power: Ultra Light
MSRP: $109.95

GFS 64
Length: 6'6"
Power: Medium Light
MSRP: $109.95

GPLS 65
Length: 6'6"
Power: Medium
MSRP: $109.95

GFS 70
Length: 7'0"
Power: Medium Light
MSRP: $114.95

HMX™ FRESHWATER RODS

Ever notice as the wind picks up, so does the traffic headed back to the boat landing? Many forget that increased wave action mottles the water's surface, allowing you to get even closer to skittish fish. Like that idea? Then here's your rod, the dual-tapered Fenwick HMX.

Created with fast actions that punch baits straight into stiff headwinds, the HMX's crisp tip also creates quick hooking power. And when the fish decides it's not quite time to quit, you'll find a wealth of power in the butt section to help them reconsider that decision.

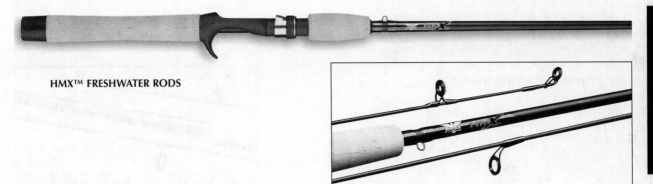

HMX™ FRESHWATER RODS

HMX™ FRESHWATER RODS (DETAIL)

SPECIFICATIONS
1-Piece Spinning
HMX S49UL
Length: 4'9"
Power: Ultra Light
MSRP: $69.95

HMX S53L
Length: 5'3"
Power: Light
MSRP: $69.95

HMX S53ML
Length: 5'3"
Power: Medium Light
MSRP: $69.95

HMX S59M
Length: 5'9"
Power: Medium
MSRP: $69.95

HMX S60ML
Length: 6'0"
Power: Medium Light
MSRP: $69.95

HMX S60MH
Length: 6'0"
Power: Medium Heavy
MSRP: $69.95

HMX S60M
Length: 6'0"
Power: Medium
MSRP: $69.95

HMX S66ML
Length: 6'6"
Power: Medium Light
MSRP: $69.95

HMX S66M
Length: 6'6"
Power: Medium
MSRP: $69.95

HMX S610MH
Length: 6'10"
Power: Medium Heavy
MSRP: $74.95

HMX S70ML
Length: 7'0"
Power: Medium Light
MSRP: $74.95

HMX S70M
Length: 7'0"
Power: Medium
MSRP: $74.95

HMX S70H
Length: 7'0"
Power: H
MSRP: $74.95

2-Piece Spinning
HMX S56UL-2
Length: 5'6"
Power: Ultra Light
MSRP: $69.95

HMX S60L-2
Length: 6'0"
Power: Light
MSRP: $69.95

HMX S66L-2
Length: 6'6"
Power: Light
MSRP: $69.95

HMX S66ML-2
Length: 6'6"

Power: Medium Light
MSRP: $69.95

HMX S66M-2
Length: 6'6"
Power: Medium
MSRP: $69.95

HMX S70M-2
Length: 7'0"
Power: Medium
MSRP: $74.95

HMX S76L-2
Length: 7'6"
Power: Light
MSRP: $74.95

1-Piece Triggerstik®
HMX T60M
Length: 6'0"
Power: Medium
MSRP: $69.95

HMX T60MH
Length: 6'0"
Power: Medium Heavy
MSRP: $69.95

HMX T66M
Length: 6'6"
Power: Medium
MSRP: $79.95

HMX T66MH
Length: 6'6"
Power: Medium Heavy
MSRP: $79.95

HMX T66H
Length: 6'6"
Power: H
MSRP: $79.95

HMX T610XH
Length: 6'10"
XPower: H
MSRP: $79.95

HMX T70MH
Length: 7'0"
Power: Medium Heavy
MSRP: $79.95

HMX T70H
Length: 7'0"
Power: H
MSRP: $79.95

1-Piece Triggerstik® With Carboloy Tip Tops
HMX T66XHC
Length: 6'6"
XPower: H
MSRP: $89.95

HMX T70XHC
Length: 7'0"
XPower: H
MSRP: $89.95

1-Piece Telescopic Flippin'stik™ (collapses to 6')
HMX T76XH-T
Length: 7'6"
XPower: H
MSRP: $89.95

FENWICK® RODS

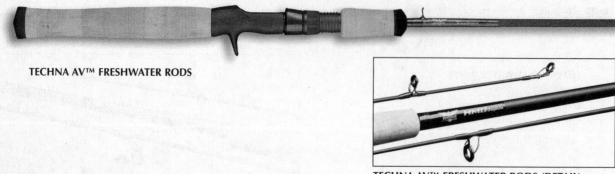

TECHNA AV™ FRESHWATER RODS

TECHNA AV™ FRESHWATER RODS (DETAIL)

TECHNA AV™ FRESHWATER RODS

Designed with extra-fast and fast actions, the Aramid Veil hoop fiber technology allows for blurring casting speeds and distance, while offering ultra-fast line recovery on the hookset. Up to four times more impact-resistant than ordinary graphites, these rods are durable, yet featherlight.

We've significantly reduced the rod's weight, while increasing lateral strength with the Aramid Veil. The lighter tip weights, with the help of the Fuji New Concept Guide Spacing System, diminish wobble--providing perfect tracking for straighter casts that retain energy. This also results in a responsive, balanced touch for pin-point accuracy with everything from light trout and panfish lures to rod-testing jigs or live bait rigs.

You'll notice every pebble, every grain of sand and the lightest takes because the Fenwick Techna AV is the most sensitive rod we've ever developed. You also might notice a faint hum as the rod whips past your ear. Don't be startled. That's just the sound of a record in the making.

SPECIFICATIONS
Model: AVS 59MLF
Length: 5'9"
Power: Medium Light
MSRP: $249.95

Model: AVS 60MF
Length: 6'0"
Power: Medium
MSRP: $249.95

Model: AVS 60LF
Length: 6'0"
Power: Light
MSRP: $249.95

Model: AVS 66LF
Length: 6'6"
Power: Light
MSRP: $249.95

Model: AVS 66MF
Length: 6'6"
Power: Medium
MSRP: $249.95

Model: AVS 70LM
Length: 7'0"
Power: Light
MSRP: $249.95

LAMIGLAS

CERTIFIED PRO FIBERGLASS

Fiberglass rods have pretty much been relegated to two locations: the dusty corner of the garage and the hands of old-school crankbait fishermen like Gerald Beck. Years ago he insisted we not give in to graphite with this series. Many anglers prefer the soft, slow action of glass and know how to use the extra weight to their advantage. So we're glad to keep making them the same way we have for decades, with gloss black blanks and Fuji Alconite guides.

SPECIFICATIONS
Model: XCF 665
Length: 6' 6"
Sections: 1
Lure Weight: ⅜-1 oz.
Line Weight: 10-20 lb.
Action: Fast
Lamiglas Visual Power Rating: 5, Medium Heavy—Ultimate Spinnerbait Rod, Topwater, Rippin', Jerkbaits, Jigs, Worms, Pitchin' and Carolina rig
Type: Crankin' (Gerald Beck)
MSRP: $176.00

Model: XCF 705
Length: 7'
Sections: 1
Lure Weight: ⅜-1 oz.
Line Weight: 10-20 lb.
Action: Fast
Lamiglas Visual Power Rating: 5, Medium Heavy—Ultimate Spinnerbait Rod, Topwater, Rippin', Jerkbaits, Jigs, Worms, Pitchin' and Carolina rig
Type: Crankin' (Gerald Beck)
MSRP: $176.00

Model: XCF 705R
Length: 7'
Sections: 1
Lure Weight: ⅜-1½ oz.
Line Weight: 8-20 lb.
Action: Fast
Lamiglas Visual Power Rating: 5, Medium Heavy—Ultimate Spinnerbait Rod, Topwater, Rippin', Jerkbaits, Jigs, Worms, Pitchin' and Carolina rig
Type: Rippin'
MSRP: $176.00

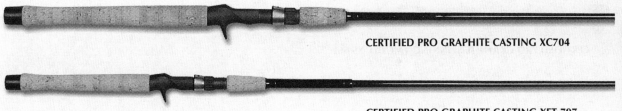

CERTIFIED PRO GRAPHITE CASTING XC704

CERTIFIED PRO GRAPHITE CASTING XFT 797

CERTIFIED PRO GRAPHITE CASTING

These are the kinds of sticks every bass angler should have in their bag of tricks. Certified Pro rods have quietly established themselves as some of the finest moderately-priced rods on the market today. They dominate the western bass scene, and now that they've etched a few tournament wins into the cork, the rest of the country is taking notice. The blanks feature an unbelievably small diameter, yet retain uncompromising strength. They're extremely light, incredibly sensitive and well known for their ability to display a serious backbone when they need to. Each was designed with a specific technique in mind. All are single-piece, casting rods in lengths of 6' 6" to 7', with the exception of four XFT rods. These are longer rods for those situations where longer casts are preferred. The XFTs feature our unique telescoping design so they'll still fit in your rod lockers. All Certified Pro rods utilize the Fuji Concept Guide System with Fuji Alconite guides, top-grade cork and Fuji reel seats.

SPECIFICATIONS

Model: XC 661
Length: 6' 6"
Sections: 1
Lure Weight: ¼-⅝ oz.
Line Weight: 6-17 lb.
Action: Fast
Lamiglas Visual Power Rating: 1, Light—Drop Shot, Split Shot, Topwater, Grubs, Small Spinnerbaits, Small Crankbaits, Jerkbaits, Light Rippin'
MSRP: $170.00

Model: XC 664
Length: 6' 6"
Sections: 1

Lure Weight: ⅜-1 oz.
Line Weight: 6-17 lb.
Action: Fast
Lamiglas Visual Power Rating: 4, Medium—Spinnerbaits, Topwater, Buzzbaits, Larger Tube Baits, Worms
MSRP: $170.00

Model: XC 665
Length: 6' 6"
Sections: 1
Lure Weight: ⅜-1½ oz.
Line Weight: 15-40 lb.
Action: Fast
Lamiglas Visual Power Rating: 5, Medium Heavy—Ultimate Spinnerbait Rod, Topwater, Rippin', Jerkbaits, Jigs, Worms, Pitchin' and Carolina rig (E-Glass version—Ultimate Crankin' Rods)
MSRP: $170.00

Model: XC 687
Length: 6' 8"
Sections: 1
Lure Weight: 1½-3 oz.
Line Weight: 15-30 lb.
Action: Fast
Lamiglas Visual Power Rating: 7, Extra Heavy—Pitchin' Carolina Rig, Texas Rig, Worms, Jigs (Ultimate Heavy Cover Rod)
MSRP: $190.00

Model: XC 704
Length: 7'
Sections: 1
Lure Weight: ⅜-¾ oz.
Line Weight: 8-17 lb.
Action: Moderate/Fast
Lamiglas Visual Power Rating: 4, Medium—Spinnerbaits, Topwater, Buzzbaits, Larger Tube Baits, Worms
Type: Graphite Crankin'
MSRP: $190.00

Model: XC 704C

Length: 7'
Sections: 1
Lure Weight: ⅜-¾ oz.
Line Weight: 8-17 lb.
Action: Moderate/Fast
Lamiglas Visual Power Rating: 4, Medium—Spinnerbaits, Topwater, Buzzbaits, Larger Tube Baits, Worms
Type: Tri-Flex Composite
MSRP:

Model: XC 704J
Length: 7'
Sections: 1
Lure Weight: ⅜-1¼ oz.
Line Weight: 12-20 lb.
Action: Fast
Lamiglas Visual Power Rating: 4, Medium—Spinnerbaits, Topwater, Buzzbaits, Larger Tube Baits, Worms
Type: Jig Special
MSRP:

Model: XC 705
Length: 7'
Sections: 1
Lure Weight: ⅜-1½ oz.
Line Weight: 12-25 lb.
Action: Fast
Lamiglas Visual Power Rating: 5, Medium Heavy—Ultimate Spinnerbait Rod, Topwater, Rippin', Jerkbaits, Jigs, Worms, Pitchin' and Carolina rig
MSRP: $190.00

Model: XC 705C
Length: 7'
Sections: 1
Lure Weight: ⅜-1½ oz.
Line Weight: 12-25 lb.
Action: Fast
Lamiglas Visual Power Rating: 5, Medium Heavy—Ultimate Spinnerbait Rod, Topwater, Rippin', Jerkbaits, Jigs, Worms, Pitchin' and Carolina rig
MSRP: $190.00

LAMIGLAS RODS

CERTIFIED PRO GRAPHITE SPINNING - MODEL XS 661

Model: XC 807
Length: 8'
Sections: 1
Lure Weight: ¾-3½ oz.
Line Weight: 15-30 lb.
Action: Fast
Lamiglas Visual Power Rating: 7, Extra Heavy—Pitchin' Carolina Rig, Texas Rig, Worms, Jigs (Ultimate Heavy Cover Rod)
Type: Big Bait Special
MSRP: $210.00

Model: XPC 703
Length: 7'
Sections: 1
Lure Weight: ¼-½ oz.
Line Weight: 6-15 lb.
Action: Fast
Type: Finesse
MSRP:

Model: XPC 704
Length: 7'
Sections: 1
Lure Weight: ⅜-¾ oz.
Line Weight: 8-17 lb.
Action: Fast
Type: Finesse
MSRP:

Model: XPC 763
Length: 7' 6"
Sections: 1
Lure Weight: ¼-½ oz.
Line Weight: 6-15 lb.
Action: Fast
Type: Finesse
MSRP:

Model: XFT 764
Length: 7' 6"
Sections: 1
Lure Weight: ⅜-¾ oz.
Line Weight: 8-17 lb.
Action: Fast
Type: Finesse
MSRP:

Model: XFT 766
Length: 7' 6"
Sections: 1 (telescopic)
Lure Weight: ⅜-2½ oz.
Line Weight: 15-30 lb.
Action: Fast
Lamiglas Visual Power Rating: 6, Heavy—Pitchin' Carolina Rig, Texas Rig, Worms, Jigs, Soft Jerkbaits, Flippin' (Ultimate Rod for Carolina Rig and Flippin' Techniques)
Type: Flippin'
MSRP:

Model: XFT 797
Length: 7' 9"
Sections: 1 (telescopic)
Lure Weight: 1/2-2 oz.
Line Weight: 12-30 lb.
Action: Fast
Lamiglas Visual Power Rating: 7, Extra Heavy—Pitchin' Carolina Rig, Texas Rig, Worms, Jigs (Ultimate Heavy Cover Rod)
Type: Magnum Grass Rod
MSRP:

Model: XFT 806
Length: 8'
Sections: 1 (telescopic)
Lure Weight: ½-2 oz.
Line Weight: 12-30 lb.
Action: Fast
Lamiglas Visual Power Rating: 6, Heavy—Pitchin' Carolina Rig, Texas Rig, Worms, Jigs, Soft Jerkbaits, Flippin' (Ultimate Rod for Carolina Rig and Flippin' Techniques)
Type: Flippin'
MSRP:

CERTIFIED PRO GRAPHITE SPINNING

Like the casting series, these rods feature small-diameter, fast-action blanks. They're extremely light, incredibly sensitive and well known for their ability to display a serious backbone when they need to. Here, too, the Fuji Concept Guide System really shines. It dramatically cuts down on line twist and gives you far greater line control while casting, retrieving and long, drawn out battles.

SPECIFICATIONS

Model: XS 66 DH
Length: 6' 6"
Sections: 1
Lure Weight: ⅛-⅜ oz.
Line Weight: 4-10 lb.
Action: Extra Fast
Lamiglas Visual Power Rating: 1, Light—Drop Shot, Split Shot, Topwater, Grubs, Small Spinnerbaits, Small Crankbaits, Jerkbaits, Light Rippin'
Type: Darter Head
MSRP: $170.00

Model: XS 661
Length: 6' 6"
Sections: 1
Lure Weight: ¼-⅝ oz.
Line Weight: 6-17 lb.
Action: Fast
Lamiglas Visual Power Rating: 1, Light—Drop Shot, Split Shot, Topwater, Grubs, Small Spinnerbaits, Small Crankbaits, Jerkbaits, Light Rippin'
MSRP: $170.00

Model: XS 663
Length: 6' 6"
Sections: 1
Lure Weight: ⅜-¾ oz.
Line Weight: 8-20 lb.
Action: Fast
Lamiglas Visual Power Rating: 3, Medium Light—Spider Jigs, Grubs, Worms, Rippin', Topwater, Tube Baits, Spinnerbaits
MSRP: $170.00

CERTIFIED PRO GRAPHITE SPINNING - MODEL XS 703

COMPETITOR SERIES - MODEL CC 661

Model: XS 663-2
Length: 6' 6"
Sections: 2
Lure Weight: ⅛-⅜ oz.
Line Weight: 4-10 lb.
Action: Extra Fast
Lamiglas Visual Power Rating: 1,
Light—Drop Shot, Split Shot,
Topwater, Grubs, Small Spinnerbaits,
Small Crankbaits, Jerkbaits, Light
Rippin'
MSRP: $180.00

Model: XS 664
Length: 6' 6"
Sections: 1
Lure Weight: ⅜-1 oz.
Line Weight: 10-20 lb.
Action: Fast
Lamiglas Visual Power Rating: 4,
Medium—Spinnerbaits, Topwater,
Buzzbaits, Larger Tube Baits, Worms
MSRP: $170.00

Model: XS 703
Length: 7'
Sections: 1
Lure Weight: ⅜-¾ oz.
Line Weight: 10-20 lb.
Action: Fast
Lamiglas Visual Power Rating: 3,
Medium Light—Spider Jigs, Grubs,
Worms, Rippin', Topwater, Tube Baits,
Spinnerbaits
Type: Drop Shot
MSRP: $180.00

Model: XPS 703
Length: 7'
Sections: 1
Lure Weight: ¼-½ oz.
Line Weight: 6-15 lb.
Action: Fast
Type: Finesse
MSRP:

Model: XPS 704
Length: 7'
Sections: 1

Lure Weight: ⅜-¾ oz.
Line Weight: 8-17 lb.
Action: Fast
Type: Finesse
MSRP:

Model: XPS 763
Length: 7' 6"
Sections: 1
Lure Weight: ¼-½ oz.
Line Weight: 6-15 lb.
Action: Fast
Type: Finesse
MSRP:

Model: XPS 764
Length: 7' 6"
Sections: 1
Lure Weight: ⅜-¾ oz.
Line Weight: 8-17 lb.
Action: Fast
Type: Finesse
MSRP:

COMPETITOR SERIES
You're always competing against
something. It might be 100 other tournament pros all battling for first place,
or your son or daughter for the day's
bragging rights. Either way, you'll
have a measurable edge with a
Lamiglas Competitor rod. These are
all fast-action rods with well-balanced
light tips and a full range of power,
line and lure ratings. CC rods are
casting models. CS rods are spin models. All are made with ultra-sensitive
graphite with one exception. Model
CFC 685 is made of forgiving E-Glass.
It's for all you die-hards who just can't
go graphite for serious crankin' and
rippin' waters. All Competitor rods
include Fuji Concept guides, cush-
ioned-hood graphite reel seats, and
premium-grade grips.

SPECIFICATIONS
Model: CC 661
Length: 6' 6"
Sections: 1
Lure Weight: ¼-⅝ oz.
Line Weight: 6-17 lb.
Action: Fast
Lamiglas Visual Power Rating: 1,
Light—Drop Shot, Split Shot,
Topwater, Grubs, Small Spinnerbaits,
Small Crankbaits, Jerkbaits, Light
Rippin'
MSRP: $130.00

Model: CC 664
Length: 6' 6"
Sections: 1
Lure Weight: ⅜-1 oz.
Line Weight: 8-20 lb.
Action: Fast
Lamiglas Visual Power Rating: 4,
Medium—Spinnerbaits, Topwater,
Buzzbaits, Larger Tube Baits, Worms
MSRP: $130.00

Model: CC 665
Length: 6' 6"
Sections: 1
Lure Weight: ⅜-1½ oz.
Line Weight: 10-25 lb.
Action: Fast
Lamiglas Visual Power Rating: 5,
Medium Heavy—Ultimate Spinnerbait
Rod, Topwater, Rippin', Jerkbaits, Jigs,
Worms, Pitchin' and Carolina rig
MSRP: $130.00

Model: CC 703
Length: 7'
Sections: 1
Lure Weight: ¼-½ oz.
Line Weight: 6-15 lb.
Action: Fast
Lamiglas Visual Power Rating: 3,
Medium Light—Spider Jigs, Grubs,
Worms, Rippin', Topwater, Tube Baits,
Spinnerbaits
MSRP: $130.00

LAMIGLAS RODS

COMPETITOR SERIES - MODEL CC 705

Model: CC 705
Length: 7'
Sections: 1
Lure Weight: ⅜-1½ oz.
Line Weight: 12-25 lb.
Action: Fast
Lamiglas Visual Power Rating: 5,
Medium Heavy—Ultimate Spinnerbait
Rod, Topwater, Rippin', Jerkbaits, Jigs,
Worms, Pitchin' and Carolina rig
MSRP: $130.00

Model: CC 706
Length: 7'
Sections: 1
Lure Weight: ½-2 oz.
Line Weight: 12-30 lb.
Action: Fast
Lamiglas Visual Power Rating: 5,
Medium Heavy—Ultimate Spinnerbait
Rod, Topwater, Rippin', Jerkbaits, Jigs,
Worms, Pitchin' and Carolina rig
MSRP: $130.00

Model: CS 661
Length: 6' 6"
Sections: 1
Lure Weight: ⅛-⅜ oz.
Line Weight: 4-10 lb.
Action: Fast
Lamiglas Visual Power Rating: 1,
Light—Drop Shot, Split Shot,
Topwater, Grubs, Small Spinnerbaits,
Small Crankbaits, Jerkbaits, Light
Rippin'
MSRP: $130.00

Model: CS 663
Length: 6' 6"
Sections: 1
Lure Weight: ¼-¾ oz.
Line Weight: 6-12 lb.
Action: Fast
Lamiglas Visual Power Rating: 3,
Medium Light—Spider Jigs, Grubs,
Worms, Rippin', Topwater, Tube Baits,
Spinnerbaits
MSRP: $130.00

Model: CS 681
Length: 6' 8"
Sections: 1
Lure Weight: ⅛-⅜ oz.
Line Weight: 4-10 lb.
Action: Fast
Lamiglas Visual Power Rating: 1,
Light—Drop Shot, Split Shot,
Topwater, Grubs, Small Spinnerbaits,
Small Crankbaits, Jerkbaits, Light
Rippin'
MSRP: $130.00

Model: CS 701
Length: 7'
Sections: 1
Lure Weight: ⅛-⅜ oz.
Line Weight: 4-10 lb.
Action: Fast
Lamiglas Visual Power Rating: 1,
Light—Drop Shot, Split Shot,
Topwater, Grubs, Small Spinnerbaits,
Small Crankbaits, Jerkbaits, Light
Rippin'
MSRP: $130.00

Model: CFC685
Length: 6' 8"
Sections: 1
Lure Weight: ⅜-1½ oz.
Line Weight: 8-20 lb.
Action: Moderate Fast
Lamiglas Visual Power Rating: 5,
Medium Heavy—Ultimate Spinnerbait
Rod, Topwater, Rippin', Jerkbaits, Jigs,
Worms, Pitchin' and Carolina rig
MSRP: $130.00

G200 GRAPHITE SPIN & CAST

These incredibly affordable rods have
high-quality graphite, components
and features not normally found in
this category. You'll find aluminum
oxide guides, cushioned hood
graphite reel seats, premium cork
grips, hook keepers and a stealth
black finish. G200 rods are perfect for
kids or gifts, or if you're just looking
to save some cash to fill up the boat.
SPECIFICATIONS

Model: MBC 603
Length: 6'
Sections: 1
Lure Weight: ⅜-¾ oz.
Line Weight: 8-17 lb.
Action: Moderate Fast
Power: Medium
MSRP: $69.95

Model: MBC 661
Length: 6' 6"
Sections: 1
Lure Weight: ¼-⅝ oz.
Line Weight: 6-15 lb.
Action: Moderate Fast
Power: Light
MSRP: $69.95

Model: MBC 663
Length: 6' 6"
Sections: 1
Lure Weight: ⅜-¾ oz.
Line Weight: 8-17 lb.
Action: Moderate Fast
Power: Medium
MSRP: $69.95

Model: MBC 703
Length: 7'
Sections: 1
Lure Weight: 3/8-3/4 oz.
Line Weight: 8-17 lb.
Action: Moderate Fast
Power: Medium
MSRP: $69.95

Model: MBC 705
Length: 7'
Sections: 1
Lure Weight: ⅝-1¼ oz.
Line Weight: 10-20 lb.
Action: Moderate Fast
Power: Medium/Heavy
MSRP: $69.95

TI2000 TITANIUM/IM700 - MODEL TBS 661

Model: MBS 603
Length: 6'
Sections: 1
Lure Weight: ⅜-¾ oz.
Line Weight: 8-17 lb.
Action: Moderate Fast
Power: Medium
MSRP: $69.95

Model: MBS 703
Length: 7'
Sections: 1
Lure Weight: ⅜-¾ oz.
Line Weight: 8-17 lb.
Action: Moderate Fast
Power: Medium
MSRP: $69.95

Ti2000 TITANIUM/IM700

There's nothing we can say about these trend-setting rods that's more powerful than what the press has already said about them. "Best of Show" at ASA and "Best of Show-Editor's Choice Award" by Sport Fishing magazine. Pros currently fishing them include Robert Lee, West Coast Bass Angler of the Year, Skeet Reese, Roland Martin, Ish Monroe and many others. Ti2000 rods feature pure-titanium shafts integrated with our exclusive IM700 graphite blanks

to create a rod that is lightweight, powerful and so sensitive it actually amplifies whatever is going on at the end of your line. The Fuji Concept Guide System enhances them even further by reducing line twist, improving line control and dramatically increasing castability. Ti2000 rods don't look like anything else out there. Because there simply isn't anything else out there that measures up.

SPECIFICATIONS

Model: TBS 661
Length: 6' 6"
Sections: 1
Lure Weight: ¼-⅝ oz.
Line Weight: 6-17 lb.
Action: Fast
Lamiglas' Visual Power Rating: 1, Light—Drop Shot, Split Shot, Topwater, Grubs, Small Spinnerbaits, Small Crankbaits, Jerkbaits, Light Rippin'
MSRP: $420.00

Model: TBS 663
Length: 6' 6"
Sections: 1
Lure Weight: ⅜-¾ oz.
Line Weight: 8-20 lb.
Action: Fast
Lamiglas' Visual Power Rating: 3,

Medium Light—Spider Jigs, Grubs, Worms, Rippin', Topwater, Tube Baits, Spinnerbaits
MSRP: $420.00

Model: TBS 703
Length: 7'
Sections: 1
Lure Weight: ⅜-¾ oz.
Line Weight: 8-20 lb.
Action: Fast
Lamiglas' Visual Power Rating: 3, Medium Light—Spider Jigs, Grubs, Worms, Rippin', Topwater, Tube Baits, Spinnerbaits
MSRP: $420.00

Model: TBS 705
Length: 7'
Sections: 1
Lure Weight: ⅜-1½ oz.
Line Weight: 12-25 lb.
Action: Fast
Lamiglas' Visual Power Rating: 5, Medium Heavy—Ultimate Spinnerbait Rod, Topwater, Rippin', Jerkbaits, Jigs, Worms, Pitchin' and Carolina rig (E-Glass version—Ultimate Crankin' Rods)
MSRP: $420.00

Opt For Lightweight Rods
You'll make better casts if you use a lightweight rod that becomes like an extension of your arm. Lightweight rods—not to be confused with light action rods—increase response time and sensitivity while reducing fatigue, thus improving overall efficiency.

PFLUEGER RODS

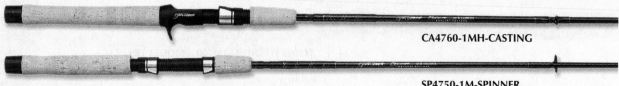

CA4760-1MH-CASTING

SP4750-1M-SPINNER

TRION IM-8 GRAPHITE

- 98% IM-8 graphite construction. (CAC 4770-1M cranking rod is fiberglass.)
- Features Aramid braid for extra strength.

- Premium Fuji® guides with Fuji® New Guide Concept on all models.
- Blank-through-handle construction for added strength and sensitivity.
- Fuji® conventional reel seats with cushioned stainless steel hoods.

- Top grade cork grips with protective rubber butt.
- Hook keeper.
- 17 new actions.
- Five year limited warranty.
MSRP:$49.95 to $59.95

SPECIFICATIONS

Model#	Length	Pcs.	Handle	Action	Lb.-Test	Lure-Wt.-Oz.	Guides
CA4760-1MH	6'0"	1	A	MH	10-20	¼-¾	7+tip
CA4766-1M	6'6"	1	A	M	8-15	⅛-⅝	8+tip
CA4766-1MH	6'6"	1	A	MH	10-20	¼-¾	8+tip
CA4770-1MH	7'0"	1	A	MH	10-20	¼-¾	9+tip
SP4750-1ML	5'0"	1	B	ML	4-10	1⁄16-¼	6+tip
SP4759-1ML	5'9"	1	B	ML	4-10	1⁄16-¼	6+tip
SP4756-2L	5'6"	2	B	L	4-8	1⁄16-⅜	6+tip
SP4762-1L	6'2"	1	C	L	4-8	1⁄16-⅜	6+tip
SP4760-1MH	6'0"	1	C	MH	8-15	¼-⅝	6+tip
SP4760-2M	6'0"	2	C	M	6-12	⅛-½	6+tip
SP4766-1MH	6'6"	1	C	MH	8-15	¼-⅝	7+tip
SP4766-2L	6'6"	2	C	L	4-8	1⁄16-⅜	7+tip
SP4766-2M	6'6"	2	C	M	6-12	⅛-½	7+tip'
SP4770-2M	7'0"	2	C	M	6-12	⅛-½	8+tip
SP4770-1MH	7'0"	1	C	MH	8-15	⅛-⅝	8+tip

L—Light; ML—Medium Light; M—Medium; MH—Medium-Heavy

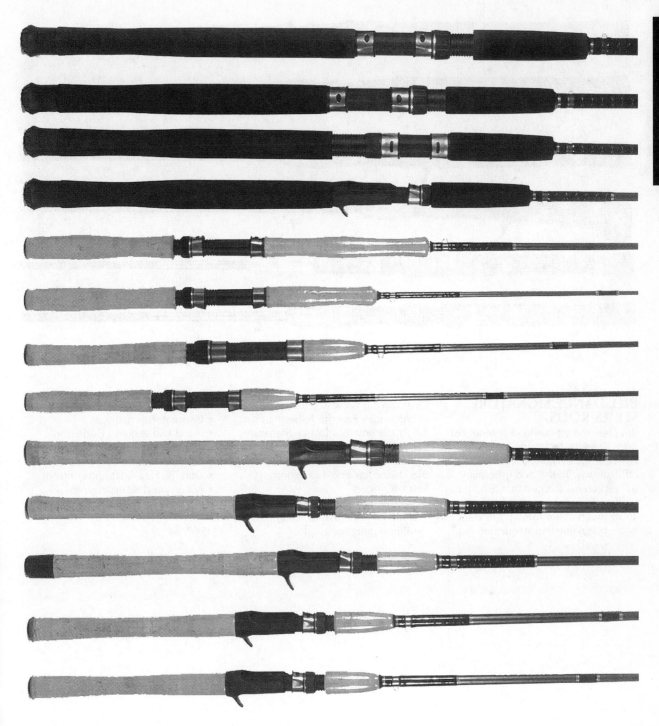

AFFINITY™ RODS

Quantum Affinity™ rods are perfectly balanced for value and performance. Whether you're an amateur or professional, there's a model for just about every type of fisherman's need.

SPECIFICATIONS

- IM7 graphite blanks for sensitivity and light weight
- Quantum low-profile progressive guide system
- Contoured stainless steel reel seat
- Comfortable natural cork handles
- 21 actions available

MSRP: $44.95

QUANTUM® RODS

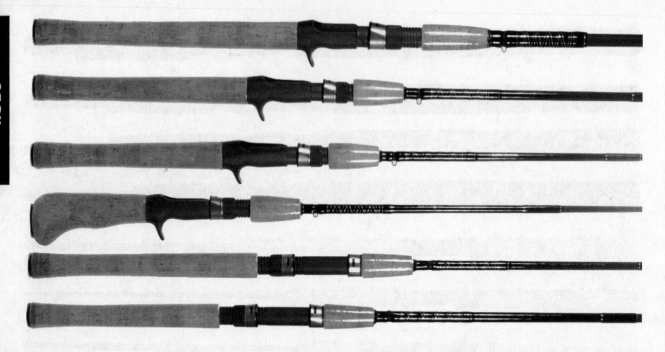

BILL DANCE SIGNATURE SERIES RODS

Bill Dance is an outdoors legend. For over 30 years, he has delivered fishing advice on television in his humorous, off-beat way. To the avid fisherman, Bill represents the best that fishing has to offer. Even for people who don't know much about fishing, Bill Dance is the one name that stands out. Now,

Quantum has harnessed the knowledge of "America's Favorite Fisherman" in the totally new Bill Dance Signature Series line of rods. Actions, tapers, guides, seats and overall quality that Bill Dance has come to expect.

SPECIFICATIONS

- Custom-designed HSX44 high-strain graphite blanks featuring 44 million modulus graphite

- Genuine Fuji guides
- Genuine Fuji reel seat
- Hand-laid genuine Gudebrod thread wraps
- Grade-A natural cork handles
- Durable Flex Coat epoxy finish
- Actions and tapers custom-designed by Bill Dance
- 17 actions available

MSRP: $49.95

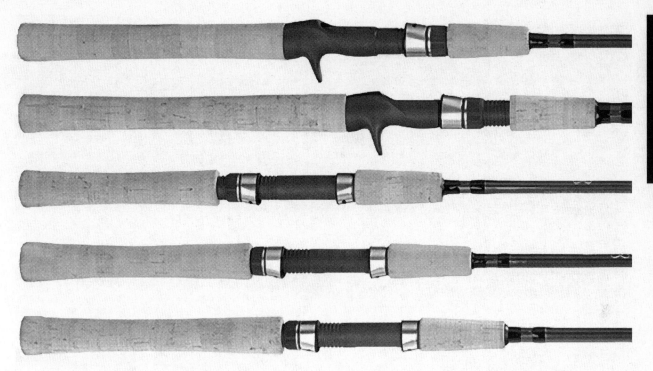

TORSION™ RODS

Quantum Torsion™ rods are perfectly balanced for value and performance. Whether you're an amateur or professional, there's a model for just about every type of fisherman's need.

SPECIFICATIONS

- IM6 graphite blanks for sensitivity and light weight
- Contoured stainless steel reel seat
- Comfortable natural cork handles
- 7 actions available

MSRP: $19.95

QUANTUM® RODS

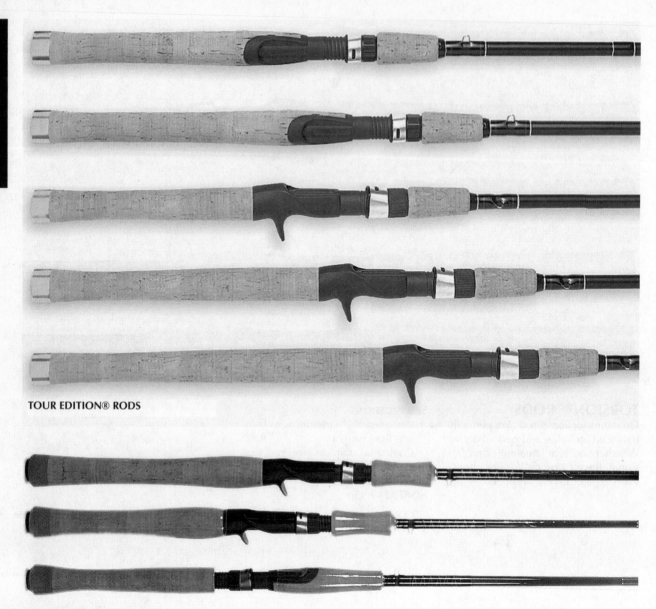

TOUR EDITION® RODS

TOUR EDITION® PT RODS

TOUR EDITION® RODS

Quantum's top of the line Tour Edition rod series combines the years of fishing experience of our Advisory Staff with the art of custom rod building. These legendary rods have been helping tournament pros earn a living on the top bass and walleye trails for years. Now, this NEW Tour Edition series takes its proven performance to an even higher level. Thanks to technological advances and continued input from America's top fishing professionals, these rods feature lighter and more sensitve blanks. And they are fitted with Fuji Hardloy Concept Guides for the ultimate in line flow during casting and retrieval. Tour Edition rods are designed with the serious fisherman in mind...give them a try and see what all the pros are talking about.

SPECIFICATIONS
• 44 million PSI tensile strength, custom-designed HSX44 Hi-Strain graphite blanks
• Power-rated tapers for specific angling situations
• Fuji Hardloy Concept Guides strategically places more smaller-size guides along the blank to minimize weight and increase casting distance
• Hand-laid thread wraps
• Durable Flex Coat epoxy finish
• Actions custom-designed by Quantum Professional Advisory Staff
• 18 actions available
MSRP: $69.95

SHAKESPEARE RODS

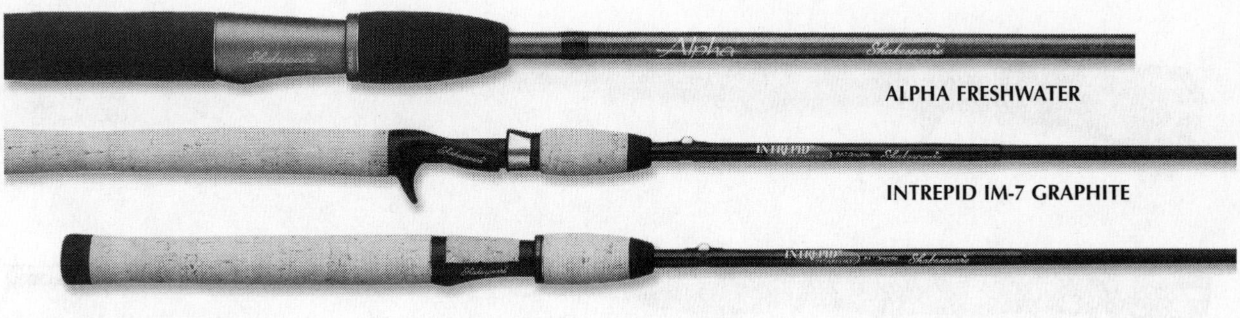

ALPHA FRESHWATER

INTREPID IM-7 GRAPHITE

ALPHA FRESHWATER

- Tubular glass construction.
- Stainless steel guides with ceramic inserts.
- Graphite twist-lock reel seat.
- Comfortable EVA foam grips.
- Matte finish.

MSRP: $12.99

SPECIFICATIONS

Model#	Length	Pcs.	Handle	Action	Lb.-Test	Lure-Wt.-Oz.	Guides
BC2156-1M	5'6"	1	A	M	8-15	⅛-⅝	4+Tip
CA2160-1MH	6'0"	1	B	MH	10-20	¼-¾	5+Tip
CA2166-1MH	6'6"	1	B	MH	10-20	¼-¾	5+Tip
SC2156-2M	5'6"	2	A	M	6-12	⅛-⅝	4+Tip
SC2160-2M	6'0"	2	A	M	6-12	⅛-¾	4+Tip
SP2150-2UL	5'0"	2	C	UL	2-6	1/32-¼	4+Tip
SP2156-2L	5'6"	2	C	L	4-8	1/16-⅜	4+Tip
SP2160-2M	6'0"	2	D	M	6-12	⅛-½	4+Tip
SP2166-2M	6'6"	2	D	M	6-12	⅛-½	4+Tip
SP2170-2M	7'0"	2	D	M	6-12	⅛-½	5+Tip

UL—Ultra-light | L—Light | M—Medium | MH—Medium-heavy | BC—Pistol Grip Baitcast | CA—Straight Handle Casting | SC—Spincasting | SP—Spinning Rod

INTREPID IM-7 GRAPHITE

- IM-7 graphite construction for lightweight, sensitive blanks.
- Lightweight stainless steel guides with long lasting titanium guide inserts for reduced line wear.
- Comfortable top grade cork handles.
- Matte finish with eye-catching holographic labels.
- Spinning models feature new graphite twist-lock reel seat with cushioned stainless steel hood.
- Casting models feature "Comfort-Fit" exposed blank reel seat for added sensitivity and cushioned stainless steel twist-lock hood.
- Blank-through-handle construction for added strength and sensitivity.
- Complete with hook keeper.
- Downrigger model features graphite reel seat with cushioned stainless steel hoods and EVA grips.
- 8'6" models feature graphite reel seat with cushioned stainless steel hoods and top grade cork handles with rubber butt cap.

MSRP: $29.99 to $44.99

SPECIFICATIONS

Model #	Lgth.	Pcs.	Handle	Action	Lb.-Test	Lure-Wt.-Oz.	Guides
BC3056-1M	5'6"	1	A	M	8-15	⅛-⅝	5+Tip
CA3060-1MH	6'0"	1	B	MH	10-20	¼-¾	6+Tip
CA3066-1M	6'6"	1	B	M	8-15	1/16-⅜	6+Tip
CA3066-1MH	6'6"	1	B	MH	10-20	¼-¾	6+Tip
CA3066-2MH	6'6"	2	B	MH	10-20	¼-¾	6+Tip
CA3070-2UL	7'0"	2	C	UL	2-8	1/32-¼	7+Tip
CA3070-1MH	7'0"	1	C	MH	10-20	¼-¾	7+Tip
CAF3076-1MH	7'6"	1	J	MH	10-20	¼-¾	7+Tip
SP3050-1ML	5'0"	1	E	ML	4-10	1/16-¼	4+Tip
SP3050-2UL	5'0"	2	E	UL	2-6	1/32-¼	4+Tip
SP3056-2L	5'6"	2	E	L	4-8	1/16-⅜	4+Tip
SP3060-1MH	6'0"	1	F	MH	8-15	¼-⅝	5+Tip
SP3060-2L	6'0"	2	F	L	6-12	1/16-⅜	5+Tip
SP3060-2M	6'0"	2	F	M	6-12	⅛-½	5+Tip
SP3066-2L	6'6"	2	F	L	4-10	⅛-½	5+Tip
SP3066-2M	6'6"	2	F	M	6-12	⅛-½	5+Tip
SP3070-2M	7'0"	2	F	M	6-12	⅛-½	5+Tip
SP3070-2ML	7'0"	2	F	ML	4-10	1/16-¼	5+Tip
SPI3070-1MH	7'0"	1	F	MH	8-15	¼-⅝	5+Tip

UL—Ultra-light | L—Light | ML—Medium-light | M—Medium | MH—Medium-heavy | H—Heavy | BC—Pistol Grip Baitcast | CA—Straight Handle Casting | SP—Spinning Rod

SHAKESPEARE RODS

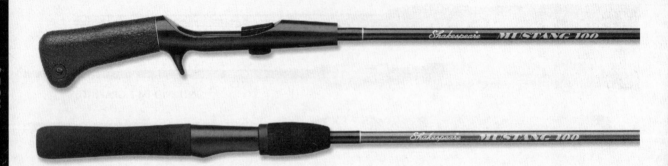

MUSTANG

SPECIFICATIONS
- High-strength tubular glass blanks.
- Packed in assorted colors (Red, Green, Dark Blue).

SPECIFICATIONS

Model#	Length	Pcs.	Handle	Action	Lb.-Test	Lure-Wt.-Oz.	Guides
MSC56	5'6"	2	A	L	4-8	¹⁄₁₆-³⁄₈	3+Tip
MSC60	6'0"	2	A	M	6-12	¹⁄₈-¹⁄₂	3+Tip
MSP56	5'6"	2	B	L	4-8	¹⁄₁₆-³⁄₈	3+Tip
MSP60	6'0"	2	B	M	6-12	¹⁄₈-¹⁄₂	3+Tip

L—Light | M—Medium

SYNERGY SS IM-6 GRAPHITE

- IM-6 graphite construction for added sensitivity.
- Stainless steel guides with stainless steel inserts are lighter and more durable than standard guides.
- Top grade cork handles with protective EVA butt cap.
- Spinning models feature graphite twist-lock reel seat with cork insert.
- Casting models feature "Comfort-Fit" exposed blank reel seat for added sensitivity.
- Complete with hook keeper.
- Blank-through-handle construction for strength and sensitivity.
- Matte finish rod with holographic label.
- New walleye actions now available.
- Perfect match for all Synergy reels.

MSRP: $19.99 to $24.99

SPECIFICATIONS

Model#	Length	Pcs.	Handle	Action	Lb.-Test	Lure-Wt.-Oz.	Guides
BC2956-1M	5'6"	1	A	M	8-15	¹⁄₈-⁵⁄₈	6+Tip
CA2960-1M	6'0"	1	B	M	8-15	¹⁄₈-⁵⁄₈	6+Tip
CA2966-1M	6'6"	1	B	M	8-15	¹⁄₈-⁵⁄₈	6+Tip
CA2970-1ML	7'0"	1	B	ML	8-17	¹⁄₄-⁵⁄₈	7+Tip
SP2946-1UL	4'6"	1	C	UL	2-6	¹⁄₃₂-¹⁄₄	4+Tip
SP2950-1UL	5'0"	1	C	UL	2-6	¹⁄₃₂-¹⁄₄	4+Tip
SP2950-2UL	5'0"	2	C	UL	2-6	¹⁄₃₂-¹⁄₄	4+Tip
SP2956-2L	5'6"	2	C	L	4-8	¹⁄₁₆-³⁄₈	4+Tip
SP2960-1MH	6'0"	1	D	MH	8-15	¹⁄₄-⁵⁄₈	5+Tip
SP2960-2L	6'0"	2	D	L	4-8	¹⁄₁₆-³⁄₈	5+Tip
SP2960-2M	6'0"	2	D	M	6-12	¹⁄₈-¹⁄₂	5+Tip
SP2966-2	6'6"	2	D	L		4-8	¹⁄₈-¹⁄₂	5+Tip
SP2966-1MH	6'6"	1	D	MH	8-15	¹⁄₄-⁵⁄₈	5+Tip
SP2966-2M	6'6"	2	D	M	6-12	¹⁄₈-¹⁄₂	5+Tip
SP2970-1MH	7'0"	1	D	MH	8-15	¹⁄₄-⁵⁄₈	5+Tip
SP2970-2M	7'0"	2	D	M	6-12	¹⁄₈-¹⁄₂	5+Tip

CAL—Straight Handle Casting | SPL—Spinning Rod | UL—Ultra-light | L—Light | ML—Medium-light | M—Medium | MH—Medium-heavy

SHAKESPEARE RODS

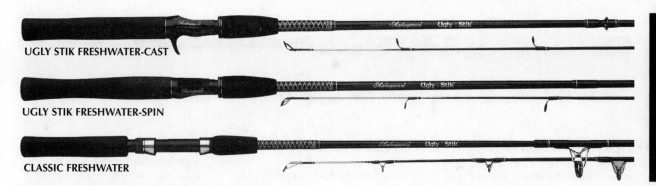

UGLY STIK FRESHWATER-CAST

UGLY STIK FRESHWATER-SPIN

CLASSIC FRESHWATER

UGLY STIK FRESHWATER & CLASSIC FRESHWATER

- Exclusive quick-taper Clear Tip® design.
- All Ugly Stik rods feature blank-through-handle construction for added strength and sensitivity.
- Durable and lightweight EVA grips. Spinning models have an EVA insert on top of reel seat for added comfort.

- Graphite twist-lock reel seats are standard on most models.
- Ugly Stik Classic models feature conventional reel seats with cushioned stainless steel hoods on spinning models.
- Guides feature black stainless steel frames and aluminum oxide inserts.
- Ugly Stik Classic models feature

double-footed, chrome-plated stainless steel wire frame guides with aluminum oxide inserts.
- Ferruless design on two-piece models for the strength and feel of a one-piece rod.
- Over 30 actions to choose from for all freshwater fishing applications.
  MSRP: $27.95 to $31.95

SPECIFICATIONS FOR FRESHWATER RODS

Model#	Length	Pcs.	Handle	Action	Lb-Test	Lure-Wt.-Oz.	Guides
BCL1100	5'6"	1	A	M	8-20	¼-¾	5+Tip
BCL1100	6'0"	1	A	M	12-20	¼-¾	5+Tip
CAL1100	6'0"	1	B	M	8-20	¼-¾	6+Tip
CAL1101	6'0"	1	B	MH	10-25	¼-¾	6+Tip
CAL1100	6'6"	1	B	M	8-20	¼-¾	6+Tip
CAL1101	6'6"	1	C	MH	10-25	¼-¾	6+Tip
CAL1102	6'6"	2	C	MH	10-25	¼-¾	6+Tip
CALM1100	6'6"	1	E	H	8-20	¼-¾	6+Tip
CAL1100	7'0"	1	C	M	8-20	¼-¾	7+Tip
CAL1101	7'0"	1	F	MH	10-25	⅜-1	7+Tip
CAL1100	7'6"	1	C	ML	6-17	¼-¾	7+Tip
CAL1102	7'0"	2	C	M	8-20	¼-¾	7+Tip
CALB1102	7'0"	2	C	ML	8-20	¼-¾	7+Tip
SCL1102	5'0"	2	A	UL	2-6	¹⁄₃₂-¼	4+Tip
SCL1100	5'6"	2	A	M	6-12	⅛-⅜	5+Tip
SCL1100	6'0"	2	A	M	6-12	⅛-⅜	5+Tip
SPL1100	5'0"	1	G	UL	2-6	¹⁄₃₂-¼	4+Tip
SPL1102	5'0"	2	G	UL	2-6	¹⁄₃₂-¼	4+Tip
SPL1100	5'6"	1	H	M	6-15	⅛-⅝	5+Tip
SPL1101	5'6"	2	G	L	4-10	⅛-¼	4+Tip
SPL1100	5'10"	1	I	M	6-15	⅛-⅝	5+Tip
SPL1102	5'10"	2	I	M	6-15	⅛-⅝	5+Tip
SPL1102	6'0"	2	I	M	6-15	⅛-⅝	5+Tip
SPL1100	6'0"	1	I	MH	8-20	¼-¾	5+Tip
SPL1100	6'6"	2	I	M	6-15	⅛-⅝	5+Tip
SPL1100	7'0"	2	I	M	6-15	⅛-⅝	5+Tip

UL—Ultra-light | L—Light | ML—Medium-light | M—Medium | MH—Medium-heavy | H—Heavy | BCL—Pistol Grip Baitcast | CAF—Flipping | CAL—Straight Handle Casting | CALB—Straight Handle Live Bait Rod | CALM—Straight Handle Musky Rod | SCL—Spincasting Rod | SPL—Spinning Rod

SPECIFICATIONS FOR CLASSIC FRESHWATER RODS

Model#	Length	Pcs.	Handle	Action	Lb-Test	Lure-Wt.-Oz.	Guides
SP1102	5'10"	2	I	M	6-15	⅛-⅝	5+Tip
SP1100	6'0"	1	I	H	8-20	¼-¾	5+Tip
SP1100	6'6"	2	I	M	6-15	⅛-⅝	5+Tip
SP1101	6'6"	1	J	MH	8-20	¼-¾	5+Tip
SP1100	7'0"	2	I	M	6-15	⅛-⅝	5+Tip
SP1101	7'0"	1	J	MH	8-20	¼-⅝	5+Tip

M—Medium | MH—Medium-heavy | SP—Spinning Rod

SHAKESPEARE RODS

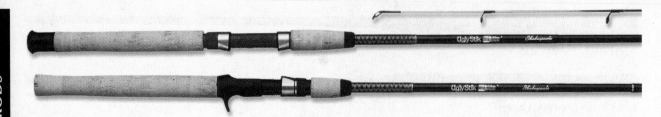

UGLY STIK GRAPHITE
- Howald Process construction.
- Double-Built 100% graphite blank.
- Extra strong solid graphite tip.
- Top-grade cork handles with rubber butt cap.
- Blank-through-handle construction for added strength and sensitivity.
- Black stainless steel frame guides with aluminum oxide inserts.
- Ugly Back 60-day/5-year warranty.

MSRP: $59.95

SPECIFICATIONS

Model#	Lgth	Pcs.	Handle	Action	Lb.-Test	Lure-Wt.	Guides
GBC1160-1M	6'0"	1	A	M	8-15	¼-⅝	7+Tip
GCA1160-1M	6'0"	1	B	M	8-15	¼-⅝	7+Tip
GCA1160-1MH	6'0"	1	B	MH	10-20	¼-¾	7+Tip
GCA1166-1M	6'6"	1	B	M	8-15	¼-⅝	8+Tip
GCA1166-1MH	6'6"	1	B	MH	10-20	¼-¾	8+Tip
GCA1170-1ML	7'0"	1	B	ML	8-17	⅛-⅝	9+Tip
GCA1170-1MH	7'0"	1	B	MH	10-20	⅛-¾	9+Tip
GCAF1176-1MH	7'6"	1	C	MH	10-25	⅛-¾	9+Tip
GSP1150-1UL	5'0"	1	D	UL	2-6	¹⁄₃₂-¼	4+Tip
GSP1160-1M	6'0"	1	E	M	6-12	⅛-¾	6+Tip
GSP1160-2M	6'0"	2	E	M	6-12	⅛-¾	6+Tip
GSP1166-1M	6'6"	1	E	M	6-12	⅛-¾	7+Tip
GSP1166-1MH	6'6"	1	E	MH	8-15	⅛-¾	7+Tip
GSP1166-2M	6'6"	2	E	M	6-12	⅛-¾	7+T
GSP1170-1M	7'0"	1	F	M	6-12	⅛-⅝	8+Tip
GSP1170-2M	7'0"	2	F	M	6-12	⅛-¾	8+Tip

UL—Ultra-light | ML—Medium-light | M—Medium | MH—Medium-heavy | GCA—Casting Rod | GSP—Spinning Rod | GBC—Pistol Grip Baitcast Rod | GCAF—Flipping stick with telescoping handle

Rod Saver
When motoring from one spot to another on a river or lake, always lay your rods flat. If you lean a rod against a sharp edge, the bouncing of the boat may "score" the blank, causing it to break when a fish is on.

SHAKESPEARE RODS

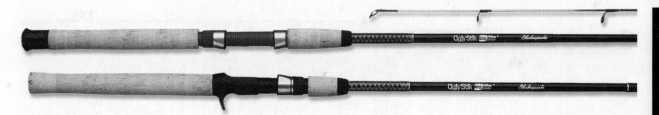

UGLY STIK
LITE FRESHWATER

- Howald Process Triple-Built blank featuring graphite/glass/graphite construction making the Ugly Stik Lite thinner, lighter and more sensitive.
- Exclusive quick-taper Clear Tip® design.

- Top-grade cork handles with conventional reels seats on casting models and twist-lock reel seats with cushioned stainless steel hoods on spinning models.
- Lightweight guides feature black stainless steel frames with durable polished stainless steel inserts.

- Blank-through-handle construction for added strength and sensitivity.
- Fly Rod features aluminum oxide guides, stainless steel snake guides and top-grade cork handles.

MSRP: $39.95 to $59.95

SPECIFICATIONS

Model#	Length	Pcs.	Handle	Action	Lb.-Test	Lure-Wt.-Oz.	Guides
BC1156-1M	5'6"	1	B	M	10-17	¼-⅝	6+Tip
CA1160-1M	6'0"	1	C	M	10-17	¼-⅝	6+Tip
CA1166-1M	6'6"	1	D	M	10-17	¼-⅝	7+Tip
SP1150-1UL	5'0"	1	H	UL	2-6	¹⁄₃₂-¼	4+Tip
SP1150-2UL	5'0"	2	H	UL	2-6	¹⁄₃₂-¼	4+Tip
SP1159-1ML	5'9"	1	H	ML	4-10	¹⁄₁₆-¼	4+Tip
SP1156-2L	5'6"	2	H	L	4-8	¹⁄₃₂-¼	4+Tip
SP1162-1L	6'2"	1	I	L	4-8	⅛-½	5+Tip
SP1160-2M	6'0"	2	I	M	6-15	⅛-⅝	5+Tip
SP1160-1MH	6'0"	1	I	MH	8-17	⅛-¾	5+Tip
SP1166-2M	6'6"	2	I	M	6-15	⅛-⅝	5+Tip
SP1170-2M	7'0"	2	I	M	6-15	⅛-⅝	5+Tip

UL—Ultra-light | L—Light | M—Medium | MH—Medium-heavy | BC—Pistol Grip Baitcast | CA—Straight Handle Casting | FY—Fly Rod | SP—Spinning Rod

Select the Right Action

When buying new rods, consider the size of lures you intend to use when deciding which action is best. For example, smaller topwater lures often work best on a rod with light tip action. Heavy jigs will work best on a long heavy rod.

SHAKESPEARE RODS

XTERRA FRESHWATER

- Graphite composite construction.
- Stainless steel guides with aluminum oxide inserts.
- Graphite twist-lock reel seat.
- Comfortable composite cork rear grip.
- Matte finish with holographic label.

MSRP: $14.99 to $18.99

SPECIFICATIONS

Model#	Length	Pcs.	Handle	Action	Lb.-Test	Lure-Wt.-Oz.	Guides
BC2156-1M	5'6"	1	A	M	8-15	⅛-⅝	4+Tip
CA2160-1MH	6'0"	1	B	MH	10-20	¼-¾	5+Tip
CA2166-1MH	6'6"	1	B	MH	10-20	¼-¾	5+Tip
SC2156-2M	5'6"	2	A	M	6-12	⅛-⅝	4+Tip
SC2160-2M	6'0"	2	A	M	6-12	⅛-¾	4+Tip
SP2150-2UL	5'0"	2	C	UL	2-6	1/32-¼	4+Tip
SP2156-2L	5'6"	2	C	L	4-8	1/16-⅜	4+Tip
SP2160-2M	6'0"	2	D	M	6-12	⅛-½	4+Tip
SP2166-2M	6'6"	2	D	M	6-12	⅛-½	4+Tip
SP2170-2M	7'0"	2	D	M	6-12	⅛-½	5+Tip

UL—Ultra-light | L—Light | M—Medium | MH—Medium-heavy | BC—Pistol Grip Baitcast | CA—Straight Handle Casting | SC—Spincasting | SP—Spinning Rod

The Right Rod Selection Easier Than Ever

Selecting a rod for a specific purpose was once difficult, but many of today's rods are labeled for the technique they are best suited for, such as cranking, flipping, pitching, worming or spinnerbait fishing. These rods have the proper action built into them and the correct range of line sizes is printed on the rod. Match the rod you select with a well-balanced reel, and you're ready to fish.

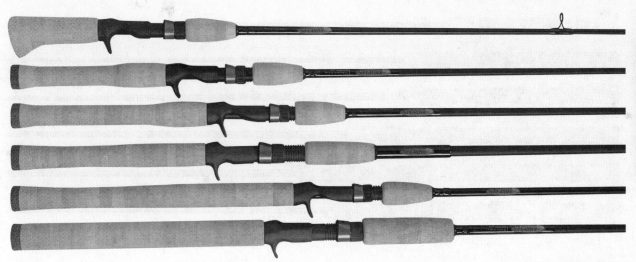

AVID AC60MF, AC66MF, AC70MF BAITCASTING RODS

AVID AC56MF CASTING ROD
SPECIFICATIONS
A classic 5'6" pistol grip casting rod found in the Avid series. The ergonomically-shaped cork handle allows for day-long casting comfort. Great model for fishing docks, topwater, and spinnerbaits. Recommended for 10-17 lb. line and ³⁄₁₆-⁵⁄₈ oz. lures.
MSRP: $140.

AVID AC60MF, AC66MF, AC70MF BAITCASTING RODS
SPECIFICATIONS
Three medium power, fast action baitcasting rods in the Avid series. These 6', 6'6", and 7' rods are rated for 10-17 lb. line and ¼-¾ oz. lures. Applications include plastics, jigs, spinnerbaits and topwater. Very versatile models.
MSRP: $150-155.

AVID AC60MHF, AC66MHF, AC70MHF BAITCASTING RODS
SPECIFICATIONS
Three medium-heavy power, fast action baitcasting rods in the Avid series. These 6', 6'6", and 7' rods are rated for 10-20 lb. line and ³⁄₈-1 oz. lures. Great for jigs, Carolina rigs, spinnerbaits, and fishing in heavy cover.
MSRP: $150-165.

AVID AC610MHF, AC73MHF BAITCASTING RODS
SPECIFICATIONS
This duo of medium-heavy power, fast action Avid telescoping baitcasting rods are 6'10" and 7'3" in length. Rated for 12-25 lb. line and ³⁄₈-1¼ oz. lures, they are ideal for pitching jigs and Carolina rigs.
MSRP: $170.

ST. CROIX RODS

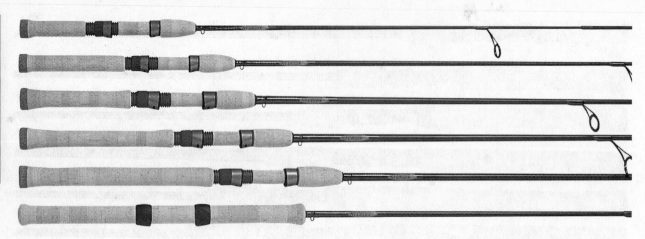

AVID AS60MF, AS66MF, AS70MF SPINNING RODS

AVID AS60MF, AS66MF, AS70MF SPINNING RODS

Specifications

Three medium-power, fast action spinning rods in the Avid series. This trio of 6', 6'6", and 7' rods are rated for 6-12 lb. line and ³⁄₁₆-⅝ oz. lures. Perfect for plastic worms, tubes, and grubs. *MSRP*: $140-160.

AVID AC62MXF ROD

SPECIFICATIONS

A medium-power, extra-fast action Avid series model in a 6'2" length. A perfect rod for fishing topwater lures and smaller spinnerbaits. Rated for 8-14 lb. line and ³⁄₁₆-⅝ oz. lures. Retail is $150.

AVID AC66MM, AC70MM BAITCASTING RODS

SPECIFICATIONS

A pair of medium-power, moderate-action baitcasting rods designed specifically for fishing crankbaits. These 6'6" and 7' rods are rated for 8-14 lb. line with ¼-⅝ oz. lures, and are ideal for small to medium size crankbaits. *MSRP*: AC66MM, $150; AC70MM, $160

AVID AC66MHM, AC70MHM BAITCASTING RODS

SPECIFICATIONS

Two medium-heavy power, moderate action, 6'6" and 7' baitcasting rods designed specifically for fishing crankbaits. Each is rated for 10-20 lb. line, ³⁄₈-1 oz. lures, and are ideal for medium to large crankbaits including deep divers. *MSRP*: $150 and $160 respectively.

AVID AC68MXF BAITCASTING ROD

SPECIFICATIONS

Medium power, extra-fast action baitcasting rod in the Avid series. This 6'8" rod is ideal for plastic worms, tubes, topwater baits, and dropshotting. Designed for 8-14 lb. line and ³⁄₁₆-⅝ oz. lures. *MSRP*: $150.

AVID AC710HF FLIPPING STICK

SPECIFICATIONS

This 7'10" heavy power, fast action flipping stick in the Avid series is ideal for working thick cover with heavy jigs. It's rated for 12-30 lb. line with ½-2 oz. lures. *MSRP*: $175.

RODS

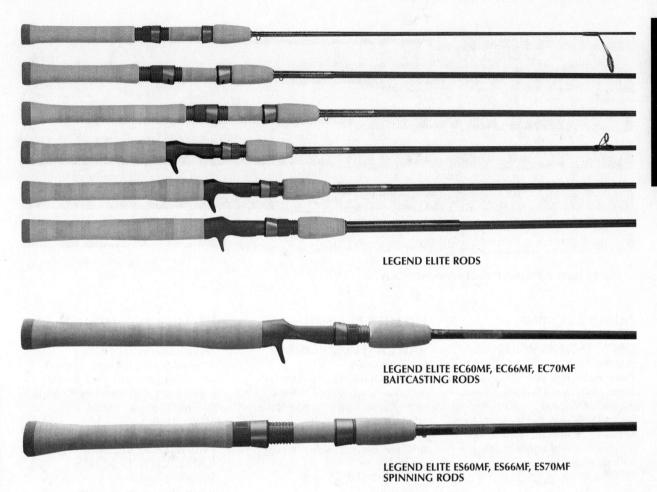

LEGEND ELITE RODS

LEGEND ELITE EC60MF, EC66MF, EC70MF
BAITCASTING RODS

LEGEND ELITE ES60MF, ES66MF, ES70MF
SPINNING RODS

LEGEND ELITE EC60MF, EC66MF, EC70MF BAITCASTING RODS

SPECIFICATIONS

Three medium power, fast action bait-casting rods in the Legend Elite series. These 6', 6'6", and 7' rods are rated for 10-17 lb. line and ¼ - ¾ oz.. lures. Applications include plastics, jigs, spinnerbaits, and topwater. Very versatile models.
MSRP: $290-300.

LEGEND ELITE ES60MF, ES66MF, ES70MF SPINNING RODS

SPECIFICATIONS

A trio of medium power, fast action spinning rods found in the Legend Elite series in 6', 6'6", and 7' lengths.

All three are rated for 6-12 lb. line and ³⁄₁₆-⅝ oz. lures. Great rods for fishing plastic worms, tubes, and grubs.
MSRP: $290-300.

LEGEND ELITE EC66MHF, EC70MHF BAITCASTING RODS

SPECIFICATIONS

Two medium-heavy power, fast action baitcasting rods in the Legend Elite series. Both the 6'6" and 7' model are rated for 10-20 lb. line and ⅜-1 oz. lures. Perfect for jigs, Carolina rigs, spinnerbaits, and fishing in heavy cover.
MSRP: $310.

LEGEND ELITE EC68MXF BAITCASTING ROD

SPECIFICATIONS

Medium power, extra-fast action baitcasting rod in the Legend Elite series. This 6'8" rod won the Outdoor Life Editor's Choice award in May 2002. Excellent for plastic worms, tubes, topwater baits, and dropshotting. Recommended for 8-14 lb. line and ³⁄₁₆-⅝ oz. lures.
MSRP: $300.

ST. CROIX RODS

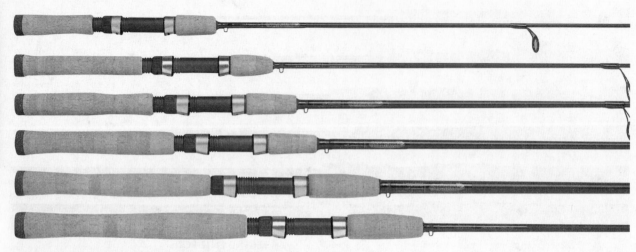

PREMIER PS60MF, PS66MF, PS70MF SPINNING RODS

PREMIER PC60MF, PC66MF, PC70MF BAITCASTING RODS
SPECIFICATIONS
Three medium-power, fast-action baitcasting rods in the Premier series. These 6', 6'6", and 7' rods are rated for 10-17 lb. line and ¼ - ¾ oz. lures. Applications include plastics, jigs, spinnerbaits, and topwater. Very versatile models.
MSRP: $80-90.

PREMIER PS60MF, PS66MF, PS70MF SPINNING RODS
SPECIFICATIONS
Three medium-power, fast-action spinning rods in the Premier series. These rods, in 6', 6'6", and 7' lengths, are rated for 6-12 lb. line and ¼-⅝ oz. lures. Designed for fishing plastic worms, tubes, and grubs.
MSRP: $80-90.

PREMIER PC60MHF, PC66MHF, PC70MHF BAITCASTING RODS
SPECIFICATIONS
Three medium-heavy power, fast-action baitcasting rods in the Premier series. These 6', 6'6", and 7' rods are rated for 10-20 lb. line and ⅜-1 oz. lures. Ideal for jigs, Carolina rigs, spinnerbaits, and fishing in heavy cover.
MSRP: $90-100.

PREMIER PC66MF2, PC66MHF2 BAITCASTING RODS
SPECIFICATIONS
A couple of Premier series baitcasting rods in 6'6" lengths that feature two-piece construction for the traveling bass fisherman. The PC66MF2 is rated for 10-17 lb. line and ¼-¾ oz. lures, while the PC66MHF2 is best with 10-20 lb. line and ⅜-1 oz. lures.
MSRP: $95 and $105 respectively.

PREMIER PC76HF FLIPPING STICK
SPECIFICATIONS
A heavy-power, fast-action Premier series flipping stick. This 7'6" telescoping rod is designed for 12-25 lb. line and ½-1½ oz. lures.
MSRP: $120.

PRO-GLASS GC66M, GC70M BAITCASTING RODS
SPECIFICATIONS
A pair of medium-power, moderate-action baitcasting rods in the Pro-Glass series. The moderate blank actions are ideal for fishing crankbaits. Available in 6'6" and 7' lengths, they are rated for 10-17 lb. line and ¼-¾ oz. lures.
MSRP: $75.

RODS

ABU GARCIA® REELS

ABUMATIC 275 SPINCASTING REEL

AMBASSADEUR ANTI-BACKLASH BAITCASTING REEL

AMBASSADEUR C3 BAITCASTING REELS5500C3 AND 5501C3

ABUMATIC 275 SPINCASTING REEL

Children and adults will appreciate the comfortable fit the Abumatic 275 spincast reel offers. The downsized version of the classic Abumatic also has the ability to handle the light fishing line conditions needed for clear water bass fishing. The Abumatic 275 offers such big reel features as two steel bearings on the drive system providing pure cranking performance. The 4.1:1 gear ratio allows the angler to fish a wide range of lure retrieval speeds. The instant anti-reverse assists with solid hooksets while the multi-disk star drag system lets the angler adjust the drag to match the fish. Dual swing-arm stainless steel pins, instead of the conventional plastic single pin most spincast reels offer, provide certain line release on casts and pick up the line quickly for even winding on the graphite spool. The anodized metal front cover and single piece graphite gearbox deliver years of fishing enjoyment. And there's no backlash with the easy, one-touch casting on the AbuMatic 275. The reel weighs only 8.3 ounces, can be arranged for left and right hand retrieve and is spooled at the factory with 110 yards of 8-pound Berkley Trilene fishing line.

SPECIFICATIONS
Gear Ratio: 4.1:1 *Weight:* 8.3 oz.
Capacity: 110 yards of 8-pound-test monofilament
MSRP: $29.95.

AMBASSADEUR 5000B AND 6000B BAITCASTING REELS

The B-Series Ambassadeurs are available in three sizes, the 5000B, 6000B and 7000B, and have an eye-catching sunset orange finish. The reels feature bushings for low-maintenance upkeep with Swedish cut brass gears and Abu Garcia construction to provide a durable and dependable baitcast reel that can take a lifetime of abuse.

SPECIFICATIONS
Model: 5000B
Gear Ratio: 5.3:1
Line Alarm Clicker: No *Weight:* 9.5 oz.
Capacity: 205 yards of 12-pound test monofilament *Left-hand available:* Yes
Aluminum spool: Yes
MSRP: $59.95

Model: 6000B
Gear Ratio: 5.3:1
Line Alarm Clicker: Yes *Weight:* 10.5 oz.
Capacity: 245 yards of 14-pound test line
Left-hand available: Yes
Aluminum spool: Yes
MSRP: $69.95

Model: 7000B
Gear Ratio: 5.3:1
Line Alarm Clicker: Yes *Weight:* 17.7 oz.
Capacity: 325 yards of 17-pound test monofilament *Left-hand available:* No
Aluminum spool: Yes
MSRP: $109.95

AMBASSADEUR ANTI-BACKLASH BAITCASTING REEL

Simply put, the Anti-Backlash takes the frustration out of baitcasting—backlashes! It's the perfect reel for the anglers who's concerned about a baitcaster's learning curve, yet wants to step up from a spinning or spincast. Unique anti-backlash technology inspires confidence no matter what the conditions, and whenever you're ready for a traditional baitcasting reel, simply switch off the backlash control.

SPECIFICATIONS
Ball bearings: 3 *Gear Ratio:* 5.3:1

Capacity: 205 yards of 12-pound-test monofilament *Weight:* 11.3 oz.
MSRP: $109.95

AMBASSADEUR C3 BAITCASTING REELS

The C3 may be the most widely used baitcaster in the world. It's the standard for baitcasting dependability, thanks to years of continual improvement at the hands of Swedish engineers. Brass and steel, combined with lighter tolerances, make this more than a working man's reel. It's an heirloom.

SPECIFICATIONS
Model: 4600C3 and 4601C3
Gear Ratio: 5.3:1
Capacity: 170 yards of 10-pound-test monofilament *Weight:* 9.2 oz.
MSRP: $69.95

Model: 5500C3 and 5501C3
Gear Ratio: 5.3:1
Capacity: 205 yards of 12-pound-test monofilament *Weight:* 9.5 oz.
MSRP: $69.95

Model: 6500C3 and 6501C3
Gear Ratio: 5.3:1
Capacity: 245 yards of 14-pound-test monofilament *Weight:* 10.5 oz.
MSRP: $79.95

Model: 7000C3
Gear Ratio: 4.1:1
Capacity: 325 yards of 17-pound-test monofilament *Weight:* 17.8 oz.
MSRP: $169.95

Model: LD6600C3
Gear Ratio: 5.3:1
Capacity: 245 yards of 14-pound-test monofilament *Weight:* 14.6 oz.
MSRP: $164.95

REELS

AMBASSADEUR C3
BAITCASTING REEL
WITH LINE COUNTER

AMBASSADEUR C4
BAITCASTING REELS
5600C4

AMBASSADEUR C4
BAITCASTING REELS
6500C4

AMBASSADEUR C3 BAITCASTING REEL WITH LINE COUNTER

The Ambassadeur® 6500C3 LC reel is equipped with the new Abu Garcia line counter, located on the end opposite the crank handle and star drag. The water-proof sealed unit is built for fresh and salt water conditions. All controls for setting zero and operating the menu of the line counter are easy to use. For many anglers, it is a matter of setting to zero and fishing.

Sophisticated line counter users will appreciate how easy it is to program their unit to accommodate line type and size and spool fill. The menu walks the angler through a short series of options to adjust the line counter for the type of line being used, the line's size and even for spool fill. Now line is accurately measured and displayed in either feet or meters on the electronic LCD readout.

The battery-operated line counter works up to a year on an over-the-counter watch battery available everywhere. The unit has a battery-saving automatic shut-off feature. Night anglers will appreciate the line counter's backlight.

The smooth casting 6500C3 reel features Instant Anti-Reverse and aluminum spool.

REEL SPECIFICATIONS
Gear Ratio: 5.3:1
Bearings: 3 stainless steel
Capacity: 245 yards of 14-pound test monofilament
MSRP: $139.95

AMBASSADEUR C4 BAITCASTING REELS

The legendary toughness you expect from the C series, yet with varying gear ratios to perfectly tune retrieval speed. The high-speed C4 is ideal for buzzbaits, spinnerbaits and rattle baits. The C4 Winch features a lower gear ratio perfect for crankbaits or slower retrieves. Instant anti-reverse and on-slip spool, featured on both the C4 and C4 Winch, provide solid hooking power. Each reel in the series has four ball bearings.

SPECIFICATIONS
Model: 4600C4
Gear Ratio: 6.3:1
Capacity: 170 yards of 10-pound-test monofilament
Weight: 9.6 oz.
MSRP: $84.95

Model: 4601C4
Gear Ratio: 6.3:1
Capacity: 170 yards of 10-pound-test monofilament
Weight: 9.6 oz.
MSRP: $84.95

Model: 5600C4
Gear Ratio: 6.3:1
Capacity: 205 yards of 12-pound-test monofilament
Weight: 10.6 oz.
MSRP: $84.95

Model: 5601C4
Gear Ratio: 6.3:1
Capacity: 205 yards of 12-pound-test monofilament
Weight: 10.6 oz.
MSRP: $84.95

Model: 6500C4
Gear Ratio: 6.3:1
Capacity: 245 yards of 14-pound-test monofilament
Weight: 11.3oz.
MSRP: $94.95

Model: 6501C4
Gear Ratio: 6.3:1
Capacity: 245 yards of 14-pound-test monofilament
Weight: 11.3 oz.
MSRP: $94.95

Model: 4600C4W
Gear Ratio: 3.8:1
Capacity: 170 yards of 10-pound-test monofilament
Weight: 9.6 oz.
MSRP: $84.95

Model: 4601C4W
Gear Ratio: 3.8:1
Capacity: 170 yards of 10-pound-test monofilament
Weight: 9.6 oz.
MSRP: $84.95

Model: 5600C4W
Gear Ratio: 3.8:1
Capacity: 205 yards of 12-pound-test monofilament
Weight: 10.6 oz.
MSRP: $84.95

Model: 5601C4W
Gear Ratio: 3.8:1
Capacity: 205 yards of 12-pound-test monofilament
Weight: 10.6 oz.
MSRP: $84.95

ABU GARCIA® REELS

AMBASSADEUR C5 MAG-X BAITCASTING REELS 5600C5 MAG-X

AMBASSADEUR EON BAITCASTING REELS E5600 AND E501

AMBASSADEUR EON™ PRO BAITCASTING REEL

AMBASSADEUR C5 MAG-X BAITCASTING REELS

The newest incarnation of the legendary C series. A convenient magnetic brake has been added to fine-tune outgoing spool friction and significantly lessen the possibility of overrun, especially when casting lighter baits. The five-bearing construction results in the smoothest casting C series reel yet.

SPECIFICATIONS

Model: 4600C5 MAG-X
Gear Ratio: 5.3:1
Capacity: 170 yards of 10-pound-test monofilament
Weight: 10.0 oz.
MSRP: $99.95

Model: 5600C5 MAG-X
Gear Ratio: 5.3:1
Capacity: 205 yards of 12-pound-test monofilament
Weight: 10.6 oz.
MSRP: $99.95

AMBASSADEUR EON BAITCASTING REELS

In-line planetary gears distribute cranking power through five gears, giving you the ability to cast, retrieve and control a lure unlike anything you've ever experienced. The unique design allows for the convenient repositioning of the drag and brakes, and the free-floating levelwind reduces outgoing line friction for smoother casting.

SPECIFICATIONS

Model: E3600 and E3601
Ball bearings: 4
Gear Ratio: 6.3:1
Capacity: 105 yards of 12–pound-test monofilament
Weight: 10 oz.
MSRP: $119.95

Model: E5600 and E501
Ball bearings: 4
Gear Ratio: 6.3:1
Capacity: 175 yards of 12–pound-test monofilament
Weight: 10 oz.
MSRP: $119.95

Model: E6600 and E6601
Ball bearings: 4
Gear Ratio: 6.3:1
Capacity: 195 yards of 14–pound-test monofilament
Weight: 10 oz.
MSRP: $129.95

AMBASSADEUR EON™ PRO BAITCASTING REEL

Abu Garcia has taken the popular EON baitcast reel, ICAST winner when introduced, and with added features created the new EON Pro. The EON Pro is also a winner of the ICAST Best New Reel Award and the smoothest operating baitcast reel on the market.

The unique advanced design of the original EON has been taken a few steps forward with the new premium EON Pro. The hybrid shape, a cross between a round barrel and low profile shape, is more comfortable to grip than any other baitcast reel. The planetary gears, a pinion gear surrounded by three orbital gears and a large ring gear gives the reel a totally different cranking scheme. As a result, the cranking handle is inline with the spool. This handle placement allows for oversized graphite impregnated Teflon drag washers with an easy to use oversized ribbed aluminum drag adjustment ring.

The new EON Pro is built for serious anglers with magnesium and graphite construction for lightweight durable performance for a lifetime of fishing. InfiniSpool® is added for the smoothest operation and longest casting ever. Even the spool has bearings with this technology. This results in lightweight, long-lasting reels that can handle the lightest of lures.

SPECIFICATIONS

Gear Ratio: 6.2:1
Weight: 8.47 oz.
Capacity: 105 yards of 12-pound test monofilament
MSRP: $419.95.

AMBASSADEUR
MORRUM
BAITCASTING
REELS
M5600C

AMBASSADEUR
MÖRRUM® IVCB
BAITCASTING REEL

AMBASSADEUR
STAR SERIES
FIVE STAR

AMBASSADEUR TGC
BAITCASTING REELS
TGC5000C AND
TGC5001C

AMBASSADEUR MORRUM BAITCASTING REELS

The Morrum employs the height in Swedish engineering for the kind of smoothness serious envy is made of. If you demand the ultimate in performance and durability, Morrum deserves a long, hard look. Anti-distortion spool (ADS) technology and ultra-tight tolerances keep the spool and bearings perfectly aligned for a precise, solid feel.

SPECIFICATIONS
Model: M5600C
Gear Ratio: 5.1:1
Capacity: 175 yards of 14-pound-test monofilament
Weight: 11.5 oz.
MSRP: $219.95

Model: M6600C
Gear Ratio: 5.1:1
Capacity: 220 yards of 17-pound-test monofilament
Weight: 12.4 oz.
MSRP: $229.95

AMBASSADEUR MÖRRUM® IVCB BAITCASTING REEL

Mörrum IVCB reels provide ultimate braking control with the new infinity variable centrifugal brake (IVCB) system. A control dial on the end cap adjusts the brakes by actually moving the brakes in and out for precision tension control. The reel features five Instant Anti-Reverse, stainless steel bearings to create smooth cranking power and a balanced aluminum spool for long accurate casts.

SPECIFICATIONS
Gear Ratio: 6.3:1
Weight: 7.2 oz.
Capacity: 155 yards of 10-pound test monofilament
MSRP: $339.95.

AMBASSADEUR STAR SERIES

Rugged, dependable and versatile, the Star series have a non-slip aluminum spool and a mult-disc star drag to protect your line from breakage no matter what the technique. The Siz Star includes a line-out alarm.

SPECIFICATIONS
Model: FIVE STAR
Gear ratio: 5.3:1
Capacity: 205 yards of 12–pound-test monofilament
Weight: 9.5 oz.
MSRP: $54.95

Model: SIX STAR
Gear ratio: 5.3:1
Capacity: 245 yards of 14–pound-test monofilament

Weight: 10.3 oz.
MSRP: $64.95

AMBASSADEUR TGC BAITCASTING REELS

Modeled after the legendary C series, this one-bearing baitcaster proves it's truly possible to get something great for a great price.

SPECIFICATIONS
Model: TGC4000c
Gear Ratio: 5.3:1
Capacity: 170 yards of 10-pound-test monofilament
Weight: 9.5 oz.
MSRP: $54.95

Model: TGC5000C and TGC5001C
Gear Ratio: 5.3:1
Capacity: 205 yards of 12-pound-test monofilament
Weight: 9.9 oz.
MSRP: $54.95

Model: TGC6000C
Gear Ratio: 5.3:1
Capacity: 245 yards of 14-pound-test monofilament
Weight: 10.5 oz.
MSRP: $59.95

ABU GARCIA® REELS

**CARDINAL® 100 SERIES
SPINNING REELS
103 AND 103R**

CARDINAL® 100 SERIES SPINNING REELS

Three ball bearings for smooth operation and long lasting brass pinion gear give the Cardinal 100 Series of reels the feel of more expensive models offered by the competition. Line twists are eliminated with the oversized line roller and the aluminum-skirted spool prevents line tangles under the spool. Other standard features on the 100 Series include a durable graphite body, Instant Anti-Reverse for positive hook sets and aluminum handle that folds away for convenient storage and is finished with a comfortable soft-touch knob. Anglers can choose between a front or rear precision-click drag. Both drag adjustment locations are positioned for easy-to-reach drag tension changes even with a fighting fish on the line. Each Cardinal 100 has an attractive metallic silver and blue finish.

SPECIFICATIONS
Model: 100U
Weight: 6.3 oz.
Capacity: 80 yards of 4-pound test monofilament

Model: 101
Weight: 9 oz.
Capacity: 175 yards of 6-pound test

Model: 102 and 102R
Weight: 9.5 oz.

Capacity: 175 yards of 8-pound test

Model: 103 and 103R
Weight: 10.1 oz.
Capacity: 160 yards of 10-pound test line

Model: 104 and 104R
Weight: 12.2 oz.
Capacity: 180 yards of 12-pound test line

Model: 105 and 105R
Weight: 12.8 oz.
Capacity: 320 yards of 12-pound test line

Model: 106
Weight: 12.8 oz.
Capacity: 245 yards of 14-pound test monofilament

MSRP (all reels in series): $34.95

CARDINAL® 300 SERIES SPINNING REELS

The Cardinal 300 spinning reels are designed to give the angler a comfortable fishing reel with the confidence to cast long and accurately. Five bearings and a brass pinion gear provide a smooth operation that can be depended on for a lifetime of fishing. Line twists are eliminated with the oversized line roller and line tangles under the spool are no longer a problem with the aluminum skirted spool. Instant Anti-Reverse comes in handy

for positive hook sets. Changing the drag tension, even in the midst of fighting a chunky fish, is easy with the precision-click front drag. The reversible aluminum handle is finished with a comfortable soft-touch knob. The graphite body is built tough.

SPECIFICATIONS
Model: 300U
Gear Ratio: 5.1:1
Weight: 6.3 oz.
Capacity: 100 yards of 4-pound test monofilament

Model: 301
Gear Ratio: 5.1:1
Weight: 7.7 oz.
Capacity: 110 yards of 6-pound test monofilament

Model: 302
Gear Ratio: 5.1:1
Weight: 10.2 oz.
Capacity: 175 yards of 6-pound test monofilament

Model: 303
Gear Ratio: 5.1:1
Weight: 10.8 oz.
Capacity: 180 yards of 8-pound test monofilament.

MSRP (all reels in the series): $44.95 (includes a spare graphite spool.)

CARDINAL® 500 SERIES SPINNING REELS

Every Cardinal 500 reel is built with the features anglers depend on for a full day of hassle-free fishing. Built to last a lifetime, Cardinal 500 reels start with a graphite body. The six-bearing drive and brass pinion provide smooth and reliable operation cast after cast. The oversized line roller prevents line twist and fatigue during take up and the anodized aluminum is performance for feather light comfort & performance. The easy to reach precision-click front drag lets the angler adjust the reel's operation to fit the ever-changing conditions while fighting fish. Instant Anti-Reverse comes in handy for positive hook sets. The reversible aluminum handle is finished with a sure-grip wooden knob. The handle features one-touch folding. The metallic champagne reels with gold accents are available in three sizes.

SPECIFICATIONS
Model: 501
Gear Ratio: 5.1:1
Weight: 7.7-oz.
Capacity: 110 yards of 6-pound test monofilament

Model: 502
Gear Ratio: 5.1:1
Weight: 10.2 oz.
Capacity: 175 yards of 6-pound test monofilament

Model: 504
Gear Ratio: 5.1:1
Weight: 11.4 oz.
Capacity: 210 yards of 10-pound test monofilament
MSRP (all reels in the series): $54.95 (includes a spare painted graphite spool)

CARDINAL® 600 SERIES SPINNING REELS

The Cardinal 600 combines an outstanding appearance with the latest technology that delivers an extremely strong reel that is 20% lighter than comparable reels. The Cardinal 600 features the patented Stamina drag system, with 240 percent more drag surface than conventional drags. Located at the base of the spool, the easy-access Stamina drags produce 35 percent less heat than competitive models. The smooth and powerful drag is created with multi-disc Teflon and graphite with stainless components.

The one-piece aluminum stem/gear box maintains gear alignment for the life of the reel. Five, bearings enhance the reels ultra-smooth performance. Line is evenly placed on the spool with the even-line-lay oscillation system. The oversized line roller prevents line twist and fatigue during take up.

Each reel comes with the Mega-Distance™ casting system, including an aluminum spool with the quick-disconnect feature. Spools are skirted to prevent line tangles along the shaft. Anglers will appreciate powerful hooksetting advantage of the Instant Anti-Reverse, which can instantly be turned off or on, and the EZ Access gearing. Removing only three screws allows easy maintenance without losing gear alignment. The reversible aluminum handle is finished with a comfortable soft touch knob.

SPECIFICATIONS
Model: 600U
Gear Ratio: 4.8:1
Weight: 6 oz.
Capacity: 100 yards of 4-pound-test monofilament
MSRP: $54.95

Model: 602
Gear Ratio: 5.1:1
Weight: 7.8 oz.
Capacity: 110 yards of 8-pound test monofilament.
MSRP: $54.95

CARDINAL AGENDA SPINNING REELS

Instant anti-reverse and a front drag give you the confidence to excel in any situation, while an oversized line roller reduces line twist and fatigue.

SPECIFICATIONS
Model: AGULF
Gear ratio: 5.2:1
Capacity: 80 yards of 4–pound-test monofilament
Weight: 6.3 oz.
MSRP: $34.95

CARDINAL AGENDA SPINNING REELS

Model: AG1F
Gear ratio: 5.2:1
Capacity: 130 yards of 8–pound-test monofilament
Weight: 9.0 oz.
MSRP: $34.95

Model: AG2F
Gear ratio: 5.2:1
Capacity: 140 yards of 10–pound-test monofilament
Weight: 9.5 oz.
MSRP: $34.95

Model: AG3F
Gear ratio: 5.2:1
Capacity: 130 yards of 12–pound-test monofilament
Weight: 10.1 oz.
MSRP: $34.95

Model: AG4F
Gear ratio: 5.2:1
Capacity: 140 yards of 14–pound-test monofilament
Weight: 12.2 oz.
MSRP: $34.95

Model: AG5F
Gear ratio: 5.2:1
Capacity: 250 yards of 14–pound-test monofilament
Weight: 12.8 oz.
MSRP: $34.95

Model: AG6F
Gear ratio: 5.2:1
Capacity: 250 yards of 17–pound-test monofilament
Weight: 13.2 oz.
MSRP: $34.95

ABU GARCIA® REELS

CARDINAL
ASCENT
SPINNING
REELS
ASUL

CARDINAL
ENDEUR
EN2F

SUVERAN SPINNING REELS
S200M

CARDINAL ASCENT SPINNING REELS

Four bearings keep the Ascent spinning reel moving free of friction for the smooth dependability you can bet a fishing trip on. Instant anti-reverse gives you solid hooksets, and if you'd rather backreel than play the fish with the Ascent's burly front drag, simply switch the instant anti-reverse off. Four ball bearings. Spare spool included.

SPECIFICATIONS
Model: ASUL
Gear ratio: 5.2:1
Capacity: 80 yards of 4–pound-test monofilament
Weight: 6.3 oz.
MSRP: $44.95

Model: AS1F
Gear ratio: 5.2:1
Capacity: 130 yards of 8–pound-test monofilament
Weight: 9 oz.
MSRP: $44.95

Model: AS2F
Gear ratio: 5.2:1
Capacity: 140 yards of 10–pound-test monofilament
Weight: 9.5 oz.
MSRP: $44.95

Model: AS3F
Gear ratio: 5.2:1
Capacity: 130 yards of 12–pound-test monofilament
Weight: 10.1 oz.
MSRP: $44.95

CARDINAL ENDEUR

The Cardinal Endeur is ultralight, ultra-smmoth, with five bearings and AccuBalanced rotor. A perforated, anodized aluminum spool keeps the reel featherlight, your arm fresh and reaction time to a minimum. Instant Anti-Reverse gives you confident hooksets every time. A multi-disc front drag gives you the power to turn any fish. And the oversized line roller reduces line twist. Spare spool included.

SPECIFICATIONS
Model: EN1F
Gear ratio: 5.2:1
Capacity: 130 yards of 8–pound-test monofilament
Weight: 9 oz.
MSRP: $54.95

Model: EN2F
Gear ratio: 5.2:1
Capacity: 140 yards of 10–pound-test monofilament
Weight: 9.5 oz.
MSRP: $54.95

Model: EN4F
Gear ratio: 5.2:1
Capacity: 140 yards of 14–pound-test monofilament
Weight: 12.2 oz.
MSRP: $54.95

SUVERAN SPINNING REELS

Suveran is the first spinning reel with the drag repositioned in the center. This convenient location helps put the brakes on a running bass by giving you the power to make split-second precision tuning of the drag pressure. Magnum drag washers dissipate heat without pulsating. A sturdy, one-piece gearbox helps prevent gear torque, and seven ball bearings ensure lasting smoothness.

SPECIFICATIONS
Model: S200M
Gear Ratio: 5.2:1
Capacity: 120 yards of 8-pound-test monofilament
Weight: 12.8 oz.
MSRP: $219.95

Model: S400M
Gear Ratio: 5.2:1
Capacity: 180 yards of 8-pound-test monofilament
Weight: 13.6 oz.
MSRP: $21.9.95

www.StoegerIndustries.com

REELS

**TÖRNO ™
BAITCASTING REELS
3003**

**TÖRNO™ BAITCASTING
REELS WITH
INFINISPOOL®
3006 HSI**

TÖRNO ™
BAITCASTING REELS

The Törno low-profile baitcast reels are designed with state-of-the-art Swedish technology and an ergonomic shape for comfort. Törno reels palm better and feel great while casting, cranking and fighting fish. Three Törno baitcast reels are available. All feature Instant Anti-Reverse, aluminum spools, easy-out spool system, comfort thumb bars, star drag, a ceramic insert in the level wind guide and a one-piece polymeric body with internal aluminum support. Törno low profile baitcasters are equipped with crowned precision-cut worm gears. Törno reels have a line capacity of 105 yards of 12-pound test line.

SPECIFICATIONS
Model: 3003
Gear Ratio: 5.3:1
Weight: 9 oz.
Bearings: 3 stainless-steel Swedish construction bearings
Features: centrifugal brakes and soft-touch rubber grips on the cranking handle
MSRP: $89.95

Model: 3004HS
Gear Ratio: 6.3:1
Weight: 9.1 oz.
Bearings: 4 stainless steel Swedish construction bearings
Features: externally-adjusted magnetic brakes and soft-touch rubber grips
MSRP: $109.95

Model: 3006HS
Gear Ratio: 6.3:1
Weight: 9.1 oz.
Bearings: 6 stainless-steel Swedish construction bearings
Features: externally-adjusted magnetic brakes and ergonomically-designed crank handle grips
MSRP: $129.95

TÖRNO™ BAITCASTING
REELS WITH INFINISPOOL®

Törno reels with InfiniSpool have premium reel features, including Ballant C treatment on the crowned internal hardened-brass gears, precision-cut worm gears and aluminum V-spool for enhanced casting. Abu Garcia InfiniSpool has been developed jointly with SKF, a leading bearing manufacturer. The patented design results in the smoothest operating spool possible. The free-spinning spool gives long smooth cast time after time, even with the lightest jigs. Both models are built on a one-piece polymeric body and feature externally-adjusted magnetic brakes, a ceramic insert in the level wind, comfort thumb bars and Instant Anti-Reverse.

SPECIFICATIONS
Model: 3004 HSI
Gear Ratio: 6.3: 1
Weight: 9.1 oz.
Bearings: 4
Grips: Soft Touch
MSRP: $149.95

Model: 3006 HSI
Gear Ratio: 6.3:1
Weight: 9.1 oz.
Bearings: 6
Grips: Ergonomic
MSRP: $169.95

Use Mono Backing With Superlines
When spooling a reel with one of today's superlines, it helps to add a short length of monofilament backing between the superline and the reel spool to keep the superline from slipping on the spool.

CABELA'S REELS

REELS

**ALL-PRO
BAITCASTING REEL**

**BLACK LABEL II
BAITCASTING REEL**

**CLASSIC
BAITCASTING REEL**

ALL-PRO BAITCASTING REEL

For the cost-conscious angler who wants a quality baitcasting reel but doesn't want to drop a pile of money, we offer a low-profile, one-piece graphite frame reel. Magnetic anti-backlash and flipping switch.
Specifications
Gear ratio: 5.1:1
Line capacity: 150 yds./10 lb.
Weight: 8.6 oz.
Available: Left or Right Hand.
MSRP: $29.99

BLACK LABEL II BAITCASTING REEL

Every component on this workhorse has been tested to the extreme to ensure its durability and dependability under any circumstance. Torque-resistant frame. Brass main and pinion gears. One-way anti-reverse, aluminum spool and handle. Magnetic cast control. Thumb-bar/flippin' feature. Aluminum oxide line guide. Available Right or Left Hand.
Specifications
Gear ratio: 5.1:1
Ball bearings: 6
Line capacity: 100 yds./12 lb.
Weight: 9.5 oz.
MSRP: $49.99

CLASSIC BAITCASTING REEL

With a superior design and outstanding features, this reel deserves to be called a classic. The frame and spool are constructed of machine-cut anodized aluminum for exceptional strength and lasting reliability. An Unlimited Anti-Reverse™ eliminates handle play for rock-solid hooksets. And the cast control adjustment combines with a Spool Inertia Brake™ for precise casting in all conditions. Convenient star drag and super-smooth Teflon washers ensure even drag performance. The Titanium-Shielded™ line guide protects your line from damaging abrasion.
Specifications
Model: CL-100
Gear ratio: 5.6:1
Ball bearings: 4
Line capacity: 150/10
Weight: 11.2 oz.
Price: $49.99

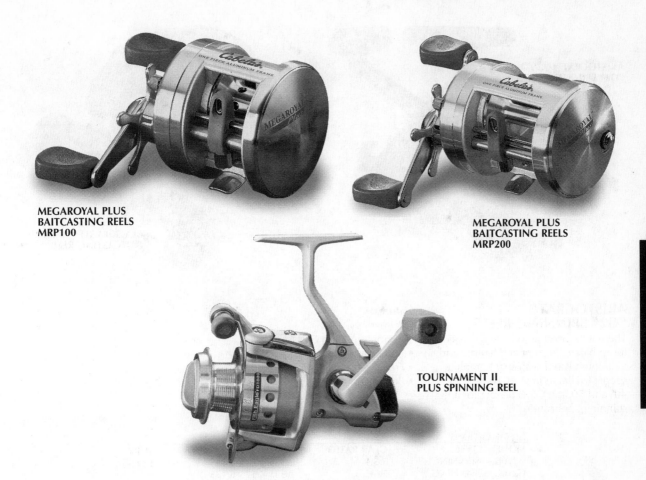

**MEGAROYAL PLUS
BAITCASTING REELS
MRP100**

**MEGAROYAL PLUS
BAITCASTING REELS
MRP200**

**TOURNAMENT II
PLUS SPINNING REEL**

MEGAROYAL PLUS BAITCASTING REELS

Megaroyal Plus reels take the tournament-tested reliability of Cabela's popular Megaroyal reels and add even more performance-enhancing features—without the high-performance cost. Features include: all-new titanium line guide; titanium-coated spool; multi-disc drag system; comfortable, non-slip thumb bar; sleek one-piece aluminum frame; and high-performance ball bearing system.

SPECIFICATIONS
Model: MRP100
Gear ratio: 5.2:1
Ball bearings: 6
Line capacity: 125/12
Weight: 10.5 oz.
MSRP: $89.99

Model: MRP101 (left-handed)
Gear ratio: 5.2:1
Ball bearings: 6
Line capacity: 125/12
Weight: 10.5 oz.
MSRP: $89.99

**Model: MRP200
(features reel clicker)**
Gear ratio: 5.2:1
Ball bearings: 6
Line capacity: 185/20
Weight: 12.2 oz.
MSRP: $89.99

TOURNAMENT II PLUS SPINNING REEL

The unmatched precision of our Fish Eagle Tournament II Plus reel begins with a one-piece aluminum body that keeps the gears and drive train held solidly in place for superior strength and lasting reliability. Instant anti-reverse and a one-way clutch bearing provide rock-solid hook sets. The machined aluminum spool is ported to reduce weight without affecting strength. A titanium coating on the spool lip and line roller reduces wear and friction during line pay-out and retrieve and greatly increases the life of your line. Nine ball bearings (8 BB + 1 roller) provide silky-smooth operation. The fold-down, one-touch handle allows for convenient, compact travel and storage. Spare aluminum spool included. Four models from which to choose.
MSRP: $69.99

EAGLE CLAW® REELS

ARISTOCRAT™
"G2" SPINNING REELS

BLACK EAGLE™ BRBC10
BAITCASTING REEL

ARISTOCRAT™ "G2" SPINNING REELS

The new 2 bearing XG™ series features: balanced rotor and handle and aluminum spool with spare graphite spool. Available in sizes 10, 20, 30, 40, and 50, the G2 is perfect for any spinning application.

Features:
- 2 Bearings
- Aluminum Long Cast Spool
- Balanced Handle
- Free Graphite Spool
- Balanced Rotor

SPECIFICATIONS

MODEL	TYPE	GEAR RATIO	LINE SIZE	MSRP
G210B	SPINNING	5.5:1	2/335-4/175-6/135	$20.95
G210C	SPINNING	5.5:1	2/335-4/175-6/135	$20.95
G220B	SPINNING	5.5:1	6/195-8/135-10/115	$21.95
G220C	SPINNING	5.5:1	6/195-8/135-10/115	$21.95
G230B	SPINNING	5.5:1	8/220-10/200-12/180	$22.95
G230C	SPINNING	5.5:1	8/220-10/200-12/180	$22.95
G240B	SPINNING	5.5:1	10/270-12/250-14/220	$23.95
G240C	SPINNING	5.5:1	10/270-12/250-14/220	$23.95
G250B	SPINNING	5.1:1	10/250-12/230-14/180	$24.95
G250C	SPINNING	5.1:1	10/250-12/230-14/180	$24.95

BLACK EAGLE™ BRBC10 BAITCASTING REEL

The low profile Black Eagle baitcast reel makes baitcasting fun and effortless. Featuring magnetic spool control, ball bearing smoothness and level wind guide system.

Features:
- 1 Ball Bearing
- Magnetic Spool Control
- Level Wind Guide System
- One-Piece Graphite Frame
- Adjustable Star Drago

SPECIFICATIONS

MODEL	TYPE	GEAR RATIO	WEIGHT	LINE SIZE	MSRP
BRBC10B	BAITCAST	5.1:1	8.5 oz.	8/170-10/150-12/100	$35.95

GOLD EAGLE™ SPINNING REELS

"XG"™ SPINNING REELS

GOLD EAGLE™ SPINNING REELS

The new Gold Eagle™ reel is an exceptional value. With an aluminum spool, one ball bearing, and balanced handle, the front drag Gold Eagle™ comes in sizes 10, 20, 30, 40, and 50.

Features:
- One Bearing
- Aluminum Spool
- Balanced Handle
- Front Drag

SPECIFICATIONS

MODEL	TYPE	GEAR RATIO	LINE SIZE	MSRP
GE110B	SPINNING	5.5:1	2/370-4/235	$15.45
GE110C	SPINNING	5.5:1	2/370-4/235	$15.45
GE120B	SPINNING	5.5:1	4/330-6/215-8/160	$15.95
GE120C	SPINNING	5.5:1	4/330-6/215-8/160	$15.95
GE130B	SPINNING	4.5:1	8/205-10/185-12/100	$16.95
GE130C	SPINNING	4.5:1	8/205-10/185-12/100	$16.95
GE140B	SPINNING	4.5:1	10/185-12/105-15/95	$17.95
GE140C	SPINNING	4.5:1	10/185-12/105-15/95	$17.95
GE150B	SPINNING	4.5:1	10/285-12/180-15/150	$18.95
GE150C	SPINNING	4.5:1	10/285-12/180-15/150	$18.95

"XG"™ SPINNING REELS

The new 6 bearing XG™ series of spinning reels feature one-way clutch for instant anti-reverse, balanced rotor, one touch handle, aluminum spool with free graphite spool. Available in sizes 20, 30, and 40, the XG™ is perfect for any spinning application.

Features:
- 6 Bearings
- One Way Clutch
- Aluminum Long Cast Spool
- Sensi-touch Drag
- Free Graphite Spool
- Balanced Rotor

SPECIFICATIONS

MODEL	TYPE	GEAR RATIO	LINE SIZE	MSRP
XG620B	SPINNING	5.5:1	6/195-8/135-10/115	$39.95
XG620C	SPINNING	5.5:1	6/195-8/135-10/115	$39.95
XG630B	SPINNING	5.5:1	8/220-10/200-12/180	$39.95
XG630C	SPINNING	5.5:1	8/220-10/200-12/180	$39.95
XG640B	SPINNING	5.5:1	10/270-12/250-14/220	$39.95
XG640C	SPINNING	5.5:1	10/270-12/250-14/220	$39.95

JOHNSON REELS

CENTURY REELS
C100B

CENTURY REELS
C100BDLX

JAVELIN GOLD
BAITCASTING
REEL
JG-SC

JAVELIN
BAITCASTING
REEL
J-SC

CENTURY REELS

Not only is this the reel your dad grew up with, it's the reel the industry went to school on. Simple. Rugged. All-metal. Now it's back with its classic design, robust construction and trouble-free performance. You won't find any tinny metal or brittle plastics here – this reel is made to last a lifetime. Features include full-metal construction, precision metal gears, die-cast metal spool, Infinite-setting top-mounted slipping-spool drag, exclusive over/under retrieve. Pre-spooled with 10 lb. mono.

SPECIFICATIONS
Model: C100B
Gear ratio: 3.6:1
Capacity: 10 lb./60 yds.
Bearings: 0
Weight: 11 oz.
MSRP: $24.95

Model: C100BDLX
Gear ratio: 3.1:1
Capacity: 10 lb./60 yds.
Bearings: 1
Weight: 11 oz.
MSRP: $29.95

JAVELIN BAITCASTING REEL
Features:
- Precision-bearing operation for smooth handling.
- Dual-roller pickup pins ensure instant line pick-up for better response and reduced line wear.
- Large crank handle for fighting leverage.
- Star drag is easy-to-adjust, even during a battle.
- Pre-spooled with 8-lb. mono.

SPECIFICATIONS
Model: J-SC
Gear ratio: 3.3:1
Capacity: 8 lb./80 yds.
Bearings: 1
MSRP: $24.95

JAVELIN GOLD BAITCASTING REEL
Features:
- Triple-bearing system provides the smoothest, most trouble-free spincast handling you've ever experienced.
- Instant anti-reverse for bone-jarring hook sets.
- Twin roller pickup pins collect the line instantly and reliably, resulting in faster response time and decreased line wear.
- Big, easy-to-use star drag adjusts to match your fish and conditions.
- Pre-spooled with 10 lb. mono

SPECIFICATIONS
Model: JG-SC
Gear ratio: 3.3:1
Capacity: 10 lb./65 yds.
Bearings: 3
Weight: 9.2 oz.
MSRP: $24.95

REELS

MAXXUM
PRO REEL

TANGLEFREE™
SPINCAST REELST
F10M

TANGLEFREE™
SPINCAST REELS
TF20M

MAXXUM PRO REEL

The Maxxum Pro is the future of large capacity spincast reels. It holds an incredible 150 yards of 20 pound mono so you're always ready for the big ones. The sleek body-forward design allows easy access to the casting button for any size hands. Performance-engineered for unparalleled fishing. Inside the Maxxum Pro are precision-cut brass helical pinion for durability, twin pick-up pins, and dual bearings.

Features:

- Dual pick-up pins for ultra quick engagement
- Infinite anti-reverse
- Titanium Nitride line guide for smooth pinpoint casts
- Twin bearings provide fluid retrieves
- Oscillating spool design with 150 yards of 20 pound mono
- Sleek, comfortable body forward design
- Polished aluminum cover

Specifications

Gear ratio: 4.1:1
Capacity: 20 lb./150 yds.
Bearings: 2
Weight: 12.5 oz.
MSRP: $34.95

TANGLEFREE™ SPINCAST REELS

The newly-redesigned Tanglefree reels make line twists and tangles a bad memory. The high-tech Drivetrain Drag System eliminates line twists and tangles and lets you focus on what's important—catching fish. Johnson's exclusive DriveTrain drag prevents line from twisting against the drag once a fish is hooked. It's one of the great innovations in the history of reels.

Features:

- Heavy-duty composite frame
- Exclusive Drivetrain Drag™ System with easy-to-adjust star drag wheel
- Ball-bearing Camdrive™ improves cranking power
- Low friction roller pick-up pin

SPECIFICATIONS

Model: TF10M
Gear ratio: 3.4:1
Capacity: 10 lb./65 yds.
Bearings: 1
Weight: 7.7 oz.
MSRP: $14.95

Model: TF20M
Gear ratio: 3.4:1
Capacity: 14 lb./85 yds.
Bearings: 1
Weight: 10.8 oz.
MSRP: $16.95

LEW'S REELS

BB® SPEED SPOOL® BAITCASTING REELS B19GS

BB® SPEED SPOOL® BAITCASTING REELS BB25SW

BB® SPEED SPOOL® BAITCASTING REELS BB25SS

GOLD SPEED SPIN® SPINNING REELS GSS2F

GOLD SPEED SPIN® SPINNING REELS GSS3F

BB® SPEED SPOOL® BAITCASTING REELS

Features:
- Original Lew's Tournament-Tested Mechanism
- Original Lew's centrifugal brake system
- One-piece, die-cast aluminum frame
- Continuous Anti-Reverse
- Thumb bar spool release
- Titanium-Nitride line guide
- 125 yds/14 lb. capacity

SPECIFICATIONS
Model: B19GS: 4.3:1 low-speed gear ratio; 19 in./turn retrieval
MSRP: $119.95
Model: BB25SS: 5.5:1 high-speed gear ratio, 25 inches per turn retrieval
MSRP: $119.95
Model: BB25SW: 5.5:1 hi-speed gear ratio; 25 in./turn retrieval
MSRP: $134.95

GOLD SPEED SPIN® SPINNING REELS

A true tournament angler finds his edge from skills long developed and tested. Only the experienced, winning angler can determine what equipment will satisfy the demands placed on it week in and week out. Lew's has proven itself as the right tackle for tournament anglers for more than a quarter of a century. The new Speed Spin reels are certainly no exception. Smooth, accurate casts and retrieves with an unmatched drag reliability are the hallmarks of these tournament workhorses.

SPECIFICATIONS
- 5 Stainless Steel Ball Bearings
- Continuous Anti-Reverse
- Aluminum Long Stroke Spool
- Balanced Handle and Rotor
- Smooth, Wide Range Front Drag
- 5.2:1 gear ratio
- Spare aluminum spool included

Model: GSS2F: 140 yards/6 pound capacity
Model: GSS3F: 160 yards/8 pound capacity
MSRP: $49.95

LEW'S REELS

LASER™ BAITCASTING REELS LB300HS

LASER™ BAITCASTING REELS LB300

SPEED SPIN® SPINNING REELS LSS2R

SPEED SPIN® SPINNING REELS LSS3R

LASER™ BAITCASTING REELS

Laser™ by Lew's is the perfect low-profile baitcast reel for the value-conscious, experienced angler who needs the quality and durability in the tradition of Lew's with more affordable features.

SPECIFICATIONS
Model: LB300HS
- 6.2:1 high-speed gear ratio
- 3 Bearing Drive
- Continuous Anti-Reverse
- High-strength brass gears
- Magnetic cast control

- Quick-release side cover
- 25 inches per turn retrieve
- 165 yards/12 lb. line capacity

MSRP: $54.95

Model: LB300
- 5.1:1 high-speed gear ratio
- 3 Bearing Drive
- Continuous Anti-Reverse
- High-strength brass gears
- Magnetic cast control
- Quick-release side cover
- 21 inches per turn retrieve
- 165 yards/12 lb. line capacity

MSRP: $54.95

SPEED SPIN® SPINNING REELS

SPECIFICATIONS
- 5 Stainless Steel Ball Bearings
- 60-Stop Anti-Reverse
- Aluminum Long Stroke Spool
- Balanced Handle and Rotor
- Smooth, Wide Range Rear Drag
- Spare graphite spool included

Model: LSS2R: 140 yards/6 pound capacity

Model: LSS3R: 160 yards/8 pound capacity

MSRP: $39.95

MITCHELL REELS

300X SERIES SPINNING REELS

300X SERIES SPINNING REELS 308X

GOLD SERIES SPINNING REELS 300XG

GOLD SERIES SPINNING REELS 308XG

COPPERHEAD MCH20 IAR

COPPERHEAD MCH40 IAR

300X SERIES AND 300X GOLD SERIES SPINNING REELS

The Mitchell 300X and 300X Gold Series spinning reels exemplify Mitchell's heritage of innovation with advanced patented technology to make fishing easier and more enjoyable. The revolutionary cartridge spool system enables you to change your line in seconds. The worm gear oscillation provides perfect line lay.

Features:
- Durable, lightweight graphite body
- Instant anti-reverse for instant hooksets.
- Patented cartridge spool system.
- Spare spool for quick line changes.
- Worm gear oscillation feature provides perfect line winding.
- Durable aluminum handle with right- or left-hand retrieve; gold handle with wooden knob on Gold Series (XG) reels.

SPECIFICATIONS
Model: 300X
Gear ratio: 6.1:1
Capacity: 8 lb./240 yds.
Bearings: 5
Weight: 11.1 oz.
MSRP: $44.95

Model: 308X
Gear ratio: 5.5:1
Capacity: 6 lb./160 yds.
Bearings: 5
Weight: 8.6 oz.
MSRP: $44.95

Model: 300XG
Gear ratio: 6.0:1
Capacity: 8 lb./240 yds.
Bearings: 10
Weight: 11.1 oz.
MSRP: $64.95

Model: 308XG
Gear ratio: 5.5:1
Capacity: 6 lb./160 yds.
Bearings: 10
Weight: 8.6 oz.
MSRP: $64.95

COPPERHEAD MCH20 IAR AND MCH40 IAR SPINNING REELS

These Copperhead rear-drag spinning reels are popular performers all over the country. They're smooth, fast, and built to provide years of trouble-free service.

Features:
- Instant anti-reverse for solid hooksets.
- Patented cartridge spool system and spare spool for quick line changes.
- 5 bearings for smooth performance.
- Patented elliptic oscillation feature provides perfect line winding.

SPECIFICATIONS
Model: MCH20 IAR
Gear ratio: 5.1:1
Capacity: 8 lb./100 yds.
Bearings: 5
Weight: 9.3 oz.
MSRP: $44.95

Model: MCH40 IAR
Gear ratio: 5.6:1
Capacity: 12 lb./145 yds.
Bearings: 5
Weight: 11.4 oz.
MSRP: $44.95

COPPERHEAD MCH220
SPINNING REEL

COPPERHEAD
PRO SPINNING REEL
MCHP20

COPPERHEAD MCH220 SPINNING REEL

Weighing a mere 9.1 ounces, the new MCH220 is the lightest, liveliest reel in the Copperhead line - with refined styling that looks as great as it performs. Smooth, powerful, balanced and comfortable, it's quickly becoming one of the most popular Mitchell models.

Features:

- Instant anti-reverse for solid hook-sets.
- 4 bearings for smooth performance.
- Aluminum spool.
- Smooth, oversized drag.
- Lightweight for easy handling.

SPECIFICATIONS

Model: MCH220
Gear ratio: 4.8:1
Capacity: 10 lb./155 yds.
Bearings: 4
Weight: 9.1 oz.
MSRP: $34.95

COPPERHEAD PRO SPINNING REEL

Beautiful in both action and appearance, the Copperhead Pro is the ultimate in spinning reel design. It casts farther, thanks to the exclusive Tri-Lobe spool that reduces friction and allows the line to peel off faster and easier. The patented recessed drag knob prevents the line from catching in windy conditions. Back that up with plenty of raw, quick-strike power and a reinforced mounting strut, and you've got one mean, pro-action fishing reel.

Features:

- Instant anti-reverse for solid hooksets.
- Patented cartridge spool system and spare spool for quick line changes.
- Patented recessed drag knob system.
- Patented elliptic oscillation feature provides perfect line winding.

SPECIFICATIONS
Model: MCHP20
Gear ratio: 5.4:1
Capacity: 8 lb./160 yds.
Bearings: 5
Weight: 9.9 oz.
MSRP: $54.95

Fill Your Baitcasting Reel Just Right
When putting new line on your baitcasting reel, fill the reel to approximately 1/16 inch from the top edge of the spool. This optimizes casting performance.

MITCHELL REELS

EPIC® SPINNING REELS
E20

EPIC®
SPINNING
REELS
E10

EPIC® SPINNING REELS
E20T

EPIC®
SPINNING
REELS
E40

EPIC®
SPINNING
REELS
E10T

EPIC® SPINNING REELS

Epic spinning reels, with graphite bodies, perform like much more expensive spinning reels with features anglers can depend on. Smooth operation is secured by four drive bearings, hooksets are aided with Instant Anti-Reverse, the skirted aluminum spool prevents line tangles on the shaft and the automatic bail spring provides immediate line pick-up. The soft-touch reversible handle can be positioned for right or left hand cranking and the smooth front drag is dependable for playing any size fish.

The wide range of reel sizes gives the angler a choice for matching the right reel to the type of light to medium action fishing enjoyed. Each Epic reel, finished in gunmetal gray with gold accents, provides a full day of comfortable angling without arm and wrist fatigue. The Epic 10T and Epic 20T are trigger reels with self-centering bails.

SPECIFICATIONS
Model: E20 and E20T
Gear ratio: 4.8:1
Capacity: 8 lb./180 yds.
Bearings: 4

Weight: 9.1 oz.
MSRP: $24.95

Model: E10 and E10T
Gear ratio: 4.8:1
Capacity: 6 lb./110 yds.
Bearings: 4
Weight: 8.4 oz.
MSRP: $24.95

Model: E40
Gear ratio: 5.14:1
Capacity: 14 lb./145 yds.
Bearings: 4
Weight: 13.8 oz.

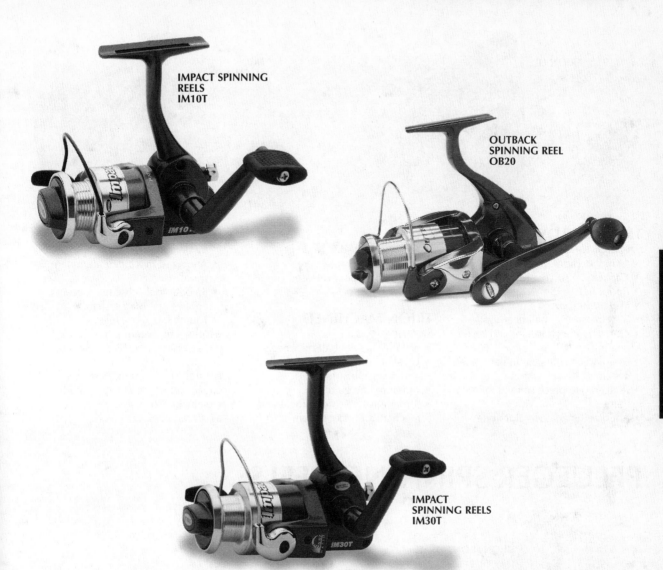

IMPACT SPINNING REELS IM10T

OUTBACK SPINNING REEL OB20

IMPACT SPINNING REELS IM30T

IMPACT SPINNING REELS

For those who prefer a self-centering, trigger-style bail, Impact is the reel for you. Silky-smooth action and plenty of power features, including four ball bearings, brass pinion gear, and an innovative long-life spring bail system are sure to have a serious impact on you... and the fish. Choose from the mid-sized 30T or the lightweight 10T.

SPECIFICATIONS
Model: IM10T
Gear ratio: 4.9:1
Capacity: 6 lb./110 yds.

Bearings: 4
Weight: 7.2 oz.
MSRP: $34.95

Model: IM30T
Gear ratio: 5.6:1
Capacity: 6 lb./150 yds.
Bearings: 4
Weight: 9.7 oz.
MSRP: $34.95

OUTBACK SPINNING REEL

Take hold of the Mitchell Outback reel and... no worries, mate! You're all set to take on anything that swims in the light-to-medium action class. With a three-bearing drive, our powerhouse brass pinion gear and multi-stop anti-reverse, the Outback is designed for years of dependable service.

SPECIFICATIONS
Model: OB20
Gear ratio: 5.0:1
Capacity: 6 lb./175 yds.
Bearings: 3
Weight: 9.5 oz.
MSRP: $24.95

PFLUEGER BAITCAST REELS

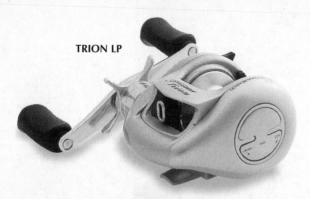

TRION LP

TRION
MACHINED

TRION LP (LOW PROFILE)
SPECIFICATIONS
- *Class*: Medium, freshwater
- *Capacity*: 120 yds./12 lb.
- *Ratio*: 6.3:1
- *Weight*: 9.8 oz.
- 5 stainless steel ball bearings.
- One-way clutch instant anti-reverse bearing.
- 6-pin adjustable centrifugal brake system.
- Rugged one-piece solid aluminum frame.
- Anodized machined aluminum spool.
- Smooth multi-disc main gear applied star drag system.
- Thumb bar spool release.

MSRP: $99.95

TRION MACHINED
SPECIFICATIONS
- 5 stainless steel ball bearings.
- Uni-Lok, one-way clutch instant anti-reverse bearing.
- Titanium line guide.
- 4-pin adjustable centrifugal and mechanical brake system.

- Rugged one-piece solid aluminum frame and side plates.
- Anodized machined aluminum spool.
- Smooth multi-disc main gear applied star drag system.
- Thumb bar spool release.

Model 46: medium, freshwater; capacity 125 yds./12 lb.; ratio 5.3:1; weight 10.4 oz.

Model 56: medium, freshwater; capacity 180 yds./14 lb.; ratio 5.2:1; weight 11.2 oz.

MSRP: $79.95

PFLUEGER SPINNING REELS

TRION FRONT DRAG

TRION FRONT DRAG
SPECIFICATIONS
- 6 ball bearings.
- Uni-Lok, one-way clutch instant anti-reverse bearing.
- Lightweight graphite body, side-plate and rotor.
- Large diameter titanium line roller.
- Smooth six-disc drag system with stainless steel and oiled felt washers.
- Anodized machined aluminum spool.
- Left/right convertible quick release fold down handle.
- Rosewood T Knob.
- Spare aluminum spool included.
- Ratio: 5.2:1

Model 4725: ultralight, freshwater; capacity 125 yds./4 lb.; weight 9 oz.

Model 4730: light, freshwater; capacity 130 yds./6 lb.; weight 10.2 oz.

Model 4735: medium-light, freshwater; capacity 160 yds./8 lb.; weight 12.7 oz.

Model 4725: medium, freshwater; capacity 180 yds./10 lb.; weight 13.6 oz.

MSRP: $39.95

**ACCURIST™ ACS
BAITCASTING REELS
AC500PT**

**ACCURIST™ ACS
BAITCASTING REELS
AC501CX**

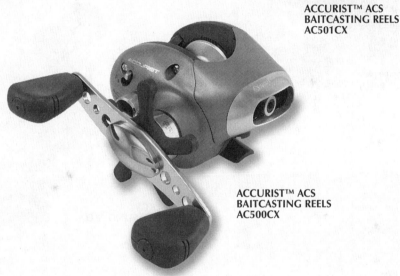

**ACCURIST™ ACS
BAITCASTING REELS
AC500CX**

ACCURIST™ ACS BAITCASTING REELS

Features:
- ACS cast control
- Ultra-low profile design
- 4 or 5 stainless steel bearings
- Lightweight machined aluminum spool
- Continuous Anti-Reverse
- Thumb bar spool release
- Quick-release bayonet sidecover
- Flippin' switch
- Left-hand models available

SPECIFICATIONS
Model AC500PT: 5 Bearings, 6.2:1 gear ratio
MSRP: $99.95
Model AC500CX: 5 Bearings, 6.2:1 gear ratio
MSRP: $94.95
Model AC501CX: 5 Bearings, left-hand, 6.2:1 gear ratio
MSRP: $94.95
Model AC400C: 4 Bearings, 5.1:1 gear ratio
MSRP: $89.95
Model AC401C: 4 Bearings, left-hand, 5.1:1 gear ratio
MSRP: $89.95
Model AC501PT: 5 Bearings, 6.2:1 gear ratio, left-handed
MSRP: $99.95

Long Cast Spools
If you can't cast as far as you need to, switch to a spinning reel with "long cast" style spool that is longer and shallower. On most reels, line starts flows freely when you first cast, but as the line level drops on the spool, the line must climb a steeper grade over the spool lip. This increased friction reduces the distance can cast. With a "long cast" type spool, the shallower design keeps the lip to a minimum, thus casting distances are improved.

QUANTUM® REELS

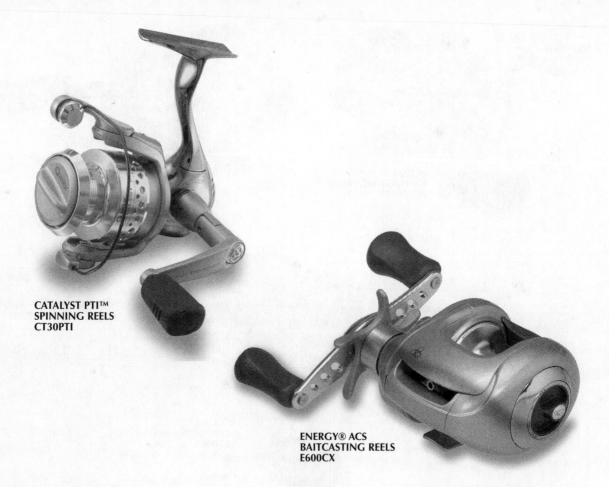

**CATALYST PTI™
SPINNING REELS
CT30PTI**

**ENERGY® ACS
BAITCASTING REELS
E600CX**

CATALYST PTI™
SPINNING REELS

As we all know, magnets either attract or repel each other depending on how they are positioned to one another. The TiMAG™ System uses these inherent magnetic forces to exert the exact same amount of bail force each and every time, making the need for a spring obsolete. No spring - no stretching, breaking or wearing out. Ever. And it's backed up by a Lifetime Guarantee.

Features:
- One-piece ThinLine™ aluminum body and side cover
- "Screwless" aluminum side cover
- TiMAG™ II bail system with LIFE-TIME WARRANTY
- 8 stainless steel bearings
- Low-friction Continuous Anti-Reverse™ II
- MaxCast™ Longstroke® aluminum spool
- Ceramic Magnum Drag System

- Spare aluminum spool
- Oversized Twist-Reducer™ line roller
- TRU-Balance® offset rotor design
- Counter-balancing FootForward™ design

SPECIFICATIONS
Model CT20PTi: 8 Bearings, 5.2:1 gear ratio, 140 yds./6 lb. line capacity
Model CT30PTi: 8 Bearings, 5.2:1 gear ratio, 160 yds./8 lb. line capacity
Model CT40PTi: 8 Bearings, 5.2:1 gear ratio, 230 yds./10 lb. line capacity
MSRP: $89.95 (all models)

ENERGY® ACS
BAITCASTING REELS

Features:
- Upgraded ACS II™ cast control
- 4 and 6 bearing models
- Our lowest profile design ever
- One-piece aluminum frame
- Stainless steel ball bearings
- Continuous Anti-Reverse™
- Forged aluminum spool
- Super Free Spool pinion gear

- Low-profile Zirconia line guide
- Quick-release bayonet side cover
- Precision-calibrated drag

SPECIFICATIONS
Model: E600PT
- Proprietary polymer/stainless hybrid hi-speed 6 bearings
- Ceramic level-wind worm shaft
- Zirconia level-wind pawl
- Ultralight MaxCast™ spool
- Upgraded Super Free Spool II
- Upgraded ACS II™
- Harder brass gear system
- Scratch-resistant vacuum-deposition plating
- Hot-Sauce™ molecular lubrication

MSRP: $159.95

SPECIFICATIONS
Model E600CX: 6 Bearings, 6.2:1 gear ratio, 25.4 inches per turn
MSRP: $109.95
Model E400C: 4 Bearings, 5.1:1 gear ratio, 20.6 inches per turn
MSRP: $99.95

QUANTUM® REELS

ICON™ BAIT-CASTING REEL
IC300C

ICON™ SPINNING REELS
IC20

IRON® ACS BAITCASTING REELS
IR1300C

IRON® ACS BAITCASTING REELS
IR400CX

ICON™ BAITCASTING REEL
Features:
- 3 Stainless steel bearings
- One-piece composite frame
- DynaMag™ magnetic cast control
- Lightweight aluminum spool
- Machined brass gears
- Continuous Anti-Reverse™

SPECIFICATIONS
Model IC300C: 3 Ball bearings, 5.1:1 gear ratio, 165 yds./12 lb. line capacity
MSRP: $44.95

ICON™ SPINNING REELS
Features:
- One-piece ThinLine™ aluminum body and side cover
- 4 bearing system
- Low-friction Continuous Anti-Reverse™ II
- Oversized Twist-Reducer™ line roller
- MaxCast™ Longstroke® aluminum spool
- Counter-balancing FootForward™ design
- "Springless" bi-polar magnetic bail trip
- TRU-Balance® offset rotor design

SPECIFICATIONS
Model IC20: 4 bearings, 5.2:1 gear ratio, 140yds./6lb. line capacity
Model IC30: 4 bearings, 5.2:1 gear ratio, 160yds./8lb. line capacity
Model IC40: 4 bearings, 5.2:1 gear ratio, 230yds./10lb. line capacity

MSRP: $49.95 (all models)

IRON® ACS BAITCASTING REELS
Features:
- ACS cast control
- 3 or 4 stainless steel bearings
- One-piece aluminum frame
- Continuous Anti-Reverse
- Thumb bar spool release
- Quick-release bayonet sidecover

SPECIFICATIONS
Model IR400CX: 4 Bearings, 6.3:1 gear ratio
MSRP: $104.95
Model IR300C: 3 Bearings, 5.2:1 gear ratio
MSRP: $89.95

QUANTUM® REELS

**KINETIC PTI™
SPINNING REELS
KT20PTI**

**MG BAITCASTING REELS
1310MGC**

KINETIC PTI™
SPINNING REELS

Features:

- One-piece ThinLine™ aluminum body and side cover
- "Screwless" aluminum side cover
- 6 stainless steel bearings
- TiMAG™ II bail system with LIFE-TIME WARRANTY
- MaxCast™ Longstroke® aluminum spool
- Ceramic Magnum Drag System
- Low-friction Continuous Anti-Reverse™ II
- Oversized Twist-Reducer™ line roller
- Spare aluminum spool
- TRU-Balance® offset rotor design
- Counter-balancing FootForward™ design

Model KT20PTi: 6 bearings, 5.2:1 gear ratio, 140 yds./6 lb. line capacity
Model KT30PTi: 6 bearings, 5.2:1 gear ratio, 160 yds./8 lb. line capacity
Model KT40PTi: 6 bearings, 5.2:1 gear ratio, 230 yds./10 lb. line capacity
MSRP: $69.95 (all models)

MG BAITCASTING REELS

Features:

- One-piece aluminum frame
- DynaMag cast control
- TRU-Balance spool with perimeter-weighted outside rim and counter-balance shaft
- Multi-disc drag
- Continuous Anti-Reverse
- Capacity: 165 yard/12 lb line capacity

SPECIFICATIONS
Model: 1310MGC
Bearings: 2
Gear ratio: 5.1:1

Model: 1310CX
Bearings: 3
Gear ratio: 6.0:1

Model: 1310CP
Bearings: 3
Gear ratio: 3.8:1

QUANTUM® REELS

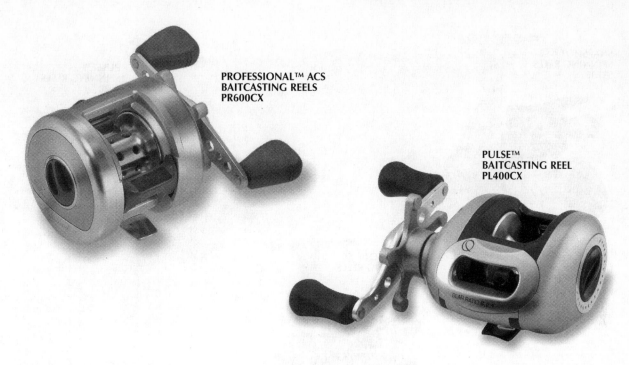

PROFESSIONAL™ ACS BAITCASTING REELS PR600CX

PULSE™ BAITCASTING REEL PL400CX

PROFESSIONAL™ ACS BAITCASTING REELS

Features:
- ACS cast control
- 6 stainless steel bearings
- One-piece aluminum frame
- Continuous Anti-Reverse
- Thumb bar spool release
- Quick-release bayonet sidecover
- Titanium-nitride levelwind guide
- Ultralight MaxCast spool

SPECIFICATIONS
Model PR600CX: Hi-speed, 6.3:1 gear ratio
MSRP: $127.95
Model PR600C: Standard speed, 5.2:1 gear ratio
Model PR600CXS: Large Capacity, 6:3:1 gear ratio

PULSE™ BAITCASTING REEL

Features:
- 4 Stainless steel ball bearings
- One-piece composite frame
- DynaMag™ magnetic cast control
- Lightweight aluminum spool
- High-speed machined brass gears
- Continuous Anti-Reverse™

SPECIFICATIONS
Model PL400CX: 4 Bearings, 6.2:1 gear ratio, 165 yds./12 lb. line capacity
MSRP: $64.95

Proper Brake Adjustment Equals Fewer Backlashes
You'll make more accurate casts with fewer backlashes if you adjust your baitcasting reel's mechanical brake according to the weight of the lure you're casting. Look for the brake adjustment knob on the side-plate beneath the handle. With the lure attached to your line, depress the free-spool button. When the brake knob is properly adjusted, the lure should descend slowly to the ground and stop without any spool overrun. If the lure falls too quickly or slowly, adjust the brake knob to compensate.

QUANTUM® REELS

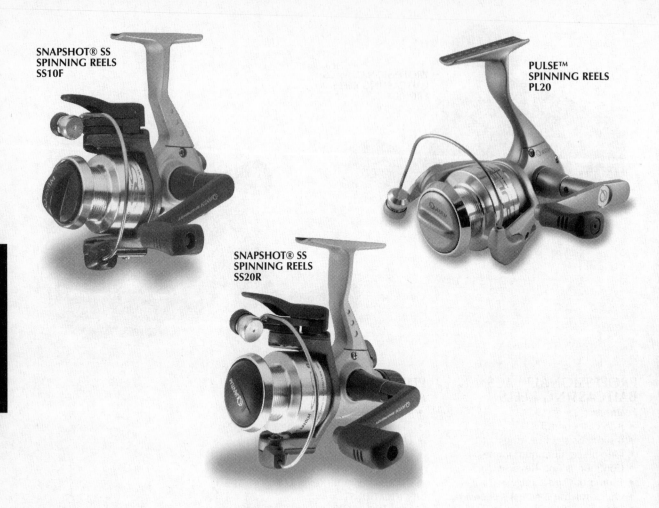

SNAPSHOT® SS SPINNING REELS SS10F

PULSE™ SPINNING REELS PL20

SNAPSHOT® SS SPINNING REELS SS20R

PULSE™ SPINNING REELS

Features:
- One-piece ThinLine™ aluminum body and side cover
- 5 bearing system
- Low-friction Continuous Anti-Reverse™ II
- Oversized Twist-Reducer™ line roller
- MaxCast™ Longstroke® aluminum spool
- Spare aluminum spool
- Counter-balancing FootForward™ design
- "Springless" bi-polar magnetic bail trip
- TRU-Balance® offset rotor design

SPECIFICATIONS
Model PL20: 5 ball bearings, 5.2:1 gear ratio, 140 yds./6 lb. line capacity
Model PL30: 5 ball bearings, 5.2:1 gear ratio, 160 yds./8 lb. line capacity
Model PL40: 5 ball bearings, 5.2:1 gear ratio, 230 yds./10 lb. line capacity
MSRP: $59.95 (all Models)

SNAPSHOT® SS SPINNING REELS

Quantum's exclusive Snapshot2 casting system employs a unique trigger that allows you to cast without ever touching the line. Also, the patented Firing Pin grabs, holds and then releases the line accurately…cast after cast.

Features:
- Snapshot casting system
- Ball-bearing drive
- Twist Reducer line roller
- Aluminum Long Stroke spool
- Strong, composite body

SPECIFICATIONS
Model SS10F: 4.4:1 gear ratio, 125 yds./4 lb. line capacity, front drag
MSRP: $19.95
Model SS20R: 4.4:1 gear ratio, 140 yds./6 lb. line capacity, rear drag
MSRP: $19.95
Model SS30R: 4.0:1 gear ratio, 160 yds./8 lb. line capacity, rear drag
MSRP: $19.95
Model SS40F: 4.0:1 gear ratio, 270 yds./8 lb. line capacity, front drag
MSRP: $19.95

QUANTUM® REELS

SNAPSHOT® SX

XR®

VECTOR™

SNAPSHOT® SX SPINNING REELS

Features:
- Snapshot2 casting system
- 4 stainless steel bearings
- Twist Reducer line roller
- TRU-Balance handle and rotor
- Aluminum Long Stroke spool
- Quantum Magnum Gears
- Spare graphite spool

SPECIFICATIONS

Model SX20F: Front drag, 4 bearings, 5.2:1 gears, 140 yds./6 lb.
Model SX10F: Front drag, 4 bearings, 5.3:1 gears, 125 yds./4 lb.
Model SX20R: Rear drag, 4 bearings, 5.2:1 gears, 140 yds./6 lb.
Model SX30F: Front drag, 4 bearings, 5.2:1 gears, 160 yds./8 lb.
Model SX30R: Rear drag, 4 bearings, 5.2:1 gears, 160 yds./8 lb.
Model SX40F: Front drag, 4 bearings, 5.2:1 gears, 270 yds./8 lb.
MSRP: $29.95 (all models)

VECTOR™ SPINNING REELS

Features:
- Ball-bearing drive
- Aluminum Longstroke® spool
- Twist-Reducer™ line roller
- Selective 3-position on/off/center anti-reverse
- Convenient front drag

SPECIFICATIONS

Model VR10F: 1 bearing, 4.4:1 gears, 125 yds./4 lb.
Model VR20F: 1 bearing, 4.4:1 gears, 140 yds./6 lb.
Model VR30F: 1 bearing, 4.0:1 gears, 160 yds./8 lb.
MSRP: $14.95

XR® SPINNING REELS

These beginning price point spinning reels have just re-defined what today's customers expect to get for their money. They will be pleased with the added-value features and the stylish good-looks usually found only on those products selling at higher prices.

Features:
- Ball-bearing drive
- Twist Reducer line roller
- Aluminum Long Stroke spool

SPECIFICATIONS

Model XR30R: 4.0:1 gear ratio, 160 yds. w/ 8 lb. line capacity, rear drag
Model XR00F: 5.2:1 gear ratio, 80 yds. w/ 4 lb. line capacity, front drag
Model XR10F: 4.4:1 gear ratio, 125 yds. w/ 4 lb. line capacity, front drag
Model XR20R: 4.4:1 gear ratio, 140 yds. w/ 6 lb. line capacity, rear drag
Model XR40F: 4.0:1 gear ratio, 270 yds. w/ 8 lb. line capacity, front drag
Model XR60F: 4.7:1 gear ratio, 225 yds. w/ 14 lb. line capacity, front drag
Model XR70F: 4.7:1 gear ratio, 320 yds. w/ 17 lb. line capacity, front drag
Model XR20F: 4.4:1 gear ratio, 140 yds. w/ 6 lb. line capacity, front drag
Model XR30F: 4.0:1 gear ratio, 160 yds. w/ 8 lb. line capacity, front drag
MSRP: $17.95 (all models)

SHAKESPEARE BAITCAST REELS

ALPHA 110

CATERA LP

SKP 3000/4000
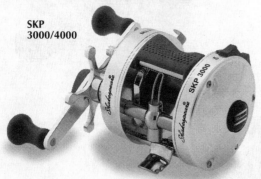

SKP 3000A/4000A

ALPHA 110
SPECIFICATIONS
Class: medium, freshwater
Capacity: 120 yds./14 lb.
Ratio: 5.1:1
Weight: 8.6 oz.
- Ball bearing design.
- Graphite reinforced frame and side plates.
- High strength graphite spool.
- Flip-up hood.
- Adjustable magnetic cast control to help eliminate backlash.
- E-Z Cast® thumb bar spool release.
- Machined brass gears.
- Smooth main gear applied star drag system.
- Flipping switch.
MSRP: $19.99

CATERA LP
SPECIFICATIONS
Class: medium, freshwater
Capacity: 120 yds./14 lb.
Ratio: 5.5:1
Weight: 8.5 oz.
- 3 ball bearings.
- One-way clutch instant anti-reverse bearing.

- Anodized machined aluminum spool.
- Reinforced graphite frame and side plates.
- Adjustable magnetic cast control to help eliminate backlash.
- E-Z Cast® thumb bar spool release.
- Machined brass gears.
- Smooth main gear applied star drag system.
MSRP: $29.99

SKP 3000/4000
SPECIFICATIONS
- Ball bearing.
- Rigid chrome-plated brass frame with anodized aluminum side plates.
- Smooth main gear applied star drag system.
- Lightweight graphite spool.
- Selective on/off bait clicker.
- Push button spool release.
- Adjustable spool tension knob.
- Dual pin centrifugal brake system.
- Machine cut brass gears.
- *Ratio*: 5.3:1
Model 3000: medium, freshwater; capacity 200 yds./12 lb.; weight 9.9 oz.

Model 4000: heavy, freshwater; capacity 160 yds./20 lb.; weight 10.3 oz.
MSRP: $29.99

SKP 3000A/4000A
SPECIFICATIONS
- Ball bearing.
- One-way clutch instant anti-reverse bearing.
- Rigid chrome-plated brass frame with anodized aluminum side plates.
- Anodized machined aluminum spool.
- Smooth main gear applied star drag system.
- Selective on/off bait clicker.
- Push button spool release.
- Adjustable spool tension knob.
- Dual pin centrifugal brake system.
- Precision machined brass gears.
- *Ratio*: 5.3:1
Model 3000A: medium, freshwater; capacity 200 yds./12 lb.; weight 11 oz.
Model 4000A: heavy, freshwater; capacity 160 yds./20 lb.; weight 11.4 oz.
MSRP: $39.99

REELS

SHAKESPEARE SPINCASTING REELS

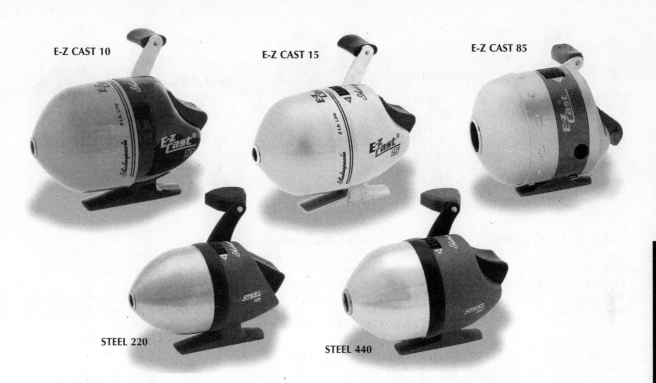

E-Z CAST 10
E-Z CAST 15
E-Z CAST 85
STEEL 220
STEEL 440

E-Z CAST 10
SPECIFICATIONS
- **Class**: Light, freshwater
- **Capacity**: 100 yds./8 lb.
- **Ratio**: 3.2:1
- **Weight**: 5.6 oz.
- Graphite frame and painted ABS cone.
- Star drag system.
- Precision metal gears.
- Multi-point pickup housing.
- Filled with 8-lb. test line.

MSRP: $4.99

E-Z CAST 15
SPECIFICATIONS
- **Class**: Light, freshwater
- **Capacity**: 100 yds./8 lb.
- **Ratio**: 3.2:1
- **Weight**: 6.3 oz.
- Reinforced graphite frame and painted ABS cone.
- Three color assortment (Red, Gold and Silver).
- Spool applied disc drag system.
- Precision metal gears.
- Stainless steel pickup pin.
- Filled with 8-lb. test line.

MSRP: $5.99

E-Z CAST 85
SPECIFICATIONS

- Oversized spincasting reel.
- **Class**: Heavy, freshwater
- **Capacity**: 85 yds./20 lb.
- **Ratio**: 3.2:1
- **Weight**: 13.5 oz.
- Ball bearing.
- Reinforced graphite frame.
- Left/right convertible retrieve.
- Comfort grip power handle.
- Adjustable disc drag system.
- Heavy duty metal gears.
- Stainless steel Insta-Grab' pickup pins and "Largemouth" line guide.
- Selective silent anti-reverse.
- Features selective bait clicker.
- Filled with 20-lb. test line.

MSRP: $14.99

STEEL 220
SPECIFICATIONS
- **Class**: Light, freshwater
- **Capacity**: 85 yds./6 lb.
- **Ratio**: 3.1:1
- **Weight**: 6.1 oz.
- Stainless steel front cones.
- Strong graphite frame.
- Comfort grip power handle.
- Adjustable disc drag system.
- Stainless steel Insta-Grab' pickup pin.
- Filled with 6-lb. test line.

MSRP: $7.99

STEEL 440
SPECIFICATIONS
- **Class**: Medium, freshwater
- **Capacity**: 65 yds./10 lb.
- **Ratio**: 3.4:1
- **Weight**: 7.2 oz.
- Stainless steel front cone.
- Strong graphite frame.
- Adjustable disc drag system.
- Comfort grip power handle.
- Stainless steel Insta-Grab pickup pins.
- Filled with 10-lb. test line.

MSRP: $7.99

STEEL MICROCAST
SPECIFICATIONS
- **Class**: Ultralight, freshwater
- **Capacity**: 60 yds./4 lb.
- **Ratio**: 4.1:1
- **Weight**: 5.1 oz.
- One ball bearing.
- Strong graphite frame.
- Smooth, spool-applied disc drag system.
- Soft rubber pinch ring on rotor for reduced line wear.
- Stainless steel Insta-Grab' pickup pin.
- Left/right hand retrieve.
- MicroSpin features selective silent anti-reverse.
- Filled with 6-lb. test line.

MSRP: $11.99

SHAKESPEARE SPINCASTING REELS

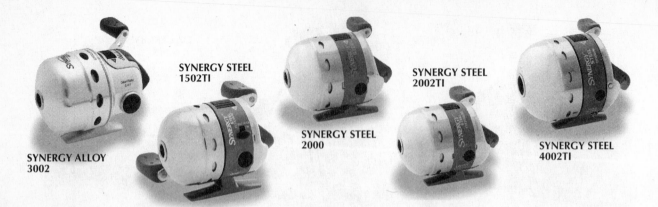

SYNERGY STEEL 1502TI

SYNERGY STEEL 2002TI

SYNERGY ALLOY 3002

SYNERGY STEEL 2000

SYNERGY STEEL 4002TI

SYNERGY ALLOY 3002
SPECIFICATIONS
- **Class**: Medium-heavy, freshwater
- **Capacity**: 110 yds./10 lb.
- **Ratio**: 3.4:1
- **Weight**: 14 oz.
- 2 bearing design.
- One-way clutch instant anti-reverse bearing.
- Machined aluminum front cone and rear cover.
- Oscillating spool for more even line lay and casting distance.
- Dual rolling stainless steel Insta-Grab pickup pins.
- Durable metal foot.
- Gear-driven adjustable disc drag system.
- Left/right convertible retrieve.
- Heavy-duty metal gears.
- Soft, durable elastomer pinch ring for reduced line wear.
- Filled with 10-lb. test line.

MSRP: $24.99

SYNERGY STEEL 1502TI
SPECIFICATIONS
- **Class**: Light, freshwater
- **Capacity**: 70 yds./6 lb.
- **Ratio**: 3.4:1
- **Weight**: 8 oz.
- 2 ball bearings.
- Polished stainless steel front cone and rear cover with Secure-Lock securing screw in the rear cover.
- Titanium line guide.
- Dual titanium Insta-Grab' pickup pins.
- Durable lightweight graphite frame.
- Gear-driven adjustable disc drag system.
- Strong, lightweight, gold chrome-plated steel handle with textured soft rubber knob.
- Left/right convertible retrieve.
- Soft, durable elastomer pinch ring for reduced line wear.
- Filled with 6-lb. test line.

MSRP: $14.99

SYNERGY STEEL 2000
SPECIFICATIONS
- **Class**: Medium, freshwater
- **Capacity**: 75 yds./10 lb.
- **Ratio**: 3.8:1
- **Weight**: 10.3 oz.
- Polished stainless steel front cone and rear cover with Secure-Lock securing screw in the rear cover.
- Durable lightweight graphite frame.
- "Gear-driven" adjustable disc drag system.
- Strong, lightweight, chrome-plated steel dual-grip handle with textured soft rubber knobs.
- Left/right convertible retrieve.
- Heavy-duty metal gears.
- Dual stainless steel Insta-Grab' pickup pins.
- Soft, durable elastomer pinch ring for reduced line wear.
- Selective silent anti-reverse and bait clicker.
- Filled with 10-lb. test line.

MSRP: $9.99

SYNERGY STEEL 2002TI
SPECIFICATIONS
- **Class**: Medium, freshwater
- **Capacity**: 75 yds./10 lb.
- **Ratio**: 3.8:1
- **Weight**: 10.3 oz.
- 2 ball bearings.
- Polished stainless steel front cone and rear cover with Secure-Lock securing screw in the rear cover.
- Titanium line guide.
- Dual titanium Insta-Grab' pickup pins.
- Durable lightweight graphite frame.
- Gear-driven adjustable disc drag system.
- Strong, lightweight, gold chrome-plated steel handle with textured soft rubber knob.
- Left/right convertible retrieve.
- Heavy-duty metal gears.
- Soft, durable elastomer pinch ring for reduced line wear.
- Features selective silent anti-reverse and bait clicker.
- Filled with 10-lb. test line.

MSRP: $14.99

SYNERGY STEEL 4002TI
SPECIFICATIONS
- Oversized spincasting reel.
- **Class**: Heavy, freshwater
- **Capacity**: 85 yds./20 lb.
- **Ratio**: 3.2:1
- **Weight**: 17.4 oz.
- 2 ball bearings.
- Dual titanium-coated Insta-Grab' pickup pins and Largemouth line guide.
- Polished stainless steel front cone and rear cover with Secure-Lock securing screw in the rear cover.
- Durable lightweight graphite frame.
- "Gear-driven" adjustable disc drag system.
- Strong, lightweight, gold chrome-plated steel dual-grip handle with textured soft rubber knobs.
- Left/right convertible retrieve.
- Heavy-duty metal gears.
- Soft, durable elastomer pinch ring for reduced line wear.
- Selective silent anti-reverse and bait clicker.
- Filled with 20-lb. test line.

MSRP: $19.99

SHAKESPEARE SPINNING REELS

ALPHA

ALPHA LX

CATERA' REAR DRAG

CATERA' FRONT DRAG

ALPHA

SPECIFICATIONS

- Ball bearing.
- Reinforced graphite body and spool.
- Spool applied, six-disc drag system.
- Precision die-cast gears.
- E-Z Cast® trigger with self-centering bail (25-40 size).
- Selective silent anti-reverse.
- Left/right hand retrieve with fold down handle.
- *Ratio*: 4.8:1 (4.9:1 on Models 2525 and 2530)

Model 2525: ultralight, freshwater; capacity 125 yds./4 lb.; weight 5.5 oz.
Model 2530: light, freshwater; capacity 130 yds./6 lb.; weight 8 oz.
Model 2535: medium-light, freshwater; capacity 160 yds./8 lb.; weight 8.5 oz. **Model 2540:** medium, freshwater; capacity 180 yds./10 lb.; weight 10.5 oz.
Model 2550: medium-heavy, freshwater; capacity 210 yds./12 lb.; weight 11.2 oz.
MSRP: $12.99

ALPHA LX

SPECIFICATIONS

- Ball bearing.
- Graphite reinforced frame and machined aluminum spool.

- Spool applied, six-disc drag system.
- E-Z Cast® trigger with self-centering bail (25-40 size).
- Selective silent anti-reverse.
- Left/right hand retrieve with fold down handle.
- *Ratio*: 4.9:1

Model 2425: ultralight, freshwater; capacity 125 yds./4 lb.; weight 8.3 oz.
Model 2430: light, freshwater; capacity 130 yds./6 lb.; weight 8.5 oz.
Model 2435: medium-light, freshwater; capacity 160 yds./8 lb.; weight 11.2 oz.
Model 2440: medium, freshwater; capacity 180 yds./10 lb.; weight 12.1 oz.
MSRP: $12.99

CATERA' FRONT DRAG

SPECIFICATIONS

- 4 ball bearings.
- One-way clutch instant anti-reverse bearing.
- Large diameter titanium line roller.
- Smooth six-disc drag system with stainless steel and oiled felt washers.
- Anodized machined aluminum spool.
- Left/right convertible fold down counter-balanced handle.
- *Ratio* 5.2:1

Model 4525: ultralight, freshwater; capacity 125 yds./4 lb.; weight 9 oz.

Model 4530: light, freshwater; capacity 130 yds./6 lb.; weight 10.2 oz.
Model 4535: medium-light, freshwater; capacity 160 yds./8 lb.; weight 12.7 oz.
Model 4540: medium, freshwater; capacity 180 yds./10 lb.; weight 13.6 oz.
MSRP: $29.99

CATERA' REAR DRAG

SPECIFICATIONS

- 4 ball bearings.
- One-way clutch instant anti-reverse bearing.
- Large diameter titanium line roller.
- Smooth six-disc drag system with stainless steel and oiled felt washers.
- Anodized machined aluminum spool.
- Left/right convertible fold down counter-balanced handle.
- *Ratio* 5.2:1 (4.8:1 on Model 4540R)

Model 4530R: light, freshwater; capacity 130 yds./6 lb.; weight 12.1 oz.
Model 4535R: medium-light, freshwater; capacity 160 yds./8 lb.; weight 12.7 oz.
Model 4540R: medium, freshwater; capacity 180 yds./10 lb.; weight 15 oz.
MSRP: $29.99

SHAKESPEARE SPINNING REELS

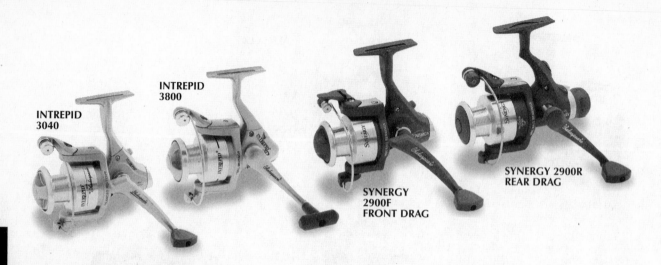

INTREPID 3040

INTREPID 3800

SYNERGY 2900F FRONT DRAG

SYNERGY 2900R REAR DRAG

INTREPID 3000 SERIES
SPECIFICATIONS
- 4 ball bearings.
- 45-point anti-reverse system.
- Large diameter line roller with shielded stainless steel ball bearing.
- Large diameter titanium line roller.
- Smooth six-disc drag system with stainless steel and oiled felt washers.
- Anodized machined aluminum spool.
- Spare aluminum spool
- Left/right convertible fold-down counterbalanced aluminum handle.

Ratio: 5.2:1

Model 3025: ultralight, freshwater; capacity 125 yds./4 lb.; weight 8.2 oz.
Model 3030: light, freshwater; capacity 130 yds./6 lb.; weight 8.9 oz.
Model 3035: medium-light, freshwater; capacity 160 yds./8 lb.; weight 11.6 oz.
Model 3040: medium, freshwater; capacity 180 yds./10 lb.; weight 12.7 oz.
MSRP: $36.39

INTREPID 3800 SERIES
SPECIFICATIONS
- 4 stainless steel ball bearings (3860, 70 & 80 have 2).
- Exclusive 60-point anti-reverse system (3870 & 80 have 72-point).
- Large diameter titanium-coated line roller.
- Reinforced graphite frame and rotor.
- Six-disc drag system with stainless steel and oiled felt washers.
- Machined and anodized aluminum spool.
- Corrosion resistant stainless steel components.
- Left/right convertible fold down handle with barrel knob.

Model 3835: light, freshwater; capacity 160 yds./8 lb.; ratio 5.1:1; weight 12 oz.
Model 3840: medium, freshwater; capacity 180 yds./10 lb.; ratio 4.9:1; weight 15.2 oz.
Model 3850: heavy, freshwater; capacity 210 yds./12 lb.; ratio 4.9:1; weight 16 oz.
MSRP: $36.39

SYNERGY 2900F FRONT DRAG
SPECIFICATIONS
- 3 ball bearings. .
- One-way clutch instant anti-reverse bearing.
- Anodized machined aluminum spool.
- Spare graphite spool.
- E-Z Cast® trigger system with self-centering bail.
- Smooth multi-disc drag system.
- Precision metal gears.
- Selective silent anti-reverse.
- Left/right convertible fold-down handle.

Ratio: 5.1:1

Model 2925F: ultralight, freshwater; capacity 125 yds./4 lb.; weight 9 oz.
Model 2930F: light, freshwater; capacity 130 yds./6 lb.; weight 10.5 oz.
Model 2935F: medium-light, freshwater; capacity 160 yds./8 lb.; weight 12 oz.
Model 2940F: medium, freshwater; capacity 180 yds./10 lb.; weight 15.5 oz.
MSRP: $28.99

SYNERGY 2900R REAR DRAG
SPECIFICATIONS
- 3 ball bearings.
- Anodized machined aluminum spool.
- Spare graphite spool.
- E-Z Cast® trigger system with self-centering bail.
- 45-point anti-reverse.
- Smooth multi-disc drag system.
- Precision metal gears.
- Selective silent anti-reverse.
- Left/right convertible fold-down handle.

Ratio: 4.9:1

Model 2925R: ultralight, freshwater; capacity 125 yds./4 lb.; weight 8.6 oz.
Model 2930R: light, freshwater; capacity 130 yds./6 lb.; weight 9.4 oz.
Model 2935R: medium-light, freshwater; capacity 160 yds./8 lb.; weight 12.2 oz.
Model 2940R: medium, freshwater; capacity 180 yds./10 lb.; weight 13.1 oz.
MSRP: $28.99

REELS

www.StoegerIndustries.com

SHAKESPEARE ULTRALIGHT SPINNING REELS

ALPHA 250
SPECIFICATIONS
- *Capacity*: 125 yds./4 lb.
- *Ratio*: 4.9:1
- *Weight*: 6 oz.
- 2 ball bearings.
- Machined and anodized aluminum spool.
- Left/right retrieve with fold-down handle.
- Graphite body.
- Precision die-cast gears.
- Selective silent anti-reverse.
- Spool applied disc drag system.
MSRP: $12.99

SYNERGY 200
SPECIFICATIONS
- *Capacity*: 90 yds./4 lb.
- *Ratio*: 5.2:1
- *Weight*: 4.8 oz.
- 3 ball bearings.
- Machined and anodized aluminum spool.
- Left/right retrieve with fold-down rosewood handle.
- Machine cut brass pinion gear.
- Graphite body.
- Selective silent anti-reverse.
- Spool applied disc drag system.
MSRP: $19.99

250UL
SPECIFICATIONS
- *Capacity*: 125 yds./4 lb.
- *Ratio*: 4.9:1
- *Weight*: 5.7 oz.
- Ball bearing.
- Left/right retrieve with fold-down handle.
- Graphite body and spool.
- Precision die-cast gears.
- Selective silent anti-reverse.
- Spool applied disc drag system.
MSRP: $19.99

ALPHA 250

SYNERGY 200

SHAKESPEARE UNDERSPIN REELS

STEEL MICROSPIN
SPECIFICATIONS
- *Class*: Ultralight, freshwater
- *Capacity*: 60 yds./4 lb.
- *Ratio*: 4.1:1
- *Weight*: 5.6 oz.
- One ball bearing.
- Strong graphite frame.
- Smooth, spool-applied disc drag system.
- Soft rubber pinch ring on rotor for reduced line wear.
- Stainless steel Insta-Grab' pickup pin.
- Left/right hand retrieve.
- Selective silent anti-reverse.
- Filled with 6-lb. test line.
MSRP: $11.99

SYNERGY STEEL 1402TI
SPECIFICATIONS
- *Class*: Light, freshwater
- *Capacity*: 70 yds./6 lb.
- *Ratio*: 3.4:1
- *Weight*: 8 oz.
- 2 ball bearings.
- Polished stainless steel front cone and rear cover with Secure-Lock securing screw in the rear cover.
- Titanium line guide.
- Dual titanium Insta-Grab' pickup pins.
- Durable lightweight graphite frame.
- Gear-driven adjustable disc drag system.
- Strong, lightweight, gold chrome-plated steel handle with textured soft rubber knob.
- Left/right convertible retrieve.
- Soft, durable elastomer pinch ring for reduced line wear.
- Filled with 6-lb. test line.
MSRP: $14.99

SYNERGY STEEL 1802TI
SPECIFICATIONS
- *Class*: Medium, freshwater
- *Capacity*: 75 yds./10 lb.
- *Ratio*: 3.8:1
- *Weight*: 10.3 oz.
- 2 ball bearings.
- Polished stainless steel front cone and rear cover with Secure-Lock securing screw in the rear cover.
- Titanium line guide.

STEEL MICROSPIN

- Dual titanium Insta-Grab' pickup pins.
- Durable lightweight graphite frame.
- Gear-driven adjustable disc drag system.
- Strong, lightweight, gold chrome-plated steel handle with textured soft rubber knob.
- Left/right convertible retrieve.
- Soft, durable elastomer pinch ring for reduced line wear.
- Features selective silent anti-reverse and bait clicker.
- Filled with 10-lb. test line.
MSRP: $14.99

SPIDERCAST™ REELS

300 PRO BAITCASTING REEL SC300P

400 PRO BAITCASTING REELS C400P

ALLOY SPINNING REELS SCA10

ALLOY SPINNING REELS SCA30

ALLOY SPINNING REELS SCA50

LOW PROFILE 300 BAITCASTING REEL SCL300

300 PRO BAITCASTING REEL
Features:
- Instant Anti-Reverse for instant hooksets
- Machine aluminum frame and side-plates
- Machined aluminum high performance spool
- Fully adjustable 6-position centrifugal cast control for easy precise casting
- Patented ergonimic body styling with soft touch grip pad
- Titanium nitride line guide
- Cross-web line weave for even line winding
- Custom laser-etched sideplate

SPECIFICATIONS
Model: SC300P
Bearings: 3
Capacity: 10 lb./120 yds.
Weight: 10.1 oz.
Gear ratio: 5.1:1
MSRP: $94.95

400 PRO BAITCASTING REEL
Features:
- Ergonomic round reel with built-in thumb rest and thumb pad
- Instant Anti-Reverse for instant hooksets
- Crank tool for quick adjustment and cleaning
- Machine aluminum frame

- Machined aluminum high performance spool
- Oversized titanium nitride line guide reduces line wear and allows for easier casting
- Cross-web line weave for even line winding

SPECIFICATIONS
Model: SC400P
Bearings: 4
Capacity: 12 lb./135 yds.
Weight: 10.2 oz.
Gear ratio: 5.2:1
MSRP: $84.95

ALLOY SPINNING REELS
Features:
- Durable aluminum alloy die-cast body
- Instant Anti-Reverse for instant hooksets
- Heavy duty, long stroke oscillation
- Smooth teflon/stainless steel multi-disk drag system
- Nickel-plated steel mainshaft
- Hardened brass pinion gear

SPECIFICATIONS
Model: SCA10
Bearings: 5
Capacity: 6 lb./140 yds.
Weight: 11.9 oz.
Gear ratio: 5.2:1
MSRP: $74.95

Model: SCA30
Bearings: 5
Capacity: 8 lb./240 yds.
Weight: 14.6 oz.
Gear ratio: 5.3:1
MSRP: $74.95

Model: SCA50
Bearings: 5
Capacity: 10 lb./310 yds.
Weight: 18.2 oz.
Gear ratio: 4.6:1
MSRP: $74.95

LOW PROFILE 300 BAITCASTING REEL
Features:
- Instant Anti-Reverse for instant hooksets
- Easy access aluminum spool
- Fully adjustable 6-position centrifugal cast control for easy precise casting
- Flippin' switch
- Soft-handle knobs

SPECIFICATIONS
Model: SCL300
Bearings: 3
Capacity: 12 lb./110 yds.
Weight: 8.2 oz.
Gear ratio: 5.1:1
MSRP: $64.95

REELS

SPIDERCAST™ REELS

LOW PROFILE
500
BAITCASTING
REEL

LOW PROFILE
500 PRO
BAITCASTING
REEL
SCL500P

SLC200 LOW
PROFILE
BAITCASTING
REELS
SCL200

SLC200 LOW
PROFILE
BAITCASTING
REELS
SCL201

LOW PROFILE 500 BAITCASTING REEL

Features:
- Instant Anti-Reverse for instant hooksets
- Patented cartridge spool system
- Aluminum spool and spare graphite spool
- Fully adjustable 6-position centrifugal cast control for easy precise casting
- Flippin' switch
- Soft-handle knobs

SPECIFICATIONS
Model: SCL500
Bearings: 5
Capacity: 12 lb./110 yds.
Weight: 8.5 oz.
Gear ratio: 5.1:1
MSRP: $74.95

LOW PROFILE 500 PRO BAITCASTING REEL

Features:
- Instant Anti-Reverse for instant hooksets
- Patented cartridge spool system
- Aluminum frame
- Aluminum spool and spare graphite

spool
- Fully adjustable 6-position centrifugal cast control for easy precise casting
- Patented ergonimic body styling with soft touch grip pad
- Titanium nitride line guide
- Cross-web line weave for even line winding

SPECIFICATIONS
Model: SCL500P
*Bearings:*5
Capacity: 12 lb./120 yds.
Weight: 10.2 oz.
Gear ratio: 6.1:1
*MSRP:*94.95

SLC200 LOW PROFILE BAITCASTING REELS

Bringing the rare combination of performance and value out of the shadows and into the light, SpiderCast SCL200 & SCL201 baitcast reels deliver incredible power, sleek design and dynamic good looks. Available in both right and left-hand versions, these reels are packed with features and exceptionally priced for anglers who are fiercely competitive and

wickedly smart.
Features:
- Dual bearing drive for smooth performance
- Instant Anti-Reverse for solid hooksets
- Ergonomic design reduces hand fatigue
- User-friendly magnetic brake adjustment system
- Available in left- and right-hand versions

SPECIFICATIONS
Model SCL200
(Right hand retrieve)
Bearings: 2
Capacity: 12 lb./120 yds
Weight: 8.8 oz
Gear ratio: 6.1:1
MSRP: $54.95

Model SCL201
(Left hand retrieve)
Bearings: 2
Capacity: 12 lb./120 yds.
Weight: 8.8 oz
Gear ratio: 6.1:1
MSRP: $54.95

ZEBCO® REELS

33® CLASSIC SPINCAST

33® GOLD SPINCAST

33® SPINCAST

GENESIS™ GEN100 BAITCAST

GENESIS™ GEN20 AND GEN 30 SPINNING

REELS

33® CLASSIC SPINCAST REEL

Features:

- Helical-cut, extra-hard all-metal Zebco Magnum Gears
- Zebco Magnum Drag System
- Cut-proof ceramic pickup pin
- New "burnt gold" powder-coated stainless steel cover
- Improved dual bearing drive system
- Continuous Anti-Reverse for instant hooksets

SPECIFICATIONS
Ball bearings: 2
Gear ratio: 3.5:1
Continuous Anti-Reverse
Rhino Dual-Cam drag
Pre-spooled with 90 yds./10 lb. line
MSRP: $23.95

33® GOLD SPINCAST REEL

Features:

- Stainless steel covers
- Left/right retrieve
- Dual cam all-metal Zebco Magnum drag
- Positive Pickup

SPECIFICATIONS
Ball bearings: 2

Gear ratio: 3.5:1
Pre-spooled with 90 yds./10-pound line
MSRP: $18.95

33® SPINCAST REEL

Everyone who fishes knows the Zebco 33. It's been in production longer than any other spincast reel. As anyone, "What was the first reel you ever fished with?" The answer will, more often than not, be "the Zebco 33." Zebco's newest 33 still features corrosion-resistant all-metal gears and polished stainless steel covers, but also has a smooth ball-bearing drive system and a dual-cam all-metal drag. It's also convertible for left or right-handed retrieve.

SPECIFICATIONS

- Ball bearing drive
- Dual-cam adjustable drag
- Changeable right or left retrieve
- All-metal gears
- QuickSet anti-reverse
- Pre-spooled with 10-pound line

MSRP: $16.95

GENESIS™ GEN100 BAITCAST REEL

The Genesis model GEN100 baitcast reel features a ball-bearing drive, star-adjustable drag system, sturdy graphite frame and a DynaMag™ magnetic cast control. It comes pre-spooled with 12 pound line.

SPECIFICATIONS
Gear ratio: 5.1:1
MSRP: $19.95

GENESIS™ GEN20 AND GEN 30 SPINNING REELS

Genesis spinning reels, models GEN20 and GEN30 offer great versatility. Both have a ball-bearing drive, front-adjustable smooth drag, Continuous Anti-Reverse™, a Twist-Reducer™ line roller and an aluminum Long Stroke® spool. The GEN20 comes pre-spooled with 8 pound test line, and the GEN30 is pre-spooled with 10 pound test line.

SPECIFICATIONS
Gear ratio: 4.7:1
MSRP: $11.95

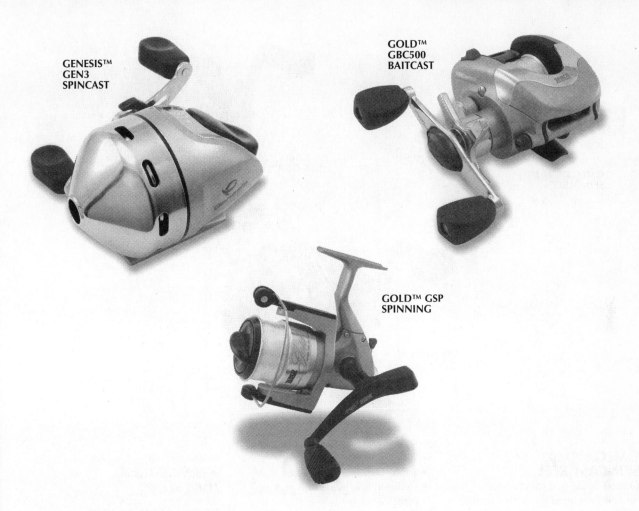

GENESIS™
GEN3
SPINCAST

GOLD™
GBC500
BAITCAST

GOLD™ GSP
SPINNING

GENESIS™ GEN3 SPINCAST REEL

The Genesis model GEN3 spincast reel features a large, easy-to-use thumb button, steel front cover for long-lasting durability and a star-adjustable full-range drag system that prevents line twist found in traditional spincast reels. The GEN3 features a Positive Pickup™, steel front cover, quick-change spool system, star-adjustable Twist-Reducer™ drag system, and comes pre-spooled with 10 pound line.

SPECIFICATIONS
Gear ratio: 3.8:1
MSRP: $9.99

GOLD™ GBC500 BAITCAST REEL

Performance is the key to the success of the Gold GBC500 baitcasting reel, with professional features for the smoothest possible feel and adjustable magnetic braking for the ultimate in cast control. The GBC500 features corrosion resistant all-metal gears, a star-adjustable Zebco Magnum drag system and a Flippin' Switch™ for fishing with finesse. It is built on a solid and lightweight graphite frame.

Features:
• Continuous Anti-Reverse
• Magnetic spool braking system
• Flippin' Switch
• Aluminum spool

SPECIFICATIONS
Ball bearings: 4
Gear ratio: 5.1:1
Capacity: 100 yds with 12 lb. line
Pre-spooled with 12-lb. line
MSRP: $29.95

GOLD™ GSP SPINNING REELS

These 5-bearing reels feature the Twist-Reducer line rooler and are designed for the serious angler, to battle serious fish.

Features:
• 4 ball bearings plus clutch bearing
• Aluminum Long Stroke spool
• Ultra-smooth front drag
• Selective Continuous Anti-Reverse
• TRU-Balance handle and rotor
• Spare graphite spool

SPECIFICATIONS
Model GSP40: Front drag, 4 ball bearings, 5.5:1 gear ratio, 120 yds./12 lb.
Model GSP20: Front drag, 4 ball bearings, 5.5:1 gear ratio, 110 yds./6 lb.
Model GSP30: Front drag, 4 ball bearings, 5.5:1 gear ratio, 150 yds/8 lb.
MSRP: $17.95

ZEBCO® REELS

OMEGA™ Z03 SPINCAST

ONE GOLD™

PROSTAFF® 2030™

OMEGA™ Z03 SPINCAST REEL

Omega is the first spincast reel to feature six ball bearings. It also features a unique and comfortable design unlike any ever seen before. The materials selected for this reel provide reliability and performance that are unmatched. And it has a feel that tells you immediately that this is the reel that will do the job right.

Features:

- 6 stainless steel ball bearings
- 3X positive line pick-up system
- Level wind oscillating spool system
- Quick-change spare spool
- Diecast aluminum body and reel foot
- Continuous anti-reverse

- Aircraft aluminum covers
- Triple cam multi-disk drag
- Ceramic line guide and pick-up pins
- Power crank reversible handle
- Sealed soft-touch rubber thumb button
- Pre-spooled with 10-pound line

SPECIFICATIONS
Gear ratio: 3.7:1
MSRP: $50.00

ONE GOLD™

SPECIFICATIONS
- Ball bearing drive
- *Gear ratio:* 3.6:1
- Zebco Star Magnum Drag
- Selective on/off anti-reverse
- Pre-spooled with 100 yds./14 lb.

line
- Right-hand retrieve
MSRP: $22.99

PROSTAFF® 2030™

SPECIFICATIONS
- Ball bearing drive
- Lightweight, durable graphite frame
- Star-actuated fade-free drag
- Zebco Magnum Gears
- Pro-style paddle handle
- Silent Anti-Reverse
- Star Magnum Drag
- Gear ratio: 3.6:1
- Pre-spooled with 90 yds./14-lb. line
MSRP: $16.95

Degrease Your Reel
If you purchased a new fishing reel and found it a little stiff when casting, take it apart and remove some of the grease on the gears. Old reels work better, too, if you clean out gummed-up grease and replace it with fresh. Most reels come with a tube of grease; use it.

LURES

CRANKBAITS

ABU GARCIA® TORMENTORS

ARBOGAST MUD-BUG® G22

ARBOGAST MUD-BUG® G20

BASS PRO SHOPS® CHOW HOUND

ABU GARCIA® TORMENTORS

Minnow-shaped lures have been catching fish worldwide for decades. The more realistic the finish and the action the baits have, the better job they've done. One lure, Abu Garcia's Tormentor, in Europe has been getting a lot of attention the last few years and, now for the first time, is available in North America. The attention has been due mostly to the custom look of each bait and the fact that Tormentors really catch fish. It matches the food chain of game fish like no other. The torpedo shape creates rocket-like long-distance casts with pinpoint accuracy.

SPECIFICATIONS

Sizes: floating 2" weighing ⅛ oz.; floating 3" weighing ⁵⁄₁₆ oz.; floating 3.5" weighing ⅜ oz.; sinking 3" weighing ⁵⁄₁₆ oz., sinking 3" weighing ⅝ oz.

Finishes (hand-painted by airbrush): Black and Silver, Silver with Copper and Blue, Rainbow Trout, Green Shad,

Black Back.
MSRP: $3.99.

ARBOGAST MUD-BUG®

Bearing a remarkable resemblance in appearance and action to a crawfish, the Mud-Bug® is a deep-running bottom digger that will haul in the big ones. Its unique design enables it to "back out" of potential hang-up situations, and its durability is unparalleled.

SPECIFICATIONS

Model: G22
Size: 3½"
Weight: ⅝ oz.
Hook Size: #2
Cranking Depth: 7-9'*
MSRP: $3.99

Model: G20
Size: 3"
Weight: ¼ oz.
Hook Size: #4
Cranking Depth: 4-6'*
MSRP: $3.99

Colors: Perch, Crayfish/Orange Belly, Bone/Orange Belly, Chrome/Blue Back, Fire Tiger, Red Glitter/Black Back Bar
* *Depths approximate using 12-lb. test Silver Thread line*

BASS PRO SHOPS® CHOW HOUND

The Chow Hound was added to the Avoidance Behavior Lure Collection by Dr. Loren Hill due to the unique lip spinner blade configuration, which creates an awesome flash. The bait also delivers a tight, frantic wiggle, eliciting an immediate feeding response in bass.

SPECIFICATIONS

Size: 4"
Weight: ⅝ oz
MSRP: $5.99.
Colors: Bleeding Tennessee Shad, Natural Brown Craw, Baby Bass, Albino Shad, Green Shad, River Minnow, Bleeding Bass, Chrome/Black Back.

LURES

**BASS PRO SHOPS®
XPS SHALLOW CRANKBAIT**

**BERKLEY
FRENZY™ DIVER**

**BASS PRO SHOPS®
XPS SUSPENDING MINNOW**

BERKLEY FRENZY™ DIVING MINNOW

BASS PRO SHOPS® XPS EXTREME SHALLOW CRANKBAIT

When black bass are in a shallow water pattern, the new XPS (Extreme Performance Series) Shallow Crankbait will be an excellent addition to your tackle box. One of the many new XPS baits by Bass Pro Shops, the XPS Shallow Crankbait features a multi-chambered plastic body with a variegated rattle chamber with a range of 0' to 2'. Offering incredibly fine-scale detail on holographic laser tape finish for ultimate flash and coloration, the XPS Shallow Crankbait is perfect for fishing murky or stained water. Lifelike 3-D eyes and quality Mustad® hooks complete this bait.

SPECIFICATIONS
Size: 2¼".
MSRP: $4.99.
Colors: Bleeding Tennessee Shad, Firetiger, Natural Brown Craw, Green Shad, River Minnow, Chrome/Black Back, Bone Hologram, Watermelon, Chartreuse/Black Back.

BASS PRO SHOPS® XPS SUSPENDING MINNOW

This suspending minnow is designed with a multi-chambered plastic body with a variety of rattles strategically placed throughout the lure. Each lure has fine-scale detail and a layer of extremely thin holographic laser tape and 3-D eyes. A great lure to throw to bass when the water is cool and they're feeding on shad.

SPECIFICATIONS
Size: 4¾"
Weight: 9⁄16 oz.
MSRP: $4.99
Colors: Bleeding Tennessee Shad, Gold/Black Back, Chrome/Blue Back, Clown, Green Shad, Bleeding Bass, Copper Shad, Chrome/Black Back, Aurora, Silver/Chartreuse Back, Gray Shad and Purple Shad.

BERKLEY FRENZY™ DIVER

The Frenzy Diver's internal weight transfer system shifts weight to the rear for bullet-like casting into the wind. The weight moves to the nose during retrieve for a steep dive that keeps the lure in the strike zone longer and creates actions that turn fish on! Add to that a variety of lifelike finishes and you've got a crankbait ideal for attracting fish in stained or muddy water conditions. Each Frenzy hardbait is made of polycarbonate and is finished with an extra-hard clear-coat for years of trouble-free fishing. Frenzy Divers come standard with top quality, super-sharp VMC® Cone Cut treble hooks.

Specifications
Model: Shallow Diver and Medium Diver
Weight: ⅜ oz.
MSRP: $5.49

Models: Medium Mag Diver and Deep Mag Diver
Weight: ⅞ oz.
MSRP: $6.49

Colors: Firetiger, Crawdad, Treadfin Shad, Perch, Blue Gill, Blue Chartreuse, Chrome Bluegill, Chrome/Black, Chrome/Blue, Chrome Perch, Chrome Threadfin Shad (Medium and Deep Mag Divers available only in Blue Chartreuse, Bluegill, Fire Tiger and Tennessee Shad)

BERKLEY FRENZY™ DIVING MINNOW

The hard-durable coat on each minnow takes the abuse of rocks, logs and sharp teeth, while the attention-getting rattle attracts fish through sound and vibrations. Ideal for both trolling and casting, the minnows are built with VMC Cone Cut hooks to stick to the fish fast and hold 'em tight.

SPECIFICATIONS
Model: Shallow
Size: 4"
Depth: 0-4'
MSRP: $6.49

Model: Medium
Size: 4"
Depth: 8-10'
MSRP: $6.49
Colors: Baby Bass, Chrome Black, Chrome Blue, Chrome Perch, Chrome Rainbow, Chrome Threadfin Shad, Clown, Gold/Black, Rainbow Trout, Perch, Fire Tiger, Silver Shad, Threadfin Shad

LURES

CRANKBAITS

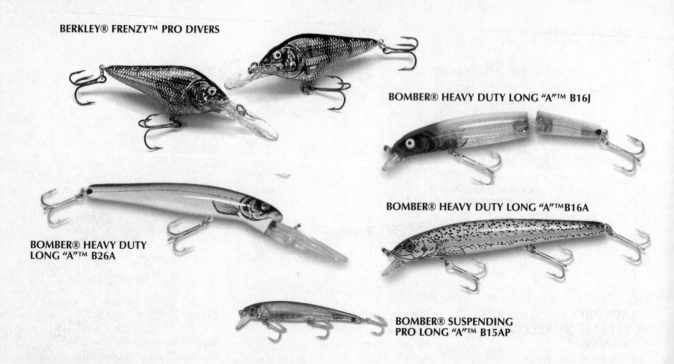

BERKLEY® FRENZY™ PRO DIVERS

BOMBER® HEAVY DUTY LONG "A"™ B16J

BOMBER® HEAVY DUTY LONG "A"™ B16A

BOMBER® HEAVY DUTY LONG "A"™ B26A

BOMBER® SUSPENDING PRO LONG "A"™ B15AP

BERKLEY® FRENZY™ PRO DIVER

Frenzy Pro Divers are available in seven popular colors and each lure has a holographic finish with life-like features found on real baitfish. The patterns and texturing of the body include the finite details of scales and gills. The 3-D eyes add another dimension to the Frenzy look. Available in medium and shallow diving models

SPECIFICATIONS
MSRP: $5.49
Colors: Pro Perch, Pro Bluegill, Pro Threadfin Shad, Lime Blue Chartreuse, Golden Shiner, Emerald Shiner, Silver Blue Shad

BOMBER® HEAVY DUTY LONG "A"™

When you need a heavy-duty lure to go down and get 'em, that's when you put on the 26A. Effective when casting or trolling. The 16A is a shallow-water producer in saltwater and for bigger freshwater game fish. This lure features extra-thick walls for durability and 3X strong hooks to pull in the big ones. This Jointed Heavy Duty Long "A"™ will perform just like the 16A with the added action of a jointed tail.

SPECIFICATIONS
Model: B26A
Size: 6"
Weight: 1½ oz.
Hook Size: 1/0
Cranking Depth: 15-20'*
Trolling Depth: 20-25'*
MSRP: $5.99

Model: B16J (Jointed)
Size: 6"
Weight: 1 oz.
Hook Size: 1/0
Cranking Depth: 2-3'*
Trolling Depth: 4-6'*
MSRP: $6.99

Model: B16A
Size: 6"
Weight: ⅞ oz.
Hook Size: #1
Cranking Depth: 2-3'*
Trolling Depth: 4-6'*
MSRP: $5.99
Colors: Black, Mother of Pearl, Yellow Baby Striper, Silver Flash/Pink Back & Belly, Rainbow Trout, Baby Striper, Chartreuse Flash/Orange Belly, Silver Flash/White Back & Belly/Red Head, Silver Prism/Blue Back, Silver Flash, Pearl/Yellow, White/Yellow, Fire River Minnow/Orange Belly, Silver Chrome Minnow/Black Back, Gold Chrome Minnow/Black Back, Silver Flash/

Green Back/White Belly, Silver Flash/Blue Back, Bonita, Spanish Mackerel, Silver Flash/Chartreuse Back & Belly
 * *depths approximate using 20-25lb test Silver Thread® line*

BOMBER® SUSPENDING PRO LONG "A"™

Tournament pros like Tim Horton and Mark Menendez say this is the "Ultimate Bomber® Jerkbait." The Suspending Pro Model Long "A"™ features proven jerkbait color patterns, a realistic fish eye and is weighted to suspend out of the package. An extremely true-running lure, the Suspending Pro Model Long "A"™ is all about performance, whether it's cast or trolled.

SPECIFICATIONS
Model: B15AP
Size: 4⅝"
Weight: ⁹⁄₁₆ oz.
Hook Size: #4
Cranking Depth: 4-6'*
MSRP: $4.99
Colors: Clown Flash, Blue Flash, Chartreuse Flash/Orange Belly, Silver Flash/Blue Back, Silver Flash/Red Head, Silver Flash/Orange Belly
 * *depths approximate using 10-14lb test Silver Thread® line*

BOMBER® LONG "A"™ B25A

BOMBER® LONG "A"™ B15J

BOMBER® LONG "A"™ B15A

BOMBER® LONG "A"™ B24A

BOMBER® LONG "A"™ B14A

BOMBER® LONG "A"™

The Long "A" trademark tight wiggle and rolling action create a life-like swimming action. It produces the same productive action whether fished with a slow retrieve on top or at a faster trolling speed using a downrigger. The molded-in lip design gives the lure added strength and true-running performance.

SPECIFICATIONS
Model: B25A (Deep Long "A")
Size: 4½"
Weight: ½ oz.
Hook Size: #2
Cranking Depth: 12-15'*
Trolling Depth: 20-25'*
MSRP: $4.29

Model: B15A (Long "A")
Size: 4½"
Weight: ⅜ oz.
Hook Size: #4
Cranking Depth: 2-3'*
Trolling Depth: 4-8*
MSRP: $3.69

Model: B15J (Jointed Long "A")
Size: 4½"
Weight: ⅜ oz.
Hook Size: #4
Cranking Depth: 3-4'**
Trolling Depth: 4-8'*
MSRP: $4.99

Model: B24A (Deep Long "A")
Size: 3½"
Weight: ½ oz.
Hook Size: #4
Cranking Depth: 10-12'**
Trolling Depth: 15-20'*
MSRP: $3.69

Model: B14A (Long "A")
Size: 3½"
Weight: ½ oz.
Hook Size: #6
Cranking Depth: 2-3'***
Trolling Depth: 4-8'*
MSRP: $3.69
Colors: Silver Flash/Green Back/White Belly, Silver Flash/Blue Back, Gold Chrome/Orange Belly, Rainbow Trout,

Baby Striper, Baby Pike, Fire Tiger Bass, Baby Bass/Orange Belly, Clear/Blue Nose, Pearl/Black to Gray Back/ Orange Belly, Fire River Minnow, Gold Chrome, Chartreuse Flash/ Orange Belly, Chartreuse Flash, Silver Flash/Orange Belly, Silver Flash, Silver Flash/Red Head, Chrome/Black Back/ Orange Belly, Chrome/Black Back, Chartreuse Flash/Blue Back/ Orange Belly, Bengal Fire Tiger, Silver Prism/ Blue Back, Silver Prism/Black Back, Gold Prism/Black Back & Bars/Orange Belly, Silver Flash/ Chartreuse Back & Belly. Model B15A also available in Wonderbread, Silver Insert/Pink/ Chartreuse/Pink, Gold Chrome/ Charteuse/Pink, Chrome/Blue/ Pink/White, Purple/Black, Yellow Perch, Mother of Pearl, Clown, Chrome/ Chartreuse, Gold Chrome/ Fluorescent Orange/White, Trout/Green/Pink
* using 12-lb. test line, **using 10-20lb test line, ***using 10-14lb test line. Depths are approximate and achieved using Silver Thread® line.

Watch Your Line
Bass often inhale a crankbait, then swim off to one side or the other. You won't always feel these hits, but you will notice the line moving sideways if you pay attention to your line at all times.

CRANKBAITS

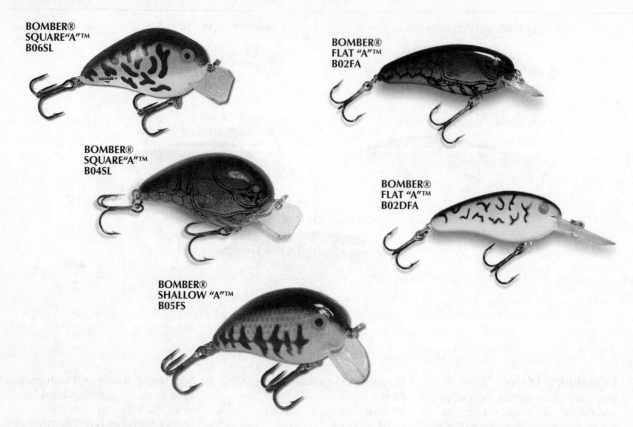

BOMBER®
SQUARE"A"™
B06SL

BOMBER®
FLAT "A"™
B02FA

BOMBER®
SQUARE"A"™
B04SL

BOMBER®
FLAT "A"™
B02DFA

BOMBER®
SHALLOW "A"™
B05FS

BOMBER® SQUARE"A"™

The Bomber® Square "A"™ features a square paddle with chamfered corners that allows this bait to run over fallen timber and through heavy cover. It produces a wide wobble and is built Bomber® tough.

SPECIFICATIONS
Model: B06SL
Size: 2⁵⁄₁₆"
Weight: ½ oz.
Hook Size: #3
Cranking Depth: 0-3'*
MSRP: $3.69

Model: B05SL
Size: 2"
Weight: ⅜ oz.
Hook Size: #6
Cranking Depth: 0-3'*
MSRP: $3.69

Model: B04SL
Size: 1⅝"
Weight: ¼ oz.
Hook Size: #8
Cranking Depth: 0-3'*
MSRP: $3.69
Colors: Oxbow Bream, Tennessee Shad, Chrome/Blue Back/Black Bars,
Red Apple Crawdad, Chartreuse/Black Scales, Silver Flash, Bengal Fire Tiger, Dark Brown Crawdad, Baby Bass/Orange Belly, Brown on Yellow, Lemon Lime/ Orange Belly, Fire Tiger/Orange Belly
* using 12-lb. test Silver Thread® line

BOMBER® SHALLOW "A"™

The Bomber® Shallow "A"™ is designed for shallow water and "wake" fishing. It produces a wide wobble and is built Bomber® tough.

SPECIFICATIONS
Model: B05FS
Size: 2"
Weight: ⅜ oz.
Hook Size: #6
Cranking Depth: 0-1'*
MSRP: $3.69
Colors: Oxbow Bream, Tennessee Shad, Chrome/Blue Back/Black Bars, Red Apple Crawdad, Chartreuse/Black Scales, Silver Flash, Bengal Fire Tiger, Dark Brown Crawdad, Baby Bass/Orange Belly, Brown on Yellow, Lemon Lime/Orange Belly, Fire Tiger/Orange Belly
* using 12-lb. test Silver Thread® line

BOMBER® FLAT "A"™

This flat-sided, near-neutral buoyancy crankbait generates a tight, vibrating action with a slow rise.

SPECIFICATIONS
Model: B02FA (Flat "A")
Size: 2½"
Weight: ⅜ oz.
Hook Size: #4
Cranking Depth: 3-5'*
Trolling Depth: 5-6'*
MSRP: $3.69

Model: B02DFA (Deep Flat "A")
Size: 2½"
Weight: ⅝ oz.
Hook Size: #4
Cranking Depth: 0-8'*
Trolling Depth: 12-15'*
MSRP: $3.69
Colors: Fire Tiger, Coppernose Bluegill, Bream/Orange, Silver Flash, Bengal Fire Tiger, Apple Red Crawdad, Black/Chartreuse, Tennessee Shad, Dark Brown Crawdad, Baby Bass/Orange Belly
* using 10-12-lb. test Silver Thread® line

BOMBER® MODEL "A"® B07A

BOMBER® MODEL "A"® B02A

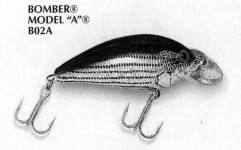

BOMBER® MODEL "A"® B06A

BOMBER® MODEL "A"® B05A

BOMBER® MODEL "A"®

The Model "A"® is a little slimmer, trimmer, has a faster wiggle and dives deeper than the ordinary crankbait. The bill of the Model "A"® is molded-in to ensure extra strength and true-running capabilities.

SPECIFICATIONS

Model: B07A
Size: 2⅝"
Weight: ½ oz.
Hook Size: #4
Cranking Depth: 8-10'*
MSRP: $3.69

Model: B06A
Size: 2⅛"
Weight: ⅜ oz.
Hook Size: #6
Cranking Depth: 8-10'*
MSRP: $3.69

Model: B05A
Size: 1⅞"
Weight: ⅕ oz.
Hook Size: #6
Cranking Depth: 4-6'*
MSRP: $3.69

Model: B02A
Size: 2⅛"
Weight: ¼ oz.
Hook Size: #6
Cranking Depth: 3-5'*
MSRP: $3.69

Colors: Silver Shad, Tennessee Shad, Oxbow Bream, Dull Fluorescent, White, Baby Striper, Apple Red Crawdad, Dark Brown Crawdad, Chrome/Blue/Black Bars, Silver Flash, Lemon Lime, Baby Bass/Chartreuse Belly, Bream, Black Herringbone, Baby Bass/OB, Dark Green Crawdad, Fire Crawdad, Metachrome Black Back, Baby Threadfin Shad, Black Chartreuse, Brown on Yellow, Baby Bass, Fire River Minnow, Chartreuse Herringbone, Fire Tiger, G-Fleck Brown Crawdad, G-Fleck Bengal Fire Tiger
* using 12-lb. test Silver Thread® line

Pump and Drop
When fishing deep-running crankbaits, try working your rod with a pump-and-drop action, pulling the rod forward and dropping it back. This allows the lure to "tread water," giving bass the chance to catch up and inhale it.

LURES

CRANKBAITS

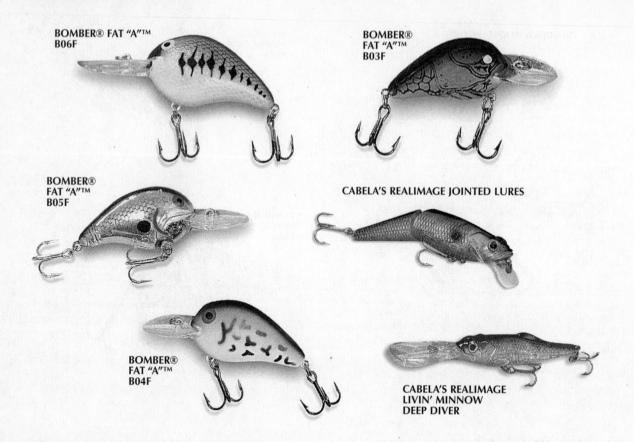

BOMBER® FAT "A"™
B06F

BOMBER®
FAT "A"™
B03F

BOMBER®
FAT "A"™
B05F

CABELA'S REALIMAGE JOINTED LURES

BOMBER®
FAT "A"™
B04F

CABELA'S REALIMAGE
LIVIN' MINNOW
DEEP DIVER

BOMBER® FAT "A"™

The Fat "A"™ series is designed to deliver a buoyancy characteristic equal to or greater than balsa crankbaits.

SPECIFICATIONS
Model: B06F
Size: 2¼"
Weight: ⅝ oz.
Hook Size: #3
Cranking Depth: 8-10'*
MSRP: $3.69

Model: B05F
Size: 2"
Weight: ⅜ oz.
Hook Size: #6
Cranking Depth: 6-8'*
MSRP: $3.69

Model: B04F
Size: 1½"
Weight: ⅛ oz.
Hook Size: #8
Cranking Depth: 4-6'*
MSRP: $3.69

Model: B03F
Size: 1¼"
Weight: ⅛ oz.
Hook Size: #10
Cranking Depth: 4-6'*
MSRP: $3.69
Colors: Lemon Lime/Orange Belly, Baby Bass/Orange Belly, Chrome/Blue Back/Black Bars, Brown on Yellow, Red Apple Crawdad, Silver Tennessee Shad W/Red Eyes, Chartreuse Baby Bass, Silver Flash, Oxbow Bream, Dark Brown Crawdad, Bengal Fire Tiger, G-Fleck Bengal Fire Tiger, Chartreuse/Black Scales, Fire Tiger/Orange Belly, Baby Threadfin Shad
* *using 12-lb. test Silver Thread® line*

CABELA'S REALIMAGE JOINTED LURES

The jointed body of these incredibly lifelike baits gives an erratic action on a wide-wobbling shallow dive that's absolutely deadly on bass and other gamefish. The slender body mimics a minnow perfectly to entice big fish into striking. Just as deadly cranked on a straight or stop-and-go retrieve as twitched on top of the water.

SPECIFICATIONS
Size: 3¾"
Weight: ⁵⁄₁₆ oz.
MSRP: $3.99
Colors: Shad, Perch, Baby Bass, Rainbow Trout, Golden Shiner, Blue Shad

CABELA'S REALIMAGE LIVIN' MINNOW DEEP DIVER

You know they're down there, hiding out in the cool deep water. So go after them with one of these deep-diving/floating crankbaits. The RealImage finish is just what it takes to pull them out of hiding and lure them in for a bite. VMC needle cone-cut hooks.

SPECIFICATIONS
Sizes/Weights: 2¾", ³⁄₁₆ oz.; 3½", ⅜ oz.; 4½", ⅞ oz. (Length excludes 1½" diving bill.)
MSRP: $3.99
Colors: Shad, Golden Shiner, Sunfish, Blue Shad, Baby Bass, Rainbow Trout

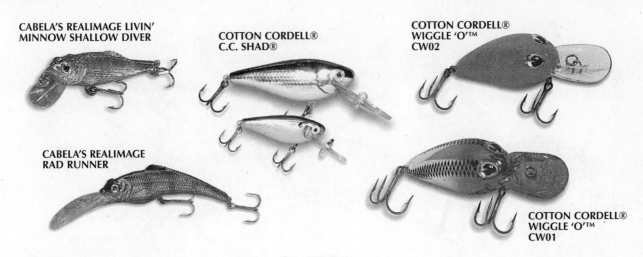

CABELA'S REALIMAGE LIVIN' MINNOW SHALLOW DIVER

CABELA'S REALIMAGE RAD RUNNER

COTTON CORDELL® C.C. SHAD®

COTTON CORDELL® WIGGLE 'O'™ CW02

COTTON CORDELL® WIGGLE 'O'™ CW01

CABELA'S REALIMAGE LIVIN' MINNOW SHALLOW DIVER

The Shallow Diver can be used as a floater for steady retrieves or as a suspending bait for a stop-and-go retrieve.

SPECIFICATIONS

Model: Floater for steady retrieves
Sizes/Weights: 2¾", ³⁄₁₆ oz.; 3½", ⅜ oz.; 4⅜", ¾ oz.
MSRP: $3.99
Colors: Shad, Golden Shiner, Blue Shad, Baby Bass, Rainbow Trout, Sunfish

Model: Suspending for stop-and-go retrieve
Sizes/Weights: 2¾", ³⁄₁₆ oz.; 3½", ⅜ oz.
MSRP: $3.99
Colors: Shad, Golden Shiner, Blue Shad, Baby Bass, Rainbow Trout, Sunfish

CABELA'S REALIMAGE RAD RUNNER

The curved profile of the Rad Runner adds a wider wobble to the action of the RealImage series for trolling or slow cranking for bass and other gamefish that key in on the speed and motion of the lure. The loud rattle chamber signals out to fish and begs them to "come and get it." The bright, flashy finish is highly visible and drives fish crazy on this floater/diver.

SPECIFICATIONS
Size: 3 ½"
Weight: ½ oz.
MSRP: $3.99

Colors: Shad, Perch, Firetiger, Chartreuse/Silver, Golden Shiner, Blue Shad

COTTON CORDELL® C.C. SHAD®

The deep-running C.C. Shad is a favorite of bass anglers. It can be trolled to depths up to 20 feet with 150 feet of 10-pound-test line. The Wee Shad delivers pulsating action on spinning or spincast gear. The small profile means it is a great producer in ponds, streams, rivers and lakes.

SPECIFICATIONS
Model CD12 (C.C. Shad)
Size: 2½"
Weight: ⅓ oz.
Hook size: 6
Cranking depth: 6-8'
Trolling depth: 20'

Model C11 (Wee Shad)
Size: 1½"
Weight: ⅛ oz.
Hook size: 10
Cranking depth: 2-4

Colors: Chrome/Black, Shad, Black/Orange/Chartreuse, Chrome/Blue, Arkansas Shiner, Blue/Chartreuse/Orange, Smoky Joe, Chartreuse Shad, Metalized Perch

COTTON CORDELL® WIGGLE 'O'™

The new Wiggle 'O' and Big Wiggle 'O' crankbait by Cotton Cordell is true running at high cranking speeds with a wide wobble action that fish can't resist. The Wiggle O's hooks will not "foul" each other or on the paddle. It cranks and trolls straight, right out of the package — no tuning required!

SPECIFICATIONS
Model: CW02 (Big Wiggle "O")
Size: 2½"
Weight: ¾ oz.
Hook Size: #2
Cranking Depth: 8-10'*
Trolling Depth: 14-18'*
MSRP: $3.99
Colors: Flaky Doctor, Simba, Green Pirate, Blue Pirate, Chrome Silver Shad, Chrome Gold Shad, Chrome Blue Shad, Baby Bass, Pearl Purple Splatter, Pearl Gold Shad, Clown, Kryptonite, Yellow Fever, Hummingbird, Chartreuse Gold Shad, Chartreuse Green Shad, Black Gold, Bone Black Splatter, Fire Tiger, Orange Craw Bug, Silver Tongue, Valdez Shad, Sunkissed, Electric Banana, Chartreuse Craw Bug, Golden Craw Bug, Watermelon Seed, Ghost Brown Craw, Ghost Green Craw

Model: CW01 (Wiggle "O")
Size: 2"
Weight: ⁷⁄₁₆ oz.
Hook Size: #4
Cranking Depth: 8-10'*
Trolling Depth: 14-18'*
MSRP: $3.99
Colors: Tickled Pink, Scarlet Polly, Lemon Lime, Sun Fire, Silver Shad, Passion Polly, Blue Polly, Copper Polly, Black Widow, Red Dog, Panda, Fluorescent Orange, Flakey Docctor, Green Pirate, Blue Pirate
* using 12-lb. test line

LURES

CRANKBAITS

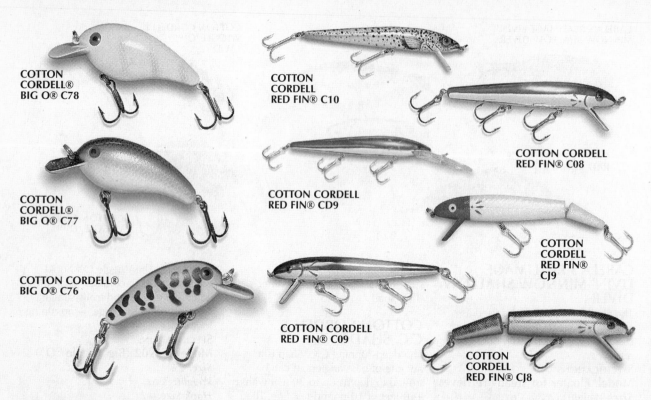

COTTON CORDELL® BIG O® C78

COTTON CORDELL® BIG O® C77

COTTON CORDELL® BIG O® C76

COTTON CORDELL RED FIN® C10

COTTON CORDELL RED FIN® CD9

COTTON CORDELL RED FIN® C09

COTTON CORDELL RED FIN® C08

COTTON CORDELL RED FIN® CJ9

COTTON CORDELL RED FIN® CJ8

COTTON CORDELL®
BIG O®

In 1967, when Fred Young carved the first Big O from a block of balsa wood, he created a legacy that has endured for decades. The three inch C78 launched thousands of crankbaits — the size that actually matches the size, shape and weight of the original Big O. The C77 2¼" Big O is a favorite lure of the bass tournament pros.

SPECIFICATIONS
Model: C78
Size: 3"
Weight: ⅜ oz.
Hook Size: #4
Cranking Depth: 4-6'*
MSRP: $3.69

Model: C77
Size: 2¼"
Weight: ⅓ oz.
Hook Size: #6
Cranking Depth: 3-5'*
MSRP: $3.69

Model: C76
Size: 2"
Weight: ¼ oz.
Hook Size: #8
Cranking Depth: 2-4'**
MSRP: $3.69

Colors: Chrome/Black, Pearl/Red Eye, Smoky Joe, Super Shad, Perch, Crawdad, Chartreuse Perch, Fire Tiger, Natural Crawdad
* using 10lb test line,
**using 6lb test line

COTTON CORDELL
RED FIN®

The Cordell Red Fin is the classic "V-wake" lure. Its hollow head allows it to be twitched and worked on the surface like no other minnow lure.

SPECIFICATIONS
Model: C10 (Red Fin)
Size: 7"
Weight: 1 oz.
Hook Size: #3/0
Cranking Depth: 0-1'*
MSRP: $3.99

**Model: CD9
(Deep Diving Red Fin)**
Size: 5"
Weight: ⅝ oz.
Hook Size: #2
Cranking Depth: 8-10'*
MSRP: $4.79

Model: C09 (Red Fin)
Size: 5"
Weight: ⅝ oz.

Hook Size: #2
Cranking Depth: 0-3'*
MSRP: $3.99

Model: CJ9 (Jointed Red Fin)
Size: 5"
Weight: ⅝ oz.
Hook Size: #2
Cranking Depth: 0-3'*
MSRP: $4.79

Model: C08 (Red Fin)
Size: 4"
Weight: ⅜ oz.
Hook Size: #4
Cranking Depth: 0-2'**
MSRP: $3.99

Model: CJ8 (Jointed Red Fin)
Size: 4"
Weight: ⅜ oz.
Hook Size: #4
Cranking Depth: 0-2'**
MSRP: $3.99
Colors: Gold/Black, Chrome/Black, Chrome/Blue, Smoky Joe, Pearl/Blue, Pearl/Red, Arkansas Shiner, Rainbow Trout, Gold/Orange
* using 12-lb. test line, **using 8lb test line

LURES

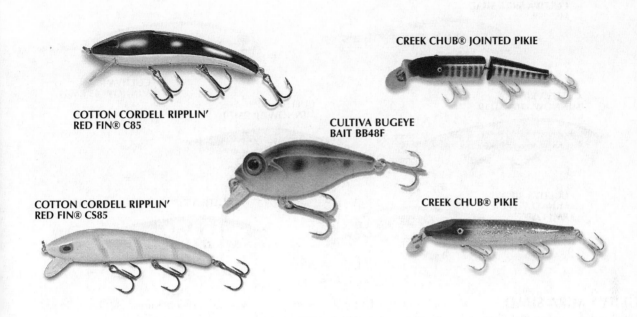

COTTON CORDELL RIPPLIN' RED FIN® C85

CREEK CHUB® JOINTED PIKIE

CULTIVA BUGEYE BAIT BB48F

COTTON CORDELL RIPPLIN' RED FIN® CS85

CREEK CHUB® PIKIE

COTTON CORDELL RIPPLIN' RED FIN®

The Ripplin' Red Fin's molded-in wavy sides give the illusion of constant movement when the lure is in the water.

SPECIFICATIONS
Model: C85 (Ripplin' Red Fin)
Size: 4½"
Weight: ⅜ oz.
Hook Size: #4
Cranking Depth: 0-3'*
MSRP: $3.99

CS85 (Suspending Ripplin' Red Fin)
Size: 4½"
Weight: ⅜ oz.
Hook Size: #4
Cranking Depth: 0-3'*
MSRP: $3.99
Colors: Chrome/Black, Chrome/Blue, Smoky Minnow, Chartreuse Perch, Chartreuse, Fire Tiger, Gold/Orange
* using 10lb test line

CREEK CHUB® PIKIE

These steady, high-profile floater/divers attain depths of 4-7' when casting and up to 11' when trolling. The extended lip model dives 5' deeper. The hardware of each Pikie is selected for lasting strength and durability.

SPECIFICATIONS
Model: I3000P (Jointed Pikie)
Size: 6"
Weight: 1¾ oz.
Hook size: 1/0
Cranking depth: 4-7'
Trolling depth: 11'
MSRP: $5.99
Model: I2600DDP (Jointed Pikie)
Size: 4½"
Weight: ⅞ oz.
Hook size: 2
Cranking depth: 9-12'
Trolling depth: 16'
MSRP: $5.99

Model: I2600P (Jointed Pikie)
Size: 4½"
Weight: ¾ oz.
Hook size: 2
Cranking depth: 4-7'
Trolling depth: 11'
MSRP: $5.99

Model: I2300P (Pikie)
Size: 5-¾"
Weight: 1-½ oz.
Hook size: 1/0
Cranking depth: 4-7'
Trolling depth: 11'
MSRP: $5.99

Model: I700DDP (Pikie)
Size: 4¼"
Weight: ¾ oz.

Hook size: 2
Cranking depth: 9-12'
Trolling depth: 16'
MSRP: $5.99

Model: I700P (Pikie)
Size: 4¼"
Weight: ¾ oz.
Hook size: 2
Cranking depth: 4-7'
Trolling depth: 11'
MSRP: $5.99
Colors: Red/White, Silver Flash, Perch, Pikie, Black/Red Eye, Yellow Striper

CULTIVA BUGEYE BAIT

A small-profile crankbait that is a shallow runner when retrieved. Stop, and the little lure pops to the surface, where twitching it is sure to drive big bass crazy. Features include Cultiva's exclusive "Living Eyes," chattering rattles, and beautifully painted finishes. Each lure is rigged with two Owner ST-36 Super Needle Point treble hooks (#8 on the front and #10 on the rear).
SPECIFICATIONS
Model: BB48F
Size: 2"
Weight: ¼ oz.
MSRP: $12.00
Colors: (06) Shiner, (13) Baby Bass, (53) Bull Frog, (57) Baby Frog

CRANKBAITS

CULTIVA MIRA SHAD MS50SP

CULTIVA RIP'N MINNOW 65 RM65

CULTIVA RIP'N MINNOW 110 RM110

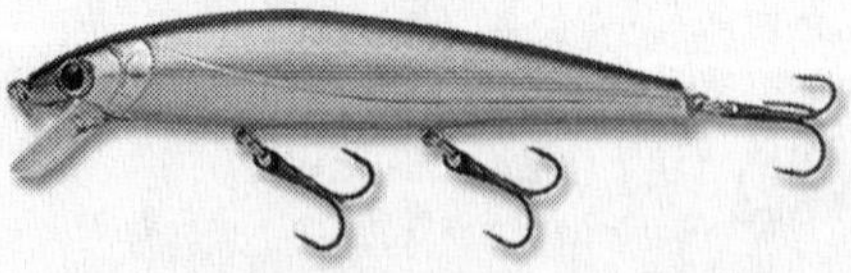

CULTIVA RIP'N MINNOW 70 RM70

CULTIVA RIP'N MINNOW 112 RM112SP

CULTIVA RIP'N MINNOW 90 RM90

CULTIVA MIRA SHAD

A small, forge-size bait that dives when trolled or retrieved, or stop the retrieve and twitch or jerk the bait as it suspends. Features include Cultiva's exclusive "Living Eyes," chattering rattles and a transparent, highly-reflective holographic finish. Each lure is rigged with two #10 Owner Stinger-36 Super Needle Point treble hooks.

SPECIFICATIONS

Model: MS50SP
Size: 2"
Weight: 1/7 oz.
MSRP: $12.00
Colors: (01) Gold Shad, (02) Black Pearl (06) Shiner, (11) Brown Trout, (13) Baby Bass, (30) Flame

CULTIVA RIP'N MINNOW 110

Large profile version that rips to three-foot depths. Features reflective foil finish, and rigged with three Owner Stinger-31 hooks.

SPECIFICATIONS

Model: RM110
Size: 4¼"
Weight: ½ oz.
MSRP: $12.00
Colors: (01) Gold Shad, (02) Black Pearl, (03) Pearl Green, (07) Tennessee Shad, (08) Fire Tiger, (13) Baby Bass, (27) Rainbow Trout

CULTIVA RIP'N MINNOW 112

With an enticing wobbling action, this minnow bait dives when retrieved, then stop and jerk the bait as it suspends. Cast or slow-troll the bait. Features include Cultiva's "Living Eyes" moving weight system with "thunder" rattles, and highly reflective textured, holographic and foil finishes. Each lure is rigged with two #4 Owner Stinger-41 Cutting Point treble hooks.

SPECIFICATIONS

Model: RM112SP
Size: 4½"
Weight: ¾ oz.
MSRP: $12.00
Colors: (02) Black Pearl, (06) Shiner, (13) Baby Bass, (15) Blue Back, (27) Rainbow Trout, (32) Golden Shiner, (67) Golden Ghost.

CULTIVA RIP'N MINNOW 65

Dives when retrieved, but then stop and twitch or jerk the bait as it suspends. Features exclusive "Living Eyes," rattling moving weight system, and reflective foil finish. Rigged with two Owner Stinger-31 Cutting Point™ treble hooks.

SPECIFICATIONS

Model: RM65
Size: 2⅗"
Weight: ¼ oz.
MSRP: $12.00
Colors: (02) Black Pearl, (04) Green Tiger, (06) Shiner, (11) Brown Trout, (13) Baby Bass, (15) Purple Magic, (32) Golden Shiner, (33) Blue Ghost, (50) Rainbow Ghost.

CULTIVA RIP'N MINNOW 70

Crank and twitch this tantalizing forage-size bait to five-foot depths. Features reflective foil finish, and rigged with two Owner ST-31 Cutting Point™ treble hooks.

SPECIFICATIONS

Model: RM70
Size: 2⅗"
Weight: ¼ oz.
MSRP: $12.00
Colors: (06) Shiner, (11) Brown Trout, (13) Baby Bass, (25) Blue Scales, (27) Rainbow Trout, (31) Green Scales

CULTIVA RIP'N MINNOW 90

For surface twitching or sub-surface ripping to two-foot depths. Dances and darts. Features reflective foil finish, and rigged with two Owner Stinger-31 hooks.

SPECIFICATIONS

Model: RM90
Size: 3⅗"
Weight: ¼ oz.
MSRP: $12.00
Colors: (01) Gold Shad, (02) Black Pearl, (03) Pearl Green, (07) Tennessee Shad, (08) Fire Tiger, (13) Baby Bass, (27) Rainbow Trout, (50) Rainbow Ghost

LURES

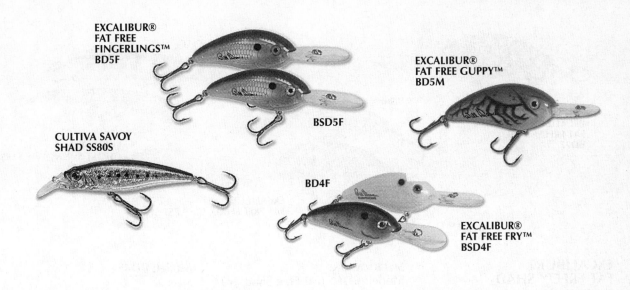

EXCALIBUR®
FAT FREE
FINGERLINGS™
BD5F

EXCALIBUR®
FAT FREE GUPPY™
BD5M

BSD5F

CULTIVA SAVOY
SHAD SS80S

BD4F

EXCALIBUR®
FAT FREE FRY™
BSD4F

CULTIVA SAVOY SHAD

A thick-bodied, shallow-diving bait that wobbles when retrieved, then sinks when it's stopped. Features include Cultiva's exclusive "Living Eyes," chattering rattles and highly-reflective textured, holographic and foil finishes. Each lure is rigged with two #4 Owner ST-47 Cutting Point™ treble hooks.

SPECIFICATIONS
Model: SS80S
Size: 2⅛"
Weight: ½ oz.
MSRP: $12.00
Colors: (06) Shiner, (15) Blue Back, (22) Green Back, (30) Flame, (32) Golden Shiner, (38) Pink Head

EXCALIBUR® FAT FREE FINGERLINGS™

Fat Free Fingerlings™ are just the right size for most crankbait situations. The suspending model, unlike other Fat Free Shads™, features a precision sound chamber with a "clicker" that reproduces the natural sounds of baitfish.

SPECIFICATIONS
Model: BD5F (Fat Free Fingerling)
Size: 2⅜"

Weight: ⅜ oz.
Hook Size: #6
Cranking Depth: 8-10'*
MSRP: $4.99

Model: BSD5F (Suspending Fat Free Fingerling)
Size: 2⅜"
Weight: ½ oz.
Hook Size: #6
Cranking Depth: 10-12'*
MSRP: $4.99
Colors: Coppernose Bluegill, Fire Tiger, Crawfish, Pearl White, Citrus Shad, Tennessee Shad, Threadfin Shad
* using 12-lb. Silver Thread® line

EXCALIBUR® FAT FREE FRY™

The Fat Free Fry™ is the perfect crankbait choice when the average size of shad and other baitfish are smaller than two inches.

SPECIFICATIONS
Model: BD4F (Fat Free Fry)
Size: 2"
Weight: ¼ oz.
Hook Size: #6
Cranking Depth: 4-6'*
MSRP: $4.99

Model: BSD4F (Suspending Fat Free Fry)
Size: 2"
Weight: ⁷⁄₁₆ oz.
Hook Size: #6
Cranking Depth: 4-6'*
MSRP: $4.99
Colors: Coppernose Bluegill, Fire Tiger, Crawfish, Pearl White, Citrus Shad, Tennessee Shad, Threadfin Shad
*using 12-lb. Silver Thread® line

EXCALIBUR® FAT FREE GUPPY™

The Fat Free Guppy™ is an easy-pulling crankbait that casts for distance and is made for medium to shallow waters.

SPECIFICATIONS
Model: BD5M
Size: 2⅜"
Weight: ⅜ oz.
Hook Size: #6
Cranking Depth: 4-6'*
MSRP: $4.99
Colors: Coppernose Bluegill, Fire Tiger, Crawfish, Pearl White, Citrus Shad, Tennessee Shad, Threadfin Shad
* using 12-lb. Silver Thread® line

A Varied Selection for Crankbait Success
If you often fish with crankbaits, stock your tackle box with a variety of crankbaits that exhibit different characteristics–crankbaits with and without rattles, crankbaits with tight wobbles and some with wide wobbles, crankbaits that run deep, shallow and in-between. By carrying lures with slightly different features, you're prepared for any crankbait situation that develops.

LURES

CRANKBAITS

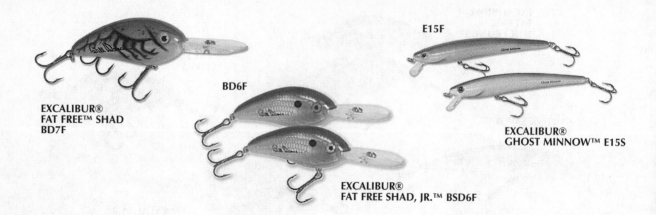

EXCALIBUR®
FAT FREE™ SHAD
BD7F

BD6F

EXCALIBUR®
FAT FREE SHAD, JR.™ BSD6F

E15F

EXCALIBUR®
GHOST MINNOW™ E15S

EXCALIBUR® FAT FREE™ SHAD

The Original Fat Free Shad is the "granddaddy" of the Fat Free™ Shad Family that took the 1995 B.A.S.S. Master's Classic Championship. The Fat Free Shad's® flat-sided design is unique to deep-running lures, providing easy control and almost-effortless retrieves. Fat Free Shads® feature kick-out paddles that "kick out" of hang-ups and work through cover. All Fat Free™ lures have an enticing action and a life-like reflective finish enhanced by realistic 3-D eyes and Excalibur® Rotating Treble Hooks.

SPECIFICATIONS
Model: BD7F (Fat Free Shad)
Size: 3"
Weight: ¾ oz.
Hook Size: #2
Cranking Depth: 14-18'*
MSRP: $4.99

Model: BSD7F (Suspending Fat Free Shad)
Size: 3"
Weight: 1 oz.
Hook Size: #2
Cranking Depth: 14-18*
MSRP: $4.99
Colors: Coppernose Bluegill, Fire Tiger, Crawfish, Pearl White, Citrus Shad, Tennessee Shad, Threadfin Shad
using 12-lb. Silver Thread® line

EXCALIBUR® FAT FREE SHAD, JR.™

The Fat Free Shad, Jr.™ has great castability, a tight wiggle and a pulsating vibration that is unmatched for its size.

SPECIFICATIONS
Model: BD6F (Fat Free Shad, Jr.)
Size: 2½"
Weight: ½ oz.
Hook Size: #4
Cranking Depth: 8-14'*
MSRP: $4.99

Model: BSD6F (Suspending Fat Free Shad, Jr.)
Size: 2½"
Weight: ⅝ oz.
Hook Size: #4
Cranking Depth: 10-14'*
MSRP: $4.99
Colors: Coppernose Bluegill, Fire Tiger, Crawfish, Pearl White, Citrus Shad, Tennessee Shad, Threadfin Shad
using 12-lb. Silver Thread® line

EXCALIBUR® FAT FREE SHALLOWS™

Fat Free Shallows™ are square-lipped, shallow to medium running crankbaits. These deflective-type baits are more weedless than most crankbaits and are designed to be retrieved in shallow waters with heavy cover.

SPECIFICATIONS
Model: BD6SL
Size: 2½"
Weight: ½ oz.
Hook Size: #4
Cranking Depth: 0-3'*
MSRP: $4.99

Model: BD5SL
Size: 2¼"
Weight: ⅜ oz.
Hook Size: #6
Cranking Depth: 0-3'*
MSRP: $4.99

Model: BD4SL
Size: 2"
Weight: ¼ oz.
Hook Size: #8
Cranking Depth: 0-3'*
MSRP: $4.99
Colors: Coppernose Bluegill, Fire Tiger, Crawfish, Pearl White, Citrus Shad, Tennessee Shad, Threadfin Shad
using 12-lb. Silver Thread® line

EXCALIBUR® GHOST MINNOW™

The Excalibur® Ghost Minnow™ has a captured weight and rattle system that other minnows lack. The wobbling, rolling action of the Ghost Minnow™ and the realistic look and small profile fill the need for a jerk-bait of its size.

SPECIFICATIONS
Model: E15F (Floating Ghost Minnow™)
Size: 4"
Weight: ¹¹⁄₃₂ oz.
Hook Size: #6
Cranking Depth: 0-2'*
MSRP: $4.99
Colors: Blue Shad, Natural Shad, River Shad

Model: E15S (Suspending Ghost Minnow™)
Size: 4"
Weight: ⅜ oz.
Hook Size: #6
Cranking Depth: 0-2'*
MSRP: $4.99
Colors: Blue Shad/Orange Belly, Natural Shad/Orange Belly, River Shad/Orange Belly
using 12-lb. Silver Thread® line

LURES

EXCALIBUR SWIM'N IMAGE® X9230

HEDDON HELL-BENDER™ W0800

W0800-D

HEDDON TADPOLLY® X9900

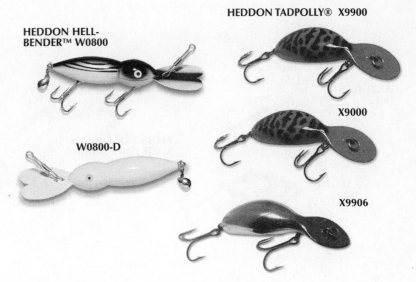

X9000

X9906

EXCALIBUR SWIM'N IMAGE®

This shallow-running crankbait closely resembles a three-inch threadfin shad. This natural-acting lure has a productive tight wiggle, snagless action and swims where many other lures can't.

SPECIFICATIONS
Model: X9230
Size: 3"
Weight: ⁷⁄₁₆ oz.
Hook Size: #6
Cranking Depth: 0-18"*
MSRP: $4.99
Colors: Fire Tiger, Threadfin Shad, Tennessee Shad, Gizzard Shad
* using 12-lb. Silver Thread® test line

HEDDON HELLBENDER™

The Magnum Hellbender is one of the original deep-diving crankbaits. When tied ahead of a lure, the Magnum Downrigger (no hooks) can take it down to 40 feet, depending on length of line and trolling speed.
SPECIFICATIONS

Model: W0800 (Magnum)
Size: 5½"
Weight: ⅞ oz.
Hook Size: #1
MSRP: $4.99

Model: W0800-D (Magnun Downrigger)
Size: 5½"
MSRP: $4.99
Colors: White, Silver, Striper

HEDDON TADPOLLY®

The Tadpolly… Heddon's all-time favorite lure for bass, salmon and steelhead trout alike. As a crankbait lure, it was one of Heddon's earliest crankbaits. Troll it or cast it. The Tadpolly is one of the most versatile baits from Heddon.
SPECIFICATIONS
Model: X9906 (Clatter Mag Tadpolly)
Size: 3¾"
Weight: ⅝ oz.
Hook Size: #6

Cranking Depth: 8'*
Trolling Depth: 11'*
MSRP: $4.99

Model: X9900 (Clatter Tad)
Size: 2⁵⁄₁₆"
Weight: ½ oz.
Hook Size: #4
Cranking Depth: 6'*
Trolling Depth: 9'*
MSRP: $4.99

Model: X9000 (Tadpolly)
Size: 2⁵⁄₁₆"
Weight: ½ oz.
Hook Size: #4
Cranking Depth: 6'*
Trolling Depth: 9'*
MSRP: $4.99
Colors: Tickled Pink, Scarlet Polly, Lemon Lime, Green Pirate, Flaky Doctor, Sun Fire, Silver Shad, Passion Polly, Blue Pirate, Blue Polly, Copper Polly, Black Widow, Red Dog, Panda
* using 12-lb. Silver Thread® line

LURES

Coming Off of Snags
You can sometimes unsnag a floating, deep-diving crankbait by allowing the line to go slack if the lure catches in timber. The lure should float upward and backward, freeing itself. Anglers sometimes remove the front treble hook to make the lure more snag-resistant.

CRANKBAITS

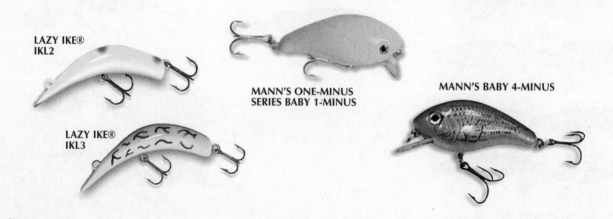

LAZY IKE®
IKL2

LAZY IKE®
IKL3

MANN'S ONE-MINUS
SERIES BABY 1-MINUS

MANN'S BABY 4-MINUS

LAZY IKE®

There are three periods of Lazy Ike production. From 1938 to 1940, the entire production was hand-made by Newell Daniels. Daniels left the company in 1940, turning over rights to the lure to Joseph Kautzky, founder of the Kautzky Company. It was primarily a gun and gunsmith shop and over the years expanded to include fishing and hunting supplies as well. Kautzky hired a man named "Pop" Shuck to fashion the lures. He used a jigsaw to cut out the blanks and finished them by hand. By 1945, demand had outstripped Shuck's ability to turn them out and they went to a lathe production. The era of the wooden Lazy Ike ended in 1960 with the advent of the plastic version. The Lazy Ike remains one of the most versatile lures ever created. Whether trolled for walleye, salmon or steelhead or cast for bass or pike, the Lazy Ike's action says it all!

Designed for spinning/spincast or light baitcasting, the Lazy Ike can be used for either casting or trolling.

SPECIFICATIONS
Model: IKL3 (Mighty Ike)
Size: 3"
Weight: ⅓ oz.
Hook Size: #6
Cranking Depth: shallow
MSRP: $4.39

Model: IKL2 (Lazy Ike)
Size: 2½"
Weight: ¼ oz.
Hook Size: #6
Cranking Depth: shallow
MSRP: $4.39
Colors: Metallic Blue, Pink, Fire Tiger, Red Eye, Red Spot, Yellow Spot, Red/White

MANN'S ONE-MINUS SERIES (TINY 1-, BABY 1-, MID 1- AND 1-)

Shallow water worldwide is home to the One-Minus series. From a maximum of 12 inches deep to the surface, there are seven different sizes and shapes to suit any fisherman. Twitch 'em, crank 'em, jerk 'em. They won't run any deeper than one foot. Fish them over weedbeds, stump field, shallow flats and other lunker holding areas. Wide wobbling action plus rattles. Includes Tiny 1-, Baby 1-, Mid 1- and 1- lures.

SPECIFICATIONS
Length: Tiny 1-, 1-1/2"; Baby 1-, 2-1/4"; Mid 1-, 2-3/4"; 1-, 3-1/4"
MSRP: $6.14 (Holographic $6.88)
Colors: Fire Red Fluorescent, Bone/Orange Belly, Brown Crawfish, Foil Flake Shad, Chrome/Blue Back, Blue Shad, Chrome/Black Back, Black Nite Glow, Baby Bass, Blue Shad Crystaglow, Pearl/Black Back Crystaglow, Bronze Back Crystaglow, Desert Sunset Crystaglow, Aqua Shad Crystaglow, Brown Crawfish Crystaglow, Alabama Shad Crystaglow, Pearl/Black Back, Tennessee Shad, Fire Shad, Alabama Shad, Grey Ghost, Green Shad Chartreuse, Rainbow Trout, Wild Shiner, Chartreuse Craw Crystaglow, Lemon Shad Crystaglow, Tennesse Shad Crystaglow, Bluegill Crystaglow, Blue Green Sunfish, White Crappie Crystaglow, Fire Shad Crystaglow, Gray Ghost Crystaglow. Holographic Patterns: Parakeet, Splatterback Sunfish, Orange Tiger, Chartreuse Threadfin, Copper Shad, Wounded Alewife, Red Shiner, Autumn Brown, Silver/Black Back. (Not all colors available for all sizes/models.)

MANN'S BABY 4-MINUS

The Baby 4- has the identical size, noise, and fish catching action as the Baby 1-, America's premier shallow crankbait, but it utilizes a new unique lip. This new lip not only provides a depth of 3 to 4 feet, but it also gives the Baby 4- the ability to be fished through shallow structure with reduced hang-ups.

SPECIFICATIONS
Length: 2¼"
Weight: ¼ oz.
MSRP: $6.14
Colors: Brown Craw, Splatterback Sunfish, Firetiger, Chrome/Blue, Chrome/Black, Wounded Alewife, Red Shiner, Autumn Brown, Silver/Black, Lemon Shad

LURES

CRANKBAITS

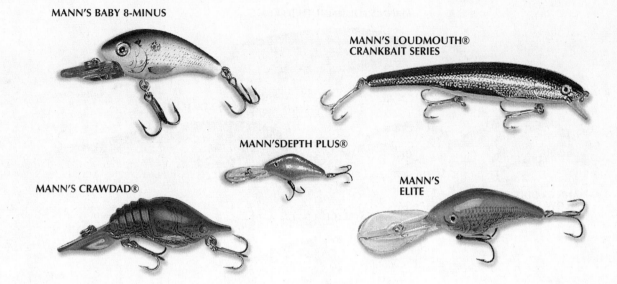

MANN'S BABY 8-MINUS

MANN'S LOUDMOUTH®
CRANKBAIT SERIES

MANN'SDEPTH PLUS®

MANN'S CRAWDAD®

MANN'S
ELITE

MANN'S BABY 8-

The new Baby 8- has the identical size, noise, and fish-catching abilities as its tournament winning predecessors, the Baby 1- and the Baby 4-. The Baby 8- utilizes a slightly longer lip that the Baby 4-. This new lip allows the Baby 8- to dive to a depth of just under 8 feet and gives it the ability to be fished through structure with reduced hang-ups. Designed for covering a lot of water in a hurry, the Baby 8- casts great into the wind, runs true at all retreive speeds and the special shape of the lip makes it bounce off stumps, logs, and treetops while providing extra protection for the hooks.

SPECIFICATIONS
Length: 2¼"
Weight: ¼ oz.

Colors: Brown Craw, Splatterback Sunfish, Firetiger, Chrome/Blue, Chrome/Black, Wounded Alewife, Red Shiner, Autumn Brown, Silver/Black, Lemon Shad

MANN'S CRAWDAD®

Gives a detailed imitation of fresh water's most delicious crustaceans with rattling and diving. Preferred by bass everywhere.

SPECIFICATIONS
Weight: ⅛, ¼ oz.
Length: 2⅜", 3⅛"
Depth: ⅛ oz. dives 3-5'; ¼ oz. dives 5-7'
MSRP: $5.56

Colors: Fire Red Fluorescent, Soft Shell Bone, Brown Crawfish, Chartreuse Crawfish, Green Crawfish

MANN'S DEPTH PLUS® SERIES

These floating, rattling divers run where their names say they do. Trolling and long casts with lighter line assure deeper operating ranges. Exclusive Davis System Lip allows greater depth with less resistance. 5+, 10+ and 15+ are ideal for smallmouth and white bass, plus finicky or clear water large-mouths. The 20+, the first to break the elusive 20-foot mark, is a favorite of bass tournament anglers. The 30+ is the deepest diver in its class.

SPECIFICATIONS
5+: ¹/₁₀ oz., 1½". Dives to 5 feet.
10+: ⅛ oz., 1¾". Dives to 10 feet.
15+: ¼ oz., 2¼". Dives to 15 feet.
20+: ⅝ oz., 3". Dives to 20 feet.
30+: ¾ oz., 3¼". Dives to 30 feet.
MSRP: $5.56 (Holographic $6.14)
MSRP: $6.14
Colors: Tennessee Shad, Brown Crawfish, Fire Shad, Chrome/Blue Back, Grey Ghost Crystaglow, Pearl/Blue Back Crystaglow, Parakeet Holographic, Splatterback Sunfish Holographic, Orange Tiger Holographic, Chartreuse Threadfin Holographic, Copper Shad Holographic, Wounded Alewife Holographic, Red Shiner Holographic, Autumn Brown Holographic, Silver/Black Back Holographic,

MANN'S ELITE SERIES

A series of lures featuring new and unique paint schemes, special Eagle Claw Kahle style treble hooks and bulging eyes. Available in Baby 1-, Mid 1-, Depth 15+ and 20+.

SPECIFICATIONS
MSRP: $6.14
Colors: Parakeet, Splatterback Sunfish, Orange Tiger Shad, Chartreuse Threadfin, Copper Shad, Wounded Alewife, Red Shiner, Autumn Brown, Pearl/Black

MANN'S LOUDMOUTH® CRANKBAIT SERIES

Precise combinations of steel shot inside a body made of a special, harder plastic makes these lures the loudest in the world. That noise attracts fish from further away and makes them attack. Paul Elias caught the heaviest stringer of the 1993 BASS Masters Classic with a Loudmouth Crankbait.

SPECIFICATIONS
Loudmouth 1: ⅝ oz., 3"
Loudmouth 2: ⅜ oz., 2¾"
Loudmouth 3: ¼ oz., 2"
MSRP: $6.14
Colors: Chartreuse/Blue Back Holographic, Pearl/Black Back Holographic, Brown Craw Holographic, Grey Ghost Holographic, Pearl/Blue Back Holographic, Icicle Holographic

LURES

CRANKBAITS

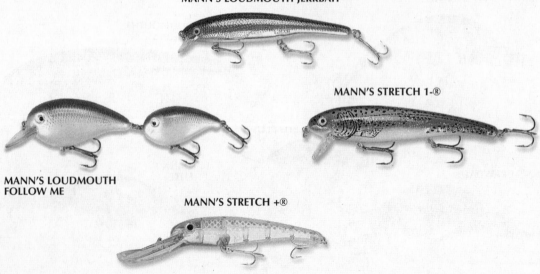

MANN'S LOUDMOUTH JERKBAIT

MANN'S STRETCH 1-®

MANN'S LOUDMOUTH FOLLOW ME

MANN'S STRETCH +®

MANN'S LOUDMOUTH FOLLOW ME

The appearance of two fish following each other triggers the natural aggressive instinct that makes a gamefish automatically attack. The Follow Me gives twice the look, action, sound, and vibration for a single lure without losing the castability or depth of a single lure.

SPECIFICATIONS
Weight: ⅝ oz.
Length: 4½"
MSRP: $9.43
Colors: Lemon Shad, Chrome/Blue Back, Brown Crawfish, Fire Shad, Tennessee Shad, Grey Ghost

MANN'S LOUDMOUTH® JERKBAIT

It casts into the wind and almost suspends. Great action and super noise whether jerked or cranked.

SPECIFICATIONS
Weight: ½ oz.
Length: 4⅜"

MSRP: $5.56
Colors: Chrome/Black Back, Tennessee Shad, Wild Shiner, Yellow Perch, Fire Tiger, Grey Ghost, Chrome/Blue Back, Baby Bass

MANN'S STRETCH 1-® SERIES

Explosive on top, dynamite just under the surface, deadly over the weeds. Retrieve them with a slow wobble, erratic jerks, or steady swim – they won't dive deeper than 1 foot. Equipped with rattles.

SPECIFICATIONS
Baby Stretch 1-: ⅛ oz., 3¼"
Stretch 1-: ½ oz., 4½"
Super Stretch 1-: ⅞ oz., 6"
MSRP: $5.56 (Super Stretch 1-, $7.94)
Colors: Pearl/Black Back, Tennessee Shad, Green Mackerel, Chrome/Blue Back, Redhead, Green Shad Chartreuse, Wild Shiner Crystaglow, Fire Tiger Crystaglow, Yellow Perch Crystaglow, Desert Sunset Crystaglow, Blue/Green Sunfish Crystaglow, Aqua

Shad Crystaglow, Grey Ghost Crystaglow, Rainbow Trout Crystaglow

MANN'S STRETCH +® SERIES

Stretch+ lures dive almost vertically for maximum time at their designated running depths. They track true without speed sensitivity, and their impressive performance is consistent from one lure to the next. High-impact plastic construction, internal rattles, two-stage David System Lip, and strong one piece lip/body design.

SPECIFICATIONS
Stretch 5+: 1/10 oz., 2½".
Dives to 5 feet.
Stretch 10+: ⅛ oz., 3⅜".
Dives to 10 feet.
Stretch 15+: ½ oz., 4⅝".
Dives to 15 feet.
Stretch 20+: ½ oz., 4⅝".
Dives to 20 feet.
MSRP: $5.56

Bend to Tune
If you're using a crankbait that tracks to the side instead of running straight as it should, bend or turn the line attachment eye. If the lure tracks to the left, bend the eye to the right (when looking at the lure head-on) and vice versa.

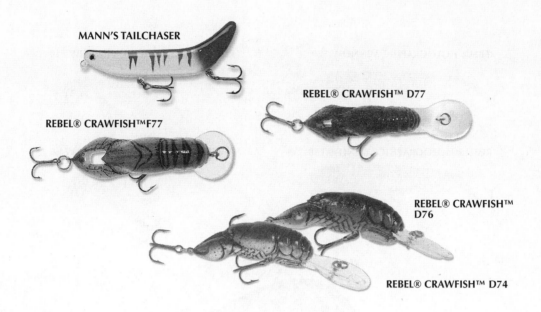

MANN'S TAILCHASER

REBEL® CRAWFISH™ F77

REBEL® CRAWFISH™ D77

REBEL® CRAWFISH™ D76

REBEL® CRAWFISH™ D74

MANN'S TAILCHASER

The Tailchaser walks-the-dog easily, just by twitching it. The nose swings back and forth, 90 degrees to one side and then all the way around to the other. It sinks slowly at 1 ft. in 2 seconds and rattles. Invented by Florida bass guide Joe Jenkins.

SPECIFICATIONS
Weight: ⅝ oz.
Length: 3¾"
MSRP: $3.07
Colors: Chartreuse/Blue Back, Chartreuse Firetail, Fire Red Fluorescent, Gold/Black Back, Chrome/Blue Back, Grey Ghost

REBEL® CRAWFISH™

The Rebel® Crawfish is the original realistic crawfish crankbait. These baits mimic a fleeing crawfish. The distinct, pulsating action is irresistible and extremely effective in rivers and streams.

SPECIFICATIONS
Model: D74 (Big Craw)
Size: 2½"
Weight: ⅜ oz.
Hook Size: #4
Cranking Depth: 8-10'*
MSRP: $3.99

Colors: Chartreuse/Green Back, Cajun Crawdad, Stream Crawfish, Nest Robber, Ditch (brown)

Model: D76 (Deep Wee)
Size: 2⅜"
Weight: ⅜ oz.
Hook Size: #6
Cranking Depth: 8-10'*
MSRP: $3.99
Colors: Chartreuse/Green Back, Cajun Crawdad, Texas Red, Pumpkinseed, Stream Crawfish, Devil Red, Shrimp Crawfish, Nest Robber, Chartreuse/Brown, Softshell Crawfish, Ditch (brown), Moss Crawfish

Model: F76 (Wee-Crawfish)
Size: 2"
Weight: ⅕ oz.
Hook Size: #8
Cranking Depth: 5-7'**
MSRP: $3.99
Colors: Chartreuse/Green Back, Cajun Crawdad, Texas Red, Pumpkinseed, Stream Crawfish, Devil Red, Shrimp Crawfish, Nest Robber, Chartreuse/Brown, Softshell Crawfish, Ditch (brown), Moss Crawfish, Fire Tiger, Chrome/Black Back

Model: D77 (Deep Teeny Wee)
Size: 1½"
Weight: ⅛ oz.
Hook Size: #14
Cranking Depth: 4-5'***
MSRP: $3.99
Colors: Chartreuse/Green Back, Cajun Crawdad, Texas Red, Pumpkinseed, Stream Crawfish, Devil Red, Shrimp Crawfish, Nest Robber, Chartreuse/Brown, Softshell Crawfish, Ditch (brown), Moss Crawfish

Model: F77 (Teeny Wee-Crawfish)
Size: 1½"
Weight: ⅒ oz.
Hook Size: #14
Cranking Depth: 2-3'***
MSRP: $3.99
Colors: Chartreuse/Green Back, Cajun Crawdad, Texas Red, Pumpkinseed, Stream Crawfish, Devil Red, Shrimp Crawfish, Nest Robber, Chartreuse/Brown, Softshell Crawfish, Ditch (brown), Moss Crawfish, Fire Tiger, Chrome/Black Back
* using 10-12-lb. test line, **using 10.-lb test line, ***using 6.-lb. test line. Depths approximate, results achieved using Silver Thread® fishing line.

LURES

CRANKBAITS

REBEL® HOLOGRAPHIC MINNOW F20

REBEL® HOLOGRAPHIC MINNOW F10

REBEL® HOLOGRAPHIC MINNOW F50

REBEL® HOLOGRAPHIC MINNOWF49

REBEL® HUMPBACK® F25

LURES

REBEL® HOLOGRAPHIC MINNOW

Rebel® color technicians have designed 10 brilliant patterns that adorn four popular sizes of its Holographic Minnows. These trend-setting colors carry on the tradition of excellence set by Rebel® minnows for over four decades. Complete with realistic fish eyes, the Holographic Rebel® Minnows feature a "live-bait" look that offers broken-scale patterns and touches of iridescence. Rebel® Holographic Minnows. A new finish for a great tradition!

SPECIFICATIONS

Model: F20
Size: 4½"
Weight: ⅜ oz.
Hook Size: #4
Cranking Depth: 0-3'*
MSRP: $3.99
Colors: Perch Hologram, Baby Bass Hologram, Tennessee Shad Hologram, Purple/Chartreuse Hologram, Clown Hologram, Silver/Blue Hologram, Gold/Black Hologram, Silver/Black Hologram

Model: F10
Size: 3½"
Weight: ⁵⁄₁₆ oz.
Hook Size: #6
Cranking Depth: 0-3'**
MSRP: $3.99
Colors: Perch Hologram, Baby Bass Hologram, Tennessee Shad Hologram, Purple/Chartreuse Hologram, Clown Hologram, Silver/Blue Hologram, Gold/Black Hologram, Silver/Black Hologram

Model: F50
Size: 2½"
Weight: ⅛ oz.
Hook Size: #10
Cranking Depth: 0-2'***
MSRP: $3.99
Colors: Rainbow Trout Hologram, Brown Trout Hologram, Silver/Blue Hologram, Gold/Black Hologram, Silver/Black Hologram

Model: F49
Size: 1⅝"
Weight: ³⁄₃₂ oz.
Hook Size: #12

Cranking Depth: 0-2'****
MSRP: $3.99
Colors: Rainbow Trout Hologram, Brown Trout Hologram, Silver/Blue Hologram, Gold/Black Hologram, Silver/Black Hologram

* using 10-lb. test line, **using 8-lb. test line, ***using 6-lb. test line, ****using 4-lb. test line. Silver Thread® line used for all results.

REBEL® HUMPBACK®

The classic shape of the Humpback produces fish year after year. As a shallow runner, the Humpback is effective when fished above or around aquatic vegetation and is great for schooling fish.

SPECIFICATIONS

Model: F25
Size: 1¾"
Weight: ¼ oz.
Hook size: 6
Cranking depth: 2-4'
MSRP: $3.69
Colors: Silver/Black, Gold/Black, Silver/Blue

REBEL® MINNOW F40S

REBEL® MINNOW F30S

REBEL® MINNOW J30S

REBEL® MINNOW

The 3½" Rebel® Minnow (Model F10) was the first hard plastic Rebel® lure produced. Its success came almost overnight. Demand quickly grew for other sizes and styles of the now legendary Rebel® Minnow. For traditional, dependable, true-running action, nothing compares to the one that started it all — the Rebel® Minnow.

SPECIFICATIONS

Model: F40S (Minnow)
Size: 7"
Weight: 2 oz.
Hook Size: 3/0
Cranking Depth: 0-4'*
MSRP: $4.99
Colors: Silver/Black, Gold/Black, Silver/Blue, Green Mackerel

Model: F30S (Minnow)
Size: 5½"
Weight: 1 oz.
Hook Size: #2
Cranking Depth: 0-4'**
MSRP: $3.99
Colors: Silver/Black, Gold/Black, Silver/Blue, Green Mackerel

Model: J30S (Jointed Minnow)
Size: 5-1/2"
Weight: 1/2 oz.
Hook Size: #2
Cranking Depth: 0-4'**
MSRP: $4.99
Colors: Silver/Black, Gold/Black, Silver/Blue, Green Mackerel

Model: F20S (Minnow)
Size: 4½"

Weight: ⅜ oz.
Hook Size: #4
Cranking Depth: 0-3'**
MSRP: $3.99
Colors: Silver/Black, Gold/Black, Silver/Blue

Model: J20S (Jointed Minnow)
Size: 4½"
Weight: ⅜ oz.
Hook Size: #4
Cranking Depth: 0-3'**
MSRP: $3.99
Colors: Silver/Black, Gold/Black, Silver/Blue, Tennessee Shad, Brown Trout, Rainbow Trout, Bass, Perch

Model: F10 (Minnow)
Size: 3½"
Weight: 5/16 oz.
Hook Size: #6
Cranking Depth: 0-3'***
MSRP: $3.99
Colors: Silver/Black, Gold/Black, Silver/Blue

Model: J10 (Jointed Minnow)
Size: 3½"
Weight: ¼ oz.
Hook Size: #6
Cranking Depth: 0-3'***
MSRP: $3.99
Colors: Silver/Black, Gold/Black, Silver/Blue, Tennessee Shad, Brown Trout, Rainbow Trout, Bass, Perch

Model: F50 (Minnow)
Size: 2½"
Weight: ⅛ oz.
Hook Size: #10

Cranking Depth: 0-2'****
MSRP: $3.99
Colors: Silver/Black, Gold/Black, Silver/Blue

Model: J50 (Jointed Minnow)
Size: 2½"
Weight: ⅛ oz.
Hook Size: #10
Cranking Depth: 0-2'****
MSRP: $3.99
Colors: Silver/Black, Gold/Black, Silver/Blue, Tennessee Shad, Brown Trout, Rainbow Trout, Bass, Perch

Model: F49 (Minnow)
Size: 1⅝"
Weight: 3/32 oz.
Hook Size: #12
Cranking Depth: 0-2'*****
MSRP: $3.99
Colors: Silver/Black, Gold/Black, Silver/Blue

Model: J49 (Jointed Minnow)
Size: 1¾"
Weight: 1/12 oz.
Hook Size: #14
Cranking Depth: 0-2'*****
MSRP: $3.99
Colors: Silver/Black, Gold/Black, Silver/Blue, Tennessee Shad, Brown Trout, Rainbow Trout, Bass, Perch

* using 14-lb. test line, **using 10-lb. test line, ***using 8-lb. test line, ****using 6-lb.-test line, *****using 4-lb. test line. Silver Thread® line used for all results.

CRANKBAITS

REBEL® SHAD-R® S33

REBEL SPOONBILL MINNOW D22S

REBEL SPOONBILL MINNOW M93

REBEL SPOONBILL MINNOW D20S

REBEL SPOONBILL MINNOW DJ30S

REBEL SPOONBILL MINNOW F93

REBEL SPOONBILL MINNOW D30S

REBEL SPOONBILL MINNOW D93

REBEL® SHAD-R®

The Shad-R, an all-time favorite mid-range suspending lure, is designed to deliver top fishing performance to trolling and casting anglers alike. It delivers a tight swimming action whether cast or trolled.

SPECIFICATIONS

Model: S33
Size: 2¾"
Weight: ⅓ oz.
Hook size: 4
Cranking depth: 8'
MSRP: $3.99
Colors: Kryptonite, Doctor "D", Silver Shadow, Sunrise, Bleeding Alewife, Aztec Gold

REBEL SPOONBILL MINNOW

The Rebel® Spoonbill Minnow is equipped with super-strong corrosion-resistant hooks and a tight-defined wiggling action. It digs down into a variety of waters, catching several species.

SPECIFICATIONS

Model: D20S (Spoonbill)
Size: 4½"
Weight: ½ oz.
Hook Size: #4
Cranking Depth: 7-9'*
Trolling Depth: 14.4'*
MSRP: $3.99

Model: D22S (Suspending Rattlin' Spoonbill)
Size: 4½" *Weight:* ½ oz.

Hook Size: #4
Cranking Depth: 7-9'*
Trolling Depth: 14.4'*
MSRP: $3.99

Model: D30S (Spoonbill)
Size: 5½"
Weight: ¾ oz.
Hook Size: #2
Cranking Depth: 8-10'*
Trolling Depth: 15.7'*
MSRP: $4.69

Model: DJ30S (Jointed Spoonbill)
Size: 5½"
Weight: ¾ oz.
Hook Size: #2
Cranking Depth: 8-10'*
Trolling Depth: 16.9'*
MSRP: $5.49
Colors: Silver/Black, Gold/Black, Silver/Blue, Silver/Blue/Orange Belly, Tennessee Shad, Fire Tiger

* depths are approximate and obtained using 10-lb. test Silver Thread® line (trolling depths measured 120 ft. back with .0134" diameter line)

REBEL® WEE-R®

A long time classic, the Wee-R® has a great wiggle and is easy to retrieve. Bass anglers use the Wee-R® as a fish locator around rocks, stumps and submerged timber.

SPECIFICATIONS

Model: D93 (Deep Wee-R®)
Size: 2"

Weight: ⅜ oz.
Hook Size: #6
Cranking Depth: 8-10'*
MSRP: $3.49

Model: M93 (Medium Deep Wee-R®)
Size: 2"
Weight: ⅜ oz.
Hook Size: #6
Cranking Depth: 5-7'*
MSRP: $3.69

Model F93 (Wee-R®)
Size: 2"
Weight: ⅜ oz.
Hook Size: #6
Cranking Depth: 4.5-6'*
MSRP: $3.49
Colors: Silver/Black, Gold/Black, Silver/Blue, Fire Tiger, Baby Bass, Tennessee Shad, Crawfish/Orange Belly, Bumble Bee, Tiger, Yellow Spring Crawfish, Blue Chartreuse, Red Craw, Splatter Back Black, Crawfish/Chartreuse Belly, Spring Crawfish Chartreuse, Chartreuse/Black Back, Pearl/Blue Back, Splatter Back Blue, Plum Shad, Plum Tiger, Swamp Shad, Pearl, Tequila Sunrise, Softshell Crawfish, Summer Craw, Fire Craw, Lemon Splatter, Golden Craw, Chartreuse Shad, Lemon Tiger, Muddy Pup

* depths are approximate and obtained using 12-lb. test Silver Thread® line.

LURES

REBEL® WINDCHEATER

SNAG PROOF
FROGZILLA 6900

SNAG PROOF
HELLGRAMMITE
100

SNAG PROOF
HARRY'S ROUND
FROG 2500

SNAG PROOF MOSS
MASTER CRANKBAIT
9000

REBEL® WINDCHEATER®

Windcheater minnows are known for distance and accuracy. Their stability, durability and extra-strong hardware make these baits ideal for both freshwater and salt water.

SPECIFICATIONS
Model: F86
Size: 6"
Weight: 1⅞ oz.
Hook size: 3/0
Cranking depth: 0-5'
MSRP: $5.29

Model: F85
Size: 4½"
Weight: ¾ oz.
Hook size: #2
Cranking depth: 0-6'
MSRP: $4.99
Colors: Silver/Black, Silver/Blue, Rainbow Trout, Silver/Red Head/White Belly, Silver/Green Back/White Belly, Gold/Black Orange Belly, Silver/Black Back/White Belly, Silver/Blue Back/White Belly, Blue Mackerel, Green Mackerel, Silver/Yellow

SNAG PROOF FROGZILLA

If you want to catch the really big fish, you've got to have the right approach. Think like a big fish. You want to hang out in the cover, yet

near deep water. You don't want to spend the energy to chase some fast-moving, shiny little thing that wouldn't even be a mouthful. You want something that looks like dinner instead of a snack. And, you want it to come to you. You want Frogzilla. Frogzilla is big, weedless and effective in open water, as well as heavy cover. Sporting a very big, very sharp 7/0 Gamakatsu hook, Swimmin' Legs and a rattle.

SPECIFICATIONS
Model: 6900
Weight: ¾ oz.
Length: 6" nose-to-toe
MSRP: $8.50 ea., 3 for $24.00
Colors: Black, Brown, green, chartreuse, Firetiger, white

SNAG PROOF HARRY'S ROUND FROG

Featuring Mustad treble hooks, the Round Frog gives you triple the hooking power in a weedless presentation. The oval shape gives this lure a more erratic wobble than other frog shapes. The soft, hollow body lends itself to the use of attractant gels or pastes, leaving a scent trail. TIP: Try it as a tandem lure, tying two on the line with 6" spacing.

SPECIFICATIONS
Model: 2500

MSRP: $3.55 ea., 3 for $9.25
Colors: Black, chartreuse, white, silver

SNAG PROOF HELLGRAMMITE

The secret to savage strikes. Nothing else like it. Dozens of wiggling, swimming legs give it a live cilia action that game fish can't resist. Use like a jig for bass. Casts well. Weighted tail, sinks rapidly.

SPECIFICATIONS
Model: 100
Weight: ¼ oz.
MSRP: $3.00 ea., 3 for $7.75
Colors: Black, Brown, Green

SNAG PROOF MOSS MASTER CRANKBAIT

At last, a totally weedless crankbait. The power to fish the heaviest cover where big fish lie and ordinary crank-baits can't go. The soft, hollow body fools fish completely and protects the double hook, while the adjustable link/guard keeps the lip clear of weeds. 8-to-10 foot diving range.

SPECIFICATIONS
Model: 9000
Weight: ¼ oz.
MSRP: $5.00 ea., 3 for $13.50
Colors: Black, Brown, Chartreuse, Silver

LURES

CRANKBAITS

SNAG PROOF SK SERIES WEED DEMON 8000

SNAG PROOF PRO SERIES TOURNAMENT FROG 6700

SNAG PROOF MOSS MASTER TOURNAMENT POPPER 4500

SNAG PROOF MOSS MASTER TOURNAMENT FROG 6500

SNAG PROOF MOSS MASTER TOURNAMENT FROG

Featuring a specially weighted body for more accurate casting, chemically sharpened knife edge double hook for the best hookset, and a built-in rattle to attract the big ones. The silicone-coated rubber skirt provides colorful action and won't mat or melt in your tackle box.

SPECIFICATIONS
Model: 6500
Weight: ¼ oz.
MSRP: $5.00 ea., 3 for $13.50
Colors: Black, Brown, Green, Chartreuse, White, Pumpkinseed, Plum, Baby Coot

SNAG PROOF MOSS MASTER TOURNAMENT POPPER

The first popping, diving, floating, weedless, tournament-fish catching popper ever. Fish it in short twitching slurps for attracting scattered fish. Give it a big pull, and it pops, then dives and wriggles back to the surface like a struggling baitfish, frog or other prey.

SPECIFICATIONS
Model: 4500
Weight: ¼ oz.
MSRP: $5.00 ea., 3 for $13.50
Colors: Black, Moss Green, Hot Orange, Silver, Chartreuse, Pearl White, Red Hot, Candy Green

SNAG PROOF PRO SERIES TOURNAMENT FROG

All the style of the original Tournament Frog plus premium Owner double hooks and special colors hand-picked by the pros. This Frog increases your hookset percentage by 30% and is your ticket to a winning catch.

SPECIFICATIONS
Model: 6700
Weight: ½ oz.
MSRP: $6.50 ea., 3 for $18.75
Model: 6600
Weight: ¼ oz.
MSRP: $6.50 ea., 3 for $18.75
Colors: Black with red diamond, Black with blue diamond, Firetiger, Pearl White, Watermelon, Junebug

SNAG PROOF SK SERIES SK FROG ULTRA

The original skirted frog. Made especially for use in thick lily pads, shoreline willows, cattails and moss. Work it over hydrilla and matted weedbeds with a lively twitch-and-pause action and be prepared for an explosion. Tear-drop shape gives excellent hooking action. Now with attention-getting rattle and chemically sharpened knife-edge double hook.

SPECIFICATIONS
Model: 2000
Weight: ¼ oz.
MSRP: $3.55 ea., 3 for $9.25
Colors: Black, Green, Chartreuse, White, Hot Pink, Pumpkinseed

SNAG PROOF SK SERIES WEED DEMON

Now you can "walk the dog" anywhere. Drive fish crazy in any type of structure or cover and enjoy some of the most exciting fishing found anywhere. The Weed Demon lures them in from far away and won't hang up on the job. Dance the Sidewinder on and off the edges of weeds or zigzag it through stands of lily pads, reeds or tulles. Check out blowholes in matted vegetation. The possibilities are endless and the fishing fantastic. The soft, hollow plastic body protects the hook from snags and feels natural to the fish. The "walk-the-dog" action can be attained by holding the rod tip down and making short rhythmic twitches with just the tip of the rod. Try different cadences, or twitch and pause, letting it set for 3-to-4 seconds before moving it again.

SPECIFICATIONS
Model: 8000
Weight: ¾ oz.
MSRP: $3.55 ea., 3 for $9.25
Colors: Green, Chartreuse, Firetiger, Black, Mossback, Silver shad, Blue Shad

SMITHWICK RATTLIN' ROGUE®

The Rattlin' Rogues are equipped with attractive rattles and a wounded action that will produce fish year-round. Rogues are very effective, cast or trolled. Smithwick's Suspending Rattlin' Rogue is the original suspending minnow. Rogues are equipped with loud rattles and suspend right out of the package. No lead tape or drilling required.

SPECIFICATIONS
Model: ADRB1200
(Rattlin' Rogue)
Size: 4½"
Weight: ⅓ oz.
Hook Size: #6
Cranking Depth: 0-4'*

LURES

SMITHWICK RATTLIN' ROGUE® ARB1200

SMITHWICK RATTLIN' ROGUE® ASDRB1200

SMITHWICK RATTLIN' ROGUE® ARA1200

STRIKE KING® SPENCE SCOUT™ RATTLIN' CRANKBAITS

Trolling Depth: 4-10'*
MSRP: $3.99
Colors: Tiger Roan, Silver Shiner, Chrome/Black Back, Chrome/Black Back/Orange Belly, Chrome/Blue Back, Chrome/Blue Back/Orange Belly, Clown (chrome/yellow back), Gold Rogue, Silver w/Black Stripes, Log Perch (Tiger Minnow)

Model: ARB1200 (Rattlin' Rogue)
Size: 4½"
Weight: ⅓ oz.
Hook Size: #6
Cranking Depth: 0-2'**
Trolling Depth: 2-6'*
MSRP: $3.99
Colors: Tiger Roan, Silver Shiner, Chrome/Black Back, Chrome/Black Back/Orange Belly, Chrome/Blue Back, Chrome/Blue Back/Orange Belly, Clown (chrome/yellow back), Gold Rogue, Silver w/Black Stripes, Log Perch (Tiger Minnow), Blue Rib, Bream, Golden Bass, Gold Dust

Model: ARA1200 (Rattlin' Rogue)
Size: 3½"
Weight: ¼ oz.
Hook Size: #6
Cranking Depth: 0-1'**
Trolling Depth: 1-4'*
MSRP: $3.99
Colors: Tiger Roan, Silver Shiner, Chrome/Black Back, Chrome/Black Back/Orange Belly, Chrome/Blue Back, Chrome/Blue Back/Orange Belly, Clown (chrome/yellow back), Gold Rogue, Silver w/Black Stripes, Log Perch (Tiger Minnow)

Model: ASDRB1200 (Suspending Rattlin' Rogue)
Size: 4½"
Weight: ⅜ oz.

Hook Size: #6
Cranking Depth: 0-10'***
Trolling Depth: 10-14'*
MSRP: $3.99
Colors: Tiger Roan, Silver Shiner, Chrome/Black Back, Chrome/Black Back/Orange Belly, Chrome/Blue Back, Chrome/Blue Back/Orange Belly, Clown (chrome/yellow back), Gold Rogue, Silver w/Black Stripes, Log Perch (Tiger Minnow), Tequila, Avocado Shad, Red Sunrise, Threadfin Shad, Red Bream, Purple Darter

Model: ASSRB1200 (Deep Suspending Rattlin' Rogue)
Size: 6"
Weight: ⅜ oz.
Hook Size: #4
Cranking Depth: 10'***
Trolling Depth: 10-18'*
MSRP: $3.99
Colors: Tiger Roan, Silver Shiner, Chrome/Black Back, Chrome/Black Back/Orange Belly, Chrome/Blue Back, Chrome/Blue Back/Orange Belly, Clown (chrome/yellow back), Gold Rogue, Silver w/Black Stripes, Log Perch (Tiger Minnow)
* using 8-12 lb. test line, **using 6-10 lb. test line, ***using 8-17 lb. test line

SMITHWICK SPOONBILL SUPER ROGUE®
This is a Spoonbill version of the five-inch Super Rogue. It features a reinforced built-in paddle, which gives the Spoonbill Super Rogue true-running and true-trolling action. The Spoonbill Super Rogue is very durable and features a precision brass rattle system with a steel ball, which creates an enticing sound and helps the castability of the lure. The Spoonbill Super Rogue

features an attractive realistic etching on the body and is decorated with Smithwick's patented 3-D eye.
SPECIFICATIONS
Model: ASSRD1200 (Suspending Spoonbill Super Rogue)
Size: 5"
Weight: ⅝ oz.
Hook Size: #6
Cranking Depth: 10-12'*
Trolling Depth: 18-24'*
MSRP: $4.29

Model: ASRD1200 (Floating Spoonbill Super Rogue)
Size: 5"
Weight: ½ oz.
Hook Size: #6
Cranking Depth: 8-10'*
Trolling Depth: 16-20'*
MSRP: $4.29
Colors: Chrome/Black, Chrome/Black Back/Orange Belly, Chrome/Blue Back, Orange Belly, Clown, Gold Rogue
* using 12-lb.-test line

STRIKE KING® SPENCE SCOUT™ RATLIN CRANKBAITS
Two line tie positions allow for two different actions and run depths - shallow with medium wobble or super shallow with wide wobble. It has internal rattles, new style color-coordinated hook skirt, virtually snag free and line tie snap.
SPECIFICATIONS:
Model: 245
Weight: ⅜ oz.
Colors: Pearl Blue Eyes, Chartreuse White, Blue Chartreuse, Gold Shiner, Gizzard Shad, Fire Tiger, Tennessee Shad, Baby Bass, Black Chartreuse, Gray Ghost.

LURES

LIPLESS CRANKBAITS

BERKLEY® FRENZY™
PRO RATTL'R

BASS PRO SHOPS® UNCLE
BUCK'S® RATTLE SHAD

BASS PRO SHOPS®
VERIFIER SHAD

BERKLEY FRENZY™ RATTL'R

BASS PRO SHOPS® UNCLE BUCK'S® RATTLE SHAD

If you're looking for a never-fail bass lure, try Uncle Buck's Rattle Shad by Bass Pro Shops. This lure has eye-popping 3-D eyes for a realistic appearance and fish-enticing noisy rattle.

SPECIFICATIONS

Size: 3"
Weight: ½ oz.
MSRP: $2.49
Colors: Firetiger, Watermelon, Silver Shad, Tennessee Shad, Lemon-Lime, Red Crawfish, Bleeding Shiner, Blue/Silver Shad and Green Shore Minnow.

BASS PRO SHOPS® VERIFIER SHAD

The Verifier Shad, one of a series of Avoidance Behavior Lures developed by Dr. Loren Hill, suspends and then sinks slowly. It offers the natural configurations of this natural bait fish, including the dramatic features of action, sound (rattles), scent, color patterns and body shape which stimulates all the senses of predatory game

fish like black bass.

SPECIFICATIONS

Size: 3"
Weight: ¾ oz.
MSRP: $5.99
Colors: Bleeding Tennessee Shad, Baby Bass, Albino Shad, Green Shad, River Minnow, Bleeding Bass and Chrome/Black Back.

BERKLEY® FRENZY™ PRO RATTL'R

The Frenzy Rattl'r has 3-D eyes, a textured surface that looks like real scales and gills, and "Pro" colors. The new holographic finish has life-like features found on real bait fish. The patterns and texturing of the body include the finite details of scales and gills. The 3-D eyes add another dimension to the Frenzy look. These features actually contribute to a more frenzied motion, with a wider action and more rattle than before.

SPECIFICATIONS

Weights: ¼ oz., ½ oz.
MSRP: $4.75
Colors: Pro Perch, Pro Bluegill, Pro

Threadfin Shad, Lime Blue Chartreuse, Chartreuse Shinner, Gold Blaze, Silver Blue Shad

BERKLEY FRENZY™ RATTL'R

The Frenzy Rattl'r is a versatile search tool for finding lone fish spread across a wide area. The vibrant finishes and rattling sound trigger more strikes. You can cast the Frenzy Rattl'r long to blanket the water, or let it sink and jig it to pull fish out of different depths. The Frenzy Rattl'r is constructed of durable ABS with incredibly realistic fish patterns and an extra-hard clear coat finish that will stand up to years of use. Every Frenzy hardbait comes standard with top quality, extra sharp VMC® Cone Cut™ treble hooks.

SPECIFICATIONS

Size: ¼ oz., ½ oz.
MSRP: $4.49
Colors: Bluegill, Chrome Blue, Chrome Bluegill, Chrome Perch, Chrome Threadfin Shad, Fire Tiger, Gold/Black, Perch, Threadfin Shad

LURES

LIPLESS CRANKBAITS

BILL LEWIS LURES RAT-L-TRAP SERIES

BILL LEWIS LURES SPIN-TRAP

BILL LEWIS LURES 2000 RAT-L-TRAP SERIES

BILL LEWIS LURES RAT-L-TRAP SERIES

America's #1 selling lure. The Rat-L-Trap has earned its place in history as the most productive lure ever to come along. Its versatility is unmatched.

SPECIFICATIONS
Model: MT (Mini-Trap)
Model: MTB (Mini-Trap with Freedom Barbless Hooks)
Weight: ¼ oz.
MSRP: $3.79

Model: RT (Original Rat-L-Trap)
Model: RTB (Original Rat-L-Trap with Freedom Barbless Hooks)
Weight: ½ oz
MSRP: $4.69

Model: MG (Magnum Trap)
Weight: ¾ oz.
MSRP: $3,89

Model: MF (Magnum Force)
Weight: 1 oz.
MSRP: $4.79

Model: ST (Super-Trap)
Weight: 1½ ozs.
MSRP: $8.75

Model: FST (Floating Super-Trap)
Weight: 1½ ozs.
MSRP: $8.95

Model: TT (Tiny Trap)
Weight: 1/8 oz.

MSRP: $3.79
Colors: Grasshopper LSU Tiger Trap™, Orange Crawdad, Tennessee Shad, Blue Crawfish, Wild Shiner, Pearl Blue Eye, Fire Tiger, Yearling Bass, Silver Tennessee Shad, White Crawfish, Natural Fire Tiger, Pearl/Pink Eye, Chartreuse Crawdad, Yearling Bass Orange Belly, Crappie, Red Crawfish Chartreuse Belly, Red Ghost, Smokey Joe, Chrome Black Back, Limon, Striper, Chartreuse Shiner, Silver Ghost, Bone Orange Belly, Chrome Blue Back, Limon Orange Belly, Bull Bream, Diamond Dust, Tequila Sunrise, Orange Black Back, Chrome Green Back, Bluegill, Brown Crawfish, Honey Bee, Pumpkin Seed, Red Dog Red, Chrome Purple Back, Bleeding Shiner®, Chartreuse Crawfish, Apricot, Pumpkin Pepper, Chartreuse Black Back, Chrome Plain, Bleeding Shiner® Chrome, Natural Crawfish, Watermelon, Red Halo, Parrot, Lake Fork Special, Gold Tennessee Shad, Red Crawfish, Shad, Clown Halo, Rainbow Trout, Gold, Tennessee Shad on Chrome, Original Crawfish, Silver Shad, Copper Brown (Note: Not all sizes are available in all colors.)

BILL LEWIS LURES 2000 SERIES RAT-L-TRAP

The 2000 Series is the most dynamic Rat-L-Trap® ever produced. Realistic scale patterns make this Trap so life-like, it jumps in the box. Comes with advanced Eagle Claw® Kahle® treble hooks with Nickel TEFLON coating. It's the sharpest hook ever put on a Rat-L-Trap. The Kahle® design makes it almost impossible for a fish to throw the hook.

SPECIFICATIONS
Model: TX
MSRP: $4.69
Colors: Margarita, Yellow Bass, Golden Boy, Jade Stone, Lavender Gem, Sailfin Shiner, Silver Shiner, Baby Bass, Redfish, Greenie

BILL LEWIS LURES SPIN-TRAP®

The Spin-Trap® is effective when worked in shallow water and when used as a drop bait in deep water. The blade adds action and flash to the lure.

SPECIFICATIONS
Model: MS
Weight: ¼ oz.
MSRP: $4.09

Model: TS
Weight: ⅛ oz.
MSRP: $4.09
Colors: Chrome Blue Back, Gold Black Back, Bleeding Shiner®, Natural Crawfish, Fire Tiger, White Red Head, Chrome Chartreuse, Chrome Hot Pink, Gold Chartreuse, Gold Mullet

LURES

LIPLESS CRANKBAITS

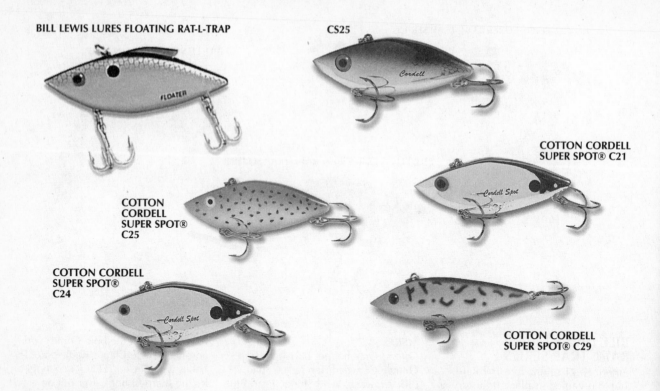

BILL LEWIS LURES FLOATING RAT-L-TRAP

CS25

COTTON CORDELL SUPER SPOT® C21

COTTON CORDELL SUPER SPOT® C25

COTTON CORDELL SUPER SPOT® C24

COTTON CORDELL SUPER SPOT® C29

BILL LEWIS LURES FLOATING RAT-L-TRAP

The Floating Rat-L-Traps are designed to work along weedbeds, grass lines and all types of shallow structure. Retrieves can be varied to a crawl in 3 inches of water, or burned down to 3 feet. Now when you need to go shallow, go with the top producing lure ever... the Rat-L-Trap!

SPECIFICATIONS
Model: FR
Weight: ½ oz.
MSRP: $3.79
Colors: Smokey Joe, Fire Tiger, Chrome Black Back, Chrome Blue Back, Gold, Bleeding Shiner®, Tennessee Shad, Crawfish Natural, Chartreuse Shiner, Red Shad

CABELA'S REALIMAGE RAT-TLIN DIVING RAD-SHAD

There is nothing quite like a fat juicy shad to excite a hungry lunker. No other bait looks, sounds and swims like a shad better than this lure in Cabela's RealImage line. Its deep profile and diving lip has what it takes to coax lunkers out of the depths. VMC needle cone-cut hooks.

SPECIFICATIONS
Sizes/Weights: 2¾", ⅜ oz.; 3¼", ½ oz.;

3½" ¾ oz.
MSRP: $3.79
Colors: Shad, Firetiger, Crawdad, Baby Bass, Clown, Sunfish

COTTON CORDELL SUPER SPOT®

The Super Spot is the lipless, big sound, vibrating-action lure that can be fished at any depth.

SPECIFICATIONS
Model: C25 (Super Spot)
Size: 3"
Weight: ½ oz.
Hook Size: #4
Cranking Depth: sinker
MSRP: $2.99
Colors: Gold/Black, Chrome/Black, Chrome/Blue, Fire Tiger, Rayburn Red, Watermelon Seed

Model: CS25 (Suspending Super Spot)
Size: 3"
Weight: ⅜ oz.
Hook Size: #4
Cranking Depth: 0-3'*
MSRP: $2.99
Colors: Chrome Black/3D Eye, Chrome Blue/3D Eye, Fire Tiger/3D Eye, Texas Red/3D Eye

Model: C24 (Super Spot)
Size: 2½"
Weight: ¼ oz.
Hook Size: #4
Cranking Depth: sinker
MSRP: $2.99
Colors: Gold/Black, Chrome/Black, Chrome/Blue, Fire Tiger, Rayburn Red, Watermelon Seed

Model: C21 (Super Spot)
Size: 2"
Weight: ³⁄₁₆ oz.
Hook Size: #8
Cranking Depth: sinker
MSRP: $2.99
Colors: Gold/Black, Chrome/Black, Chrome/Blue, Fire Tiger, Rayburn Red, Watermelon Seed

Model: C29 (Spot Minnow)
Size: 1⅞"
Weight: ⅛ oz.
Hook Size: #14
Cranking Depth: 1-8'**
MSRP: $2.99
Colors: Chrome Black/3D Eye, Chrome Blue/3D Eye, G-Finish Blue Shad, G-Finish Smokey Joe, Fire Tiger/3D Eye
* using 10-17 lb. test line, **using 2-8 lb. test line

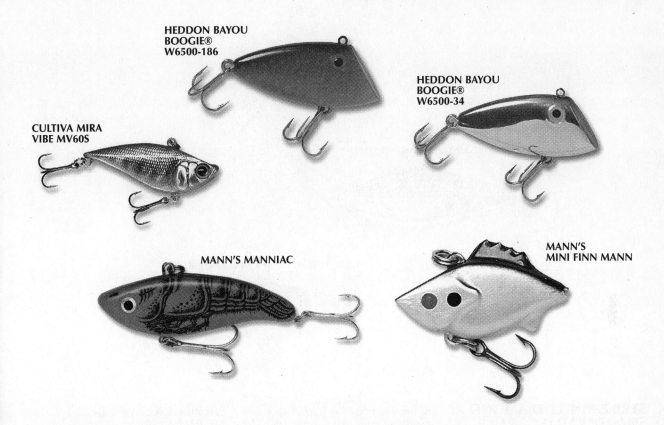

HEDDON BAYOU BOOGIE® W6500-186

CULTIVA MIRA VIBE MV60S

HEDDON BAYOU BOOGIE® W6500-34

MANN'S MANNIAC

MANN'S MINI FINN MANN

CULTIVA MIRA VIBE

A lipless, "super-sonic" crankbait that rides nose-down and vibrates and rattles with an enticing tight wiggle when retrieved or slow trolled. It casts like a bullet and has a classic baitfish profile, with lifelike features that include X-large "Living Eyes" and a fine scale reflective finish, with color patterns that duplicate the look of small baitfish and juvenile game fish. Each lure is rigged with two #6 Owner ST-36 Super Needle Point treble hooks.

SPECIFICATIONS
Model: MV60S
Size: 2⅜"
Weight: ⅓ oz.
MSRP: $12.00
Colors: (01) Fire Tiger, (02) Black Pearl (06) Shiner, (13) Baby Bass, (24) Chartreuse, (59) Perch

HEDDON BAYOU BOOGIE®

An old standard for 45 years that continues to catch all species of fish for millions of fishermen. The Bayou Boogie is a "count-down" type lure that can be fished at any depth. This lure has a fast vibrating action that makes it a versatile lure, performing well for both trolling and casting.

SPECIFICATIONS
Model: W6500
Size: 2"
Weight: ⅓ oz.
Hook Size: #6
Cranking Depth: sinking
MSRP: $2.99
Colors: Threadfin Shad, Barfish, Bream, Striper, Black Silver, Chrome Blue, Bass, Blazing Tiger, Tennessee Shad, Rayburn Red

MANN'S MANNIAC

A rattling, vibrating, sinking bait with our superior self-centering line-tie system for a better running lure. "Sparkle" finish adds a realistic bait-fish flash.

SPECIFICATIONS
Weight: ½ oz.
Length: 3"
MSRP: $3.07
Colors: Chartreuse, Pearl/Black Back, Tennessee Shad, Pearl/Blue Back, Fire Shad, Alabama Shad, Chrome/Blue Back, Fire Red (Brown) Craw, Chartreuse Craw, Fire Red Fluorescent

MANN'S MINI FINN MANN

These 2-pack, ultralight, rattling sinkers deliver convenience, value and fun. The Mini Finn Mann catches numbers of bass, plus large panfish, just by casting and reeling it in.

SPECIFICATIONS
Weight: ⅛ oz.
Length: 1¼"
MSRP: $4.66 per 2-pack
Colors: Clear Water Assortment, Stained Water Assortment

LURES

LIPLESS CRANKBAITS

STRIKE KING® DIAMOND SHAD™

STRIKE KING®PREMIER DIAMOND SHAD™

STRIKE KING® DIAMOND SHAD™ RATLIN CRANKBAITS

Rattling lipless crankbait with super loud fish-attracting interior rattles.

SPECIFICATIONS:
Model: DS12P
Weight: ½ oz.
MSRP: $2.49

Model: DS14
Weight: ¼ oz.
MSRP: $2.49

Model: DS34
Weight: ¾ oz.
MSRP: $2.49

Colors: Chrome Blue Back, Chrome Black Back, Metallic Gold/Black Back, Chrome/Green Back, Chartreuse/White, Blue/Chartreuse, Golden Shiner, Chartreuse Crawfish, Green Back/Chartreuse, Gizzard Shad, Fire Tiger, Crawfish, Tennessee Shad, Red Crawfish, Watermelon Shad, Arkansas Shiner, Neon Shad, Baby Bass, Ghost, Black Back/Chartreuse.

STRIKE KING® PREMIER DIAMOND SHAD™ RATLIN CRANKBAITS

It has smooth sides with holographic scales, 3-D eyes and Premier finishes.

SPECIFICATIONS:
Model: DS12P
Weight: ½ oz.
MSRP: $2.49
Colors: Chartreuse/White, Blue/Chartreuse, Golden Shiner, Chartreuse Crawfish, Green Back/Chartreuse, Gizzard Shad, Fire Tiger, Crawfish, Tennessee Shad, Blue/Pearl, Red Crawfish, Watermelon Shad, Arkansas Shiner, Neon Shad, Baby Bass, Ghost, Black Back/Chartreuse, Gray Ghost, Chrome/Black Back, Chrome/Blue Back, Metallic Gold/Black Back.

Try Trolling

Trolling over creek channels and other underwater structure is another excellent way to fish lipless crankbaits. Toss the lure far out behind the boat and let it sink free-spooled for several feet. Then lock on the anti-reverse. Move slowly in a zig-zag pattern over bass structure, using an electric motor or drifting in the wind. When bass are suspended at 9-10 foot depths, you can usually pinpoint them by trolling a 1/2-ounce lipless crankbait 120 feet behind the boat with 12-pound line. If you go to heavier line, subtract a foot for every pound test you move up to. If you troll with line lighter than 12-pound-test, add a foot of depth for every pound test you drop in line size. Troll at approximately 3 m.p.h.

LURES

BOMBER® FLAIR HAIR JIG

**CABELA'S 31-PIECE
BASS JIG KIT**

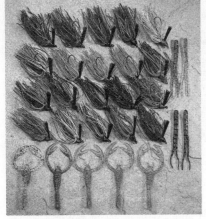

**CHARLIE BREWER
SPIDER WEB JIG**

**BULLET WEIGHTS®
ULTRA STEEL™
INTERCHANGEABLE
JIG KIT**

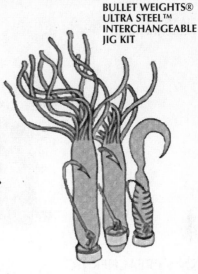

BOMBER® FLAIR HAIR JIG™

The Flair Hair Jig provides an irresistible target when retrieved with sharp jerks.

SPECIFICATIONS
Model B05J
Weight: 1 oz.
MSRP: $1.59

Model B04J
Weight: ¾ oz.
MSRP: $1.59

Model B03J
Weight: ½ oz.
MSRP: $1.59
Colors: White/Chartreuse, White/White

BULLET WEIGHTS® ULTRA STEEL™ INTERCHANGEABLE JIG KIT

Bullet Weights®, Inc. offers the Ultra Steel™ Interchangeable Jig with a patented weight-changing system that eliminates constant line tying.The weights (or jig heads) that come with the 66-piece Ultra Steel jig kit are slotted so that they can be added or removed from the specially designed Eagle Claw" hooks without retying the line. As is the case with all Ultra Steel

products, the new jig weights leave no residue in tackle trays, are non-toxic and pose no threat to waterfowl. Because of the "hardness" quality of steel, the weights offer more sensitivity, less deformation and have more fish-attracting noise.

With all the different components, each kit offers a total of 120 different color and size combinations.
SPECIFICATIONS
Each kit includes:
12 Eagle Claw size #4, style 570 hooks in three colors–gold, bronze and black pearl; 24 Ultra Steel weights in three sizes (¹⁄₃₂, ¹⁄₁₆ and ⅛ oz.). Five colors in each size weight: 2 natural steel, 2 yellow, 2 white, 1 red and 1 black; 30 high-quality 2" grubs that have been specially processed to prevent any color bleeding.; 1 plastic compart-mental container

CABELA'S 31-PIECE BASS JIG KIT

Get Terminator and Hornet jigs in one handy pack. Terminators feature a pointed, conical head and a subtle rattle. Hornet Jigs have a slightly rounded head. Both sport Eagle

Claw® hooks, Kaleidoscope metal flake finish, and silicone skirts.
Specifications
Kit includes: five Terminator Rattlin' Weedless Jigs, 15 Hornet Weedless Jigs, five split-tail trailers, five crawfish trailers and a plastic tackle box.
MSRP: $19.99

CHARLIE BREWER SPIDER WEB JIG

The Spider Web Jig is built with Charlie Brewer's class spider head, with a larger 3/0 hook and bigger bite. The silicone skins are available in the most popular colors. Charlie recommends jigs be rigged weedless with worms or grubs. Pork rind also can be added. Charlie designed the Spider Web Jig especially for light tackle fishermen.
Specifications
MSRP: $1.50
Colors: Black & Red/Red & Silver Glitter, Brown/Orange/Orange Glitter, Pumpkin Black/Chartreuse/Black & Gold Glitter, Purple/Clear/Chartreuse/Black & Purple Glitter, Black/Chartreuse/Gold Glitter, Black/Black/Chartreuse/Silver Glitter

JIGS

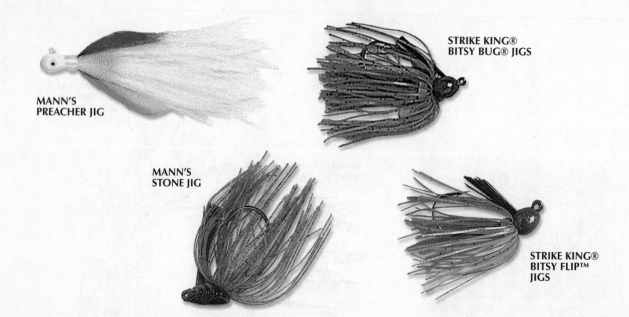

MANN'S
PREACHER JIG

STRIKE KING®
BITSY BUG® JIGS

MANN'S
STONE JIG

STRIKE KING®
BITSY FLIP™
JIGS

MANN'S PREACHER JIG

The ultimate bass jig! Fly-tied buck-tail, for Icelandic sheep wool, duck feathers, and tinsel – the Preacher Jig is one of the finest jigs on the market. Each component used to make up the patterns are hand-wrapped one item at a time so that the finished jig resembles a distressed gizzard shad in the water. Although designed initially for freshwater fishing, many saltwater anglers call the Preacher Jig a tremendous asset for a variety of species.

SPECIFICATIONS
Weight: ½ oz.
MSRP: $5.93
Colors: Original, Deluxe, Grey Ghost, Green Back Shad, Perch

MANN'S STONE JIG

Developed by Mike Iaconelli, one of the leading pros on the BASS and FLW circuits, the Stone Jig features a ridged head. The ridges cause more water displacement and causes the bait to throw off a different vibration than that of a smooth head design. It also gives the jig a natural craw look and texture. Stand-up head makes the Stone Jig great for skipping, and the bait features an integrated line tie which makes it better for weeds and helps protect the knot. It features a 30-strand fiber guard and premium silicone skirt.

SPECIFICATIONS
Weights: ¼, ⅜, ½, ¾ oz.

MSRP: $3.49
Colors: Black/Blue , Black/Brown, Black/ Chartreuse, Green Pumpkin, Natural, White/Silver, Hot Craw, Mike's Special

STRIKE KING® BITSY BUG® JIGS

Features include:

• Snagless/weedless head design helps prevent jig from getting wedged in rocks
• Inverted line tie on the upper part of head helps keep line from being frayed on rocks
• Premium silicone skirt gives more action than a soft plastic body
• Fiber weedguard helps prevent line from being cut like it can on wire guards

SPECIFICATIONS:
Model: BBJ14
Weight: ¼ oz.
MSRP: $1.49

Model: BBJ316
Weight: ³⁄₁₆ oz.
MSRP: $1.49

Model: BBJ118
Weight: ⅛ oz.
MSRP: $1.49

Model: BBJ116
Weight: ¹⁄₁₆ oz.
MSRP: $1.49

Colors: Black, Black/Blue, Plum, White, Pumpkin, Green Crawfish, Cajun Crawfish, Watermelon, Pumpkin Craw, Copper/Pumpkin, Camouflage, Smoke/Pepper/Red

STRIKE KING® BITSY FLIP™ JIGS

The Bitsy Bug™ has become a favorite jig for thousands of fishermen around the country. It's one of the best fish "catchingest" lures of all time. Some avid fans of the Bitsy Bug™ have asked for one with a beefier hook so they can throw it into heavy cover with big line. Strike King's team has come up with the answer - the Bitsy Flip™. It's a Bitsy Bug™ with a bigger, super-strong, black nickel Mustad hook and beefier weed-guard.

SPECIFICATIONS
Model: BFJ14
Weight: ¼ oz.
Colors: Black, Black/Blue, Pumpkin, Green Crawfish, Cajun Crawfish, Watermelon, Pumpkin Craw, Camouflage

STRIKE KING® BOOTLEGGER RATLIN JIGS

Features include:

• Single barrel rattler with two BB's
• Mirage, silicone skirt
• Fiber weedguard

SPECIFICATIONS:
Model: BLJ12

STRIKE KING® DENNY BRAUER DESIGN PRO-MODEL®

STRIKE KING® BOOTLEGGER RATLIN JIGS

STRIKE KING® DENNY BRAUER DESIGN PRO-GLO PRO-MODEL®

STRIKE KING® PREMIER ELITE™

Weight: ½ oz.
MSRP: $1.99

Model: BLJ38
Weight: ⅜ oz.
MSRP: $1.99

Model: BLJ14
Weight: ¼ oz.
MSRP: $1.99
Colors: Black/Red, Black/Blue, Texas Craw, Black, Tequila Sunrise, Pro-White Shad, Watermelon, Chameleon Craw, Cajun Craw

STRIKE KING® DENNY BRAUER DESIGN PRO-GLO PRO-MODEL® JIGS
Features include:
- Premium scale pattern silicone glow-in-the-dark skirt
- Same features as standard Pro-Model® jigs

SPECIFICATIONS:
Model: PMJ12
Weight: ½ oz.
MSRP: $1.99

Model: PMJ38
Weight: ⅜ oz.
MSRP: $1.99
Colors: Black/Blue, Black/Chartreuse, Green Crawfish, Watermelon

STRIKE KING® DENNY BRAUER DESIGN PRO-MODEL® JIGS
Features include:
- Extra-loud double-barrel rattler that also helps keep pork bait trailers in proper position and has "keeper"

for soft plastics
- Mirage, silicone skirt
- Black nickel hook
- Fiber weedguard

SPECIFICATIONS:
Model: PMJ1
Weight: 1 oz.
MSRP: $1.99

Model: PMJ12
Weight: ½ oz.
MSRP: $1.99

Model: PMJ38
Weight: ⅜ oz.
MSRP: $1.99

Model: PMJ14
Weight: ¼ oz.
MSRP: $1.99
Colors: Black, Black/Blue, Black/Chartreuse, Black/Red, Tequila, Texas Craw, Red Craw, Pro-White, Green Pumpkin, Green Crawfish, Chameleon Crawfish, Cajun Crawfish, Watermelon, Electric Blue, Copper/Pumpkin, Camouflage, Black/Brown/Amber, Smoke/Silver and Red Flake, Chartreuse/White

STRIKE KING® PREMIER ELITE™ JIGS
Strike King set out to design the ultimate jig and the result is the new Premier ELITE™. If you are an uncompromising jig fisherman, this is the jig for you!
Features include:
- Gamakatsu, black nickel hook with horizontal line tie
- Camo-flash silicone skirt

- Multi-color, chip-proof paint
- Reflective, lifelike eyes

SPECIFICATIONS:
Model: PEJ1
Weight: 1 oz.
MSRP: $1.99

Model: PEJ34
Weight: ¾ oz.
MSRP: $1.99

Model: PEJ12
Weight: ½ oz.
MSRP: $1.99

Model: PEJ38
Weight: ⅜ oz.
MSRP: $1.99

Model: PEJ14
Weight: ¼ oz.
MSRP: $1.99
Colors: Black/Blue Flash, Black/Green/Chartreuse Flash, Pumpkin Green Flash, Watermelon Flash, Camouflage Flash, Black/Brown/Amber Flash, Brown Sugar Flash, Black/Blue/Purple Flash

STRIKE KING® PRO-GLO BITSY BUG® JIGS
Features include:
- Premium scale pattern silicone glow-in-the-dark skirt
- Same features as standard Bitsy Bug®

SPECIFICATIONS:
Model: BBJ316
Weight: ³⁄₁₆ oz.
MSRP: $1.99
Colors: Black/Blue, Pumpkin, Watermelon, Smoke/Pepper/Red

SOFT PLASTIC

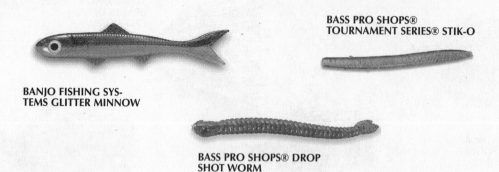

BANJO FISHING SYS-TEMS GLITTER MINNOW

BASS PRO SHOPS® TOURNAMENT SERIES® STIK-O

BASS PRO SHOPS® DROP SHOT WORM

BANJO FISHING SYSTEMS BANJO MINNOW

The Banjo Minnow is a soft plastic jerk bait designed to look and swim exactly like a real injured, crippled or dying minnow. It employs a unique weedless hooking system called a "Nosehook" that screws directly into the nose of the minnow and allows the bait to perfectly duplicate that exact action. These lures, introduced in 1996, have finely-detailed eyes, gills, scales and fins and have evolved into the most realistic-looking lure on the market today. The 3" and 4" sizes are ideal for spinning rods. The original 5" size is heavy enough to be used with a baitcaster.

SPECIFICATIONS
Model: Banjo Glitter Minnow
Size: 3", 4" or 5"
MSRP: $2.49 (3"), $3.29 (4"), $4.99 (5")
Colors: Pink Shad, Dark Blue Shad, Clear Black Pepper Shad, Chartreuse Shad, Rainbow Shad, Black Silver Shad, Silver Shiner, Emerald Shiner, Golden Shiner, Purple Blue Shad, Glow Shad, Bolack Red Shad, Red Smoke Shad
Pack Count: 10

Model: Banjo Natural Minnow
Size: 3", 4" or 5"
MSRP: $1.50 (3"), $1.95 (4"), $2.65 (5")
Colors: Natural Perch, Natural Shad, Rainbow Trout, Fire Tiger
Pack Count: 3

BASS PRO SHOPS® DROP SHOT WORM

Designed with deep water drop-shotting in mind, this split-tail worm is a dead ringer for a small bait fish. The Drop Shot Worm features small eyes and a large, extra-fat head, making hook placement easy.

SPECIFICATIONS
Size: 4"
MSRP: $2.99 per 10 pack
Colors: Green Pumpkin, Watermelonseed, Watermelon Red, Purple Flake, Light Smoke/Purple Flake, Pumpkin Blue Flake and Albino Shad

BASS PRO SHOPS® TOURNAMENT SERIES® STIK-O

Bass Pro Shops® new Tournament Series® Stik-O is the ticket to driving black bass crazy. The ultimate soft jerkbait is one of the most enticing and versatile finesse baits a fisherman will use. Not only does the lure have incredible darting-diving action, it also casts like a rocket and gets into the strike zone quickly. Loaded with salt, the Stik-O also doubles nicely as a Carolina-rig bait. It will also produce strikes when fished wacky-style.

SPECIFICATIONS
Size: 4", 6" and 7"
MSRP: $4.99 per 20-pack.
Colors: Green Pumpkinseed, Watermelonseed, Watermelon Red/Purple Flake, Clear Silver Flake, Pearl, Chartreuse Silver Flake, Albino, Bubblegum, Junebug and Bubblegum/Yellow

Versatile Floating Worm
A weedless floating worm rig is ideal for fishing matted vegetation in shallow water. You can work it in the same areas where rubber frogs or rats are fished, but the worm offers more versatility because it sinks into holes. To enhance the sinking trait, insert a small piece of nail into the lure's mid-section to make it fall slowly and enticingly.

LURES

BERKLEY® BUBBLE UP CRAWFISH

BERKLEY® BUNGEE™ POWER HAWG

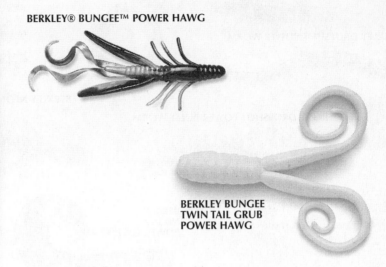

BERKLEY BUNGEE
TWIN TAIL GRUB
POWER HAWG

BERKLEY® BUBBLE UP POWER BAITS

It was fun, although not very fishable, to insert a piece of Alka Seltzer into the cavity of a tube bait before casting. If the bait didn't throw the Alka Seltzer on the cast, the tube would hopefully discharge bubbles as it was retrieved back to the boat. Berkley has taken all the guesswork out of this picture with the introduction of the new "Bubble Up" Power Baits.

Available in three popular fish-catching shapes, Bubble Up Tournament Strength Power Baits are built with a pre-formed pocket to hold another new Berkley product, the Bubble Up Pellet. This reliable combination is sure to catch more fish.

Bubble Up Power Baits shapes include a 4-inch crawfish shape, a 3-inch minnow grub and a 4-inch minnow tube. The baits are coated with Power Scales, a poly-graphic finish of thousands of tiny hexagonally-shaped pieces of holographic fleck. Power Scales gradually fall from the lure
during the retrieve for a life-like look of a wounded baitfish loosing its scales.

Placed into the pre-formed pocket of the crawfish and grub or the cavity of the tube, the Bubble Up Pellet begins to create bubbles as it dissolves in water. These bubbles have addition-al Power Bait attractant for scent and flavor and also create a bubbling sound. In the tube, for example, the bait actually rises as bubbles are momentarily trapped inside the cavity. As the bubbles escape, the tube drops. This combination of bubbles, sounds, scent, flavor and motion create bait that bass and other game fish simply can't resist. A single Bubble Up Pellet lasts approximately 15 minutes in the water and replacement is easy. Each pellet visually contains a red dye, which simulates a blood trail. Each bait has a realistic laminate colored finish with a lighter bottom and darker top.

Specifications
Model: Crawfish
Size: 4"
Colors: Watermelon, Crawdad, Pumpkin Chartreuse, Pumpkin Fluorescent Orange, Black Blue

Model: Minnow Tube
Size: 4"
Colors: Pearl White, Emerald Shiner, Pearl Blue Shad, Chartreuse Shad, Smelt

Model: Minnow Grub
Size: 3"
Colors: Blue Shad, Emerald Shiner, Pearl Blue Shad, Chartreuse Shad, Smelt
MSRP: Bubble Up Power Baits, 3.99
MSRP: Power Pellets (pkg. of 16), $4.49

BERKLEY® BUNGEE™ POWER HAWG

The Bungee Power Hawg has two large side appendages with the proven Bungee curling shape that work as flippers. These react with a different motion after each twitch of the rod tip with an unbelievable motion that never seems to stop. Available both in original Power Bait formula and in Tournament Strength.

Specifications
Size: 4"
Pack size: 7
MSRP: $4.49
Colors: Blue Fleck, June Bug, Green Pumpkin, Pumpkinseed, Watermelon

BERKLEY BUNGEE TWIN TAIL GRUB

A tail that coils back "automatically" gives the Bungee Twin Tail added action and more fish appeal. A fantastic spinnerbait trailer, or fish it on the bottom as a Carolina rig.

Specifications
Size: 4"
Pack size: 8
MSRP: $3.99
Colors: Chartreuse with Silver Fleck, Green Chartreuse, Pumpkinseed, White, Yellow Orange

LURES

SOFT PLASTIC

BERKLEY BUNGEE WORM

BERKLEY NEONZ POWER CRAW®

BERKLEY DROPSHOT POWER WORM

BERKLEY NEONZ POWER LIZARD®

BERKLEY DROPSHOT POWER PULSE WORM

BERKLEY NEONZ POWER GRUB®

LURES

BERKLEY BUNGEE WORM

With its slender, tapered body, the Bungee Worm looks AND MOVES like a live nightcrawler. Unique recoiling action generates more strikes.

SPECIFICATIONS
Size: 4"
Pack size: 12
MSRP: $3.99

Size: 7"
Pack size: 10
MSRP: $3.99
Colors: Black, Black Neon Shad, Blue Fleck, Blue Fleck Firetail, Camo, Motor Oil, Pumpkinseed, Red Shad, Red Shad Green Glitter, Tequila Sunrise

BERKLEY DROPSHOT POWER WORM

The Dropshot Worm was specially designed for dropshotting. A great bait for fish that feed on small minnows.

SPECIFICATIONS
Size: 4"
Pack size: 15
MSRP: $4.49
Colors: Clear Gold Black Back, Emerald Shiner, Natural Pro Blue, Pearl Blue Shad, Pearl Olive Shad, Pearl Watermelon Shad, Rainbow Silver Fleck

BERKLEY DROPSHOT POWER PULSE WORM

An effective finesse bait for bass. Ideal for very light presentations in deep water and great for dropshotting.

SPECIFICATIONS
Size: 3"
Pack size: 15
MSRP: $4.49
Colors: Clear Gold Black Back, Emerald Shiner, Natural Pro Blue, Pearl Blue Shad, Pearl Olive Shad, Pearl Watermelon Shad, Rainbow Silver Fleck

BERKLEY NEONZ POWER CRAW®

The NEONZ™ Power Craw combines bright neon colors with a lifelike craw design. Its floating craws simulate a defensive position of a real crawfish, making it great for vertical techniques. Its lifelike look and feel and Power Bait scent and flavor enhancers join together to create a truly irresistible bait.

SPECIFICATIONS
Size: 4"
Pack size: 8
MSRP: $3.99
Colors: Crawdad, Pumpkin Green

BERKLEY NEONZ POWER GRUB®

The NEONZ™ Power Grub offers an exciting swimming action that's effective across the board – from crappie to walleye and bass to pike. Its curly tail design combines with our rich NEONZ™ coloration to create a lively presentation fish can't resist.

SPECIFICATIONS
Size: 2"
MSRP: $3.99
Pack size: 24

Size: 3"
Pack size: 18
MSRP: $3.99
Colors: Chartreuse, Fluorescent Orange, Merthiolate, Sherbet, Smoke Red Glitter, White, Yellow

BERKLEY NEONZ POWER LIZARD®

The NEONZ Power Lizard realistically imitates a spawning salamander or spring lizard – both natural forage to bass. Lifelike texture and action combined with Power Bait scent ingredients and bright NEONZ coloration makes for a great underwater presentation.

SPECIFICATIONS
Size: 6"
Pack size: 10
MSRP: $3.99
Colors: Pumpkin Green Fleck, Pumpkin/Chartreuse Pepper, Smoke Red Glitter, Watermelon Red Glitter

BERKLEY NEONZ POWER TUBE®

BERKLEY POWER GRUB®

BERKLEY NEONZ POWER WORM®

BERKLEY POWER LIZARD®

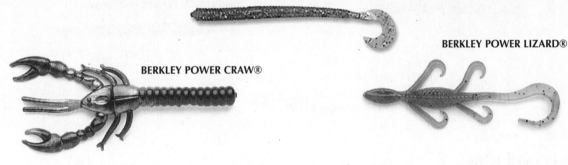

BERKLEY POWER CRAW®

BERKLEY NEONZ POWER TUBE®

THE NEONZ™ Power Tube is designed with lifelike tentacles to imitate small baitfish. Exciting colors offer additional fish-catching effectiveness to this tried and true shape. Can be filled with PowerBait Attractant to create an even more powerful presentation.

SPECIFICATIONS
Size: 3"
Pack Size: 10
MSRP: $3.99
Colors: Chartreuse Pepper, Melon Pepper, Pumpkin Green Fleck, Smoke Red Glitter, Watermelon Red Glitter

BERKLEY NEONZ POWER WORM®

Our most popular Power Bait shape, available in exciting NEONZ™ colors. The ribbontail design of the NEONZ™ Power Worm lets it swim naturally on the fall, with twitches, short hops, or from currents when lying motionless. Ideal for all your favorite fishing lakes, rivers, streams and conditions.

SPECIFICATIONS
Size: 4" (sickle tail)
Pack size: 12
MSRP: $3.99

Colors: Christmas Cider, Electric Green Pumpkin, Salt and Pepper, Watermelon Red Glitter

Size: 7" (swimming tail)
Pack size: 10
MSRP: $3.99
Colors: Black Neon Shad, Electric Grape, Electric Green Pumpkin, Red Shad Green Glitter, Watermelon Red Glitter

BERKLEY POWER CRAW®

The Power Craw features a realistic design with floating claws to simulate a defensive posture. The lifelike craw-worm design provides the ability to use many techniques, like worming, jigging, flipping and pitching.

SPECIFICATIONS
Size: 4"
Pack size: 8
MSRP: $3.99
Colors: Black/Blue, Black/Chartreuse, June Bug, Pumpkin/Chartreuse, Pumpkinseed

BERKLEY POWER GRUB®

Curly-tail grub with Berkley scent and flavor ingredients features an enticing swimming action and small profile to stimulate feeding. Ideal for a variety of rigging applications, including jigs

and spinnerbait trailers.

SPECIFICATIONS
Size: 2"
Pack size: 20
MSRP: $3.99

Size: 3"
Pack Size: 15
MSRP: $3.99
Colors: Black, Chartreuse, Pearl White, Pumpkinseed

BERKLEY POWER LIZARD®

The salamander is a natural forage to bass and therefore a perfect bait. Realistic shape of the Power Lizard imitates a salamander shape with Power Bait scent and flavor ingredients, and multiple leg and tail action. Great for Texas or Carolina rigging, or as a trailer for skirted jigs and spinnerbaits.

SPECIFICATIONS
Size: 4"
Pack Size: 12
MSRP: $3.99

Size: 6"
Pack size: 10
MSRP: $3.99
Colors: Black, Black/Blue, Blue Fleck, Pumpkin/Chartreuse, Pumpkinseed, Purple

SOFT PLASTIC

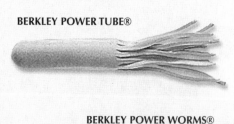

BERKLEY POWER TUBE®

BERKLEY T.S. POWER CRAW

BERKLEY POWER WORMS®

BERKLEY T.S. POWER FINESSE WORM

BERKLEY T.S. POWER CAROLINA SLUG

BERKLEY POWER TUBE®

An all-purpose bait for bass and other game fish, the Power Tube is your secret weapon for baiting of inactive fish in clear water. Molded-in tentacles provide subtle or lively motion of small shad or minnows. A hollow tube design can be filled with attractant to create a more powerful presentation.

SPECIFICATIONS
Size: 3"
Pack Size: 10
MSRP: $3.99
Colors: Blue Fleck, Camo, Motor Oil, Pumpkinseed, Smoke, White

BERKLEY® POWER WORMS

The most popular and widely used plastic worms are Berkley Power Worms. These Power Bait-flavored worms are created with a special attractant additive, a secret formula based on scientific research that entices more bites than other worms. Fish also hold Power Bait worms in their mouth up to 18 times longer, giving the angler a better chance for a positive hookset.

SPECIFICATIONS
Sizes: 4" (sickle tail), 7" (swimming tail), 10" (swimming tail)
Pack size: 6, 10, 12 or 100
MSRP: 12-pack of 4", $3.99; 10-pack of 7", $3.99; 6-pack of 10", $3.99; 100-pack of 4" $19.99; 100-pack of

7", $23.99; 100-pack of 10" $39.99
Colors: Black, Camo, Pumpkinseed, Purple, Red Shad, Blue Fleck, Blue Fleck Firetail, Motor Oil, Tequila Sunrise, Black/Blue, June Bug, Green Pumpkin, Watermelon (different sizes available in different colors)

BERKLEY TOURNAMENT STRENGTH POWER CAROLINA SLUG

The Carolina Slug glides through the water with the slightest motion. ribbed belly lines keep the body in a constant flexing action that looks alive to hungry bass.

SPECIFICATIONS
Size: 5"
Pack size: 8
MSRP: $4.49
Colors: Baby Bass, Black Red Fleck, Bullfrog, Camo, Pumpkinseed

BERKLEY TOURNAMENT STRENGTH POWER CRAW

Lifelike crawfish design provides ability to use many techniques, like worming, jigging, flipping and pitching.

SPECIFICATIONS
Size/Pack size: 3", 12; 4", 8
MSRP: $4.49
Colors: Black Neon/Chartreuse, Black/Blue, Black/Chartreuse, Crawdad, Green Pumpkin/Orange (3" only). June Bug, Pearl Watermelon Shad (4" only). Pumpkin Green Fleck,

Pumpkin/Chartreuse, Pumpkin/Fluorescent Orange, Pumpkinseed, Red Shad

BERKLEY TOURNAMENT STRENGTH POWER FINESSE WORM

Great for inactive fish. Looks like easy prey to slower moving fish. Great for clear water situations where a less active lure presentation is desired.

SPECIFICATIONS
Size: 4"
Pack size: 12
MSRP: $4.49
Colors: Black/Chartreuse, Blue Fleck, Camo, Electric Grape, Pumpkinseed, Purple, Smoke Black Glitter, Watermelon, Watermelon Red Glitter

BERKLEY TOURNAMENT STRENGTH POWER FATHEAD TUBE

The ultimate flippin' tube. The tapered ribs of this bait deliver a softer presentation for spooky bass. Super-sized body helps to penetrate cover. Designed to be rigged Texas style and for flippin' and pitchin' into holes.

SPECIFICATIONS
Size: 4"
Pack size: 8
MSRP: $4.49
Colors: Camo, Green Pumpkin, Pumpkin Green Fleck, Sour Grape

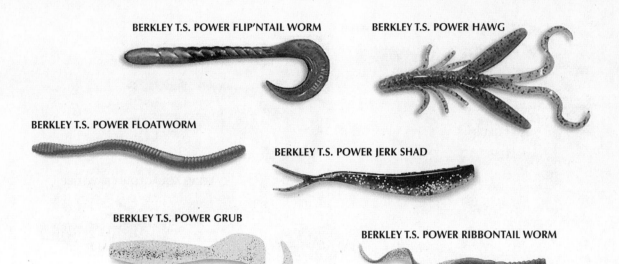

BERKLEY T.S. POWER FLIP'NTAIL WORM

BERKLEY T.S. POWER HAWG

BERKLEY T.S. POWER FLOATWORM

BERKLEY T.S. POWER JERK SHAD

BERKLEY T.S. POWER GRUB

BERKLEY T.S. POWER RIBBONTAIL WORM

BERKLEY TOURNAMENT STRENGTH POWER FLIP'NTAIL WORM

The Flip'ntail creates a vibration and thump that bass can't ignore.

SPECIFICATIONS
Size: 6"
Pack size: 10
MSRP: $4.49
Colors: Black, Black/Chartreuse, Blue Fleck, Camo, Green Pumpkin, June Bug, Pumpkin Chartreuse, Pumpkinseed, Red Shad Green Glitter, Tequila Green Glitter

BERKLEY TOURNAMENT STRENGTH POWER FLOATWORM

Great for topwater or surface fishing. Cast it alongside docks or heavy weeds and draw the big bass out. Also an ideal split-shot and Carolina rigging bait.

SPECIFICATIONS
Size: 6"
Pack size: 10
MSRP: $4.49
Colors: Bubble Gum, Merthiolate, Natural Blue, Sherbet, White, Yellow

BERKLEY TOURNAMENT STRENGTH POWER GRUB

Great for jigs and spinners. This swimming tail grub features a fast action tail that simulates live bait. Specifically formulated to appeal to a bass' sense of taste and smell.

SPECIFICATIONS
Size: 4"
Pack size: 12
MSRP: $4.49
Colors: Camo, Chartreuse with Silver Fleck, Clear with Silver Fleck, Glow with Silver Fleck, Pumpkin Green Fleck, Pumpkinseed, Rootbeer Gold/Red Fleck, Smoke, Watermelon, White, Yellow

BERKLEY TOURNAMENT STRENGTH POWER HAWG

Versatile, great for flipping, or cast it long to cover more water. Trim off the double tail to create a darting action on the fall.

SPECIFICATIONS
Size: 4"
Pack size: 7
MSRP: $4.49

Size: 5"
Pack size: 6
MSRP: $4.49
Colors: Black Blue Laminate, Black Grape/Red & Green Glitter, Black Neon Shad, Black Red Fleck, Green Pumpkin, June Bug, Pumpkinseed, Pumpkin Green Fleck, Sour Grape, Watermelon, Watermelon Red Glitter

BERKLEY TOURNAMENT STRENGTH POWER JERK SHAD

A killer bait for suspended bass. The erratic darting motion imitates a struggling baitfish. Looks like an easy meal for a hungry bass.

SPECIFICATIONS
Size: 5"
Pack size: 8
MSRP: $4.49
Colors: Albino, Amber Watermelon, Arkansas Shiner, Black Neon Shad, Chartreuse with Silver Fleck, Clear with Gold Fleck, Glow with Silver Fleck, Pearl White, Rainbow, Smoke

BERKLEY TOURNAMENT STRENGTH POWER RIBBONTAIL WORM

The Ribbontail's quick wide swimming action is ideal for most techniques, including Texas or Carolina rigs.

SPECIFICATIONS
Sizes: 6", 7"
Pack size: 10
MSRP: $4.49
Colors: Black, Black/Chartreuse, Black Grape, Black Grape/Red & Green Glitter (6" only). Black Neon Shad (7" only). Blue Fleck, Camo, Electric Grape, Electric Green Pumpkin (6" only). Green Pumpkin, June Bug, Motor Oil, Natural, Pumpkin/Chartreuse, Pumpkinseed, Purple, Red Shad Green Glitter, Smoke Black Glitter (7" only). Tequila Green Glitter, Watermelon Red Glitter, White/Glow (6" only).

LURES

SOFT PLASTIC

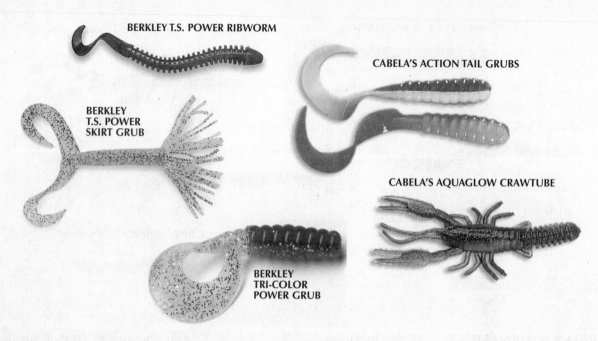

BERKLEY T.S. POWER RIBWORM

BERKLEY T.S. POWER SKIRT GRUB

CABELA'S ACTION TAIL GRUBS

CABELA'S AQUAGLOW CRAWTUBE

BERKLEY TRI-COLOR POWER GRUB

BERKLEY TOURNAMENT STRENGTH POWER RIBWORM

Attracts fish by creating a stir. This popular design with flexible ribs offers soft texture for more consistent hooksets. Attracts fish in dingy or stained water where visibility is low.

SPECIFICATIONS
Size: 4"
Pack size: 12
MSRP: $4.49
Colors: Black/Chartreuse, Blue Fleck, Camo, Pumpkinseed, Red Shad

BERKLEY TOURNAMENT STRENGTH POWER SKIRT GRUB

The living end for bass. Unique swimming action attracts big bass with the slightest movement.

SPECIFICATIONS
Size: 4"
Pack size: 6
MSRP: $4.49
Colors: Amber Watermelon, Chartreuse Pepper, Green Pumpkin, June Bug, Pumpkin Green Fleck, Pumpkinseed, Rootbeer Gold with Red Fleck, Smoke Clear, Watermelon Red Glitter

BERKLEY® TRI-COLOR POWER GRUB

The Tri-Color Power Grub has a body made with two colors laminated together and a third color that makes up the tail. These curly-tailed grubs can be rigged and fished in the same manner as any other grub.

SPECIFICATIONS
Sizes: 2", 3"
Pack size: 20 per bag for 2", 15 per bag for 3"
MSRP: $3.99
Colors: Firetiger, Captain America, Black Marble and Christmas Lights

CABELA'S ACTION TAIL GRUBS

When Texas-rigged on a slider, Cabela's Action Tail Grubs will talk fish right out of the weeds. Jig these grubs any kind of black bass and virtually all other game fish.

SPECIFICATIONS
Sizes: 2", 3", 4"
Pack size: 25
MSRP: $1.79-$1.99
Colors: Black, Yellow, White, Shad, Firetiger, Orange/Yellow, Chartreuse Shad, Chartreuse, Black/Red, White Firetail, White/Pink, Pink/Silver Flake, Chartreuse/Glitter, Motor Oil/Red Flake, Pumpkin Pepper, Sour Grape

CABELA'S AQUAGLOW SOFT PLASTICS

AquaGlow™ soft plastics are infused with a super glow coloring process that gives these baits the ability to retain their bright glow 10 times longer than other glow baits, for never-before-attained levels of fishing success. The AquaGlow™ Baits are extremely visible under normal conditions. The special fish-catching colors are truly eye-popping in the low light conditions of early morning or late evening, and in dark, stained waters, as well as overcast days. The innovative ringed-body design enhances their action and sends out fish-attracting vibrations. A long lasting, specially-formulated menhaden minnow scent is injected into each lure. All of these features combine to produce a highly-visible lure with a realistic, lifelike feel, taste and texture that fish grab and hang on to.

SPECIFICATIONS
Model: Lizard
Ringed body lizard shape combined with the AquaGlow™ colors.
Sizes: 4", 6"
MSRP: $2.99
Colors: Firetiger, Crawfish, Brown Crawdad, Starry Night, Green Pumpkin, Tomato, Black Blue, Red Bug.

Model: Crawtube
This new design in soft plastics is absolutely deadly on big bass.
Size: 4¼"
MSRP: $2.99
Colors: Crawfish, Starry Night, Green Pumpkin, Blue Bug, Tomato, Red Bug.

CABELA'S AQUAGLOW TUBE

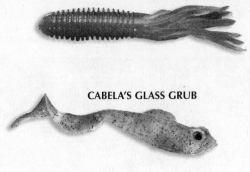

CABELA'S BASS WORM BUCKET

CABELA'S GLASS GRUB

CABELA'S LIVIN' EYE CHUB

CABELA'S DOUBLE TAIL GRUB

Model: Tube
Classic tube style with tantalizing tentacles for a slow fall.
MSRP: $2.99
Colors: Crawfish, Starry Night, Green Pumpkin, Blue Bug, Tomato, Red Bug.

Model: Grub
Traditional grub with the added color, scent and feel of our new AquaGlow™ series.
Length: 4"
MSRP: $2.99
Colors: Firetiger, Crawfish, Brown Crawdad, Starry Night, Green Pumpkin, Sour Grape, Blue Bug, Tomato, Black Blue, Red Bug.

CABELA'S BASS BUCKETS
Bass Buckets keep you supplied with enough soft-plastic baits to carry you through a successful season.
SPECIFICATIONS
Worm Bucket: includes 195 pieces, including 13 each of 15 different worms in a variety of colors
MSRP: $10.99
Bass Tube Bucket: includes 110 pieces of your favorite tube lures. You get 11 each of five different colors of the 2½" and five colors in the 3½".
MSRP: $10.99

Shad/Grub Bucket: includes a 420-piece assortment of fish-catching grubs and shads
MSRP: $10.99

Gallon Bucket: the best assortment of worms, frogs, lizards and grubs
MSRP: $21.99

CABELA'S GLASS GRUB
The addition of a flashy mylar insert that reflects light gives these translucent baits a glistening shine that duplicates the scales of a baitfish for freshwater fishing. The large 3-D eyes give a prowling predator a target to lock onto.
SPECIFICATIONS
Size: 4½"
Pack size: 12
MSRP: $3.99
Colors: Clear Glitter/Black, Black/Red Fleck, Clear, Purple Halo, Emerald Glitter, Clear Glitter, Chartreuse Black/Red Fleck, Pearl Glitter

CABELA'S LIVIN' EYE CHUB
The thicker body with an elongated tail section of the Chub imitates a wounded chub to entice strikes. Hook pocket puts the hook in the best position on the bait for positive hooksets.
SPECIFICATIONS
Size: 3"
MSRP: $3.99
Colors: Firetiger, Pumpkinseed Pepper, Black Shad, Purple Shad, Tennessee Shad, Emerald Shiner, Baby Bass, Fathead Minnow, Glass Minnow

CABELA'S LIVIN' EYE DOUBLE TAIL GRUB
The double ribbon tail produces lots of flutter and undulation underwater. These lures feature a hook pocket on 3" and 4" length for easy rigging and proper action.
SPECIFICATIONS
Sizes: 1", 2", 3", 4" (with tail)
Pack size: 12
MSRP: $3.99
Colors: Firetiger, Pumpkinseed Pepper, Black Shad, Purple Shad, Tennessee Shad, Emerald Shiner, Baby Bass, Glass Minnow, Fathead Minnow

LURES

SOFT PLASTIC

CABELA'S GLASS MINNOWS

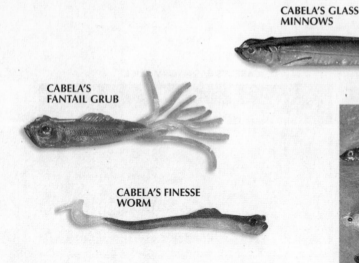

CABELA'S FANTAIL GRUB

CABELA'S FINESSE WORM

CABELA'S GLASS MINNOW KIT

CABELA'S LIVIN' EYE FANTAIL GRUB

The extra-wide tail on these grubs waves and undulates through the water, enticing fish to bite.

SPECIFICATIONS
Sizes: 2", 3', 4'
Pack size: 12
MSRP: $3.99
Colors: Firetiger, Purple Shad, Tennessee Shad, Emerald Shiner, Fathead Minnow, Baby Bass

CABELA'S LIVIN' EYE FINESSE WORM

The lifelike design and shape of the Finesse Worm is irresistible to fish. Great for bass, the colors and action from the slim body and small curly tail have a realistic look. With its thin profile, the finesse worm is good for doodling or shallow-water Texas rigging.

SPECIFICATIONS
Size: 4½"

Pack size: 12
MSRP: $3.99
Colors: Shad, Pumpkinseed Pepper, Black Shad, Red Shad, Purple Shad, Watermelon Seed, Glass Minnow, Baby Bass

CABELA'S LIVIN' EYE GLASS MINNOWS

A reflective mylar insert gives these jerk-type baits the extra flash needed to catch everything from all bass species. Realistically-molded heads and eyes add even more lifelike detail. Rig them with a jig or Texas-style. Either way, they do a convincing imitation of a dying baitfish.

SPECIFICATIONS
Sizes: 6", 8"
MSRP: $3.69
6" Colors: Clear Rainbow Foil, Emerald Green Foil, Purple Halo, Chartreuse Foil, Pearl Rainbow Foil, Firecracker Foil, Salt & Pepper Rainbow Foil, Blue Foil, Gold Foil,

Natural Shad Foil
8" Colors: Clear Rainbow Foil, Emerald Green Foil, Chartreuse Foil, Pearl Foil, Blue Foil, Gold Foil, Natural Shad Foil

CABELA'S LIVIN' EYE GLASS MINNOW KIT

If you want the most colorful plastic baits or if you're just restocking your tackle box for the upcoming fishing season, you need this all-new collection from Cabela's. These soft-plastic baits are meticulously crafted and tested to look and move just like a real minnow. What sets them apart from other soft plastics is a unique foil insert that gives them glitter and flash.

SPECIFICATIONS
Kit includes: 36 lures in six assorted colors (six each), six Mustad offset worm hooks and one tackle box (7⅝" x 5¼" x 1¾").
MSRP: $14.99

Polarized Glasses Help Line Watchers
When fishing plastic worms, it helps to watch your line for unusual movements that indicate a bass has inhaled the lure. You'll see your line better if you wear polarized sunglasses that reduce surface glare and help you see the line at the point of entry. If the line moves, set the hook.

CABELA'S LIVIN' EYE MINNOW KIT

CABELA'S LIVIN' EYE SINGLE TAIL GRUB

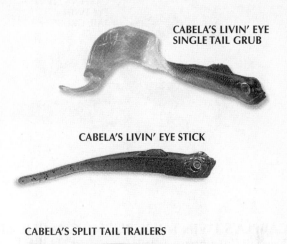

CABELA'S LIVIN' EYE STICK

CABELA'S LIVIN' EYERIBBON TAIL WORM

CABELA'S SPLIT TAIL TRAILERS

CABELA'S LIVIN' EYE MINNOW KIT

These minnow baits look so real you'll be tempted to dump them in a bait bucket. The 3-D lifelike detail is nothing short of amazing. The natural shape of the heads, with detailed gills and mouths, give these baits lifelike appeal and the realistic eyes are proven fish-catchers. Plus, they've been impregnated with SX76 for added attraction. Each kit contains a complete fish-catching set of minnows, jigheads and hooks. You'll be ready to hit the water as soon as your kit arrives.

SPECIFICATIONS
Kit includes: six 3" Single-Tail Grubs; six 4" Single-Tail Grubs; six 3" Double-Tail Grubs; six 4½" Finesse Worms; six 5" Stick Minnows; six 3" Chubs; six ¼ oz. Jigheads; eight ⅛ oz. Jigheads; three ¹⁄₁₆ oz. Insider Jigheads; eight Offset Worm Hooks; one Plano 3500 Tackle Box; and instructions for rigging and fishing techniques.
MSRP: $12.99

CABELA'S LIVIN' EYE RIBBON TAIL WORM

The classic 5" ribbon-tail worm is now available with all the lifelike realism of Cabela's Livin' Eyes™ design.

SPECIFICATIONS
Size: 5"
Pack size: 12
MSRP: $3.99
Colors: Shad, Pumpkinseed Pepper, Black Shad, Red Shad, Purple Shad, Watermelon Seed

CABELA'S LIVIN' EYE SINGLE TAIL GRUB

Cabela's took their highly realistic Classic Single Tail Grub and gave it a 21st-century look with even more fish-attracting colors. Versatile and reliable, this is the perfect soft plastic for bass and other fish. The unique color-coating and the amazing action from the oversized, extra-wide single ribbon tail makes it so realistic that it often outperforms live bait. The hook pocket is built-in for perfect rigging every time.

SPECIFICATIONS
Sizes: 1", 2", 3", 4"
Pack size: 12
MSRP: $3.99
Colors: Firetiger, Pumpkinseed Pepper, Black Shad, Purple Shad, Tennessee Shad, Emerald Shiner, Baby Bass, Glass Minnow, Fathead Minnow.

CABELA'S LIVIN' EYE STICK

Cabela's Livin' Eye lures perfectly imitate wounded baitfish to provoke strikes from aggressive bass. The Stick has an extra-wide, extra-thick body that moves a lot of water and undulates like a dying baitfish.
Specifications
Size: 5"
MSRP: $3.99
Colors: Firetiger, Pumpkinseed Pepper, Tennessee Shad, Glass Minnow, Watermelon Seed, Shad, Emerald Shiner, Baby Bass

CABELA'S SPLIT TAIL TRAILERS

The 4" Split Tail's extra-soft construction gives it a fish-attracting pulsation that's superior to any regular trailer you could add.
SPECIFICATIONS
Size: 4"
Pack size: 20
MSRP: $1.99
Colors: Clear Silver, Black, White, Pearl/Chartreuse, Blue/Blue Flake, Chartreuse/Silver Flake, Pumpkin/Pepper

SOFT PLASTIC

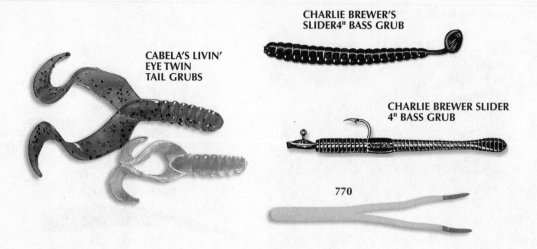

CABELA'S LIVIN' EYE TWIN TAIL GRUBS

CHARLIE BREWER'S SLIDER 4" BASS GRUB

CHARLIE BREWER SLIDER 4" BASS GRUB

770

CABELA'S TWIN TAIL GRUBS

Twin Tail Grubs have twin tails for double the lure action. All the versatility of single-tail grubs, but the twin tail is especially effective during murky water situations when visibility is poor and the fish need a little more action and vibration to zero in on.

SPECIFICATIONS
Sizes: 2", 4"
Pack size: 25
MSRP: $2.99
Colors: Black, Yellow, White, Shad, Firetiger, Orange/Yellow, Chartreuse Shad, Chartreuse, Black/Red, White Firetail, White/Pink, Motor Oil/Red Flake, Chartreuse Glitter, Pumpkin Pepper, Pink/Silver Flake, Sour Grape

CHARLIE BREWER'S SLIDER 4" BASS GRUB

The 4" Bass Grub with its vibra-tail causes an irresistible wobble that imitates nature. This grub can be fished weedless and effectively with the Slider Classic Spider Head or opened hook using the regular Slider Head. Very good for larger bass.

SPECIFICATIONS
Size: 4"
Pack Count: 10
MSRP: $2.75
Colors: Watermelon/Red/Copper/ Black Flake, Natural Pro Blue, Pearl, Cotton Candy, Brown Orange/Red Flake, Black/Red Flake/Chartreuse Tail

CHARLIE BREWER SLIDER 4" TUBE LURE

This is a very soft Tube Lure and Crawfish combination which has crawfish scent. This makes the lure irresistible to bass and other fish.
Specifications
Size: 4"
Pack Count: 4
MSRP: $2.50
Colors: Pearl Pepper, Natural/Blue Glitter, Green Pumpkin/Black Flake, Glass Minnow, Watermelon/Red Flake, Black/Red Flake

CHARLIE BREWER SLIDER WORM

The 4" Slider Worm was specially designed for Slider fishing. It is a straight worm with a small paddle tail that will not over-act nature. The 4" worm will match the size of the food that bass eat 80% to 90% of the time. As this worm is smaller, the bass can inhale it easier and quicker. As a result, you won't miss as many strikes while fishing the Slider techniques, "sliding" or "pull'n drop" methods.

SPECIFICATIONS
Size: 4"
Pack Count: 20
MSRP: $3.25
Colors: Black, Purple, Chartreuse, Smoke, Watermelon Green, Grape, Motor Oil, Black/Fluorescent Pink Tail, Purple/Fluorescent Pink Tail, Black/Chartreuse Tail, Black/Blue, Brown/Orange Tail, Grape/Fluorescent Pink Tail, Motor Oil Glitter/Orange Tail, Plum Glitter/Chartreuse Tail, Pumpkin/Chartreuse Tail, Junebug/Chartreuse Tail, Purple/Glitter, Electric Blue, Smoke/Glitter, Green/Gold Glitter, Strawberry/Glitter, Grape/Glitter, Motor Oil/Glitter, Plum/Glitter, Salt & Pepper, Pumpkin/Black Flake, Avocado Green, June Bug, Irish Whiskey, Cotton Candy, Watermelon Seed, Black/Pumpkin, Stardust, Black/Cherry, Tequila Sunrise, Chameleon Purple, Grape Neon, Plum Glitter/Chartreuse Glitter, Tennessee Shad, Camouflage, Shrimp/Mean Green Core, Chartreuse/Black Core, Smoke/Yellow Red Glitter Core, Smoke/Red Core, Creamy Green/Red Core, Creamy Green/Pumpkin Core

CREME LURES BURKE® SPLIT TAIL TRAILERS

This highly productive trailer is made of a specially formulated plastic that gives it an action unequaled by any other product. It's tough so it will last cast after cast, yet is extremely supple in any water. This has made it a favorite of successful tournament fishermen across the country.

SPECIFICATIONS:
Model: 770
Size: 4" (approximately)
Package Count: 6 spares
MSRP: $2.16
Colors: White Hot Tip, Clear Chartreuse/Hot Tip, Chartreuse/ Hot Tip, Black, Yellow, White, Clear Chartreuse, Chartreuse, Pearl

SOFT PLASTIC

CREME LURES LIT'L FISHIE® SHAD

CREME LURES SCOUNDREL®

CREME LURES CURL TAIL WORM

CREME LURES DEVIL'S TONGUE®

This hand-poured, high-floating lure is excellent for both smallmouth and largemouth bass. The unique manufacturing process, which allows pure air to be injected into the soft plastic during the molding process makes, this lure a phenomenal floater. This new air-filled lure has perfect coloration and will float most hooks for true Carolina rigging. The Devil's Tongue can also be rigged Texas, Split Shot, Drop Shot or as a jig trailer.

SPECIFICATIONS
Model: 9900-8
Size: 4" (approximately)
Package count: 8 spares
MSRP: $4.32
Colors: Chartreuse Pepper, Watermelon Red Flake, Black, Watermelon, Motor Oil/Red Flake, Ice Tea, June Bug, Red Bug, Smokin' Green, Pumpkin

CREME LURES LIT'L FISHIE® SHAD

This lure swims like a real fish because the head and body remain stable, but the tail moves with the most natural action you'd ever want to see. This, coupled with the hand-painted soft plastic body, results in the most versatile, eye-appealing shad around.

SPECIFICATIONS:
Model: 24100
Size: 4" (approximately)
Package Count: 1 rigged
MSRP: $6.74

Model: 4100
Size: 4" (approximately)

Package Count: 2 spares
MSRP: $10.04

Model: 34100
Size: 3" (approximately)
Package Count: 1 rig/2 spares
MSRP: $6.74

Model: 22200
Size: 2" (approximately)
Package Count: 1 jig/3 spares
MSRP: $3.19
Colors: Black Back, Green/Black Back, Gold/Blue Back, Red Fin, Milk Char/Black Back, Gray Back, Croaker

CREME LURES PRE-RIGGED CURL TAIL WORM

Creme Lure was the originator of the plastic worm and the first to pre-rig this same straight tail worm with a reusable rig. Creme is now the first lure company to pre-rig a curled tail worm with the reusable rig. This is an item that will soon become a staple in any tackle box.

SPECIFICATIONS:
Model: 6CT00-3
Size: 6" (approximately)
Package count: 1 rigged curled tail worm
Colors: Pumpkin/Char Pepper, Black/Blue, Grape/Fire, Electric Grape/Fire, Black/Fire

Model: 4CT00-3
Size: 4" (approximately)
Package count: 1 rigged curled tail worm
Colors: Purple/Fire, Grape/Fire, Black/Char, Black/fire, Pumpkin/Chartreuse Pepper

CREME LURES SCOUNDREL® WORM RIGS

These tournament-proven performers come pre-rigged and ready to use in a variety of color options. The 6" Scoundrel is the first plastic worm ever produced. All Creme's rigs are designed to be deadly so long as you fish them SLOW. Featuring a wire leader and propeller, they are available in a weedless variety with #1 hooks and wire weedguards to prevent snags and hang-ups.

SPECIFICATIONS:
Model: 100-3
Size: 6" (approximately)
Package Count: 1 rig/1 spare
MSRP: $2.28
Colors: Live, Red, Black, Yellow, Cotton Candy, White, Motor Oil/Red Flake, Purple/Silver Flake, Black Neon, Black/Blue Tail, Shad, Crawfish, Camo, Grass Snake, Plum, Orange Crunch, June Bug, Smoke Pepper, Electric Blue, Purple, Powder Blue, Blk/Chartreuse, Blk/Red Tail, Watermelon, Fluorescent Orange, Lime Green, Ice Tea, Kudzu, Red Bug, Merthiolate, Watermelon Red, Blue, Fluorescent Green, Grape/Glo Pink Tail, Purple/White Dot, Dirty White, Black/White Dots, Chartreuse Pumpkin, Purple/Red Tail, Pumpkin, Pumpkin Seed, Purple/Yellow, Purple/White Tail, Pumpkin/Green, Chameleon/Blue, Motor Oil, Chartreuse Milk, Black/Fire Tail, Bubble Gum, Purple/Glo Pink Tail, Lime/Glo Pink Tail, Tequila, Little Bass, Grape, Purple/Fire Tail

LURES

SOFT PLASTIC

CREME LURES SCREMER®

CREME LURES SUPER TUBE®

CREME LURES WHACKY WORM®

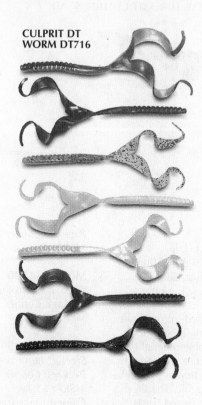

CULPRIT DT WORM DT716

CREME LURES SCREMER®

The SCREMER has it all. The unique body design provides 43% more underwater sound than other soft plastic worms. The unusual back and forth rotation action creates a movement that cannot be ignored by bass. The ridges also allow greater compression, which increases the catch-to-strike ratio.

SPECIFICATIONS:
Model: 600-99
Size: 6" (approximately)
Package Count: 12 spares
Colors: Little Bass, Pumpkin, Red Shad, Black/Blue, Tequila Sunrise, Plum Watermelon/Chartreuse, Junebug, Sour Grape, Black, Black Neon/Chartreuse, Ice Tea, Watermelon, Black/White, Black/Chartreuse, Black Neon

CREME LURES SUPER TUBE® HEAVY

This lure's coloration duplicates what these baits were originally designed for – to imitate forage fish. Its patented, internally-colored body design

allows coloration as never before seen in this type lure. This coloration duplicates what a predator fish sees just prior
to engulfing his food – gills.

SPECIFICATIONS:
Model: 78800
Size: 3.5" (approximately)
Package Count: 8 spares
MSRP: $4.82
Colors: Pearl Black Glitter, Black Neon, Trout, Black/Blue Glitter, Shad, Watermelon Seed, Pumpkin Watermelon, Moss Watermelon, Watermelon Blend, Gray Back Shad, Bluegill, Sunperch, Crawfish, Red Head

CREME LURES WHACKY WORM®

The Whacky Worm is perhaps the ultimate finesse rig for bass in a neutral or negative feeding mode. This hand-poured, soft-plastic worm has the perfect combination of flexibilty and durability, which are essential. Fishing slow or even completely still is the key to the rig's success.

SPECIFICATIONS:
Model: WW-00
Size: 6" (approximately)
Package Count: 12 spares
MSRP: $3.16
Colors: Live Color, School Bus Yellow, June Bug, Smoke Pepper, Watermelon, Ice Tea, Red Bug, Merthiolate, Watermelon, Red Flake, Chartreuse Pumpkin, Pumpkin, Chameleon Blue

CULPRIT DT WORM

Combining the Culprit worm body with an awesome double-kicking tail, this lure can be retrieved slower to keep it in the strike zone longer. Also a great flipping bait, with increased action in short bursts.

Specifications
Model: DT716
Size: 7"
Pack Count: 16
MSRP: $3.79
Colors: Black Shad, Red Shad, Pumpkin Seed, Chartreuse Shad, Pearl, Tequila Shad, June Bug

LURES

CULPRIT FINESSE WORM TK515

CULPRIT FROG SF310

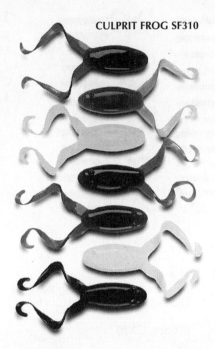

CULPRIT JERK WORM JW610

CULPRIT FINESSE WORM

The 5-inch Finesse worm quietly grabs attention. Ribbed for slight vibrations in the water and with a spade tail to provide a subtle flutter action, it will "finesse" stubborn fish to bite. Great for most fishing rigs, including Texas, Carolina and even wacky-style. Culprit offers the lure in a wide range of color combinations, including unique tail-colors not available to the industry until now.

SPECIFICATIONS
Model: TK515
Size: 5"
Pack Count: 15
MSRP: $2.59
Colors: Red Shad, Black, Green

Pumpkin/Watermelon Pepper Tail, Watermelon Red/Watermelon Pepper Tail, Black/Blue Tail, Tequila Shad, June Bug, White, Pumpkin Seed/Chartreuse Tail, Blue Shadow and Kudzu Shad

CULPRIT FROG

Features a flat sled-like belly for a slow horizontal descent or for gliding across the water's surface. The forward-facing legs produce an incredible kicking action.

SPECIFICATIONS
Model: SF310
Size: 3"
Pack Count: 10
MSRP: $3.79
Colors: Red Shad, Green Shad,

Chartreuse Shad, Bull Frog, Tequila Shad, White Hi-Floater, Black Hi-Floater

CULPRIT JERK WORM

Exciting wounded-baitfish action produced by the Jerk Worm provides aggressive strikes when worked near the surface. The V-shaped body provides the unique motion, while the hook pocket enables the angler to set the hook faster and easier.

SPECIFICATIONS
Model: JW610
Size: 6"
Pack Count: 10
MSRP: $3.79
Colors: Speckled B.G., Pearl, Red Shiny Shad, Shadflash, New Penny, Arkansas Shiner

LURES

Tube Bait Fix-up
Tube baits are excellent black bass catchers, but you can improve these lures with one simple modification. Most manufacturers put too many tentacles on each lure, which inhibits their full range of motion. You can change this by removing 6-8 tentacles from the lure at spaced intervals. This allows the remaining tentacles to move freely in the water, giving more life to the bait.

SOFT PLASTIC

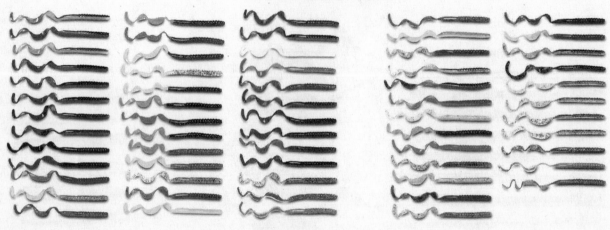

CULPRIT ORIGINAL WORM
SPECIFICATIONS
Model: C425
Size: 4.5"
Pack Count: 20
MSRP: $3.79
Colors: Black Shad, Red Shad, Grape Shad, Crawdad, Moccasin, Red Shad/Green Flake, Black, Grape, Tequila Shad, June Bug, Watermelon Pepper, Tomato, Fire Tiger, Red, Hot Watermelon

Model: C625
Size: 6"
Pack Count: 20 (18*)
MSRP: $3.79
Colors: Black Shad, Red Shad, Blue Shad, Grape Shad, Crawdad, Moccasin, Red Shad/Green Flake, Black, Grape, Purple, Motor Oil Flake, Electric Blue Lightnin', Grape/Red Tail*, Black/Chartreuse Tail*, Black/Blue Tail*, Pumpkin Seed, Chartreuse Shad, Tequila Shad/Green Flake, Pearl, Fire & Ice, Tequila Shad, June Bug, Plum Crazy, Red Shiny Shad, Watermelon Pepper, Tomato, Motor Oil Shad, Pumpkin Seed/Chartreuse Tail*, Purple Neon, Fire Tiger, Red, Hot Watermelon

Model: C720
Size: 7.5"
Pack Count: 20 (15*)
MSRP: $3.79
Colors: Black Shad, Red Shad, Green Shad, Blue Shad, Grape Shad, Crawdad, Moccasin, Red Shad/Green Flake, Black, Grape, Purple, Motoroil Flake, Electric Blue Lightnin', Grape/Firetail*, Grape/Red Tail*, Grape/Chartreuse Tail*, Salt & Pepper/Chartreuse Tail*, Black/Chartreuse Tail*, Black/Blue Tail*, Black/Red Tail*, Black/Firetail*, Blue/Chartreuse Tail*, Pumpkin Seed, Pumpkin Seed/Firetail*, Chartreuse Shad, Tequila Shad/Green Flake, Blue Moccasin Shad, Pearl, Bull Frog, Fire & Ice, Tequila Shad, June Bug, Christmas, Plum Crazy, Red Shiny Shad, Watermelon Pepper, Bloody Mary, Tomato, Blue Blood, Motoroil Shad, Pumpkin Seed/Chartreuse Tail*, Black Shad/Green Flake, Crawdad/Green Flake, Purple Neon, Fire Tiger, June Bug/Blue Tail*, Red, Hot Watermelon, Tiger Tail*, Green Pumpkin, Chartreuse Pumpkin, Watermelon Red Flake, Motoroil/Chartreuse Tail*, Wtr. Red Flake Shad, Blue Shadow, Green Pumpkin Red Mist, Kudzu Shad, Blueberry, Redberry, Goby, Wtr. Red Flake Core, Chili Pepper

Model: C1010
Size: 10"
Pack Count: 10
MSRP: $3.79
Colors: Black Shad, Red Shad, Blue Shad, Crawdad, Moccasin, Pumpkin Seed, Tequila Shad, June Bug, Plum Crazy, Blueberry, Redberry

Model: C125
Size: 12"
Pack Count: 5
MSRP: $3.79
Colors: Black Shad, Red Shad, Crawdad, Black, Pumpkin Seed, Tequila ShadSalt & Pepper Shad, Smoke Silver Shad

Crayfish Rigging and Retrieve
Soft-plastic crayfish often come pre-rigged. Those that aren't can be outfitted with a weighted hook or leadhead jig, with the hook point turned in to make the lure weedless. Be sure to insert the hook so the crayfish will be retrieved backward in the same way that a live crayfish scoots backward across the bottom.

CULPRIT SALTY TUBES

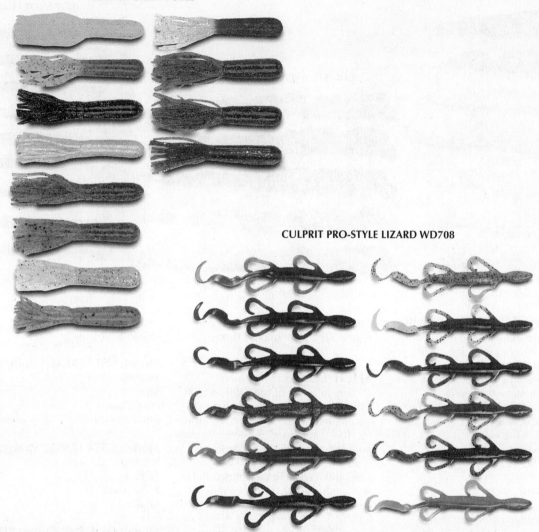

CULPRIT PRO-STYLE LIZARD WD708

CULPRIT PRO-STYLE LIZARD

A classic-styled bait, this lizard is the perfect choice for year-round catching of big bass. A wide range of colors and features like the "kicking" tail and the high-action legs help to produce bigger fish catches. The slim profile allows it to slither into heavy vegetation. It has the perfect flotation response, when Carolina-rigged, compared to other salt-filled brands that do not float naturally.

SPECIFICATIONS
Model: WD708
Size: 7"
Pack Count: 8
MSRP: $2.99
Colors: Black Shad, Red Shad, Crawdad, Electric Blue Lightnin', Pumpkin Seed/Firetail, June Bug, Watermelon Pepper, Pumpkin Seed/Chartreuse Tail, Green Pumpkin, Chartreuse Pumpkin, Watermelon Red Flake, Motor Oil/Chartreuse Tail

CULPRIT SALTY TUBES

Salty Tubes are perfect for flipping. They're heavy, compact and packed with salt. They're also great with a jighead for big smallmouths. These tubes catch numbers of quality fish year-round – a great tournament bait.

SPECIFICATIONS
Model: CST
Size: 4"
Pack Count: 10
MSRP: $4.29
Colors: Chartreuse/Silver Flake, Melon/Chartreuse Pepper, Black Neon, Pearl/Silver Flake, Smoke/Black & Red Flake, Orange Pumpkin, Salt & Pepper, Yellow Pumpkin, Smoke Silver/Clear Silver Flake, Dark Melon Pepper, Green Pumpkin, Goby

LURES

SOFT PLASTIC

CULPRIT SWIM FIN GRUB SG312

CULPRIT SWIM FIN WORM SW610

CULPRIT SPECIALTY DROP SHOT LURES

CULPRIT SWIM FIN GRUB

This is one bait you don't want to be without. It's got incredible action, even at slow speeds. It requires nothing more than a little current or slow retrieve to make it come to life. This bait perfectly imitates a bowfin resting in the water with its back fin undulating through the water.

SPECIFICATIONS
Model: SG312
Size: 3"
Pack Count: 12
MSRP: $3.79
Colors: Red Shad, Black, Pearl, Chartreuse, Solid Motor Oil, Pink, Perch

CULPRIT SWIM FIN WORM

Swim Fins feature a rippled fin that runs the entire length of the lure, producing a unique undulating action. A slow retrieve produces maximum action so you can keep this lure in the strike zone longer.

Model: SW610
Size: 6"
Pack Count: 10
MSRP: $3.79

Colors: Red Shad, Black, June Bug, Plum Crazy, Watermelon Pepper

CULPRIT SPECIALTY DROP SHOT LURES

Offering a series of specialty baits, Culprit now provides lures that work exceptionally well with the drop shot rig. The "Drop Shot" is becoming very popular with both the professional tournament fisherman and the weekend angler. Three distinct shapes and unique color selections provide versatility when trying to "match the hatch."

The ZEAL brand is the Japanese equivalent to the Culprit brand. Made here for the Japanese market under the most stringent quality guidelines.

SPECIFICATIONS
Model: CR3 (ZEAL "Culrin" Worm)
Size: 3"
Pack Count: 10
MSRP: $3.79

Model: CR4 (ZEAL "Culrin" Worm)
Size: 4"

Pack Count: 10
MSRP: $3.79

Model: CST3 (ZEAL "Straight" Worm)
Size: 3"
Pack Count: 10
MSRP: $3.79

Model: CST4 (ZEAL "Straight" Worm)
Size: 4"
Pack Count: 10
MSRP: $3.79

Model: DSW410 (Culprit "Drop Shot" Worm)
Size: 4"
Pack Count: 10
MSRP: $3.79
Colors: Red Shad, Black, Green Pumpkin/ Watermelon/Pepper Tail, Watermelon Red/Watermelon Pepper Tail, Black/Blue Tail, Tequila Shad, June Bug, White, Pumpkin Seed/ Chartreuse Tail, Blue Shadow and Kudzu Shad

Topwater Worm
By leaving off the slip-sinker, you can fish a Texas-rigged worm as a surface lure. Larger worms are especially effective this way when worked over vegetation, around brushtops and along weedy shorelines.

LURES

CULPRIT TASSEL TAIL WORM TT712

CULPRIT TASSEL LIZARD TTL708

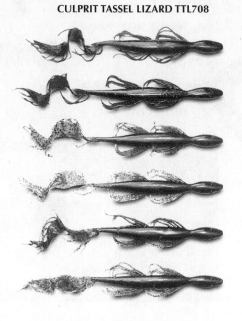

CULPRIT TK WORMTW615

CULPRIT TASSEL LIZARD

This lure combines the skirt tentacles of a tube bait with the legs and tail of the Culprit Pro-style Lizard, creating a wild lizard imitation. The Tassel Lizard produces lots of action in the water. The tassels create an enticing flotation response with very little water current or movement of the bait.

SPECIFICATIONS
Model: TTL708
Size: 7"
Pack Count: 8
MSRP: $3.79
Colors: Red Shad, June Bug, Blue Shadow, Green Pumpkin, Goby and Chili Pepper

CULPRIT TASSEL TAIL WORM

Culprit has combined the tantalizing skirt tentacles of a tube bait and the kicking action of the Culprit worm and lizard to provide a series of lures that produces a fantastic and unique action in the water. The tentacles flow with the perfectly balanced body and tail while retrieved in the water, producing a wave of action. The tassels also produce an enticing flotation response with very little movement of the bait while "dead-sticking" the lure on the water's bottom. This tentacle skirt and lure combination has never been successfully accomplished before now!

SPECIFICATIONS
Model: TT712
Size: 7"
Pack Count: 12
MSRP: $3.79
Colors: Red Shad, Crawdad, Tequila Shad, June Bug, Hot Watermelon, Blue Shadow, Blueberry, Redberry, Goby and Chili Pepper

CULPRIT TK WORM

The TK Worm is an awesome worm for fishing weightless (floating style). It has a spade-type tail that really produces "walk the dog" action and sways on descent. This worm is heavy enough to throw with baitcasting gear when you need to use heavier rods and line. It's perfect to use with spinning tackle when you need to skip it into tight spots, such as overhanging trees and docks.

SPECIFICATIONS
Model: TW615
Size: 6"
Pack Count: 15
MSRP: $3.69
Colors: Red Shad, Christmas, Watermelon Pepper, White, Chartreuse Pumpkin

LURES

Scent Holder for Tubes
When using bass attractant with tube lures, insert a piece of cotton or packing foam through the bottom and push it to the top of the tube before rigging Texas style. When the hook is inserted, it will keep this material in place. The attractant then can be applied inside the tube, and the scent will hold much longer.

SOFT PLASTIC

CULPRIT WOOLLY BOOGER WB310

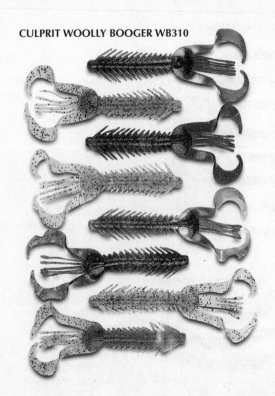

FISHTEK JELLTEX SHADS

FISHTEK JELLY WORMS

FISHTEK TWINTAILS

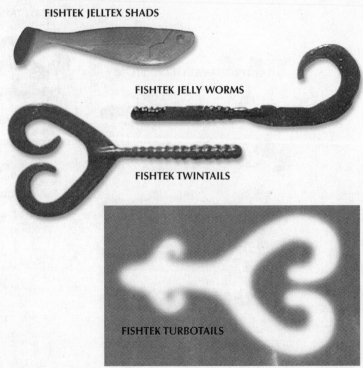

FISHTEK TURBOTAILS

CULPRIT WOOLLY BOOGER

Featuring wild appendages and two kicking tails for the ultimate in lure action, the Woolly Booger produces maximum action with a slow retrieval speed to help keep it in the strike zone longer. Perfect for flipping or for fishing Carolina-rigged just above the weed line.

SPECIFICATIONS
Model: WB310
Size: 3"
Pack Count: 10
MSRP: $3.79

Model: WB408
Size: 4"
Pack Count: 8
MSRP: $3.79
Colors: Red Shad/Green Flake, Pumpkin Seed, June Bug, Watermelon Pepper, Black Shad/Green Flake, Black Neon, Hot Watermelon, Chartreuse Pumpkin

FISHTEK JELLTEX SHADS

These highly detailed fish shads have a paddle-shaped tail that thumps out vibrations, even at low retrieval speeds. They are virtually indestructible and will still be landing fish long after conventional soft baits would

have fallen to bits.
SPECIFICATIONS
Sizes: 4" to 9"
MSRP: $5.25 to $9.95

FISHTEK JELLTEX SOFTBAITS

All Fishtek softbaits are made of Jelltex. This is a revolutionary new latex like material developed by Fishtek that has many unique properties resulting in a lure that is far superior to other softbaits on the market. Jelltex stretches rather than snaps – in fact it can stretch to ten times its original length! In fishing terms, this means that a fish keeps striking the lure until you get a hook up. Conventional softbaits will tear and break after a few strikes. Jelltex lures are virtually indestructible and can be used again and again. Fishtek lures have a superb action, even when worked very slowly. This is due to the inherent suppleness of Jelltex – so with very little water movement our lures produce an incredibly lifelike action in the water. Compare them to standard softbaits and you will see the difference immediately.

Chemically safe! Unlike most softbaits, Jelltex has full FDA approval and is completely harmless to you and the environment.

Available in a range of sizes and colors including Lumo.

FISHTEK JELLY WORMS

Super strong Jelltex worms. The curly tail mimics the swimming action of baitfish. Because Jelltex is so flexible, the tail wiggles tantalisingly even at low retrieval speeds. And because Jelltex is so tough, they keep on wiggling, strike after strike.
SPECIFICATIONS
Sizes: 4" and 7"
MSRP: $2.25 (4"), $3.75 (7")

FISHTEK TWINTAILS

Twintails produce twice the vibration, and benefit from all the advantages of Jelltex. Irresistible to predators. Pull these lures nice and slowl through the water – even at very low retrieval speeds, these lures flutter irresistibly!
SPECIFICATIONS
Sizes: 4" and 7"
MSRP: $4.95

FISHTEK TURBOTAILS

This 4" twintail has rippler fins to produce more vibration. A suberb lure for bass. Available in a range of colors.
MSRP: $3.50

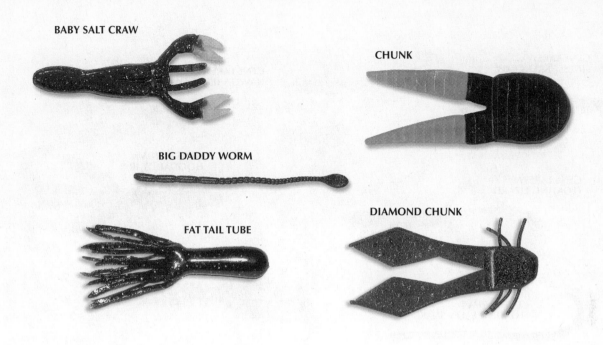

BABY SALT CRAW

CHUNK

BIG DADDY WORM

DIAMOND CHUNK

FAT TAIL TUBE

GENE LAREW®
BABY HOODADDY

This little salt-impregnated, garlic-scented "creature" bait has all the looks and action of its larger namesakes, the Hoodaddy and Hoodaddy Jr., but in a more compact size. It's perfect for split-shotting, and it's great for drop-shotting. Or, rig it on a jig head and swim it around docks or other cover. It's also the perfect size for use in small creeks and rivers. But don't think small necessarily means small waters and small fish. The Baby Hoodaddy is ideal for tough fishing conditions as a result of cold fronts and/or heavy fishing pressure. And there are just certain times of the year that big fish prefer small baits.

SPECIFICATIONS
Size: 3"
Pack Count: 15
MSRP: $3.50.
Colors: Black Blue, Black Neon, Black Neon/Silver, Pearl Silver, Chartreuse Silver, Clear Silver, Green Cotton Candy, Junebug, Dark Plum, Pumpkin Pepper Green, Purple Silver/Clear Silver, Red Shad, Pumpkin Seed, Green Pumpkin, Green Pumpkin/Watermelon Pepper, Smoke Silver, Watermelon Pepper, Watermelon Pepper Neon

GENE LAREW®
BABY SALT CRAW
SPECIFICATIONS
Length: 2.75"
MSRP: $1.99
Colors: Black Neon, Smoke Cracker, Butterscotch, Watermelon Cracker, Junebug, Black Blue/Blue, Pumpkin Pepper, Black Neon/Chartreuse, Pumpkin Pepper Green, Black Neon/Fire, Pumpkin Seed, Pumpkin Pepper Green/Orange Green, Pumpkin Seed/Chartreuse, Black Silver/Chartreuse, Green Pumpkin, Junebug/Chartreuse, Watermelon Pepper, Melon Pepper Neon/Orange Green, Natural Craw, Pumpkin Pepper/Orange, Pumpkin Candy

GENE LAREW®
BIG DADDY WORM
SPECIFICATIONS
Length: 10.5"
MSRP: $3.89
Colors: Black Electric Blue (Lam), Pumpkin Pepper Green, Black Neon, Red Shad (Lam), Cherry Pepper, Green Pumpkin, Electric Blue, Tequila Sunrise, Grape Big Red, Dark Watermelon, Junebug, Tomato Red, Pumpkin Pepper

GENE LAREW® CHUNK
SPECIFICATIONS
Length: 3"
MSRP: $3.29
Colors: Black Neon, Black Blue/Blue, Blue, Black Neon/Fire, Bone White, Black Neon /Silver, Pearl White, Black Silver/Chartreuse, Pumpkin Pepper Green, White Silver/Silver, Watermelon Pepper

GENE LAREW®
DIAMOND CHUNK
SPECIFICATIONS
Length: 3.5"
MSRP: $3.29
Colors: Black Blue, Black Blue/Blue, Black Neon, Black Neon/Fire, Bone White, Black Neon/Sliver, Pearl White, Black Silver/Chartreuse, Pumpkin Pepper Green, White Silver/Silver, Watermelon Pepper

GENE LAREW®
FAT TAIL TUBE
SPECIFICATIONS
Length: 4.5"
MSRP: $3.29
Colors: Black Shad, Natural Craw (Lam), Black Blue, Pumpkinseed, Black Neon, Green Pumpkin, Junebug, Smoke Red, Red Shad (Lam), Watermelon Pepper, Salt and Pepper, Smoke Blue

LURES

SOFT PLASTIC

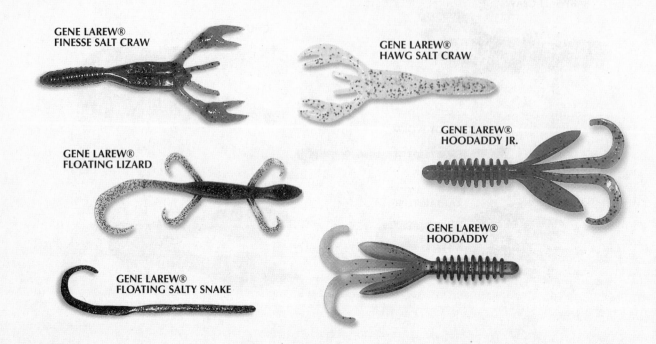

GENE LAREW®
FINESSE SALT CRAW

GENE LAREW®
HAWG SALT CRAW

GENE LAREW®
FLOATING LIZARD

GENE LAREW®
HOODADDY JR.

GENE LAREW®
HOODADDY

GENE LAREW®
FLOATING SALTY SNAKE

GENE LAREW®
FINESSE SALT CRAW
SPECIFICATIONS
Length: 3"
MSRP: $3.50 - 15-count ziplock bag
Colors: Black Blue, Mellon Pepper, Black Blue/Blue, Pumpkin Pepper, Black Neon, Pumpkin Pepper/Orange, Gr. Pumpkin Green, Pumpkin Pepper/Green, Black Neon/Chart, Pumpkin Seed, Natural Craw, Pumpkin Seed . Chart, Black Neon/Fire, Green :umpkin, Black Neon/Silver, Smoke Red, Chartreuse Pepper, Watermelon Pepper, Junebug, Watermelon Pepper/Chartreuse, Junebug/Chartreuse, Watermelon Pepper

GENE LAREW®
FLOATING LIZARD
SPECIFICATIONS
Length: 6"
MSRP: $3.75
Colors: Black Blue, Black Neon, Gr. Pumpkin Green, Junebug, Pumpkin Seed, Green Pumpkin, Watermelon Pepper

GENE LAREW®
FLOATING SALTY SNAKE
SPECIFICATIONS
Length: 11"

MSRP: $4.50
Colors: Black Blue, Black Neon, Gr. Pumpkin Green, Junebug, Pumpkin Seed, Green Pumpkin, Watermelon Pepper

GENE LAREW®
HAWG SALT CRAW
SPECIFICATIONS
Length: 6"
MSRP: $4.50
Colors: Black Blue/Blue, Pumpkin Pepper, Black Blue/Powder Blue, Pumpkin Pepper/Orange, Black Neon, Pumpkin Pepper Green, Natural Craw, Pumpkin Pepper Green/Chartreuse, Pumpkin Candy, Pumpkin Pepper Green/Green, Smoke Cracker, Pumpkin Pepper Green/Orange Green, Watermelon Cracker, Pumpkin Seed, Black Neon/Chartreuse, Pumpkin Seed/Chartreuse, Black Neon/Fire, Green Pumpkin, Bone White, Smoke Blue Orange, Chartreuse Pepper, Smoke Green Orange, Huckleberry, Watermelon Pepper, Junebug, Watermelon/Chartreuse, Junebug/Blue, Watermelon Pepper Blue, Mean Pumpkin Green/Chartreuse Neon, Watrmelon Neon, Melon Pepper Neon/Orange Green, Sour Grape (Lam), Plum

GENE LAREW®
HOO-DADDY
SPECIFICATIONS
Length: 6"
MSRP: $4.00
Colors: Black Blue, Pumpkin Pepper Green, Black Neon, Purple Silver/Clear Silver, Black Neon/Silver, Red Shad (Lam), Pearl Silver, Pumpkin Seed, Firetiger (Lam) 6 Ct. Only, Green Pumpkin, Green Cotton Candy, Green Pumpkin/Watermelon Pepper, Junebug, Watermelon Pepper, Kudzu, Watermelon Neon, Dark Plum

GENE LAREW®
HOO-DADDY JR.
SPECIFICATIONS
Length: 4.5"
MSRP: $3.50
Colors: Black Blue, Pumpkin Pepper Green, Black Neon, Purple Silver/Clear Silver, Black Neon/Silver, Red Shad (Lam), Bluegill, Pumpkin Seed, Pearl Silver, Green Pumpkin, Green Cotton Candy, Green Pumpkin/Watermelon Pepper, Junebug, Watermelon Pepper, Kudzu, Watermelon Neon, Dark Plum

GENE LAREW® HOOK TAIL WORM

GENE LAREW® MEGA RING SHAD

GENE LAREW® KOMODO LIZARD

GENE LAREW® MEGA RING SNAKE

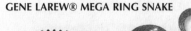

GENE LAREW® RIBBON TAIL WORM

GENE LAREW® LONG JOHN MINNOW

GENE LAREW®
HOOK TAIL WORM
SPECIFICATIONS
Length: 8"
MSRP: $2.99
Colors: Black Neon, Grape Big Red, Black Neon/Chartreuse, Junebug, Black Neon/Fire, Motor Oil Neon, Brown Blue, Plum, Cameleon Neon, Pumpkin Pepper Green, Cameleon Neon/Fire, Red Clear, Cherry Pepper, Red Gold, Electric Blue, Red Silver, Electric Blue/Fire, Tomato Red, Electric Blue/Pearl White, Black Blue/Blue

GENE LAREW®
KOMODO LIZARD
SPECIFICATIONS
Length: 7.5
MSRP: $2.99
Colors: Black Blue, Pumpkinseed, Black Blue/Blue, Pumpkinseed/Chartreuse, Black Blue/Powder Blue, Green Pumpkin, Black Neon, Green Pumpkin/Chartreuse, Black Neon/Chartreuse, Watermelon Pepper, Huckleberry (Lam), Watermelon Pepper/Chartreuse, Pumpkin Pepper Green, Sour Grape (Lam), Pumpkin Pepper Green/Chartreuse

GENE LAREW®
LONG JOHN MINNOW
SPECIFICATIONS
Length: 3.5
MSRP: $2.39
Colors: Chartreuse Silver/Black Back, Pearl White/Black Back, Pearl White/Blue Back, Smoke Silver, Pearl Orange/ Black Back, Chartreuse Silver, Pearl Chartreuse/Black Back, Clear Silver

GENE LAREW®
MEGA RING SHAD
SPECIFICATIONS
Length: 3.5", 4.5"
MSRP: $3.75
Colors (2.5"): Black Blue/Blue, Dark Plum, Black Neon, Pumpkin Pepper Green, Green Pumpkin Green, Red Shad (Lam), Black Neon/Chartreuse, Pumpkin Seed, Pearl Silver, Pumpkin Seed/Chartreuse, Chartreuse Silver, Green Pumpkin, Clear Silver, Smoke Silver, Green Cotton Candy, Tequila Sunrise (Lam), Junebug, Watermelon Pepper, Junebug/Chartreuse, Watermelon Neon
Colors (4.5"): Black Blue/Blue, Dark Plum, Black Neon, Pumpkin Pepper Green, Green Pumpkin Green, Red Shad (Lam), Black Neon/Chartreuse, Pumpkin Seed, Natural Craw, Pumpkin Seed/Chartreuse, Pumpkin Candy, Green Pumpkin, Smoke Cracker, Tequila Sunrise (Lam), Watermelon Cracker, Dark Watermelon, Pearl Silver, Watermelon Pepper, Junebug, Watermelon Neon, Junebug/Chartreuse, Sour Grape, Green Cotton Candy

GENE LAREW®
MEGA RING SNAKE
SPECIFICATIONS
Length: 7.5"
MSRP: $3.49
Colors: Black Blue/Blue, Green Pumpkin, Black Neon, Smoke Red, Black Neon/Chartreuse, Tequila Sunrise (Lam), Junebug, Watermelon Pepper, Pumpkin Pepper Green, Sour Grape (Lam), Red Shad (Lam), Natural Craw, Salt and Pepper, Pumpkin Candy, Pumpkin Seed, Smoke Cracker, Pumpkin Seed/Chartreuse, Watermelon Cracker

GENE LAREW®
RIBBON TAIL WORM
SPECIFICATIONS
Length: 8"
MSRP: $3.49
Colors: Black Blue, Pumpkin Seed, Black Neon, Green Pumpkin, Red Bug, Tequila Sunrise, Camo, Tomato Red, Electric Blue, Watermelon Seed, Green Cotton Candy, Watermelon Neon, Junebug, Green Pumpkin Green, Plum, Ultimate Green, Red Shad, Green Christmas Tree, Red Silver, Baby Bass

SOFT PLASTIC

GENE LAREW® SALT CRAW

GENE LAREW® SALTY SNAKE

GENE LAREW® SALT FRY

GENE LAREW® SALTY RING TAIL

GENE LAREW® SKIRTED SALT CRAW

GENE LAREW® SALT CRAW
SPECIFICATIONS
Length: 4", 5"
MSRP: $2.99
Colors (4"): Black Blue, Watermelon Cracker, Black Neon, Black/Tomato Red, Bluegill, Black/Yellow, Bone White, Black Blue/Blue, Butterscotch, Black Blue/Powder Blue, Chartreuse Pepper, Black Green/Green, Cranapple, Black Neon/Chartreuse, Electric Blue, Black Neon/Fire, Huckleberry, Black Neon/Silver, Glow, Black Silver/Chartreuse, Junebug, Bluegill/Chartreuse, Plum, Electric Blue/Chartreuse, Pumpkin Pepper, Junebug/Blue, Pumpkin Pepper Green, Junebug/Chartreuse, Pumpkin Seed, Mean Pumpkin Green/Chartreuse Neon, Pumpkin Seed/Chartreuse, Melon Pepper Neon/Orange Green, Green Pumpkin, Pumpkin Pepper/Orange, Tequila Sunrise (Lam), Pumpkin Pepper Green/Chartreuse, Tomato Red, Pumpkin Pepper Green/Green, Watermelon Pepper, Pumpkin Pepper Green/Orange Green, Sour Grape (Lam), Root Beer Pepper/Orange, Natural Craw, Smoke Silver/Chartreuse, Pumpkin Candy, Watermelon Pepper/Chartreuse, Smoke Cracker
Colors (5"): Black Neon, Natural Craw, Chartreuse Pepper, Pumpkin Candy, Plum, Smoke Cracker, Pumpkin Pepper Green, Watermelon Cracker, Pumpkinseed, Black Blue/Blue, Pumpkinseed/Chartreuse, Black Neon/Chartreuse, Green Pumpkin, Black Neon/Fire, Tequila Sunrise (Lam), Pumpkin Pepper/Orange, Watermelon Pepper

GENE LAREW® SALT FRY
SPECIFICATIONS
Length: 4"
MSRP: $2.39
Colors: Black Blue/Blue, Green Pumpkin, Chartreuse Pepper, Tequila Sunrise (Lam), Cotton Candy, Watermelon Pepper, Green Cotton Candy, Watermelon Pepper/Chartreuse, Junebug, Watermelon Neon, Red Shad (Lam)

GENE LAREW® SALTY RING TAIL
SPECIFICATIONS
Length: 4", 7.5"
MSRP: $2.39 (4"), $2.99 (7.5")
Colors (4"): Black Overshot Red, Black Blue/Blue, Bluegill, Black Neon/Fire, Cranapple, Black Neon/Pearl White, Plum, Black Silver/Chartreuse, Plum Apple, Grape/Powder Blue, Pumpkin Pepper, Junebug/Blue, Pumpkin Pepper Green, Pumpkin Pepper/Orange, Salt and Pepper, Purple Silver/Bone White, Watermelon Pepper
Colors (7.5"): Camouflage (Lam), Sour Grape (Lam), Cranapple, Black Blue/Blue, Plum, Black Neon/Fire, Pumpkin Pepper, Black Neon/Pearl White, Pumpkin Pepper Green, Black Silver/Chartreuse, Red Shad (Lam), Junebug/Blue, Tequila Sunrise, Purple Silver/Bone White,

GENE LAREW® SALTY SNAKE
SPECIFICATIONS
Length: 11"
MSRP: $3.49
Colors: Black Electric Blue (Lam), Plum, Black Neon, Red Shad (Lam), Camouflage (Lam), Green Pumpkin, Fire and Ice (Lam), Tequila Sunrise, Huckleberry (Lam), Tomato Red, Grape Big Red, Watermelon Pepper, Junebug, Watermelon Pepper Blue, Dark Plum, Sour Grape (Lam)

GENE LAREW® SKIRTED SALT CRAW
SPECIFICATIONS
Length: 4"
MSRP: $4.49
Colors: Butterscotch, Chartreuse Pepper, Pumpkin Candy, Pumpkin Pepper, Smoke Cracker, Pumpkin Pepper Green, Watermelon Cracker, Pumpkin Pepper Neon, Black Blue/Blue, Green Pumpkin, Black Silver/Chartreuse, Smoke Pepper, Electric Blue/Black Blue, Watermelon Pepper, Beige Pepper/Chartreuse Pepper

LURES

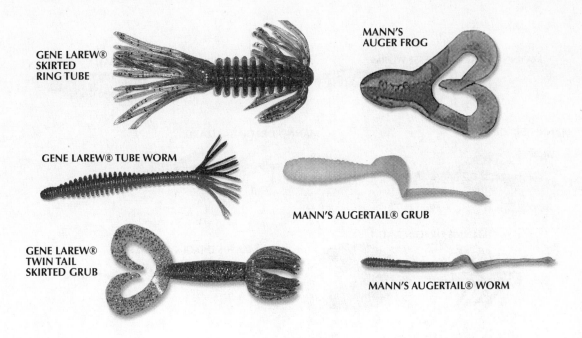

GENE LAREW® SKIRTED RING TUBE

MANN'S AUGER FROG

GENE LAREW® TUBE WORM

MANN'S AUGERTAIL® GRUB

GENE LAREW® TWIN TAIL SKIRTED GRUB

MANN'S AUGERTAIL® WORM

GENE LAREW® SKIRTED RING TUBE
SPECIFICATIONS
Length: 4"
MSRP: $4.49 - 10-bait ziplock bag
Colors: Black Shad (Lam), Green Pumpkin, Black Blue, Smoke Red, Black Neon, Dark Watermelon, Green Cotton Candy, Watermelon Pepper, Junebug, Watermelon Neon, Dark Plum, Smoke Blue, Red Shad (Lam)

GENE LAREW® TUBE WORM
SPECIFICATIONS
Length: 4", 6"
MSRP: 4", 10-count ziplock bag, $3.75; 6", 8 count bag, $3.75
Colors (4"): Black Blue, Pumpkin Seed, Black Neon, Green Pumpkin, Red Bug, Smoke Red, Camo, Tequila Sunrise, Electric Blue, Watermelon Seed, Junebug, Green Pumpkin Green, Plum, Ultimate Green, Red Shad, Green Christmas Tree, Red Silver, Baby Bass
Colors: (6"): Black Blue, Green Pumpkin, Black Neon, Smoke Red, Red Bug, Tequila Sunrise, Camo, Tomato Red, Electric Blue, Watermelon Seed, Junebug, Green Pumpkin Green, Plum, Ultimate Green, Red Shad, Green Christmas Tree, Red Silver, Baby Bass

GENE LAREW® TWIN TAIL SKIRTED GRUB
SPECIFICATIONS
Length: 2.5", 4"
MSRP: $4.49
Colors (2.5"): Bluegill, Salt and Pepper, Cherry Chartreuse, Pumpkinseed, Clear Pepper, Green Pumpkin, Green Cotton Candy, Smoke Red, Mauve Pepper, Smoke Silver, Pumpkin Pepper Green, Watermelon Pepper, Pumpkin Pepper Neon, Smoke Pepper Purple
Colors (4"): Bluegill, Pumpkin Pepper Neon, Cherry Chartreuse, Salt and Pepper, Clear Pepper, Pumpkinseed, Mauve Pepper, Green Pumpkin, Pumpkin Pepper, Smoke Red, Pumpkin Pepper Green, Watermelon Pepper

MANN'S AUGER FROG
Twisting, kicking legs and a natural shape make predator fish target these active frogs.
SPECIFICATIONS
Size: 1½", 2", 3"
Pack size: 20 or 100 lures per pack
MSRP: 1½" 20-pack, $2.75; 1½" 100-pack, $11.00; 2" 20-pack, $3.08; 2" 100-pack, $13.00; 3" 20-pack, $4.45; 3"100-pack, $17.80
Colors: Black, Brown/Orange, Chartreuse, Chartreuse/Black, Frog, Pearl

MANN'S AUGERTAIL® GRUB
It's a subtle, finesse grub with more action than most.
SPECIFICATIONS
Size: 2", 4"
Pack size: 20 or 100 lures per pack
MSRP: 2" 20-pack, $2.11; 2" 100-pack, $8.45; 4" 20-pack, $2.75; 4"100-pack, $13.50
Colors: Amber, Avocado, Green, White, White Fluorescent, Yellow

MANN'S AUGERTAIL® WORM
It was one of *Sports Afield* magazine's "Top 100 Bass lures" in 1989 and was still catching state record largemouth in 1999. Its special "auger" feature makes the tail kick and flicker.
SPECIFICATIONS
Size: 4", 6", 8", 12"
Pack size: 10 or 100
MSRP: 4": $1.60 (10-pack), $13.50 (100-pack); 6": $1.79 (10-pack), $14.30 (100-pack); 8": $1.90 (10-pack), $15.25 (100-pack); 12": $2.85 (10-pack), $22.80 (100-pack)
Colors: Blackberry, June Bug, Red Shad, Watermelonseed, Tequila Sunrise, Motor Oil/Red MF, Pumpkinseed/Chartreuse Tail, Arkansas Shiner, Sour Grape, Kudzu, Smoke/Green MF Violet

LURES

SOFT PLASTIC

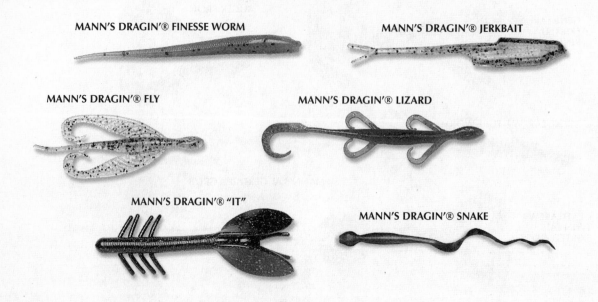

MANN'S DRAGIN'® FINESSE WORM

MANN'S DRAGIN'® JERKBAIT

MANN'S DRAGIN'® FLY

MANN'S DRAGIN'® LIZARD

MANN'S DRAGIN'® "IT"

MANN'S DRAGIN'® SNAKE

MANN'S DRAGIN'® FINESSE WORM

"Awesome" and "it looks so real" are the main comments Mann's has received on the Dragin Finesse Worm. It took some time, but it was worth the wait for these "awesome" color patterns and sizes, for the finest in finesse fishing.

SPECIFICATIONS
Size: 4", 6"
Pack size: 15
MSRP: $3.08
Colors: Chartreuse Pumpkin, Blue Ice, Sand, Arkansas Shiner, Smoke/Green Flake/Violet, Red Pepper, Blue Pearl, Watermelon/Violet, Kudzu, June Bug

MANN'S DRAGIN'® FLY

Dragonfly wings flutter with the slightest input. It is the hottest Carolina-rigged lure in the trend-setting western bass tournaments. Or Texas-rig it, hook it on a weedless jig, or work it like a buzzbait on top.

SPECIFICATIONS
Size: 3", 5", 7½"
Pack size: 15 (3"), 10 (5"), 8 (7-1/2")
MSRP: $3.08
Colors: Pumpkinseed/Chartreuse, Whiskey Ice, Red Shad, Electric Grape, Watermelonseed, Albino Shad,

Chartreuse Candy, Tequila Green, Green Pumpkin, June Bug

MANN'S DRAGIN'® "IT"

"It" has a unique shape that works several "creature" situations. Pitching, flipping, or dragging it through the water "Carolina-style", this bait has plenty of action.

SPECIFICATIONS
Size: 6"
Pack size: 8
MSRP: $3.08
Colors: Green Pumpkin, Pumpkinseed, Root Beer Pepper/Green Flake, Watermelonseed/Red Flake, Red Shad, Tequila/Green Flake, June Bug, Chartreuse/Green/Gold/Flake, Black/Blue Flake

MANN'S DRAGIN'® JERKBAIT

A hollow tube design incorporating a unique "hump back" weed guard that guarantees better hook penetration and weedless performance.

SPECIFICATIONS
Size: 4", 6"
Pack size: 15 (4"), 10 (6")
MSRP: $3.08
Colors: Watermelonseed, Albino Shad, Lemon Shad, Baby Bass, Pearl White, Smokin Shad,

Gold Fish, Bubble Gum, Blue Ice

MANN'S DRAGIN'® LIZARD

Ultra thin legs and long curly tail makes this lizard perform well with either a slow or fast retrieve. Mann's has carefully selected colors that are sure to attract the attention of even the most reluctant fish.

SPECIFICATIONS
Size: 6", 8"
Pack size: 8 (8"), 10 (6")
MSRP: $3.08
Colors: Tequila/Green Flake, Watermelon/Chartreuse, Green Pumpkin, Cotton Candy, Red Bug, Smoke/Blue/Chartreuse Flake, Sour Grape, Chartreuse/Blue/Black/Green Flake, Kudzu, Pumpkinseed, June Bug

MANN'S DRAGIN'® SNAKE

The Dragin'® Snake has lifelike action and detail. The flat, augured tail produces the wiggling action of a real snake.

SPECIFICATIONS
Size: 9"
Pack size: 10
MSRP: $3.08
Colors: Green Pumpkin, Copperhead, Black Snake, Green Snake, Moccasin, Indigo, Red Shad

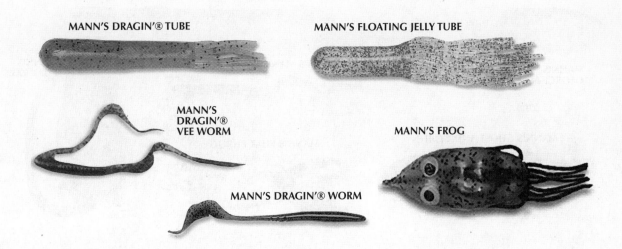

MANN'S DRAGIN'® TUBE

MANN'S FLOATING JELLY TUBE

MANN'S DRAGIN'® VEE WORM

MANN'S FROG

MANN'S DRAGIN'® WORM

MANN'S DRAGIN'® SUPER FINESSE WORM

The Super Finesse Worm features a unique action on the fall and retrieve. Its great fished dropshot, Carolina-rig or weightless as a Wacky Worm-style rig. Special plastic blend and extra salt added.

SPECIFICATIONS
Size: 4", 5"
Pack size: 8
MSRP: $3.08
Colors: Green Pumpkin, Watermelonseed, Rootbeer Flake, Bluegill, Salt and Pepper, Black, Pearl, Chartreuse/Black Flake, Red Shad, June Bug

MANN'S DRAGIN'® TUBE

Unique injected-molded tentacles provide life-like action for flipping, pitching, or when used with a Carolina-rigged system. Thicker walls and greater color selection provide more fishing choices. We have also made the head thicker, just like the Pros suggested. The realistic features and greater color selection provide more fishing choices.

SPECIFICATIONS
Size: 4½"
Pack size: 8
MSRP: $3.08
Colors: Green Pumpkin, Watermelonseed, Cherry Seed, Pearl/Silver Flake, Smoke Pepper/Red Flake, Chartreuse/Green/Blue Flake, Dark Smoke/Blue Flake, Sour Grape, Chartreuse Pumpkin

MANN'S DRAGIN' VEE WORM

Made from Mann's super-soft plastic formula, the Dragin'® Vee Worm has factory-locked legs to preserve the action of the bait. Two unique appendages work against each other as the bait swims through the water to simulate one bait fish chasing the other.

SPECIFICATIONS
Size: 6"
Pack size: 12
MSRP: $3.08
Colors: Green Pumpkin, Watermelonseed/Red Metal Flake, Electric Grape, June Bug, Gold Shiner, Red Shad

MANN'S DRAGIN'® WORM

The Dragin Worm is the perfect plastic curltail worm. Unique color patterns and the great action of this bait makes it a must for every soft plastic tackle box.

SPECIFICATIONS
Size: 5½", 7½"
Pack size: 12 (5½"), 10 (7½")
MSRP: $3.08
Colors: Green Pumpkin, Watermelonseed/Red Flake, Tequila/Green, Sour Grape, Pumpkinseed, Watermelon/Purple Pearl, Chartreuse/Green/Blue Flake, Smoke/Blue/Chartreuse/Black Flake, Red Shad, June Bug

MANN'S FLOATING JELLY TUBE

Using a special plastic containing garlic and a flotation insert that is resistant to attack, Mann's has created the next generation of the tube lure. The molded-in tentacles provide more realistic action and feel, while the thicker body offers more fishing options. Great for flipping or pitching without the insert, the Floating Jelly Tube is a deadly weapon when fished Carolina-rigged-style for suspended fish.

SPECIFICATIONS
Size: 4" (8 tubes/8 floats), 6" (4 tubes/4floats)
Pack size: : 4", 8 tubes/8 floats; 6", 4 tubes/4floats
MSRP: $3.07 (4"), $3.17 (6")
Colors: Pumpkinseed, Watermelonseed, Green Gourd, Smoke Red Pepper, Pearl MF, Chartreuse Green Flake, Pearl/Gold Green Flake, Black Red Flake/Blue Pepper, Pearl MF/Smoke Blue Flake, Gold Fish

MANN'S FROG

The wider profile of a frog with the weedless performance of the Rat. In areas where gamefish feed on frogs, this is a natural choice.

SPECIFICATIONS
Length: 2½"
MSRP: $2.85
Colors: Black, Chartreuse, Chewin' Gum, Frog, Grey, Pumpkinseed, White, Brown

SOFT PLASTIC

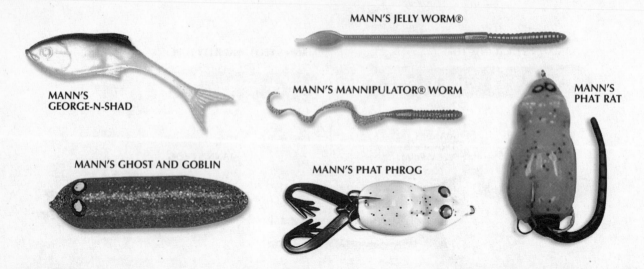

MANN'S JELLY WORM®

MANN'S MANNIPULATOR® WORM

MANN'S PHAT RAT

MANN'S GEORGE-N-SHAD

MANN'S GHOST AND GOBLIN

MANN'S PHAT PHROG

MANN'S GEORGE-N-SHAD

You may not know much about this bait. Fishermen who use it won't tell, but we can tell you – it's one of the best lead/plastic baits around. Colors are easy to change by simply popping the plastic body off the lead.

SPECIFICATIONS
Size/Weight: 3", ¼ oz; 4", ½ oz.; 5", 1 oz.
MSRP: $1.54
Colors: Pearl, Pearl/Black, Pearl/Blue Back, Chartreuse/Blue Back

MANN'S GHOST AND GOBLIN

Weedless, hollow body, floating baits with an easy "walk-the-dog" action. Work them over heavy vegetation, skip them under docks, or tempt open-water fish. They cast like missiles. Twin hooks are exposed when fish strike.

SPECIFICATIONS
Length: Ghost, 3¾", Goblin 2½"
MSRP: $2.85
Colors: Black, Blue Metal Flake, Frog, Red Metal Flake, Silver Metal Flake, White, Nite Glow, White Shad, Golden Shad

MANN'S JELLY WORM®

The #1 selling plastic worm of all time! Introduced in 1967, its soft, life-like texture has never been surpassed. Slow-waving tail coaxes bass to strike, and the straight design comes through grass and brush without hanging up. In original fruit flavors and colors.

SPECIFICATIONS
Size: 4", 6", 8", 9"
Pack size: 20 or 100
(10-packs only for 12")
MSRP: 4": $2.11 (20-pack), $9.85 (100-pack); 6": $2.11 (20-pack), $10.00 (100-pack); 8": $2.96 (20-pack), $13.50 (100-pack); 9": $3.91 (20-pack), $16.00 (100-pack); 12": $4.21 (10-pack)
Colors: Blackberry, Blueberry, Grape, Marmalade (Motor Oil), Watermelonseed/Red MF, Cherry Seed, Scuppernong, Tequila/Green, Watermelonseed/Chartreuse, Black Grape, Grape Firetail, Strawberry (12" worms not available in fire tails.)

MANN'S MANNIPULATOR® WORM

When locked in place, the curly tail makes two revolutions. When released, it has three action points for triple the motion and vibration. Hammered tail pattern flashes as it reflects light.

SPECIFICATIONS
Size: 5", 7", 9"
Pack size: 15 or 100
MSRP: 5": $2.11 (15-pack), $8.69 (100-pack); 7": $2.64 (15-pack), $10.82 (100-pack); 9": $3.39 (15-pack), $14.20 (100-pack)
Colors: Blackberry, Electric Grape, June Bug, Red Shad, Tequila Green, Green Gourd/Black MF, Mossy Pumpkin, Pearl/Blue/Green, Arkansas Shiner, Watermelonseed Red Metal Flake

MANN'S PHAT PHROG

The Phat Phrog uses the same features of its cousin the Phat Rat to increase hook-ups, be more weedless, and reduce water entry into the lure. The Phat Phrog also has 2 realistic swimming legs to imitate a real frog. The Phat Phrog incorporates these great fish-catching features: A treble hook to increase hook-ups by 87 percent, totally weedless design, Superseal legs to dramatically reduce water entry and provide lifelike action, lead-free bismuth belly weight always rolls body right-side up, fish-catching rattle, and excellent castablility to reach far into vegetation.

SPECIFICATIONS
Length: 2½"
Weight: ¼ oz.
MSRP: $3.42
Colors: White Frog, Chartreuse Frog, Black, Brown, Grey

MANN'S PHAT RAT

The Phat Rat solves the number one problem encountered when fishing hollow body soft baits – poor hook-up-to-strike ratios. The combination of treble hooks incorporated into a body specifically designed to keep the hook barbs from contact with grass and hydrilla results in a dramatic improve-ment in catch ratios. The Phat Rat is guaranteed to be the best hollow body soft bait you will ever fish.

SPECIFICATIONS
Size: ¼ oz. (Baby Phat Rat), ⅜ oz. (Phat Rat)

LURES

MANN'S POPPER

MANN'S SPITTIN' SHAD

MANN'S RAT

MANN'S SKIRTED FROG

MANN'S SWIMMIN' RAT

MANN'S STING RAY GRUB®

MSRP: $3.42
Colors: White, Chartreuse/Black Black Back, White/Green Black Metal Flake, Dark Green/ Black Metal Flake, Silver/Blue Back, Chartreuse, Grey, Black,

MANN'S POPPER

The splashing commotion of a popping face plus the weedlessness of a soft hollow body with upright hooks. It crawls and hops over obstacles easily.
SPECIFICATIONS
Length: 1¾"
MSRP: $2.85
Colors: Black, Chartreuse, Chewin' Gum, Frog, Grey, Pumpkinseed, White, Brown,

MANN'S RAT

The original and most famous hollow body weedless "Rat" lure. The imitations just don't hold up as well, or hook as well as the Mann's Rat. It excels on heavy mats of vegetation where other baits can't go.
SPECIFICATIONS
Length: 2½"
MSRP: $2.85
Colors: Black, Chartreuse, Chewin'

Gum, Frog, Grey, Pumpkinseed, White, Brown,

MANN'S SINGLE HOOK SWIMMIN' RAT AND SKIRTED FROG

Same dependable action as the double hook version, but the single hook may help avoid lost strikes. Weedless baits that can be worked over even the heaviest vegetation.
SPECIFICATIONS
Length: 2½"
MSRP: $3.09
Colors: Green Frog, Disco, Clear Silver MF/Blue Back, White Frog,

MANN'S SKIRTED FROG

Silicone spinnerbait-style skirt quivers and flares as you retrieve this weedless frog.
SPECIFICATIONS
Length: 2½"
MSRP: $2.85
Colors: Black, Chartreuse, Chewin' Gum, Frog, Grey, Pumpkinseed, White, Brown,

MANN'S SPITTIN' SHAD

Concave disk chugs water as the bait glides over vegetation. Soft, hollow

body collapses when fish bite to expose the twin hook points.
SPECIFICATIONS
Length: 2½"
MSRP: $2.85
Colors: Frog, Chartreuse/Metal Flake, Golden Shiner, White Shad, Silver/Blue Flake

MANN'S STING RAY GRUB®

The original flat tail artificial grub. Although the 2" size makes a great trailer bait, the Sting Ray Grub is excellent for both fresh water and saltwater species when used with leadhead jigs. Excellent for bass. Good for surface feeding fish and just as effective when bounced off bottom.
SPECIFICATIONS
Size: 3", 4"
Pack size: 20, 100 or 1000 lures per pack
MSRP: 3" 8-pack, $1.69; 3" 20-pack, $2.43; 3" 100-pack, $10; 4" 6-pack, $1.90; 4" 20-pack, $3.49; 4"100-pack, $14
Colors: avocado, green, green/metal flake, smoke, white firetail, yellow firetail, chartreuse, green firetail, shrimp, white, yellow

LURES

SOFT PLASTIC

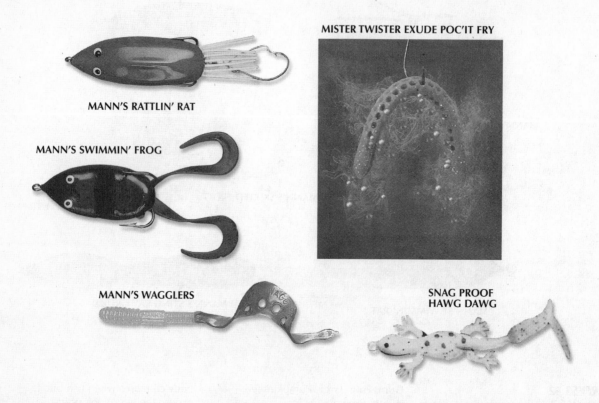

MANN'S RATTLIN' RAT

MANN'S SWIMMIN' FROG

MISTER TWISTER EXUDE POC'IT FRY

MANN'S WAGGLERS

SNAG PROOF HAWG DAWG

MANN'S SUPER RATTLIN' RAT

We made the original Rat bigger, inserted rattles, and added a "free swivieling" weedless trailer hook for extra attraction and hooking power.

SPECIFICATIONS
Length: 3"
MSRP: $2.85
Colors: Black, Chartreuse, Chewin' Gum, Frog, Grey, Pumpkinseed, White, Brown,

MANN'S SWIMMIN' FROG

The slightest rod twitch brings this bait to life, making it look like the real thing.

SPECIFICATIONS
Length: 2½"
MSRP: $2.85
Colors: Black, Chartreuse, Chewin' Gum, Frog, Grey, Pumpkinseed, White, Brown,

MANN'S WAGGLERS

Prized by bass anglers as a flipping worm. Big tail has plenty of motion-holes and turbulence.

SPECIFICATIONS
Size: 6"
Pack size: 10 or 100
MSRP: $3.70 (10-pack), $25.35 (100-pack)
Colors: White Grape, Chartreuse Pearl, Night Glow, Chartreuse/MF, Green Firetail, Yellow Firetail, White Firetail

MISTER TWISTER EXUDE POC'IT FRY

The Exude™ Poc'it Fry features a "double whammy" – Poc'it bubbles and the exclusive Exude formulation. Exude™ is the most powerful scent-releasing system ever developed for soft plastic lures. Every Exude™ lure explodes when it hits the water, oozing a slime coating of scents, minerals, proteins and amino acids. So, the Poc'it Fry, like all Exude™ brand lures, has both a supreme feel and texture. Big fish grab on and won't let go.

Fishermen will also appreciate the Poc'it Fry's versatility. It can be rigged and fished just about any way you wish, making it the ideal lure for fishing strange water or difficult weather patterns.

SPECIFICATIONS
Size: 5"
MSRP: $4.19 (8-pack)

SNAG PROOF HAWG DAWG

Leapin' lizards. Bass can't resist it. Looks, feels and swims like a mud-puppy or salamander. Pre-rigged for bottom fishing, it's great for getting into and around spawning beds, rocks, weeds and stumps.

SPECIFICATIONS
Model: 300
MSRP: $3.00 ea., 3 for $7.75
Colors: Black, Purple, Chartreuse, White, Hot Pink, Pumpkinseed

Model: 400
(Floating Hawg Dawg Lite)
MSRP: $3.00 ea., 3 for $7.75
Colors: Black, Purple, Chartreuse, White, Hot Pink, Pumpkinseed

SNAG PROOF LEECH 900

SNAG PROOF SOFT CRAW

SNAG PROOF SUPER CURLY 1000

SNAG PROOF WORM 7000

SNAG PROOF MINI-MINNOW 3000

STRIKE KING® BITSY TUBE™ BT2.75

SNAG PROOF MOSS MASTER SWIMMIN' SHAD

SNAG PROOF LEECH

Big bass love a leech. Weighted tail and hinged reflex body makes it come alive. Retrieval in slow twitches gives it action just like a swimming leech. Steady retrieve gives it a writhing action. Deadly.

SPECIFICATIONS
Model: 900
Weight: ¼ oz.
MSRP: $3.00 ea., 3 for $7.75
Colors: Black, Brown, Purple

SNAG PROOF MINI-MINNOW

Savage strikes are guaranteed with the life-like frantic action of the Mini-Minnow. Hollow, air-filled body makes it dart, dive, swim and float to the surface like a wounded minnow. Flashy, silver glitter body attracts trout, bass and walleye. Runs medium depth.

SPECIFICATIONS
Model: 3000
Length: 3¼"
MSRP: $3.00 ea., 3 for $7.75
Colors: Clear, glittery body with Black, orange, Purple, or Blue top stripe.

SNAG PROOF MOSS MASTER SWIMMIN' SHAD

The first weedless, swimming crankbait. Realistic swimming action combined with the flash of holographic glitter, a writhing tail, and the vibration of the large rattling eyes draw fish in like a magnet.

SPECIFICATIONS

Model: 3700
Weight: ½ oz.
MSRP: $5.00 ea., 3 for $13.50

Model: 3600
Weight: ¼ oz.
MSRP: $5.00 ea., 3 for $13.50
Colors: Silver w/black stripe, Chartreuse w/Green Stripe, Red w/Black Stripe, Gold w/Green Stripe, Silver w/blue Stripe, Gold w/Black Stripe

SNAG PROOF SOFT CRAW

The most natural feel, looks, action available in any artificial craw. Hinged "reflex" tail makes it move like a live craw. Bass pick it up without hesitation.

SPECIFICATIONS
Model: 5000
Weight: ¼ oz.
MSRP: $3.00/ea., 3 for $7.75
Model: 5200
Weight: ⅛ oz.
MSRP: $3.00/ea., 3 for $7.75
Colors: Black, Brown, Moss Green, Pumpkinseed

SNAG PROOF SUPER CURLY

Triggers the strike reflex. The slightest retrieve makes the entire lure come alive. Writhing, squirming, swimming like a struggling minnow, leech or eel. Good in open water, or for even more strikes.

SPECIFICATIONS
Model: 1000
Weight: ¼ oz.
MSRP: $3.00 ea., 3 for $7.75

Colors: Black, Purple, Yellow

SNAG PROOF WORM

Deadly. Air-filled tail and weighted head make it wriggle like a swimming eel. No other worm has its writhing action. The soft, hollow body protects double hook against all snags.

SPECIFICATIONS
Model: 7000
Weight: ¼ oz.
MSRP: $3.00 ea., 3 for $7.75

SNAG PROOF

Frogzilla, Harry's Round Frog, Hellgramite, Moss Master Tournament Frog, Moss Master Tournament Popper, Pro Series Tournament Frog, SK Series SK Frog Ultra, SK Series Weed Demon (see pages 283-284)

STRIKE KING® BITSY TUBE™

Our new salt-impregnated Bitsy Tube™, is great when the bite requires finesse.

SPECIFICATIONS:
Model: BT2.75
Size: 2¾ in.
MSRP: $1.69
Colors: Black Blue Flake/Blue Tail, Pumpkin Green Flake, Watermelon/Chartreuse Tail, Smoke with Red and Black Flake, Black Neon, Junebug, Pearl Pepper, Green Pumpkin, Pumpkin/Chartreuse Tail, Chartreuse Pepper, Pumpkin Red/Green Flake, Mustard, Watermelon Blue Flake, Watermelon Gold Flake.

SOFT PLASTIC

STRIKE KING® DENNY BRAUER'S PRO-MODEL FLIP-N-TUBE™ FLPT4.5

STRIKE KING® POP'N GRASS FROGS GRASS FROGS P300

STRIKE KING® KEVIN VANDAM KVD PRO-MODEL TUBE™ PMT3.5

YUM® AIR FRY™ YAFY4

STRIKE KING® DENNY BRAUER'S PRO-MODEL FLIP-N-TUBE™

The Denny Brauer model designed especially for flippin' and pitching. Although the body is hollow to trap air and to feel life-like to fish, these tubes feature a solid head, which makes the bait easier to rig and not tear up as easily as other tubes. This will enable the angler to catch more fish during the life of the lure. These tubes are heavily impregnated with salt. It is perfect for a Mustad, Megabite or similar hook. The design works well Texas rigged with a slip or screw type sinker.

SPECIFICATIONS:
Model: FLPT4.5
Size: 4½ in.
MSRP: $1.99
Colors: Black Blue Flake/Blue Tail, Pumpkin Green Flake Chameleon Craw, Chameleon Craw/ Orange Tail, Watermelon/Chartreuse Tail, Electric Blue, Smoke with Red and Black Flake, Smoke with Blue and Black Flake, Bluegill, Sand, Black Neon, Black Neon/Chartreuse Tail, Junebug, Pearl Pepper, Green Pumpkin, Pumpkin/Chartreuse Tail, Chartreuse Pepper, Black Neon Firetail, Pumpkin Red/Green Flake, Mustard, Watermelon Blue Flake, Watermelon Gold Flake.

STRIKE KING® KEVIN VANDAM KVD PRO-MODEL TUBE™

Strike King's salt-impregnated Kevin VanDam KVD Pro-Model, Tube™ is great when the bite requires a little more finesse. It's an inch shorter than Denny's Pro-Model, Flip-N-Tube™ and does not have the solid head. It is a great all around size. Lead-head jig hooks can be slipped up inside the tube and then the line tie can be poked through. This is a great natural presentation and is perfect for light line and spinning rod applications. This KVD tube works great Texas rigged for flippin' and pitchin' too.

SPECIFICATIONS:
Model: PMT3.5
Size: ³⁄₁₆ in.
MSRP: $1.99
Colors: Black Blue Flake/Blue Tail, Pumpkin Green Flake Chameleon Craw, Chameleon Craw/Orange Tail, Watermelon/Chartreuse Tail, Electric Blue, Smoke with Red and Black Flake, Smoke with Blue and Black Flake, Bluegill, Sand, Black Neon, Black Neon/Chartreuse Tail, Junebug, Pearl Pepper, Green Pumpkin, Pumpkin/Chartreuse Tail, Chartreuse Pepper, Black Neon Firetail, Pumpkin Red/Green Flake, Mustard, Watermelon Blue Flake, Watermelon Gold Flake.

STRIKE KING® POP'N GRASS FROGS GRASS FROGS

If you're looking for topwater action, these Strike Hyde™ foam frogs with their leg kicking action are what you need. The Grass Frog can be fished in almost anything and the Pop'n Frog's unique sound will get the attention of even the most stubborn Bass.

Features include:
- Sensational top-water vegetation or open water bait
- Feels life-like to fish
- Unique leg action serves as weed-guard for trailer hook
- Durable Strike Hyde‰ foam
- Eagle Claw, lazer sharp hook and trailer hook
- Pop'n model produces loud fish attracting popping sounds when pulled through water

SPECIFICATIONS:
Model: P300 (Pop'n Grass Frog)
Weight: ¼ oz.
MSRP: $2.99

Model: 300 (Grass Frog)
Weight: ³⁄₁₆ oz.
MSRP: $2.99
Colors: Chartreuse Coachdog, Green Frog/Black Coachdog, Yellow/Black Coachdog, Black Coachdog, White/Black Coachdog

YUM® AIR FRY™

This is a bait for a Carolina rig. For those times when fish suspend and a high-floating bait is required, the Air Fry will stay off the bottom and in the strike zone.

SPECIFICATIONS
Model: YAFY4
Length: 4"
Bag Count: 10
MSRP: $2.99
Colors: Green Pumpkin, Watermelon Seed, Pumpkin Pepper Green Flake, Chartreuse Pepper

YUM® CHUNK

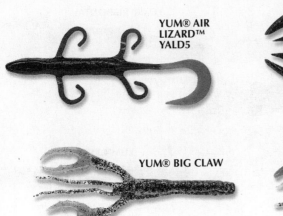

YUM® AIR LIZARD™ YALD5

YUM® CRAW BUG

YUM® BIG CLAW

YUM® AIR LIZARD™

The Air Lizard's patented design traps air, making it the highest-floating lizard you can buy. It's great on a Carolina rig over grass, or when fish are suspended. If you have a strong heart, rig it weightless and fish the grass mats.

SPECIFICATIONS
Model: YALD5
Length: 5"
Bag Count: 10
MSRP: $2.99
Colors: Green Pumpkin, Watermelon Seed, Black Blue, Carolina Pumpkin Chartreuse

YUM® BIG CLAW™

The Big Claw is durable, yet velvety soft to the touch. It has one of the most realistic shapes of any slim profile crawfish imitation. With its natural oversized pincers, it makes a great jig trailer and can be equally effective on a Carolina or Texas rig.

SPECIFICATIONS
Model: YBC3
Length: 3"
Bag Count: 10
MSRP: $2.49

Model: YBC4
Length: 4"
Bag Count: 10
MSRP: $2.49

Model: YBC5
Length: 5"
Bag Count: 8
MSRP: $2.49
Colors: Junebug, Carolina Pumpkin, Green Pumpkin, Watermelon Seed, Pumpkin Pepper Green Flake, Black Blue, Black Neon Chartreuse, Texas Smoke, Plum, Pumpkin Green Flake Orange

YUM® CHUNK™

Loaded with salt, this chunk adds bulk to your favorite jig, slowing its fall rate. The Chunk also features oversized swimming legs and a small head that won't interfere with the hook.

SPECIFICATIONS
Model: YC2
Length: 2.75"
Bag Count: 8
MSRP: $2.49

Model: YC3
Length: 3.5"
Bag Count: 8
MSRP: $2.49
Colors: Black Neon, Green Pumpkin, Watermelon Seed, Pumpkin Pepper Green Flake, Black Blue Flake, White Silver Flake, Ozark Smoke, Sky Blue Flake

YUM® CRAW BUG™

A crawfish is to a bass what a steak is to a cowboy – the ultimate meal. The YUM CrawBug is nature re-created. This bait is designed with three-dimensional features never before seen in a soft plastic lure. Amazingly realistic detail, a specially designed hollow body and super-soft texture combine to imitate a fleeing crawfish perfectly. Add in our exclusive YUM Crawfish Formula Attractant plus salt and you have the most lifelike crawfish imitation ever designed. Flip it, rig it or jig it. This bait does its job.

SPECIFICATIONS
Model: YCB2
Size: 2.5"
Bag Count: 10
MSRP: $3.49

Model: YCB3
Size: 3.25"
Bag Count: 8
MSRP: $3.49

Model: YCB4
Size: 4"
Bag Count: 8
MSRP: $3.49
Colors: Black Neon, Watermelon Red Flake, Tequila Sunrise, Junebug, Red Shad Green Flake, Crawdad, Carolina Pumpkin, Green Pumpkin, Watermelon Seed, Green Pumpkin Texas Red, Pumpkin Pepper Green Flake, Black Blue

LURES

SOFT PLASTIC

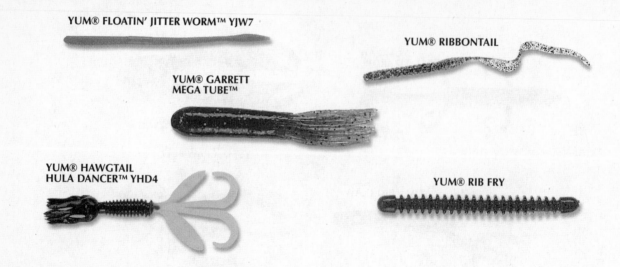

YUM® FLOATIN' JITTER WORM™ YJW7

YUM® GARRETT MEGA TUBE™

YUM® HAWGTAIL HULA DANCER™ YHD4

YUM® RIBBONTAIL

YUM® RIB FRY

YUM® FLOATIN' JITTER WORM™

The Floating Jitter Worm can be worked over, around and in any type of cover. It gives you the perfect option when hard baits simply aren't practical.

SPECIFICATIONS
Model: YJW7
Length: 7"
Bag Count: 15
MSRP: $2.49

Colors: Green Pumpkin, Watermelon Seed, Firetiger, Bullfrog, Bubble Gum, Sherbet, Lemon, Limetreuse

YUM® GARRETT MEGA TUBE™

There can be only one original and this is it. Doug Garrett designed it and put it on the map by winning back-to-back Bassmaster Megabucks. This is the bait that started the oversized tube craze, now the most popular category of soft plastics. We've added YUM with LPT and heavy-grain salt to make this the elite oversized tube in all of fishing.

SPECIFICATIONS
Model: YMT3
Size: 3"
Bag Count: 10
MSRP: $2.99

Model: YMT4
Size: 4"
Bag Count: 10, 50
MSRP: $2.99
Colors: Black Neon, Junebug,

Carolina Pumpkin, Watermelon Seed, Pumpkin Pepper Green Flake, Black Blue, Green Pumpkin, Smoke Red Pepper, Black Blue Flake, White Silver Flake, Ozark Smoke, Green Pumpkin Chartreuse, Crawfish Green Flake, Watermelon Neon, Green Pumpkin Firecracker, Watermelon Copper Flake, Bluegill, Smoke Silver Flake

YUM® HAWGTAIL HULA DANCER™

The Hawgtail Hula Dancer possesses all of the great fish catching features of the Woolly Hawgtail with the addition of a skirt to slow its rate of fall. This is a bait for those times when the fish aren't quite as aggressive.

SPECIFICATIONS
Model: YHD4
Length: 4"
Bag Count: 8
MSRP: $2.49

Colors: Carolina Pumpkin, Junebug, Green Pumpkin, Watermelon Seed, Pumpkin Pepper, Green Flake, Dark Watermelon, Black Blue, Black Neon Chartreuse

YUM® RIBBONTAIL™

This is the classic by which all other worms are measured. A fantastic bait for fishing brush piles, ledges or points, the action in the easy-to-rig Ribbontail is built-in. Just sit back, relax, and let the worm do the work.

SPECIFICATIONS
Model: YRT6
Size: 6"

Bag Count: 15
MSRP: $2.49

Model: YRT7
Size: 7.5"
Bag Count: 15
MSRP: $2.49

Model: YRT10
Size: 10"
Bag Count: 10
MSRP: $2.49
Colors: Black Neon, Tequila Sunrise, Junebug, Red Shad Green Flake, Watermelon Seed, Pumpkin Pepper Green Flake, Red Shad, Tequila Green, Grape Red Flake, Green Pumpkin Purple Flake

YUM® RIB FRY™

The Rib Fry can be Carolina-rigged, Texas-rigged or rigged wacky-style. The secret is its subtleness. Its ribs capture air bubbles and release them under the water. A solid head ensures the hook stays in place.

SPECIFICATIONS
Model: YRF4
Length: 4.5"
Bag Count: 15
MSRP: $2.49
Colors: Carolina Pumpkin, Green Pumpkin, Watermelon Seed, Pumpkin Pepper Green Flake, Dark Grasshopper, Firetiger, Rainbow Trout, Red Shad Chartreuse, Chartreuse Pepper, Watermelon Candy, Texas Smoke, Sour Grape

LURES

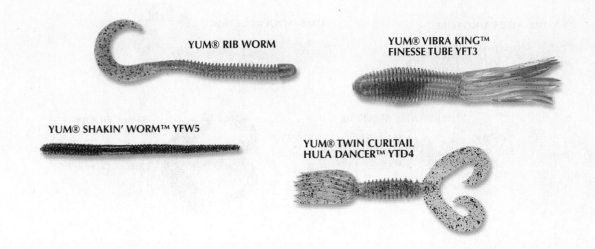

YUM® RIB WORM

YUM® VIBRA KING™ FINESSE TUBE YFT3

YUM® SHAKIN' WORM™ YFW5

YUM® TWIN CURLTAIL HULA DANCER™ YTD4

YUM® RIB WORM™

The Rib Worm's ringed segments capture air bubbles and release them, creating a very lifelike presentation. A thick head adds more hooking power, and the oversized curl tail creates vibration. This bait works great in any water clarity and fishes best on a Texas rig.

SPECIFICATIONS
Model: YRW4
Size: 4"
Bag Count: 15
MSRP: $2.49

Model: YRW6
Size: 6"
Bag Count: 15
MSRP: $2.49
Colors: Junebug, Red Shad Green Flake, Green Pumpkin, Pumpkin Pepper Green Flake, Black Neon Chartreuse, Texas Smoke, Sour Grape, Plum, Red Bug, Watermelon Seed

YUM® SHAKIN' WORM™

Don't tie on a drop shot without this finesse worm. There's no better bait for a deep-water vertical presentation. The uses for this worm are virtually limitless, whether it be Texas rigging, Carolina rigging, "shaking" on a lead head or wacky style.

SPECIFICATIONS
Model: YFW5
Length: 5"
Bag Count: 20
MSRP: $2.49
Colors: Watermelon Red Flake, Junebug, Green Pumpkin, Watermelon Seed, Pumpkin Pepper Green Flake, Firetiger, Rainbow Trout, Red Shad Chartreuse, Fall Crawfish, Chartreuse Pepper, Sour Grape, Green Pumpkin Purple Flake, Spring Crawfish, Grasshopper

YUM® TWIN CURLTAIL HULA DANCER™

Ideal for rigging on a jig head, the Hula Dancer is the only spider grub featuring a ribbed body. This bait is best fished on a slow fall for deep, clear-water smallmouths and spotted bass.

SPECIFICATIONS
Model: YTD4
Length: 4"
Bag Count: 8
MSRP: $2.49
Colors: Junebug, Green Pumpkin, Watermelon Seed, Pumpkin Pepper Green Flake, Black Blue, Black Neon Chartreuse

YUM® VIBRA KING™ FINESSE TUBE

The new Vibra King Finesse Tube possesses all of the great fish-catching qualities of the original Vibra King Tube, but presents a more slender profile in the water. This bait features fine ribs that create an awesome vibration with an incredibly realistic feel. Fish it on a light wire, wide gap hook and it's the perfect offering for clear-water smallmouths and sight-fishing for largemouths. It comes in an array of vibrant colors to cover any water condition.

SPECIFICATIONS
Model: YFT3
Size: 3.5"
Bag Count: 10
MSRP: $2.49
Colors: Black Neon, Tequila Sunrise, Junebug, Red Shad Green Flake, Carolina Pumpkin, Watermelon Seed, Pumpkin Pepper Green Flake, Red Shad, Dark Grasshopper, Dark Watermelon, Dark Smoke Blue, Firetiger, Green Pumpkin, Smoke Red Pepper, Black Blue Flake, Arkansas Shiner, Rainbow Trout, Red Shad Chartreuse, Alewife, White Silver Flake

Don't Get Hung Up on a Few Favorite Colors
All bass anglers have their favorite colors and shades when it comes to soft-plastic lures, such as worms and lizards. But it's a mistake to assume that bass share your preferences. Carry a wide variety of colors, and keep throwing different ones until the bass tell you what they want that day.

LURES

SOFT PLASTIC

YUM® VIBRA KING TUBE

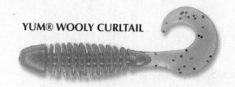

YUM® WOOLY CURLTAIL

YUM® WOOLY BEAVETAIL

YUM® WOOLY HAWGTAIL

YUM® VIBRA KING™ TUBE

The most unique oversized tube on the market, Vibra King Tubes are fully injected for excellent product consistency. The fine ribs create a unique feel and vibration and this bait also features a solid head for added durability and use with a Florida-rig weight. Fish it on heavy line and punch it through the grass or pitch it in the bushes. Either way this tube will produce.

SPECIFICATIONS
Model: YVK3
Size: 3.5"
Bag Count: 8
MSRP: $2.49

Model: YVK4
Size: 4.25"
Bag Count: 8
MSRP: $2.49
Colors: Black Neon, Junebug, Red Shad Green Flake, Green Pumpkin, Watermelon Seed, Pumpkin Pepper Green Flake, Dark Grasshopper, Dark Watermelon, Firetiger, Tequila Sunrise, Smoke Red Pepper, Black Blue Flake, Rainbow Trout, Alewife, White Silver Flake, Red Shad Chartreuse

YUM® WOOLY BEAVERTAIL™

Ideal for flipping, the Beavertail creates an unusual profile in the water. It features a unique large-rib design for great vibration and a very thick head for easy rigging.

SPECIFICATIONS
Model: YWC2
Size: 2"

Bag Count: 10
MSRP: $2.49

Model: YWC3
Size: 3"
Bag Count: 9
M*SRP:* $2.49

Model: YWC4
Size: 4"
Bag Count: 8
MSRP: $2.49
Colors: Black Neon, Tequila Sunrise, Junebug, Green Pumpkin, Watermelon Seed, Red Shad, Dark Grasshopper, Dark Watermelon, Firetiger, Black Blue, Red Shad Chartreuse, Carolina Pumpkin Chartreuse

YUM® WOOLY CURLTAIL™

For those days when the fish want something just a little different, this Wooly Bait® is designed to be flipped, pitched or Carolina rigged. The curltail features a unique large-rib design for greater vibration, and a solid head for easy rigging and durability. This is the bait to tie on when you need a kicker fish.

SPECIFICATIONS
Model: YWB2
Size: 2"
Bag Count: 10
MSRP: $2.49

Model: YWB3
Size: 3"
Bag Count: 8
MSRP: $2.49

Model: YWB4
Size: 4"
Bag Count: 8
MSRP: $2.49
Colors: Black Neon, Tequila Sunrise, Junebug, Green Pumpkin, Watermelon Seed, Pumpkin Pepper Green Flake, Red Shad, Dark Grasshopper, Dark Watermelon, Firetiger, Black Blue, Red Shad Chartreuse, Fall Crawfish, Carolina Pumpkin Chartreuse

YUM® WOOLY HAWGTAIL™

As the only creature bait you'll ever need, the Hawgtail fits its name. This is a big-time big-fish bait. It works equally well on a Carolina rig, or pitched and flipped on a Texas rig. The Hawgtail produces massive action and the Wooly body makes it truly unique.

SPECIFICATIONS
Model: YWH2
Size: 3"
Bag Count: 10
MSRP: $2.49

Model: YWH3
Size: 4.5"
Bag Count: 8
MSRP: $2.49
Colors: Black Neon, Tequila Sunrise, Junebug, Red Shad Green Flake, Green Pumpkin, Watermelon Seed, Pumpkin Pepper Green Flake, Red Shad, Dark Grasshopper, Dark Watermelon, Firetiger, Tequila Green, Black Blue, Rainbow Trout, Red Shad Chartreuse, Fall Crawfish, Carolina Pumpkin Chartreuse, Gobee

SPINNERBAITS, SPINNERS, BUZZBAITS

**ABU GARCIA®
REFLEX SPINNER**

**BERKLEY®
SCENT VENT
SPINNERS**

**ABU GARCIA®
ROULETTE SPINNER**

ABU GARCIA® REFLEX SPINNER

The Abu Garcia Reflex Spinner has a simple design that's easy to use and catches bass of all species. The streamlined Reflex casts long and accurately, even against the wind. It's an all-purpose lure that consistently catches fish in lakes, ponds, rivers and streams. The solid elongated body is matched with a balanced oval blade with a wavy or corrugated shape and a holographic finish. During the retrieve the blade may rotate clockwise and then shift to counterclockwise; either way the Reflex repels line twist. The ultra-sharp treble hook is hidden behind hand-tied feathers.

SPECIFICATIONS
Weights: ¼-, ⅜- and ⅝-oz.
MSRP: $3.08
Colors: Silver, Zebra, Blue Gold, Green on Green

ABU GARCIA® ROULETTE SPINNER

The streamlined Roulette's unusual design has the ability to bend in the middle. The body has the appearance of two worm weights strung back to back on the spinner's jointed wire shaft. The joint is equipped with a metal cylinder that clicks against the body during the retrieve, as the bait flexes. The free-spinning French blade attracts fish from a distance with its flash and movement. During the retrieve, the blade repels line twist by rotating both ways; clockwise one time, counterclockwise another. The ultra-sharp treble hook is accented with hand-tied select rooster neck. The all-purpose Roulette is easy to use and consistently catches bass and other fish.

SPECIFICATIONS
Weights: 3/16-, 5/16- and ⅜-oz.
MSRP: $3.08
Colors: Blue, Red, Black on White

BERKLEY® SCENT VENT SPINNERS

Scent Vent Spinners are the only in-line spinners that release a scent when retrieved. The design includes a quality spinner with a custom scent basket as the lure's body between the blade and hook. The barrel-shaped basket has brass caps on both ends to facilitate spinning. Power Bait Jelly or Dough can be rubbed in to the waffle-like perforations in the basket. As the bait is retrieved, the basket spins, gradually discharging the Power Bait scent and taste. The attractant can be restocked any time. A hand-tied marabou tail gives the lure a life-like motion. A silver blade model without the marabou tail is also available.

SPECIFICATIONS
Weight: ⅛ oz., 1/16-oz.
Reflective spinner blade colors: silver, gold, chartreuse, firetiger, rainbow
MSRP: $2.99

SPINNERBAITS, SPINNERS, BUZZBAITS

**BOMBER®
BUSHWHACKER™
B12S**

**BOMBER®
BUSHWHACKER™
B12T**

**BOMBER®
MINI-WHACKER™
B02M**

**BOMBER®
MINI-WHACKER™
B12M**

x

LURES

BOMBER®
BUSHWHACKER™

Bushwhacker spinnerbaits feature the pulsating vibration of live-rubber skirts. Bushwhackers are crafted of chip-resistant head finishes, high-grade stainless wire and a tangle-free line-tie.

SPECIFICATIONS
Model B12S
(Single Colorado Blade)
Weight: ½ oz.
MSRP: $1.59 - $1.69

Model B38S
(Single Colorado Blade)
Weight: ⅜ oz.
MSRP: $1.59 - $1.69

Model B14S
(Single Colorado Blade)

Weight: ¼ oz.
MSRP: $1.59 - $1.69

Model B12T (Tandem Colorado/Willow Leaf)
Weight: ½ oz.
MSRP: $1.59 - $1.69

Model B38T (Tandem Colorado/Willow Leaf)
Weight: ⅜ oz.
MSRP: $1.59 - $1.69

Model B14T (Tandem Colorado/Willow Leaf)
Weight: ¼ oz.
MSRP: $1.59 - $1.69
Colors: White, Chartreuse, Chartreuse/Blue, Black, Chartreuse/White, Chartreuse/Black

BOMBER®
MINI-WHACKER™

The Mini-Whacker™ is an ultra-light lure, but it is heavy enough to be fished with spincast or baitcast gear.
SPECIFICATIONS
Model: B02M
(Single Colorado Blade)
Weight: ⅛ oz
MSRP: $1.79

Model: B12M
(Tandem Colorado Blades)
Weight: ⅛ oz.
MSRP: $2.21
Colors: White, Black, Green/Yellow, Chartreuse/Lime, Brown/Orange, Chartreuse, Chartreuse/Orange, Yellow/Black, Black/White, Chartreuse/Black

310 • 2003 Bassing Bible

www.StoegerIndustries.com

SPINNERBAITS, SPINNERS, BUZZBAITS

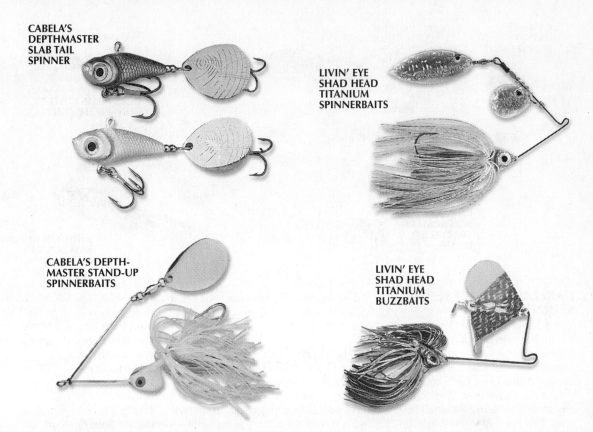

CABELA'S DEPTHMASTER SLAB TAIL SPINNER

LIVIN' EYE SHAD HEAD TITANIUM SPINNERBAITS

CABELA'S DEPTH-MASTER STAND-UP SPINNERBAITS

LIVIN' EYE SHAD HEAD TITANIUM BUZZBAITS

CABELA'S DEPTHMASTER SLAB TAIL SPINNER

Depthmaster Spinnerbaits have a highly visible, shad-shaped lead body with engraved detail and a 3D Livin' Eye™ get the attention of bass. A slow-fluttering Colorado blade entices them to strike. VMC hooks are up front and on back for those short-striking fish.

SPECIFICATIONS
Sizes: 1 oz., 2 oz.
MSRP: $2.89
Colors: Shad, Pearl, Chartreuse Shad, Gold/Orange, Golden Shiner, Firetiger.

CABELA'S DEPTHMASTER STAND-UP SPINNERBAITS

Depthmaster Spinnerbaits, with their unique designs and unbeatable action, are sure to produce when ordinary spinners won't. With its stand-up jighead design, this spinner is perfect for slow rolling and stair-stepping up or down deep-water

structure. It's equipped with a slow-fluttering single Colorado blade and flashy metal-flake silicone skirts. Features a Mustad Needlepoint hook.

SPECIFICATIONS
Sizes: 1 oz., ½ oz., ¾ oz.
MSRP: $2.99
Colors: White, Firetiger, Chartreuse, Glow Blue, Green Craw, Black/Blue/Purple.

CABELA'S LIVIN' EYE SHAD HEAD TITANIUM SPINNER-BAITS AND BUZZBAITS

Shad-profiled spinnerbaits and buzzbaits add an extra sense of realism to their overall appearance when running through the water. The shad heads match with the blade to look like baitfish swimming in a small cluster. The two-tone finish matches with the metal-flake silicone skirt for a shocking appearance that looks like the real thing. Large, 3-D eyes give fish a place to target on the strike. The aluminum blades are finished

with a hologram appearance to give the shadows of even more baitfish swimming around the lure. The titanium wire won't bend or break under the stress of heavy fish. The spinnerbaits have ball-bearing swivels and an extra eye on the blade. Both use Mustad needlepoint hooks for incredible penetration.

SPECIFICATIONS
Spinnerbaits: ball-bearing swivels and an extra eye on the blade
Size: ⅜ oz.
MSRP: $5.99
Colors: White, Shad, Firetiger, Chartreuse, Chartreuse/White, Baby Bass

Buzzbaits: shad heads match with the blades to look like baitfish swimming in a small cluster
Size: ⅜ oz.
MSRP: $5.99
Colors: White, Shad, Firetiger, Chartreuse, Chartreuse/White, Baby Bass

SPINNERBAITS, SPINNERS, BUZZBAITS

CABELA'S LIVIN' EYE SPINNERBAITS

JOHNSON BASS BUSTER® RATTLIN' BEETLE SPIN®

JOHNSON BASS BUSTER® CRAZYTAIL™ BEETLE

JOHNSON GENUINE BASS BUSTER® BEETLE SPIN®

CABELA'S LIVIN' EYE SPINNERBAITS

It's no secret among anglers that bass key on the eyes of baitfish, triggering strikes and attacks. Cabela's fishing experts used this knowledge in developing the Livin' Eye Spinnerbait, to take advantage of the bass's predatory instincts. Each spinnerbait features Cabela's 3-D Livin' Eyes™ on the head, with 3-D eyes also attached to each blade, giving the single bait the appearance of a group of tasty baitfish. The molded body of each bait is highly-detailed with lifelike gills, mouths and scales. The tandem Colorado and Willowleaf blades are finished with the same rich detail as the body, further enhancing the baitfish-like appearance of each lure. Premium skirts add to the realistic swimming motion.

SPECIFICATIONS
Sizes: ¼ oz., ⅜ oz., ½ oz.
MSRP: $3.99
Colors: White, Perch, Firetiger, Red Shad, Chartreuse, Clown

JOHNSON BASS BUSTER® CRAZYTAIL™ BEETLE SPIN®

Soft Beetle Spin body with crazytail action and a bright flashing spinner. Features include a new lead-free head, scented Beetle body to fool fish.

SPECIFICATIONS
Size: 1½"
Weight: ¹⁄₃₂, ⅛ ounce
MSRP: $0.99
Colors: (all colors not available in all sizes): Red Sparkle w/Chartreuse Tail,

Silver Sparkle w/Chartreuse Tail, Silver Sparkle w/White Tail, Black w/Chartreuse Tail

JOHNSON BASS BUSTER® RATTLIN' BEETLE SPIN®

A Genuine Beetle Spin with full features. Color-coordinated translucent polycarbonate jighead. Steel shot adds weight for better jigging. Shot creates a louder, harder rattle that calls in fish from farther away.

SPECIFICATIONS
Sizes: 1½", 2"
Weights: ⅛, ¼ ounce
MSRP: $1.15
Colors: (all colors not available in all sizes): Chartreuse, Pearl, Smoke

JOHNSON BEETLE SPIN® CREATURES WITH POWER BAIT

For nearly 50 years, the traditional Johnson Beetle Spin kept the same body shape as the one created by Fishing Hall-of-Famer Virgil Ward when he invented the lure. The round grubby-shaped body with short forked tail adorned the Beetle Spin with great success. Now Johnson has added the new Beetle Spin Creature baits with a frog and a minnow-shaped body. To further enhance the fish-catching ability, the Berkley Power Bait scent and flavor has been added to the bait.

Beetle Spin Creatures are sure to attract the most vicious strikes from bass. The Beetle Spin Creature has the body of the new Power Bait Micro shapes from Berkley, either the frog

or minnow. The Micro Frog has a wide body with large hind legs and short front legs. The Micro Minnow has the traditional minnow shape with a split tail.

SPECIFICATIONS
Weight: ⅛ oz.
Length: 2"
MSRP: $1.15
Colors: Bullfrog, Toad, Green Frog, Black, White, Chartreuse with Silver Fleck (Micro Frog); Chartreuse with Silver Fleck, Clear with Gold Fleck, Glow, Black Shad, Rainbow with Silver Fleck, Chartreuse Pearl, Smelt Colors (Micro Minnow)

JOHNSON GENUINE BASS BUSTER® BEETLE SPIN®

This is the direct ancestor of the spinner grub fishing Hall-of-Famer Virgil Ward created more than 50 years ago. Today's Beetle Spin has a slightly softer body for livelier action. It's made out of a real fish-fooling formula that sends a fish-attracting scent into the water. Now, when fish bite, the tasty body keeps them holding on and on and on, and that gives you more time to set the hook.

Features:
- New lead-free head and genuine Beetle Spin body
- Beetle body is scented to fool fish. Fish hang on longer to set the hook
- Bright, matching, flashing spinner

SPECIFICATIONS
Sizes: 1", 1½", 2"
Weight: ¹⁄₆₀, ¹⁄₃₂, ⅛, ¼ ounce
MSRP: $0.99

SPINNERBAITS, SPINNERS, BUZZBAITS

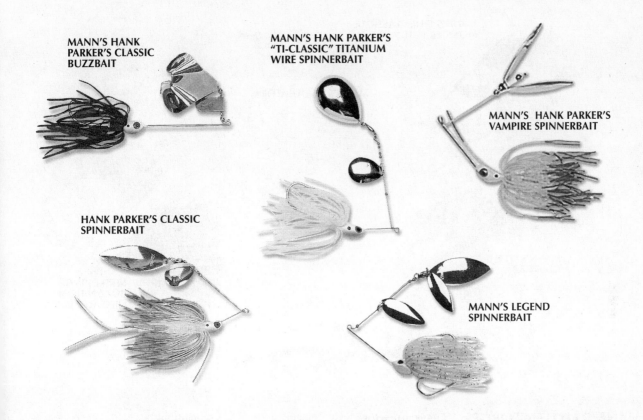

MANN'S HANK PARKER'S CLASSIC BUZZBAIT

MANN'S HANK PARKER'S "TI-CLASSIC" TITANIUM WIRE SPINNERBAIT

MANN'S HANK PARKER'S VAMPIRE SPINNERBAIT

HANK PARKER'S CLASSIC SPINNERBAIT

MANN'S LEGEND SPINNERBAIT

Colors: (all colors not available in all sizes) Purple, Fluorescent Chartreuse, Catalpa w/ Black Stripes, Yellow w/Black Stripes, Black w/Yellow Stripes, Brown/Orange, Black/Chartreuse/Orange, Yellow w/Black Dots, Yellow w/Red Dots, Red Sparkle w/White Tail, Purple Sparkle w/Chartreuse Tail, White w/Chartreuse Tail, Fire Orange w/Chartreuse Tail

MANN'S HANK PARKER'S CLASSIC SPINNERBAITS AND BUZZBAIT

The number one selling spinnerbait series in the U.S. since Hank Parker won the 1989 B.A.S.S. Masters Classic with the original version. All have high vibration ultra-thin wire forms, ball bearing swivels, chip-resistant paint and Hank's custom trailer.

SPECIFICATIONS
Weights: ⅛, ¼, ⅜, ¾ oz. (¼ and ½ oz. buzzbait)
MSRP: $4.55
Colors: white, chartreuse, chartreuse/white, fire tiger, chartreuse/ blue, gold fire tiger, silver chartreuse/white, silver white, black

MANN'S HANK PARKER'S "TI-CLASSIC" TITANIUM WIRE SPINNERBAIT

This Hank Parker design features a small titanium wire that allows the use of an "R" bend for increased vibration, and it never needs tuning. A Nickel TEFLON©-coated Eagle Claw Lazer-Sharp hook provides faster penetration and the unique skirt provides extra flash. The "Ti-Classic" features 24K gold-plated Willow or Indiana blades.

SPECIFICATIONS
Size: ⅛ oz.
Blades: Single Colorado gold and single willowleaf gold
Size: ⅜ oz.
Blades: Double Indiana or willowleaf gold
Size: ½ oz.
Blades: Double Indiana or willowleaf gold
MSRP: $7.99
Colors: white, chartreuse, chartreuse/white

MANN'S HANK PARKER'S VAMPIRE SPINNERBAIT

The Vampire Spinnerbait blade concept is a real breakthrough in blade design. The blade adjusts to fit any spinnerbait condition. Even with the blade bent completely out of balance, this bait will still run true.

SPECIFICATIONS
Weight: ½ oz.
MSRP: $4.55
Colors: White, Chartreuse, Chartreuse/White, Fire Tiger

MANN'S LEGEND SPINNERBAIT

The "Legend" spinnerbait features a unique head shape and combination of blades. Three willowleaf blades with two combined on a Sampo swivel, plus a special divider, gives 3 distinct areas and sizes of maximum flash. Available in Gold and Silver Willow.

SPECIFICATIONS
Weight: ½, 1 oz.
MSRP: $4.62
Colors: White, Chartreuse, Chartreuse/White, Fire Tiger

SPINNERBAITS, SPINNERS, BUZZBAITS

MANN'S "THE CLASSIC" MONSTER BAIT

MANN'S UNDULATOR®

MANN'S LITTLE GEORGE®

STRIKE KING®
BUZZ-N-DROP™
SPECIALTY LURES

MANN'S WINGER

MANN'S LITTLE GEORGE®

Little George may be one of the oldest lures on the market today, but it still works just as well today as it used to, and it's one of the top lures of all times. This sinking tailspinner has earned the right to be in every angler's tackle box. The ripping technique is deadly near the bottom, and nothing is better in schooling fish.

SPECIFICATIONS
Weight: ⅛, ¼, ½, ¾, 1 oz.
MSRP: $2.21 (⅛, ¼,½ oz.),
$2.33 (¾ and 1 oz., $2.33); $2.46
(Holographic colors)
Colors: Chartreuse, Silver, Silver/Black Back, Hammered Silver, White/Black, White/Blue, White/Green, White/Pink Eye, Yellow/Black, Gold/Gold Blade

MANN'S "THE CLASSIC" MONSTER BAIT

Specially designed for deepwater fishing, the 1½ oz. Hank Parker's "Classic Monster" uses the same thin wire as the original Classic for better vibration and fish appeal. The large willowleaf blade gives off flash and vibration, while the reduced lift allows the lure to hug the bottom on retrieve. Gold Willow.

SPECIFICATIONS
Weight: 1½ oz.
MSRP: $5.19
Colors: White, Chartreuse, Chartreuse/White

MANN'S UNDULATOR®

Patented, segmented blade flaps up and down, rather than spin, for more flash and vibration on the drop and release. It practically planes on top as it kicks up a splashy noisy commotion. Available in "Gold Blade" only.

SPECIFICATIONS
Weight: ¼, ½ oz.
MSRP: $4.55
Colors: White, Chartreuse, Chartreuse/White, Fire Tiger

MANN'S WINGER

Colorado lure designer Bud Bates' innovative double-blade assembly products twice the fish-attracting flash and vibration as standard spinners. Rotating eyes add realism and a target for strikes. Because the balanced blade assembly creates less torque, line twist is reduced. The Winger catches all gamefish, including trout, panfish, walleye, pike, and salmon. Plated with genuine silver or gold.

SPECIFICATIONS
Weight: ¹⁄₁₆, ⅛, ¼ oz.
MSRP: $3.28
Colors: Silver, Gold, Black, Chartreuse, Yellow, White

STRIKE KING® BUZZ-N-DROP™ SPECIALTY LURES

This unique lure is designed to be a new type of buzzbait that can be stopped and dropped by cover. The free-swinging blade arm causes the lure to fall slowly and in a horizontal position. This gives a more realistic presentation than regular buzzbaits and spinnerbaits that may tilt unnaturally as they fall and it falls slower than most spinnerbaits. Since the blade assembly swings freely, it is pushed up out of the way as a fish clamps down, thus enabling better hook-ups than regular buzzbaits.

SPECIFICATIONS
Model: BND14
Weight: ¼ oz.
MSRP: $3.99
Model: BND38
Weight: ⅜ oz.
MSRP: $3.99
Colors: Chartreuse, White, Standby, Tequila

SPINNERBAITS, SPINNERS, BUZZBAITS

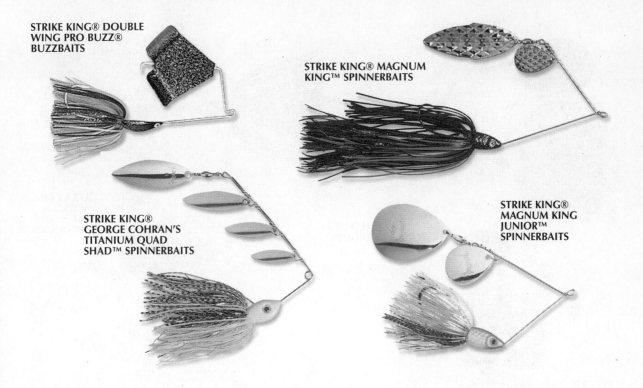

STRIKE KING® DOUBLE WING PRO BUZZ® BUZZBAITS

STRIKE KING® MAGNUM KING™ SPINNERBAITS

STRIKE KING® GEORGE COHRAN'S TITANIUM QUAD SHAD™ SPINNERBAITS

STRIKE KING® MAGNUM KING JUNIOR™ SPINNERBAITS

STRIKE KING® DOUBLE WING PRO BUZZ® BUZZBAITS

Mirage, blade and Mirage, skirt

SPECIFICATIONS

Model: 12PBM

Weight: ½ oz.

Model: 14PBM

Weight: ¼ oz.

Colors: Chartreuse Shiner, White Shiner, Emerald Shiner, Texas Red, Gold Shiner, Sun Perch

STRIKE KING® GEORGE COHRAN'S TITANIUM QUAD SHAD™ SPINNERBAITS

It's a four-bladed George Cochran Titanium Quad Shad™ featuring premium titanium wire. We at Strike King® can't remember when George has ever been more excited about a spinnerbait. Take it from him, "it will outfish any other spinnerbait in certain conditions. It's awesome!"

SPECIFICATIONS

Model: GCQ38

Weight: ⅜ oz.

MSRP: $5.99

Colors: Chartreuse, White, Emerald Shad, Alpha Shiner

STRIKE KING® MAGNUM KING™ SPINNERBAITS

Features include:

• Available in 6 colors
• A large size spinnerbait designed for muskie and pike
• Diamond blades for sensational flash
• 6/0 super strong Mustad, needle point main hook
• Special .55 stainless steel wire
• Removable 3/0 treble trailer hook attached to this wire
• Realistic Premier Elite‰ sculptured head with 3-D holographic eyes and custom paint scheme
• Custom silicone glitter skirt
• Additional skirt on the trailer hook
• Heavy-duty ball-bearing swivel

SPECIFICATIONS

Model: MAG15

Weight: 1½ oz.

Model: MAG2

Weight: 2 oz.

Colors: Chartreuse/Blue Back (Copper/Silver Blades), Tequila (Copper/Gold Blades), Fire Tiger (Copper/Gold Blades), White (Copper/Silver Blades), Orange/Black Back (Copper/Copper Blades), Black/Red (Copper/Silver Blades)

STRIKE KING® MAGNUM KING JUNIOR™ SPINNERBAITS

The "Junior" was created to fill the gap between the Magnum King™ and ordinary sized spinnerbaits. It is irresistible to Largemouth Bass. Bass fishermen are using the Mag Junior to probe deep ledges, flooded timber and other locations, and they're catching some of the biggest bass of their lives.

SPECIFICATIONS

Model: MAGJR125CW (Colorado/Willow)

Weight: 1¼ oz.

Model: MAGJR125CI (Colorado/Indiana)

Weight: 1¼ oz.

Colors: Chartreuse Shad (Gold/Silver Blades), Golden Shiner (Gold/Gold Blades), Bream (Gold/Silver Blades), Rainbow Trout (Silver/Gold Blades), White Shad (Silver/Silver Blades), Perch (Gold/Silver Blades)

SPINNERBAITS, SPINNERS, BUZZBAITS

**STRIKE KING®
MIDNIGHT PREMIER™
RATLIN SPINNERBAITS**

**STRIKE KING®
MINI PRO BUZZ®
BUZZBAITS**

**STRIKE KING®
MIDNIGHT SPECIAL™
RATLIN SPINNERBAITS**

**STRIKE KING®
MIRAGE®
PRO-SERIES™
SPINNERBAITS**

STRIKE KING® MIDNIGHT PREMIER™ RATLIN SPINNERBAITS

Features include:
- ½ ounce shortarm spinnerbait with double barrel rattler
- Chemically-sharpened black nickel hook
- Premium #7 Indiana blades

SPECIFICATIONS
Model: MP12 (Black Nickel Single)
Weight: ½ oz.

Model: MP12 (24K Gold Single)
Weight: ½ oz.
Colors: Black/Chartreuse, Black/Blue, Black/Red

STRIKE KING® MIDNIGHT SPECIAL™ RATLIN SPINNERBAITS

Features include:
- ⁷⁄₁₆ ounce shortarm spinnerbait with single barrel rattler designed for low light and night fishing

SPECIFICATIONS
Model: MS716 (Silver Single Colorado)

Weight: ⁷⁄₁₆ oz.
MSRP: $1.99

Model: MS716 (Gold Single Colorado)
Weight: ⁷⁄₁₆ oz.
MSRP: $1.99

Model: MS716 (Black Nickel Single Colorado)
Weight: ⁷⁄₁₆ oz.
MSRP: $0.00
Colors: Chartreuse, White, Red Shad, Black/Blue, Black/Red, Black/Silver

STRIKE KING® MINI PRO BUZZ® BUZZBAITS

Diamond Dust Head with Diamond Dust silicone skirt
SPECIFICATIONS
Model: 18PBM
Weight: ⅛ oz.
MSRP: $1.99
Colors: Black Head with Black Skirt, Chartreuse Head with Chartreuse Skirt, White Head with White skirt, Chartreuse Head with White/Chartreuse Skirt

STRIKE KING® MIRAGE® PRO-SERIES™SPINNERBAITS

Favorites of the Pros, these spinnerbaits produce super vibration and maximum flash. The Ratlin version is great in heavy cover and its rattler calls 'em in from long distances in murky waters.

Features include:
- Tennessee Diamond blades
- Mirage, painted Diamond Dust head
- Scale pattern silicone skirt
- Eagle Claw, Laser-Sharp hook
- American-made "Spin-Eze" ball-bearing swivel

SPECIFICATIONS
Model: MPS38
Weight: ⅜ oz.

Model: MPS14
Weight: 1-4 oz.
Colors: Chartreuse (Silver/Silver Blades), White (Silver/Silver Blades), Standby (Silver/Silver Blades), Fire Tiger (Gold/Gold Blades), Tequila Sunrise (Silver/Silver Blades)

LURES

SPINNERBAITS, SPINNERS, BUZZBAITS

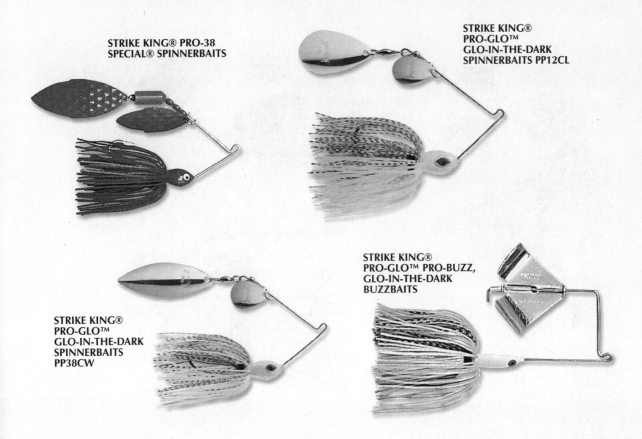

STRIKE KING® PRO-38 SPECIAL® SPINNERBAITS

STRIKE KING® PRO-GLO™ GLO-IN-THE-DARK SPINNERBAITS PP12CL

STRIKE KING® PRO-GLO™ GLO-IN-THE-DARK SPINNERBAITS PP38CW

STRIKE KING® PRO-GLO™ PRO-BUZZ, GLO-IN-THE-DARK BUZZBAITS

STRIKE KING® PRO-38 SPECIAL® SPINNERBAITS

Features include:
- Diamond Dust head
- "Spin-Eze" ball-bearing swivel
- Grass Bell®

SPECIFICATIONS

Model: PRO38

Weight: ⅜ oz.

MSRP: $1.99

Colors: Silver Double Willow

Diamond Blades: Chartreuse Head Chartreuse Skirt, White Head White Skirt *Painted Diamond Dust Double Willow Blades:* Red Shad Head Red Shad Skirt, Chartreuse Head Chartreuse Skirt, White Head White Skirt, Orange Head Orange/ Chartreuse Skirt, Silver Head Clear/ Silver/Red Skirt, Blue Head Black/ Blue Skirt

STRIKE KING® PRO-GLO™ GLO-IN-THE-DARK SPINNERBAITS

24k gold and/or nickel-plated premium blades engraved with "Strike King" and blade size. Mustad, double-hardened premium black nickel chemically-sharpened hook. Premium scale-pattern silicone glow-in-the-dark skirt. Superior quality "Spin-Eze," ball bearing swivel. Premier Vibra-Max wire for maximum blade vibration

SPECIFICATIONS

Model: PP38CW (Colorado/Willow)

Weight: ⅜ oz.

MSRP: $3.89

Model: PP12CI (Colorado/Indiana)

Weight: ½ oz.

Colors: Chartreuse Shiner (Silver/Gold Blades), White Shiner (Silver/Silver Blades), Emerald Shad (Silver/Silver Blades), Alpha Shad (Silver Gild Blades), Gold Shiner (Gold/Gold Blades), Fire Tiger (Gold/Gold Blades).

STRIKE KING® PRO-GLO™ PRO-BUZZ, GLO-IN-THE-DARK BUZZBAITS

Premium scale-pattern silicone glow-in-the-dark skirt. Boat-shaped planing head designed to help the bait come up quicker and stay on top. Eyes add extra fish-catching appeal. Large, super sharp Eagle Claw hook. Center axis blade to help reduce torque and straighten out the direction of the retrieve.

SPECIFICATIONS

Model: 14PBM

Weight: ¼ oz.

MSRP: $3.89

Model: 12PBM

Weight: ½ oz.

MSRP: $3.89

Colors: Chartreuse Shiner, White Shiner.

SPINNERBAITS, SPINNERS, BUZZBAITS

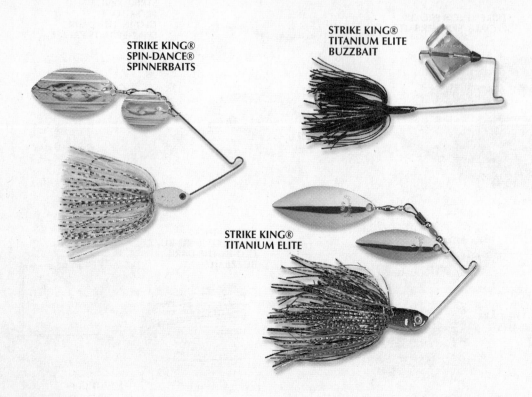

**STRIKE KING®
SPIN-DANCE®
SPINNERBAITS**

**STRIKE KING®
TITANIUM ELITE
BUZZBAIT**

**STRIKE KING®
TITANIUM ELITE**

STRIKE KING® SPIN-DANCE® SPINNERBAITS

Features include:
- Scale pattern silicone skirt
- American-made "Spin-Eze" ball-bearing swivel
- Eagle Claw® Laser-Sharp hook
- Tennessee Diamond Prism Bar blades

SPECIFICATIONS
Model: SDD38
Weight: ⅜ oz.

Model: SDD14
Weight: ¼ oz.
Colors: Chartreuse (Silver/Silver Blades), White (Silver/Silver Blades), Standby (Silver/Silver Blades), Fire Tiger (Silver/Gold Blades), Tequila Sunrise (Silver/Silver Blades)

STRIKE KING® TITANIUM ELITE BUZZBAIT™ SPINNERBAITS

These new high-tech buzzbaits are loaded with features. The combination of a flexible premium titanium wire and a long, super sharp black nickel hook helps increase the strike-to-hook-up ratio. The center-axis blade with "gurgle holes" helps the bait run true, produce a unique sound, and leave an enticing bubble trail. Perhaps the neatest feature is the exclusive new "grass cone" in front of the blade which helps keep trash from fouling the blade.

SPECIFICATIONS
Model: TEB12
Weight: ½ oz.
MSRP: $3.99

Model: TEB38
Weight: ⅜ oz.
MSRP: $3.99

Model: TEB14
Weight: ¼ oz.
MSRP: $3.99
Colors: Chartreuse, Fire Tiger, White, Black/Silver

STRIKE KING® TITANIUM ELITE™ SPINNERBAITS

The ultimate titanium spinnerbaits has all the features of our top-of-the-line Premier™ Elite™ plus a new-style head design with some of the most beautiful finishes you've ever seen.

Features include:
- Superior titanium nickel alloy wire
- Beautiful lifelike sculpted head.
- Holographic 3-D eyes
- Black nickel, chemically-sharpened hook
- Premium scaled pattern silicone skirt that matches the head.
- Premier blades of the best nickel and/or 24K gold plating.
- Spin-Eze ball bearing swivel.

SPECIFICATIONS
Model: TE38CW (Colorado/Willow)
Weight: ⅜ oz.
MSRP: $4.99

Model: TE12CW (Colorado/Willow)
Weight: ½ oz.
MSRP: $4.99

Model: TE38WW (Willow/Willow)
Weight: ⅜ oz.
MSRP: $4.99

SPINNERBAITS, SPINNERS, BUZZBAITS

STRIKE KING®
TITANIUM
PRO MODEL

STRIKE KING®
TRI-WING
BUZZ KING®

Model: TE12WW (Willow/Willow)
Weight: ½ oz.
MSRP: $4.49
Model: TE38CC
(Colorado/Colorado)
Weight: ⅜ oz.
MSRP: $4.49
Colors: Chartreuse Shad (Silver/Gold Blades), Golden Shiner (Gold/Gold Blades), Bream (Silver/Gold Blades), Rainbow Trout (Gold/Silver Blades), White Shad (Silver/Silver Blades), Shad (Gold/Silver Blades), Sunfish (Gold/Silver Blades), Perch (Silver/Gold Blades)

STRIKE KING® TITANIUM PRO-MODEL™ SPINNERBAITS

This lure enables you to obtain the characteristics of a titanium wire at a reduced cost.

Features include:
• Superior titanium nickel alloy wire
• Mirage painted Diamond Dust head with Diamond eye
• Premier Mirage silicone skirt
• Laser-sharp hook
• Spin-Eze ball bearing swivel
SPECIFICATIONS
Model: TPM38CW
(Colorado/Willow)
Weight: ⅜ oz.
MSRP: $4.49
Model: TPM12WW
(Willow/Willow)
Weight: 1/2 oz.
MSRP: $4.49

Model: TPM38TDP (Tennessee Diamond Prism)
Weight: ⅜ oz.
MSRP: $4.49
Colors: Chartreuse Shiner (Silver/Gold Blades), White Shiner (Silver/Silver Blades), Emerald Shad (Silver/Silver Blades), Alpha Shiner (Silver/Gold Blades), Gold Shiner (Gold/Gold Blades)

STRIKE KING® TRI-WING BUZZ KING® BUZZBAITS

Diamond Dust head with Diamond Dust silicone skirt
SPECIFICATIONS
Model: 516BM
Weight: ⁵⁄₁₆ oz.
MSRP: $2.99

Model: 316BM
Weight: ³⁄₁₆ oz.
MSRP: $2.99
Colors: Chartreuse Head and Chartreuse Skirt, Chartreuse Head and Chartreuse/Blue/Silver Skirt, White Head and White Skirt, Black/Blue Head and Black/Blue Skirt

Buzzbait Features
Buzzbaits come in a wide variety of colors and sizes to suit your bassing needs. Many have additional bits of hardware (blades, bearings, etc.) that add clacks, purrs, squeals, and other bass-attracting sounds to the bait's normal spitting and sputtering. Many anglers will tell you that the more noise a buzzbait produces, the more readily it will attract bass coming in to investigate.

SPOONS AND OTHER METAL LURES

ABU GARCIA®TOBY

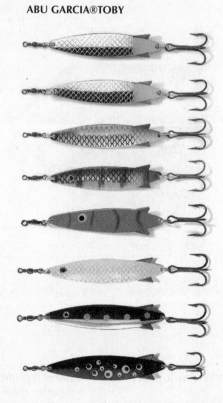

ABU GARCIA® LINK LURE

ABU GARCIA® SLANDAN

ABU GARCIA® LINK LURE

The Link Lure from Abu Garcia is unlike any lure on the market. Swedish inventor Vidar Thorbjornsen had this crazy idea to make a fishing lure from a flexible watchband by adding a snap swivel on the head and a treble hook on the tail. The Link Lure has been a proven bait in Europe and the Nordic countries for over ten years.

The Link Lure's flexible body changes shape continuously, giving the bait a new look with each crank of the reel. During the retrieve, the lure wobbles and undulates, giving the fish a look they've never seen before. When jigged vertically, the Link Lure will flatten out on the rod, twitch, and then collapse into a multitude of shapes during the drop. The action of the Link Lure never stops and bass can't resist the dancing temptation of this bait.

SPECIFICATIONS
Size: 2½"
Weight: ⁵/₁₆ oz.
MSRP: $3.99.
Colors: Gold, Silver, Copper

ABU GARCIA® SLANDAN

The new Slandan from Abu Garcia resembles a typical spoon when first given a glance. But on closer inspection, the shape is found not to be symmetrical. One side is relatively straight, while the opposite side has a smooth curve, creating a slender head and wider body. The spoon is also created with an undulating shape, giving the Slandan an action that will draw bass into striking. Comes equipped with a high-quality snap swivel and nickel-plated hooks and split rings. A red bead on the hook adds to the spoon's appeal. Each bait is finished with a large prominent eye.

SPECIFICATIONS
Size: 3½"
Weight: ¹¹/₁₆ oz.
MSRP: $ 2.92.
Colors: Silver, Blue, Green, Green with yellow

ABU GARCIA® TOBY

Back in the 50s and 60s, the Toby was a legend. Hardly a tackle box could be found that didn't have a few Toby spoons ready and waiting. Although not available in the United States for the past thirty years, anglers in Europe and around the globe never stopped catching fish with the classic lure. Now Abu Garcia has brought the Toby back to America.

The Toby is a narrow spoon-type bait valued for both deep and shallow presentations. When retrieved with rod tip high, the Toby wobbles and thrashes along the surface, causing fish from below to rise to the occasion. Drop the rod tip and the bait has an erratic motion that mimics a baitfish that can't decide which way to swim. Slow the retrieve and the Toby drops even deeper. Fished vertically, the Toby can be jigged up and down with a motion that is sure to result in a strike.

The Toby is distinguished by the two red fins along the sides of the lure near the tail and an undulating body shape. It is this body shape that gives the Toby its erratic motion when retrieved. The lure is packaged with a high-quality snap swivel.

SPECIFICATIONS
Sizes/Weights: 3", ⅜ oz. and 3.5", ⅝ oz.
MSRP: $ 2.69
Colors (holographic): Silver, Copper, Silver with Blue, Green with a yellow pattern, White

LURES

SPOONS AND OTHER METAL LURES

BASS PRO SHOPS® XPS STRIKE SPOON

BOMBER® SLAB SPOON

CABELA'S REALIMAGE JIGGING SPOON

CABELA'S REALIMAGE WEEDLESS

COTTON CORDELL® C.C. SPOON®

BASS PRO SHOPS® XPS STRIKE SPOON

Solid brass with high-polish nickel or 14K gold plating and a hand-tied white feather hook with red accent makes this spoon great for fishing deep water impoundments in the summer when bass go deep. Fish this bait straight down in 30' to 60' of water and jig the spoon up and down.

SPECIFICATIONS
Weight: ¼ oz. and ½ oz.
MSRP: $2.49.
Colors: Gold, Silver, Silver/Black and Chartreuse/Silver

BOMBER® SLAB SPOON®

The Slab Spoon's shape and heavy weight make it possible to fish rapidly and allows the lure to hold tight to the bottom.

SPECIFICATIONS
Model: B8900
Weight: 1¼ oz.
MSRP: $1.89

Model: B8800
Weight: ⅞ oz.
MSRP: $1.89
Colors: White, Silver Back, Plain Metachrome, Metachrome Black Back, Metachrome Blue Back, Fluorescent Yellow

CABELA'S REALIMAGE JIGGING SPOON

The realistic look of Cabela's Jig-N-Spoons generates a following any time you drop them in the water. These lures imitate the movement of a dying baitfish when you're jigging for bass and most predator fish. By lifting your rod tip and dropping it, these spoons flutter gracefully downward in the water and mimic a baitfish falling to the bottom. The fins, gills and mouth also have a lifelike appearance that, combined with the bait's action, invite a strike.

SPECIFICATIONS
Weights: ½ oz., 1 oz., 1½ oz., 2 oz.
MSRP: $1.99 - $2.59
Colors: Shad, Perch, Chartreuse Shad, Glow, Rainbow Trout

CABELA'S REALIMAGE WEEDLESS SPOONS

Fish this lunker spoon in the toughest places and never get hung up. Add a trailer and you have a unique combo that's unbeatable in cover for bass. Enticing wobble to draw those lunkers out of thick weedbeds.

SPECIFICATIONS
Sizes/Weights: 2⅜", ¼ oz.; 2⅝", ½ oz.; 3⅜", ¾ oz.
MSRP: $2.99

Colors: Shad, Firetiger, Golden Shiner, Tennessee Shad, Blue Shad, Baby Bass, Perch

COTTON CORDELL® C.C. SPOON®

C.C. Spoons deliver a fluttering descent that gets the desired depth, even in swift current or windy conditions. These lures feature sturdy hardware and strong rust-proof hooks. 2 per package.

SPECIFICATIONS
Model: K7034 (C.C. Spoon)
Size: 3"
Weight: ¾ oz.
Hook size: 2
MSRP: $2.39

Model: K7038 (C.C. Spoon)
Size: 2"
Weight: ⅜ oz.
Hook size: 8
MSRP: $2.39

Model: K7114 (Little Mickey)
Size: 1½"
Weight: ¼ oz.
Hook size: 8
MSRP: $2.39

SPOONS AND OTHER METAL LURES

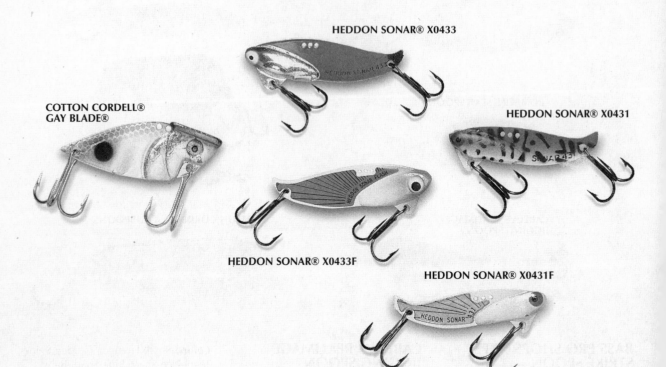

HEDDON SONAR® X0433

COTTON CORDELL®
GAY BLADE®

HEDDON SONAR® X0431

HEDDON SONAR® X0433F

HEDDON SONAR® X0431F

COTTON CORDELL® GAY BLADE®

The Gay Blade's "flathead" action plane creates a tight, pulsating action that lets the angler feel the lure working.

SPECIFICATIONS
Model: C38
Size: 2"
Weight: ⅜ oz.
Hook size: 6
Cranking depth: sinker
MSRP: $2.99

Model: C14
Size: 1½"
Weight: ¼ oz.
Hook size: 8
Cranking depth: sinker
MSRP: $2.99
Colors: Chrome/Black, Chrome/Blue, Smoky Joe, Chartreuse

HEDDON SONAR®

This is the original action-adjustable lure. The three line-tie holes allow adjustment of the running depth and action. The front hole is for shallow running and high vibration. The rear

hole produces deep running and a wide, slower, wobbling action. The center hole is perfect for jigging. The Sonar Flash has a flash finish that enhances visibility and the Rattling Sonar Flash has the added sound of a one-eighth steel ball between a brass eye chamber.

SPECIFICATIONS
Model: X0433 (Sonar)
Size: 2⅜"
Weight: ½ oz.
Hook Size: #4
Cranking Depth: sinker
MSRP: $3.29

Model: X0431 (Sonar)
Size: 1⅞"
Weight: ¼ oz.
Hook Size: #6
Cranking Depth: sinker
MSRP: $3.29

Model: X0433F
(Rattling Sonar Flash)
Size: 2⅜"
Weight: ½ oz.
Hook Size: #4

Cranking Depth: sinker
MSRP: $3.29
Model: X0431F (Sonar Flash)
Size: 1⅞"
Weight: ¼ oz.
Hook Size: #6
Cranking Depth: sinker
MSRP: $3.29
Colors: Blue Flitter Shad, Gray Shad, Fluorescent Green, Silver Shiner, Gold Shiner, Perch, Red Head, Chrome. Flash Colors: Chartreuse, Green, Pink, Silver, Gold, Blue.

JOHNSON SILVER MINNOW®

After 80 years, most lures are just a fading memory. But not the Silver Minnow. This is no ordinary weedless lure; this one works. Crank it through thick hydrilla, cabbage grass or milfoil. The Weedless Wonder comes up clean and weed-free. Fish can't resist its patented 35-degree wobble. It rocks back and forth, but it won't roll and twist line.

The mid sizes have been some of the best largemouth bass lures of all

SPOONS AND OTHER METAL LURES

JOHNSON SILVER MINNOW®

MANN'S MANN-O-LURE®

**JOHNSON SILVER MINNOW®
SPINNER SPOON**

STRIKE KING® JIG-N-SPOONS™

time. They allow fishermen to fish in the slop and work the open pockets of water where the big hawgs hide. And the largest Silver Minnows are as potent as any oversized lure for exciting big, big Bass.

Features:
- Patented 35-degree wobble
- Hand-soldered hook
- No-twist eye
- Unique shape produces bullet casts
- Thicker in the middle than at the edges. This creates the patented 35-degree wobble. No other spoon is built like this, which is why no other lure has worked so well for so long.

SPECIFICATIONS
Sizes: 1"-3¾"
Weights: ¹⁄₂₄, ⅛, ¼, ½, ¾, 1⅛ oz.
MSRP: $2.92-$4.62
Colors: (not available in all sizes) silver, gold, black, rainbow, firetiger flash, chartreuse flash, red flash, red shad gold, red & white, firetiger, diamond back

JOHNSON SILVER MINNOW® SPINNER SPOON
When the big predators are deep in hiding, the Silver Minnow Spinner Spoon is the lure to pull 'em out. It has the flash and wobble of the famous Silver Minnow, plus the irresistible action of a spinner. Think of it as the Weedless Wonder Plus.

Features:
- A full featured genuine Silver Minnow
- Matching silver or gold spinner
- Extra-action rattle beads on spinner stem

SPECIFICATIONS
Size: 2½"
Weight: ½ oz.
MSRP: $4.58
Colors: silver, gold

MANN'S MANN-O-LURE®
This hefty bait is made for heavy-duty fishing. Some use it for big inland fish, while others attest to its tremendous abilities in saltwater. Either way,

it's a great bait for jigging or going down deep for the big ones.

SPECIFICATIONS
Weight/Length: ¼ oz., 1⅝";
½ oz., 2¼"; 1 oz., 2¾";
2 oz., 4¼", 4 oz., 5½"
MSRP: $2.64 (¼, ½ oz.), $2.75 (1 oz.), $2.96 (2 oz.), $5.99 (4 oz.)
Colors: Chartreuse, Pearl/Blue Back, Pearl/Green Back, Pearl/Black Back, Silver, Silver/Black, Back, Hammered Silver, Hammered 24K Gold Plated, Pearl

STRIKE KING® JIG-N-SPOONS™
- Diamond stamped for extra flash
- Split ring line tie and treble hook
- Spin-Eze™ ball-bearing swivel on front line tie

SPECIFICATIONS
Model: 500-7 (Silver)
Weight: ¾ oz.

Model: 500-7G (Gold)
Weight: ¾ oz.

TOPWATER HARD BAITS

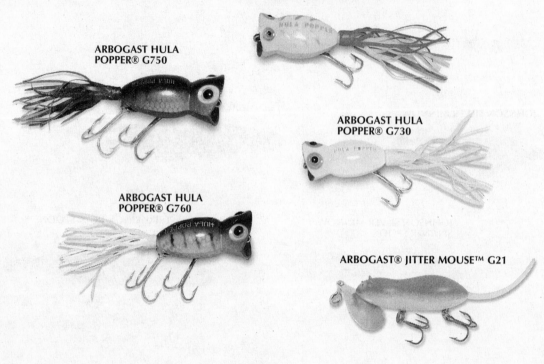

ARBOGAST HULA POPPER® G770

ARBOGAST HULA POPPER® G750

ARBOGAST HULA POPPER® G730

ARBOGAST HULA POPPER® G760

ARBOGAST® JITTER MOUSE™ G21

ARBOGAST HULA POPPER®

This topwater lure features a Hula Skirt and a uniquely-shaped popping head that causes a lot of commotion and a Hula Skirt trailer.

SPECIFICATIONS
Model: G750
Size: 2¼"
Weight: ⅝ oz.
Hook Size: #1
MSRP: $4.49

Model: G760
Size: 2"
Weight: ⅜ oz.
Hook Size: #4
MSRP: $4.49

Model: G770
Size: 1¾"
Weight: ¼ oz.
Hook Size: #5
MSRP: $4.49

Model: G730
Size: 1¼"
Weight: 1/16 oz.
Hook Size: #8
MSRP: $4.49
Colors: White/Red Head, Black, Yellow, Perch, Frog/White Belly, Frog/Yellow Belly, Coach Dog/Orange Belly, Coach Dog, Yellow Coach Dog, Chartreuse, Flame Red/Black Belly, Fire Tiger, Bass, Brown Parrot

ARBOGAST® JITTER MOUSE™

Same dependable, "plodding" Jitterbug action in an ultralight size. A smaller cousin of the most productive nighttime lure ever designed, the Jitter Mouse provides excitement at your favorite lake or pond.

SPECIFICATIONS
Model: G21
Size: 1¾"
Weight: 3/16"
Hook size: #8
MSRP: $4.49

Early and Late is Great
Fish early and late hours religiously when using topwater lures, especially during hot weather. Near dawn and dusk, surface water has cooled, forage animals are more prone to move on top, and bass feed actively near the surface. The water is generally calmer, too, so prop bait vibrations attract bass over greater distances.

ARBOGAST
JITTERBUG®
G700

ARBOGAST
JITTERBUG®
G650/655

ARBOGAST
JITTERBUG®
G670/675

ARBOGAST JITTERBUG®
G600/605

ARBOGAST
JITTERBUG®
G680

ARBOGAST JITTERBUG®
G620/625

ARBOGAST
JITTERBUG®
G610

ARBOGAST
JITTERBUG®
G690

ARBOGAST JITTERBUG®

This is the No.1 night-time topwater lure of all time. The Jitterbug's® double-loped lip, placed at an angle to ensure proper action, creates a loud, paddling sound.

SPECIFICATIONS

Model: G700 (XL Jitterbug)
Size: 4½"
Weight: 1¼ oz.
Hook Size: 2/O
MSRP: $5.49

Model: G650 (Jitterbug)
Size: 3"
Weight: ⅝ oz.
Hook Size: #1
MSRP: $4.49

Model: G655 (Jitterbug, clicker)
Size: 3"
Weight: ⅝ oz.
Hook Size: #1
MSRP: $4.49

Model: G600 (Jitterbug)
Size: 2½"
Weight: ⅜ oz.
Hook Size: #5
MSRP: $4.49

Model: G605 (Jitterbug, clicker)
Size: 2½"

Weight: ⅜ oz.
Hook Size: #5
MSRP: $4.49

Model: G630 (Jitterbug)
Size: 2"
Weight: ¼ oz.
Hook Size: #6
MSRP: $4.49

Model: G635 (Jitterbug, clicker)
Size: 2"
Weight: ¼ oz.
Hook Size: #6
MSRP: $4.49

Model: G680 (Jitterbug)
Size: 2"
Weight: ¼ oz.
Hook Size: #6
MSRP: $4.49

Model: G670 (Jointed Jitterbug)
Size: 3½"
Weight: ⅝ oz.
Hook Size: #1
MSRP: $4.59

Model: G675 (Jointed Jitterbug, clicker)
Size: 3½"
Weight: ⅝ oz.
Hook Size: #1

MSRP: $4.59

Model: G620 (Jointed Jitterbug)
Size: 2½"
Weight: ⅜ oz.
Hook Size: #5
MSRP: $4.59

Model: G625 (Jointed Jitterbug, clicker)
Size: 2½"
Weight: ⅜ oz.
Hook Size: #5
MSRP: $4.59

Model: G610 (Weedless Jitterbug)
Size: 2½"
Weight: ⅝ oz.
Hook Size: 1/O
MSRP: $4.49

Model: G690 (Weedless Jitterbug)
Size: 2"
Weight: ⅜ oz.
Hook Size: 2/O
MSRP: $4.49
Colors: White/Red Head, Black, Yellow, Perch, Frog/White Belly, Frog/Yellow Belly, Coach Dog/Orange Belly, Coach Dog, Yellow Coach Dog, Chartreuse, Flame Red/Black Belly, Fire Tiger, Bass, Brown Parrot, Tennessee Shad

TOPWATER HARD BAITS

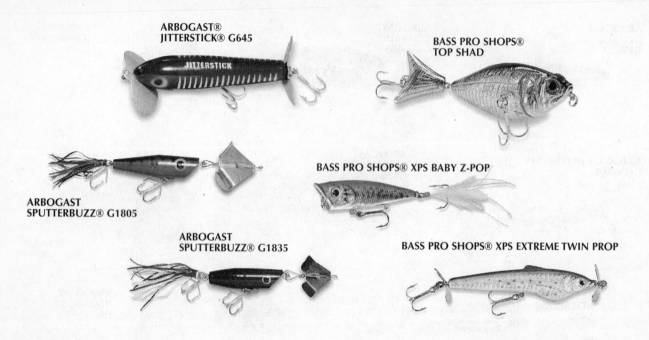

ARBOGAST®
JITTERSTICK® G645

BASS PRO SHOPS®
TOP SHAD

ARBOGAST
SPUTTERBUZZ® G1805

BASS PRO SHOPS® XPS BABY Z-POP

ARBOGAST
SPUTTERBUZZ® G1835

BASS PRO SHOPS® XPS EXTREME TWIN PROP

ARBOGAST® JITTERSTICK®

This is the longer, action-packed version of the world-famous Jitterbug. The Jitterstick boasts a large, surface-bursting prop that chops the water at the slightest movement of the lure. This adds an extra measure of lunker-tempting action to the lure's popular and proven effectiveness.

SPECIFICATIONS
Model: G645
Size: 4"
Weight: ⅝ oz.
Hook size: #1
MSRP: $4.69
Colors: White/Red Head, Black w/Ribs, Yellow, Perch, Frog/White Belly, Flame Red/Black Belly, Fire Tiger, Tennessee Shad

ARBOGAST SPUTTERBUZZ®

The floating design of this lure keeps the large blade on top of the water regardless of the retrieved speed.

SPECIFICATIONS
Model: G1805
Size: 5"
Weight: ⅝ oz.
Hook Size: #1
MSRP: $4.49

Model: G1835
Size: 3½"
Weight: ⅜ oz.
Hook Size: #4

MSRP: $4.49
Colors: White/Red Head, Black, Perch, Frog/White Belly, Fire Tiger, Tennessee Shad

BASS PRO SHOPS® TOP SHAD

Since the shad is the number one forage fish eaten by predatory game species, such as black bass, Dr. Loren Hill developed the Top Shad, another addition to his Avoidance Behavior Lure series. The Top Shad lure creates unique actions by flipping back and forth when it is near the water's surface. Game fish recognize this as "avoidance behavior" and will strike and consume this bait.

SPECIFICATIONS
Size: 4¾"
Weight: ⅝ oz
MSRP: $5.99.
Colors: Bleeding Tennessee Shad, Baby Bass, Albino Shad, Green Shad, River Minnow, Bleeding Bass and Chrome/Black Back.

BASS PRO SHOPS® XPS BABY Z-POP

Bass Pro Shops' own pro staff has designed the new XPS (Extreme Performance Series) Baby Z-Pop to catch bass when a small presentation topwater technique is required. The XPS Baby Z-Pop comes in amazingly fine-scale detail colors on a holographic laser tape finish for ultimate flash and coloration. Other features include lifelike 3-D eyes, variegated rattle chambers and quality Mustad® hooks.

SPECIFICATIONS
Size: 2"
Weight: ³⁄₁₆ oz.
MSRP: $4.99
Colors: Bleeding Tennessee Shad, Baby Bass, Albino Shad, Chrome/Black Back, Bone Hologram, Chartreuse/Black Back/Orange Belly, Aurora, Redhead White/Black Back, Lakefork Shad, Black Shore Minnow and Frog.

BASS PRO SHOPS® XPS EXTREME TWIN PROP

The new Extreme Performance Series (XPS) Lazer Eye Twin Prop is an exciting lure that causes a lot of commotion on the surface water, but its unique deep-bodied profile acts like a keel to keep it from rolling on a quick "walking" retrieve.

SPECIFICATIONS
Size: 4½"
Weight: ½ oz.
MSRP: $4.99
Colors: Bleeding Tennessee Shad, Firetiger, Gold/Black Back, Albino Shad, Chrome/Black Back, Aurora, Frog and Watermelon.

TOPWATER HARD BAITS

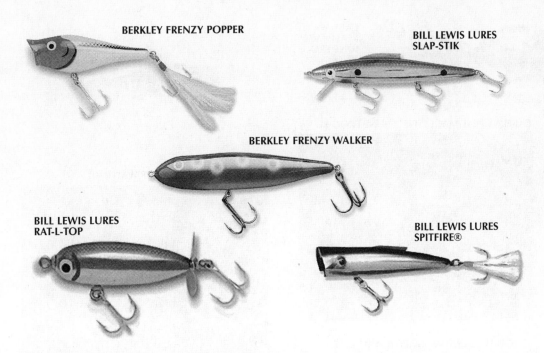

BERKLEY FRENZY POPPER

BILL LEWIS LURES SLAP-STIK

BERKLEY FRENZY WALKER

BILL LEWIS LURES RAT-L-TOP

BILL LEWIS LURES SPITFIRE®

BERKLEY FRENZY POPPER

The Popper's unique balanced design allows it to be fished two ways. Snap and pop it, and it splits water like a big fish chasing a little one. Slow it down with soft jerking action, and it walks with the best of 'em. This makes it the perfect bait for drawing big bass out from under docks and vegetation. Pop it hard or walk it slow - bass can't resist it!

SPECIFICATIONS
Size: 2¾"
MSRP: $7.29
Colors: Bullfrog, Grey Ghost, Purple Ghost, Rainbow Trout, Threadfin Shad

BERKLEY FRENZY WALKER

Cast this big, slow-moving bait long and it'll draw fish from up to twenty feet away. The slow, lazy action resembles a big frog sloshing through the water and stimulates big fish to feed. Its specially designed balance system makes this bait easy to walk with very little effort from the angler. Also offers incredible casting distance. Great for fishing in deep water off rocky bluffs or off the shady side of a dock.

SPECIFICATIONS
Size: 4"
MSRP: $6.99
Colors: Clown, Fire Tiger, Bullfrog, Grey Ghost, Rainbow Trout, Threadfin Shad

BILL LEWIS LURES RAT-L-TOP

The improved Rat-L-Top is about 10% bigger than the old model. We also used stronger split rings and larger, beefier hooks. We reshaped the lure, giving it a more stealth-like design. It's sleeker and holds in the water extremely well for better action than other lures of its kind. Sonic weld technology gives the Rat-L-Top additional strength and a seamless outer finish. Most important, the Rat-L-Top comes with lightweight rattles, giving it that famous fish-calling sound.

SPECIFICATIONS
Model: TP
Weight: ¼ oz.
MSRP: $3.79
Colors: Fire Tiger, Smokey Joe, Chrome Black Back, Chrome Blue Back, Lake Fork Special, Gold Orange Belly, Tennessee Shad, Clear, Frog, Black Minnow

BILL LEWIS LURES SLAP-STIK

The Slap-Stik sits upright at water level because of its shifted tail weight. Sound chambers contain "Rattlers" which produce an irresistible vibrating, chattering noise. The Slap-Stik combines the actions of a minnow and jerk bait for incredible results.

SPECIFICATIONS
Model: SS (Slap-Stik)
Weight: ⅜ oz.
MSRP: $3.89

Model: MSS (Magnum Slap-Stik)
Weight: ⅝ oz.
MSRP: $3.89
Colors: Red Head White, Fire Tiger, Chrome Blue Back, Chrome Black Back, Chrome Chartreuse, Chrome Hot Pink, Gold Orange Belly, Gold Chartreuse, Gold Tennessee Shad, Gold Mullet, Chartreuse Shiner

BILL LEWIS LURES SPITFIRE®

With its unique bucket-mouth, the SpitFire actually splashes and sprays water in front of the lure as you work it along the surface. You can control the amount of spray with your rod tip and speed of retrieve.

SPECIFICATIONS
Model: SF
Weight: ⅜ oz.
MSRP: $4.29
Colors: Smokey Joe, Redhead White, Bone Orange Belly, Chrome Chartreuse, Chrome Blue Back, Chrome Pink, Gold Orange Belly, Gold Mullet, Chartreuse Shiner, Diamond Dust, Classic Baby Bass, Fire Tiger

LURES

TOPWATER HARD BAITS

CABELA'S REALIMAGE JUNE FROG

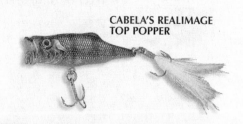

CABELA'S REALIMAGE TOP POPPER

CABELA'S REALIMAGE 7-PIECE JUNE FROG KIT

CABELA'S REALIMAGE TOP WATER KIT

CABELA'S REALIMAGE PENCIL WALKER

CABELA'S REALIMAGE JUNE FROG

Few bass can pass up these realistic topwater baits. Cast one of these light-weight baits near lily pads, and brace yourself for a belt. The RealImage™ June Frog™ resembles and behaves like a frog scooting across the water surface when you rip your line. The feathers over the rear hooks provide stability in the water, and the dual VMC needle, cone-cut hooks won't let a big fish get away.

SPECIFICATIONS
Size: 1¾"
Weight: ⅛ oz.
MSRP: $3.99
Colors: Frog, Shad, Firetiger, Blue Pearl, Clear, Yellow Frog

CABELA'S REALIMAGE 7-PIECE JUNE FROG KIT

There's nothing quite like the sight of a bass exploding on an unsuspecting frog. The lipped body of this frog-like lure sputters and splashes just like a kicking frog. Just toss one into the water, give it a twitch or two and hold on tight.

SPECIFICATIONS
Kit includes one each of the follow-ing RealImage June Frog colors:
Blue Pearl, Frog, Clear, Firetiger, Shad, Yellow Frog. All come packaged in a handy utility tackle box.
MSRP: $18.99

CABELA'S REALIMAGE PENCIL WALKER

Combine walkin'-the-dog motion with the realistic flash and luster of the patented RealImage finish and you've got a top-water bait that's guaranteed to trip the trigger of any hungry fish. VMC needle cone-cut hooks.

SPECIFICATIONS
Sizes/Weights: 2¾", ³⁄₁₆ oz.; 3½", ¼ oz.
MSRP: $3.99
Colors: Frog, Shad, Golden Shiner, Clear, Baby Bass

CABELA'S REALIMAGE TOP POPPER

The Top Popper delivers all the popping and chugging action of baits costing twice as much. With its RealImage finish, this bait will be your go-to weapon anytime the top-water action is hot. VMC needle cone-cut hooks give them the bite to land more fish.

SPECIFICATIONS
Sizes/Weights: 2⅜", ¼ oz.; 3", ⅜ oz.
MSRP: $3.99
Colors: Perch, Pearl, Clear, Baby Bass, Sunfish

CABELA'S REALIMAGE TOP WATER KIT

When the topwater bite is on, you'll be armed with the right weapons when you have this assortment on board. Just pick your weapon and start casting. Be ready, because bass can't resist the action and flash of RealImage baits.

SPECIFICATIONS
Kit includes: three 2⅜" Top Poppers in Baby Bass, Perch and Pearl, three Pencil Walkers (one 2¾" Golden Shiner, one 3½" Frog and one 3½" Shad) and a rugged plastic utility box to keep it all organized.
MSRP: $21.99

TOPWATER HARD BAITS

COTTON CORDELL
BOY HOWDY® C41

CREEK CHUB® DARTER IF2000P

COTTON CORDELL
CRAZY SHAD™
C04

CREEK CHUB KNUCKLE-HEAD™ I6600JP

COTTON CORDELL PENCIL POPPER™ C67

CULTIVA GOBO POPPER GP60

COTTON CORDELL BOY HOWDY®

The long, slender profile of the Boy Howdy draws strikes from all game species. Spinning blades at the front and rear suggests an injured and easily consumed baitfish.

SPECIFICATIONS
Model: C41
Size: 4½"
Weight: ⅜ oz.
Hook Size: #6
MSRP: $3.99
Colors: Gold/Black, Chrome/Black, Chrome, Chrome/Blue, Smoky Joe, Clear/Blue Nose, Frog, Bone/Orange .

COTTON CORDELL CRAZY SHAD™

The spinning blades chop the surface, simulating a baitfish in distress. This lure is easily cast on spinning or baitcasting equipment.

SPECIFICATIONS
Model: C04
Size: 3"
Weight: ⅜ oz.
Hook Size: #4
MSRP: $3.99
Colors: Gold/Black, Chrome/Black, Chrome, Chrome/Blue, Smoky Joe, Clear/Blue Nose, Frog, Bone/Orange

COTTON CORDELL PENCIL POPPER™

The Pencil Popper is equipped with super-strong rust-resistant hooks. Added weight in the tail of these lures allows for long casts and the lure's famous bobbing-and-weaving topwater action.

SPECIFICATIONS
Model: C67
Size: 7"
Weight: 2 oz.
Hook Size: 3/0
MSRP: $4.79

Model: C66
Size: 6"
Weight: 1 oz.
Hook Size: 1/0
MSRP: $4.79
Colors: Chrome/Black, Pearl/Red, Chrome/Blue, Pearl/Blue, Mackerel, Rainbow Trout

CREEK CHUB® DARTER

The efficient, high-floating Darter was first introduced in 1920. It is known for its long, accurate casts and multi-species capabilities in both fresh and saltwater.

SPECIFICATIONS
Model: IF2000P
Size: 3¾"
Weight: ½ oz.
Hook size: #2
MSRP: $5.99
Colors: Black/Red Eye, Yellow Striper, Silver Flash, Frog, Pike, Red/White

CREEK CHUB KNUCKLE-HEAD™

This unique jointed topwater popper is designed with the big-fish angler in mind. Featuring super-strong saltwater hooks, the Knuckle-Head™ is a floating lure that casts super-long distances. Creek Chub's® patent-pending "Hold-Tite™" link holds the head of the lure to the body and gives the lure its "injured gill" look.

SPECIFICATIONS
Model: I6600JP
Size: 5"
Weight: 1½ oz.
Hook Size: 1/0
MSRP: $9.99
Colors: Chrome/Blue Back, Red/White, Parrot, Yellow Croaker, Chrome/Black Back, Baby Striper, Black/Red Eye, Mackerel

CULTIVA GOBO POPPER

Great topwater action, accented by feathered trailing treble hook. Pops, spits and chugs when retrieved. "Living Eyes," rattling moving weight system, foil finish and rigged with two Owner Stinger-31 Cutting Point™ trebles.

SPECIFICATIONS
Model: GP60
Size: 2⅜ inches
Weight: ⅕ ounce
MSRP: $12.00
Colors: (02) Black Pearl, (06) Shiner, (13) Baby Bass, (34) Green/Chartreuse, (49) Smoke, (51) Golden Bass

LURES

TOPWATER HARD BAITS

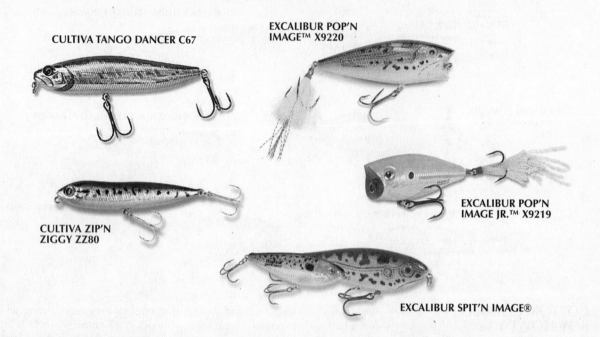

CULTIVA TANGO DANCER C67

EXCALIBUR POP'N IMAGE™ X9220

CULTIVA ZIP'N ZIGGY ZZ80

EXCALIBUR POP'N IMAGE JR.™ X9219

EXCALIBUR SPIT'N IMAGE®

CULTIVA TANGO DANCER

A thick-bodied, topwater bait that walks, dances and darts enticingly at the surface, even in hard-to-fish windy and rough-water conditions. Features include Cultiva's exclusive "Living Eyes," resonating "thunder" rattles and highly reflective textured, holographic and foil finishes. Each lure is rigged with two #2 Owner ST-41 Cutting Point treble hooks.

SPECIFICATIONS
Model: TD115
Size: 4⅝ inches
Weight: ⅞-ounce
MSRP: $12.00
Colors: (01) Gold Shad, (02) Black Pearl, (06) Shiner, (13) Baby Bass, (15) Blue Back, (27) Rainbow Trout

CULTIVA ZIP'N ZIGGY

Skips, slides, darts and walks as slightly arched body maximizes topwater action. Features reflective foil finish, and rigged with two Owner ST-31 Cutting Point™ treble hooks.

SPECIFICATIONS
Model: ZZ80
Size: 3⅕ inches
Weight: ⅓-ounce
MSRP: $12.00
Colors: (01) Gold Shad, (02) Black Pearl, (06) Shiner, (11) Brown Trout, (12) Ivory Chartreuse, (13) Baby Bass, (47) Natural Minnow

EXCALIBUR POP'N IMAGE™

Designed for castability, easy walk-the-dog action and a "pop" that's unmatched, the Pop'n Image features Excalibur's® realistic finish, fish-like eyes and Excalibur® Rotating Treble Hooks.

SPECIFICATIONS
Model: X9220
Size: 3"
Weight: ⅝ oz.
Hook Size: #4
MSRP: $4.99
Colors: Red Ear Sunfish, Gizzard Shad, Baby Bass, Threadfin Shad, Bull Frog, Tennessee Shad

EXCALIBUR POP'N IMAGE JR.™

The Pop'n Image's™ unique design gives anglers the ability to walk-the-dog or "pop" with the same topwater bait. Now the versatile lure is available in a smaller version – the Pop'n Image Jr.™ The Junior features the same realistic finish, fish-like eyes and Excalibur® Dressed Rotating Hooks and a fish attracting rattle.

SPECIFICATIONS
Model: X9219
Size: 2⅜"
Weight: ⁵⁄₁₆ oz.
Hook Size: #6
MSRP: $4.99
Colors: Red Ear Sunfish, Citrus Shad, Baby Bass, Threadfin Shad, Bull Frog, Tennessee Shad

EXCALIBUR SPIT'N IMAGE®

The original Spit'n Image® set the world on fire in 1997. It's the "spit'n" image of a fleeing shad. The Spit'n Image® has a unique walking action. When retrieved, it will move from side to side; when sitting still, the bottom sits down in the water. The Spit'n Image®, Jr. is a little more rounded and has more "bounce" than the original Spit'n Image®.

SPECIFICATIONS
Model: X9270 (Spit'n Image®)
Size: 3¼"
Weight: ⁷⁄₁₆ oz.
Hook Size: #4
MSRP: $4.99

Model: X9250 (Spit'n Image®, Jr.)
Size: 3"
Weight: ⁵⁄₁₆ oz.
Hook Size: #6
MSRP: $4.99
Colors: Baby Bass, Bull Frog, Gizzard Shad, Hickory Shad, Threadfin Shad, Tennessee Shad, Citrus Shad, Punkinseed

TOPWATER HARD BAITS

EXCALIBUR SUPER SPOOK

HEDDON CRAZY CRAWLER® X9120

HEDDON DYING FLUTTER™ X9205

GREEN DRAGON'S "SP"CHUGGER™

HEDDON CRAZY CRAWLER® X0320

HEDDON LUCKY 13 X2500

EXCALIBUR SUPER SPOOK®

The Super Spook® and Super Spook, Jr.® feature the most advanced decoration application on the market today. Realistic scale patterns, highly reflective finishes and three dimensional eyes combine to produce an amazingly life-like flash. Every Super Spook® is equipped with a super strong body structure.

SPECIFICATIONS
Model: X9256 (Super Spook®)
Size: 5"
Weight: ⅞ oz.
Hook Size: #4
MSRP: $4.99

Model: X9236 (Super Spook, Jr.®)
Size: 3½"
Weight: ½ oz.
Hook Size: #6
MSRP: $4.99
Colors: Florida Bass, Okie Shad, Lake Fork Shad, Bleeding Shad

GREEN DRAGON'S "SP"CHUGGER™

The engineers at Green Dragon Lures have created the "SP" (Spring Powered) Chugger. This lure features a computer-designed, jointed body, with ultra-sharp EWG hooks, 100# braided Spectra line, ultralite skirt and 14" stainless-steel spring. Upon entering the water, the lure begins its lifelike struggling action, while emitting a loud clicking sound that calls fish to the surface. The lure can be

continuously reactivated from even the most distant casting range with a simple popping or chugging retrieve, producing up to five seconds of audible clicking and body-shaking action.

SPECIFICATIONS
Colors: Golden Tiger, Blue Shad, Frog, Baby Bass, Aqua Tiger, Yellow Coachdog, White Coachdog, Rainbow, Classic Bullfrog, Night Glow, Chartreuse
MSRP: $9.99

HEDDON CRAZY CRAWLER®

The Crazy Crawler's wings create a wild, crawling, water-throwing action. It's an excellent choice for bass any time the top water bite is on, but is especially effective at night.

SPECIFICATIONS
Model: X9120 (Crazy Crawler)
Size: 2⅜"
Weight: ⅝ oz.
Hook Size: #2
MSRP: $5.39

Model: X0320 (Tiny Crazy Crawler)
Size: 1¾"
Weight: ¼ oz.
Hook Size: #6
MSRP: $4.99
Colors: Glo Black Frog, Bullfrog, Black Hornet, Fluorescent Green Crawdad, Red Shore Minnow, Yellow Hornet

HEDDON DYING FLUTTER™

The Dying Flutter has a long, slender body with dual propellers that create a loud, whirring sound and a commotion that stimulates even non-feeding gamefish into a strike.

SPECIFICATIONS
Model: X9205
Size: 3¾"
Weight: ⅜ oz.
Hook Size: #4
MSRP: $3.99
Colors: Brown Crawdad, Baby Bass, Bullfrog, Fluorescent Green Crawdad, Black, Coach Dog

HEDDON LUCKY 13

The Lucky 13 has likely caught as many or more fish than any other artificial lure in history. Since its creation in 1920, the Lucky 13's unique action has drawn topwater strikes from many generations of anglers. Available in six new colors, a new generation now can discover the lure that has turned more anglers into lucky anglers.

SPECIFICATIONS
Model: X2500
Size: 3¾"
Weight: ⅝ oz.
Hook Size: #2
MSRP: $4.59
Colors: Black Shiner, Nickel Rainbow Shiner, Baby Bass, Bullfrog, Red Head, Fluorescent Green Crawdad

LURES

TOPWATER HARD BAITS

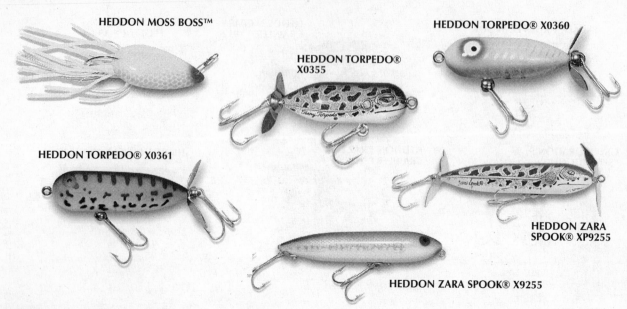

HEDDON MOSS BOSS™

HEDDON TORPEDO® X0355

HEDDON TORPEDO® X0360

HEDDON TORPEDO® X0361

HEDDON ZARA SPOOK® XP9255

HEDDON ZARA SPOOK® X9255

HEDDON MOSS BOSS™

The Heddon Moss Boss is a weedless lure designed to glide easily over all types of matted vegetation.

SPECIFICATIONS
Model: X0515
Size: 3"
Weight: ⅜ oz.
Hook Size: 6/0
MSRP: $3.59

Model: X0510
Size: 2½"
Weight: 1/4 oz.
Hook Size: 4/0
MSRP: $3.59
Colors: Black Shad, Bull Frog, Chartreuse Scaled, White Scaled

HEDDON TORPEDO®

The Torpedo's aerodynamic shape, along with its balance and weight, allow anglers to cast them like a bullet. The Torpedos create a wild splashing surface disturbance.

SPECIFICATONS
Model: X0361 (Baby Torpedo)
Size: 2½"
Weight: ⅜ oz.
Hook Size: #4
MSRP: $3.99
Colors: Brown Crawdad, Bullfrog, Flourescent Green Crawdad, Clear, Red Head, Shad, Baby Bass, Perch, Natural Leopard Frog, Natural Perch, Yellow Shore Minnow, Red Shore Minnow, Black Shiner, Blue Shiner, Nickel Plate, Silver Shore Minnow,

Black Shore Minnow.
"G" Finish: Gold Bass, Pearl/Red Eye, Shad, Blue Shad.

Model: X0360 (Tiny Torpedo)
Size: 1⅞"
Weight: ¼ oz.
Hook Size: #6
MSRP: $3.99
Colors: Brown Crawdad, Bullfrog, Flourescent Green Crawdad, Clear, Red Head, Shad, Baby Bass, Perch, Natural Leopard Frog, Natural Perch, Yellow Shore Minnow, Red Shore Minnow, Black Shiner, Blue Shiner, Nickel Plate, Silver Shore Minnow, Black Shore Minnow.
"G" Finish: Gold Bass, Pearl/Red Eye, Shad, Blue Shad. G-Fleck: G-Fleck Rainbow, G-Fleck Blue Shore Minnow

Model: X0355 (Teeny Torpedo)
Size: 1½"
Weight: ⅛ oz.
Hook Size: #10
MSRP: $3.99
Colors: Baby Bass, Bull Frog, Brown Crawdad, Fluorescent Green Crawdad, Black Shiner, Natural Leopard Frog, Blue Shiner, Black Shore Minnow.
"G" Finish: Blue Shad, Shad.

HEDDON ZARA SPOOK®

Generations of anglers have called the Heddon Zara Spook their "secret" lure – one they can count on when the fishing gets tough. The Zara

Spook's legendary "walk-the-dog" action has been written about more than any other fishing lure. The Zara Spook's topwater fishing action prompts rod-jarring strikes in the spring and calls the lunkers up from the depths in the summer.

SPECIFICATIONS
Model: XP9255 (Wounded Zara Spook)
Size: 4½"
Weight: ¾ oz.
Hook Size: 1/0
MSRP: $4.49
Colors: Baby Bass, Bullfrog, Natural Leopard Frog, Clear, Fluorescent Green Crawdad, Black Shiner, Red Head, Flitter Shad, Blue Shore Minnow, Black Shore Minnow

Model: X9255 (Zara Spook)
Size: 4½"
Weight: ¾ oz.
Hook Size: 1/0
MSRP: $4.19
Colors: Baby Bass, Bullfrog, Natural Leopard Frog, Clear, Fluorescent Green Crawdad, Black Shiner, Red Head, Flitter Shad, Blue Shore Minnow, Black Shore Minnow, Bone, Nickel Plate, Nickel Rainbow Shiner, Yellow Shore Minnow, Flash Shad, Flash Bass, Natural Perch, Silver Shore Minnow.
"G" Finish: Gold Bass, Shad, Blue Shad, Pearl/Red Eye, G-Fleck Rainbow, G-Fleck Blue Shore Minnow

LURES

TOPWATER HARD BAITS

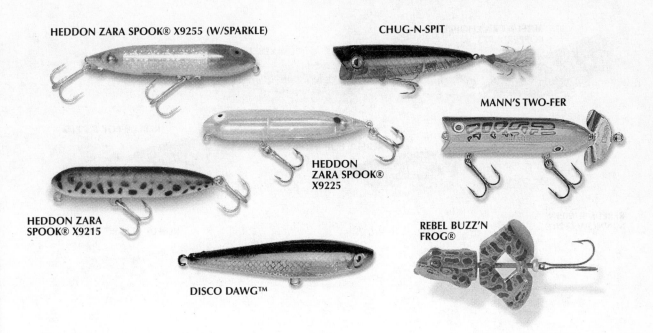

HEDDON ZARA SPOOK® X9255 (W/SPARKLE)

CHUG-N-SPIT

MANN'S TWO-FER

HEDDON ZARA SPOOK® X9225

HEDDON ZARA SPOOK® X9215

REBEL BUZZ'N FROG®

DISCO DAWG™

**Model: X9255
(Sparkle Zara Spook)**
Size: 4½"
Weight: ¾ oz.
Hook Size: 1/0
MSRP: $4.19
Colors: Silver/Black/White,
Silver/Blue/White, Gold/Green/White,
Gold/Black/Orange, Gold/Chartreuse/
Chartreuse, Silver/Red Head/White

Model: X9225 (Zara Puppy)
Size: 3"
Weight: ⅛ oz.
Hook Size: #6
MSRP: $4.19
Colors: Baby Bass, Bullfrog, Natural
Leopard Frog, Clear, Fluorescent Green
Crawdad, Black Shiner, Red Head,
Flitter Shad, Blue Shore Minnow, Black
Shore Minnow, Bone, Nickel Plate,
Nickel Rainbow Shiner, Yellow Shore
Minnow, Flash Shad, Flash Bass,
Natural Perch, Silver Shore Minnow.
"G" Finish: Gold Bass, Shad, Blue
Shad, Pearl/Red Eye, G-Fleck
Rainbow, G-Fleck Blue Shore Minnow

Model: X9215 (Zara Pooch)
Size: 2"
Weight: ⅛ oz.
Hook Size: #10
MSRP: $3.99
Colors: Baby Bass, Bullfrog, Clear,
Fluorescent Green Crawdad, Black

Shiner, Flitter Shad, Blue Shore
Minnow, Red Head

MANN'S DISCO DAWG™
The Disco Dawg is a true "walk-the-
dog"-style lure with a subtle surface
splash. It comes in new fish-catching
colors, all with holographic paint
finishes.
SPECIFICATIONS
Length: 3½"
Weight: ⅜ oz.
MSRP: $6.14
Colors: Parakeet Holographic,
Splatterback Shad Holographic,
Pearl/Black Back, Holographic,
Baby Bass Holographic, Gold/Black
Back Holographic, Grey Ghost
Holographic, Albino Shad
Holographic, Clown Holographic,
Pearl/Blue Back Holographic

MANN'S LOUDMOUTH CHUG-N-SPIT
It walks, it talks, and it spits. Deep
mouth throws water forward while
the head hole squirts water upward.
Loudmouth technology adds noisy
rattles, and special weighing lets you
walk-the-dog.
SPECIFICATIONS
Weight: ⅜ oz.
Length: 3½"
MSRP: $5.56
Colors: Yellow Perch, Chrome/Black

Back, Chrome/Blue Back, Tennessee
Shad, Frog, Pearl/Black Back, Baby Bass

MANN'S TWO-FER
Versatile and economical design
provides TWO topwater lures for the
price of one. Alabama cattleman Kenny
Childree designed this unique bait that
catches fish and saves money.
SPECIFICATIONS
Weight: ⅜ oz.
Length: 3½"
MSRP: $3.07
Colors: Frog, Chartreuse/Blue,
Chrome/Blue, Gold/Black,
Black/Silver Rib, Tennessee Shad

REBEL® BUZZ'N FROG®
The Buzz'n Frog® is a buzz bait in
disguise. The only difference is that
when you stop the retrieve, this lure
floats head up just like a frog.
The free-spinning rear legs churn the
water's surface and the semi-weedless
rear hooks easily slip through heavy
grass, weeds and moss.
SPECIFICATIONS
Model: T4
Size: 2½"
Weight: ½ oz.
Hook Size: 1/0
MSRP: $3.99
Colors: Green Bull Frog, Northern
Leopard Frog, Swamp Frog, Southern
Leopard Frog

TOPWATER HARD BAITS

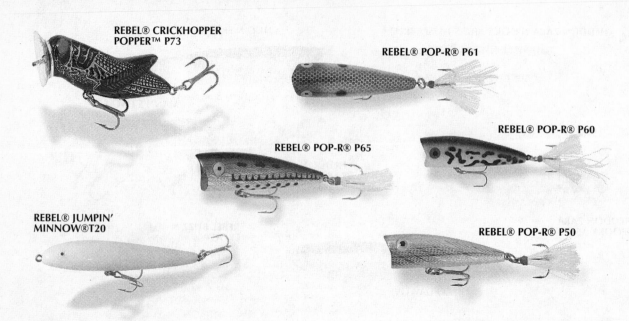

REBEL® CRICKHOPPER POPPER™ P73

REBEL® POP-R® P61

REBEL® POP-R® P65

REBEL® POP-R® P60

REBEL® JUMPIN' MINNOW® T20

REBEL® POP-R® P50

REBEL® CRICKHOPPER POPPER™

You've fished with real grasshoppers, now fish with this: the Rebel® Crickhopper Popper™. It's the first "popping" critter of its kind. This realistic ultralight will cause such a commotion that you'll catch fish all day long. Twitch it to make it "pop" across the water.

SPECIFICATIONS
Model: P73
Size: 1¾"
Weight: ³⁄₁₆ oz.
Hook Size: #10
MSRP: $3.99
Colors: Fire Tiger, Gold Pearl/Black Back, Yellow/Black Back, Chrome/Black Back, Chrome/Blue Back, Green/Chartreuse/Black Back, Black

REBEL® JUMPIN' MINNOW®

The Jumpin' Minnow® might be the easiest-to-use stick bait ever made. Its perfectly-balanced body makes it easy even for the beginner to create the lunker-enticing "walk-the-dog" action. This lure also features a single, super-

loud rattle to call up the big ones.

SPECIFICATIONS
Model: T20
Size: 4½"
Weight: ½ oz.
Hook Size: #2
MSRP: $3.99
Colors: Silver Black, Bone, Silver Blue, Copper/Orange/Orange, Copper/Black/Orange

REBEL® POP-R®

Often copied, but never duplicated, the Rebel® Pop-R® remains the standard by which all other topwater poppers are judged. Don't be fooled by the imitations. These are the original Pop-Rs®.

SPECIFICATIONS
Model: P65 (Magnum Pop-R®)
Size: 3"
Weight: ½ oz.
Hook Size: #4
MSRP: $3.99
Colors: Bone, Silver/Black, Olé Bass, Tennessee Shad, Clear, Fire Tiger, G-Fleck Rainbow. G-Finish: Purple Shad, Green Perch, Red Eye Perch, Silver Shad

Model: P61 (Pop-R® Plus)
Size: 2½"
Weight: ¼ oz.
Hook Size: #6
MSRP: $3.99
Colors (G-Finish): Purple Shad, Green Perch, Red Eye Perch, Silver Shad

Model: P60 (Pop-R®)
Size: 2½"
Weight: ¼ oz.
Hook Size: #6
MSRP: $3.99
Colors: Bone, Silver/Black, Olé Bass, Tennessee Shad, Clear, Fire Tiger, Bubble Gum, Silver/Black, Green Shiner, Silver/Blue, G-Fleck Rainbow

Model: P50 (Small Pop-R®)
Size: 2"
Weight: ⅛ oz.
Hook Size: #8
MSRP: $3.99
Colors: Bone, Silver/Black, Olé Bass, Tennessee Shad, Clear, Fire Tiger, G-Fleck Rainbow

LURES

Lighten Up on Line
Heavy line is OK when using a straight steady retrieve, but if you're working with short twitches and sputters, topwater lures baits will perform better if you use relatively light line.

SMITHWICK DEVIL'S HORSE® AF100

THORNWOOD LURES BIRD

SMITHWICK DEVIL'S HORSE®AF200

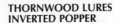

THORNWOOD LURES INVERTED POPPER

STRIKE KING®
SPIT-N-KING™ SNKP

SMITHWICK DEVIL'S HORSE®

The Devil's Horse® is a classic, prop-equipped, hand-crafted wood lure. The unique buoyancy of wood, combined with two carefully balanced, surface-churning propellers, duplicates the unique commotion of a fleeing shad to produce rod-busting strikes from surface-feeding fish.

SPECIFICATIONS
Model: AF100
Size: 4½"
Weight: ⅜ oz.
Hook Size: #6
MSRP: $4.29

Model: AF200
Size: 4½"
Weight: ½ oz.
Hook Size: #4
MSRP: $4.29
Colors: Yellow & Black Striper, Tiger Roan, Perch, White/Black Stripes, Silver Shiner, Frog, Chrome/Black Back, Chrome/Black Back, Orange Belly, Chrome/Blue Back, Chrome/Blue Back/Orange Belly, Black Back/Dark Green Scale, Bass /Orange Belly

STRIKE KING® SPIT-N-KING™

New-style face design is horizontally-oriented and cut to maximize the 'spit' and 'spray' during retrieve. It comes in premier holographic colors, has lifelike 3-D eyes, premium tinsel tail hook and internal free-floating rattles.

SPECIFICATIONS
Model: SNKP
Weight: ⅜ oz.
Size: 2½ in.
MSRP: $3.99
Colors: Blue Chartreuse, Gold Shiner, Gizzard Shiner, Tennessee Shad, Blue Shad, Watermelon Shad, Arkansas Shiner, Neon Shad, Baby Bass, Gray Ghost

THORNWOOD LURES BIRD AND BABY BIRD

Red Wing Blackbird, Blackbird, Chickadee, Northern Cardinal, House Sparrow, Song Sparrow, White Throated Sparrow, American Robin, Eastern Meadowlark, Rose Breasted Grosbeak, Goldfinch, Bluebird, Blue Jay, Baltimore Oriole, Grackle, Starling

SPECIFICATIONS
Length: 3½" (Bird); 2½" (Baby Bird)
Weight: 0.75 oz. (Bird); 0.5 oz. (Baby Bird) (Weight and length will vary slightly by species; above represents an average.)
MSRP: $12.00 to $16.00

THORNWOOD LURES INVERTED POPPER

Features:
• Inverted posture floats belly up, eyes down for injured, distressed appearance
• Hand-carved, all wood, white cedar or basswood body for unmatched, responsive action
• Deep, concave mouth for additional popping and spitting
• Longer body promotes "side to side" walking
• "Deep cut" bleeding gills (non-bleeding optional)
• Rich, vibrant colors for contrast and realism
• All premium Owner™ hooks
• Hard, enduring exterior shell doubles as fishes' natural slime coat
• 3D holographic eyes

SPECIFICATIONS
Length: 3 inches
Weight: 0.390 oz.
MSRP: $16.00
Colors: Black/White, Black/Silver, Black/Gold, All Black, Blue/White, Blue/Silver, Green/White, Green/Silver, Green/Gold, Perch, Yellow/White, Clown, Purple/White, Purple/Yellow/White, All Gold, All Silver, All White, White With Colored Scales, Gray/White, Crawdad Green, Crawdad Yellow, Arkansas Shiner, Leather/Bone, All Bone, Red/White

TOPWATER HARD BAITS

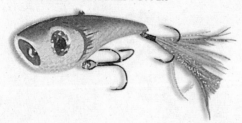

THORNWOOD LURES POPPER

THORNWOOD LURES PROP BAIT

THORNWOOD LURES POPPERS

Features:

- Hand-carved, all wood, white cedar or basswood body for unmatched, responsive action
- Deep, concave mouth for additional popping and spitting
- Longer body promotes "side to side" walking
- "Deep cut" bleeding gills (non-bleeding optional)
- Rich, vibrant colors for contrast and realism
- All premium Owner™ hooks
- Hard, enduring exterior shell doubles as fishes' natural slime coat
- 3D holographic eyes

SPECIFICATIONS
Model: Large Popper
Length: 4½"
Weight: 0.725 oz.
MSRP: $16.00

Model: Medium Popper
Length: 3¼"
Weight: 0.42 oz.
MSRP: $16.00

Model: Small Popper
Length: 2½"
Weight: 0.295 oz.
MSRP: $16.00
Colors: Black/White, Black/Silver, Black/Gold, All Black, Blue/White, Blue/Silver, Green/White, Green/Silver, Green/Gold, Perch, Yellow/

White, Clown, Purple/White, Purple/Yellow/White, All Gold, All Silver, All White, White With Colored Scales, Gray/White, Crawdad Green, Crawdad Yellow, Arkansas Shiner, Leather/Bone, All Bone, Red/White

THORNWOOD LURES PROP BAIT

Features:

- Realistic, life size profile and contour replicate real live bait fish
- Hand-carved, all wood, white cedar or basswood body for unmatched, responsive action
- Longer body promotes "side to side" walking
- "Deep cut" bleeding gills (non-bleeding optional)
- Rich, vibrant colors for contrast and realism
- All premium owner™ hooks
- Hard, enduring exterior shell doubles as fishes' natural slime coat
- 3D holographic eyes

SPECIFICATIONS
Length: 4¼"
Weight: 0.48 oz.
MSRP: $16.00
Colors: Black/White, Black/Silver, Black/Gold, All Black, Blue/White, Blue/Silver, Green/White, Green/Silver, Green/Gold, Perch, Yellow/White, Clown, Purple/White, Purple/Yellow/White, All Gold, All Silver, All White, White With Colored Scales, Gray/White, Crawdad Green,

Crawdad Yellow, Arkansas Shiner, Leather/Bone, All Bone, Red/White

THORNWOOD LURES SIDE FLOATING PROP BAIT

Features:

- Floats on its side simulating injured or dying bait fish
- Realistic, life size profile and countour replicate real live bait fish
- Hand-carved, all wood, white cedar or basswood body for unmatched, responsive action
- Longer body promotes "side to side" walking
- "Deep cut" bleeding gills (non-bleeding optional)
- Rich, vibrant colors for contrast and realism
- All premium Owner™ hooks
- Hard, enduring exterior shell doubles as fishes' natural slime coat
- 3D holographic eyes

SPECIFICATIONS
Length: 4¼"
Weight: 0.48 oz.
MSRP: $16.00
Colors: Black/White, Black/Silver, Black/Gold, All Black, Blue/White, Blue/Silver, Green/White, Green/Silver, Green/Gold, Perch, Yellow/White, Clown, Purple/White, Purple/Yellow/White, All Gold, All Silver, All White, White With Colored Scales, Gray/White, Crawdad Green, Crawdad Yellow, Arkansas Shiner, Leather/Bone, All Bone, Red/White

LURES

TERMINAL TACKLE

TERMINAL TACKLE

DAIICHI HOOKS

 DROP SHOT'N HOOK, BLEEDING BAIT RED

 DROP SHOT'N HOOK, BLACK NICKEL

 OFFSET WORM HOOK, BLEEDING BAIT RED

 OFFSET WORM HOOK, BLACK NICKEL

 OFFSET WORM HOOK BLACK NICKEL

TERMINAL TACKLE

DROP SHOT'N HOOK, BLEEDING BAIT RED

- Special light wire for 'nose hooking' plastics.
- Bleeding bait red
- Light wire
- Wide gap
- Adds Gill Flash to nose-hooked baits

SPECIFICATIONS
Model: D25Z
Hook Size: 4
Pack Count: 12
MSRP: $5.55

Hook Size: 2
Pack Count: 10
MSRP: $5.55

Hook Size: 1
Pack Count: 9
MSRP: $5.55

Hook Size: 1/0
Pack Count: 8
MSRP: $5.55

DROP SHOT'N HOOK, BLACK NICKEL

Special light wire for "nose hooking" plastics
- Black nickel
- Light wire
- Wide gap

SPECIFICATIONS
Model: D26Z
Hook Size: 4
Pack Count: 12
MSRP: $5.55
Hook Size: 2
Pack Count: 10
MSRP: $5.55

Hook Size: 1
Pack Count: 9
MSRP: $5.55

Hook Size: 1/0
Pack Count: 8
MSRP: $5.55

OFFSET WORM HOOK, BLEEDING BAIT RED

Perfect for basic worm'n.
SPECIFICATIONS
Model: D30Z
Hook Size: 1
Pack Count: 9
MSRP: $5.55

Hook Size: 1/0
Pack Count: 8
MSRP: $5.55

Hook Size: 2/0
Pack Count: 7
MSRP: $5.55

Hook Size: 3/0
Pack Count: 6
MSRP: $5.55

Hook Size: 4/0
Pack Count: 5
MSRP: $5.55

Hook Size: 5/0
Pack Count: 4
MSRP: $5.55

OFFSET WORM HOOK, BLACK NICKEL

Perfect for basic worm'n.
SPECIFICATIONS
Model: D37Z
Hook Size: 2
Pack Count: 9
MSRP: $5.55

Hook Size: 1
Pack Count: 9
MSRP: $5.55

Hook Size: 1/0
Pack Count: 8
MSRP: $5.55

Hook Size: 2/0
Pack Count: 7
MSRP: $5.55
Hook Size: 3/0
Pack Count: 6
MSRP: $5.55

Hook Size: 4/0
Pack Count: 5
MSRP: $5.55

Hook Size: 5/0
Pack Count: 4
MSRP: $5.55

OFFSET WORM HOOK

Great for wide-bodied plastics
- Wide gap
- Forged
SPECIFICATIONS
Model: D42Z
(Black nickel)
Hook Size: 2/0
Pack Count: 6
MSRP: $5.55

Hook Size: 3/0
Pack Count: 5
MSRP: $5.55

Hook Size: 4/0
Pack Count: 4
MSRP: $5.55

Hook Size: 5/0
Pack Count: 4
MSRP: $5.55

Model: D45Z
(Bleeding Bait Red)
Hook Size: 2/0
Pack Count: 6
MSRP: $5.55

Hook Size: 3/0
Pack Count: 5
MSRP: $5.55

Hook Size: 4/0
Pack Count: 4
MSRP: $5.55

Hook Size: 5/0
Pack Count: 4
MSRP: $5.55

FATGAP™ WORM/TUBE HOOK

- Bleeding Bait Red
- Medium wire
SPECIFICATIONS
Model: D46Z
Hook Size: 1/0
Pack Count: 7
MSRP: $5.55

Hook Size: 2/0
Pack Count: 6
MSRP: $5.55

Hook Size: 3/0
Pack Count: 5
MSRP: $5.55

Hook Size: 4/0
Pack Count: 4
MSRP: $5.55

Hook Size: 5/0
Pack Count: 3
MSRP: $5.55

CATCH AND RELEASE WACKY™ HOOK

Don t set the hook. Just lift the rod slowly and this hook will find home.
- Bleeding Bait Red
- Forged
- Kirbed

OFFSET WORM HOOK BLEEDING BAIT RED

FATGAP™ WORM/TUBE HOOK

CATCH AND RELEASE WACKY™ HOOK

ROUND BEND WORM HOOK

COPPERHEAD™ TWITCHBAIT/ TUBE HOOK BLACK

COPPERHEAD™ TWITCHBAIT/ TUBE HOOK BLEEDING BAIT RED

DEATH TRAP™ TREBLE HOOKS BLACK NICKEL

DEATH TRAP™ TREBLE HOOKS BLEEDING BAIT RED

SPECIFICATIONS
Model: D48Z
Hook Size: 2/0
Pack Count: 6
MSRP: $5.55

Hook Size: 3/0
Pack Count: 5
MSRP: $5.55

ROUND BEND WORM HOOK

The round bend eliminates plastic "ball ups"
- 2 slices
- Black

SPECIFICATIONS
Model: D50Z
Hook Size: 2
Pack Count: 12
MSRP: $5.55

Hook Size: 1
Pack Count: 11
MSRP: $5.55

Hook Size: 1/0
Pack Count: 10
MSRP: $5.55

Hook Size: 2/0
Pack Count: 9
MSRP: $5.55

Hook Size: 3/0
Pack Count: 8
MSRP: $5.55

Hook Size: 4/0
Pack Count: 7
MSRP: $5.55

Hook Size: 5/0
Pack Count: 6
MSRP: $5.55

COPPERHEAD™ TWITCHBAIT/TUBE HOOK

The special bend at the front of the hook allows more hook to penetrate
- 60-degree jig eye
- Hitchhiker lure holder

SPECIFICATIONS
Model: D61Z (Black)
Hook Size: 2/0
Pack Count: 6
MSRP: $5.55

Hook Size: 3/0
Pack Count: 5
MSRP: $5.55

Hook Size: 4/0
Pack Count: 5
MSRP: $5.55

Hook Size: 5/0
Pack Count: 4
MSRP: $5.55

Model: D65Z (Bleeding Bait Red)
Hook Size: 2/0

Pack Count: 5
MSRP: $5.55

Hook Size: 3/0
Pack Count: 5
MSRP: $5.55

Hook Size: 4/0
Pack Count: 4
MSRP: $5.55

Hook Size: 5/0
Pack Count: 4
MSRP: $5.55

DEATH TRAP™ TREBLE HOOKS

Extra light wire allows you to increase hook sizes on most lures
- Round bend
- Extreme welds

SPECIFICATIONS
Model: D93Q (Black nickel)
Hook Size: 8
Pack Count: 4
MSRP: $5.55

Hook Size: 6
Pack Count: 4
MSRP: $5.55

Hook Size: 4
Pack Count: 4
MSRP: $5.55

Hook Size: 2
Pack Count: 4
MSRP: $5.55

Hook Size: 1
Pack Count: 3
MSRP: $5.55

Hook Size: 1/0
Pack Count: 3
MSRP: $5.55

Model: D99Q (Bleeding Bait Red)
Hook Size: 8
Pack Count: 5
MSRP: $5.55

Hook Size: 6
Pack Count: 5
MSRP: $5.55

Hook Size: 4
Pack Count: 5
MSRP: $5.55

Hook Size: 2
Pack Count: 4
MSRP: $5.55

EAGLE CLAW® HOOKS

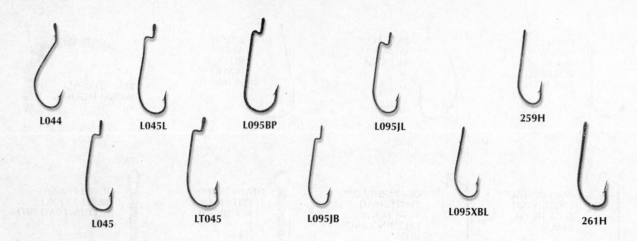

L044 L045L L095BP L095JL 259H

L045 LT045 L095JB L095XBL 261H

L044 MESSLER® AUTOMATIC ROTATING WORM HOOKS
SPECIFICATIONS
- Lazer Sharp® bronze
- Offset ringed eye

Sizes: 2, 1, 1/0, 2/0, 3/0, 4/0
MSRP: $2.25-$2.37 per vinyl bag of 8 or 10 hooks (8 hooks for "0" sizes), $5.63-$8.80 per box of 50 hooks

L045 AUTOMATIC ROTATING WORM HOOKS
SPECIFICATIONS
- Lazer Sharp® bronze
- Kinked shank
- Offset ringed eye
- Z-bend

Sizes: 1, 1/0, 2/0, 3/0, 4/0
MSRP: $2.37 per vinyl bag of 8 or 10 hooks (8 hooks for "0" sizes), $6.53-$8.80 per box of 50 hooks

L045L AUTOMATIC ROTATING WORM HOOKS
SPECIFICATIONS
- Lazer Sharp® light wire bronze
- Kinked shank
- Offset ringed eye
- Z-bend

Sizes: 1, 1/0, 2/0, 3/0, 4/0
MSRP: $2.37 per vinyl bag of 8 or 10 hooks (8 hooks for "0" sizes)

LT045 AUTOMATIC ROTATING WORM HOOKS
SPECIFICATIONS
- Lazer Sharp® bronze
- Double Barb™
- Kinked shank

- Offset ringed eye
- Z-bend

Sizes: 1/0, 2/0, 3/0, 4/0
MSRP: $3.26 per clam pack of 8 or 10 hooks (8 hooks for "0" sizes), $8.58-$12.31 per box of 50 hooks

L095BP PRO SERIES Z-BEND WORM HOOKS
SPECIFICATIONS
- Lazer Sharp® black pearl™
- Southern sproat
- Needle tip forged point
- Non-offset ringed eye

Sizes: 1/0, 2/0, 3/0, 4/0, 5/0
MSRP: $2.99 per vinyl bag of 8 or 10 hooks (8 hooks for "0" sizes), $9.99 per clam pack of 25 hooks

L095JB PRO SERIES™ Z-BEND WORM HOOKS
SPECIFICATIONS
- Lazer Sharp® bronze
- Southern sproat
- Non-offset ringed eye

Sizes: 1/0, 2/0, 3/0, 4/0, 5/0
MSRP: $2.37 per vinyl bag of 8 or 10 hooks (8 hooks for "0" sizes), $6.53-$8.80 per box of 50 hooks

L095JL PRO SERIES Z-BEND WORM HOOKS
SPECIFICATIONS
- Lazer Sharp® bronze
- Southern sproat
- Light wire
- Non-offset ringed eye

Sizes: 2, 1, 1/0, 2/0, 3/0, 4/0
MSRP: $2.37 per vinyl bag of 8 or 10

hooks (8 hooks for "0" sizes), $5.20-$7.51 per box of 50 hooks, $8.28-$12.79 per 100 pack

L095XBL PRO SERIES WIDE GAP WORM HOOKS
SPECIFICATIONS
- Lazer Sharp® black
- Southern sproat
- 2 slices
- Ringed eye

Sizes: 1, 1/0, 2/0, 3/0, 4/0, 5/0
MSRP: $2.37 per vinyl bag of 8 or 10 hooks (8 hooks for "0" sizes), $6.54-$9.83 per box of 50 hooks

259H TRAILER HOOKS
SPECIFICATIONS
- Classic bronze
- For spinnerbaits and buzzbaits
- Tubing & instructions included
- Forged
- Non-offset

Sizes: 1/0, 2/0, 3/0
MSRP: $1.83 per poly bag of 8 hooks

261H TRAILER HOOKS
SPECIFICATIONS
- Classic nickel
- For spinnerbaits and buzzbaits
- Tubing & instructions included
- Forged
- Non-offset

Sizes: 1, 1/0, 2/0, 3/0, 4/0
MSRP: $1.69 per poly bag of 10 hooks (size 1); $1.83 per poly bag of 8 hooks (1/0-4/0)

TERMINAL TACKLE

EAGLE CLAW® HOOKS

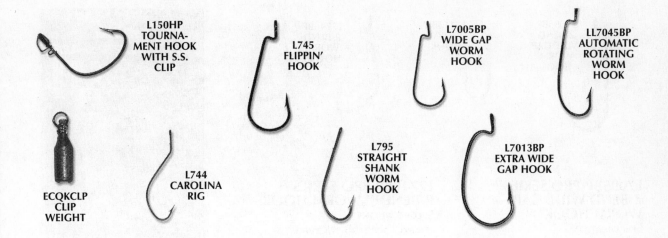

L150HP TOURNAMENT HOOK WITH S.S. CLIP

L745 FLIPPIN' HOOK

L7005BP WIDE GAP WORM HOOK

LL7045BP AUTOMATIC ROTATING WORM HOOK

L795 STRAIGHT SHANK WORM HOOK

L7013BP EXTRA WIDE GAP HOOK

ECQKCLP CLIP WEIGHT

L744 CAROLINA RIG

HP FISHHOOK SYSTEM

The HP Fishhook System is undeniably the most widely used rig on the BASSMASTER® tournament trail. Designed by bass pro Shaw Grigsby, these hooks feature Lazer Sharp® points. The SS Quik Clip® holds the bait and/or weight on the shank. Add the Quik Clip® weights, and you've got the most versatile hook system ever made.

HP TOURNAMENT HOOK WITH S.S. CLIP
SPECIFICATIONS
Model: L150
- Lazer sharp® black™
- Non-offset
- Forged
- Ringed eye
Sizes: 4, 2, 1, 1/0, 2/0, 3/0, 4/0
MSRP: $4.62 per vinyl bag of 10 hooks

QUIK CLIP WEIGHTS FOR HP HOOKS™
SPECIFICATIONS
Model: ECQKCLP
Weights: ¹⁄₃₂ oz., ¹⁄₁₆ oz., ⅛ oz.
MSRP: $2.25 per vinyl bag of 10

L744 CAROLINA RIG HOOKS
SPECIFICATIONS
- Featherlite®
- Lazer sharp
- Messler automatic rotating
- Light wire
- Wide gap
- Single slice
- Ringed eye
Sizes: 0.5/0, 1.5/0, 2.5/0
MSRP: $3.54 per vinyl bag of 8 hooks

L745BP PRO SERIES FLIPPIN' HOOK
SPECIFICATIONS
- Lazer Sharp® black pearl™
- Needle tip
- Forged point
- Flat forged
- Round bend
Sizes: 2/0, 3/0, 4/0, 5/0, 6/0
MSRP: $2.99 per vinyl bag of 8 hooks; $9.99 per clam pack of 25 hooks

L795 STRAIGHT SHANK WORM HOOK
SPECIFICATIONS
- Featherlite
- Lazer Sharp®
- 2 slices
- Ringed eye
Sizes: 2, 1, 0.5/0, 1.5/0, 2.5/0, 3.5/0
MSRP: $3.54 per vinyl bag of 10 hooks (8 hooks for 0 sizes)

L7005BP PRO SERIES WIDE GAP WORM HOOK
SPECIFICATIONS
- Lazer sharp® Black Pearl™
- Needle tip
- Forged point
- Light wire
Sizes: 2, 1, 1/0, 2/0, 3/0, 4/0
MSRP: $2.99 per vinyl bag of 6 hooks; $9.99 per bag of 25 hooks

L7013BP PRO SERIES EXTRA WIDE GAP HOOKS
SPECIFICATIONS
- Lazer Sharp® Black Pearl™
- Needle tip
- Forged point
- Non-offset
- Ringed eye
Sizes: 1, 1/0, 2/0, 3/0, 4/0
MSRP: $2.99 per vinyl bag of 6 hooks; $9.99 per bag of 25 hooks

L7045BP PRO SERIES AUTOMATIC ROTATING WORM HOOK
SPECIFICATIONS
- Lazer Sharp®Black Pearl™
- Needle tip
- Forged point
- Kinked
- Offset
- Ringed eye
- Z-bend
Sizes: 1, 1/0, 2/0, 3/0, 4/0
MSRP: $2.99 per vinyl bag of 6 hooks; $9.99 per bag of 25 hooks

TERMINAL TACKLE

EAGLE CLAW® HOOKS

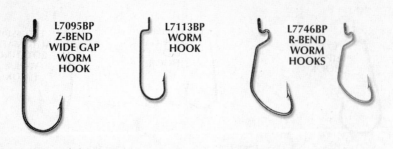

L7095BP
Z-BEND
WIDE GAP
WORM
HOOK

L7113BP
WORM
HOOK

L7746BP
R-BEND
WORM
HOOKS

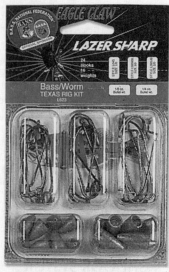

L623 TEXAS RIG ASSORTMENT

L7095BP PRO SERIES™ Z-BEND WIDE GAP WORM HOOK

SPECIFICATIONS
- Lazer Sharp® Black Pearl™
- Needle tip
- Forged point
- Round bend
- Non-offset
- Ringed eye

Sizes: 1/0, 2/0, 3/0, 4/0, 5/0
MSRP: $2.99 per vinyl bag of 6 hooks; $9.99 per bag of 25 hooks

L7113BP PRO SERIES™ WORM HOOK

SPECIFICATIONS
- Lazer Sharp®Black Pearl™
- Needle tip
- Forged point
- Light wire

Sizes: 2, 1, 1/0, 2/0, 3/0, 4/0
MSRP: $2.99 per vinyl bag of 6 hooks; $9.99 per bag of 25 hooks

L7746 R-BEND™ WORM HOOKS

- Featherlite®
- Lazer Sharp®
- Shaw Grigsby design
- Wide gap
- Non-offset
- Ringed eye

Sizes: 1/0, 2/0, 3/0, 4/0
MSRP: $4.62 per vinyl bag of 8 hooks

L7746BP PRO SERIES™ R-BEND™ WORM HOOKS

SPECIFICATIONS
- Lazer Sharp®Black Pearl™
- Needle tip
- Forged point
- Shaw Grigsby design
- Wide gap

Sizes: 1/0, 2/0, 3/0, 4/0
MSRP: $2.99 per vinyl bag of 6 hooks; $9.99 per vinyl bag of 25 hooks

CLASSIC & LAZER SHARP® HOOK ASSORTMENTS

A great convenience for the fisherman who wants a variety of different styles, sizes and finishes of fishhooks. This assortment is offered in a multi-cell, clear plastic package and contains a wide fishhook selection for plastic worm fishing.

SPECIFICATIONS
Model: 618 (Bass Worm Hooks)
Hook styles (sizes, number): L045 (1/0, 16; 2/0, 16), L095XBL (3/0, 16), 449W (1, 3), 084 (1/0, 16)
Total hooks in assortment: 67
MSRP: $5.76

Model: L619 (Bass Worm Hooks)
Hook styles (sizes, number): L095XBL (2/0, 20), L095XBL (3/0, 16), L045 (1/0, 16; 2/0, 16)
Total hooks in assortment: 69
MSRP: $6.95

Model: L623 (Texas Rig Hook & Weight Assortment)
Hook styles (sizes, number): L045 (1/0, 8), L095XBL (3/0, 8), L095JB (2/0, 8)
Total hooks in assortment: 24
Weights (size, number): Worm weight (1/8 oz., 8); worm weight (1/4 oz., 8)
Total weights in assortment: 16
MSRP: $6.95

Model: L625 (Treble Hook Upgrade)
Hook styles: L954 (5 size 2, 5 size 6), L955 (5 size 2, 5 size 4)
Total hooks in assortment: 20
Split rings: 5 each size T, 2 and 3
Total split rings in assortment: 15
MSRP: $6.95

Model: L626 (HP®Hook Assortment)
Hook styles: L150 (4 each size 1, 1/0 and 2/0)
Total hooks in assortment: 12
Munch-It®weight: four 1/4 oz.
Quik Clip®weight: four 1/8 oz.
Total weights in assortment: 8
MSRP: $10.70

EXCALIBUR HOOKS

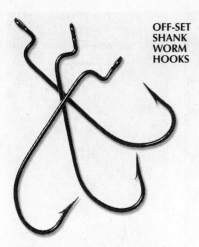

OFF-SET SHANK WORM HOOKS

EXCALIBUR® DRESSED ROTATING TREBLE HOOKS

The Excalibur®Rotating Treble Hook delivers a significant hooking advantage over standard treble hooks. Designed with a proprietary angle in each hook bend, each of the two free points of the Excalibur®Treble travel counter-clockwise once contact is made with one point. This movement of the hook points usually results in at least one other point coming into contact with a striking fish. This torque-accelerated movement when combined with the sharp, cutting

point of the hook generally will force at least two points past the barb. It is possible for this hook to increase an angler's strike-to-land ratio by as much as 30 percent.

SPECIFICATIONS

Model: XTE2
Size: #2
Hooks/Package: 4
MSRP:

Model: XTE4
Size: #4
Hooks/Package: 4
MSRP:

Model: XTE6
Size: #6
Hooks/Package: 4
MSRP:

Model: XTE8
Size: #8
Hooks/Package: 4
MSRP:

EXCALIBUR® DRESSED ROTATING TREBLE HOOKS

These Excalibur®Rotating Treble Hooks are dressed in white with a red flashabou insert and a red collar. Nothing hooks fish better than an

Excalibur Treble Hook, and now nothing will dress up a lure like an Excalibur®Dressed Treble Hook!

SPECIFICATIONS

Model: XTE4-D
Size: #4
Hooks/Package: 2

Model: XTE6-D
Size: #6
Hooks/Package: 2

EXCALIBUR® OFF-SET SHANK WORM HOOKS

These heavy wire super-sharp off-set shank worm hooks are perfect for hauling in those heavy catches.

SPECIFICATIONS

Model: XOE3
Size: 3/0
Hooks/pkg.: 6

Model: XOE4
Size: 4/0
Hooks/pkg.: 5

Model: XOE5
Size: 5/0
Hooks/pkg.: 5

MSRP: $2.59

How'd You Hook It?

When you catch a bass, pay attention to where it was hooked. Was the hook inside the fish's mouth or outside? If it was outside the mouth, you're probably missing some strikes and losing a high percentage of bass that bite. It's time to alter the appearance or action of your bait. If the fish was hooked inside the mouth, don't change anything.

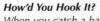

TERMINAL TACKLE

MUSTAD HOOKS

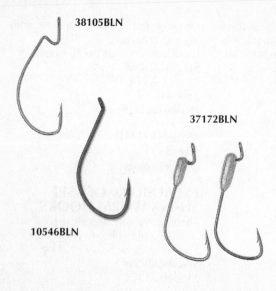

38105BLN

37172BLN

10546BLN

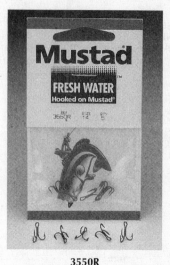

3550R

36102R

CLASSIC SERIES RED TREBLE HOOKS

With a sleek red finish and chemically sharpened point, these sharp new hooks offer fast, smooth penetration and are an outstanding replacement treble hook. They are specially tempered.

SPECIFICATIONS
Model: 3550R
Sizes: 10,12,14,16 and 18.

EXCALIBUR® OFF-SET SHANK WORM HOOKS

These heavy wire super-sharp off-set shank worm hooks are perfect for hauling in those heavy catches.

SPECIFICATIONS
Model: XOE3
Size: 3/0
Hooks/pkg.: 6

Model: XOE4
Size: 4/0
Hooks/pkg.: 5

Model: XOE5
Size: 5/0
Hooks/pkg.: 5
MSRP: $2.59

ULTRA POINT™ DROP SHOT HOOK

These wide-gap hooks feature needle-sharp points, fine wire diameters and sleek finishes for ultra-quick hooksets as well as turned-up eyes ideal for soft plastic and live bait drop shot presentation.

SPECIFICATIONS
Model: 10546BLN
Finish: Black Nickel
Sizes: 2,4,6 and 8.

ULTRA POINT™ SERIES IMPACT HOOKS

Impact hooks are perfect for finesse presentations with trick worms, grubs and other smaller soft plastic baits. Their fine wire, unique design, and weighing system give them extra action and their chemically sharpened Opti-Angle™ needle points and black nickel finish provide extra fast penetration.

SPECIFICATIONS
Model: 37172BLN
(with weed guard)
Weight: 1/32 oz.
Sizes: 1/10 and 2.
MSRP:
  Model: 37173BLN
Weight: 1/16 or 1/32 oz.
Sizes: 1/10 and 2.

ULTRA POINT™ SERIES ULTRA LOCK HOOKS

These hooks are specially designed for soft plastic baits. They feature an innovative "v-shaped bend" to "lock" soft plastic baits in place, ensuring optimum presentation and performance. Premium Ultra Lock hooks also feature an extra wide gap for better hooksets, plus a chemically sharpened Opti-Angle needle point and black nickel finish for super fast penetration.

The new ultra Lock is part of the ultra sharp, ultra strong Mustad® Ultra Point™ series of hooks. Ultra point hooks are created using state-of-the-art, three stage Opti-Angle™ sharpening technology which removes less metal from the point than traditional methods – without compromising sharpness. Ultra Point hooks also undergo Mustad's computer-controlled tempering process, Non-Tempering™, increasing the strength up to 30% compared to conventional hooks. The result is a very sharp, very strong needle point that delivers quick, easy penetration and longer performance.

SPECIFICATIONS
Model: 38105BLN
Sizes: 5/0 through1/0

ULTRA POINT™ SERIES ULTRA NP RED TREBLE HOOK

The Ultra Point series Ultra NP treble hook now has a sleek, red finish and revolutionary Opit-Angle™point for ultra-quick penetration. It's also ringed and features a round bend and short shank, making it the ultimate replacement treble hook.

SPECIFICATIONS
Model: 36102R
Sizes: 2,4,6 and 8.

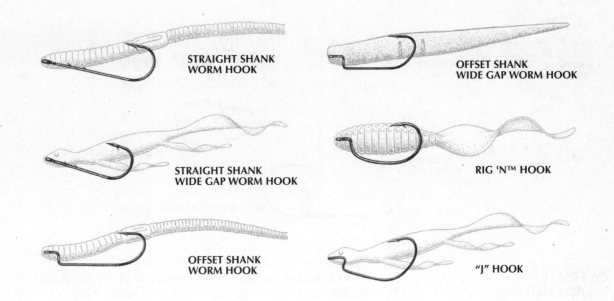

STRAIGHT SHANK WORM HOOK

OFFSET SHANK WIDE GAP WORM HOOK

STRAIGHT SHANK WIDE GAP WORM HOOK

RIG 'N™ HOOK

OFFSET SHANK WORM HOOK

"J" HOOK

STRAIGHT SHANK WORM HOOKS

Ideal for split-shotting plastic worms. Features include a round bend, Cutting Point™, black chrome finish and baitholder slices on the inside of the straight shank.

Model 5100 (Pocket Packs)
Sizes (quantity): #2 (6), #1 (6), #1/0 (6), #2/0 (6), #3/0 (5), #4/0 (5), #5/0 (5)
MSRP: $5.00 per pack

Model 5300 (Pro Packs)
Sizes (quantity): #2 (34), #1 (34), #1/0 (34), #2/0 (34), #3/0 (28), #4/0 (28), #5/0 (28).
MSRP: $25.00 per pack

STRAIGHT SHANK, WIDE GAP WORM HOOKS

Worm hooks for rigging large baits and setting the hook on big bass. Features include a round bend, Cutting Point™, black chrome finish, baitholder slices on the inside of the straight shank, and they're XXX strong.

Model 5103 (Pocket Packs)
Sizes (quantity): #1/0 (6), #2/0 (6), #3/0 (5), #4/0 (5), #5/0 (5)
MSRP: $5.00 per pack

Model 5303 (Pro Packs)
Sizes (quantity): #1/0 (34), #2/0 (34), #3/0 (28), #4/0 (28), #5/0 (28)
MSRP: $25.00 per pack

OFFSET SHANK WORM HOOKS

Hooks with a worm-holding 90° bend shoulder. Preferred by many bass anglers for straight and easy rigging of plastic worms. Features include Cutting Point™ and black chrome finish.

Model 5101 (Pocket Packs)
Sizes (quantity): #2 (6), #1 (6), #1/0 (6), #2/0 (6), #3/0 (5), #4/0 (5), #5/0 (5)
MSRP: $5.00 per pack

Model 5301 (Pro Packs)
Sizes (quantity): #2 (34), #1 (34), #1/0 (34), #2/0 (34), #3/0 (28), #4/0 (28), #5/0 (28)
MSRP: $25.00 per pack

OFFSET SHANK, WIDE GAP WORM HOOKS

Hooks with worm-holding 90° bend shoulder. Extra wide gap bend and heavy-duty XXX strong shank for rigging big baits and hauling bass from heavy cover. Ideal for jerk baits. Features include Cutting Point™ and black chrome finish.

Model 5102 (Pocket Packs)
Sizes (quantity): #1/0 (6), #2/0 (6), #3/0 (5), #4/0 (5), #5/0 (5)
MSRP: $5.00 per pack

Model 5302 (Pro Packs)
Sizes (quantity): #1/0 (34), #2/0 (34), #3/0 (28), #4/0 (28), #5/0 (28)
MSRP: $25.00 per pack

RIG 'N™ HOOKS

Engineered for Carolina Rig N, Texas Rig N and Split Shot N, these hooks ride with the point upright in an optimum striking position. Features include a short shank, huge wide bite, Cutting Point™ and black chrome finish.

Model 5137 (Pocket Packs)
Sizes (quantity): #4 (6), #2 (6), #1 (6), #1/0 (6), #2/0 (6), #3/0 (5), #4/0 (5), #5/0 (5)
MSRP: $5.00 per pack

Model 5337 (Pro Packs)
Sizes (quantity): #4 (34), #2 (34), #1 (34), #1/0 (34), #2/0 (34), #3/0 (28), #4/0 (28), #5/0 (28)
MSRP: $25.00 per pack

"J" HOOKS

"J"Hooks have an extra wide bend, perfect for Carolina and Texas rigging lizards and other larger soft plastic baits. Point surfaces quicker on hook sets, and wide bend reduces the chance of fish throwing the hook. Features include a worm-holding Z-Lock shoulder bend, Cutting Point™ and black chrome finish.

Model 5140 (Pocket Packs)
Sizes (quantity): #4 (6), #2 (6), #1 (6), #1/0 (6), #2/0 (6), #3/0 (5), #4/0 (5), #5/0 (5)
MSRP: $5.00 per pack

Model 5340 (Pro Packs)
Sizes (quantity): #4 (34), #2 (34), #1 (34), #1/0 (34), #2/0 (34), #3/0 (28), #4/0 (28), #5/0 (28)
MSRP: $25.00 per pack

TERMINAL TACKLE

OWNER HOOKS

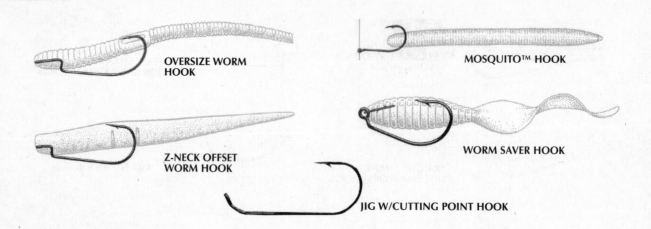

OVERSIZE WORM HOOK

MOSQUITO™ HOOK

Z-NECK OFFSET WORM HOOK

WORM SAVER HOOK

JIG W/CUTTING POINT HOOK

OVERSIZE WORM HOOKS

These hooks, with a heavy-duty forged shank, are the ideal choice for rigging king-size worms for big bass. Features include worm holding Z-Lock shoulder bend, Cutting Point™ and black chrome finish.

Model 5110 (Pocket Packs)
Sizes (quantity): #7/0 (5), #11/0 (4)
MSRP: $5.00 per pack

Z-NECK™, OFFSET WORM HOOKS

Z-Neck™, Offset worm hooks, with a radical Z-Lock shoulder bend, keep rigged soft plastics in place, while an extra wide gap accommodates bigger baits and offers greater hooking power. Features include a round bend, Super Needle Point and black matte finish.

Model 5191 (Pocket Packs)
Sizes (quantity): #1/0 (6), #2/0 (6), #3/0 (5), #4/0 (5), #5/0 (5)
MSRP: $3.00 per pack

Model 5391 (Pro Packs)
Sizes (quantity): #1/0 (25), #2/0 (25), #3/0 (25), #4/0 (25), #5/0 (25)
MSRP: $12.25 per pack

WORM SAVER HOOKS

Worm Saver hooks, with worm grippers, assure easy rigging and fewer torn baits. Hook rides upright in an optimum striking position. Ideal for Carolina Rig N, Texas Rig N and Split Shot N. Features include a 45° eye bend, short shank, huge wide bite, Cutting Point™ and black chrome finish.

Model 5132 (Pocket Packs)
Sizes (quantity): #1/0 (6), #2/0 (6), #3/0 (5), #4/0 (5), #5/0 (5)
MSRP: $5.00 per pack

MOSQUITO™ HOOKS

Fast becoming a favorite when using the down shot system for bass. For light line use, it is self-setting and the perfect hook for windy conditions or turbulent water where it is difficult to keep a tight line. Ideal for rigging small live baits, for nose-hooking soft plastics and for wacky wormin' (hooking through middle of the worm and letting the ends dangle equally). Features include a black chrome finish and a fine-wire forged shank with offset Super Needle Point.

Model 5177 (Pocket Packs)
Sizes (quantity): #10 (12), #8 (11), #6 (10), #4 (10), #2 (9), #1 (8), 1/0 (7), 2/0 (6)
MSRP: $2.50 per pack

DOWN SHOT™, OFFSET HOOKS

With its eye in the "down" position, this hook is ideal for the down shot fishing system, as it's engineered to ride perfectly horizontal when tied into a line that is to be fished straight up and down. Use any kind of knot, but pull the tag end of the line up and over through the hook's eye one additional time before attaching sinker. Rig any kind of soft plastic bait and use as a deadly presentation for suspended game fish. Light wire, forged and includes a 90-degree shoulder bend, Cutting Point and black chrome finish.

Model 5133 (Pocket Packs)
Sizes (quantity): #4 (6), #2 (6), #1 (6), 1/0 (6), 2/0 (6), 3/0 (6)
MSRP: $5.00 per pack

90 JIG HOOKS

Round bend, and X strong, forged shank. Versatile for molding jigheads of varying designs. Features include a 90° eye-bend, short shank, curved in point and a corrosion-resistant black chrome finish.

Model 5313 (Pro Packs)
Sizes (quantity): #1 (63), #1/0 (57), #2/0 (51), #3/0 (46)
MSRP: $25.00 per pack

JIG HOOKS w/CUTTING POINTTM

Round bend, and XX strong, forged shank. Ideal for molding low-profile jigheads designed for fishing in heavy cover. Features include 30° eye-bend, crossed eye, and black matte finish.

Model 5383 (Pro Packs)
Sizes (quantity): #3/0 (52)
MSRP: $25.00 per pack

DEEP THROAT, WIDE GAP JIG HOOKS

Flip 'n' pitch jig hooks, with a reverse sproat bend that s ideal for fishing porkrind and other trailing baits. Additional features include Cutting Point™, 60° eye-bend, wide gap, XX strong shank and black finish.

Model 5304 (Pro Packs)
Sizes (quantity): #1 (66), #1/0 (66), #2/0 (59), #3/0 (52), #4/0 (45), #5/0 (40)
MSRP: $25.00 per pack

TERMINAL TACKLE

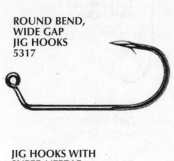

ROUND BEND, WIDE GAP JIG HOOKS 5317

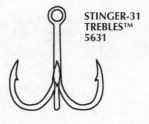

STINGER-31 TREBLES™ 5631

SPINNERBAIT TRAILER HOOKS 5131

JIG HOOKS WITH SUPER NEEDLE POINT 5318

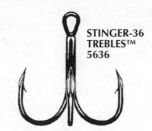

STINGER-36 TREBLES™ 5636

SPINNERBAIT HOOKS 5320

ROUND BEND, WIDE GAP JIG HOOKS

Flip 'n' pitch jig hooks, with a 60° eye-bend and a heavy-duty, forged XXX strong shank, ideal for horsing big bass out of heavy cover. Features include Cutting Point™ and black finish.

Model 5317 (Pro Packs)
Sizes (quantity): #3/0 (52), #4/0 (45), #5/0 (40)
MSRP: $25.00 per pack

JIG HOOKS WITH SUPER NEEDLE POINT

Round bend and light wire shank that encourages deep hook penetration and makes it easy to bend hook enough to pull free of sunken stumps. Features include 90° eye-bend and black finish.

Model 5318 (Pro Packs)
Sizes (quantity): #4 (90), #2 (85), #1 (80), #1/0 (78), #2/0 (73), #3/0 (68), #4/0 (63), #5/0 (58)
MSRP: $25.00 per pack

STINGER-31 TREBLES™

These are the perfect stinger replacement hooks for improving the hooking power of freshwater lures. In fact, these are the same hooks found factory-rigged on Owner's small profile Cultiva™ hard baits. Features include round bends, three slightly curved in Cutting Points™ and a bright nickel finish.

Model 5631 (Pocket Packs)
Sizes (quantity): #8 (8), #6 (8), #4 (8), #2 (7), #1 (6), #1/0 (6)
MSRP: $5.00 per pack

STINGER-36 TREBLES™

With a corrosion-resistant black chrome finish, these are ideal either as replacement hooks for smaller profile lures or as a "stinger" when bait fishing. Features include round bends, plus three straight Super Needle Points for wide-gap hooking efficiency.

Model 5636 (Pocket Packs)
Sizes (quantity): #10 (8), #8 (8), #6 (8), #4 (7), #2 (6), #1 (6), #1/0 (5)
MSRP: $5.00 per pack

STINGER-41 TREBLES™

2X strong with a corrosion-resistant black chrome finish, these are the ideal replacement hooks for improving the hooking power of heavy freshwater plugs, spoons and die-cast jigs. Lethal when used as a stinger for rigging natural baits. Features include a short shank, round bends and three slightly curved in Cutting Points™.

Model 5641 (Pocket Packs)
Sizes (quantity): #6 (8), #4 (8), #2 (7), #1 (6). #1/0 (6), #2/0 (6)
MSRP: $6.00 per pack

SPINNERBAIT HOOKS

With a wide gap, round bend and a heavy-duty, forged XXX strong shank, these hooks are ideal for stabilizing spinnerbait action and leveraging big fish. Features include Cutting Point™ and nickel finish.

Model 5320 (Pro Packs)
Sizes (quantity): #1/0 (60), #2/0 (55), #3/0 (50), #4/0 (44), #5/0 (39)
MSRP: $25.00 per pack

SPINNERBAIT TRAILER HOOKS

These hooks have a wide gap, round bend, oversized eye, and a heavy-duty, forged short shank. Ideal for rigging as a trailer on spinnerbaits and jigs, or as a replacement hook for spoons. Skinned eye keeps rigged hook from slipping off. Features include Cutting Point™ and nickel finish.

Model 5131 (Pocket Packs)
Sizes (quantity): #2/0 (7), #3/0 (6), #4/0 (5)
MSRP: $5.00 per pack

DOUBLE FROG HOOK

With 3X-strong shanks and super sharp points, these frog hooks allow for easier hookups and more leverage in pulling big bass from heavy cover. Quickly and easily replace inferior hooks typically found on factory-rigged frog baits. Features are Super Needle Points and black chrome finish.

Model 5671 (Pocket Packs)
Sizes (quantity): 4/0 (5), 6/0 (4)
MSRP: $6.00 per pack

TERMINAL TACKLE

TRU-TURN HOOKS

THE BRUTE™

BRONZE BASS WORM HOOK

BLOOD RED BASS WORM HOOK

ULTRA SHARP BASS HOOK

THE BRUTE™
Ideal for Spectra® Super Lines.
- Big bite design
- Forged
- Ringed eye
- Two slices
- Spear point
- Bronze

SPECIFICATIONS
Model: 007ZS
Hook Size: 1/0
Pack Count: 7
MSRP: $2.25

Hook Size: 2/0
Pack Count: 6
MSRP: $2.25

Hook Size: 3/0
Pack Count: 5
MSRP: $2.25

Hook Size: 4/0
Pack Count: 4
MSRP: $2.25

Hook Size: 5/0
Pack Count: 4
MSRP: $2.25

Model: 007Z
Hook Size: 1/0
Pack Count: 18
MSRP: $5.65

Hook Size: 2/0
Pack Count: 17
MSRP: $5.65

Hook Size: 3/0
Pack Count: 14
MSRP: $5.65

Hook Size: 4/0
Pack Count: 12
MSRP: $5.65

Model: 007BL
Hook Size: 1/0
Pack Count: 50
MSRP: $8.90

Hook Size: 2/0
Pack Count: 50
MSRP: $10.10

Hook Size: 3/0
Pack Count: 50
MSRP: $10.90

Hook Size: 4/0
Pack Count: 50
MSRP: $12.80

Hook Size: 5/0
Pack Count: 50
MSRP: $14.80

BRONZE BASS WORM HOOK
The #1 bass worm hook in the world.
- Sproat design
- Ringed eye
- Two slices
- Spear Point

SPECIFICATIONS
Model: 047ZS
Hook Size: 2
Pack Count: 8
MSRP: $2.25

Hook Size: 1
Pack Count: 8
MSRP: $2.25

Hook Size: 1/0
Pack Count: 8
MSRP: $2.25

Hook Size: 2/0
Pack Count: 7
MSRP: $2.25

Hook Size: 3/0
Pack Count: 6

MSRP: $2.25

Hook Size: 4/0
Pack Count: 5
MSRP: $2.25

Hook Size: 5/0
Pack Count: 4
MSRP: $2.25

Model: 047Z
Hook Size: 1/0
Pack Count: 22
MSRP: $5.65

Hook Size: 2/0
Pack Count: 20
MSRP: $5.65

Hook Size: 3/0
Pack Count: 17
MSRP: $5.65

Model: 047BL
Hook Size: 2
Pack Count: 50
MSRP: $7.80

Hook Size: 1
Pack Count: 50
MSRP: $7.80

Model: 047BL
Hook Size: 1/0
Pack Count: 50
MSRP: $7.90

Hook Size: 2/0
Pack Count: 50
MSRP: $8.90

Hook Size: 3/0
Pack Count: 50
MSRP: $10.10

Hook Size: 4/0
Pack Count: 50
MSRP: $10.90

Hook Size: 5/0

Pack Count: 50
MSRP: $12.80

BLOOD RED BASS WORM HOOK
- Sproat design
- Ringed eye
- Two slices
- Spear point
- Blood Red finish

SPECIFICATIONS
Model: 063ZS
Hook Size: 1
Pack Count: 6
MSRP: $2.25

Hook Size: 1/0
Pack Count: 6
MSRP: $2.25

Hook Size: 2/0
Pack Count: 5
MSRP: $2.25

Hook Size: 3/0
Pack Count: 4
MSRP: $2.25

Hook Size: 4/0
Pack Count: 3
MSRP: $2.25

ULTRA SHARP BASS HOOK
Super sharp for even more hookups.
- Forged
- Tapered point with cutting edges
- Low profile barb
- Black

SPECIFICATIONS
Model: 069ZS
Hook Size: 1/0
Pack Count: 6
MSRP: $2.25

Hook Size: 2/0
Pack Count: 5
MSRP: $2.25

TERMINAL TACKLE

TRU-TURN HOOKS

BLUE BASS WORM HOOK

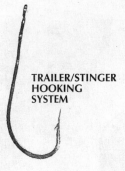

TRACER® BASS HOOK

TRAILER/STINGER HOOKING SYSTEM

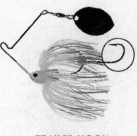

TRAILER HOOK, BLOOD RED®

Hook Size: 3/0
Pack Count: 4
MSRP: $2.25

Hook Size: 4/0
Pack Count: 4
MSRP: $2.25

Hook Size: 5/0
Pack Count: 3
MSRP: $2.25

BLUE BASS WORM HOOK
- Sproat design
- Ringed eye
- Two slices
- Spear point

SPECIFICATIONS
Model: **077ZS**
Hook Size: 2
Pack Count: 8
MSRP: $2.25

Hook Size: 1
Pack Count: 8
MSRP: $2.25

Hook Size: 1/0
Pack Count: 8
MSRP: $2.25

Hook Size: 2/0
Pack Count: 7
MSRP: $2.25

Hook Size: 3/0
Pack Count: 6
MSRP: $2.25

Hook Size: 4/0

Pack Count: 5
MSRP: $2.25

Hook Size: 5/0
Pack Count: 4
MSRP: $2.25

Model: 077BL
Hook Size: 1/0
Pack Count: 50
MSRP: $7.90

Hook Size: 2/0
Pack Count: 50
MSRP: $8.90

Hook Size: 3/0
Pack Count: 50
MSRP: $10.10

Hook Size: 4/0
Pack Count: 50
MSRP: $10.90

TRACER® BASS HOOK
- Vanadium
- Forged with tapered piercing point
- Black

SPECIFICATIONS
Model: 090Z
Hook Size: 1/0
Pack Count: 8
MSRP: $3.75

Hook Size: 2/0
Pack Count: 7
MSRP: $3.75

Hook Size: 3/0
Pack Count: 6

MSRP: $3.75

TRAILER/STINGER HOOKING SYSTEM
Features removable, replacable GrassMaster Weedguards. Contains PVC tubing and surgical tubing in addition to the hooks.
- Forged
- Large ringed eye
- Spear point
- Nickel

SPECIFICATIONS
Model: 101ZS
Hook Size: 2/0
Pack Count: 5
MSRP: $2.25

Hook Size: 3/0
Pack Count: 5
MSRP: $2.25

TRAILER HOOK, BLOOD RED®
- Medium
- Large ringed eye
- Spear point
- Tubing included

SPECIFICATIONS
Model: 183ZS
Hook Size: 2/0
Pack Count: 5
MSRP: $2.25

Hook Size: 3/0
Pack Count: 4
MSRP: $2.25

EZ LINK® HOOKING SYSTEM
Featuring Super Baitholder

Coils.
- Ultra sharp
- Forged
- Big bite design
- Special jig-type eye
- Spear point
- Blue, with snap on, snap off wormholders

SPECIFICATIONS
Model: 240ZS
Hook Size: 1/0
Pack Count: 4
MSRP: $2.25

Hook Size: 2/0
Pack Count: 4
MSRP: $2.25

Hook Size: 3/0
Pack Count: 4
MSRP: $2.25
Hook Size: 4/0
Pack Count: 3
MSRP: $2.25

Model: 240Z
Hook Size: 1/0
Pack Count: 7
MSRP: $5.65

Hook Size: 2/0
Pack Count: 7
MSRP: $5.65

Hook Size: 3/0
Pack Count: 7
MSRP: $5.65

Hook Size: 4/0
Pack Count: 7
MSRP: $5.65

TERMINAL TACKLE

BERKLEY LINE

GORILLA
LINE

IRONSILK

TRILENE®
BIG GAME®

TRILENE® BIG GAME®

Trilene Big game has the muscle and shock strength to handle even the worst punishment. It features an abrasion resistant formula that runs through the guides with less friction, but has the power to handle big fish in saltwater marathons. In key tensile strength tests, Trilene Big Game outperforms both Ande®and Maxima®.

SPECIFICATIONS

Colors: Ultra Clear, Green, Solar Collector

Line size: 10, 12, 15, 20, 25, 30, 40, 50 pound test
Spool size: ¼ pound
MSRP: $8.49

Line size: 10, 12, 15, 20, 25, 30, 40, 50 pound test
Spool size: ½ pound
MSRP: $16.99

Line size: 10, 12, 15, 20, 25, 30, 40, 50, 60, 80 pound test
Spool size: 1 pound
MSRP: $31.49

Line size: 12, 15, 20, 25, 30, 40, 50, 60, 80, 100, 125, 150, 200 pound test
Spool size: 3 pounds
MSRP: $89.99

Solar Collector only available in ¼ pound spools and 3 pound spools up to 80 pound test. Green only available in sizes up to 125 pound test.

GORILLA TOUGH BRAIDED LINE

Compared to monofilament fishing lines, Gorilla Tough delivers half the diameter and twice the strength at a price that is sure to please anglers. Gorilla Tough is a bi-component micro braid consisting of high tenacity microfiber Dyneema backbone with a colored polyester tracer filament. The combination creates an incredibly thin fishing line that is brutally tough and extremely strong yet is soft, with no memory and low stretch characteristics for a great handling line. The line is resistant to side cutting, an important feature when hard fighting fish twist and turn and test the line and angler to the limits. It cuts thru weeds and vegetation, has zero water absorption and is extremely long lasting.

SPECIFICATIONS

Color: Camo-Green
Spool size: 125 yards
Line size: 10-, 20-, 35-, 50-, 80-pound-test
MSRP: $8.95 per spool

IRONSILK™

Polymer chemists working within the state of the art laboratories at Berkley have discovered a technical breakthrough that allows a way to molecularly reinforce nylon molecules. They refer to this chemistry as Reinforced Polymer Matrix. The easiest way to visualize Reinforced Polymer Matrix technology is to think of it as being akin to the using of steel rebar to reinforce concrete. Only this reinforcing system is done at the molecular level and is so incredibly complex that not even electron microscopes can detail the process. Berkley IronSilk is the first fishing line ever made using this truly breakthrough technology.

Tough as iron, IronSilk is 200% - 300% more abrasion resistant than other leading tough-lines. The reinforcing network of the line's construction adds greater resistance to nicks, cuts and line wear. Knots tie strong and tight. With IronSilk the angler has the confidence needed to seek aggressive fish that live in impossible locations and are hard fighting on the hook.

IronSilk casts smooth as silk, not because of some slick coating of silicone or fluorocarbon. The smooth feel of IronSilk is due to the reinforcing polymer mixture used to create the line. The low co-efficient of friction allows IronSilk to travel through rod guides 10-25% faster improving casting distance and accuracy. With no line memory like other tough lines, IronSilk lays out flat on the water, giving the angler more control over bait action whether using baitcasting or spinning tackle. The low stretch of IronSilk creates a sensitivity unlike monofilament yet the line maintains the shock resistance needed for hard hooksets.

SPECIFICATIONS

Colors: Low Visibility Green, Solar Mint
Line/spool size: 4- to 30-pound test in 330-yard filler spools; 25-pound test in a 275-yard filler spool; 30-pound test in a 250-yard filler spool
MSRP: $10.49 for the 4-, 6- and 8-pound spools; $12.19 in 10-pound test and heavier

BIG GAME SUPREME

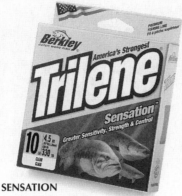

SENSATION

FIRELINE

TRILENE® BIG GAME® SUPREME

The complex polymer alloy technology that was first used in Trilene Sensation is incorporated into Improved Big Game Supreme. Improved Big Game Supreme is now 20 percent stronger per diameter or PSI than standard Big Game monofilament and up to 40 percent stronger than other high strength brands. Even with all the new strength attributes built in, Improved Big Game Supreme is still 25 to 100 percent more flexible than other high strength brands and is more sensitive. Improved Big Game Supreme is a good choice when ultimate shock strength is critical.

SPECIFICATIONS
Colors: Low-vis green, steel gray
Line/spool size: ¼-pound spools in line strengths from 10- to 50-pound test; 1-pound spools with 30-, 40-, 50- and 80-pound test line
MSRP: $ 12.95 for a ¼-pound spool, $ 44.95 for the 1-pound spool

TRILENE® SENSATION

Berkley Trilene Sensation delivers up to 30 percent greater sensitivity than competitive monofilaments, is 25 percent stronger and up to 70 percent more flexible for greater control. The line features low stretch manageability, small diameter and super strength. Sensation has less memory and increased casting control and is one of the strongest monofilaments in the Trilene line. It incorporates five different and unique polymers and a newly engineered extrusion process to deliver its enhanced properties.

New colors have optical additives unique to Berkley. The Photochromic line appears gold on the reel spool but has a fluorescent demeanor to the angler on the water. Beneath the surface the line looks clear, a big advantage when dealing with line shy fish. The new solar color is proven to be the most visible color to the human eye, even more visible than the popular hunter orange. The line will fluoresce in sunlight or under a black light for nighttime fishing.

SPECIFICATIONS
Colors: Clear, Photochromic, Solar
Line size: 2, 4, 6, 8 pound test
Spool size: 330 yards
MSRP: $8.49

Line size: 10, 12, 14, 17 pound test
Spool size: 330 yards
MSRP: $10.19

Line size: 20 pound test
Spool size: 330 yards
MSRP: $12.99

Line size: 25 pound test
Spool size: 275 yards
MSRP: $12.99

Line size: 30 pound test
Spool size: 250 yards
MSRP: $12.99

Line size: 4, 6, 8 pound test
Spool size: 3000 yards
MSRP: $54.99

Line size: 10, 12, 14, 17 pound test
Spool size: 3000 yards
MSRP: $74.99

Line size: 20 pound test
Spool size: 3000 yards
MSRP: $82.59

Line size: 25 pound test
Spool size: 2600 yards
MSRP: $82.59

Line size: 30 pound test
Spool size: 2400 yards
MSRP: $82.59

(Photochromic color available in 4 to 20 pound test; solar color available in 4 to 14 pound test. Both colors in 330 yard spools only.)

FIRELINE®

Berkley FireLine is stronger than monofilament. It casts farther. And it handles as well -- even better in some situations. It doesn't create birds nests by digging into your spool. And it ties easier knots, makes smoother casts, and stays hassle free in any kind of weather. And FireLine is as durable as it is versatile. It won't deteriorate over a lifetime. Ultra-light rays or sunlight won't affect it. And neither will the cold.

SPECIFICATIONS
Colors: Fluorescent Flame Green, Smoke
Line size: 4, 6, 8, 10, 14, 20, 30
Spool size: 125 yards
MSRP: $15.45

Line size: 4, 6, 8, 10, 14, 20, 30
Spool size: 300 yards
MSRP: $29.45

Line size: 4, 6, 8, 10, 14, 20, 30
Spool size: 1000 yards
MSRP: $92.45

BERKLEY LINE

TRILENE XL

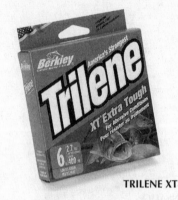

TRILENE XT

TRILENE PREMIUM STRENGTH

TRILENE XL®
Trilene XL's high-performance, low-memory formulation delivers outstanding handling characteristics. It won't kink. Won't coil. Won't let you down.
SPECIFICATIONS
Colors: Clear, Fluorescent Clear/Blue, Low-Vis Green

Line size: 1, 2, 3, 4, 6, 8, 10, 12 pound test
Spool size: 20 yards
MSRP: $1.09

Line size: 2, 4, 6, 8 pound test
Spool size: 110 yards
MSRP: $2.69

Line size: 10, 12, 14, 17 pound test
Spool size: 110 yards
MSRP: $3.49

Line size: 20 pound test
Spool size: 110 yards
MSRP: $4.59

Line size: 2, 4, 6, 8 pound test
Spool size: 400 yards
MSRP: $7.19

Line size: 10, 12, 14, 17 pound test
Spool size: 400 yards
MSRP: $8.59

Line size: 20
Spool size: 400 yards
MSRP: $10.99

Line size: 25

Spool size: 330 yards
MSRP: $10.99

Line size: 30
Spool size: 300 yards
MSRP: $10.99

Line size: 4, 6, 8 pound test
Spool size: 1000 yards
MSRP: $16.29

Line size: 10, 12, 14, 17 pound test
Spool size: 1000 yards
MSRP: $21.29

Line size: 20 pound test
Spool size: 1000 yards
MSRP: $25.99

Line size: 2, 4, 6, 8 pound test
Spool size: 3000 yards
MSRP: $38.99

Line size: 10, 12, 14, 17 pound test
Spool size: 3000 yards
MSRP: $52.99

Line size: 20 pound test
Spool size: 3000 yards
MSRP: $58.29

Line size: 25 pound test
Spool size: 2600 yards
MSRP: $58.29

Line size: 30 pound test
Spool size: 2400 yards
MSRP: $58.29

TRILENE XT®
Abrasion-resistant XT is unmatched in its ability to resist friction. In key strength tests, XT outperforms other lines by over 20%. You'll be ready for the roughest underwater terrain with America's strongest, Trilene XT, on your reel.
SPECIFICATIONS
Colors: Clear, Green

Line size: 2, 4, 6, 8 pound test
Spool size: 400 yards
MSRP: $7.19

Line size: 10, 12, 14, 17 pound test
Spool size: 400 yards
MSRP: $8.59

Line size: 20 pound test
Spool size: 400 yards
MSRP: $10.99

Line size: 25 pound test
Spool size: 330 yards
MSRP: $10.99

Line size: 30 pound test
Spool size: 300 yards
MSRP: $10.99

Line size: 4, 6, 8 pound test
Spool size: 1000 yards
MSRP: $16.29

Line size: 10, 12, 14, 17 pound test
Spool size: 1000 yards
MSRP: $21.29

Line size: 20 pound test
Spool size: 1000 yards
MSRP: $25.99

Line size: 4, 6, 8 pound test
Spool size: 3000 yards
MSRP: $38.99

Line size: 10, 12, 14, 17 pound test
Spool size: 3000 yards
MSRP: $52.99

Line size: 20 pound test
Spool size: 2800 yards
MSRP: $56.99

Line size: 25 pound test
Spool size: 2400 yards
MSRP: $56.99

Line size: 30 pound test
Spool size: 1800 yards
MSRP: $56.99

TRILENE PREMIUM STRENGTH
The most versatile Trilene ever made. It's super-strong, super-tough and casts like a champ. Features a unique photochromic coloration that maximizes line visibility above the surface but still creates a low-vis underwater presentation.
SPECIFICATIONS
Colors: Photochromic, Phantom Green

Line size: 4, 6, 8, 10 pound test
Spool size: 275 yards
MSRP: $6.45

Line size: 12, 14, 17, 20 pound test
Spool size: 275 yards
MSRP: $7.45

TERMINAL TACKLE

RIPCORD SI PLUS

NO-VIS

VIVID

RIPCORD SI PLUS

This addition to Cabela's popular Ripcord line offers significant advantages over other multifilament lines available today. Manufactured using Micro-Dyneema fibers that are stronger than steel and more advanced than the Spectra material found in other superlines, it's perfectly suited for spinning and casting. The "Plus" is a unique microfilament polyester tracer that adds even more body for longer casts, less rod tip wraps, increased abrasion resistance and improved knot strength. Add in extra-thin diameter, minimal stretch and a silicone coating for less friction, and you have a line that's the next generation of superlines.

SPECIFICATIONS

Colors: Bronze or Green color
Spool size: 150-yard or 400-yard
MSRP: $21.99-$54.99

NO-VIS & VIVID FLUOROCARBON LINES

This fluorocarbon line is nearly invisible and highly abrasion-resistant. The light refractive index is nearly identical to that of water, making 100% fluorocarbon disappear in water. Because of its heavier density, it sinks faster than mono of the same diameter, giving you better lure control and sensitivity. Minimal water absorption means greater knot strength, better abrasion resistance and quicker hook sets. Because of 100% fluorocarbon's high UV resistance, you'll be fishing it long after monofilament has given up. Fluorocarbon leader material is designed to be used strictly for leaders or spinner rigs, as it's extra stiffness and hard finish make it unsuitable for use on reels. Fluorocarbon fishing line is extruded to be softer and limper, making it suitable for use with spinning or casting reels.

Cabela's No-Vis™ line is virtually invisible underwater, and its abrasion resistance, knot strength and tensile strength exceeded expectations. The extra-soft properties and minimal stretch make No-Vis™ the most castable 100% Fluorocarbon line on the market.

Vivid™ Fluorocarbon offers higher visibility for those times when you need to see your line to detect light strikes and bites. Just like the original, Vivid™ sinks faster than traditional monofilament for increased lure control and sensitivity. Not only does Vivid offer great castability, but it's much less visible under water than other high visibility monofilaments.
MSRP: $9.99-$29.99

TERMINAL TACKLE

CABELA'S LINE

PROLINE

PROLINE PREMIUM MONOFILAMENT

All the features you would expect in a premium line at a fraction of the cost. Designed to help you catch the biggest fish in the toughest conditions. That means a line with high performance as well as high strength.

SPECIFICATIONS
Colors:
- Root Beer, a coloration that virtually disappears under a wide variety of fishing situations
- Clear Blue Fluorescent for those times when you need to detect the most subtle line twitch

- Natural Clear for underwater invisibility and completely natural presentations. Ultra-low
- Ultra-low Visibility Green for superior light-dampening characteristics in bright sunlight
MSRP: $6.99

POWERPRO LINE

MICROFILAMENT

MICRO FILAMENT LINE

PowerPro is the ultimate combination of modern technology and old-fashioned fishing knowledge. We begin with ultra-strong braided Spectra®Fiber, then use Enhanced Body Technology™ to create an incredibly round, smooth, and sensitive line. PowerPro outperforms monofilament lines in any situation and leaves other superlines in the dust.

SPECIFICATIONS
Colors: Moss Green, Hi-Vis Yellow, White

Strength (Lb.-Test): 10, 20, 30, 50, 65, 80, 100, 150, 200, 250
Spool size (yds.): 100, 150, 300, 500, 1500
MSRP: $12.00-$433

**SIGMA
MONOFILAMENT**

**OUTCAST
MONOFILAMENT**

**APLHA
MONOFILAMENT**

SIGMA MONOFILAMENT
SPECIFICATIONS
- Premium co-polymer monofilament construction.
- Low memory for better cast control.
- Color(s): Clear Blue Fluorescent.
- Tensile and Knot Strength balanced for maximum performance.
- Special self-lubricating formula for resistance to abrasion.
- Constricted diameter and low coil set for long, lean casting.
- Calculated stretch for hooking power without brittleness.
- Made in the U.S.A.
- Sizes (lb.-test): 4, 6 8, 10, 12, 15, 20, 25, 30
- Available in 300-yard Filler Spools or variable capacity Magnum Spools

ALPHA MONOFILAMENT
SPECIFICATIONS
- Less stretch for improved hook setting.
- Improved tensile strength and smaller diameter.
- Color(s): Blue; Clear (25, 30 & 50 lb. only)
- Made in the U.S.A.
- Sizes (lb.-test): 4, 6 8, 10, 12, 15, 20, 25, 30, 50
- Available in variable capacity spools

OUTCAST MONOFILAMENT
SPECIFICATIONS
- Less stretch for improved hook setting.
- Improved tensile strength and smaller diameter.
- Color(s): Blue; Clear (25, 30 & 50 lb. only)
- Sizes (lb.-test): 4, 6 8, 10, 12, 15, 20, 25, 30, 50
- Available in variable capacity spools

TERMINAL TACKLE

SPIDERWIRE LINE

BRAID

FUSION

SUPER MONO LS

BRAID

Designed with high-tech Spectra material, SpiderWire Braid s strength and sensitivity is legendary. In fact, SpiderWire Braid is the strongest, thinnest, most sensitive fishing line in the world. Period.
Features:

- Highest strength-to-diameter ratio in the world
- 5 times stronger than conventional mono for the most extreme fishing structure
- Ultra sensitive to feel more fish strikes
- Near zero stretch for instant hook sets
- Specially-designed coating to increase durability and line body
- Works well on any quality fishing rod with ceramic or titanium guides
- Works on any quality fishing reel
- Easy to tie using a double or triple palomar knot
- Easy to spool: apply heavy tension and use a cloth rag when spooling

SPECIFICATIONS

ULTRA-LITE
Model: SB10G-100
Test: 10 lb.
Mono equivalent: 2
Color: Moss Green

Length: 100 yds.

Model: SB10G-150
Test: 10 lb.
Mono equivalent: 2
Color: Moss Green
Length: 150 yds.

SPIDERWIRE BRAID
Model: SB20G-100
Test: 20 lb.
Mono equivalent: 6
Color: Moss Green
Length: 100 yds.

Model: SB20G-150
Test: 20 lb.
Mono equivalent: 6
Color: Moss Green
Length: 150 yds.

Model: SB20G-300
Test: 20 lb.
Mono equivalent: 6
Color: Moss Green
Length: 300 yds.

Model: SB30G-100
Test: 30 lb.
Mono equivalent: 6
Color: Moss Green
Length: 100 yds.

Model: SB30G-150
Test: 30 lb.
Mono equivalent: 6
Color: Moss Green
Length: 150 yds.

Model: SB30G-300
Test: 30 lb.
Mono equivalent: 6

Color: Moss Green
Length: 300 yds.

Model: SB40G-100
Test: 40 lb.
Mono equivalent: 8
Color: Moss Green
Length: 100 yds.

Model: SB40G-150
Test: 40 lb.
Mono equivalent: 8
Color: Moss Green
Length: 150 yds.

Model: SB40G-300
Test: 40 lb.
Mono equivalent: 8
Color: Moss Green
Length: 300 yds.

Model: SB50G-100
Test: 50 lb.
Mono equivalent: 10
Color: Moss Green
Length: 100 yds.

Model: SB50G-150
Test: 50 lb.
Mono equivalent: 10
Color: Moss Green
Length: 150 yds.

Model: SB50G-300
Test: 50 lb.
Mono equivalent: 10
Color: Moss Green
Length: 300 yds.

Model: SB60G-100
Test: 60 lb.
Mono equivalent: 12

Color: Moss Green
Length: 100 yds.

Model: SB60G-150
Test: 60 lb.
Mono equivalent: 12
Color: Moss Green
Length: 150 yds.

Model: SB60G-300
Test: 60 lb.
Mono equivalent: 12
Color: Moss Green
Length: 300 yds.

Model: SB80G-150
Test: 80 lb.
Mono equivalent: 15
Color: Moss Green
Length: 150 yds.

Model: SB80G-300
Test: 80 lb.
Mono equivalent: 15
Color: Moss Green
Length: 300 yds.†

MSRP: $15.99-$19.99 (100-yd. spool); $21.99-$26.99 (159-yd. spool); $41.99-$49.99 (300-yd. spool)

FUSION

SpiderWire Fusion's patented production process delivers the world's most sensitive fishing line with traditional handling characteristics. High-tech, Spectra microfilaments enable you to feel every rock, every turn of the

SPIDERWIRE LINE

spinner blade, every light bite.

Features:
- Up to 2 times stronger than conventional mono
- Sensitive, to feel more fish
- Low stretch for instant hook sets!
- Ties easily with any fishing knot.
- Works well for crankbaits, plainer boards/downriggers and terminal tackle.

SPECIFICATIONS
Model: SF10G-150
Test: 10 lb.
Mono equivalent: 6 lb.
Color: Ghost Green
Length: 150 yds.

Model: SF10G-300
Test: 10 lb.
Mono equivalent: 6 lb.
Color: Ghost Green
Length: 300 yds.

Model: SF12G-150*
Test: 12 lb.
Mono equivalent: 8 lb.
Color: Ghost Green
Length: 150 yds.

Model: SF12G-300*
Test: 12 lb.
Mono equivalent: 8 lb.
Color: Ghost Green
Length: 300 yds.

Model: SF14G-150
Test: 14 lb.
Mono equivalent: 10 lb.
Color: Ghost Green
Length: 150 yds.

Model: SF14G-300
Test: 14 lb.
Mono equivalent: 10 lb.
Color: Ghost Green
Length: 300 yds.

Model: SF24G-150
Test: 24 lb.
Mono equivalent: 12 lb.
Color: Ghost Green
Length: 150 yds.

Model: SF24G-300
Test: 24 lb.
Mono equivalent: 12 lb.
Color: Ghost Green
Length: 300 yds.

MSRP: $6.49-$7.59 (150-yd. spool); $12.99-$14.59 (300-yd. spool)

SUPER MONO LS
New SpiderLine Super Mono LS is extra limp with low memory for long, easy casts every time.

SPECIFICATIONS
Model: SMLS4G-110
Test: 4 lb.
Color: Lo Vis Green
Length: 110 yds.

Model: SMLS4G-400
Test: 4 lb.
Color: Lo Vis Green
Length: 350 yds.

Model: SMLS4G-2500
Test: 4 lb.
Color: Lo Vis Green
Length: 2500 yds.

Model: SMLS6G-110
Test: 6 lb.
Color: Lo Vis Green
Length: 110 yds.

Model: SMLS6G-400
Test: 6 lb.
Color: Lo Vis Green
Length: 350 yds.

Model: SMLS6G-2500
Test: 6 lb.
Color: Lo Vis Green
Length: 2500 yds.

Model: SMLS8G-110
Test: 8 lb.
Color: Lo Vis Green
Length: 110 yds.
Model: SMLS8G-400
Test: 8 lb.
Color: Lo Vis Green
Length: 350 yds.

Model: SMLS8G-1200
Test: 8 lb.
Color: Lo Vis Green
Length: 1200 yds.

Model: SMLS10G-110
Test: 10 lb.
Color: Lo Vis Green
Length: 110 yds.

Model: SMLS10G-400
Test: 10 lb.

Color: Lo Vis Green
Length: 350 yds.

Model: SMLS12G-110
Test: 12 lb.
Color: Lo Vis Green
Length: 110 yds.

Model: SMLS12G-400
Test: 12 lb.
Color: Lo Vis Green
Length: 350 yds.

Model: SMLS12G-1200
Test: 12 lb.
Color: Lo Vis Green
Length: 1200 yds.

Model: SMLS14G-110
Test: 14 lb.
Color: Lo Vis Green
Length: 110 yds.

Model: SMLS14G-400
Test: 14 lb.
Color: Lo Vis Green
Length: 350 yds.

Model: SMLS17G-110
Test: 17 lb.
Color: Lo Vis Green
Length: 110 yds.

Model: SMLS17G-400
Test: 17 lb.
Color: Lo Vis Green
Length: 350 yds.

Model: SMLS17G-700
Test: 17 lb.
Color: Lo Vis Green
Length: 700 yds.

Model: SMLS20G-400
Test: 20 lb.
Color: Lo Vis Green
Length: 350 yds.

Model: SMLS20G-700
Test: 20 lb.
Color: Lo Vis Green
Length: 700 yds.

MSRP: $2.99-$3.49 (110-yd. spool); $7.29-$10.19 (350-yd. spool); $12.69-$16.49 (700-yd. spool); $15.79-$20.09 (1200-yd. spool); $32.99-$51.99 (2500-yd. spool)

TERMINAL TACKLE

FISHTEK LEAD HEADS

MIRROR JIG HEADS

LUMINOUS JIG HEAD

MIRROR JIG HEADS

Fishtek's mirror technology has enabled us to develop a highly reflective jig head that reflects more light than any other jig available. You won't find a brighter lure than this. Rattle heads are mirror heads with rattle chamber and stainless steel rattle bead. Combines a highly reflective mirror finish with fish attracting vibrations from the rattle bead. Use Mirror heads as a jig, or put a Jelltex softbait onto the hook to get the benefits of the highly reflective mirror finish of the Mirror head and the alluring action of a Jelltex lure.

SPECIFICATIONS
Weight: 1.5 or 4 ozs.
MSRP: $1.50 (1.5 oz.) or $1.95 (4 oz.)

LUMINOUS JIG HEADS

How about fishing those dark and murky depths where there is very little light available? Even Fishtek lures might go unnoticed where there is no light to reflect! Fishing below 200 feet or so, even in clear water, is fishing in the dark. Even our super-reflective lures can only reflect the light that is around them. The answer: luminous heads!

SPECIFICATIONS
Weight: 1.5 or 4 ozs.
MSRP: $1.75 (1.5 oz.) or $2.50 (4 oz.)

OWNER LEAD HEADS

BULLET TYPE ULTRAHEAD™

Super slider design makes these ideal for Slider Rig'N and Texas Rig'N. Light wire hook features 90° bend shoulder, Super Needle Point and black matte finish.

Model 5146 (Pocket Packs)
Quantity and Sizes: Available 4 per pack in following weights in oz. **(hook sizes):** ¹⁄₁₆ (1/0), ⅛ (1/0), ³⁄₁₆ (1/0)
MSRP: $4.50 per pack

ROUND TYPE NATURAL™ ULTRAHEAD™

Features a versatile round jig head molded around an Owner 5318 light wire jig hook, with round bend, Super Needle Point and black matte finish.

Model 5145 (Pocket Packs)
Quantity and Sizes: Available 5 per pack in the following weights in oz. **(hook sizes):** ¹⁄₁₆ (2/0), ⅛ (2/0), ³⁄₁₆ (2/0), ¼ (3/0), ⅜ (3/0)
MSRP: $4.50 per pack

DARTER TYPE ULTRAHEAD™

Features a popular darter-shape jig head molded around an Owner 5318 light wire jig hook, with round bend, Super Needle Point and black matte finish.

Model 5147 (Pocket Packs)
Quantity and Sizes: Available 5 per pack in the following weights in oz. **(hook sizes):** ¹⁄₁₆ (1), ⅛ (1/0), ³⁄₁₆ (1/0), ¼ (2/0), ⅜ (2/0)
MSRP: $4.50 per pack

FINESSE TYPE ULTRAHEAD™

Eye at front of head encourages swimming action. Ideal for Texas Rig'N finesse worms, small grubs and tube baits. Round head molded around a "J" bend hook with worm-holding Z-Lock shoulder, Super Needle Point and black chrome finish.

Model 5149 (Pocket Packs)
Quantity and Sizes: Available 5 per pack in the following weights in oz. **(hook sizes):** ¹⁄₃₂ (4), ¹⁄₁₆ (4), ⅛ (4), 1/32 (1), ¹⁄₁₆ (1), ⅛ (1)
MSRP: $4.50 per pack

FOOTBALL TYPE ULTRAHEAD™

Designed for a fast, vertical drop. Perfect for crawfish-type baits, which roll upright and side-to-side when jig is slowly retrieved along rocky bottoms. Molded around an Owner Super Needle Point jig hook, with round bend and black matte finish.

Model 5143 (Pocket Packs)
Quantity and Sizes: Available 5 per pack (4 per pack for ⅜-oz.) in the following weights in oz. (hook sizes): ⅛ (1), ¼ (1/0), ⅜ (1/0)
MSRP: $4.50 per pack

STAND-UP TYPE ULTRAHEAD™

Perfect for tubes and crawfish-type baits. Features a popular stand-up style jig head molded around an Owner 5318 light wire jig hook, with round bend, Super Needle Point and black matte finish.

Model 5144 (Pocket Packs)
Quantity and Sizes: Available 5 per pack in the following weights in oz. **(hook sizes):** ⅛ (2/0), ¼ (3/0), ⅜ (3/0)
MSRP: $4.50 per pack

EXCALIBUR WEIGHTS

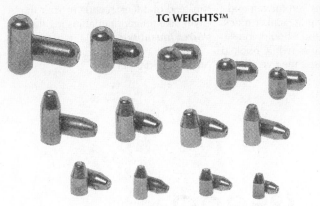

TG WEIGHTS™

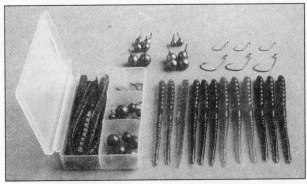

BULLET WEIGHTS™ DROP-SHOT KIT

TG WEIGHTS™

Excalibur has worked closely with our ProTeam to develop professional grade Tungsten (Tg) weights. Available in both bullet and barrel versions, these are the most technologically advanced weights available. Excalibur Tg weights transmit twice the sound of lead and are extremely sensitive, allowing fisherman to better define structure. Excalibur Tg weights are also 25% smaller than conventional lead weights, greatly increasing hookup percentages. Excalibur Tg weights include a plastic insert to ensure there are no nicks or abrasions to your line.

SPECIFICATIONS

Model: XTG100B (Barrel Weight)
Weight: 1 oz.
Weights/Package: 2

Model: XTG340B (Barrel Weight)
Weight: ¾ oz.
Weights/Package: 2

Model: XTG120B (Barrel Weight)
Weight: ½ oz.
Weights/Package: 4

Model: XTG380B (Barrel Weight)
Weight: ⅜ oz.
Weights/Package: 5

Model: XTG140B (Barrel Weight)
Weight: ¼ oz.
Weights/Package: 6

Model: XTG100W (Bullet Weight)
Weight: 1 oz.
Weights/Package: 2

Model: XTG340W (Bullet Weight)
Weight: ¾ oz.
Weights/Package: 2

Model: XTG580W (Bullet Weight)
Weight: ⅝ oz.
Weights/Package: 3

Model: XTG120W (Bullet Weight)
Weight: ½ oz.
Weights/Package: 4

Model: XTG380W (Bullet Weight)
Weight: ⅜ oz.
Weights/Package: 5

Model: XTG140W (Bullet Weight)
Weight: ¼ oz.
Weights/Package: 6

Model: XTG180W (Bullet Weight)
Weight: ⅛ oz.
Weights/Package: 8

Model: XTG316W (Bullet Weight)
Weight: ³⁄₁₆ oz.
Weights/Package: 6

BULLET WEIGHTS™ DROP-SHOT KIT

Drop-shot rigging has become the fastest-growing bass fishing technique in the world and Bullet Weights™ has responded to consumers looking for an easy way to include drop-shot rigging in their tackle box. Bullet Weights Drop-Shot Kit includes the appropriate weights, worms and hooks needed for this newly popular bass fishing technique. The package also includes easy rigging instructions for anglers who have not tried drop-shotting before.

Drop-shot rigs differ from most commonly used bass fishing rigs in that the sinker is tied to the end of the fishing line with the hook positioned above the sinker at varying lengths (usually in a range of six inches to two feet) in an effort to horizontally suspend the bait. The Drop-Shot Kit includes different weight sizes, hook sizes and worm colors so anglers can adjust the pattern as, conditions warrant.

The round-shaped lead sinkers included in the Bullet Weights Drop-Shot Kit feature a swivel line-tie that reduces line twist. There is also a line clip at the top of the weight that makes it easy to change the distance between the jig and weight without re-tying.

SPECIFICATIONS

Each kit includes:
Weights (12 total): ⅛ ounce (2), ¼ ounce (4), ⅜ ounce (4), ½ ounce (2)Culprit® 4 Worms (12 total) in these colors: Pumpkin/Blue/Black Fleck(3), Smoke/Black/Purple Fleck (3), Watermelon (3), Super Ayu (3)Gamakatsu® Hooks (6 total): G-lock worm hook size 1/0 (3), Split/drop-shot hook size #2 (3)
MSRP: $9.99

OWNER WEIGHTS

DOWNSHOT™ SINKERS

Small and lightweight, these bell-shaped sinkers are just right for use with the Down Shot System. The unique eye "pinches" on the tag end of your line - making the sinker quick to rig and adjust - and, should you hang up on the bottom (while hooked to a fish or otherwise), the eye allows you to pull back and quick-release from the snagged sinker with ease. If you decide that you want your bait suspending 3 feet off the bottom instead of 2 feet, reeling in your line will take longer than adjusting the rig. *Sizes (quantity):* 1/16 oz. (7), 1/8 oz. (7), 3/16 oz. (6), 1/4 oz. (6)
MSRP: $4.50 per pack

BERKLEY SWIVELS

CROSS-LOK SNAP/SWIVELS

BALL BEARING CROSS-LOK SNAP/SWIVELS

CROSS-LOK® SNAP/SWIVELS

These unique extra-strong Cross-Lok snap with McMahon swivel combos are finished in black.

SPECIFICATIONS
Pocket Packs
Size: 12
Lb. Test: 30
Pack Size: 5
MSRP: $2.49

Size: 7
Lb. Test: 60
Pack Size: 4
MSRP: $2.49

Size: 5
Lb. Test: 80
Pack Size: 4
MSRP: $2.49

Size: 3
Lb. Test: 100
Pack Size: 3
MSRP: $2.49

Size: 1
Lb. Test: 150
Pack Size: 3
MSRP: $2.49

Size: 1/0
Lb. Test: 175
Pack Size: 3
MSRP: $2.49

Size: 3/0
Lb. Test: 275
Pack Size: 3
MSRP: $2.49

Gross Packs
Size: 12
Lb. Test: 30
Pack Size: 144
MSRP: $38.99

Size: 7
Lb. Test: 60
Pack Size: 144
MSRP: $41.19

Size: 5
Lb. Test: 80

Pack Size: 144
MSRP: $44.39

Size: 3
Lb. Test: 100
Pack Size: 144
MSRP: $45.59

Size: 1
Lb. Test: 150
Pack Size: 144
MSRP: $53.89

Size: 1/0
Lb. Test: 175
Pack Size: 144
MSRP: $55.19

Size: 3/0
Lb. Test: 275
Pack Size: 144
MSRP: $68.39

BALL-BEARING CROSS-LOK® SNAP/SWIVELS

Wire-over-wire locking snap with ball bearing swivel. Matte black finish.

SPECIFICATIONS
Size: 2
Lb. Test: 25
Pack Size: 3
MSRP: $5.29

Size: 3
Lb. Test: 30
Pack Size: 3
MSRP: $5.29

Size: 4
Lb. Test: 100
Pack Size: 2
MSRP: $5.29

Size: 5
Lb. Test: 175
Pack Size: 2
MSRP: $5.29

Size: 6
Lb. Test: 275
Pack Size: 2
MSRP: $5.29

BERKLEY ACCESSORIES

BASS FORMULA POWER BAIT® ATTRACTANT

PowerBait® Attractant's exclusive liquid scent and flavor formula strategically disperses to create a "smell path" to attract bass. Helps to stimulate strikes in inactive fish, and mask offensive odors. Handy squeeze bottle with applicator tip makes use fast, neat and easy.

SPECIFICATIONS
Size: 2 oz.
MSRP: $2.79

Size: 8 oz.
MSRP: $4.25

BASS FORMULA POWERBAIT® JELLY

PowerBait® Jelly enhances lures, soft-baits, dough baits and even live bait with the exclusive scent and flavors of PowerBait. Squeeze tube with special tip offers easy application. Includes color and glitter to give the illusion of baitfish scales and enhance visibility.

SPECIFICATIONS
Size: 2.5 oz.
Colors: Glitter Fluorescent Orange, Glitter Chartreuse
MSRP: $4.25

BASS FORMULA POWER BAIT® ATTRACTANT

BASS FORMULA POWERBAIT® JELLY

EAGLE CLAW FISH KITS

EAGLE CLAW® READY TO FISH KITS

Here it is! The one kit designed by the pros and ready to go. Fish for your favorite freshwater fish with one simple kit that matches what you want to fish for. All kits come with a Plano® tackle box.

Bass Rigging Kit Specifications
Model: BRK60
Includes 24 hooks (8 L045, 8 L095JB, 8 L095XBL), 5 black barrel swivels, 3 red beads, 2 worm rattles, 13 worm weights
MSRP: $8.99

EXCALIBUR RATTLES

RATTLES

Excalibur soft bait Rattles are made with a patened glass construction for durability and chrome steel alloy rattle beads.

SPECIFICATIONS
Model: EWR4 (Finesse Rattle)
Size: 4mm
Rattles/Package: 10

Model: EWR5 (Worm Rattle)
Size: 4mm
Rattles/Package: 10

Model: EWR6 (Thunder Rattle)
Size: 4mm
Rattles/Package: 10

Model: EREA (Rattle Eye)
Size: 5mm, 6mm
Rattles/Package: 8, 1 coring tool

QUANTUM ACCESSORIES

SCENT WAX

HOT SAUCE LUBRICANT

HOT SAUCE™ REEL LUBRICANTS

Proper reel lubrication, or lack thereof, has always had a role in a reel's performance, corrosion and deterioration. Quantum Hot Sauce reel oil has unique qualities not found in other reel oils. With lower viscosity properties and a special formulation, the Quantum oil actually bonds with metal surfaces, creating a permanent lubrication barrier. Permanent lubrication translates into better performance and longer-life of all metal parts. There's also Quantum Hot Sauce grease.

Unlike most reel greases that break-down with heat and wear, Quantum's special version is formulated to resist structural breakdown. The super-low-friction polymers, along with exclusive tackifiers hold the grease on the wear surfaces of metal parts, and prevent migration in the gears and drags. Quantum's hydrophobic grease formulation forces water away to prevent corrosion and structural breakdown. The lubricant's bright red color provides a visual reference for placement on reel parts.
MSRP (oil and grease): $6.95

SNAG PROOF SCENT WAX

Makes fish bite and hang on. A† blend of concentrated attractants embodies the essence of a soft-shell craw in a paste form that stays on cast after cast. Leaves a scent trail fish instantly recognize as food.
SPECIFICATIONS
Model: **500**
MSRP: $3.50

Avoid Crowds
Big bass get cagey when people and boats are swarming. Fish when fewer are on the water--weekdays, in winter, at night. Better yet, fish fertile backcountry bass waters that seldom see other anglers.

TERMINAL TACKLE

STRIKE KING ACCESSORIES

BO-HAWG™ FROG PORK BAITS

SENIOR

JUNIOR

BABY

**PRO-GLO™ CORKSCREW™
SILICONE TRAILER**

PORK-O™ PORK BAITS

FISHERMAN'S TOOL

**DENNY BRAUER GLO
AND NON-GLO
SILICONE FROG
CHUNK™ TRAILER**

PIG TAIL TRAILER

BO-HAWG™ FROG PORK BAITS
Features include:
Pre-punched and pre-scented natural pork trailer with Diamond Dust
Available in Senior, Junior and Baby Bo-Hawg™ sizes
SPECIFICATIONS:
Model: BHSDD
Size: 3½" long x 1⅛" wide

Model: BHJDD
Size: 2¾"long x 1" wide

Model: BHBDD
Size: 1½" long x ½" wide
Colors: White, Brown, Black, Olive/Green, Black/Blue

FISHERMEN'S TOOL WITH LANYARD
Stainless steel tool with 9 functions:
• Reel Wrench
• Jig-Eye Cleaner
• Hook File
• Flat-Head Screwdriver
• Spring-Loaded Handle
• Wire Cutters
• Needle Nose Pliers
• Knife Blade
• Scissors
SPECIFICATIONS:
Model: FT-1
Size: 2½ in.

PIG TAIL TRAILER™ PORK BAITS
Features include:
Pre-punched and pre-scented natural pork trailer with Diamond Dust

Lifelike leg action
SPECIFICATIONS:
Model: PTT
Colors: White, Chartreuse, Black, Black/Blue

PORK-O™ PORK BAITS
Features include:
Pre-punched and pre-scented natural pork trailer with Diamond Dust
Tremendous BIG BASS bait
Unequaled lifelike action
Feels and tastes alive
SPECIFICATIONS:
Model: PO714DD
Size: 7¼ in.
Model: PO514DD
Size: 5¼ in.
Colors: White, Chartreuse, Black/Blue

DENNY BRAUER GLO AND NON-GLO SILICONE FROG CHUNK™ TRAILER
Revolutionary silicone frog style jig/spinnerbait trailer has a realistic feeling to the fish, yet is much more durable than traditional plastic trailers. Its durability enables you to fish in heavy cover; set the hook hard and catch more fish without it tearing up or tearing off! Colors do not bleed like plastic and they don't "dry out." Each lure is impregnated with garlic scent that fish can't resist. Also, there are two scent chambers that you can inject your favorite scent.
SPECIFICATIONS:
Model: TF
Size: 3¼" x ⅞ in.
Model: **TFJR**

Size: 2⅛" x ¾ in.
Colors: Black & Blue, Electric Grape, White, Pumpkin Green, Pumpkinseed, Brown/Orange, Black/Olive, Watermelon, Electric Blue, Camouflage, Chartreuse Pepper, Black Neon

Model: TFG
Size: 3¼" x ⅞ in.

Model: TFJRG
Size: 2⅛" x ¾ in.
Colors: White, Pumpkinseed, Watermelon, Chartreuse Pepper

PRO-GLO™ CORKSCREW™ SILICONE TRAILER
Revolutionary silicone snake-like glow-in-the-dark spinnerbait trailer has an incredible swimming action that will make your spinnerbaits and buzzbaits more attractive. The silicone material is much more durable than traditional plastic trailers. Its durability enables you to fish in heavy cover; set the hook hard and catch more fish without it tearing up or tearing off! Colors do not bleed like plastic and they don't "dry out". Simply put your hook through the pre-punched hole. To "charge" them to glow, expose them to the sun or hold in front of a bright light. The length of time the glow lasts depends on the length and strength of the "charge". New technology enables this material to glow longer than previous materials.
SPECIFICATIONS:
Model: TT
Colors: Chartreuse, Gold, Silver, White, Lime, Pearl

TOP SECRET/YUM ACCESSORIES

TOP SECRET AMINOGEL®

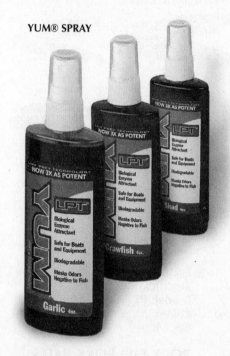

YUM® SPRAY

YUM HAND BALM

TOP SECRET AMINOGEL®

AminoGel® is a unique bait powder whose revolutionary attributes place it a step above the competition. It reliably clings to rough, porous and smooth surfaces; to rubber, plastic, fabric, glass, metal and to all natural baits. Once submerged, AminoGel assumes a gelatinous consistancy, gradually permeating surrounding waters with a fragrant cloud. Predatory fish from even the farthest distances are drawn to it not only by its bright color, but also by its aromatic intensity. Of particular value in mirky, deep, or dark waters, AminoGel®'s bright, eye-catching pigments will lead to lasting success. Each container is 1.4 oz.

YUM® HAND BALM

Be sure to use Yum Hand Balm to cover up human skin odors and chemical odors such as gasoline, tobacco and sunscreen.
SPECIFICATIONS
Model: YRY HB
MSRP: $2.69

YUM® SPRAY

YUM spray attractant features our exclusive Live Prey Technology™ (LPT) with the new 3X-as-potent formula. Developed and tested through laboratory research, YUM is proven to attract more fish, make them strike harder, and hold on longer. Available in three popular scents: Garlic, Crawfish, and Shad, YUM spray gives you an extra edge with its ability to recharge plastics, jigs, spinnerbait skirts and hardbaits. YUM is the only fish attractant that simulates the release of live baitfish enzymes.

YUM spray is available in a 4 oz. fine mist spray bottle and a 2 oz. flip top bottle. Be sure to also use YUM Hand Balm to cover up human skin odors and chemical odors such as gasoline, tobacco and sunscreen.
SPECIFICATIONS
Model: YRY401
Type: ShadSize: 4 oz.
MSRP: $4.99

Model: YRY402
Type: Crawfish
Size: 4 oz.
MSRP: $4.99

Model: YRY403
Type: Garlic
Size: 4 oz.
MSRP: $4.99

Model: YRY201
Type: Shad
Size: 2 oz.
MSRP: $2.99

Model: YRY202
Type: Crawfish
Size: 2 oz.
MSRP: $2.99

Model: YRY203
Type: Garlic
Size: 2 oz.
MSRP: $2.99

Model: YRYHB (Hand Balm)

BATTERIES/BATTERY CHARGERS

ACCESSORIES

MAX-PRO II

MAX-PRO III

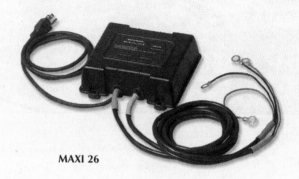

MAXI 16

MAXI 26

BATTERY CHARGERS

Every MotorGuide® charging system gives your battery precisely the power advertised. Whether it's the Max-Pro II or III, 15 amps means just that – 15 amps of output per bank. The same goes for the new and affordable Maxi™ 16 and Maxi™ 26 which deliver a solid 6 amps per battery. It's power you can take to the bank.

Features:

• An honest 15 amps or 6 amps per bank output for fast charging.
• All MotorGuide chargers automatically shut off when batteries are fully charged and turn back on when a charge is needed, preventing battery damage.
• Color-coded leads for easy installation and trouble shooting.
• Short circuit and reverse polarity protection.
• 100% waterproof and 24-month warranty.

SPECIFICATIONS

Max-Pro II
2-bank (15 amps per bank), 10.5 lbs., 10" x 6.6" x 3"
MSRP: $239

Max-Pro III
3-bank (15 amps per bank), 13.9 lbs. 13.4" x 6.6" x 3"
MSRP: $259

Max-Pro II (Remote)
2-bank (15 amps per bank w/remote), 10.5 lbs., 10" x 6.6" x 3"
MSRP: $259

Max-Pro III (Remote)
3-bank (15 amps per bank w/remote), 13.9 lbs., 13.4" x 6.6" x 3"
MSRP: $299

Maxi 16
1-bank (6 amps), 3.8 lbs., 3.8" x 4.8" x 2.3"
MSRP: $79

Maxi 26
2-bank (6 amps per bank), 5.1 lbs., 6.7" x 6" x 2.3"
MSRP: $99

BATTERIES/BATTERY CHARGERS

MINN KOTA GEL CELL TROLLING MOTOR BATTERY

Delivers ultimate starting and deep-cycle reserve power in one package. Totally sealed, 100% spillproof, vibration resistant and maintenance free.

SPECIFICATIONS
Model: MK27
Ampere-hours: 105 max at 20-hr. rate
Reserve Capacity: 160 minutes

MINN KOTA ON-BOARD BATTERY CHARGERS

Over-charging can damage the useful life of your battery. Under-charging, over time, will reduce fishing time by as much as 20% and shorten battery life. Minn Kota's MK 220 and MK 330 chargers are simply the most advanced, easy-to-use chargers on the water. Virtually "goof-proof," no other battery charger offers consistent, reliable and precision charging capabilities. Features include Smart Charger Microprocessor-controlled charging to assure the proper charge each and every time; watertight and corrosion-proof; on-demand equalization to prevent and reverse internal sulfation; rugged anodized aluminum enclosure.

SPECIFICATIONS
Model MK 220:
Multi-stage charging for up to 3 batteries, 3 banks at 10 amps per bank
Size: 7" x 8½" x 3½"
MSRP: $260

Model MK 330:
Multi-stage charging for up to 2 batteries, 2 banks at 10 amps per bank
Size: 10½" x 8½" x 3½"
MSRP: $215

ROD RACKS, HOLDERS, ETC.

BERKLEY BOAT ROD HOLDER

BERKLEY VERTICAL ROD RACK

ERKLEY HORIZONTAL ROD RACK

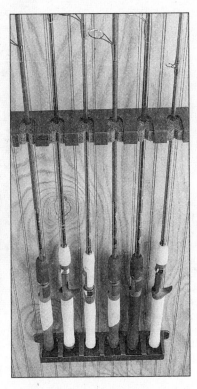

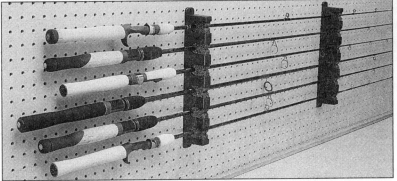

BERKLEY BOAT ROD HOLDER

Fully adjustable with two mounting brackets. Holds both spinning and casting rods.
MSRP: $13.95

BERKLEY HORIZONTAL ROD RACK

Conveniently stores up to six rods. Features long-lasting polypropylene construction and damage-resistant foam grip pads.
MSRP: $9.95

BERKLEY VERTICAL ROD RACK

Excellent for small spaces. Vertical design holds up to six rods. Features durable polypropylene construction and foam grip pads that won't mar rod finish.
MSRP: $9.95

ROD RACKS, HOLDERS, ETC.

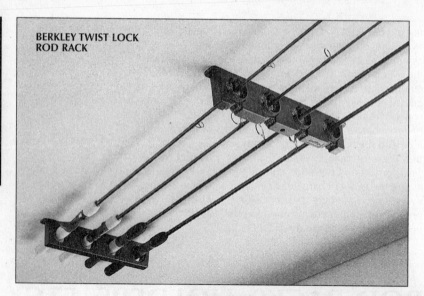

BERKLEY TWIST LOCK
ROD RACK

BERKLEY BOAT
ROD RACK

BERKLEY TWIST LOCK ROD RACK

Special twist lock design holds four rods securely in place. Great for the underside of campertops or van roofs.
MSRP: $11.95

BERKLEY BOAT ROD RACK

Designed to hold up to four rods. Made of durable polypropylene. Foam grip pads resist taking a set and won't damage finish.
MSRP: $8.95

Gel Packs Keep Tackle Boxes Dry
Save those little packets of silica gel that come packaged with so many products. A few placed in your tackle box will absorb moisture and help prevent mildew.

ROD AND REEL CASES, BAGS

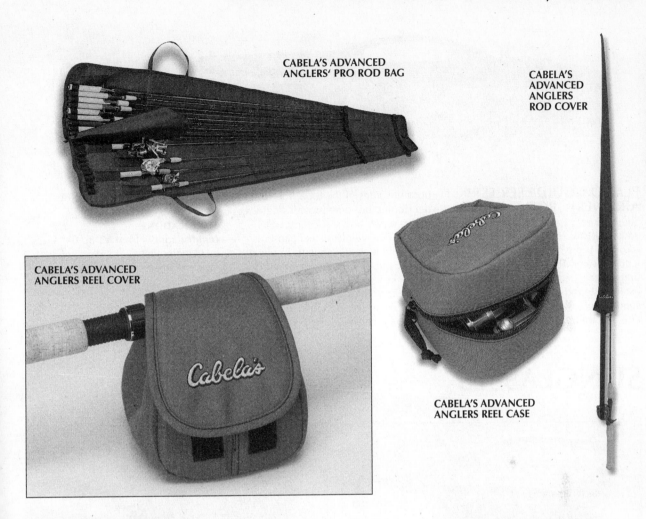

CABELA'S ADVANCED ANGLERS' PRO ROD BAG

CABELA'S ADVANCED ANGLERS ROD COVER

CABELA'S ADVANCED ANGLERS REEL COVER

CABELA'S ADVANCED ANGLERS REEL CASE

CABELA'S ADVANCED ANGLERS' PRO ROD BAG

Never again fumble with a handful of rods when going to and from your boat or favorite fishing spot. Keep eight rod and reel combos up to 7' long (casting or spinning) protected and ready to go with Cabela's Pro Rod Bag. Each side holds four rods and reels, and a padded divider prevents damage. Rod butts fit into staggered security pockets, while the tops are held securely in place by a hook-and-loop closure strap. The shell is rugged, snag-resistant nylon, and the interior is smooth fabric over foam padding. A full-length zipper allows quick, complete access. Carry straps are 1" wide and the tip end has a strap and hang tab for convenient storage. Two year warranty. Made in USA.

SPECIFICATIONS
Color: Black
8-Rod Bag: Holds eight rod and reel combos or 20 rods.
MSRP: $54.99.
4-Rod Bag: Holds four rod and reel combos or 10 rods.
MSRP: $59.99.

CABELA'S ADVANCED ANGLERS ROD COVER

No more tangled rods, line and lures with Cabela's Advanced Angler Pro Rod Cover. Protects and separates your valuable rigged fishing rods during storage and transport. Easy-to-use sleeve slides over your rigged rod and secures to rod handle just beneath the reel seat with an elastic strap. Keeps rods from tangling in your boat's rod locker, too. Rugged sleeve is constructed of lightweight nylon for years of use.

SPECIFICATIONS
Medium Size: Fits rods up to 6'
Large Size: Fits rods up to 7'
Color: Black
MSRP: $4.99

CABELA'S ADVANCED ANGLERS REEL CASE

These bags are padded with ¼" foam and covered with a 600-denier nylon shell. Zippered top opens wide for easy access. Nylon lined. Two sizes to choose from. Medium holds most bass-sized baitcasters and small to medium-sized spinning reels with folding handles. Large accommodates large spinning, saltwater and trolling reels.
MSRP: Medium: $6.99 Large: $8.99

CABELA'S ADVANCED ANGLERS REEL COVER

It's convenient to leave your reels on your rods and protect them from damage and road dust. Simply slip the cover over the reel and rod handle and Velcro® it shut. Padded with ¼" foam and covered with rugged 600-denier nylon. Sizes: Medium or Large.
MSRP: Medium: $6.99 Large: $8.99

ROD TUBES, ETC.

PLANO® GUIDE SERIES™ AIRLINER™ ROD TUBE

The Airliner™ is built tough to deliver your finest fishing rods safe and sound on every trip whether travel is by air, land or water. The exceptional durability of this heavy-duty, three-piece extendable rod tube comes from super tough, blow-molded construction and unique channel ribbing on opposite sides of the tube. The channel ribbing not only provides rigidity, it also serves as a track for tube length. Two stainless steel clip-pins positively lock adjustments in place. Or, the pins can be replaced with padlocks for even more security for airline travel. And since the tube is totally encapsulated when all three pieces are engaged, there are no latches to accidentally come open and no hinges to break.

SPECIFICATIONS
Length: adjusts from 48" to 84", in 3" increments
Inside diameter: 4¾" (will safely carry up to eight 7' rods)
Color: black
MSRP: around $29.99

SUNGLASSES

ATLANTIC

LAGUNA

H2OPTIX SUNGLASSES

The H2Optix Marine Vision System is engineered and tested to protect against extreme marine conditions. Blocking glare from the sun above and water below these polarized sunglasses perform in freshwater or saltwater environments. H2Optix offers three polarized lenses choices that are designed to cut glare and enhance visual clarity:

• Dark Grey is the preferred lens for offshore fishing and general water activities. It offers true color transmission in moderate to bright conditions.

• Amber is the optimum lens for sight fishing and high performance racing. It offers high contrast and improved depth perception.

• Dark Grey with Silver gradient flash coating. The Silver top gradient flash coating helps provide extra protection from harsh glare. All lenses possess a hydrophobic coating that reduces lens spotting and are made of durable polycarbonate that is tough enough to withstand the impact of a hammer. The frames weigh less than an ounce and are made from an impact-resistant nylon material. The frames feature H2Optix's Flex-Grip system that softly grips the contours of your face to hold the frame comfortably in place no matter how wet they get. Each pair of H2Optix comes complete with an adjustable floating sport strap to keep the sunglasses securely in place during times of high activity and a clip on neoprene case for easy storage.

SPECIFICATIONS
Style: Atlantic

Model	Lens	Frame
H91555	Dark Grey*	Crystal Olive
H91400	Dark Grey	Matte Black
H91601	Amber	Tortoise

*with silver top gradient flash coating

Style: Laguna

Model	Lens	Frame
H88555	Dark Grey*	Crystal Olive
H88400	Dark Grey	Matte Black
H88601	Amber	Tortoise

*with silver top gradient flash coating
MSRP: $99.99 (any model)

SUNGLASSES

LIDO

SANTA MARTA

THRESHER

TIBURON

STRIKE KING, KEVIN VANDAM POLARIZED

STRIKE KING, DENNY BRAUER POLARIZED

Style: Lido

Model	Lens	Frame
H95601	Amber	Tortoise
H95400	Dark Grey	Matte Black
H95555	Dark Grey*	Crystal Olive

*with silver top gradient flash coating

Style: Santa Marta

Model	Lens	Frame
H94501	Amber	Tortoise
H94300	Dark Grey	Matte Black
H94333	Dark Grey*	Matte Red

*with silver top gradient flash coating

Style: Thresher

Model	Lens	Frame
H96333	Dark Grey*	Matte Red
H96400	Dark Grey	Matte Black
H96601	Amber	Tortoise

*with silver top gradient flash coating

Style: Tiburon

Model	Lens	Frame
H97400	Dark Grey	Matte Black
H97600	Amber	Matte Black

MSRP: $99.99. (any model)

STRIKE KING, KEVIN VANDAM POLARIZED SUNGLASSES

Features include:

- Polarized polycarbonate lens
- Floating lanyard
- Protective pouch
- Blocks 99% of the sun's harmful UVA/UZ rays

SPECIFICATIONS:
Model: SG-KDV1
Color: Gray lens

Model: SG-KVDB
Color: Blue Mirror lens

Model: SG-KVDG
Color: Breakwater Green lens
MSRP: $44.99

STRIKE KING, DENNY BRAUER POLARIZED SUNGLASSES

Features include:

- Scratch-resistant lightweight polarized lens
- Sleek and stylish lightweight design
- Matte black frame
- Removable lanyard
- Blocks 99% of the sun's harmful UVA/UZ rays

SPECIFICATIONS:
Model: SG-DB1
Color: Gray lens

Model: SG-DB4
Color: Amber lens
MSRP: $7.99

SUNGLASSES

STRIKE KING, POLARIZED PROS, GLASS

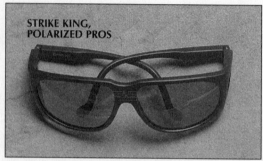

STRIKE KING, POLARIZED PROS

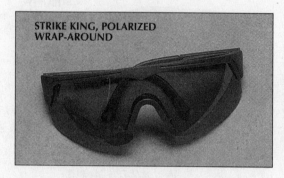

STRIKE KING, POLARIZED WRAP-AROUND

STRIKE KING, POLARIZED STRIKE KING, MODEL

STRIKE KING, POLARIZED PROS, GLASS SUNGLASSES

Features include:
- High quality polarized glass lens
- Spring loaded temple and built-in side shields
- Blocks UVA and UVB sunlight rays
- Removable lanyard
- Deluxe carrying case
- Endorsed by Strike King's All-Pro Touring Team

SPECIFICATIONS:
Model: SG-11
Color: Gray lens

Model: SG-12
Color: Pro Blocker Amber glass lens

Model: SG-13
Color: Pro Yellow glass lens
MSRP: $29.99

STRIKE KING, POLARIZED PROS, SUNGLASSES

Features include:
- Scratch-resistant lightweight polarized lens
- Spring loaded temple and built-in side shields
- Removable lanyard
- Blocks 99% of the sun's harmful UVA/UZ rays

SPECIFICATIONS:
Model: SG-9
Color: Gray lens

Model: SG-10
Color: Pro Blocker Amber lens
MSRP: $29.99

STRIKE KING, POLARIZED WRAP-AROUND SUNGLASSES

Features include:
- 1.1 mm lens
- Wrap-around lens designed for unobstructed vision
- Slip-resistant nose piece
- Absorbent sweatband
- Adjustable temple

SPECIFICATIONS:
Model: SG-21
Color: Gray lens

Model: SG-24
Color: Amber lens
MSRP: $29.99

STRIKE KING, POLARIZED STRIKE KING, MODEL SUNGLASSES

Features include:
- Scratch-resistant lightweight polarized lens
- Curved continental design and removable side shield virtually eliminate glare
- Spot fish and underwater objects
- Ideal for fresh and saltwater fishing
- Endorsed by Strike King's All-Pro Touring Team

SPECIFICATIONS:
Model: SG-1B
Color: Soft Gray lens

Model: SG-3B
Color: Pro Yellow lens

Model: SG-4B
Color: Pro Blocker Amber lens
MSRP: $29.99

Model: YM-1 (Youth Model)
Color: Gray lens

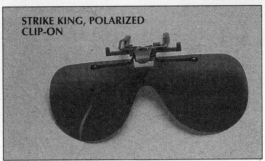

STRIKE KING, POLARIZED STRIKE EYES™ SUNGLASSES

Features include:
- Scratch-resistant lightweight polarized lens
- Sleek and stylish lightweight design
- Matte black frame
- Blocks 99% of the sun's harmful UVA/UZ rays

SPECIFICATIONS:
Model: SG-31
Color: Gray lens

Model: SG-32
Color: Reflective Blue lens
MSRP: $12.99

STRIKE KING, POLARIZED CLIP-ON SUNGLASSES

Features include:
- Bridge design allows proper fit for any facial contour
- Spring loaded tension clip with rubber tipped feet holds securely
- Doesn't scratch prescription lenses

SPECIFICATIONS:
Model: CO-1
Color: Soft Gray lens

Model: CO-4
Color: Pro Blocker Amber lens
MSRP: $5.99

Play it Right

In most situations, it's best to play the bass as hard as tackle and conditions allow, landing it as soon as possible. The longer the fish is in the water and the less pressure you apply, the more there is to go wrong and the greater likelihood of losing it. If you're near deeper, open water, however, and the fish heads that way, it may be best to let the fish wear itself down before bringing it in.

TACKLE BOXES, BAGS, ETC.

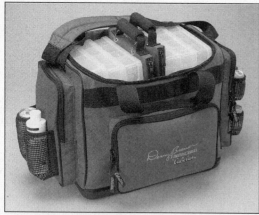

CABELA'S DENNY BRAUER SIGNATURE SERIES TACKLE BAG

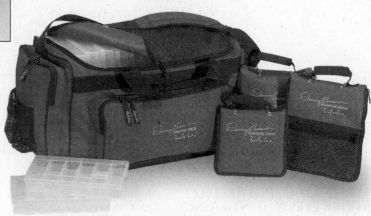

CABELA'S DENNY BRAUER TOURNAMENT SYSTEM BAGS

CABELA'S DENNY BRAUER SIGNATURE SERIES TACKLE BAG

Bass Master Classic Champion Denny Brauer knows that time is money. And there's no bigger time wasted than rummaging through an unorganized tackle box looking for the right lure. That's why you need a tackle system like our Denny Brauer Signature Series. It lets you organize your lures how you want, maximizing your time to spend more of it fishing. The bags are crafted from incredibly tough 600-denier waterproof nylon using rot-resistant thread. All critical seams are bar-tacked. Plus, a high-impact water-proof plastic bottom helps support extremely heavy loads and keeps equipment dry in wet conditions. Oversized, no-fail zippers make accessing gear easy. Three zippered outside pockets. Plus, there's a mesh pouch that holds up to six pork rind jars and one big enough for two bottles of fish scent or 12-oz. beverage can. Zippered top flap features a mesh pocket for topo maps and licenses. Three elastic tool pouches for added storage. Two-year warranty.

Color: Royal Blue with custom embroidered Denny Brauer logo.
SPECIFICATIONS
Large Bag: Holds up to six Cabela's Standard adjustable boxes plus one in the front compartment. Measures: 14"L x 11"H x 10"W.
MSRP: $44.99.

Large Bag Tournament Kit: Kit comes complete with bag and six Cabela's adjustable standard boxes.
MSRP: $59.99.

Magnum Bag: Holds up to eight Cabela's Magnum utility boxes in the main compartment and three Cabela's Standard boxes in the outside pockets.
Measures: 21"L x 14"H x 12"D.
MSRP: $54.99.

Magnum Bag Tournament Kit: Includes the Magnum Bag and eight Cabela's Magnum adjustable utility boxes.
MSRP: $79.99.

Super Magnum Bag: Holds 12 Cabela's Magnum utility boxes in the main compartment and one Cabela's

Standard box in each side pocket.
Measures: 27"L x 14"H x 12"D.
MSRP: $64.99.

Super Magnum Bag Tournament Kit: Includes the bag and 12 Cabela's Magnum utility boxes.
MSRP: $89.99.

CABELA'S DENNY BRAUER TOURNAMENT SYSTEM BAGS

If you are serious about your fishing and tackle, you need the convenience of Cabela's Denny Brauer tournament systems. System 1 starts with a Super Magnum Denny Brauer bag and added eight Cabela's Magnum utility boxes in the main compartment plus two standard boxes for the side pockets. Then Cabela's added a Jig & Pig Binder, a spinnerbait binder and a worm binder for a complete tournament quality system. The System II includes a Magnum Denny Brauer Bag, six Cabela's Magnum utility boxes, one worm binder and one spinnerbait binder.
MSRP: System 1: $99.99
System 2: $89.99

CABELA'S DENNY BRAUER TACKLE BINDERS

FINOVATIONZ TACKLE-RACK™ LURE MANAGEMENT SYSTEM

CABELA'S DENNY BRAUER TACKLE BINDERS

Organize your tackle like fishing pro Denny Brauer. Constructed of tough 1000-denier waterproof nylon, these wraps allow you to sort baits by style, size or color. The possibilities for tackle coordination are endless. Heavy-duty zipper, metal grommets and EVA handles assure a long life. Sewn-on ID card holders let you customize your baits. Standard and Jumbo worm binders feature 10 worm-proof pages. Tournament binder has ten, 8½" x 8" pages and five, 7" x 7" pages. Spinnerbait binder has six zipper-lock spinnerbait sheets, each with two compartments. For total lure management, the Magnum binder has ten, 9-1/2" x 11" worm pages and five zipper-lock spinnerbait sheets, each with two compartments. Replacement pages available. Two year warranty.

MSRP:
- *Worm Binder:* $9.99
- *Jumbo Worm Binder:* $12.99
- *Spinnerbait Binder:* $14.99
- *Pig/Jig Binder:* $14.99
- *Tournament Binder:* $24.99
- *Magnum Binder:* $29.99

FINOVATIONZ TACKLE-RACK™ LURE MANAGEMENT SYSTEM

Tackle-Rack is an open, two-sectioned tackle box that keeps lures virtually tangle-free and easily accessible. It holds up to 70 lures and has built-in storage for other fishing tools and items. The lures hang in the organizer, rather than being placed in a tray or box, which allows the lures to dry after each use, significantly reducing the possibility of lures tangling by the treble hooks, diminishes the possibility of injuring oneself while untangling crankbaits, and increases lure visibility. The handle is designed to accept an optional six-inch fluorescent light, further increasing the visibility of the Tackle-Rack™ LMS and its contents. The handle shape will accommodate bobbers, floats or small tools, such as pliers or hemostats, when not used for the light. A small open rectangular storage area is on each end of the handle. These two areas can be used to store hooks, weights, or other small parts. A slot space to place a knife or hemostat accompanies each storage area. Each unit comes with a hinged snap-on lid that can be lifted from either side. When the angler does not want to use the lid, it can be fully detached for snap-on storage on the underside.

SPECIFICATIONS
- Patented "Hook-Nook" beveled notches around the perimeter to hang over 40 fishing lures
- Four dividers with patented "Hook-Nook" beveled notches to hang an additional 28 lures
- Approximately 17" x 12" x 10" high at the handle
- Hangs lures up to 7" long from tail hook to bill
- Handle shaped to accommodate tools or light
- Spinnerbait rack under the handle hangs 14 spinnerbaits or jigs
- Additional storage areas with drain holes for hooks and weights
- Made out of durable translucent polypropylene
- Nonreactive to plasticizers in plastic bait (worm-proof)
- Punch out drainage holes in the corners of the main compartments
- Both product and packaging are made using recyclable materials
- Designed in America, using tooling and components made 100% in the USA
- 1 Year Limited Warranty

MSRP: $37.99 (includes Tackle-Rack, lid and four dividers)

TACKLE BOXES, BAGS, ETC.

PLANO® "GRAB & GO" HANGING BAIT BOX

PLANO® LARGE SPINNERBAIT BOX

PLANO® 737-001 TACKLE BOX

PLANO® STOWAWAY™ BOXES MODEL: 3715

PLANO® STOWAWAY™ BOXES MODEL: 3705

PLANO® "GRAB & GO" HANGING BAIT BOX

This tackle box measures a roomy 20.25" long x 10.88" wide x 11.25" high. Its bait racks are designed to hold 32-64 baits up to 7.5" long. The lid is fitted with two removable "Grab & Go" utility boxes that are ideal for holding terminal tackle and other accessories.

SPECIFICATIONS
Model: 7653-00
Color: Sandstone with a blue lid
Size: 20.25" long x 10.88" wide x 11.25" high
MSRP: $29.99

PLANO® LARGE SPINNERBAIT BOX

Inside this tackle box are six bait racks to hold up to 66 spinnerbaits or buzzbaits, with each rack having a patented Lurlock™ feature to hold the baits in place. On the outside and fitted to the lid are two "Grab & Go" StowAway™ utility boxes that are perfect for carrying additional skirts, blades, trailer hooks and other items.

SPECIFICATIONS
Model: 7452-00
Color: sandstone and blue
Size: 16" long x 9.5" wide x 7.75" high
MSRP: $19.99

PLANO® 737-001 TACKLE BOX

If you need one, large hard system that can take your spinnerbaits, your big baits and virtually everything else you might possibly need, then the model 737-001 is the way to go. This box is big and versatile. It has three large pull-out drawers with front access. Three model 3500 series StowAway™ boxes with their own front access compartment are included. Under the box's top lid is a spacious bulk storage area for everything from spare reels to bulk baits. Molded into the top lid is more storage space with its own top access and a DuraView™ lens so you can see what's there. The special spinnerbait storage area has three removable bait racks and can be accessed through the top access lid.

SPECIFICATIONS
Model: 737-001
Color: green box, beige lid
Size: 21.25" long x 12" wide x 12" high
MSRP: $29.99.

PLANO® STOWAWAY™ BOXES

It seems Plano® StowAway™ boxes are a lot like fishing licenses; you just can't go fishing without one. The StowAway™ 3700 series has become a real favorite because of its larger-sized and deeper compartments. Now anglers can get those same attributes, but in a smaller package. The new StowAway™ models 3715-00 and 3705-00 are exactly one-half the dimensions of the popular 3700 series. That means you still get those roomy compartments, but in a more compact size for even greater versatility and storage flexibility. Both models feature Plano's famous 100 percent wormproof, injection-molded construction.

SPECIFICATIONS
Model: 3715
Color: Clear
Size: 9" long x 7" wide x 2" high
Compartments: one open compartment perfect in size for maps and other harder to store items
MSRP: $2.99

Model 3705:
Color: Clear
Size: 9" long x 7" wide x 2" high
Compartments: comes with adjustable dividers to create 4–16 compartments
MSRP: $2.99

TACKLE BOXES, BAGS, ETC.

PLANO® 1120 TACKLE BOX

PLANO® 8600-02 TACKLE BOX

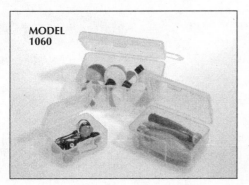

MODEL 1060

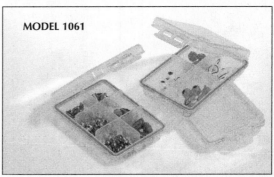

MODEL 1061

PLANO® 1120 TACKLE BOX

The model 1120-00 is a double-sided storage box just like the Plano® Magnums of yesteryear, only better. Brass bailed latches on both halves are solid and offer positive closure; hinges are strong and durable. The lids are a revolutionary new DuraView™ material to provide years of clear viewing of contents, while also protecting them from the sun and other elements.

SPECIFICATIONS
Model: 1120-00
Color: sandstone with green lids
Size: 12.63" long x 8.88" wide x 4.13" high
Compartments: 20
MSRP: $9.99

PLANO® 8600-02 TACKLE BOX

This traditional six-tray, hip-roof tackle box offers tremendous flexibility and a go-anywhere, do-anything attitude. The six-trays come with adjustable dividers to create 38–46 compartments. The rounded-corner lid features integrated lure trays and can holders for added convenience. There are tool/bait racks on the sides of the box.

SPECIFICATIONS
Model: 8600-02
Color: bottom half of box is green; the lid is beige
Size: 18.75" long x 12.13" wide x 10.25" high
Compartments: adjustable, 38-46
MSRP: $24.99

PLANO® MINI-STORAGE SYSTEMS

When it comes to storing all the tiny items associated with bass fishing, size really does matter. That's why Plano® introduced several new tiny boxes sure to have anglers saying, "that's just what I was looking for."

There are two sizes of round terminal accessory boxes perfect for small hooks, split shots and other items. Model 1040 measures 3.25" in diameter and is .75" tall. Model 1041 is 4.25" x 1.25". Both sizes are clear and have six compartments.

There are three unique rectangular mini-boxes. Model 1050 is 3.25" long x 2.25" wide x .75" high box with two adjustable dividers to create 2 – 6 compartments. Model 1051 is a 3-compartment box, but each compartment is individually accessible with its own lid. The box measures 4" long x 2.5" wide x .5" high. Model 1052 is a "one over two" box, meaning one-half is a single compartment with its own lid; the other half has two compartments, each with its own lid. Overall box size is 3.5" long x 2.5" wide x .75" high.

Model 1060 is a family of three nested boxes. Both of the smaller two fit into the largest, which measures 3.5" long x 2.25" wide x 1.75" high.

Model 1061 is a family of three waterproof mini-boxes, one each of a 1-, 4- and 6-compartment box. Each box has the same overall dimensions: 3.75" long x 2.5" wide x 3.25" high. And all three have O-ring waterproof seals.

TACKLE BOXES, BAGS, ETC.

MODEL 1070

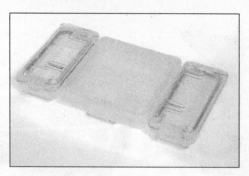

MODEL 1071

MODELS 1082

MODELS 1080-1081

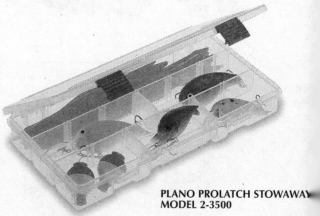

PLANO PROLATCH STOWAWAY MODEL 2-3500

Model 1070 is like a tiny opaque-gray suitcase, 4.75" x 4.25" x 1.5", but when opened, each side has its own compartment and clear lid. One-half consists of a single lid covering adjustable dividers to create as many as 24 compartments. The other half has eight compartments, each with its own lid. A hinged latch positively holds the two sides closed.

Model 1071 is a unique side by side design of three detachable, water-proof storage boxes. Each of the three boxes has an O-ring waterproof seal and an impact resistant acrylic lid. When attached, overall box dimensions are 6.6" long x 3.5" wide x 1" high.

Models 1080, 1081 and 1082 are three different sizes of round and stackable acrylic jars. Each is designed so that like-sizes screw together for user convenience and easy transport. Model 1080 consists of six 1.5" diameter jars. Model 1081 contains four 2" diameter jars. Model 1082 has six 2.75" diameter jars. All are wormproof, which is handy in this style of storage.

All of the new Plano® mini-storage systems are clear, except the model 1070, which is opaque-gray.
MSRP: Varies by size and model, ranging from $1.99 to $3.99.

PLANO® PROLATCH™STOWAWAYS™

Although the Plano® StowAways™ have been around for a long time, they have just now taken on a professional edge – literally. And it's the edge with the latches. The new ProLatch™ system is a more positive and stable locking system for anglers who are in and out of their utility boxes a lot. ProLatches™ are designed to take a better "bite" to hold lids closed tight. And they are independently molded to be more resistant to warping and stress.

The special construction process also allows ProLatches™ to be made in different colors than the boxes. As a result, the new ProLatch™ StowAways™ come with four different color sets of latches (blue, yellow, sandstone and red) so anglers can color code their boxes as to contents for quick and easy reference, while the boxes remain clear for perfect visibility. The latches are easy to remove and replace by simply snapping them in and out of the molded-in latch areas.

SPECIFICATIONS
Model 2-3500:
Size: 9.13" long x 5" wide x 1.25" high
Compartments: Four dividers create 5–9 compartments
MSRP: $2.49

Model: 2-3620
Size: 11" long x 7.25" wide x 1.75"

MODEL: 2-3620

MODEL: 2-3700

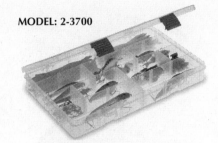

MODEL: 2-3705

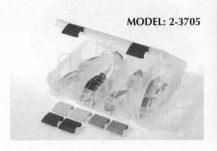

MODEL: 2-3715

**PLANO® 3376
LOWER UNIT™
SOFTSIDER TACKLE BAG**

**PLANO® 3377
EXCURSION™
SOFTSIDER TACKLE BAG**

Model: 2-3620
Size: 11" long x 7.25" wide x 1.75" high
Compartments: 20 dividers create up to 24 compartments
MSRP: $3.49

Model: 2-3700
Size: 14" long x 9.13" wide x 2" high
Compartments: adjustable dividers to create 4–24 compartments
MSRP: $4.49

Model: 2-3705
Size: 9" long x 7" wide x 2" high
Compartments: adjustable dividers to create 4–16 compartments
MSRP: $3.49

Model: 2-3715
Size: 9" long x 7" wide x 2" high
Compartments: a single open compartment
MSRP: $3.49

PLANO® 3376 LOWER UNIT™ SOFTSIDER TACKLE BAG

This tackle storage system with its gold cross-weave and leather accents looks like a fine travel bag, but it's fishing-functional all the way. The bag not only has room for the four 3700 Series StowAways™ that come in it, but also has a roomy, zippered storage compartment on each end. There's also a flap in front that covers two pouches and a mesh-covered outer that is ideal for frequently-used items and an internal one for maps, etc. A totally unique feature of the 3376 is a structured-bottom, lower unit compartment with zippered access. This area provides added protection for items like favorite reels, electronic scales, portable weather radio, etc., meaning this bag is a great choice for travel and all longer trips. An adjustable padded shoulder strap and a wrapped handle make transporting easy.
SPECIFICATIONS
Size: 21" long x 11" wide x 14.5" high
MSRP: $49.99

PLANO® 3377 EXCURSION™ SOFTSIDER TACKLE BAG

This bag is definitely ready to go fishing as it comes with 10 of the 3600 Series StowAways™ boxes fitted in the primary storage area. But there's also a zippered storage compartment on each end, as well as a full-length zippered storage compartment across the front, all with structured edges. The backside has two large storage pockets that are ideal for everything from marker buoys to first aid kits. The bag has an adjustable shoulder strap and a wrapped handle for carrying convenience. The 3377 also comes with a matching companion bag, the model 3360 boat bag, that offers more softsided storage convenience with multiple zippered compartments. This bag will hold up to four of the 3600s. Perfect for a day on the water.
SPECIFICATIONS
Model 3377
Size: 23" long x 11" wide x 12" high
Color: navy
MSRP: $69.99

TACKLE BOXES, BAGS, ETC.

**PLANO® 3392
GUIDE SERIES
SOFTSIDER TACKLE BAG**

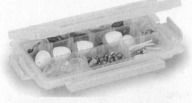

MODEL: 3540

MODEL: 3640

MODEL: 3645

MODEL: 3740

MODEL: 3741

MODEL: 3543
(SPINNERBAIT BOX)

PLANO® 3392 GUIDE SERIES SOFTSIDER TACKLE BAG

This bag has a hanging bait rack, and a lot more. Approximately two-thirds of its primary storage area consists of an injection-molded bait rack that is adjustable to hold 16–32 baits up to 7.5" in length. The remaining one-third is for the three model 3645 waterproof utility boxes that come with this tackle storage system. The bait rack is accessed through the zippered top, the boxes through a zippered front. Opening the zippered top also reveals a storage compartment over where the utility boxes are stored internally below. Each end of the bag has two additional zippered pockets, and there's a zippered pocket on the left half of the bag's front, which matches the zippered access to the waterproof boxes storage area. The bag has an adjustable, padded shoulder strap and a wrap handle.

SPECIFICATIONS
Size: 22" long x 11" wide x 9" high
Color: dark gray metallic
MSRP: $59.99

PLANO, GUIDE SERIES™ WATERPROOF STOWAWAYS™

Those who know little about fishing don't understand why it is important to have dry storage for lures and baits that are designed for use in the water. But anglers do, particularly those who have just opened a tackle box to find a favorite lure with rusted hooks and stains on the finish.

Discriminating anglers want more protection than that and get it with premium Plano, Guide Series™ Waterproof StowAways.™ Six models in all, in varying sizes and configurations, all fitted with polyurethane O-ring seals and special latches to keep water out and contents dry.

We're talking really special latches. Up-lifting, extra, extra wide latches affixed to the bottom half of the box and designed to pull the lid down tight and hold it there. The front latch is a width that equals almost 40% of the box's length. Each side latch is approximately 30% of the box's width. Closure is tight and waterproof. High quality construction utilizing durable, clear polypropylene.

SPECIFICATIONS
Model: 3540
Size: 9.13" x 5" x 1.25"

Compartments: four dividers create 5–9 compartments
MSRP: $3.99

Model: 3640
Size: 11" x 7.25" x 1.75"
Compartments: changeable dividers make 6–21 compartments, including bulk space to hold line or pliers
MSRP: $3.99

Model: 3645
Size: 9" x 7" x 2.25"
Compartments: 4
MSRP: $3.99

Model: 3740
Size: 14" x 9" x 2" with full width bulk storage
Compartments: changeable dividers create 4–27 compartments
MSRP: $4.99

Model: 3741
Size: 14" x 9" x 3.25"
Compartments: dividers create 1–3 compartments
MSRP: $5.99

Model: 3543 (spinnerbait box)
Size: 7.50" x 5.88" x 4.88" (holds up to 22 spinnerbaits and buzzbaits)
MSRP: $4.99

TACKLE BOXES, BAGS, ETC.

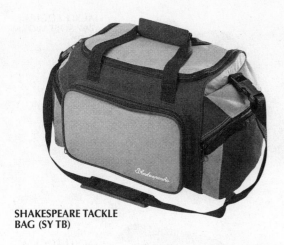

SHAKESPEARE TACKLE BAG (SY TB)

SHAKESPEARE TALL TACKLE BAG (SY TALL TB)

SHAKESPEARE DELUXE TACKLE BAG (SY DELUXE TB)

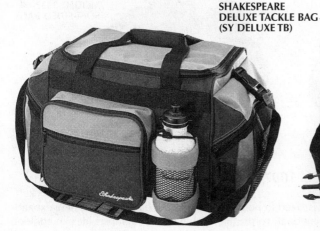

SHAKESPEARE FANNY PACK (SY FANNY)

SHAKESPEARE TACKLE BAG (SY TB)

SPECIFICATIONS

- Main compartment holds 5 standard utility boxes (not included).
- Front bellows pocket holds small utility box (not included).
- Features three external pockets.
- Waterproof zippers on all pockets.
- Velcro® carrying handle and adjustable, detachable shoulder strap.
- Durable 600D polyester fabric.
- One year limited warranty.

SHAKESPEARE TALL TACKLE BAG (SY TALL TB)

SPECIFICATIONS

- Main compartment holds 7 stan-

dard utility boxes (not included).
- Features three external pockets and water bottle holder with water bottle.
- Waterproof zippers on all pockets.
- Comes with accessory D-ring
- Velcro® carrying handle and adjustable, detachable shoulder strap.
- Durable 600D polyester fabric.
- One year limited warranty.

SHAKESPEARE DELUXE TACKLE BAG (SY DELUXE TB)

SPECIFICATIONS

- Main compartment holds 5 large utility boxes or 8 standard utility boxes (not included).
- Front bellows pocket holds small utility box (not included).
- Features three external pockets and

water bottle holder with water bottle.
- Waterproof zippers on all pockets.
- Velcro® tool loop.
- Velcro® carrying handle and adjustable, detachable shoulder strap.
- Durable 600D polyester fabric.
- One year limited warranty.

SHAKESPEARE FANNY PACK (SY FANNY)

SPECIFICATIONS

- Main compartment and two side pockets.
- Waterproof zippers throughout.
- Velcro® rod holder, D-ring and swivel hook.
- Durable 600D polyester fabric.
- Adjustable belt with quick-connect buckles.
- One year limited warranty.

TACKLE BOXES, BAGS, ETC.

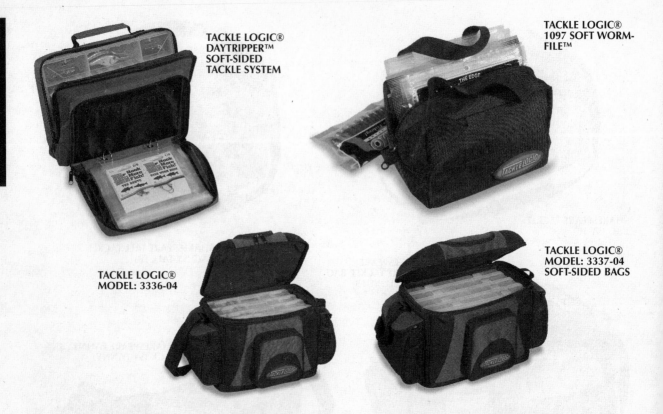

**TACKLE LOGIC®
DAYTRIPPER™
SOFT-SIDED
TACKLE SYSTEM**

**TACKLE LOGIC®
1097 SOFT WORM-
FILE™**

**TACKLE LOGIC®
MODEL: 3336-04**

**TACKLE LOGIC®
MODEL: 3337-04
SOFT-SIDED BAGS**

TACKLE LOGIC® DAY TRIPPER™SOFT-SIDED TACKLE SYSTEM

The Tackle Logic® Day Tripper™ is designed to carry everything you need for a day of fishing. It has the look and function of a small soft-sided brief case, and comes with one model 3600 Series StowAway™ in its own zippered compartment. A separate zippered compartment includes 10 patented Tackle Logic® tabs and 5 laminated bags for your own customization of contents. The wormproof bags are clear and resealable for user convenience, and are held on binder rings for easy adding and removal. Also, both compartments have multiple clear-vinyl, zippered pockets on their interior walls. On the Day Tripper's exterior are mesh pockets, one on each side. One is zippered; the other is open-topped. The bag comes with a shoulder strap.

SPECIFICATIONS
Model: 1697
Size: 12" long x 8.5" wide x 3" high
Color: royal blue
MSRP: $19.99

TACKLE LOGIC® 1097 SOFT WORMFILE™

The Soft WormFile is sized to hold up to 15 bags of conventional worm packaging. The bag's structured opening with a zipper makes for easy access. When empty, the bag stores flat, making it a handy item for suitcase travel.

Model: 1097-00
Size: 7" long x 5" wide x 1" high
Color: black
MSRP: $10.99

TACKLE LOGIC® 3336 AND 3337 SOFT-SIDED TACKLE BAGS

These bags have a new top design with fishing convenience built-in. The soft tops are actually storage pockets, supported by an interstructure system and with a top-zippered access. That means no more having to dig around or reposition bags to get into side pockets or having to get inside the bag itself for frequently used items over the course of the day – pliers, hook file, cell phone, or maybe even the soft-plastic baits of the day. With just a zip you're right there. Both

models have roomy, zippered side pockets and a zippered front pocket. And both bags feature a new expandable bottom that provides an additional 2" of room. This is a great area for storing items you don't need as often, but always want to have on every trip. Things like rain poncho, fishing regulations, cable ties, electrical tape, etc. The bags look great too, in their dark green color and cross-weave design. An adjustable shoulder strap comes with each for carrying convenience.

SPECIFICATIONS
Model: 3336-04
Size: 21.5" long x 8.25" wide x 9" high
Comes with four model 3650 bulk storage utility boxes inside
MSRP: $39.99

Model: 3337-04
Size: 23.5" long x 10" wide x 10.5" high
Comes with four model 3750 bulk storage boxes
MSRP: $49.99

BERKLEY FILLET KNIVES

BERKLEY CYCLONE LINE
SPOOLING STATION

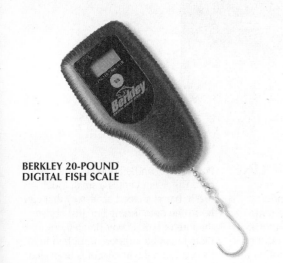

**BERKLEY 20-POUND
DIGITAL FISH SCALE**

BERKLEY PORTABLE LINE SPOOLING STATION

BERKLEY FILLET KNIVES

The folding fillet knife features a 6" stainless-steel blade, positive lock, one-piece handles construction and a non-slip grip. No sheath necessary.
MSRP: $14.95
The standard fillet knife features high-carbon, stainless-steel blades for holding a fine edge, and a graphite-reinforced handle for maximum strength. Includes a durable polypropylene sheath with compartment for spare blade storage.
MSRP: $14.95

BERKLEY CYCLONE LINE SPOOLING STATION

If you fish a lot and change line frequently, perhaps on several reels, the Cyclone can really save you time and hassle. Say goodbye to the old pencil method or holding the line spool with your foot while cranking away on a pile of reels the night before the big tournament. The Cyclone fills most small-to-medium sized casting, spinning and even fly reels in about a minute. A special hand controller lets you regulate speed and rotation direction for a smooth, even fill in a hurry. In addition, the Cyclone also removes old line in the wink of an eye with the special stripping cone attachment. Designed for use at home or on the road, the Cyclone's powerful electric motor runs on standard 110 household current, as well as the 12 volt system in your truck or boat (adapters included for both applications). The sturdy blow-molded storage case protects the unit in transit and makes it easy to keep all the attachments together.
MSRP: $269.95

BERKLEY 20-POUND DIGITAL FISH SCALE

The smaller design of this scale makes it easier to use and simpler to store. Accurate up to 20 pounds, it's completely sealed to prevent water damage and made of high impact ABS for durability.
MSRP: $24.95

BERKLEY PORTABLE LINE SPOOLING STATION

Comes complete with line stripper and built-in cutter. Sets up quickly and is easy to operate. Accommodates spinning, baitcasting and fly reels.
MSRP: $29.95

OTHER ACCESSORIES

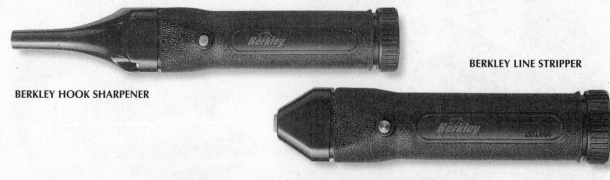

BERKLEY HOOK SHARPENER

BERKLEY LINE STRIPPER

BERKLEY BOAT LURE HOLDER

BERKLEY HOOK SHARPENER

A clean, sharp point in seconds. Uses two C batteries, not included. Sharpens sizes 6 to 10/0 hooks. Will sharpen up to 1,000 hooks. Durable, carbon steel file chips for needle point sharpening.
MSRP: $15.95

BERKLEY LINE STRIPPER

Takes the work out of changing line. Uses two C batteries, not included. Can be used on both spinning and baitcasting reels. Strips both freshwater and saltwater lines. Includes sharpening stone for hook touch-ups.
MSRP: $11.95

BERKLEY BOAT LURE HOLDER

No more fumbling through your tackle box on the water. Just pluck your lure out of this convenient foam storage unit. Attaches easily to the gunwale of your boat or in your garage. Constructed with tough polyethylene plastic to prevent warping. Comes two to a package.
MSRP: $5.95

BERKLEY® DOG BONE LINE WINDER

With the Dog Bone Line Winder, anglers can respool line onto their reel with ease. The bone-white ABS line spooler is compact and built of just three pieces. The two plastic ends separate with a simple twist for holding line spools. The tension spring keeps the spool from spinning too quickly. To operate, simply string line through the rod guides from the tip to the reel and secure the line to the reel spool. Place the spool of line onto the winder and use the curved t-shaped ends to comfortably and securely hold the spool between the feet or legs. Carefully wind up any slack line onto the reel and start cranking. The Dog Bone Line Winder works with any reel including spincast, spinning, baitcasting and fly. The lightweight Berkley Dog Bone Line Winder holds up to 1/4-pound spools of line and is easily stowed in the tackle box.
MSRP: $6.59

BERKLEY® SCENT VENT™

Anglers have long known the advantage of using Berkley Power Bait® to catch more fish. With the Scent Vent, Power Bait can be added to any lure or bait. The Scent Vent is a small tough mesh, barrel-shaped accessory that can be strung onto fishing line just above the lure or bait. Power Bait Jelly or Dough can be inserted or rubbed in to the vent and the attractant is dispersed into the water as the lure is retrieved. A propeller shaped front causes the vent to spin and a red plastic bead enhances rotation. The Scent Vent does not affect the lure's action.

The Scent Vent is reusable. The vent is simply restocked with Power Bait Jelly or Dough while still on the line. No disassembly is required to restock with attractant. This accessory can be placed in front of a spoon or spinner rig but can also be placed above a minnow or live worm rig. Filled with Power Bait, the Scent Vent will release the taste and odors of the attractant to stimulate more strikes from fish, whether you're casting, trolling or drifting.

SPECIFICATIONS
Pack size: 5 (five of single color, or five in an assortment pack)
Colors: Hot Pink, Chartreuse, Clear/Chrome, Yellow, Red
MSRP: $2.99

OTHER ACCESSORIES

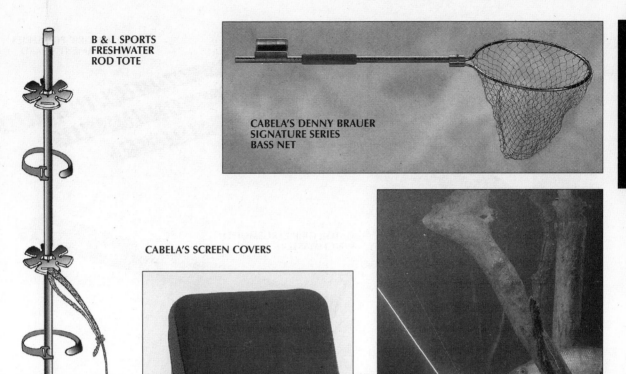

B & L SPORTS FRESHWATER ROD TOTE

CABELA'S DENNY BRAUER SIGNATURE SERIES BASS NET

CABELA'S SCREEN COVERS

CABELA'S SNAGMASTER

B & L SPORTS FRESHWATER ROD TOTE

The Rod Tote can carry and store up to six rods with reels attached. The attached shoulder strap allows it to be carried "hands free." The Rod Tote is made of durable styrene plastic, is easily assembled and may be customized to fit the length of your favorite fishing rods. Minimal assembly is required. The overall length is 72".
MSRP: $23.99

CABELA'S DENNY BRAUER SIGNATURE SERIES BASS NET

Designed with the help of Denny Brauer with the needs of the serious bass angler in mind. With an upper arm support for leverage, this extremely lightweight net makes one-handed landing easy and effortless. A 36" handle with 19" hoop lets you land the most cantankerous lunkers. PVC-coated black netting reduces tangles with hooks. Black handle and hoop. Foam-covered grip. Removable handle for easy stowage in any rod locker.
MSRP: $29.99

CABELA'S SCREEN COVERS

Cabela's screen covers protect your sonars on the water and when trailering your boat. Neoprene covers fit over most sonar units. The Eagle Lowrance small unit fits Fish ID 128, Strata 128, StrataView 128, SupraPro ID, Magna III, MagnaView, Lowrance X-28, X-48, X-49, Fisheasy and Trifinder. The Medium fits Optima, Ultra Classic and Lowrance X65, X75, X85, LCG-2400 and Accra 240, while the large size fits the Lowrance LMS-350A, X70, GlobalMap2000. For Humminbird units, the small size fits the 300TX, 200DX, 100SX, Wide One Hundred, 128, and Optic. Large size fits the 400TX, WIDE Portrait, Panorama, Paramount. A rubber mounting base cover also is available that fits all units.
MSRP: $9.99

CABELA'S SNAGMASTER

The compact, 4-oz., nickel-plated ring snaps around your line and slides quickly to the hung bait. The powerful 250-lb.-test line can bring up snag and all, if necessary. Comes complete with 30 ft. of line spooled on a heavy-duty plastic spindle. Snagmaster pays for itself with saved baits.
MSRP: $6.99

OTHER ACCESSORIES

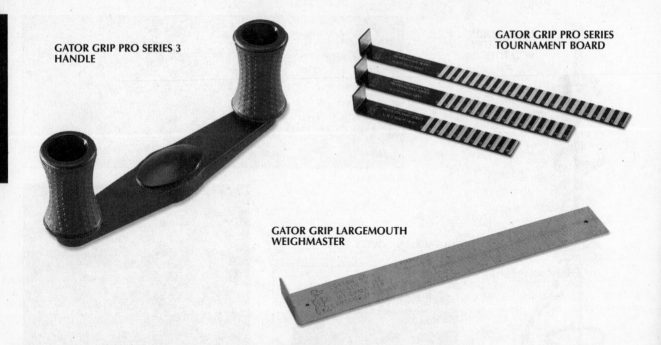

GATOR GRIP PRO SERIES 3
HANDLE

GATOR GRIP PRO SERIES
TOURNAMENT BOARD

GATOR GRIP LARGEMOUTH
WEIGHMASTER

GATOR GRIP PRO SERIES 3 HANDLE

The Professional Series Handle, a replacement reel handle for baitcasting reels, is a patented new concept, ergonomically-designed for wrist and arm relief. This new handle has multi-directional knobs that whirl around a pivot point. The knobs are covered with a textured soft outer shell assuring the ultimate in smooth movement and comfort. Constructed entirely of space-age plastic, the handle is strong enough to withstand the rigors of the serious angler. The handle fastens directly to the reel drive shaft and eliminates loose handles.

MSRP: $9.95

GATOR GRIP PRO SERIES TOURNAMENT BOARD

The new Professional Series Golden Rule tournament board is the most accurate fish measuring device ever put on the market. This board boasts durability and accuracy assuring the most precise measurement possible on a fish measuring board.

Measurements are accurate to within .003" of an inch and is achieved by computerized machinery. The board is thicker and wider than the original Golden Rule.

The black anodized rule and machined steps assure quick, accurate and precise measurement of the angler's catch. All Professional Series Boards can be personalized with the angler's name.

MSRP: $22.95 (18")
$26.95 (25")
$29.95 (32")

GATOR GRIP LARGEMOUTH WEIGHMASTER

Freshwater fisheries biologists have determined the proper length to weight formulas for Largemouth Bass. The Weighmaster displays not only inches by $\frac{1}{8}$" increments but also what the average largemouth bass would weigh at that length. The Weighmaster is anodized aluminum, gold in color, and is 3" wide. It comes with recording slips in a watertight pouch for you to record your catch and immediately release your fish. Is is used by hundreds of bass clubs that feature catch and release fishing.

MSRP: $14.95

Avoid Crowds
Big bass get cagey when people and boats are swarming. Fish when fewer are on the water—weekdays, in winter, at night. Better yet, fish fertile backcountry bass waters that seldom see other anglers.

ECS ANCHOR SUPPLY'S GRIPPER® WINDER

ECS ANCHOR SUPPLY'S GRIPPER® SPINNING WINDER

ECS ANCHOR SUPPLY'S PRO POCKET TOOL SYSTEM

ECS ANCHOR SUPPLY'S GRIPPER® WINDER

Eliminates line twist that causes wind knots, kins, line loops, loose spooling, backlashes, decreased knot strength and increased breakoffs. The Gripper® Winder's simple design fights corrosion and is practically maintenance free. The wide-stance frame ensures stability in use. Portable or permanent mount, bass to tuna, catfish to 'cuda. The Gripper® Winder ensures twist-free even tension so important to smooth, efficient and tangle-free operation of your reels. Multiple rod and reel users will appreciate the easy way to achieve uniform tension and maximum line on each outfit.

SPECIFICATIONS
Capacity: Adjusts from one 3,000-yd. spool to several smaller spools
MSRP: $14.95

ECS ANCHOR SUPPLY'S GRIPPER® SPINNING WINDER

The newest addition to the Gripper® Line Winder family is designed for filling your spinning reels. The Gripper® Spinning Winder frame is made out of

¼" steel rod, vinyl coated and has a ⁵⁄₁₆" diameter pin holding the spool at about a 68-degree angle, which will hold a spool as small as 100 yards, up to a spool of 3,000 yards. Comes with two clips to hold the spool on. The base of the holder is 5" x 5" wide. It is 5" tall from the base to the spool holder pin. It will stand on its own base or can be permanently attached to any flat surface.
MSRP: $5.99.

ECS ANCHOR SUPPLY'S PRO POCKET TOOL SYSTEM

The Pro Pocket tool system solves the problem of convenient storage for angling boats. Its patented precision design holds fishing accessories fishermen use the most, such as longnose pliers and scissors. The holder's compact, modular shape provides over 101 mounting locations (console, gunwales, seat post, inside compartments, etc.) for boat customizing. It utilizes an inverted "V" concept that stores tools in an open position that allows strap-free transporting of tools in the roughest boating conditions. With no need for cumbersome straps, tools can be removed and inserted

into the Pro Pocket with one hand, which is especially important when the other hand is occupied while holding a fish or fishing rod.

SPECIFICATIONS
Available in three mounting options: peel & stick adhesive model (no drilling holes), screw-mount model (perfect for carpeted surfaces and permanent mounting) and round post mount model (curved back to fit post 1"-3" in diameter, with adhesive and tie clamp for secure mounting. All models sold with or without tools.
Tools: 6" chromed needlenose pliers; 5" chromed diagonal cutter pliers, 5" sport stainless steel scissors. Also available with terry cloth handi-wipe towels, snap hook (to attach towel or accessories) and coiled lanyard (extends 36"/retracts to 3½")
Size: ⅞" x 1½" x 2"
Construction: injection molded ABS plastic; self-tapping stainless steel screws; premium quality acrylic adhesive specially designed for the marine environment bonds equally well to fiberglass, aluminum and other surfaces
MSRP: $19.99

OTHER ACCESSORIES

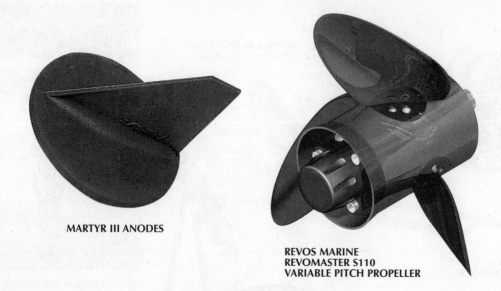

MARTYR III ANODES

REVOS MARINE
REVOMASTER S110
VARIABLE PITCH PROPELLER

MARTYR III ANODES

Many freshwater boaters sleep soundly, unaware that their boats' sacrificial zinc anodes do not fight corrosion effectively in a non-saltwater environment. Martyr solves the problem with its magnesium alloy Martyr III anode, the only aftermarket anode designed to protect outboards and outdrives in freshwater.

Traditional zinc and aluminum anodes simply do not produce the necessary voltage to work outside of saltwater, leaving the engine with little or no protection. Due to its increased activity over zinc in freshwater, magnesium provides improved protection against stray current and galvanic corrosion.

Designed to directly replace existing zincs, Martyr III anodes contain nearly 90% magnesium. Compared to a traditional zinc anode's capacity of 355 amp-hours per pound, the Martyr III's rating of 500 amp-hours per pound will provide protection for more than one year. Since the rate of magnesium's corrosion in saltwater is dramatically increased, these products should not be used in a salt- or brackish-water environment.

Martyr III magnesium anodes from Canada Metal (Pacific) Ltd. are available in limited shapes and sizes at the nearest marine retail store.
MSRP: $10.50 to $70.00

REVOS MARINE REVOMASTER S110 VARIABLE PITCH PROPELLER

The Revomaster S110 features an adjustable pitch design that allows a boater to change his propeller's performance to suit his application. In addition, its blades are replaceable, which greatly simplifies repairs. When the boater installs the Revomaster, he simply turns a pitch control knob on the propeller hub to adjust the angle of the blades. When he arrives at the pitch that provides his boat with its maximum top end speed without over-revving the engine, he locks it in place as the control knob's "max" setting. The boat is then ready for operation. Thereafter, the boater can use the knob to change pitch by ½" increments up to 2" higher or lower than the max setting. Pitches higher than "max" are marked on the knob as "eco" settings. They are ideal for long distance cruising, when greater fuel economy and reduced noise and vibration are required. Pitches lower than the max setting are marked as "ski" settings. They improve acceleration and pulling power for water skiing and other heavy load applications. This design allows a boater to use the Revomaster much like an automotive transmission. He can choose "first gear" or the ski setting for quick acceleration, "overdrive" or the eco setting for long-distance travel

and the max setting for flat-out speed, like a passing gear.

The variable pitch feature offers a number of other benefits. The boater no longer needs to carry spare propellers to change performance characteristics. He can make a heavily loaded boat plane more easily. He can also compensate for the performance changes that result from going from fresh to saltwater or from one altitude to another. He can synchronize the rpms of twin engines, or minimize pitch to allow smooth trolling. Because the blades are removable, they can be replaced right on the water if they become damaged. The procedure is quick and easy and eliminates the need to carry a complete, spare propeller.

The propeller fits Mercury, Mariner, Yamaha, Johnson and Evinrude outboards from 120 hp to 250 hp. It also works on most sterndrives up to 400 hp. The propeller is available for other engine models on request.

SPECIFICATIONS
Hub/blade construction: high-grade aluminum; black satin, corrosion-resistant finish
Available diameters: 15" to 15¾"
Pitch: adjusts from 6" to 30"
MSRP: starts at $599 (includes replacement blade and shipping to any location in the U.S.)

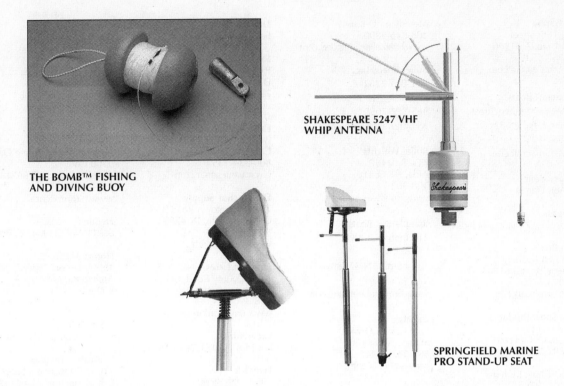

THE BOMB™ FISHING AND DIVING BUOY

SHAKESPEARE 5247 VHF WHIP ANTENNA

SPRINGFIELD MARINE PRO STAND-UP SEAT

SHAKESPEARE 5247 VHF WHIP ANTENNA

Boaters who enjoy fishing may sometimes find that their VHF antenna gets in the way of making the perfect cast. Shakespeare's 5247 VHF whip antenna provides a quick and easy solution to this problem, with a unique "Lift-N-Lay" design that allows the heavy-duty whip to fold down when not in use. Not only does this keep the 36" whip out of the way for casting, but it allows a boat to reach areas with low-hanging foliage more easily. Plus, it makes boat covering, trailering and storage more convenient. The 5247 features a new, extra-rigid, stainless steel whip for greater stability at high speeds and in rough seas. It also features a copper wire coil for superior performance. The 3dB, base-load antenna mounts by passing the SO-239 connector through horizontal surfaces up to ½" thick. 2-year warranty.
MSRP: $79.95

SPRINGFIELD MARINE PRO STAND-UP SEAT

To give anglers added comfort between hookups, Springfield Marine offers the Pro Stand-Up Seat. When fitted with the optional Pro Tilt Bracket, the seat becomes a perfect accessory for serious fishermen. Because the seat's all-plastic substrate contains no wood, the possibility of rot is virtually eliminated. To maintain a smooth and attractive appearance, its injected, V-shaped bottom completely covers all stitching and staples. The seat is finished in heavy-duty, marine-grade vinyl over plush foam padding for additional comfort and weatherability.

To provide fishermen with a variety of seating positions, Springfield also offers a six-position Pro Tilt Bracket and Kingpin seat mount that attaches easily to the Pro-Stand-Up. With its spring-loaded locking mechanism, the bracket and mount allow the seat's tilt angle to be adjusted from a flat seating position to an extreme leaning position of 50°. The seat and bracket are fully adaptable to Springfield's line of Power-Lock, Taper-Lock and Kingpin Power Rise removable pedestals.

SPECIFICATIONS

Colors: blue, black, grey, tan and white
3-year limited warranty
MSRP: $39.95 (Pro Tilt Bracket and Kingpin seat mount, $29.95 each)

THE BOMB™ FISHING AND DIVING BUOY

Whether it's a ledge, wreck or a favorite fishing or diving spot, The Bomb™ fishing and diving buoy from Seaccon Marine allows people to pinpoint important locations in the water. Designed with an emphasis on detail, The Bomb has a number of convenient features that make it easy to use.

The Bomb is constructed of closed-cell foam core with a layered outer shell of soft polyurethane for an almost indestructible composition. Even if punctured, it will not sink. Its color, international orange, provides safety and visibility.

The Bomb has 120' of line and a 300-lb. test leader. Counterweights stop the buoy at a specific depth, allowing it to let out only enough line to reach the bottom. A swivel on the end of the line reduces twisting.

A bungee cord holds a 2-lb. weight inside of the buoy when it is not in use. This means that the weight will not dent or ding a surface in case it is accidentally dropped. Using The Bomb is as simple as slipping off the bungee cord and throwing it overboard.
MSRP: $55.50.

DIRECTORY OF MANUFACTURERS

Abu Garcia
1900 18th Street
Spirit Lake,IA 51360
800-237-5539
www.abu-garcia.com.

Alumacraft Boats
315 W. Saint Julien Street
St Peter, MN, 50682
507-931-1050
www.alumacraft.com

Ambassadeur
See Abu Garcia.

Arbogast.
See PRADCO Outdoor Brands.

Astro Boats
2500 East Kearney
Springfield, MO 65803
417-873-5900
www.astroboats.com

B & L Sport Products
P.O. Box 429
Clinton, OH 44216
330-882-5362

Banjo Fishing Systems
Box 147, Route 201
Solon, ME 04979
888-646-6697
www.banjominnow.com

Bass Baby
1000 Flag Road
Adair, IA 50002
877-742-3071
www.bassbaby.com

Bass Cat
P.O. Drawer 1688
Mountain Home, AR 72654
870-481-5135
www.basscat.com

Bass Pro Shops
2500 E. Kearney
Springfield, MO 65898
800-BASS-PRO
www.basspro.com

Berkley
1900 18th Street
Spirit Lake,IA 51360
800-BERKLEY
www.berkley-fishing.com

Bill Lewis Lures
P.O. Box 7959
Alexandria, LA
800-633-4861
www.rat-l-trap.com

Bomber
See PRADCO Outdoor Brands

Bottom Line
499 E. Corporate Drive

Meredian, ID 83642
208-846-9000
www.bottomlinefishfinders.com

Bullet Boats, Inc.
P.O. Box 2202
Knoxville, TN 37901
865-577-7055
www.bulletboats.com

Bullet Weights
P.O. Box 187
Alda, NE 68810
308-382-7436
www.bulletwts.com

Bumble Bee Boats
210 Industrial Blvd.
P.O.Box 128
Tullahoma, TN 37388
931-455-9728
www.bumblebeeboats.com

Cabela's
One Cabela Drive
Sidney, NE 69160
800-237-4444
www.cabelas.com

Charger Boats, Inc.
Box 709
Richland, MO, 65556
573-765-3265
www.chargerboats.com

**Charlie Brewer's Slider
Company**
P.O. Box 130
Lawrenceburg, TN 38464
800-762-4701
www.sliderfishing.com

Connect-a-Dock
See Bass Baby

Cotton Cordell
See PRADCO Outdoor Brands

**Creek Chub World
Record Lures**
See PRADCO Outdoor Brands

Crème Lure Company
P.O. Box 6162
Tyler, TX 75711
800-445-8737
http://creme.zoovy.com

**Culprit Classic
Fishing Products**
P.O. Box 121249
Clermont, FL 34712
407-656-6133
www.culprit.com

Cultiva Lures
See Owner American

Daiichi Hooks
See TTI Companies

Eagle Claw Fishing Tackle
P.O. Box 16011
Denver, CO 80216
720-941-8700
www.eagleclaw.com

Eagle® Electronics
P.O. Box 669
Catoosa, OK 74015
800-324-1354
www.eaglesonar.com

ECS Anchor Supply
704 Waynetown Road
Crawfordsville, IN 47933
800-665-2024
www.eccecs.com

Envision Lures
2300 County Road 495
Verbena, AL 36091
888-300-9837
www.envisionlures.com

Excalibur
See PRADCO Outdoor Brands

Fenwick
1900 18th Street
Spirit Lake,IA 51360
877-336-7637
www.fenwickfishing.com.

Finovationz
900 Briggs Road,
Suite 101A
Mount Laurel, NJ 08054
877-881-3662
www.tackle-rack.com

Fisher Boats
2500 East Kearney
Springfield, MO 65803
888-669-2248
www.fisherboats.com

Fishtek
Unit 3D, Betton Way
Moretonhampstead,
Devon TQ13 8NA
United Kingdom
44-1647-441-020
www.fishtek.co.uk

G3 Boats
901 Cowan Drive
Lebanon, MO 65536
877-877-4348
www.g3boats.com

Gator Grip
P.O. Box 367
Shelbyville, IN 46176
317-398-6281
www.gatorgrip.com

Gene Larew Tackle Company
P.O. Box 1287

Owasso, OK 74055
800-YES-SALT
www.genelarew.com

Green Dragon Lures
P.O. Box 831932
Richardson, TX 75083
972-231-9398
www.spshad.com

H2Optix
Bushnell Performance Optics
9200 Cody
Overland Park, KS 66214
913-752-3400
www.h2optix.com

Heddon
See PRADCO Outdoor Brands

Honda Marine
4900 Marconi Drive
Alpharetta, GA 30005
800-426-7701
www.honda-marine.com

Humminbird
See Techsonic Industries

Innovative Textiles
2105 I-70 Business Loop
Grand Junction, CO 81501
970-242-3002
www.powerpro.com

Javelin Boats
See Stratos Boats Inc.

Johnson
1900 18th Street
Spirit Lake,IA 51360
877-508-3474
www.johnsonfishing.com.

Lamiglas
P.O. Box 1000
1400 Atlantic Avenue
Woodland, WA 98674
360-225-9436
www.lamiglas.com

Lazy Ike
See PRADCO Outdoor Brands

Legend
See Techsonic Industries

Legend Craft
2844 Cow Patty Trail
Alexander, AR 72002
501-316-4409
www.legendcraft.com

Lew's
P.O. Box 270
Tulsa, OK 74101
918-836-5581
www.lews.com

Lowrance Electronics

DIRECTORY OF MANUFACTURERS

12000 East Skelly Drive
Tulsa, OK 74128
800-324-1356
www.lowrance.com

Mann's Bait Company
1111 State Docks Road
Eufaula, AL 36027
334-687-5716
www.mannsbait.com

Martyr
Canada Metal (Pacific) Ltd.
634 Derwent Way
Delta, BC, CANADA V3M 5P7
604-525-0471
www.canmet.com

Mercury Marine
W6250 W. Pioneer Road
P.O. Box 1939
Fond du Lac, WI 54936-1939
920-929-5040
www.mercurymarine.com

Minn Kota
1326 Willow Road
Sturtevant, WI 53177
800-299-2592
www.minnkotamotors.com

Mitchell
1900 18th Street
Spirit Lake,IA 51360
877-502-6482
www.fishmitchell.com

MotorGuide
835 West 41st Street
Tulsa, OK 74107
920-929-5040
www.motorguide.com

Mustad
See O. Mustad & Son

Nitro Boats
2500 East Kearney
Springfield, MO 65803
800-41-NITRO
www.nitroboats.com

O. Mustad & Son (USA)
P.O. Box 838
Auburn, NY 13021
315-253-2793
www.mustad.no

Outboard Electric Corporation
540 Barnum Avenue,
Bldg. 2B, Box #4
Bridgeport, CT 06608
203-345-0116
www.outboardelectric.org

Owner American
3199-B Airport Loop Drive
Costa Mesa, CA 92626
714-668-9011
www.ownerhooks.com

Pflueger Fishing Tackle
3801 Westmore Drive
Columbia, SC 29223
803-754-7000
www.pflueger-fishing.com

Piranha
See Techsonic Industries

Plano Molding Company
431 East South Street
Plano, IL 60545
800-874-6905
www.planomolding.com

Polar
P.O. Box 310
Vinemont, AL 35179
256-739-4182
www.polarboats.com.

PowerPro
See Innovative Textiles

PRADCO Outdoor Brands
3601 Jenny Lind Road
Fort Smith, AR 72901
479-782-8971
www.lurenet.com

Procraft Boats
2500 East Kearney
Springfield, MO 65803
888-776-5520
www.procraftboats.com

Pure Fishing
1900 18th Street
Spirit Lake, IA 51360
877-777-3850
www.purefishing.com

Quantum
P.O. Box 270
Tulsa, OK 74101
918-836-5581
www.quantumfishing.com

Ranger Boats
P.O. Box 179
Flippin, AR 72634
870-453-2222
www.rangerboats.com

Rat-L-Trap
See Bill Lewis Lures

Rebel
See PRADCO Outdoor Brands

Revos Marine
Böhnirainstrasse 9
8800 Thalwil
Switzerland
+41-1-722-60-80
www.revosmarine.com

Saint Croix Rod
P.O. Box 279
Park Falls, WI 54552
800-826-7042
www.stcroixrods.com

SeaArk Boats
P. O. Box 803
Monticello, AR 71657
870-367-5317
www.seark.com or
www.aluminumboat.com

Seaccon Marine
13667 Automobile Boulevard
Clearwater, FL 33762
727-556-0908
(no website)

Shakespeare Fishing Tackle
3801 Westmore Drive
Columbia, SC 29223
803-754-7000
www.shakespeare-fishing.com

**Shakespeare Composites
& Electronics**
P.O. Box 733
Newberry, SC 29108
(no customer phone)
www.shakespeare-ce.com

Skeeter Boats
1 Skeeter Road
Kilgore, Texas 75662
800-753-3837
www.skeeterboats.com

Smithwick
See PRADCO Outdoor Brands

Snag Proof Manufacturing
11387 Deerfield Road
Cincinnati, OH 45242
513-489-6483
www.snagproof.com

Spider
1900 18th Street
Spirit Lake,IA 51360
877-502-6482
www.spidercast.com
www.spiderwire.com

Springfield Marine Company
P.O. Box 588
Nixa, MO 65714
417-725-2667
www.springfieldgrp.com

Stratos Boats, Inc.
880 Butler Road
Murfreesboro, TN 37127
615-895-5190

Strike King Lure Company
466 Washington Street
Collierville, TN 38017
901-853-1455
www.strikeking.com

Tackle Logic Company
431 East South Street
Plano, IL 60545
800-874-6905
www.tacklelogic.com

Techsonic Industries
108 Maple Lane
Eufaula, AL 36027
334-687-0503
www.techsonic.com

Thornwood Lures
P.O. Box 186
Thornwood, NY 10594
914-773-0523
www.thornwoodlures.com

Top Secret
Burloer Strasse
46325 Borken
Germany
01149-2861-9085811
www.top-secret-us.com

Tracker Boats
2500 East Kearney
Springfield, MO 65803
1-800-TRACKER
www.trackerboats.com

Trilene
See Berkley

Triton Boats
15 Bluegrass Drive
Ashland City, TN 37015
888-887-4866
www.tritonboats.com

TTI Companies
P.O. Box 1177
Wetumpka, AL 36092
334-567-2011
www.truturnhooks.com
www.xpointhooks.com
www.daiichihooks.com

Tru-Turn Hooks
See TTI Companies

War Eagle Boats
P.O. Box 430
Monticello, AR 71655
870-367-1554
www.eagleboats.com

X-Point Hooks
See TTI Companies

Yamaha Outboards
1270 Chastain Road
Kennesaw, GA 30144
800-88-YAMAHA
www.yamaha-motor.com

Yum Bait Company
See PRADCO Outdoor Brands

Zebco
P.O. Box 270
Tulsa, OK 74101
918-836-5581
www.zebco.com

MANUFACTURERS

BASSING BIBLE INDEX

A
ACCESSORIES
BATTERIES/BATTERY CHARGERS, 366–367
Max-Pro Battery Chargers, 366
Minn Kota Gel Cell Trolling Motor Battery, 367
Minn Kota On-Board Battery Chargers, 367
OTHER ACCESSORIES, 383–389
Berkley Fillet Knives, 383
Berkley Cyclone Line Spooling Station, 383
Berkley 20-Pound Digital Fish Scale, 383
Berkley Portable Line Spooling Station, 383
Berkley Hook Sharpener, 384
Berkley Line Stripper, 384
Berkley Boat Lure Holder, 384
Berkley Dog Bone Line Winder, 384
Berkley Scent Vent, 384
B & L Sports Freshwater Rod Tote, 385
Cabela's Denny Brauer Signature Series Bass Net, 385
Cabela's Screen Covers, 385
Cabela's Snagmaster, 385
Gator Grip Pro Series 3 Handle, 386
Gator Grip Pro Series Tournament Board, 386
Gator Grip Largemouth Weighmaster, 386
ECS Anchor Supply's Gripper Winder, 387
ECS Anchor Supply's Gripper Spinning Winder, 387
ECS Anchor Supply's Pro Pocket Tool System, 387
Martyr III Anodes, 388
Revos Marine Revomaster S110 Variable Pitch Propeller, 388
Shakespeare 5247 VHF Whip Antenna, 389
Springfield Marine Pro Stand-Up Seat, 389
Seacon Marine "The Bomb" Fishing and Diving Buoy, 389
ROD RACKS, HOLDERS, ETC., 367–368
Berkley Boat Rod Holder, 367
Berkley Horizontal Rod Rack, 367
Berkley Vertical Rod Rack, 367
Berkley Twist Lock Rod Rack, 368
Berkley Boat Rod Rack, 368
ROD AND REEL CASES, BAGS, 367

Cabela's Advanced Angler's Pro Rod Bag, 369
Cabela's Advanced Angler's Rod Cover, 369
Cabela's Advanced Angler's Reel Case, 369
Cabela's Advanced Angler's Reel Cover, 369
ROD TUBES, ETC., 370
Plano Guide Series Airliner Rod Tube, 370
SUNGLASSES, 370–373
H2Optix Sunglasses, 370
Strike King, Kevin Vandam Polarized Sunglasses, 371
Strike King, Denny Brauer Polarized Sunglasses, 371
Strike King, Polarized Pros, Glass Sunglasses, 372
Strike King, Polarized Pros, Sunglasses, 372
Strike King, Polarized Wrap-Around Sunglasses, 372
Strike King, Polarized Strike King, Model Sunglasses, 372
Strike King, Polarized Strike Eyes Sunglasses, 373
Strike King, Polarized Clip-On Sunglasses, 373
TACKLE BOXES, BAGS, ETC., 374–382
Cabela's Denny Brauer Signature Series Tackle Bags, 374
Cabela's Denny Brauer Tournament System Bags, 374
Cabela's Denny Brauer Tackle Binders, 375
Finovationz Tackle-Rack Lure Management System, 375
Plano "Grab & Go" Hanging Bait Box, 376
Plano Large Spinnerbait Box, 376
Plano 737-001 Tackle Box, 376
Plano Stowaway Boxes, 376
Plano 1120 Tackle Box, 377
Plano 8600-02 Tackle Box, 377
Plano Mini-Storage Systems, 377
Plano Prolatch Stowaways, 378
Plano 3376 Lower Unit Softsider Tackle Bag, 379
Plano 3377 Excursion Softsider Tackle Bag, 379
Plano 3392 Guide Series Softsider Tackle Bag, 380
Plano, Guide Series Waterproof Stowaways, 380
Shakespeare Tackle Bag, 381
Shakespeare Tall Tackle Bag, 381
Shakespeare Deluxe Tackle Bag, 381

Shakespeare Fanny Pack, 381
Tackle Logic Day Tripper Soft-Sided Tackle System, 382
Tackle Logic Soft Wormfile, 382
Tackle Logic Soft-Sided Tackle Bags, 382
Active bass, 50

B
Bait techniques
dead-worming, 19
doodling, 23
drop-shotting, 22–23
trick worming, 20–22
tube-jigging, 19–20
Bass
See Black bass
Bass lakes
Lake Champlain, Vermont, 8
Lake Guntersville, Alabama, 11
Lake St. Clair, Michigan, 7
Lake Texoma, Oklahoma, 10
Mississippi River oxbows, 9, 38
St. Lawrence River, New York, 6
Black bass
Guadalupe, 27
largemouth, 24–25, 27–32
redeye, 26
shoal, 26
smallmouth, 25–30, 32–33
spotted, 26–30, 33
Suwanee, 27
Black lights, 81
Bluegrass 33 reel, 14–15
BOATS
ALUMACRAFT BASS BOATS, 86
MV Super Hawk, 86
Crappie Deluxe, 86
Crappie Jon, 86
Bass Pro 165, 86
Invader 195, 86
Invader 185, 86
Invader 175, 86
Magnum 175 CS, 86
Magnum 175, 86
Magnum 165, 86
MV Tex Special CS, 87
Tournament Pro 185 CS, 87
Tournament Pro 185, 87
Tournament Pro 175 CS, 87
ASTRO BOATS, 87
1850 SF, 87
BASS CAT BOATS, 88
Cougar, 88
Jaguar, 88
Pantera Classic, 89
Antera III, 89
Phelix, 90
Sabre, 90

BASSING BIBLE INDEX

BASSING BIBLE INDEX

INDEX

BASSING BIBLE INDEX

INDEX

BASSING BIBLE INDEX

INDEX

INDEX

BASSING BIBLE INDEX

INDEX

BASSING BIBLE INDEX

INDEX

INDEX

BASSING BIBLE INDEX

PHOTOGRAPHY CREDITS

Cover: Courtesy Ranger Boats; **6, 7, 8, 10, 11**(inset images): John E. Phillips; **12-17:** Soc Clay; **18-23:** Larry Larson; **27-31:** Bob Borgwat; **34-45:** Keith B. Sutton; **46-49:** Charles Bridwell; **50-57:** Vernon Summerlin; **58-63:** Alan Clemons; **64:** Walt Rhodes; **65,67:** Jeff Samsel; **68-73:** John N. Felsher; **74-79:** Gerald A. Almy; **80-84:** Jim Spencer; **117:** Keith B. Sutton; **143:** Monte Burch; **163:** Charles Bridwell; **201:** Soc Clay; **241:** Alan Clemons; **337:** Gerald A. Almy; **365:** Keith B. Sutton